THE INFORMED ARGUMENT

A MULTIDISCIPLINARY
READER AND GUIDE

D0220050

THE INFORMED ARGUMENT

A MULTIDISCIPLINARY READER AND GUIDE

FOURTH EDITION

ROBERT K. MILLER
UNIVERSITY OF SAINT THOMAS

HARCOURT BRACE COLLEGE PUBLISHERS

FORT WORTH   PHILADELPHIA   SAN DIEGO

NEW YORK   ORLANDO   AUSTIN   SAN ANTONIO

TORONTO   MONTREAL   LONDON   SYDNEY   TOKYO

Publisher:	Ted Buchholz
Senior Acquisitions Editor:	Stephen Jordan
Senior Developmental Editor:	Sarah Helyar Smith
Manuscript Editor:	Maryan Malone, Publications Development Company of Texas
Designer:	Publications Development Company of Texas
Senior Production Manager:	Ken Dunaway
Permissions Editor:	Sheila Shutter
Cover Design:	Garry Harman

ISBN: 0-15-501482-X

Library of Congress Catalog Card Number: 94-076814

Printed in the United States of America

5 6 7 8 9 0 1 2 3   016   9 8 7 6 5 4 3 2

PREFACE FOR STUDENTS

This book has been designed to help you argue on behalf of your beliefs so that other people will take them seriously. Part 1 introduces you to basic principles of argumentation that you need to analyze the arguments you read and to compose arguments of your own. Part 2 introduces you to specific strategies for evaluating your reading and to formal conventions for supporting arguments with information that you have acquired through that reading.

The readings gathered for you in *The Informed Argument,* Fourth Edition, will give you adequate information for writing about a variety of topics. The readings that form the heart of the book are found in Part 3, "Sources for Argument." In this part of the book, you will find material on the same subject by several different writers. I hope that your reading in Part 3 will leave you better informed about the different subjects that are discussed. But whatever you learn about these subjects is a bonus. The purpose of *The Informed Argument* is not to turn you into an expert on gun control, sexual harassment, or curriculum reform; it is to help you master skills that you can apply to subjects of your own choice long after you have completed the course in which you used this book.

In choosing the various essays for Part 3, I attempted to give equal consideration to opposing viewpoints so that you can better understand different sides of the issues in question. I also included examples of different writing strategies. To fulfill these goals, I did not limit the selections to the most recent works available. You will find the date of original publication within the introductory note that comes immediately before each selection. When evaluating sources, recognize that an essay can embody a strong argument or interesting point of view many years after it was written. An old essay can include outdated information, however, so you should consider the date of each source when deciding the extent to which you can rely upon it.

If you read carefully, you will find that almost every written argument includes a point that can be questioned. This is because argument is part of an ongoing process of inquiry; a single argument is unlikely to entirely resolve any complex issue. So don't feel that an argument loses all credibility because you have discovered a flaw in it. Although you should be alert for flaws, especially in reasoning, you should consider the flaw in proportion to the argument as a whole. Some writers undermine their entire argument by contradicting themselves or by making wild charges; others are able to make a strong argument despite one or two weak points. Whatever the case, we as readers and writers learn from considering many points of view and deciding how they inform each other. Argument is not about "winning" or "losing"; it is a process devoted to finding solutions to problems. When this process is undertaken honestly, everyone stands to benefit.

I wrote this book because I saw that students often needed additional information before they could write well-supported arguments but did not always have the time to do research. Some writers, however, enjoy doing their own research, and you may want to supplement your reading in this book with material that you have discovered on your own. Part 5, "A Guide to Research," discusses how to find sources in a library. Searching for your own sources will enable you to include recently published material within your arguments. Library research may also help you discover unusual or surprising information, which will make your arguments more interesting to readers who are already familiar with the material in *The Informed Argument*. The extent to which you decide to go outside the book, if at all, is something to be decided in consultation with your instructor. The book itself has been designed to make research an option rather than a necessity.

This edition includes 13 essays written by students. These have been included to enable you to see how other students have satisfied assignments similar to those you may be asked to undertake. These essays are intended to help you rather than to impress you. Try to learn what you can from them, but do not feel that they represent some sort of perfection that is beyond your grasp. All of the student writers are serious enough about writing that they will probably see things they'd like to change as soon as they see their essays in print, for revision is a never-ending commitment essential to good writing. I want to thank these students for giving me permission to publish their work and remind them that I hope they keep on writing. I also want to thank the many students who studied the first three editions of this book and helped me to see how it could be improved.

PREFACE FOR INSTRUCTORS

The Fourth Edition of *The Informed Argument* continues to reflect my belief that learning is best fostered by encouraging students to read, reflect, and write about serious issues. Most of the readings are once again assembled into the equivalent of separate casebooks, six of which focus on important issues of the sort students often want to write about but lack adequate information to do so effectively. Instructors are free to treat each section either as a self-contained unit or as a springboard to further reading. To facilitate class discussion, every essay has its own editorial apparatus. This allows for much flexibility. Readings can be assigned in whatever sequence seems appropriate for a particular class. And there is plenty of material, so you can vary the assignments you give to different classes without undertaking the work of an entirely new preparation.

Of 85 selections, 60 are new to this edition. They are drawn from a variety of disciplines to help students master different types of writing and reading. Among the fields represented are biology, business, education, history, journalism, law, literature, political science, psychology, public health, and sociology. In selecting these readings, I have been guided by three primary concerns: (1) to give students information for writing arguments of their own, (2) to expose them to different points of view, (3) to provide them with model arguments. I have also chosen pieces that require different degrees of experience with reading. Some of the pieces—especially in the early sections—are easily accessible; others are more demanding. My goal was to give students an immediate point of entry into the issues and then encourage them to confront more difficult texts representative of the reading they will be expected to undertake on their own in college and beyond.

Although I believe in the importance of writing across the curriculum, I also believe that literature should be part of the curriculum being written across. Consequently, the book includes a section on literary criticism as a type of argumentation. The thematically organized sections in Part 3 are followed by Part 4, "Some Classic Arguments." This section increases the variety of readings made available to students through inclusion of such well-known essays as "A Modest Proposal" and "Letter from Birmingham Jail" as well as seldom-anthologized arguments by writers such as Charlotte Perkins Gilman, Margaret Sanger, and Mahatma Gandhi.

The wish to increase diversity within the book led me to include significantly more pieces by women and writers of color and to address such timely concerns as sexual harassment and immigration reform. Argument has been perceived too often as a male-dominated discourse devoted to attacking opponents and winning some kind of victory. *The Informed Argument* demonstrates that argument takes many different forms, that it is often ameliorative rather than combative, and that it is practiced by writers who differ in terms of gender, race, class, and sexual orientation.

Because books have become so expensive, I have designed *The Informed Argument* to satisfy the needs of students in a semester-long class and to be useful to them long afterward. Part 1 introduces students to the principles they need to understand for reading and writing arguments. I have kept the explanations as simple as possible. Examples are provided for each of the concepts discussed, and student essays illustrate both inductive and deductive reasoning as well as the model for reasoning devised by Stephen Toulmin. In addition, two versions of the same student essay illustrate the importance of revision, and another student essay illustrates strategies for definition. A feature new to this edition is that Parts 1 and 2 now include exercises with which students can put principles into practice immediately after they have been introduced.

Part 2 discusses the evaluation, annotation, paraphrase, summary, synthesis, and documentation of texts. For easy reference, a gray border identifies the pages devoted to documentation. The major documentation styles in use across the curriculum are illustrated—not only those of the Modern Language Association (MLA) and the American Psychological Association (APA), which are discussed in detail, but also the use of documentary footnotes and a numbered system favored in scientific writing. MLA style is also illustrated by several student essays in Part 3 and by a longer paper in Part 5. To help students using APA-style documentation, original publication dates are printed within the headnotes for selections in Parts 3 and 4. Examples of APA and other styles are provided by one or more of the essays in Part 3.

Several of the suggestions for writing in Parts 3 and 4 encourage students to do library research. How to do so is discussed in Part 5, "A Guide to Research." In keeping with the book's multidisciplinary character, I illustrate a search strategy that could be employed to locate material for many different courses. Although this information appears at the end of the book, it can be taught at any time. Rather than suggesting that research is limited to an academic exercise called "the research paper," *The Informed Argument* is designed to show that research can take many forms and, as Richard Larson has argued, "almost any paper is potentially a paper incorporating the fruits of research."

Instructors new to *The Informed Argument* might also note that the book contains a total of 13 student essays. Although student essays can be found in many textbooks, *The Informed Argument* includes essays that respond to sources that are reprinted in the book. I have included these essays because students often profit from studying the work of other students. Given the difficulty of arguing effectively and using sources responsibly, students using the Fourth Edition should welcome the chance to see how other students coped with assignments similar to their own.

In completing this edition, I have contracted many debts. I want to thank my colleagues at the University of St. Thomas for creating an atmosphere in which it is a pleasure to work. Mary Rose O'Reilley, Lon Otto, and

Joan Piorkowski deserve special thanks for their unfailing encouragement and support. I also want to thank the students with whom I've worked this year, especially Alicia Fedorczak, Christopher Lovrien, Erik Miles, Douglas Micko, Jessica Powell, and Andrew Shimek who all contributed essays to this edition.

For helpful advice in planning the Fourth Edition, I want to thank the following:

Bill Boggs, *Slippery Rock University*

Joseph Gavin, *Community College of Allegheny County*

Mary Lou Henneman, *Youngstown State University*

James Houck, *Youngstown State University*

Jerry Howard, *Northeastern Illinois University*

Sue Kelley, *Fairmont State College*

Shannon Kiser, *Shawnee State University*

Lynn Levy, *Washington State University*

Susan Lockwood, *Chattahoochee Valley Community College*

Ted McFerrin, *Collin County Community College*

Mike Moran, *University of Georgia*

Edward Palm, *Glenville State College*

Paul Perry, *Palo Alto College*

Tony Petrarca, *Community College of Allegheny County*

Barbara Roseborough, *Shelby State Community College*

Richard Tracz, *Oakton Community College*

Dede Yow, *Kennesaw State University*

At Harcourt Brace, Stephen Jordan, and Sarah Smith gave sage and helpful advice. Garry Harman designed the cover and Ken Dunaway guided the book through a tight schedule. Nancy Marcus Land, Maryan Malone, and Denise Netardus deserve many thanks for their expert help with production. Eleanor Garner was once again a model of efficiency, dedication, and good humor when negotiating permissions agreements. It was my good fortune to have so much valuable assistance.

CONTENTS

PART 4

SOME CLASSIC ARGUMENTS   477

P A R T   5

A GUIDE TO RESEARCH   583

AN INTRODUCTION
TO ARGUMENT

Argument is a means of fulfilling desire. That desire may be for something as abstract as truth or as concrete as an increase in salary. When you ask for an extension on a paper, apply for a job, propose a marriage, or recommend any change that involves someone besides yourself, you are putting yourself in a position that requires effective argumentation. You may also have occasion to argue seriously about political and ethical concerns. Someone you love may be considering an abortion, a large corporation may try to buy its chemical waste on property that adjoins your own, or you may be suddenly deprived of a benefit to which you feel entitled. By learning how to organize your beliefs and support them with information that will make other people take them seriously, you will be mastering one of the most important skills you are likely to learn in college.

Working your arguments out on paper gives you an opportunity to make changes as often as you want until you are satisfied that your words do what you want them to do. This is an important benefit because constructing effective arguments requires that you think clearly without letting your feelings dominate what you say, and this can be difficult at times. But it can also be tremendously satisfying when you succeed in making other people understand what you mean. You may not always convert others to your point of view, but you can earn their respect. This, in a way, is what argument is all about. When you argue for what you believe, you are asking others to believe in you. This means that you must prove to your audience that you are worth listening to. Instead of thinking in terms of "winning" or "losing" an argument, consider argumentation as an intellectual effort designed to solve problems by drawing people together.

Bearing this in mind, you should always be careful to treat both your audience and your opponents with respect. Few people are likely to be converted to your view if you treat them as if they are fools or dismiss their beliefs with contempt. Reason is the essence of effective argumentation, and an important part of being reasonable is demonstrating that you have given consideration to beliefs that are different from your own and have recognized what makes them appealing. Try not to be narrow-minded or overly opinionated.

The readings that form the heart of this book were chosen to make you better informed on a number of important questions so that you can argue about them more effectively. After you have read six or seven essays on the same subject, you should be able to compose an argument that shows you have considered the various views you have encountered. But remember that being "better informed" does not always mean being "well informed." Well-educated men and women recognize how little they know in proportion to how much there is to be known. Don't suppose that you've become an expert on immigration policy just because you have spent a week or two reading about it. What you read should influence what you think, but, as you read more, remember that controversial subjects are controversial because there is so much that can be said about them—much more than you may have realized at first.

CHOOSING A TOPIC

Almost anything *can* be argued, but not everything *should* be argued. You won't be taken seriously if you seem to argue indiscriminately. Argument should be the result of reflection, not reflex, and argumentation is a skill that should be practiced selectively.

When choosing a topic for a written argument, you should avoid questions that can be easily settled by referring to an authority, such as a dictionary or an encyclopedia. There is no point in arguing about how to spell "separate" or about what city is the capital of Australia: there is only one correct answer. Choose a topic that can inspire a variety of answers, any one of which can be "correct" to some degree. Your challenge is to define and support a position in which you believe even though other people do not yet share your belief.

Almost all intelligent arguments involve *opinions,* but not all opinions lead to good written arguments. There is no reason to argue an opinion with which almost no one would disagree. An essay designed to "prove" that puppies are cute or that vacations can be fun is unlikely to generate much excitement. Don't belabor the obvious. Choose a topic that is likely to inspire at least some controversy, but don't feel that you suddenly need to acquire strange and eccentric opinions.

Be careful to distinguish between opinions that are a matter of taste and those that are a question of judgment. Some people like broccoli, and some people don't. You may be the world's foremost broccoli lover, but no matter how hard you try, you will not convince someone who hates green vegetables to head quickly to the produce department of the nearest supermarket. A gifted stylist, writing in the manner of Charles Lamb or E. B. White, could probably compose an amusing essay on broccoli that would be a delight to read. But it is one thing to describe our tastes and quite another to insist that others share them. We all have firmly entrenched likes and dislikes. Persuasion in matters of taste is usually beyond the reach of what can be accomplished through the written word—unless you happen to command the resources of an unusually effective advertising agency.

Taste is a matter of personal preference. Whether we prefer green to blue or daffodils to tulips is unlikely to affect anyone but ourselves. Questions of judgment are more substantial than matters of taste because judgment cannot be divorced from logic. Our judgments are determined by our beliefs, behind which are basic principles to which we try to remain consistent. These principles ultimately lead us to decide that some judgments are correct and others are not, so judgment has greater implications than taste. Should a university require freshmen to live in dormitories? Should men and women live together before getting married? Should parents spank their children? All these are questions of judgment.

In written argumentation, questions of judgment provide the best subjects. Because they are complex, they offer more avenues to explore. This does not mean that you must cover every aspect of a question in a single essay. Good subjects have many possibilities, and the essays that are written on them will take many different directions. If you try to explore too many directions at once, you might easily get lost—or lose your readers along the way.

When planning your written argument, you may benefit from distinguishing between a *subject* and a *topic:* A topic is part of a subject. For example, "gun control" is a subject from which many different topics can be derived. Possibilities include: state laws affecting handguns, federal laws on the possession of military weapons, the constitutional right to "keep and bear arms," and gun use in crime. Each of these topics could be narrowed further. Someone interested in gun use in crime might focus on the extent to which criminals benefit from easy access to guns or on whether owning a gun serves as a deterrent to crime. Because it is easier to do justice to a well-focused topic than to a broad subject, choosing a topic is one of the most important choices writers need to make.

Some writers successfully define their topics before they begin to write. Others begin to write on one topic and then discover that they are more interested in a different topic, which may or may not be related. Still other writers use specific writing techniques for generating topics. At times, you will be required to write on a topic that has been assigned to you. But whenever you have freedom to choose your own topic, remember that writing may help you to discover what you want to write about. *Freewriting*—writing nonstop for five to ten minutes without worrying about grammar, spelling, style, organization, or repetition—often leads writers to discover that they have more ideas than they had realized. Similarly, *brainstorming*—listing as many aspects about a subject or a topic as come to mind during ten minutes or so—can help to focus an essay and to identify several essential points. In short, you do not need to choose your topic before you can even begin writing, but you should choose and develop a clearly defined topic before you submit an essay for evaluation.

Whether you choose a topic before you begin to write or use writing to discover a topic, ask yourself the following questions:

- Do I know exactly what my topic is?
- Is this topic suitable for the length of the work I am planning to write?
- Do I have an opinion about this topic?
- Would anyone disagree with my opinion?
- Can I hope to persuade others to agree with my opinion?
- Can I support my opinion with evidence?

If you answer "yes" to all of these questions, you can proceed with confidence.

Exercise I

Robert L. Rose is a staff writer for *The Wall Street Journal,* which published the following news story on February 6, 1990. After you have read it, frame at least three separate questions about the issue discussed in this piece. Then ask yourself if any of your questions are questions of judgment. Identify the question that could best lead to a written argument.

ROBERT L. ROSE

IS SAVING LEGAL?

A penny saved is a penny earned. Usually.   1

Take the case of Grace Capetillo, a 36-year-old single mother with a   2
true talent for parsimony. To save on clothing, Ms. Capetillo dresses herself
plainly in thrift-store finds. To cut her grocery bill, she stocks up on 67-cent
boxes of saltines and 39-cent cans of chicken soup.

When Ms. Capetillo's five-year-old daughter, Michelle, asked for "Li'l   3
Miss Makeup" for Christmas, her mother bypassed Toys "R" Us, where the
doll retails for $19.99. Instead, she found one at Goodwill—for $1.89. She
cleaned it up and tied a pink ribbon in its hair before giving the doll to
Michelle. Ms. Capetillo found the popular Mr. Potato Head at Goodwill, too,
assembling the plastic toy one piece at a time from the used toy bin. It cost her
79 cents, and saved $3.18.

Whose Money?

Ms. Capetillo's stingy strategies helped her build a savings account of more   4
than $3,000 in the last four years. Her goal was to put away enough to buy a
new washing machine and maybe one day help send Michelle to college. To

some, this might make her an example of virtue in her gritty North Side neighborhood, known more for boarded-up houses than high aspirations. But there was just one catch: Ms. Capetillo is on welfare—$440 a month, plus $60 in food stamps—and saving that much money on public aid is against the law. When welfare officials found out about it, they were quick to act. Ms. Capetillo, they charged, was saving at the expense of taxpayers.

Last month, the Milwaukee County Department of Social Services took   5
her to court, charged her with fraud and demanded she return the savings— and thousands more for a total of $15,545. Ms. Capetillo says she didn't know it, but under the federal program Aid to Families with Dependent Children, she was ineligible for assistance after the day in 1985 when her savings eclipsed $1,000.

Uncle Sam wanted the money back.   6

"Tax dollars are going to support a person's basic needs on the AFDC   7
program," says Robert Davis, associate director of the Milwaukee social serv- ices department. Federal rules, and the spirit of the program, don't intend for "people to take the money and put it in a savings account."

Welfare's Role

Ms. Capetillo's troubles began in 1988, when the social services department   8
discovered the savings account she had opened in 1984. The tipoff: The de- partment had matched its records with those supplied by her bank to the Inter- nal Revenue Service.

Next, the sheriff department's welfare fraud squad went into action. In-   9
vestigators contacted the M&I Bank two blocks from Ms. Capetillo's apart- ment and found she had "maintained $1,000 consistently" in her savings account from Aug. 1, 1985 through May 31, 1988.

In an interview that May with investigators, Ms. Capetillo admitted she   10
hadn't reported the savings account to the department. After doing a little arithmetic, welfare officials figured she should repay $15,545—the amount of monthly aid she received after her bank balance passed $1,000. (The assistant district attorney later considered that harsh; he lowered the figure to $3,000.)

But the judge who got her case found it hard to believe Ms. Capetillo   11
was motivated by fraud. Indeed, for Ms. Capetillo, thriftiness had been a way of life. Her father instilled the lessons of economizing, supporting his nine children on his modest income from a local tannery.

After Michelle was born, Ms. Capetillo began drawing aid—and saving   12
in earnest. She says she rents the second floor of her father's duplex for $300 a month (though the welfare department says it suspects she was able to save so much by skipping at least some rent payments). In the summer, she looks for second-hand winter clothes and in the winter shops for warm-weather outfits to snare out-of-season bargains. When Michelle's T-shirts grew tight, her mother snipped them below the underarm so they'd last longer.

"She cared for her daughter well, but simply," says Donna Paul, the   13
court-appointed attorney who defended Ms. Capetillo. "With inflation, all Grace could expect was for government aid to become more inadequate."

Now that Michelle is getting ready to enter the first grade, Ms. Capetillo   14
says she will no longer have to stay home to care for the child. She says she
plans to look for full-time work or go back to school to train to be a nurse's
aide.

But her round face, framed by shoulder-length black hair, still brightens   15
at the prospect of bargain-hunting. At her favorite supermarket, her eyes dart
from item to item. She spots the display of generic saltine crackers. "See that?
That's cheap," she pronounces, dropping a box in her grocery cart.

The total bill comes to $5.98, but Ms. Capetillo forgot the coupon that   16
entitles her to free bacon for spending more than $5. She pockets the receipt,
and vows to return for the bacon.

After the law caught up with her, Ms. Capetillo reduced her savings to   17
avoid having her welfare checks cut off. She bought her new washing machine,
a used stove to replace her hotplate, a $40 refrigerator and a new bedroom set
for Michelle. But that didn't resolve the charge of fraud.

Finally, her day in court arrived. At first, Circuit Court Judge Charles B.   18
Schudson had trouble figuring out Ms. Capetillo's crime. To him, welfare
fraud meant double dipping: collecting full benefits and holding a job at the
same time.

After the lawyers explained the rules about saving money, he made it   19
clear he didn't think much of the rules. "I don't know how much more powerfully we could say it to the poor in our society: Don't try to save," he said.
Judge Schudson said it was "ironic" that the case came as President Bush promotes his plan for Family Savings Accounts. "Apparently, that's an incentive
that this country would only give to the rich."

The Limits of Aid

Others differ. County welfare worker Sophia Partipilo says Ms. Capetillo's   20
savings raise the question of whether she needed a welfare check at all. "We're
not a savings and loan," says Ms. Partipilo, who handled the case. "We don't
hand out toasters at the end of the month. We're here to get you over the
rough times."

Ms. Capetillo could have fought the charge. Her lawyer and even the   21
judge said later that there was a good chance a jury would have sided with
the welfare mother. Even the prosecutor admits that had she simply spent
the money, rather than saving it, she could have avoided a run-in with the
law.

But for Ms. Capetillo, going to court once was enough. She was so   22
frightened and her throat was so dry that the judge could barely hear her speak.
She pleaded guilty to "failure to report change in circumstance." The judge
sentenced her to one-year probation and ordered her to repay $1,000.

A few days later, Ms. Capetillo, who remains on welfare, returns from a   23
shopping trip and is met by Michelle. Banana in hand, Michelle greets her
mother with a smile and a gingerbread man she made at half-day kindergarten.

"Now you can see why I do what I do," says Ms. Capetillo. ■   24

DEFINING YOUR AUDIENCE

Good writers remember their *audience*—the person or people with whom they are trying to communicate. For example, your audience might consist of a single professor (when no one else will be reading what you write), a group of students (your classmates or members of a writing group), or the citizens of your community (as in a letter to the editor of a newspaper or magazine). All of these are examples of "particular audiences," and you can make certain assumptions about these readers based on your own observations and experience with them.

Instead of writing for a particular audience, some writers prefer to write for a general or universal audience—one in which all readers will have the intelligence and goodwill to listen to a reasonable stranger. When you write for a general audience, a particular audience (such as your professor) may cooperate by reading your work as a member of the larger audience you have invoked. Whatever the size and particularity of the audience you envision, you should maintain the same sense of audience throughout your entire essay.

Defining your audience can help you to choose your topic because a particular audience is likely to find some topics more interesting than others. A clear sense of audience can also help you to shape your style. It would be a mistake, for example, to use complicated technical language when writing for a general audience, and it would be just as foolish to address an audience of experts as if they knew nothing about your topic. You need to avoid confusing people but you must also be careful not to insult their intelligence. Finally, a clear sense of audience will help you to choose the points you want to emphasize in order to be persuasive and to anticipate the objections that might be raised by readers who disagree with you.

Whether your audience is particular or general, you should assume that intelligent and fair-minded people are usually skeptical about sweeping generalizations and unsupported claims. Unless you are the keynote speaker at a political convention, assigned to rally the members of your party by telling them exactly what they want to hear, there is no reason to expect people to agree with you. If your audience already agrees with you, what's the point of your argument? Whom are you trying to convince? Remember that the immediate purpose of an argument is almost always to convert people to your point of view. Of course, an audience may be entirely neutral, having no opinion at all on the subject that concerns you. But by imagining a skeptical audience, you will be able to anticipate the opposition and offer counterarguments, thus building a stronger case.

Before you draft your essay, try listing the reasons why you believe as you do. You may not have the space, in a short essay, to discuss all of the points you have listed. Rank the points in order of their importance, and consider the degree to which they would probably impress the audience for whom you are writing. Once you have done this, compose another list: reasons why people might disagree with you. Having explored the opposition's point of view, ask yourself why you have not been persuaded to abandon your own beliefs. What flaw do you see in the reasoning of your opponents? Add to your second list a short rebuttal of each of your opponents' arguments.

You are likely to discover that the opposition has at least one good argument, an argument that you cannot answer. There should be nothing surprising about this. We may like to flatter ourselves by believing that Truth is on our side. In our weaker moments, we may like to pretend that anyone who disagrees with us is either ignorant or corrupt. But serious and prolonged controversies almost always continue because the opposition has at least one valid concern. Be prepared to concede a point to your opponents when it seems appropriate to do so. You must consider and respond to their views, but your responses do not always have to take the form of rebuttals. When you have no rebuttal and recognize that your opponents' case has some merit, be honest and generous enough to say so.

By making concessions to your opposition, you demonstrate to your audience that you are trying to be fair. Far from weakening your own case, an occasional concession can help bridge the gulf between you and your opponents, making it easier for you to reach a more substantial agreement. It's hard to convince opponents that your views deserve to be taken seriously when you have belligerently insisted that they are completely wrong and you are completely right. Life is seldom so simple. Human nature being what it is, most people will listen more readily to an argument that offers some recognition of their views.

You must be careful, however, not to concede too much. If you find yourself utterly without counterarguments and ready to concede numerous points, you need to reconsider the topic you have chosen. In a short essay, you can usually afford to make only one or two concessions. Too many concessions are likely to confuse readers who are uncertain about what they think. Why should they be persuaded by you when you seem half persuaded by your opponents?

Having a good sense of audience also means illustrating your case with specific examples your audience can readily understand. It's hard to make people care about abstractions; good writers try to make the abstract concrete. Remember that it is easy to lose the attention of your audience, so try to address its most probable concerns.

There is, however, a great different between responding to the interests of your audience by discussing what it wants to know and twisting what you say to please an audience with exactly what it wants to hear. The foremost responsibility of any writer is to tell the truth as she or he sees it. What we mean by "truth" often has many dimensions. When limited space forces us to be selective, it is wise to focus on those facets of our topic that will be the most effective with the audience we are attempting to sway. But it is one thing to focus and quite another to mislead. Never write anything for one audience that you would be compelled to deny before another. Hypocrites are seldom persuasive, and no amount of verbal agility can compensate for a loss of confidence in a writer's character.

To better understand the importance of audience in argumentation, consider the following essay, which was originally published as an editorial in a college newspaper.

TO SKIP OR NOT TO SKIP: A STUDENT DILEMMA

1   This is college, right? The four-year deal offering growth, maturity, experience, and knowledge? A place to be truly independent?

2   Because sometimes I can't tell. Sometimes this place downright reeks of paternal instincts. Just ask the freshmen and sophomores, who are by class rank alone guaranteed two full years of twenty-four-hour supervision, orchestrated activities, and group showers.

3   But the forced dorm migration of underclassmen has been bitched about before, to no avail. University policy is, it seems, set in stone. It ranks right up there with ingrown toe nails for sheer evasion and longevity.

4   But there's another university policy that has no merit as a policy and no place in a university. Mandatory Attendance Policy: wherein faculty members attempt the high school hall monitor–college instructor maneuver. It's a difficult trick to justify as professors place the attendance percentage of their choice above a student's proven abilities on graded material.

5   Profs rationalize out a lot of arguments to support the policy. Participation is a popular one. I had a professor whose methods for lowering grades so irritated me I used to skip on purpose. He said, "Classroom participation is a very important part of this introductory course. Obviously, if you are not present, you cannot be participating."

6   Equally obvious, though not stated by the prof, is the fact that one can be perpetually present but participate as little as one who is absent. So who's the better student—the one who makes a meaningless appearance, or the one who is busy with something else? And who gets the points docked?

7   The rest of his policy was characteristically vague, mentioning that absences "could" result in a lower grade. Constant ambiguity is the second big problem with formal policies. It's tough for teachers to figure out just how much to let attendance affect grade point. So they doubletalk.

8   According to the UWSP catalog, faculty are to provide "clear explanation" of attendance policy. Right. Based on the language actually used, ninety-five percent of UWSP faculty are functionally incapable of uttering a single binding statement. In an effort to offend no one while retaining all power of action. profs write things like (these are actual policies): "I trust students to make their own judgments and choices about coming, or not coming to class." But then continues: "Habitual and excessive absence is grounds for failure." What happened to trust? What good are the choices?

9   Or this: "More than three absences may negatively affect your grade." Then again, they may not. Who knows? And this one: "I consider every one of you in here to be mature adults. However, I reserve the right to alter grades based on attendance."

10   You reserve the right? By virtue of your saying so? Is that like calling the front seat?

11   Another argument that profs cling to goes something like, "Future employers, by God, aren't going to put up with absenteeism." Well, let's take a reality pill. I think most students

can grasp the difference between cutting an occasional class, which they paid for, and cutting at work, when they're the ones on salary. See, college students are capable of bi-level thought control, nowadays. (It's all those computers.)

In summary, mandatory attendance should be abolished because:

1. It is irrelevant. Roughly the same number of students will either skip or attend, regardless of what a piece of paper says. If the course is worth anything.

2. It is ineffective. It automatically measures neither participation, ability, or gained knowledge. That's what tests are for. Grades are what you end up knowing, not how many times you sat there to figure it out.

3. It is insulting. A college student is capable of determining a personal schedule, one that may or may not always meet with faculty wishes. An institution committed to the fostering of personal growth cannot operate under rules that patronize or minimize the role an adult should claim for himself.

4. It is arbitrary. A prof has no right and no ability to factor in an unrealistic measure of performance. A student should be penalized no more than what the natural consequence of an absence is—the missing of one day's direct delivery of material.

5. It abolishes free choice. By the addition of a factor that cannot be fought. We are not at a university to learn conformity. As adults, we reserve the right to choose as we see fit, even if we choose badly.

Finally, I would ask faculty to consider this: We have for some time upheld in this nation the sacred principle of separation of church and state; i.e., You are not God.

Karen Rivedal
Editor

Karen chose a topic that would certainly interest many college students, the audience for whom she saw herself writing. Her thesis is clear: Mandatory class attendance should not be required of college students. And her writing is lively enough to hold the attention of many readers. All this is good.

Unfortunately, Karen's argument has a number of flaws. In paragraph 6 she offers what logicians call "a false dilemma." By asking, "So who's the better student—the one who makes a meaningless appearance, or the one who is busy with something else?" she has ignored at least two other possibilities. Appearance in class is likely to be meaningful to at least some students, and cutting class may be meaningless if the "something else" occupying a student's attention is a waste of time. The comparison in paragraph 10 between reserving the right to lower grades because of poor attendance and "calling the front seat" is confusing. (In conversation after the initial publication of this essay, Karen explained to me that she was making a comparison between professors who "reserve the right to alter grades" and children who call "I got the front seat" when going out in the family car. I then pointed out that this analogy could easily be used against her. The driver *must* sit in the front seat, and surely whoever is teaching a class is analogous to the driver of a car rather than one of its passengers.) In paragraph 13 Karen claims, "Roughly the same number of students will either skip or attend, regardless of what a piece of paper says," but she offers no evidence to support this claim, which is really no more than guesswork. And since Karen herself admits that many students skip class despite mandatory attendance policies, her claim in paragraph 17 that required attendance "abolishes free choice" does not hold up.

These lapses in logic aside, the major problem with this argument is that Karen misjudged her audience. She forgot that professors, as well as students, read the school newspaper. Since students cannot change the policies of their professors, but professors themselves can usually do so, she has overlooked the very audience that she most needs to reach. Moreover, not only has she failed to include professors within her audience, but she has actually gone so far as to insult them. Someone who is told that she or he is "functionally incapable of uttering a single binding statement" (paragraph 8) is unlikely to feel motivated to change. Only in the very last paragraph of this essay does Karen specifically address the faculty, and this proves to be simply the occasion for a final insult. There may be professors who take themselves too seriously, but are there really that many who believe that they are divine?

It's a shame that it's so easy to poke holes in this argument, because Karen deserves credit for boldly calling attention to policies that may indeed be wrong. Recognizing that her original argument was flawed, but still believing strongly that mandatory class attendance is inappropriate for college students, Karen decided to rewrite her essay. Here is her revision.

Absent at What Price?
Karen Rivedal

This is college, right? A place to break old ties, solve problems, and make decisions? Higher education is, I thought, the pursuit of knowledge in a way that's a step beyond the paternal hand-holding of high school. It's the act of learning performed in a more dynamic atmosphere, rich with individual freedom, discourse, and debate.   1

Because sometimes I can't tell. Some university traditions cloud the full intent of higher education. Take mandatory attendance policies, wherein faculty members attempt the high school hall monitor–college instructor maneuver. It's a difficult trick to justify as professors place the attendance percentage of their choice above a student's proven abilities on graded material.   2

This isn't to say that the idea of attendance itself is unsound. Clearly, personal interaction between teacher and students is preferable to textbook teaching alone. It's the mandatory attendance policy, within an academic community committed to the higher education of adults, that worries me.   3

Professors, however, offer several arguments to support the practice. Participation is a popular one. I had a professor whose methods for lowering grades so irritated me that I used to skip out of spite. He said,   4

"Classroom participation is a very important part of this introductory course. Obviously, if you are not present, you cannot be participating."

Equally obvious, though, is the fact that one can be perpetually present, but participate as little as one who is absent. Participation lacks an adequate definition. There's no way of knowing, on the face of it, if a silent student is necessarily a learning student. Similarly, an instructor has no way of knowing for what purpose or advantage a student may miss a class, and therefore no ability to determine its relative validity.   5

As a learning indicator, then, mandatory attendance policy is flawed. It automatically measures neither participation, ability, or gained knowledge. That's what tests are for. A final grade should reflect what a student ends up knowing, rather than the artificial consequences of demerit points.   6

Some faculty recognize the shortcomings of a no-exceptions mandatory attendance policy and respond with partial policies. Constant ambiguity is characteristic of this approach and troublesome for the student who wants to know just where he or she stands. It's tough for teachers to figure out just how much to let attendance affect grade point. So they doubletalk.   7

This, for example, is taken from an actual policy: "I trust students to make their own judgments and choices about coming, or not coming, to class." It then continues: "Habitual and excessive absence is grounds for failure." What happened to trust? What good are the choices?   8

Or this: "More than three absences may negatively affect your grade." Then again, they may not. Who knows? And this one: "I consider every one of you in here to be mature adults. However, I reserve the right to alter grades based on attendance."   9

This seems to say, what you can prove you have learned from this class takes a back seat to how much I think you should know based on your attendance. What the teacher says goes—just like in high school.   10

Professors who set up attendance policies like these believe, with good reason, that they are helping students to learn by ensuring their attendance. But the securing of this end by requirement eliminates an important element of learning. Removing the freedom to make the decision is removing the need to think. An institution committed to the fostering of personal growth cannot operate under rules that patronize or minimize the role an adult should claim for himself.   11

A grading policy that relies on the student's proven abilities certainly takes the guesswork out of grade assigning for teachers. This take-no-prisoners method, however, also demands a high, some say unfairly high, level of personal student maturity. Younger students especially may need, they say, the extra structuring that a policy provides.   12

But forfeiting an attendance policy doesn't mean that a teacher has to resign his humanity, too. Teachers who care to can still take five minutes to   13 warn an often absent student about the possible consequences, or let the first test score tell the story. As much as dedicated teachers want students to learn, the activity is still a personal one. Students must want to.

A "real-world" argument that professors often use goes something like,   14 "Future employers aren't going to put up with absenteeism, so get used to it now." Well, let's take a reality pill. I think most students can differentiate between cutting an occasional class, which they paid for, and missing at work, when they're the ones on salary.

Students who intelligently protest an institution's policies, such as   15 mandatory attendance requirements, are proof-in-action that college is working. These students are thinking, and learning to think and question is the underlying goal of all education. College is more than its rules, more than memorized facts. Rightly, college is knowledge, the testing of limits. To be valid, learning must include choice and the freedom to make mistakes. To rely on mandatory attendance for learning is to subvert the fullest aims of that education.

In revising her essay, Karen has retained both her thesis and her own distinctive voice. Such phrases as "the high school hall monitor–college instructor maneuver," the "take-no-prisoners method," and "let's take a reality pill" are still recognizably her own. But her argument is now more compelling. In addition to eliminating the fallacies that marred her original version, Karen included new material that strengthens her case. Paragraph 3 offers a much needed clarification, reassuring readers that an argument against a mandatory attendance policy is not the same as an argument against attending class. Paragraph 7 begins with a fairly sympathetic reference to professors, and paragraph 11 opens with a clear attempt to anticipate opposition. Paragraph 12 includes another attempt to anticipate opposition, and paragraph 13, with its reference to "dedicated teachers," is much more likely to appeal to the professors in Karen's audience than any statements in the original version did. Finally, the conclusion of this essay is now much improved. It successfully links the question of mandatory attendance policies with the purpose of higher education as defined in the opening paragraph.

DEFINING YOUR TERMS

If you want your arguments to be convincing, they must be understood by your audience. To make sure that your ideas are understandable, you must be careful in your use of words. It is especially important to clarify any terms essential to your argument. Unfortunately, many writers of argument fail to define the words they use. It is not unusual, for example, to find writers advocating or opposing gun control without defining exactly what they mean by "gun control." Many arguments use words such as "censorship," "society," "legitimate," and "moral" so loosely that it is impossible to decide exactly what the writer means. When this happens, the entire argument can break down.

Don't feel that you need to define every word you use, but be certain to define any important word your audience might misunderstand. Avoid defining a word by using the same term or another term that is equally complex. For example, if you are opposed to the sale of pornography, you should be prepared to define what you mean by "pornography." It would not be especially helpful to tell your audience that pornography is "printed or visual material that is obscene" because this only raises the question: What is "obscene"? In an important ruling, the Supreme Court defined "obscene" as material that "the average person, applying community standards, would find . . . as a whole, appeals to the prurient interest," but even if you happened to have this definition at hand, you should ask yourself if "the average person" understands what "prurient" means—not to mention what the Court may have meant by "community standards." Unless you define your terms carefully, avoiding unnecessarily abstract language, you can end up writing an endless chain of definitions that require further explanation.

The easiest way to define a term is to consult a dictionary. However, some dictionaries are much better than others. For daily use, most writers usually refer to a good desk dictionary such as *The American Heritage Dictionary, The Random House Dictionary,* or *Webster's New Collegiate Dictionary.* A good general dictionary of this sort may provide you with an adequate working definition. You may also want to consider consulting the multivolume *Oxford English Dictionary,* which is available in most college libraries and is especially useful in showing how the usage of a word has changed over the years. Your audience might also appreciate the detailed information that specialized dictionaries in various subject areas can provide. Many such dictionaries are likely to be available in your college library. For example, if you are working on a paper in English literature, you might consult *A Concise Dictionary of Literary Terms* or *The Princeton Handbook of Poetic Terms.* For a paper in psychology, you might turn to *The Encyclopedic Dictionary of Psychology,* or, for a paper on a musical topic, *The New Grove's Dictionary of Music and Musicians.* There are also dictionaries for medical, legal, philosophical, and theoretical terms as well as for each of the natural sciences. When using specialized dictionaries, you will often find valuable information, but remember that the definition that appears in your paper should not be more difficult than the word or phrase you originally set out to define.

Instead of relying exclusively on dictionaries, it is often best to define a term or phrase in words of your own. You can choose from among several strategies:

- You can give synonyms.
- You can compare the term with other words with which it is likely to be confused and show how your term differs.

- You can define a word by showing what it is *not*.
- You can provide examples.

Writers frequently use several of these strategies to create a single definition; an entire essay could be devoted to defining one term. Here is an example written by a student.

Homicide
Geoff Rulland

You sit back in your lazy-boy, cold soda in hand, grab the remote control 1
and begin to flip through the channels in search of something interesting to
watch. Something on the channel nine news catches your ear. You listen
intently as the newscaster informs you that a man from a nearby town is
being charged with homicide. A lot of people would now sit back and continue the channel scan thinking that the man was a murderer. Would that
be a safe assumption?

When someone is charged with homicide it doesn't necessarily mean he 2
or she is a murderer. Homicide is classified in court as either "justifiable,"
"excusable," or "felonious." Murder, which falls into the class of felonious
homicide, is "the unlawful killing of a human being with malice afore-
thought," according to the American Heritage Dictionary. This means that
murder is always wrong, but specifying that murder is an "unlawful killing"
implies that killing a human being is not always unlawful. A justifiable
homicide would be a killing committed intentionally without any evil design
or under the circumstance of necessity. For example, when a police officer
is trying to catch a dangerous felon, using a gun to wound and possibly kill
could be justifiable. An excusable homicide would be the killing of a human
being accidentally or in self-defense, such as in the case of a burglar entering your home. Killing him may be the only thing that will save you or your
family. Manslaughter is another term often associated with killings that
aren't murders. The name gives the impression that someone was brutally
slain. Actually it is the accidental killing of one person by another, and it
may have been quite mild.

Black's Law Dictionary defines homicide as "the killing of any human 3
creature or the killing of one human being by the act, procurement, or
omission of another." In other words, it's the killing of one person by another in any manner. It doesn't matter if you hit a person accidentally with
your car, or if you purposely shot someone, or if you hired a professional
killer. Black's then goes on to state the definition as "the act of a human
being in taking away the life of another human being." The Webster's New

World Dictionary shortens all of that down to "any killing of one human being by another." The key word in this definition is "any." Webster's doesn't
say how the killing must be done; it just says that a person is killed.

Two words from the Latin language are the main composition of homi-   4
cide. The first one is homo meaning man and the other is caedere, which
ties it to killing, meaning to cut or kill. Homicida, meaning murderer, was
the form that was made from those two words which was later changed in
Latin to homicidium. After going through the Old French language, the
word then made its way into English and into its present form, homicide.

Homicide is not necessarily a crime. Even though all homicides result in   5
the loss of life, sometimes committing homicide is a person's only choice.
Homicide shouldn't be immediately judged as murder or something all-out
wrong. The word is "neutral" according to Black's Law Dictionary. It merely
states the act of killing and pronounces no judgment on its moral or legal
quality.

With this in mind, the next time you hear of a homicide on t.v. you   6
should keep your mind open and neutral. Don't immediately form the
opinion that it was a murder, because a lot of the times you may be
wrong. The word merely states that a person was killed, not necessarily
murdered.

In defining *homicide,* Geoff uses three of the strategies listed on pages
14–15: He provides examples of homicide; he compares homicide to such
terms as *murder* and *manslaughter;* and, by contrasting homicide with murder,
he clarifies what homicide is not. In addition to consulting two good desk dictionaries, *The American Heritage Dictionary* and *Webster's New World Dictionary,*
Geoff also took the trouble to consult a legal dictionary. *Black's Law Dictionary*
confirmed his sense that homicide is a much broader term than murder, and
this became the central idea of his essay. In paragraph 4, Geoff reports the
origin of the term. Any good dictionary will provide you with some information of this sort, but you must be alert for it. A brief etymology (or derivation)
usually appears in italics at either the beginning or end of dictionary definitions, and this information can often be helpful when you are trying to understand a complex term. In *Webster's New World Dictionary,* for example, the
definition of *homicide* begins:

[M.E.; O Fr.; L.L. *homicidium,* manslaughter, murder < L. *homicida,* murderer < *homo.* a man + *caedere,* to cut, kill]

Note that the arrows establish the sequence of the word's history. In this case,
they are pointing away from Latin (not toward it), indicating the Latin origin.
(Arrows pointing to the right would indicate that the earliest term came first,
with others appearing in chronological order.) A key to abbreviations used in

a dictionary can be found by consulting its table of contents. When you do so, you will probably find that your dictionary contains more information than you had realized.

Before leaving this essay, note that it reveals a good sense of audience. Writing for freshmen in an English class, Geoff recognized that many of his fellow students might find definition to be dry reading. To capture their attention, he begins with an imaginary anecdote addressed, in the second person, directly to readers. Compared with the thousands of essays that have begun "According to *Webster's* . . . ," this introduction (with which the conclusion is subsequently linked) seems original and likely to encourage further reading. But you should not assume that this strategy would be appropriate for any audience or any writing occasion.

Understanding the meaning of *homicide* could be essential in an argument on capital punishment or gun control. When writing an argument, however, you will usually need to define your terms within a paragraph or two. Even if you cannot employ all the strategies that you might use in an extended definition, remember your various options and decide which will be most effective for your purpose within the space available. (For examples of essays that incorporate definition within arguments, see pages 218–223, 272–276, and 312–318.)

In addition to achieving clarity, definition helps to control an argument by eliminating misunderstandings that can cause an audience to be inappropriately hostile or to jump to a conclusion that is different from your own. By carefully defining your terms, you limit a discussion to what you want to discuss. This increases the likelihood of your gaining a fair hearing for your views.

Exercise 2

Using the strategies listed on pages 14 and 15, write an essay of definition for one of the following terms:

feminist
society
real world
middle class
well–rounded education
affirmative action
child abuse
eating disorder
alcoholism
learning disability
civil rights
progress
liberal
family

ORGANIZING YOUR ARGUMENT

If you have chosen your subject carefully and given sufficient thought to your audience and its concerns (paying particular attention to any objections that could be raised against whatever you wish to advocate), it should not be difficult to organize an argumentative essay. Listing ideas generated by the concerns discussed in the previous sections will provide you with what amounts to a rough outline, but you must now consider two additional questions: "Where and how should I begin my argument?" and "How can I most efficiently include in my argument the various counterarguments that I have anticipated and responded to?" The answers to these questions will vary from one essay to another. But although arguments can take many forms, written arguments usually employ logic, of which there are two widely accepted types: inductive and deductive reasoning.

Reasoning Inductively

When we use *induction,* we are drawing a conclusion based on specific evidence. Our argument rests on a foundation of details that we have accumulated for its support. This is the type of reasoning that we use most frequently in daily life. We look at the sky outside our window, check the thermometer, and may even listen to a weather forecast before dressing to face the day. If the sun is shining, the temperature high, and the forecast favorable, we would be making a reasonable conclusion if we decided to dress lightly and leave our umbrellas at home. We haven't *proved* that the day will be warm and pleasant, we have only *concluded* that it will be. This is all we can usually do in an inductive argument: arrive at a conclusion that seems likely to be true. Ultimate and positive proof is usually beyond reach, and writers who recognize this and proceed accordingly will usually arrive at conclusions that are both moderate and thoughtful. Such writers recognize the possibility of an unanticipated factor undermining even the best of arguments. A lovely morning can yield to a miserable afternoon, and we may be drenched in a downpour as we hurry home on the day that began so pleasantly.

Inductive reasoning is especially important in scientific experimentation. A research scientist may have a theory that she hopes to prove. But to work toward proving this theory, hundreds, thousands, and even tens of thousands of experiments may have to be conducted to eliminate variables and gather enough data to justify a generally applicable conclusion. Well-researched scientific conclusions sometimes reach a point where they seem uncontestable. It's been many years since Congress required the manufacturers of cigarettes to put a warning on every package stating that smoking can be harmful to your health. Since then, additional research has supported the conclusion that smoking can indeed be dangerous, especially to the lungs and the heart. That "smoking can be harmful to your health" now seems to have entered the realm of established fact. But biologists, chemists, physicists, and physicians are usually aware that the history of science, and the history of medicine in particular, is an argumentative history full of debate. Methods and beliefs established over many generations can be overthrown by a new discovery. Within a few years, that "new discovery" can also come under challenge. So the serious researcher goes back to the lab and keeps on working—ever mindful that truth is hard to find.

Induction is also essential in law enforcement. The police are supposed to have evidence against someone before making an arrest. Consider, for example, the way a detective works. A good detective does not arrive at the scene of a crime already certain about what happened. If the crime seems to be part of a pattern, the detective may already have a suspicion about who is responsible. But a good investigator will want to make a careful study of every piece of evidence that can be gathered. A room may be dusted for fingerprints, a murder victim photographed as found, and if the body is lying on the floor, a chalk outline may be drawn around it for future study. Every item within the room will be cataloged. Neighbors, relatives, employers, or employees will be questioned. The best detective is usually the detective with the best eye for detail and the greatest determination to keep searching for the details that will be strong enough to bring a case to court. Similarly, a first-rate detective will also be honest enough never to overlook a fact that does not fit in with the rest of the evidence. The significance of every loose end must be examined to avoid the possibility of an unfair arrest and prosecution.

In making an inductive argument, you will reach a point at which you decide that you have offered enough evidence to support the thesis of your essay. When you are writing a college paper, you will probably decide that you have reached this point sooner than a scientist or a detective might. But whether you are writing a short essay or conducting an investigation, the process is essentially the same. When you stop citing evidence and move on to your conclusion, you have made what is known as an *inductive leap*. In an inductive essay, you must always offer interpretation or analysis of the evidence you have introduced; there will always be at least a slight gap between your evidence and your conclusion. It is over this gap that the writer must leap; the trick is to do it agilely. Good writers know that their evidence must be in proportion to their conclusion: The bolder the conclusion, the more evidence is needed to back it up. Remember the old adage about "jumping to conclusions," and realize that you'll need the momentum of a running start to make more than a moderate leap at any one time.

If you listen closely to the conversation of the people around you, the chances are good that you'll hear examples of faulty inductive reasoning. When someone says, "I don't like Chinese food," and reveals, under questioning, that his only experience with Chinese food was a frozen Chinese dinner, we cannot take the opinion seriously. A sweeping conclusion has been drawn from flimsy evidence. People who claim to know "all about" complex subjects often reveal that they actually know very little. Only a sexist claims to know all about men and women, and only a racist is foolish enough to generalize about the various racial groups that make up our society. Good writers are careful not to overgeneralize.

When you begin an inductive essay, you might cite a particular observation that strikes you as especially important. You might even begin with a short anecdote. A well-structured inductive essay would then gradually expand as the evidence accumulates, so that the conclusion is supported by numerous details. Here is an example of an inductive essay written by a student.

In Defense of Hunting
David Wagner

I killed my first buck when I was fourteen. I'd gone deer hunting with my   1
father and two of my uncles. I was cold and wet and anxious to get home,
but I knew what I had to do when I sighted the eight-point buck. Taking
careful aim, I fired at his chest, killing him quickly with a single shot.

I don't want to romanticize this experience, turning it into a noble rite of   2
passage. I did feel that I had proved myself somehow. It was important for
me to win my father's respect, and I welcomed the admiration I saw in his
eyes. But I've been hunting regularly for many years now, and earning the
approval of others no longer seems very important to me. I'd prefer to emphasize the facts about hunting, facts that must be acknowledged even by
people who are opposed to hunting.

It is a fact that hunters help to keep the deer population in balance with   3
the environment. Since so many of their natural predators have almost died
out in this state, the deer population could quickly grow much larger than
the land can support. Without hunting, thousands of deer would die slowly
of starvation in the leafless winter woods. This may sound like a self-
serving argument (like the words of a parent who beats a child and insists,
"This hurts me more than it does you; I'm only doing it for your own good").
But it is a fact that cannot be denied.

It is also a fact that hunters provide a valuable source of revenue for the   4
state. The registration and licensing fees we pay are used by the Department of Natural Resources to reforest barren land, preserve wetlands, and
protect endangered species. Also there are many counties in this state that
depend upon the money that hunters spend on food, gas, and lodging.
"Tourism" is our third largest industry, and all of this money isn't being
spent at luxurious lakeside resorts. Opponents of hunting should realize
that hunting is the most active in some of our poorest, rural counties—and
realize what hunting means to the people who live in these areas.

It is also a fact that there are hundreds of men and women for whom   5
hunting is an economic necessity and not a sport. Properly preserved, the
meat that comes from a deer can help a family survive a long winter. There
probably are hunters who think of hunting as a recreation. But all the

hunters I know—and I know at least twenty—dress their own deer and use every pound of the venison they salt, smoke, or freeze. There may be a lot of people who don't have to worry about spending $3.00 a pound for steak, but I'm not one of them. My family needs the meat we earn by hunting.

I have to admit that there are hunters who act irresponsibly by trespass-   6
ing where they are not wanted and, much worse, by abandoning animals that they have wounded. But there are many different kinds of irresponsibility. Look around and you will see many irresponsible drivers, but we don't respond to them by banning driving altogether. An irresponsible minority is no reason to attack a responsible majority.

I've listened to many arguments against hunting, and it seems to me   7
that what really bothers most of the people who are opposed to hunting is the idea that hunters <u>enjoy</u> killing. I can't speak for all hunters, but I can speak for myself and the many hunters I personally know. I myself have never found pleasure in killing a deer. I think that deer are beautiful and incredibly graceful, especially when in movement. I don't "enjoy" putting an end to a beautiful animal's life. If I find any pleasure in the act of hunting, it comes from the knowledge that I am trying to be at least partially self-sufficient. I don't expect other people to do all my dirty work for me, and give me my meat neatly butchered and conveniently wrapped in plastic. I take responsibility for what I eat.

Lumping all hunters together as insensitive beer-drinking thugs is an   8
example of the mindless stereotyping that logic should teach us to avoid. The men and women who hunt are no worse than anyone else. And more often than not, the hunting we do is both honorable and important.

David has drawn on his own experience to make an articulate defense of hunting. He begins with an anecdote that helps to establish that he knows something about the subject he has chosen to write about. The first sentence in the second paragraph helps to deflect any skepticism his audience may feel at this early stage in his argument, and the last sentence in this paragraph serves as a transition into the facts that will be emphasized in the next three paragraphs. In the third paragraph, David introduces the evidence that should most impress his audience, if we assume that his audience is unhappy about the idea of killing animals. In paragraphs 4 and 5, he defends hunting on economic grounds. He offers a concession in paragraph 5 ("There probably are hunters who think of hunting as a recreation") and another concession in paragraph 6 ("I have to admit that there are hunters who act irresponsibly"). But after each of these concessions he manages to return smoothly to his own thesis. In paragraph 7, he anticipates an argument frequently made by people who oppose hunting and offers a counterargument that puts his opponents on the defensive. The concluding paragraph may be a little anticlimactic, but within the limitations of a short essay, David has made a strong argument.

Exercise 3

The following article first appeared in the October 26, 1993 issue of *The Wall Street Journal*. Published anonymously, it can be read as an editorial representing the *Journal's* position on whether or not government should give people more choices about which schools to attend. After you have read the article, determine (1) what position it takes and (2) what pieces of evidence lead inductively to that position.

ANONYMOUS

TEACHER KNOWS BEST

About 50% of urban-area public school teachers with school-age children send their chil-   1
dren to private schools. What do they know that we ought to know? — Columnist
George Will to [U.S.] National Education Association President Keith Geiger
on "This Week With David Brinkley." Aug. 30, 1993.
     "It's about 40%." — Mr. Geiger.

     For years, many of America's public school administrators and teachers   2
haven't entrusted their own system with the education of their own children.
Nationwide, public school teachers are about twice as likely as their neighbors
to send their children to private schools. They know better than anyone else
that, even as more money is poured into them, too many of America's public
schools are delivering a substandard product.
     The issue of public school employees spurning public schools when it   3
comes to their own kids is reaching critical mass in California. Teachers'
unions there are spending some $13 million to defeat Proposition 174,
which would give parents the option of using $2,600 vouchers—less than
half of what an average public school spends—to send their kids to private
schools.
     The California State Census Data Center, after analyzing the 1990 Cen-   4
sus, found that about 18.2% of the state's public school teachers send their children to private schools. That's nearly twice the statewide average for all households, which is 9.7%. The center also found that two out of five private school
teachers, those most likely to know the most about both systems, patronize
nonpublic schools.
     Phil Angelides, former chairman of the California Democratic Party, is   5
one who warns voters not to abandon "the tradition of the common school."
He says, "I am committed to giving the public schools more time to reform
themselves." However, he sheepishly admits his own children attend private
schools, mumbling "there are a lot of problems in the Sacramento system."

Some public school advocates keep their children in the system, but still   6
use their knowledge of it to get them out of marginal schools. Bill Honig,
California's superintendent of public instruction until his conviction last year
on conflict-of-interest charges, once moved his son out of the family home in
San Francisco to a home in the suburbs so he could attend classes there.

When Nobel prize-winning economist Milton Friedman recently spoke   7
in favor of school choice at the Pacific Research Institute, he was belligerently
challenged by Assemblywoman Vivien Bronshvag, a founder of the Marin
County Alliance for Public Schools. When he asked where her own children
went to school, she replied they attended public schools. Afterward, a neighbor
approached her and noted that he knew that two of the legislator's sons had
gone to an elite private high school. Ms. Bronshvag then became flustered,
and said at *one time* they'd gone to public schools.

Polly Williams, the Wisconsin state legislator who established Milwau-   8
kee's voucher program, says she is used to such evasions. A private survey
found some 40% of Milwaukee's public school teachers wouldn't send their
own children to the school where they teach. Rep. Williams says there was an
uproar from local teachers when she merely suggested a law that would require
public school teachers to educate their kids in public schools.

"President Clinton thinks it's fine to collect tax dollars in salary and use   9
them to send Chelsea to a private school, but he thinks it's a sin to allow other
parents to get back some of their own tax dollars to do the same thing," she
told us. "President Clinton shouldn't be the only person living in public housing who has that choice."   ■

Reasoning Deductively

Sometimes it is best to rest an argument on a fundamental truth, value, or
right rather than on specific pieces of evidence. You should try to be specific
within the course of such an essay, giving examples to support your case. But
in deductive reasoning, evidence is of secondary importance. Your first concern is to define a commonly accepted value or belief that will prepare the way
for the argument you want to make.

The Declaration of Independence, written by Thomas Jefferson (pp.
485–488), is a classic example of deductive reasoning. Although Jefferson cited
numerous grievances, he rested his argument on the belief that "all men are
created equal" and that they have "certain unalienable Rights" which King
George III had violated. This was a revolutionary idea in the eighteenth century, and even today there are many people who question it. But if we accept
the idea that "all men are created equal" and have an inherent right to "Life,
Liberty, and the pursuit of Happiness," then certain conclusions follow.

The right, value, or belief from which we wish to deduce our argument
is called our *premise*. Perhaps you have already had the experience, in the
middle of an argument, of someone saying to you, "What's your premise?" If
you are inexperienced in argumentation, a question of this sort may embarrass you and cause your argument to break down—which is probably what

your opponent had hoped. But whether we recognize it or not, we almost always have a premise lurking somewhere in the back of our minds. Deduction is most effective when we think about values we have automatically assumed and deliberately build our arguments on them.

A good premise satisfies two requirements. In the first place, it is general enough that your audience is likely to accept it, thus establishing a common ground between you and the audience you hope to persuade. On the other hand, the premise must still be specific enough so that it prepares the way for the argument that will follow. It usually takes much careful thought to frame a good premise. Relatively few people have carefully articulated values always in mind. We usually know what we want or what our conclusion is going to be—but it takes time to realize the fundamental beliefs that we have automatically assumed. For this is really what a premise amounts to: the underlying assumption that must be agreed on before the argument can begin to move along.

Because it is difficult to formulate an effective premise, it is often useful to work backward when you are outlining a deductive argument. You should know what conclusion you expect to reach. Write it down, and number it as statement 3. Now ask yourself why you believe statement 3. This should prompt a number of reasons; group them together as statement 2. Now that you can look both at your conclusion and at the immediate reasons that seem to justify it, ask yourself whether you've left anything out—something basic that you skipped over, assuming that everyone would agree with that already. When you can think back successfully to what this assumption is, knowing that it will vary from argument to argument, you have your premise, at least in rough draft form.

This may be difficult to grasp in the abstract, so consider an outline for a sample argument. Suppose that the forests in your state are slowly dying because of the pollution known as acid rain—one of the effects of burning fossil fuel, especially coal. Coal is being burned by numerous industries not only in your own state, but in neighboring states as well. You hadn't even realized that there was a problem with acid rain until last summer when fishing was prohibited in your favorite lake. You are very upset about this and declare, "Something ought to be done!" But as you begin to think about the problem, you recognize that you'll have to overcome at least two obstacles in deciding what that something should be. Only two years ago, you participated in a demonstration against nuclear power, and you'd also hate to see the United States become more dependent on foreign oil. So if you attack the process of burning coal for energy, you'll have to be prepared to recommend an acceptable alternative. The other question you must answer is: "Who's responsible for a problem that seems to be springing from many places in many states?" Moreover, if you do decide to argue for a radical reduction in coal consumption, you'll have to be prepared to anticipate the opposition: "What's this going to do to the coal miners?" someone might well ask. "Will you destroy the livelihood of some of the hardest working men and women in America?"

You realize that you have still another problem. Your assessment is for a 750-word deductive argument, and it's due the day after tomorrow. You feel strongly about the problem of acid rain, but you are not an energy expert. Your primary concern is with the effects of acid rain, which you've witnessed with your own eyes. And while you don't know much about industrial chemistry, you do know that acid rain is caused principally by public utilities burning coal that has a high percentage of sulfur in it. Recognizing that you lack the expertise to make a full-scale attack on coal consumption, you decide that you can at least go so far as to argue on behalf of using low-sulfur coal. In doing so, you will be able to reassure your audience that you want to keep coal miners at work, recognize the needs of industry, and do not expect the entire country to go solar by the end of the semester.

Taking out a sheet of paper, you begin to write down your outline in reverse:

3. Public utilities should not burn coal that is high in sulfur content.
2. Burning high-sulfur coal causes acid rain, and acid rain is killing American forests, endangering wildlife, and spoiling local fishing.

Before going any further, you realize that all of your reasons for opposing acid rain cannot be taken with equal degrees of seriousness. As much as you like to fish, recreation does not seem to be in the same league with your more general concern for forests and wildlife. You know that you want to describe the condition of your favorite lake at some point in your essay, because it gave you some firsthand experience with the problem and some vivid descriptive details. But you decide that you'd better not make too much of fishing in order to avoid the risk of sounding as if you care only about your own pleasure.

You now ask yourself what lies behind the "should" in your statement 3. How strong is it? Did you say "should" when you meant "must"? Thinking it over, you realize that you did mean "must," but now you must decide who or what is going to make that "must" happen. You decide that you can't trust industry to make this change on its own because you're asking it to spend more money than it has to. You know that as an individual you don't have the power to bring about the change you believe is necessary, but you also know that individuals become powerful when they band together. Individuals band together in various ways, but the most important—in terms of power—is probably the governments we elect to represent us. You should be careful with a term like "government" and avoid such statements as "The government ought to do something about this." Not only is the "something" vague, but we don't know what kind of government you want to take charge. Most of us are subject to government on at least three levels: municipal, state, and federal. You decide to argue for *federal* legislation, because acid rain is being generated in several different states—and then carried by air to still others.

You should now be ready to formulate your premise. Your conclusion is going to demand federal regulation, so, at the very beginning of your argument, you need to establish the principle that supports this conclusion. You realize that the federal government cannot solve all problems; you therefore must define the nature of the government's responsibility so that it will be clear that you are appealing legitimately to the right authority. Legally, the federal government has broad powers to regulate interstate commerce, and this may be a useful fact in your argument because most of the industries burning coal ship or receive goods across state lines. More specifically, ever since the creation of Yellowstone National Park in 1872, the U.S. government has undertaken a growing responsibility for protecting the environment. Acid rain is clearly an environmental issue, so you would not be demanding anything new, in terms of governmental responsibilities, if you appealed to the type of thinking that led to the creation of a national park system in 1916 and the Environmental Protection Agency in 1970.

You know, however, that there are many people who distrust the growth of big government, and you do not want to alienate anyone by appealing to Washington too early in the essay. A premise can be a single sentence, a full paragraph, or more—depending on the length and complexity of the argument. The function of a premise is to establish a widely accepted value that even your opponents should be able to share. You would probably be wise, therefore, to open this particular argument with a fairly general statement— something like: "We all have a joint responsibility to protect the environment in which we live and preserve the balance of nature on which our lives ultimately depend." As a thesis statement, this obviously needs to be developed in the paragraph that follows. In the second paragraph, you might cite some popular examples of joint action to preserve the environment, pointing out, for example, that most people are relieved to see a forest fire brought under control or an oil slick cleaned up before it engulfs a long stretch of coastline. Once you have cited examples of this sort, you could then remind your audience of the role of state and federal government in coping with such emergencies, and emphasize that many problems are too large for states to handle. By this stage in your essay, you should be able to narrow your focus to acid rain, secure in the knowledge that you have laid the foundation for a logical argument. *If* the U.S. government has a responsibility to help protect the environment, and *if* acid rain is a serious threat to the environment of several states, then it follows logically that the federal government should act to bring this problem under control. A brief outline of your argument would look something like this:

1. The federal government has the responsibility to protect the quality of American air, water, soil, and so on—what is commonly called "the environment."
2. Acid rain, which is caused principally by burning high-sulfur coal, is slowly killing American forests, endangering wildlife, and polluting lakes, rivers, and streams.
3. Therefore, the federal government should restrict the use of high-sulfur coal.

Once again, this is only an *outline*. An essay that makes this argument, explaining the problem in detail, anticipating the opposition, and providing meaningful concessions before reaching a clear and firm conclusion, would amount to at least several pages.

By outlining your argument in this way, you have followed the pattern of what is called a *syllogism,* a three-part argument in which the conclusion rests on two premises, the first of which is called "the major premise" because it is the point from which the writer begins to work toward a specific conclusion. Here is a simple example of a syllogism:

MAJOR PREMISE: All people have hearts.
MINOR PREMISE: John is a person.
CONCLUSION: Therefore, John has a heart.

If the major and minor premises are both true, then the conclusion reached should be true. Note that the minor premise and the major premise share a term in common. In a written argument, the "minor premise" would usually involve a specific case that relates to the more general statement with which the essay began.

A syllogism such as the one just cited may seem very simple. And it can be simple—if you're thinking clearly. On the other hand, it's even easier to write a syllogism (or an essay) that breaks down because of faulty reasoning. Consider the following example:

MAJOR PREMISE: All women like to cook.
MINOR PREMISE: Elizabeth is a woman.
CONCLUSION: Therefore, Elizabeth likes to cook.

Technically, the *form* here is valid. The two premises have a term in common, and if we accept both the major and minor premises, then we will have to accept the conclusion. But someone who thinks along these lines may be in for a surprise, especially if he has married Elizabeth confidently expecting her to cook his favorite dishes every night just as his mother used to do. Elizabeth may *hate* to cook, preferring to go out bowling at night or read the latest issue of the *Journal of Organic Chemistry.* A syllogism may be valid in terms of its organization, but it can also be *untrue* because it rests on a premise that can be easily disputed. Always remember that your major premise should inspire widespread agreement. Someone who launches an argument with the generalization that "all women like to cook," is likely to lose many readers before making it to the second sentence. Some generalizations make sense and some do not. Don't make the mistake of confusing generally accepted truths with privately held opinions. You may argue effectively on behalf of your opinions, but you cannot expect your audience to accept an easily debatable opinion as the foundation for an argument on behalf of yet another opinion. You may have many important things to say, but nobody is going to read them if alienated by your major premise.

You should also realize that there are many arguments in which a premise may be implied but not stated. You might overhear a conversation like this:

"I hear you and Elizabeth are getting married."

"Yes, that's true."

"Well, now that you've got a woman to cook for you, maybe you could invite me over for dinner sometime."

"Why do you think that Elizabeth will be doing the cooking?"

"Because she is a woman."

The first speaker has made a number of possible assumptions. He or she may believe that all women like to cook, or perhaps that all women are required to cook whether they like it or not. If the second speaker had the patience to continue this conversation, he would probably be able to discover the first speaker's premise. A syllogism that consists of only two parts is called an *enthymeme*. The part of the syllogism that has been omitted is usually the major premise, although it is occasionally the conclusion. Enthymemes usually result when a speaker or writer decides that it is unnecessary to state a point because it is obvious. What is obvious to someone trying to convince us with an enthymeme is not necessarily obvious to those of us who are trying to understand it. Although an enthymeme might reflect sound reasoning, the unstated part of the syllogism may reveal a flaw in the argument. When you encounter an enthymeme in your reading, you will often benefit from trying to reconstruct it as a full syllogism. Ask yourself what the writer has assumed, and then ask yourself if you agree with that assumption. One sign of a faulty deductive argument is that a questionable point has been assumed to be universally true, and we may need to discover this point before we can decide that the argument is either invalid or untrue.

Deductive reasoning, which begins with a generalization and works to a conclusion that follows from this generalization, can be thought of as the opposite of *inductive reasoning,* which begins with specific observations and ends with a conclusion that goes beyond any of the observations that led up to it. So that you can see what a deductive essay might look like, here is a short essay written by a student.

Preparation for Real Life
Kerstin LaPorte

In order for all children to reach their fullest potential as adults, it is im-   1
perative that they be prepared for careers that will help them be productive
members of society. Through the school system, taxpayers are responsible
for providing the educational opportunities for the development of minds,
so that when these students become adults, they too will be able to take
their turn for supporting the education of a future generation. But many
property owners have grown increasingly angry over the continual raises in
their taxes, and this hostility is being expressed towards the school system
that these overtaxed people have to support.

Cuts in spending are made, but these cuts are not reflected in the   2
sports department. The costs of maintaining sports programs are immense. The money that is taken out of the average annual school budget
for the equipment for training players, providing uniforms, and paying
coaches is more than most taxpayers realize. I too am a taxpayer whose
taxes go up each year. It is my view that this money would be better spent
on more up-to-date textbooks, lab equipment in the science department
that is not outdated, the newest computer technology, adequate tools and
machinery for the wood and metal shops, and libraries that are stocked
with the necessary books and magazines to complement all academic subjects. These investments will help a much larger percentage of the school
population and develop skills in accord with public needs.

It would be a terrible loss to may people who gain a great deal of satis-   3
faction out of participating in sports activities if these activities were to be
completely phased out. Therefore I advocate that sports programs for adolescents be community-sponsored. Clubs, sponsored by participating members,
local merchants, and private individuals, combined with fund-raising, would
provide all the sports activities that have no place in an academic field.

Proponents of school-sponsored sports would argue that the children of   4
lower-income families would not be able to participate in a community club
due to any costs this would incur. I firmly believe that if a student from a poor
family has a special talent, clubs would probably vie for his or her membership, helping him or her with any financial deficiencies. Once the potential for
a finely tuned athlete is seen, one who can help win the game or competition
for the club, funding will be available for his or her recruitment.

The importance of physical fitness is not to be understated. Students   5
need to be physically active in order to maintain mental and physical
stamina. Therefore, a scaled-down physical education department must remain within the schools. If done for at least 30 minutes 3-5 times a week,
aerobic exercise such as running, walking, and Jazzercize raises the heart
rate sufficiently to promote physical fitness. It is not necessary to build
pools, tennis courts, football stadiums, baseball parks, and basketball
courts. Neither have I ever been able to justify the purchasing of cross-
country skis, archery, weight lifting, and gymnastic equipment with academic funding. The maintenance of all the sport grounds and equipment
involved, plus the replacement of broken or outdated equipment is also an
added annual expense to the community.

Just as students who have similar interests form clubs, which meet out-   6
side of school hours, students interested in further physical fitness can organize biking, skiing, or running clubs. This would involve the use of their
own equipment, occur on their own time, and fill the void left if sports training is taken out of the school curriculum.

If there were to be a major change in the approach to our sports pro-   7
grams, the existing buildings, equipment, and outdoor facilities in and
around the schools must not be wasted. The clubs could lease those
premises, and any member would be eligible to utilize the facilities during
club hours. This would include student members, who could go and work
out during their free hours if they wanted. In this manner, the costs would
not detract from the academic necessities, and the facilities already built
would not go to waste.

Opponents to my proposal might ask, what about funding for such extra-   8
curricular activities as band, art, drama, and choir? There too, a very basic
introduction to these fields is reasonable, just as scaled-down physical education would suffice. If a child shows promise of being a gifted musician,
artist, actor, or singer, he or she can go on to obtain private instruction.

What about some of the academic subjects that seem unrelated to the job   9
market, such as history, sociology, and psychology? Successful interaction
between people depends on some knowledge of human nature, and these
subjects are only on an introductory basis. As far as history goes, I would be
scared to death to have a generation of voters go to the polls with no knowledge of the workings of government, ours or anyone else's, and, unaware of
the mistakes of the past, try to make wise decisions for the future.

As a future teacher, I have been reminded over and over again that it is   10
imperative that I be a good role model for my students. Coaches of competitive sports are role models also. They promote healthy life styles by dis-
couraging students from smoking and drinking. They do the best they can
to make their students' experiences enjoyable by providing proper motivation and support. This need not end with the removal of the sports programs from the school. These same people can either stay in the teaching
field in another capacity or work for the community clubs.

Yes, it is true that active daily training builds a particular responsibility   11
and perseverance that will be needed in "real life." However, this "daily
training" can be accomplished within the academic field also, and will
serve to engender the school spirit that pro sports people feel is necessary
in the educational environment. Forensics, math competitions, essay contests, and history debates all contribute to build public speaking ability, alleviate math anxiety, and promote an increased ability for self-expression
in writing, which will aid students' ability to synthesize and analyze information and formulate informed opinions.

Extensive sports training through the school system prepares a very   12
small percentage of the school population for a successful future, as very
few individuals are lucky enough to go on to pro careers. Let's take the
money that goes for sports and use it to support an up-to-date, academic
education that will prepare all children for real life.

   This essay has many strengths. The topic was well chosen, not only because many people are interested in school sports, but also because Kerstin's view of sports is likely to inspire controversy—hence the need for her argument. As already noted, good writers do not belabor the obvious. Writing this essay for an audience of students (with whom she shared an earlier draft for peer review), Kerstin realized that many of her classmates believed in the importance of school sports and that their convictions on this issue could keep them from listening to what she had to say. She therefore adopted a deductive strategy in order to establish some common ground with her opponents before arguing that school systems should not fund sports. Her opening paragraph establishes the premise on which her argument is based: the function of education is to help children "reach their fullest potential as adults" and prepare them to become "productive members of society." Her minor premise appears in paragraph 12: "Extensive sports training through the school system prepares a very small percentage of the school population for a successful future . . . ." If we accept both the major and minor premises, then we should be prepared to accept the conclusion: "Let's take the money that goes for sports and use it to support an up-to-date, academic education that will prepare all children for real life."

   As you can see from this example, deduction allows a writer the chance to prepare the way for a controversial argument by strategically opening with a key point that draws an audience closer, without immediately revealing what exactly is afoot. With a genuinely controversial opinion, one must face the risk of being shouted down—especially when addressing a potentially hostile audience. Deductive reasoning increases the chance of gaining a fair hearing.

   A writer who uses deduction should still remember to address those concerns most likely to be raised by opponents. In "Preparation for Real Life," Kerstin begins paragraphs 4, 8, and 9 by anticipating opposition and then responding to it. She also makes a number of important concessions. In her third paragraph, she concedes, "It would be a terrible loss to many people who gain a great deal of satisfaction out of participating in sports activities if these activities were to be completely phased out." The fifth paragraph begins by recognizing, "The importance of physical fitness is not to be understated." Paragraph 11 also begins with a concession: "Yes, it is true that active daily training builds a particular responsibility and perseverance that will be needed in 'real life.'" And, in paragraph 10, Kerstin admits that coaches can be good role models. These are all concessions that should appeal to men and women who value sports. But Kerstin does not simply let these concessions sit on the page. In each case, she immediately goes on to show how the concession does not undermine her own argument. Whatever your own views on this topic may be, you should realize that concessions need not weaken an argument. On the contrary, they can strengthen an argument by making it more complex.

   The moment at which writers choose to anticipate opposition will usually vary; it depends on the topic, how much the author knows about it, and how easily he or she can deal with the principal counterarguments that others might raise. But whether one is writing an inductive or deductive argument, it is usually advisable to recognize and respond to the opposition fairly early in the essay. You will need at least one or two paragraphs to launch your own thesis, but by the time you are about one-third of the way into your essay, you may find it useful to defuse the opposition before it grows any stronger. If you wait until the very end of your essay to acknowledge that there are points of view different from your own, your audience may have already put your essay aside, dismissing it as "one-sided" or "narrow-minded." Also, it is usually a good idea to put the opposition's point of view at the beginning of a paragraph. By doing so, you can devote the rest of that paragraph to your response. It's not enough to recognize the opposition and include some of its arguments in your essay. You are a writer, not a referee, and you must always try to show your audience why it should not be persuaded by the counterarguments you have acknowledged. If you study the organization of "Preparation for Real Life," you will see that Kerstin begins paragraphs 3, 4, 5, 8, and 11 with sentences that acknowledge other sides to the question of public funding for school sports. But she was able to end each of these paragraphs with her own argument still moving clearly forward.

One final note: Although it is usually best to establish your premise before your conclusion, writing an essay is not the same as writing a syllogism. In "Preparation for Real Life," the minor premise does not appear until the last paragraph. It could just as easily have appeared earlier (and actually did so in a preliminary draft). Writers benefit from flexibility and the ability to make choices, depending on what they want to say. When you read or write deductive arguments, you will find that relatively few of these arguments proceed according to a fixed formula determining exactly what must happen in any given paragraph.

Exercise 4

Widely recognized as a conservative voice within the Republican Party, Barry Goldwater was that party's presidential nominee in 1964. He published the following argument in *The Washington Post* during the summer of 1993, when Congress was debating whether or not gay and lesbian Americans should be allowed to serve in the U.S. military. As you read his argument, be alert for the premise upon which it is based.

BARRY M. GOLDWATER

ENOUGH FOOLERY: LIFT THE BAN ON GAYS

Washington—After more than 50 years in the military and politics, I am still 1
amazed to see how upset people can get over nothing. Lifting the ban on gays
in the military is not exactly nothing, but it is pretty damned close.

Everyone knows that gays have served honorably in the military since at 2
least the time of Julius Caesar, and will go on doing so.

But most Americans should be shocked to know that while the country's 3
economy is going down the tubes, the military has wasted a half-billion dollars
over the past decade chasing down gays and running them out of the services.

Military studies have proven again and again that there is no valid reason 4
for keeping the ban on gays. Some thought gays were crazy, but then found
that wasn't true. Then they decided gays were a security risk, but again the
Defense Department decided that was not so—one navy study, never published, found gays to be good security risks.

We know that eventually the ban will be lifted. The only questions are 5
how much muck we will all be dragged through, and how many brave Americans like Tom Paniccia and Colonel Margarethe Cammermeyer* will have
their lives and careers destroyed in a senseless attempt to stall the inevitable.

Some in Congress think I'm wrong. They say we absolutely must con- 6
tinue to discriminate, or all hell will break loose. Who knows, they say, perhaps our soldiers may even take up arms against each other. That's just stupid.

Years ago I was a lieutenant in charge of an all-black unit. Military lead- 7
ers at the time believed that blacks lacked leadership potential. Today, every
man and woman in the U.S. military takes orders from a black man: General
Colin Powell.†

Nobody thought blacks or women could ever be integrated into the mil- 8
itary. Many thought an all-volunteer force could never protect the national
interest. Well, it has—and despite those who feared the worst, I among them,
we are still the best.

I served in the armed forces. I have flown more than 150 of the best 9
fighter planes and bombers the country manufactured. I founded the Arizona
National Guard. I chaired the Senate Armed Services Committee. And I think
it's high time to pull the curtains on this charade of policy.

We have the strongest military in the world because our service people 10
respect the chain of command and know how to follow orders. A soldier may
not like every order, or every member of his or her unit, but a good soldier
will always follow orders—and, in time, respect those who get the job done.

*Sergeant Tom Paniccia was discharged from the Air Force in 1993 because of homosexuality.
Awarded with a Bronze Star for her work in Vietnam and chosen as Nurse of the Year in 1985,
Cammermeyer was prosecuted by the Army in 1989 after disclosing her sexual orientation.
†Colin Powell was Chairman of the Joint Chiefs of Staff from 1989–1993.

What would undermine U.S. readiness would be a compromise policy   11
like "Don't ask, don't tell." That compromise doesn't deal with the issue—it
tries to hide it.

We have wasted enough precious time, money and talent trying to perse-   12
cute and pretend. It is time to deal with this straight on and be done with it.

The conservative movement, to which I subscribe, deeply believes that   13
government should stay out of people's private lives. Government governs best
when it governs least, and avoids the impossible task of legislating morality.
But legislating someone's version of morality is what we do by perpetuating
discrimination against gays.

Under the U.S. Constitution, everyone is guaranteed the right to do as   14
he pleases as long as it does not harm someone else. You don't need to be
"straight" to fight and die for the country. You just need to be able to shoot
straight.

I know that we can rise to the challenge, do the right thing and lift the   15
ban on gays in the military. Countries with far less leadership and discipline
have traveled this way, and successfully.

No American able to serve should be allowed, much less given an excuse,   16
not to serve his or her country. We need all our talent.

If I were in the Senate today, I would rise on the Senate floor in support   17
of our commander in chief. He may be a Democrat, but he happens to be right
on this question. ∎

Reasoning by Using the Toulmin Model

Although both inductive and deductive reasoning suggest useful strategies for
writers of argument, they also have their limitations. Many writers prefer not
to be bound by a prefabricated method of organization and regard the syllogism, in particular, as unnecessarily rigid. To make their case, some writers
choose to combine inductive and deductive reasoning within a single essay—
and other writers can make convincing arguments without the formal use of
either induction or deduction.

In an important book first published in 1958, a British philosopher
named Stephen Toulmin demonstrated that the standard forms of logic needed
to be reconsidered because they did not adequately explain all logical arguments. Emphasizing that logic is concerned with probability more often than
certainty, he provided a new vocabulary for the analysis of argument. In Toulmin's model, every argument consists of these elements:

CLAIM:	The equivalent of the conclusion or whatever it is a writer or speaker wants to try to prove;
DATA:	The information or evidence a writer or speaker offers in support of the claim; and
WARRANT:	A general statement that establishes a trustworthy relationship between the data and the claim.

Within any argument, the claim and the data will be explicit. The warrant may also be explicit, but it is often merely implied—especially when the arguer believes that the audience will readily agree to it.

To better understand these terms, let us consider an example adapted from one of Toulmin's:

CLAIM: Raymond is an American citizen.
DATA: Raymond was born in Puerto Rico.
WARRANT: Anyone born in Puerto Rico is an American citizen.

These three statements may remind you of the three elements in a deductive argument. If arranged as a syllogism, they might look like this:

MAJOR PREMISE: Anyone born in Puerto Rico is an American citizen.
MINOR PREMISE: Raymond was born in Puerto Rico.
CONCLUSION: Raymond is an American citizen.

The advantage of Toulmin's model becomes apparent when we realize that there is a possibility that Raymond was prematurely born to French parents who were only vacationing in Puerto Rico, and he is now serving in the French army. Or perhaps he was an American citizen but became a naturalized citizen of Russia after defecting with important U.S. Navy documents. Because the formal logic of a syllogism is designed to lead to a conclusion that is *necessarily* true, Toulmin argued that it is ill-suited for working to a conclusion that is *probably* true. Believing that the importance of the syllogism was overemphasized in the study of logic, Toulmin argued that there was a need for a "working logic" that would be easier to apply in the rhetorical situations in which arguers most often find themselves. He designed his own model so that it can easily incorporate *qualifiers* such as "probably," "presumably," and "generally." Here is a revision of the first example:

CLAIM: Raymond is probably an American citizen.
DATA: Raymond was born in Puerto Rico.
WARRANT: Anyone born in Puerto Rico is entitled to American citizenship.

Both the claim and the warrant have now been modified. Toulmin's model does not dictate any specific pattern in which these elements must be arranged, and this is a great advantage for writers. The claim may come at the beginning of an essay, or it could just as easily come after a discussion of both the data and the warrant. Similarly, the warrant may precede the data or it may follow it— or, as already noted, the warrant may be implied rather than explicitly stated at any point in the essay.

If you write essays of your own using the Toulmin model, you may find yourself making different types of claims. In one essay, you might make a claim that can be supported entirely by facts. For example, if you wanted to argue that the stock market should be subject to greater regulation, you could define the extent of current regulation, report on the laws governing overseas markets, and cite specific abuses such as scandals involving insider trading. In another essay, however, you might make a claim that is easier to support with a mixture of facts, expert opinion, and appeals to the values of your audience. If, for example, you wanted to argue against abortion, your data might consist of facts (such as the number of abortions performed within a particular clinic in 1994), testimony on which it is possible to have a difference of opinion (such as the point at which human life begins), and an appeal to moral values that you believe your audience should share with you. In short, you will cite different types of data depending on the nature of the claim you want to argue.

The nature of the warrant will also differ from one argument to another. It may be a matter of law (such as the Jones Act of 1917, which guarantees U.S. citizenship to the citizens of Puerto Rico), an assumption that one's data have come from a reliable source (such as documents published by the Securities and Exchange Commission), or a generally accepted value (such as the sanctity of human life). But whatever your warrant, you should be prepared to back it up if called on to do so. No matter how strongly you may believe in your claim, or how compelling your data may be, your argument will not be convincing if your warrant cannot be substantiated.

The Toulmin model for argumentation does *not* require that you abandon everything you've learned about inductive and deductive reasoning. These different systems of logic complement one another and combine to form a varied menu from which you can choose whatever seems best for a particular occasion. Unless your instructor specifies that an assignment incorporate a particular type of reasoning, you will often be able to choose the type of logic you wish to employ just as you might make any number of other writing decisions. And having choices is ultimately a luxury, not a burden.

For an example of a student essay that reflects the Toulmin model for reasoning, consider the following argument on the importance of studying history.

History Is for People Who Think
Ron Tackett

Can a person consider himself a thinking, creative, responsible citizen   1
and not care about history? Can an institution that proposes to foster such
attributes do so without including history in its curriculum? Many college
students would answer such a question with an immediate, "Yes!" But
those who are quick to answer do so without reflecting on what history
truly is and how and why it is important.

History is boring, complain many students. Unfortunately, a lot of people   2
pick up a bad taste of history from the primary and secondary schools. Too

may lower-level history courses (and college level, too) are just glorified Trivial Pursuit: rife with rote memorization of dates and events deemed important by the teacher and textbooks, coupled with monotone lectures that could induce comas in hyperactive children. Instead of simply making students memorize when Pearl Harbor was attacked by the Japanese, teachers should concentrate on instilling an understanding of why the Japanese felt they had no alternative but to attack the United States. History is a discipline of understanding, not memorization.

Another common complaint is that history is unimportant. But even the most fanatic antihistory students, if they were honest, would have to admit that history is important at least within the narrow confines of their own disciplines of study. Why be an artist if you are merely going to repeat the past (and probably not as expertly, since you would have to spend your time formulating theories and rules already known and recorded in Art's history)? Why write The Great Gatsby or compose Revolution again? How could anyone hope to be a mathematician, or a scientist, without knowing the field's history? Even a genius needs a base from which to build. History helps provide that base.   3

History is also important in being a politically aware citizen. Knowing that we entered World War I on the side of the Allies in part because Woodrow Wilson was a great Anglophile, as some historians charge, is not vital to day-to-day life. But it is important to know that the economic reparations imposed on Germany after the war set the stage for the rise of Hitler and World War II and that that war ended with a Russian domination of Eastern Europe that led to the Cold War, during which political philosophies were formulated that still affect American foreign and domestic policies. This type of history enables citizens to form an intelligent world view and possibly help our nation avoid past mistakes. Of course, this illustration is simplified, but the point is as valid as when Santayana said that without history, we are "condemned to repeat it." This does not mean that history will repeat itself exactly, but that certain patterns recur in history, and if we understand the patterns of what has gone before, perhaps we can avoid making the mistakes our ancestors made.   4

A person can live a long life, get a job, and raise a family without having any historical knowledge. But citizens who possess a strong knowledge of history are better prepared to contribute intelligently to their jobs and their society. Thus, knowing which Third World nations have a history of defaulting on loans can help a bank executive save his or her institution and its customers a great deal of grief by avoiding, or seeking exceptional safeguards on, such loans. And knowing the history of U.S. involvement in Central and South America, from naval incidents with Chile in the 1890s to trying to overthrow the Sandanistas in Nicaragua in the 1980s, can help   5

Americans understand why many people and nations are concerned about U.S. policies in the region. More importantly, Americans cannot intelligently determine what those policies should be without a knowledge of history.

Now, if history is important enough to be required in college, how many   6
credits are enough and what sort of history should be taught? American, European, Eastern, Latin American, or yet another? First, a course in American history must be required. Students can little appreciate the history of others, without first knowing their own. Second, since we more and more realize that we are members of a "global community," at least one world history course should be mandated. Though there is no magic number of credits that will ensure the student's becoming a thinking, creative member of society, history can help fulfill the collegiate purpose of fashioning men and women with the potential for wisdom and the ability to critically appraise political, economic, and moral issues. Thus, history should be a required part of the college curriculum.

In arguing on behalf of history, Ron shows that he is well aware that many students would like to avoid history courses. Paragraphs 2 and 3 are devoted to anticipating and responding to opposition. Although Ron concedes that history can be boring if it is badly taught, and makes an additional concession at the beginning of paragraph 5, he still insists that all college students should be required to take at least two history courses. The *claim* of this essay is "history should be a required part of the college curriculum." The *warrant* behind this claim is a value that is likely to be widely accepted: a college education should help people to think critically and become responsible members of society. This warrant underlies the entire argument, but it can be found specifically in the last paragraph where Ron refers to "the collegiate purpose of fashioning men and women with the potential for wisdom and the ability to critically appraise political, economic, and moral issues" immediately before making his claim.

Submitting *data* to support this claim presented the writer with a challenge: It would be difficult to obtain statistics or other factual evidence to prove that the claim fulfills the warrant. A reader might agree with the warrant and still doubt whether requiring college students to study history would give them the ability to think critically about political and moral issues. Ron chose to support his claim by defining history as "a discipline of understanding, not memorization" and providing several examples of historical events that are worth understanding: the Japanese attack on Pearl Harbor, the consequences of World War I, and the nature of U.S. involvement in Central and South America. Additional support for the claim is provided by appeals to other values, which Ron has assumed his audience to possess. Paragraph 3 includes an appeal to self-interest: knowing the history of your own field can save you from wasting time. This same strategy is employed in paragraph 5, where Ron suggests that the knowledge of history can lead to better job performance. All of the examples found within the essay are clearly related to the values that the argument has invoked, and within the limitations of a short essay Ron has done a good job of supporting his claim.

Exercise 5

The author of *Signs of Life: The Language and Meanings of DNA,* Robert Pollack is a biology professor at Columbia University. He published the following editorial in the *New York Times* on November 17, 1993, shortly after scientists at George Washington University Medical Center announced that they had cloned human embryos. After you have read it, identify the claim, the data, and the conclusion.

ROBERT POLLACK

BEYOND CLONING

The cloning of human embryos by Dr. Jerry L. Hall and his colleagues at the George Washington University Medical Center has brought us one step closer to Aldous Huxley's anti-utopian vision of mass-produced people—the "Brave New World" in which "the whole of a small factory" was staffed with the products of a single human egg.   1

Dr. Hall's work was based on in vitro fertilization, in which sperm and egg are joined in the laboratory to produce a human embryo. The success of that technique (which has been pursued by thousands of couples unable to conceive in the ordinary way) produces an undeniable temptation to carry out still another technique that has proved equally successful in work with mice: the creation of embryos carrying genes produced in the laboratory.   2

Because the genes of all organisms are made of the same chemical— DNA—genes of different origins can be recombined and edited in the laboratory. Genes created in this way and inserted into a new embryo were given a name in 1980 by the Yale biologist Frank Ruddle: transgenes. These genes will be present in every cell as the embryo grows, and they can exert their effects throughout an organism's lifetime. A proper transgene could replace a defective gene in an animal embryo, preventing the symptoms of an inherited disease.   3

Transgenes have been inserted into early mouse embryos for more than a decade, and from these experiments we have learned a great deal about the way genes function. Embryos no older than a few hours, and no bigger than a few dozen cells, are dislodged from a recently mated female mouse. A cell bearing   4 a new, lab-created gene is taken from a dish and inserted through a needle into the embryo, which is then implanted in the uterus of another mouse. The progeny of the new cell become normal tissue cells, and the mixed ball of cells grows into a transgenic mouse.

Transgenic mice have been produced with human genes that function   5
well enough to compensate for damaged or missing mouse genes. For instance, transgenic mice carrying a human hemoglobin gene produce functional hemoglobin; if the embryo comes from an inbred mouse strain suffering an inherited blood disease, its descendants are cured.

Why not transgenic people, then? There is no obvious technical barrier.   6
The success of in vitro fertilization has shown that the early human embryo is as accessible to transgenic manipulation as any mouse embryo.

Under current regulations, this kind of manipulation of human embry-   7
onic tissue cannot be supported by Federal research grants. But no Federal law prevents such work from receiving private support.

Can there be a transgenic medicine consistent with the Hippocratic in-   8
junction to do no harm? We will have to decide fairly soon. But the questions that must be answered before we undertake such a procedure—the ultimate in planned parenthood—are not just matters of science.

Dr. Hall's work may lead to twins or even larger numbers of children   9
born at different times—early embryos can be frozen and thawed—but it is unlikely that this advance will lead to any effort to produce a "master race"; the procedure offers no opportunity to select the inherited qualities of the cloned embryos.

Still, every new technology is imperfect. As anyone knows who has   10
tripped over the newest model of a computer or a car, the first tries are likely to have hidden flaws. This has been true of medical technology as well: the first vaccines, the first antibiotics and the first organ transplants all had dangerous, if temporary, side effects.

The first transgenic children, though, would be different in kind from   11
the first volunteers to test a new gene therapy or a new drug like AZT. These volunteers are already here, and already ill; they choose the risk of a new procedure in hopes of recovery. In contrast, a transgenic mistake means a child born with an inherited defect caused by some misstep in the procedure.

Recently, for example, scientists interested in coloring the hair and eyes   12
of an albino strain of mice injected the gene for a pigment; unexpectedly, they created a strain of mice whose viscera—heart, stomach, liver, and the like— were all turned around. These mice were unable to live long after birth; the added gene had inadvertently damaged a gene responsible for the usual positioning of the internal organs.

Beyond the risk of a fatal error, the accidental introduction of a more   13
subtle mutation in a transgenic child might present us and our descendants with the task of dealing with a new inherited disease. The potential should signal a clear boundary ahead, one that religious leaders, politicians, educators and parents have as much to say about as physicians and scientists. Before we are presented with an unregulated, ill-conceived fait accompli, we all need to

look carefully at this procedure and decide whether the first transgenic human embryos should be created.

Since responsible scientists cannot promise that all their first experiments will work, I do not see how transgenic medicine can ever be ethically launched. Many of my colleagues disagree, but we are unlikely to get the proper sort of public discussion of these issues unless the Government steps backed in and takes notice. President Clinton has removed the ban on Federal support for fetal tissue transplant research; Congress needs to hold public hearings on the matter of transgenic babies. ■   14

AVOIDING LOGICAL FALLACIES

An apparently logical argument may reveal serious flaws if we take the trouble to examine it closely. Mistakes in reasoning are called logical *fallacies*. This term comes from the Latin word for deceit, and there is some form of deception behind most of these lapses in logic. It is easy to deceive ourselves into believing that we are making a strong argument when we have actually lost our way somehow, and many fallacies are unintentional. But others are used deliberately by writers or speakers for whom "winning" an argument is more important than looking for truth. Here is a list of common fallacies that you should be careful to avoid in your own arguments and that you should be alert to in the arguments of others.

Ad Hominem Argument

An ad hominem argument is an argument that attacks the personal character or reputation of one's opponents while ignoring what they have to say. *Ad hominem* is Latin for "to the man." Although an audience often considers the character of a writer or speaker in deciding whether it can trust what he or she has to say, most of us realize that good people can make bad arguments, and even a crook can sometimes tell the truth. It is always better to give a thoughtful response to an opponent's arguments than to ignore those arguments and indulge in personal attacks.

Ad Misericordiam Argument

An ad misericordiam argument is an appeal to pity. Writers are often justified in appealing to the pity of their readers when the need to inspire this emotion is closely related to whatever they are arguing for and when the entire argument does not rest on this appeal alone. For example, someone who is attempting to convince you to donate one of your kidneys for a medical transplant would probably assure you that you could live with only one kidney and that there is a serious need for the kidney you are being asked to donate. In addition to making these crucial points, the arguer might move you to pity by describing what will otherwise happen to the person who needs the transplant.

When the appeal to pity stands alone, even in charitable appeals where its use is fundamental, the result is often questionable. Imagine a large billboard advertisement for the American Red Cross. It features a closeup photograph of a distraught (but nevertheless good-looking) man, beneath which, in large letters, runs this caption: PLEASE, MY LITTLE GIRL NEEDS BLOOD. Although we may already believe in the importance of donating blood, we should question the implications of this ad. Can we donate blood and ask that it be reserved for the exclusive use of little girls? Is the life of a little girl more valuable than the life of a little boy? Are the lives of children more valuable than the lives of adults? Few people would donate blood unless they sympathized with those who need transfusions, and it may be unrealistic to expect logic in advertising. But consider how weak an argument becomes when the appeal to pity has little to do with the issue in question. Someone who has seldom attended class and failed all his examinations but then tries to argue, "I deserve to pass this course because I've had a lot of problems at home," is making a fallacious appeal to pity. The "argument" asks the instructor to overlook relevant evidence and make a decision favorable to the arguer because the instructor has been moved to feel sorry for him. You should be skeptical of any appeal to pity that is irrelevant to the conclusion or that seems designed to distract attention from the other factors you should be considering.

Ad Populum Argument

An ad populum argument, which means "argument to the crowd," plays on the general values of an audience, often to the point where reasonable discussion of a specific issue is no longer possible. A newspaper that creates a patriotic frenzy through exaggerated reports of enemy "atrocities" is relying on an ad populum argument. But the ad populum argument can also take more subtle forms. Politicians may remind you that they were born and raised in "this great state" and that they love their children and admire their spouses—all of which are factors believed to appeal to the average man and woman but which nevertheless are unlikely to affect performance in office. When candidates linger on what wonderful family life they enjoy, it may be time to ask a question about the economy.

Argument by Analogy

An analogy is a comparison that works on more than one level, and it is possible to use analogy effectively when reasoning inductively. To do this, you must be sure that the things you are comparing have several characteristics in common and that these similarities are relevant to the conclusion you intend to draw. If you observe that isolation produces depression in chimpanzees, you could argue that isolation can cause a similar problem for human beings. The strength of this argument would depend on the degree to which chimps are analogous to humans, so you would need to proceed with care and demonstrate that there are important similarities between the two species.

When arguing from analogy, it is important to remember that you are speculating. As is the case with any type of inductive reasoning, you can reach a conclusion that is likely to be true but not guaranteed to be true. It is always possible that you have overlooked a significant factor that will cause the analogy to break down.

Unfortunately, analogies are often misused. An argument from analogy that reaches a firm conclusion is likely to be fallacious, and it is certain to be fallacious if the analogy itself is inappropriate. If a congressional candidate asks us to vote for him because of his outstanding record as a football player, he might be able to claim that politics, like football, involves teamwork. But because a successful politician needs many skills and will probably never need to run across a field or knock someone down, it would be foolish to vote on the basis of this questionable analogy. The differences between football and politics outweigh the similarities, and it would be fallacious to pretend otherwise.

Begging the Question

In the fallacy of "begging the question," a writer begins with a premise that is acceptable only to anyone who will agree with the conclusion that is subsequently reached—a conclusion often very similar to the premise itself. Thus, the argument goes around in a circle. For instance, someone might begin an essay by claiming, "Required courses like freshman English are a waste of time," and end with the conclusion that "Freshman English should not be a required course." It might indeed be arguable that freshman English should not be required, but the author who begins with the premise that freshman English is a waste of time has assumed what the argument should be devoted to proving. Because it is much easier to claim that something is true than to prove it is true, you may be tempted to beg the question you set out to answer. This is a temptation that should always be avoided.

Equivocation

Someone who equivocates uses vague or ambiguous language to mislead an audience. In argumentation, equivocation often takes the form of using one word in several different senses, without acknowledging that this has been done. It is especially easy to equivocate if you are addicted to abstract language. Watch out in particular for the abuse of such terms as "right," "society," "freedom," "law," "justice," and "real." When you use words like these, make sure you make your meaning clear. And make double sure your meaning doesn't shift when you use the term again.

False Dilemma

A false dilemma is a fallacy in which a speaker or writer poses a choice between two alternatives while overlooking other possibilities and implying that other possibilities do not exist. If a college freshman receives low grades at the end of the first semester and then claims, "What's wrong with low grades? Is cheating any better?", he is pretending that there is no other possibility—for example, that of earning higher grades by studying harder, a possibility that is recognized by most students and teachers.

Guilt by Association

This fallacy is frequently made in politics, especially toward the end of a close campaign. A candidate who happens to be religious, for example, may be maneuvered by opponents into the false position of being held accountable for the actions of all the men and women who hold to that particular faith. Nothing specific has been *argued,* but a negative association has been either created or suggested through hints and innuendos. Guilt by association may take the form of an ad hominen argument, or it may be more subtle. A careless writer may simply stumble into using a stereotype to avoid the trouble of coming up with a concrete example. Whatever its form, guilt by association is a fallacy in which prejudice takes the place of thought.

Ignoring the Question

When someone says, "I'm glad you asked that question!" and then promptly begins to talk about something else, she or he is guilty of ignoring the question. Politicians are famous for exploiting this technique when they don't want to be pinned down on a subject. Students (and teachers) sometimes use it too, when asked a question that they want to avoid. Ignoring the question is also likely to occur when friends or lovers have a fight. In the midst of a quarrel, we may hear remarks like, "What about you!" or "Never mind the budget! I'm sick of worrying about money! We need to talk about what's happening to our relationship!"

Jumping to Conclusions

This fallacy is so common that it has become a cliché. It means that the conclusion in question has not been supported by an adequate amount of evidence. Because one green apple is sour, it does not follow that all green apples are sour. Failing one test does not mean that you will necessarily fail the next. An instructor who seems disorganized the first day of class may eventually prove to be the best teacher you ever had. You should always try to have more than one example to support an argument. Be skeptical of arguments that seem heavy on opinion but weak on evidence.

Non Sequitur

This term is Latin for "it does not follow." Although this can be said of almost any faulty argument, the term "non sequitur" is usually applied more precisely.

The most common type of non sequitur is a complex sentence in which the subordinate clause does not clearly relate to the main clause, especially where causation is involved. An example of this type of non sequitur would be "Because the wind was blowing so fiercely, I passed the quiz in calculus." This is a non sequitur because passing calculus should not be dependent on the weather. A cause–and–effect relationship has been claimed but not explained. It may be that the wind forced you to stay indoors, which led you to spend more time studying than you usually do, and this in turn led you to pass your quiz. But someone reading the sentence as written could not be expected to know this. A non sequitur may also take the form of a compound sentence: "Mr. Blandshaw is young, and so he should be a good teacher." Mr. Blandshaw may indeed be a good teacher, but not just because he is young. On the contrary, young Mr. Blandshaw may be inexperienced, anxious, and humorless. He may also give you unrealistically large assignments because he lacks a clear sense of how much work most students can handle.

Non sequiturs sometimes form the basis for an entire argument: "William Henderson will make a good governor because he is a friend of the workingman. He is a friend of the workingman because he was a plumber before he became a millionaire through his contracting business." Before allowing this argument to go any further, you should realize that you've been already asked to swallow two non sequiturs. Being a good governor involves more than being "a friend of the workingman." And there is no reason to assume that Henderson is "a friend of the workingman" just because he used to be a plumber. It may be over thirty years since he last saw the inside of a union hall, and he may have acquired his wealth by taking advantage of the men and women who work for him.

Post Hoc, Ergo Propter Hoc

If you assume that an event is the result of something that merely occurred before it, you have committed the fallacy of post hoc, ergo propter hoc. This Latin phrase means "after this, therefore because of this." Superstitious people offer many examples of this type of fallacious thinking. They might tell you, "Everything was doing fine until the lunar eclipse last month; *that's* why the economy is in trouble." Or personal misfortune may be traced back to spilling salt, stepping on a sidewalk crack, or walking under a ladder.

This fallacy is often found in the arguments of writers who are determined to prove the existence of various conspiracies. They often seem to amass an impressive amount of "evidence"—but their evidence is frequently questionable. Or, to take a comparatively simple example, someone might be suspected of murder simply because of being seen near the victim's house a day or two before the crime occurred. This suspicion may lead to the discovery of evidence, but it could just as easily lead to the false arrest of the meter reader from the electric company. Being observed near the scene of a crime proves nothing by itself. A prosecuting attorney who would be foolish enough to base a case on such a flimsy piece of evidence would be guilty of post hoc, ergo propter hoc reasoning. Logic should always recognize the distinction between *causes* and what may simply be *coincidences*. Sequence is not a cause because every event is preceded by an infinite number of other events, all of which cannot be held responsible for whatever happens today.

This fallacy can be found in more subtle forms in essays on abstract social problems. Writers who blame contemporary problems on such instant explanations as "the rise of television" or "the popularity of computers" are no more convincing than the parent who argues that all the difficulties of family life can be traced to the rise of rock and roll. It is impossible to understand the present without understanding the past. But don't isolate at random any one event in the past, and then try to argue that it explains everything. And be careful not to accidentally imply a cause-and-effect relationship where you did not intend to do so.

Slippery Slope

According to this fallacy, one step will inevitably lead to an undesirable second step. An example would be claiming that legalized abortion will lead to euthanasia or that censoring pornography will lead to the end of freedom of the press. Although it is important to consider the probable effects of any step that is being debated, it is fallacious to claim that people will necessarily tumble downhill as the result of any one step. There is always the possibility that we'll be able to keep our feet firmly on the ground even though we've moved them from where they used to be.

Straw Man

Because it is easier to demolish a man of straw than to beat a live opponent fairly, arguers are sometimes tempted to pretend that they are responding to the views of their opponents when they are only setting up a type of artificial opposition which they can easily refute. The most common form of this fallacy is to exaggerate the views of others or to respond only to an extreme view that does not adequately represent the arguments of one's opponents. If you reveal flaws in the position taken by someone who has called for abolishing Social Security, you should not think that you have defended that program from all its critics. By responding only to an extreme position, you would be doing nothing to resolve specific concerns about how Social Security is financed and administered.

Exercise 6

Read a series of editorials and letters in a newspaper of your own choice. Look for examples of logical fallacies. Bring your favorite example to class and explain what is wrong in the reasoning.

UNDERSTANDING OTHER FORMS OF PERSUASION

Of the various forms of persuasive writing, logical argument is the most honorable. Although logic can be abused, its object is truth rather than manipulation. Whether we are writing a logical argument or simply trying to understand one, we have to be actively involved with ideas. To put it simply, we have to *think*. We may be influenced by what we know of the writer's credibility and whether she or he has touched our hearts within the argument as a whole. But behind any logical argument is the assumption that reasonable people should agree with its outcome—not so much because it is gracefully written (although it may be that), but because it is *true*.

There are other types of writing that rely on an indirect appeal to the mind, exploiting what is known about the psychological makeup of an audience or its most probable fears and desires. Successful advertising is *persuasive* in that it encourages us to buy one product or another, but it is not necessarily logical. Few people have the money, time, or inclination to sample every product available for consumption. When we buy a particular mouthwash, toothpaste, soap, or soft drink—and even when we make purchases as large as a car—we may simply choose the cheapest product available. But bargain hunting aside, we are frequently led to purchase brands that advertising has taught us to associate with health, wealth, and happiness. A prominent greeting card company insists that we send their cards if we really and truly care about someone. A soft drink company assures us that we will be young and have fun if we drink its best-known brand. One popular cigarette is associated with the masculinity of mounted cowboys, and another implies a dubious link with the women's movement. Almost no one really believes this sort of thing when forced to stop and think about it. But we often act without thinking, and this is one of the reasons why advertising has been able to grow into a billion-dollar industry. Through the clever use of language and visual images, advertisers can lead people into a variety of illogical and possibly ruinous acts.

This, then, is the principal distinction between argument and persuasion: argument seeks to clarify thought; persuasion often seeks to obscure it. Argument relies on evidence or widely accepted truths and does not necessarily dictate any one particular course of action. Persuasion, on the other hand, can work altogether independent of the facts as we know them (such as how much money we can afford to spend before the end of the month), and it is almost always designed to inspire action—whether it is buying a new kind of deodorant or voting for the candidate with the nicest teeth. Persuasion is thus a form of domination. Its object is to make people agree with the will of the persuader, regardless of whether the persuader is "right" or simply selling his or her services by the hour.

Argument may include an appeal to our emotions; persuasion is likely to emphasize such appeals. A persuasive writer or speaker knows how to evoke feelings ranging from love, loyalty, and patriotism to anger, envy, and xenophobia. An audience may be deeply moved even when nothing substantial has been said. With a quickened pulse or tearful eyes, we may find ourselves convinced that we've read or heard something wonderfully profound. A few days later, we may realize that we've been inhaling the intoxicating fumes of a heavily scented gasbag, rather than digesting genuine "food for thought."

Analyzing Advertisements

Although persuasion is by no means limited to advertising, advertisements represent a form of persuasion that we regularly encounter in our daily lives. Recognizing that people are often bored by ads because there are so many of them, advertisers must be doubly persuasive: Before they can persuade us to buy a particular product or engage a specific service, advertisers must begin by persuading us to pay attention to the ad. Because advertisements cannot be taken for granted, advertising agencies have attracted some highly talented people, and a successful advertising campaign usually involves much planning. Different advertisements employ different strategies, and if you think about the ads you encounter, you will find that they often include more than one message. Consider the examples on pages 49 through 56.

At first glance, the advertisement for Evian® Natural Spring Water (Figure 1) seems directed exclusively at pregnant women. The use of the second person, as in "If you plan to breast feed, experts say you should drink up to *30% more water* every day," seems to exclude anyone who is *not* planning to breast feed: a large market sector that includes women who are unable to have children, as well as many other women, and all men.

But although the written text seems to target only a small percentage of potential buyers of imported spring water, the ad as a whole is designed to persuade a much larger group. By associating their product with motherhood, the advertisers have made an appeal to feeling. According to an old adage, mothers are as American as apple pie, so by associating a European product with motherhood, the advertisers are appealing to a widely held American value. Respect for mothers is not uniquely American, however. Mother figures are revered in many different cultures, so the ad has the potential to reach a very large market. Although it is directly addressed to pregnant women, it is subconsciously directed at anyone who values motherhood. The opening line, "Mommy, can I have a drink of water?" invites readers to assume the role of children. If we are turning to our mothers for a drink of water, and good mothers are drinking Evian Natural Spring Water, then readers can hope that they will get Evian water from their mothers. If our "mommies" are no longer around to quench our thirst, then we will have to do the next best thing: head to the store for a bottle of the water good enough for mothers to give their children. To put this ad's message simply: "Mothers are good. Evian water is good for mothers. If you are a good mother, you should buy some. If you are a good child, you should also buy some."

On closer examination, we can see that the persuasive appeal of this ad involves a number of other elements. Consider the positive connotations of such italicized words as *eating, maintain, lubricate, process, cleanse,* and *life.* The

FIGURE I

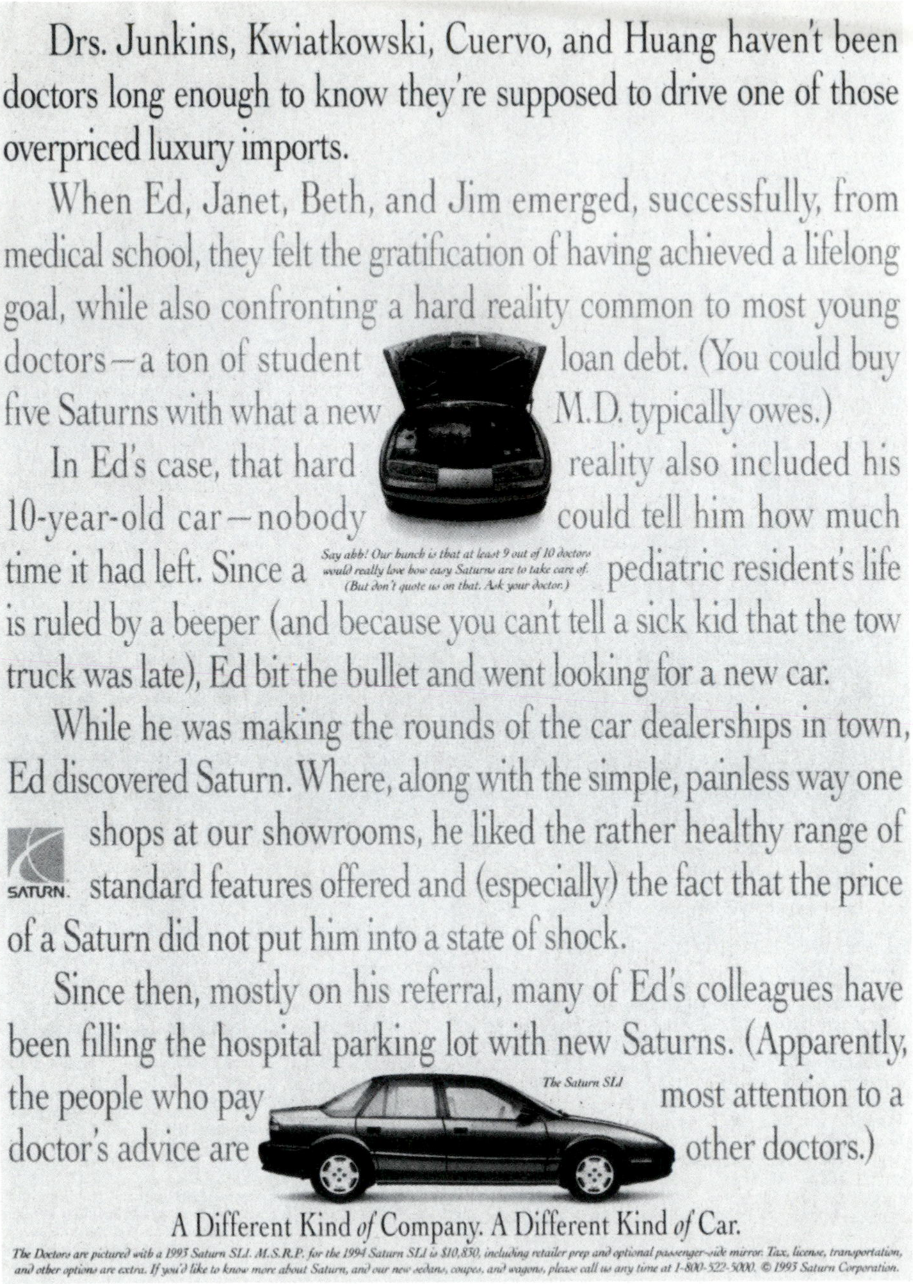
Drs. Junkins, Kwiatkowski, Cuervo, and Huang haven't been doctors long enough to know they're supposed to drive one of those overpriced luxury imports.
When Ed, Janet, Beth, and Jim emerged, successfully, from medical school, they felt the gratification of having achieved a lifelong goal, while also confronting a hard reality common to most young doctors—a ton of student loan debt. (You could buy five Saturns with what a new M.D. typically owes.)
In Ed's case, that hard reality also included his 10-year-old car—nobody could tell him how much time it had left. Since a pediatric resident's life is ruled by a beeper (and because you can't tell a sick kid that the tow truck was late), Ed bit the bullet and went looking for a new car.
Say ahh! Our hunch is that at least 9 out of 10 doctors would really love how easy Saturns are to take care of. (But don't quote us on that. Ask your doctor.)
While he was making the rounds of the car dealerships in town, Ed discovered Saturn. Where, along with the simple, painless way one shops at our showrooms, he liked the rather healthy range of standard features offered and (especially) the fact that the price of a Saturn did not put him into a state of shock.
SATURN.
Since then, mostly on his referral, many of Ed's colleagues have been filling the hospital parking lot with new Saturns. (Apparently, the people who pay most attention to a doctor's advice are other doctors.)
The Saturn SL1
A Different Kind of Company. A Different Kind of Car.
The Doctors are pictured with a 1993 Saturn SL1. M.S.R.P. for the 1994 Saturn SL1 is $10,830, including retailer prep and optional passenger-side mirror. Tax, license, transportation, and other options are extra. If you'd like to know more about Saturn, and our new sedans, coupes, and wagons, please call us any time at 1-800-522-5000. © 1993 Saturn Corporation.

FIGURE 2

Jim, Ed, Janet,
and Beth (left to right)
bought their Saturns at
Saturn of Owings Mills
and Saturn of Glen Burnie.

woman is wearing a white dress, emphasizing the purity that apparently comes with drinking the product in question. She is thoroughly at ease, reclining, a book in hand. What could be more peaceful? The image suggests the comfort that comes with wealth. After all, for every pregnant woman who can lounge in the French Alps, there are many hundreds who are working for a living. Thus, in addition to being the drink of mothers, Evian water becomes the drink of wealth and privilege. If you cannot afford a new BMW but want the illusion that you too live in a world like this, you can at least start buying what is being marketed as the right water for those who are healthy, wealthy, and cool.

Like the ad for Evian water, the ad for Saturn automobiles (Figure 2) also involves linking the product with a positive image. In this case, the association is with physicians. But rather than settling for a relatively simple message such as "Product X is the preferred brand of nine out of ten doctors," the Saturn ad conveys a message that is more complex. The doctors in question are all young and unconventional—so unconventional that they have apparently driven some distance from the hospital for an outdoor lunch without even removing their stethoscopes. Their youth and attire emphasize that these doctors are different from the stereotypical image of physicians as highly paid professionals who take themselves seriously. As such, these four doctors—perfectly balanced in terms of gender, and representing four different cultures—are perfect clients for "A Different Kind of Company. A Different Kind of Car."

Although both their clothing and the accompanying texts emphasize that Jim, Ed, Janet, and Beth are all doctors, they are also presented as good-natured and unthreatening. Three are eating simple lunches from brown paper bags, and the fourth has a plaid lunch box reminiscent of elementary school. Moreover, it is surely no accident that two of the doctors are eating fruit and the background is dominated by a large tree. These images combine to suggest that Saturn is a car for intelligent, nice, young professionals who value diversity, health, and fresh air.

The written text (in which we are quickly put on a first-name basis with strangers) reinforces the message that these unknown people—whose expertise has nothing whatsoever to do with cars—are typical of the good people who know what it's like to be in debt, drive an old car, and need reliable transportation. The informal, almost gossipy text emphasizes Ed's search for a car rather than specific features of the car on display. We read briefly about a "rather healthy range of standard features," but the details of the car are presumably less important than relating to the attractive people who are pictured as representative owners. Note that the car itself is obscured by the doctors in the photograph, and product information about the car is relegated to small print at the bottom of the left-hand page. Once again, a product is being sold because of the associations advertisers establish with it—not because of its specific qualities.

Exercise 7

Five other advertisements are reproduced on pages 54–58. Choose one and write an essay of approximately five hundred words explaining how the ad attempts to be persuasive.

Recognizing Flaws in Persuasion

Just as some advertisements are more appealing than others, so are some ads more questionable than others. Many ads are relatively straightforward, but others may approach dishonesty. When analyzing persuasion, wherever you encounter it and in whatever form, you should be alert not only for the various types of fallacious reasoning discussed earlier, but also for the following flaws.

Bogus Claims   A claim can be considered "bogus" or false whenever persuaders promise more than they can prove. If a Chicago restaurant offers "fresh country peas" in the middle of January, you might want to ask where these peas were freshly picked. And if a large commercial bakery advertises "homemade pies," try asking whose home they were made in. You'll probably get some strange looks, because many people don't really expect words to mean what they say. But good writers become good writers in part because they have eyes that see and ears that hear.

If a toothpaste promises to give your mouth "sex appeal," you'd still better be careful about whom you try to kiss. A claim of this sort is fairly crude, and therefore easily recognizable. But bogus claims can take many forms, some more subtle than others. A television advertisement for a new laxative may star a woman in a white coat, with a stethoscope around her neck. The advertisement implies—without necessarily saying so—that the product in question is endorsed by physicians. Ads of this sort are also likely to speak vaguely of "recent studies," or better yet, "recent *clinical* studies," which are declared to prove a product's value. The product may indeed have value; on the other hand, it may be indistinguishable from its competition except in price and packaging. You might like it when you try it. But well-educated people should always be a little skeptical about promises from strangers.

When writing an essay, it is easy to fall into the habit of making bogus claims when reaching for generalizations to support your point of view. Imitating the style of the advertisements with which they grew up, careless writers like to refer to those ever-popular "recent studies" that conveniently seem to support whatever is being argued. Such phrases as "recent studies have shown" enable writers to avoid identifying who did the research. A recent study may provide the evidence to prove a point, but a good writer should be prepared to cite it, especially when the claim is surprising. It is one thing to write "Recent studies have shown that nutrition plays an important role in maintaining good health," for the generalization in this case enjoys wide acceptance. It would be something else altogether to toss off a claim like "Recent studies have shown that Americans have the most nutritious diet in the

Dairy farmer Louise Ihlenfeldt values NUCLEAR ENERGY as a way to keep the *air* clean. (And the milk fresh.)

The nuclear power plant a mile up the road has been generating electricity for 19 years. The Ihlenfeldt family has been working their Wisconsin farm for 125.

Nowadays, modern electrical equipment keeps the cows milked and the milk cold. And the nuclear plant keeps creating electricity without creating air pollution. "We've never had a problem with the plant," Louise says. "It's a clean, safe power source."

There are over 100 nuclear plants in the U.S. Because they don't burn anything to make electricity, they help protect our environment and preserve our natural resources for future generations. All while providing enough electricity for 65 million homes. No single source is the whole answer to America's energy needs. But, as Louise Ihlenfeldt will tell you, nuclear energy is part of the answer.

For a free booklet, write to the U.S. Council for Energy Awareness, P.O. Box 66080, Dept. L, Washington, D.C. 20035. ©1993 USCEA

NUCLEAR ENERGY MEANS CLEANER AIR

As seen in June 1993 issues of The Washington Post and The Washington Post National Weekly Edition; July 1993 issues of The New York Times, Forbes, Christian Science Monitor and Congressional Quarterly; August 1993 issues of Newsweek, FORTUNE, The Atlantic and National Journal; September 1993 issues of National Geographic, Good Housekeeping, TIME, Parents and American Heritage; and the October 1993 issues of Reader's Digest, Ladies' Home Journal, Discover and New Choices.

FIGURE 3

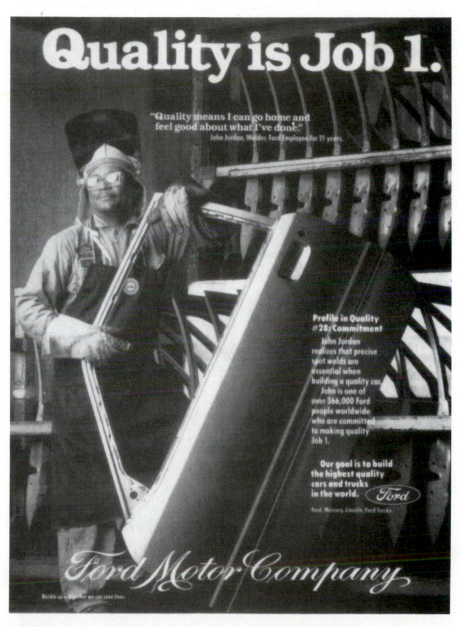

FIGURE 4

FIGURE 5

Help stop a different kind of child abuse.

This abuse is merciless. It takes innocent, fragile lives and brutalizes them
with utter poverty...with constant hunger...with relentless diseases...with no
hope for even a basic education.

As hard as parents of children
like this struggle, they simply can't
adequately provide for them.

But you can help. You can ease
the pain. Become a Save the Children
sponsor and help stop the horrible
abuse that poverty inflicts on children.

Your monthly gift of just $20 to
Save the Children will be combined
with the gifts of other caring sponsors
to benefit an entire community of
children. Instead of direct hand-outs,
your gifts will help establish community self-help programs, enabling
your girl or boy to receive the food,
medical care and education he or she
so urgently needs.

Please call or mail the coupon
below today and say you'll become a
Save the Children sponsor. Only 65¢
a day from you will help rescue a girl
or boy from the most horrible kind of

child abuse – and replace it with
vitality and hope.

**Please call 1-800-522-5558
or mail the coupon below today.**

I want to help put an end to a different kind of child abuse.

☐ My first monthly sponsorship contribution of $20 is enclosed.
   I prefer to sponsor a ☐ boy ☐ girl ☐ either in the area I've checked below.
   Please send my child's photo and personal history.

☐ Where the need is greatest
☐ Africa   ☐ Caribbean   ☐ Middle East   RS 2/10/4
☐ American Indian   ☐ Himalayas   ☐ South America
☐ Asia   ☐ Central America ☐ United States

Name_____
Address_____ Apt._____
City_____ State_____ Zip_____

☐ Instead of becoming a sponsor at this time, I am enclosing a contribution of $_____
☐ Please send me more information.

Established 1932. The original child sponsorship agency. YOUR
SPONSORSHIP CONTRIBUTIONS ARE U.S. INCOME TAX DEDUCTIBLE.
We are indeed proud of our use of funds. Our annual report and
audit statement are available upon request ©1999 Save the Children
Federation, Inc.

Save the Children.
50 Wilton Road, Westport, CT 06880

FIGURE 6

FIGURE 7

world." A specific claim requires specific support—not just a vague reference to an unidentified study. We cannot evaluate a recent study if we do not know how it was undertaken and where the results were published.

Writers who like to refer to "recent studies" are also fond of alluding to unspecified statistics, as in "statistics have shown . . ." or "According to statistics . . . ." Statistics can be of great value, but they can also be misleading. Ask yourself whether a statistic raises any unanswered questions, and note whether the source has been revealed. Similarly, turn a critical eye on claims like "It is a well-known fact that . . ." or "Everybody knows that . . . ." If the fact *is* well known, why is the writer boring us with what we already know? If the fact is *not* well known, as is usually the case when lines of this sort are thrown about, then the writer had better explain how he or she knows it.

In short, if you want to avoid bogus claims, never claim anything that would leave you speechless if you were called on to explain or defend what you have written.

Loaded Terms   Good writers have good diction; they know a lot of words and, just as important, they know how to use them accurately. They know that most words have positive or negative *connotations*—associations with the word that go beyond its standard definition or *denotation*. "Placid," "tranquil," or "serene" might all be used to describe someone who is "calm," but each word creates a slightly different impression. Experienced writers are likely to pause before choosing the adjective that best suits their subject.

A term becomes *loaded* when it is asked to carry more emotional weight than its context can legitimately support. A loaded term is a word or phrase that goes beyond connotation into the unconvincing world of the heavy handed and narrow minded. To put it simply, it is *slanted* or *biased*.

Loaded terms may appeal to the zealous, but they mislead the unwary reader and offend the critically minded. For example, when an aspiring journalist denounces the Clinton "regime" in the school newspaper, he is taking what many men and women would consider a cheap shot—regardless of their own politics. "Regime" is a loaded term because it is most frequently used to describe military dictatorships. Even someone who is politically opposed to Bill Clinton should be clearheaded enough to speak of the Clinton "Administration," which is the term best suited for a political discussion of the U.S Presidency.

Like "regime," many words have such strong connotations that they can become loaded terms very easily. In the United States, for example, terms such as "socialist," "feminist," "family," and "natural" all inspire responses that can affect how an audience responds to the context in which these words appear. Moreover, an unloaded term can become loaded within a specific context. To manipulate reader response, a writer may introduce unnecessary adjectives. A political correspondent might write "Margaret Ong, the wealthy candidate from Park Ridge, spoke today at Jefferson High School." The candidate's income has nothing to do with the news event being reported, so "wealthy" is a loaded term. It's an extra word that serves only one function: to divide the candidate from the newspaper's audience, very few of whom are "wealthy." It would not be surprising if some readers began to turn against this candidate, regardless of her platform, simply because they had been led to associate her with a background that is alien to their own.

Do not make the mistake of assuming that loaded terms occur only in political discourse. They can be found almost anywhere, if you take the trouble to read critically and intelligently. You may even find some in your textbooks.

Misrepresentation   Misrepresentation can take many forms. Someone may come right out and lie to you, telling you something you know—or subsequently discover—to be untrue. In the course of writing a paper, someone may invent statistics or alter research data that point to an unwelcome conclusion. And then there is *plagiarism*—taking someone else's words or ideas without acknowledgment and passing them off as your own.

There are always going to be people who find it easy to lie, and there isn't much we can do about this except to keep our eyes open, read well, and choose our friends with care. But we ourselves can be careful to act honorably and to follow the guidelines for working with sources that appear in Part 2 of this book. There is, however, a common misrepresentation that must be understood as part of our introduction to the principles of argument and persuasion: Dishonest writers will often misrepresent their opponents by twisting what others have said.

The most common way in which writers misrepresent opposing arguments is to oversimplify them. The ability to summarize what others have said or written is a skill that cannot be taken for granted, and we will turn to it shortly. There is always the possibility that someone may misrepresent an opponent accidentally—having failed to understand what has been said or having confused it in reporting it. But it is also possible to misreport others *deliberately*. A complex argument can be reduced to ridicule in a slogan, or an important element of such an argument could be entirely overlooked, creating a false impression.

Have the courage to ask for evidence whenever someone makes a questionable claim. When you find it necessary to quote someone, make sure you do so not only correctly but also *fairly*. The concept of "quoting out of context" is so familiar that the phrase has become a cliché. But clichés sometimes embody fundamental truths, and here is one of them: quotations should be more than accurate; they should also reflect the overall nature of the quoted source. When you select a passage that truly represents the thesis of another's work, you can use it in good conscience—as long as you remember to put it in quotation marks and reveal to your readers where you got it. If you fasten onto a minor detail and quote a line that could be misunderstood if lifted away from the sentences that originally surrounded it, then you are guilty of misrepresentation.

Bogus claims, loaded terms, and misrepresentation are almost always to be found in that extreme form of persuasion known as *propaganda*. Strictly speaking, propaganda means only the systematic use of words and images to propagate (or spread) ideas, but the abuse of propaganda within the past century has made the word widely associated with dishonesty. (For an extended definition of this term, see "The Purpose of Progaganda," by Adolf Hitler, pages 537–543.) Because the techniques of persuasion are easy to abuse, you should use them with great care. If you are trying to move an audience to action, you may find it useful to appeal to the heart as well as to the head, but you should try to avoid appealing to the heart alone. When appealing to the mind, it is always more honorable to address an audience as intelligent and thoughtful adults than to subtly exploit their subconscious hopes and fears.

An essay or speech that works primarily by inspiring an emotional response is most likely to succeed only when an audience can be called on for immediate action. If a senator can inspire her colleagues moments before a critically important vote, or an evangelist can move a congregation to generosity just as the collection plate is about to be passed, then the results of such persuasion may be significant. But opportunities of this sort are rare for most writers. Almost everything we write can be put aside and reconsidered at another time. Irrespective of the ethical importance of arguing what is true and not just what is convenient, there is also a very practical reason for trying to argue logically: The arguments that carry the greatest weight are usually the arguments that are capable of holding up under analysis. They make *more* sense as we think about them, not less. Whereas persuasion relies on impulse, argument depends on conviction. Our impulses may determine what we do this afternoon, but our convictions shape the rest of our lives. If you make a genuinely logical argument, you may make some people angry with you, but you will not be accused of dishonesty. When you abandon logic for other persuasive techniques, make sure that this is simply a change in writing strategy. Never write anything that you don't believe. This does not mean that there's anything wrong with writing fiction or satire. But it does mean that good writers shouldn't tell lies.

PART 2

WORKING WITH SOURCES

READING CRITICALLY

Although reading can be a pleasure, and many people find it relaxing to read material that provides a temporary escape from daily concerns, serious reading requires an active response on your part. When reading in college, or in whatever profession you are preparing for, you need to think about what you read. To make sure that you understand the content of what you have read, you must be able to identify key points—such as an author's thesis—and any points where you had difficulty. But beyond working to understand the material before you, you should also be prepared to *evaluate* it. As students, you will sometimes find yourself confronted with more information than you can digest with ease. You will also find that different writers will tell you different things. When this happens, inexperienced readers sometimes become confused or discouraged. Being able to recognize what material deserves the closest reading, and what sources are the most reliable, is essential to coping successfully with the many demands made on your time as students. By reading critically, and reading often, you can acquire skills that will help you in almost any college course.

As you read the material collected in this book, you will find that some articles are easier to read than others. It would be a mistake to assume that the easiest material is necessarily the most reliable. On the other hand, it would also be wrong to assume that long, difficult articles are reliable simply because they are long and difficult. Whether you are preparing to write an argument of your own or simply trying to become better informed on an issue that has more than one side, you can benefit from practicing specific strategies for critical reading.

Previewing

Even before you begin to read, there are a few steps that you can take to help you benefit from the reading you are about to undertake. A quick preview, or survey, of a written text should give you an idea of how long it will take to read, what the reading will probably reveal, and how useful the reading is likely to be. When you glance through a newspaper, identifying stories that you want to read and others that you merely want to skim over, you are practicing a simple type of preview—one that is often guided primarily by your level of interest in various issues. But when previewing reading material in college, it is usually wise to ask yourself some questions that go beyond whether you happen to find a topic appealing.

How Long Is This Work?   By checking the length of a work before you begin to read, you can estimate how much reading time this material will demand, based on the speed and ease with which you normally read. The length may also be a clue in determining how useful a text may be. Although quantity is no sure guide to quality, a long work may contain more information than a short work. When reading an article in an anthology or in a magazine, you can quickly flip ahead to see where it ends. And when doing library research (discussed in Part 6 of this book), you can usually learn the length of a work before you even hold it in your hand. This information is included in periodical indexes and most book catalogs. (See the illustrations on pages 586 and 587.)

What Can I Learn from the Title?   Although a title may be too general to give you an idea of what to expect when you read the work in question, titles often reveal an author's focus. An article called "Drugs and the Modern Athlete" will differ in focus from one called "Drug Testing and Corporate Responsibility." Moreover, a title can often indicate the author's point of view. Examples within this book include "In Defense of Hunting," "The Value of the Canon," "The Purpose of Propaganda," and "The Futility of the Death Penalty."

Do I Know Anything about the Author?   Recognizing the names of established authorities in your field becomes easier as you do more reading, but many written sources offer information that can help you estimate an author's credibility when that author is unfamiliar to you. A magazine article may identify the author at the beginning or the end of the article, or on a separate page (often called "Notes on Contributors" and listed in the table of contents). A biographical sketch of the author can usually be found on a book jacket, and a list of his or her other works may appear at either the front or the back of the book. Anthologies often include introductory headnotes for the various writers whose work has been selected. In *The Informed Argument,* the headnotes can help you to discover the authors' credentials for writing on the topic at hand. An author may have already published other works on the same subject. On the other hand, some authors choose to write about topics that are not directly related to their field of expertise. Suppose, for example, that you are about to read an argument on nuclear energy. By noting whether the article was written by a utility executive or an environmental activist, you can prepare yourself for the sort of argument you are most likely to encounter. If the article is written by a famous authority on child care, you might ask yourself whether that author will be a credible authority on nuclear power plants. Remember, however, that experts can make mistakes, and that important arguments can be written by someone new to the field. The best way to appraise an author's credibility is to read her work, noting how much evidence she provides to support her claims and how fairly she seems to treat other people.

What Do I Know about the Publisher?   An important work can be published by an obscure publisher, and a small magazine may be the first to publish an author destined to win a Pulitzer prize. The reputation of a publisher is not an automatic guide to the reliability of a source, but there are a few factors that can help you determine whether a source is likely to be worthwhile. University presses tend to expect a high degree of scholarship, and academic journals usually publish articles only after they have been examined by two or three other experts in that field. When you read an article in a popular magazine, the nature of that magazine may suggest what it is likely to publish. For example, an article on hunting in *Field & Stream* is almost certain to be very different from one on hunting in *Vegetarian Times*. If you read widely in periodicals, you will eventually find that some magazines and newspapers consistently reflect political positions that might be characterized as either "liberal" or "conservative." When you make a discovery of this sort, you can often make a pretty good guess about what kind of stand will be taken on issues discussed in one of these periodicals. This guess can prepare you to note any bias within the articles. Once again, remember that you are only making a preliminary estimate when previewing. The best way to judge a work is to read it carefully.

Is There Anything Else I Can Discover by Skimming through the Material?   A quick examination of the text can identify a number of other features that can help you orient yourself to what you are about to read. Consider the length of the average paragraph; long paragraphs may indicate a densely written text that you will need to read slowly. Are there any special features, such as tables, figures, or illustrations that will give you visual aids? Are there any subtitles? If so, they may provide you with a rough outline of the work in question and indicate points where you may be able to take a break if necessary. Quickly reading the first sentence in every paragraph may also give you a sense of the work's outline. In some cases, a writer may actually provide you with a summary. Articles from scholarly journals are often preceded by an *abstract* (or summary) that can help you understand the article and estimate the extent to which it is likely to be of use to you. (See the example on page 598.) Articles without abstracts may include a brief summary within the text itself; check the first few and last few paragraphs, the two locations where writers most often summarize their views. Finally, be sure to note whether the work includes a reference list. Scanning a bibliography—noting both how current the research seems and how extensive it is—can help you appraise a writer's scholarship and alert you to other sources that you may want to read on your own.

Annotating

Marking a text with notes, or *annotating* it, can be a great help when you are trying to understand your reading. Annotation can also help you to discover points that you might want to question when you evaluate this work. One of the advantages of owning a book—or having your own photocopy of an excerpt from a book or magazine—is that you can mark it as heavily as you wish without violating the rights of others. When you are annotating a text that is important to you, you will usually benefit from reading that text more than once and adding new annotations with each reading.

Equipped with a yellow felt-tipped pen, some students like to "highlight" the passages that seem most important to them. If this technique has worked well for you, there is no reason why you should feel compelled to abandon it. But it has two disadvantages. One is that highlighting cannot be erased. Some students find themselves with yellow-coated pages because they were initially unable to distinguish between main points and supporting details—and were later unable to remove unnecessary highlighting when they came to understand the text better. A second problem is that highlighting pens usually make broad marks ill-suited for writing. If you read with a pen like this in hand, you will need to reach for another pen or pencil whenever you want to add comments in the margin.

When reading, especially when reading a text for the first time, you might benefit from an alternative to highlighting. Try using a pen or pencil and simply marking in the margin a small check (✓) when a line seems important, an exclamation point (!) when you find surprising information or an unusually bold claim, and a question mark (?) when you have trouble understanding a particular passage or find yourself disagreeing with what it says. This simple form of annotation can be done very easily, and if you use a pencil, you will be able to erase any marks that you later find distracting.

When you are able to spend more time with a text, and want to be sure that you understand not only its content but also its strengths and weaknesses, then additional annotations are in order. Use the margins to define new words and identify unfamiliar allusions. Write comments that will remind you of what is discussed in various paragraphs. Jot down questions that you may subsequently raise in class or explore in a paper. By making cross references (like "*cf.* ¶ *3*" beside a later paragraph), you can remind yourself of how various components of the work fit together and also identify apparent contradictions within the work. Finally, whenever you are moved to a strong response—whether you are agreeing or disagreeing with what you have read—write that thought down before you lose it. An annotation of this sort can be useful when you are reviewing material before an exam, and it may very well be the seed from which a paper will later grow.

To give you an example of annotation, here is an annotated excerpt from The Declaration of Independence. (The full text, unannotated, appears in Part 4, pp. 485–488.) As you examine it, remember that readers annotate a text in different ways. Some annotations are more thorough and reflective than others, but there are no "correct" responses against which your own annotations must be measured. You may notice different aspects of a text each time you reread it, so your annotations are likely to accumulate in layers. Annotations have been reproduced here in both printing and script, to suggest how they accumulated during more than one reading.

1776 When in the Course of human events, it becomes nec- *such as Americans*
essary for one people to dissolve the political bands
which have connected them with another, and to as- *such as English*
sume among the powers of the earth, the separate and
equal station to which the Laws of Nature and of Nature's God entitle them, a decent respect to the opinions of mankind requires that they should declare the
causes which impel them to the separation.

Why should nation have "equal station" when some are more powerful than others?

Is "Nature's God" different from "God"?

We hold these truths to be self-evident, that all
men are created equal, that they are endowed by their
Creator with certain unalienable Rights, that among
these are Life, Liberty and the pursuit of Happiness.
That to secure these rights, Governments are instituted among Men, deriving their just powers from the
consent of the governed. That whenever any Form of
Government becomes destructive of these ends it is
the Right of the People to alter or to abolish it, and to
institute new Government, laying its foundation on
such principles and organizing its powers in such
form, as to them shall seem most likely to effect their
Safety and Happiness. Prudence, indeed, will dictate
that Governments long established should not be
changed for light and transient causes; and accordingly
all experience has shewn, that mankind are more disposed to suffer, while evils are sufferable, than to right
themselves by abolishing the forms to which they are
accustomed. But when a long train of abuses and
usurpations, pursuing invariably the same Object
evinces a design to reduce them under absolute
Despotism, it is their right, it is their duty, to throw
off such Government, and to provide new Guards for
their future security. Such has been the patient sufferance of these Colonies; and such is now the necessity
which constrains them to alter their former Systems of
Government. The history of the present King of Great
Britain is a history of repeated injuries and usurpations, all having in direct object the establishment of
an absolute Tyranny over these States. To prove this,
let Facts be submitted to a candid world.

Does this include women???

Why "self-evident"? Couldn't he prove them? Permanent, "not to be separates"

If the rights to life & liberty are "unalienable" how come we have capital punishment and prisons?

So the Civil War was ok?

George III (ruled from 1760 to 1820)

impartial

Why is the capitalization so weird?

SUMMARIZING

Summarizing a work is one of the best ways to demonstrate that you have understood it. On many occasions, you will be required to summarize what others have said or written—or even what you yourself have said or written. This skill is especially important in argumentation. You will have to be able to summarize the main arguments of your opponents if you want to write a convincing argument of your own. And research papers will become ridiculously long, obscure, and unwieldy if you lack the ability to summarize your reading.

There is no clear rule to determine what passages are more significant than others. Every piece of writing must be judged on its own merits, and this means that you must consider every paragraph individually. The first sentence of a paragraph may be important if it introduces a new idea. Unfortunately for writers of summary (but fortunately for readers, who would be easily bored if every paragraph followed the same mechanical pattern), the first sentence may simply be a transitional sentence, linking the paragraph with whatever has preceded it. The *topic sentence* (also called the *thesis sentence*) is the single most important sentence in most paragraphs—the exception being the very short paragraphs that serve only as transitions. (Transitional paragraphs do not advance a new idea, but simply link together longer paragraphs devoted to ideas that are related, but not closely enough so that the paragraphs can flow smoothly together.) It is important to remember that the topic sentence can occur anywhere in a paragraph.

As you read the material you want to summarize, limit yourself to marking no more than one or two sentences per paragraph. You should identify the topic sentence, and you may want to mark a line that contains an important supporting detail. At this point, you may choose to copy all the material you have noted onto a separate sheet of paper. But do not think that this means you have completed a summary. What you have are the notes for a summary: a collection of short quotations that are unlikely to flow smoothly together. A good summary should always be easy to read. After you take your notes, you must shape them into a clear, concise piece of writing.

As a writer of summary, be prepared to *paraphrase*—to restate something you've read or heard into your own words. There are many different reasons for paraphrasing, and you've probably been practicing this skill since you were a child. We frequently paraphrase the words of others to soften unpleasant truths. Sometimes we may even be tempted to restate a relatively mild statement more harshly to make trouble for someone we don't like. But in writing summary, we should paraphrase only to make complex ideas more easily understandable. A paraphrase can be as long as the original material; under some circumstances, it may even be longer. So don't confuse paraphrase with summary. Paraphrasing is simply one of the skills that we call upon to write a coherent summary.

Reading over the quotations you have compiled, look for lines that seem longer than they have to be and ideas that seem unnecessarily complicated. Lines of this sort are likely subjects for paraphrase. As you restate these ideas more simply, you may also be able to include details that appeared elsewhere in the paragraph and seem too important to leave out. You should not have to restate everything that someone else has written, although there's nothing necessarily wrong in doing so. A summary can include direct quotation, so long as the quotations are relatively short and have a clarity that you yourself cannot surpass.

You should now reread your paraphrasing and any quotations that you have included. Look for gaps between sentences, where the writing seems awkward or choppy. Rearrange any sentences that would flow more smoothly once you have done so. Eliminate any repetition and add transitional phrases wherever they can help smooth the way from one idea to the next. After you have made certain that your sentences follow in a clear and easily readable sequence and have corrected any errors in grammar, spelling, or syntax, you should have an adequate summary of the material you set out to cover. You would be wise to read over what you have written at least one more time, making sure that the content accurately reflects the nature of whatever is being summarized. Be absolutely sure that any direct quotations are recognizable as such by being placed within quotation marks.

Writing summary requires good judgment. A writer has to be able to distinguish what is essential from what is not, and the judgment that summary demands should be editorial only. If the material being summarized has a particular bias, then a good summary should indicate that that bias is part of the work in question. *But writers should not interject their own opinions into a summary of someone else's work.* The tone of summary should be neutral. You may choose to summarize someone's work so that you can criticize it later, but do not confuse summary with criticism. When summarizing, you are taking the role of helping other writers to speak for themselves. Don't let your own ideas get in the way.

Good summaries vary in length, depending on the length and complexity of the original material and on how much time or space is available for summarizing it. It's unusual, however, to need more than 500 words to summarize most material, and you may be required to summarize an entire book in less than half that length. When summary is being used as a preliminary to some other type of work—such as argument or analysis—it is especially important to be concise. For example, if you are summarizing an argument before offering a counterargument of your own, you may be limited to a single paragraph. The general rule to follow is: Try to do justice to whatever you are summarizing in as few words as possible, and make sure that you have a legitimate reason for writing any summary that goes on for more than a page or two.

Experienced writers know that summary is a skill worth practicing. If you find summary difficult, remind yourself that it combines two skills of fundamental and inescapable importance: reading and writing. Well-educated men and women must be proficient in both. Summarizing tests not only your ability to write simply and clearly, but also your ability to comprehend what you read. The selections in Parts 3 and 4 of this book will provide you with many opportunities for summarizing. You will also find an example of summary in the student essay by Sara Jenkins at the end of the section on gun control (pp. 129–130).

Exercise 8

Written by a staff reporter, the following article was first published by *The Wall Street Journal* on September 24, 1990. Write a two-paragraph summary of this article, with one paragraph devoted to why increasing numbers of teenagers are seeking plastic surgery and the second to why some experts are concerned about this trend.

SUZANNE ALEXANDER

FIXED AT A PRICE

As an eighth-grade graduation present, Kristina Olson got new ears from her   1
mother. Leigh Kane, at 17, got a new nose.

Since last month, Danielle Borngiorno, 14, has had narrower hips and   2
thinner thighs. Her mother offered to pay for breast implants, too, but
Danielle decided against that, for the time being. She is still considering chin
and nose work and a cheek implant. "Now, [it's] just like, let's go every week
and get something improved on. There are so many things you can do," says
Danielle, who lives in Brooklyn, N.Y.

Why bother with padded bras and Clearasil when silicone and dermabra-   3
sion promise permanence? Why spend one's adolescence brooding about receding chins or big ears when it is so simple to have plastic surgery?

New, Young Clientele

To the dismay of at least some psychologists and medical doctors, cosmetic   4
surgery is now hardly more exotic than orthodontics among children whose
parents have the wherewithal to pay $600 or $6,000 for a surgical procedure to
improve on nature. Statistics don't exist, but many plastic surgeons say their
teen-age clientele has doubled in the past five years and now is as much as 25%
of their business.

Nose and ear jobs remain the most popular operations. But dermabrasion   5
(sanding off layers of skin), breast augmentation and liposuction (fat sucking)
are coming on strong with kids, not just with middle-aged entertainers like
Phyllis Diller. Many Asian boys and girls, overeager to assimilate, seek to
reshape the epicanthic fold in their eyelids. Some black youths, à la Michael
Jackson, see surgeons for narrower noses and thinner lips.

Observers critical of the phenomenon see in it pampered children who   6
can't tolerate the pain of being themselves. They see a society obsessed with
appearance and with narrow-minded notions of what constitutes beauty.

"I hear doctors defend the right of teens to have face-lift surgery and eye-   7
lid surgery," says Frederick Stucker, chairman of the Otolaryngology—Head

and Neck Surgery Department at Louisiana State University, "but I think we send the wrong message when we're willing to do it for teens." Dr. Stucker maintains that a lot of operations are unnecessary because teenage acne, baby-fat, and other "problems" usually disappear on their own as kids get older.

Wanting It All

Adds Norman M. Cole, vice president of the American Society of Plastic and   8
Reconstructive Surgeons: "A real problem in our society is that parents want everything for their children. Aesthetic surgery has become a commodity. 'I want my son to have a new stereo, car, nose and chin.' This is something that deserves some careful interrogation." Surgery to change racial characteristics, Dr. Cole says, is "an inappropriate concession to Western images. The Oriental eye in China is considered the most beautiful in the world. It's a sad commentary . . . ."

Cosmetic surgeons have their own interests in the matter, and some of   9
them argue that plastic surgery is a real boon to teenagers psychologically. Insecurity, self-consciousness and a lack of self-esteem vanish once the bandages come off. Surgery can take "years off a psychiatrist's couch," says Walter Berman, a facial plastic surgeon in Beverly Hills, Calif.

"I did two kids [a 14-year-old girl and a 16-year-old boy] this week who   10
had a hereditary bagging of the upper eyelid," says Lori Hansen, a plastic surgeon in Oklahoma City, Okla. "It made them look tired all the time. So we just took the extra skin and fat away. Things are so easily fixed now. We don't have to live with them."

But critics say that in many cases parents are to blame for wanting   11
"perfect-looking" children, thus encouraging low self-esteem in their offspring. "We see it often," says Pearlman D. Hicks, a plastic surgeon in Long Beach, Calif. "The parent tells the kid, 'Your nose looks terrible. You don't even look like part of the family.' [Parents] plant the seed and get the kids worried."

Nose jobs, of course, are nothing new for teen-agers. But they once were   12
a thing of the affluent and the disfigured. Now, middle-class people get them almost willy-nilly. They are a socially acceptable mid-course correction in the life of an adolescent. New procedures, like liposuction, have been introduced in the U.S. within the past 10 years and pull in a lot of patients.

Many teen-agers who have had cosmetic surgery say they are glad they   13
did. Why put it off and prolong the agony when they are likely to have it done eventually anyway?

"My mom had the same problem. She had something done about it. I   14
could have waited years, but I did it now," says Abigail Clawson, 15, speaking of her nose and chin jobs last April. Abigail, of Westlake Village, Calif., had a bump on her nose and a receding chin. Nobody ever teased her about her profile, but for some children, ridicule from schoolmates can be merciless: "Is that your nose or a banana?" the kids in Hartshorne, Okla., used to taunt Amanda Andrews, 13. For years, Amanda would come home from school weeping.

Explains Lorraine Hollis, Amanda's grandmother and legal guardian: 15
"She had a great big snoot that slumped down—and a little, pointed chin. It
gave her a witchy look." Ms. Hollis took Amanda in for rhinoplasty (nose
surgery) on her 13th birthday a year ago this month. Now, Amanda says, "I'm
happier. A lot more guys ask me out. Even those who teased me now say,
'You're looking better.'"

Kristina Olson, 20, of Indianapolis, used to hate to go to school because   16
her "Dumbo" ears, as she refers to them, stuck out. "I couldn't enjoy life,"
says Kristina, who would sit in the back of the classroom and hold her hand
over one ear while covering the other with her hair.

Finally, her mother took her in for otoplasty—which, in effect, pins back   17
protruding ears—as a gift of "happiness and mental health." At the age of 16,
Kristina entered a new school and "no one knew the history of my ears." Her
self-esteem and self-confidence soared.

One young black woman, who doesn't want her name mentioned,   18
thought her nose was too wide. While she didn't want to change all her racial
features, the 19-year-old thought a smaller, narrower nose would "enhance"
her beauty.

So, after white friends of hers had had rhinoplasties done and her own   19
father had the surgery, the Los Angeles resident, now 21, decided to narrow
her nose, too. "I don't think I'm trying to be white," although she realizes that
"a lot of people see it that way."

Leigh Kane, of Glen Cove, N.Y., the boy who had the nose job at 17,   20
says he hadn't realized his nose was out of the ordinary until his mother told
him so two years ago. "I thought she was kidding. [She said] she noticed that
it was getting progressively worse as I got older," says Leigh, now 19. Suddenly self-conscious, Leigh had a surgeon remove a bump on his nose and fashion a new tip. And now he feels better about himself.

Despite the anecdotal evidence from satisfied young clients, medical pro-   21
fessionals worry that youngsters aren't prepared to cope with the perils—
physical and psychological—of cosmetic surgery.

"I think the psychological risk among teens is significantly higher than it   22
is among [the] more mature," says Dr. Cole. Often, teen-agers and their parents have unrealistic expectations that changing appearance will solve
deepseated problems that require psychiatric attention not cosmetic surgery.

Dr. Cole says that several years ago he performed rhinoplasty on a 16-   23
year-old girl who was ecstatic with the results at first but later returned complaining that the nose job hadn't done the trick. She couldn't, however,
articulate exactly what was bothering her. "I think psychologically . . . that
nose wasn't the problem," he says.

Since most surgical procedures are irreversible, operating on teen-agers is   24
a heavy responsibility. Patients are routinely told that things can't be put back
the way they were after the surgery has been done. Patients are counseled ex-
tensively before surgery, so they know the risks involved. In most states, an
18-year-old can get plastic surgery without parental consent. Still, some young
patients and their families have regrets.

Dr. Cole says a colleague operated on the eyelids of an 18-year-old   25
youngster of Korean ancestry who panicked because his grandparents were angry. "The family was insulted," Dr. Cole says. They felt that, in having the
surgery, the young man was rejecting his culture. He went back in desperation
seeking to have the surgery undone, but of course it wasn't possible.

Doctors say that to be unhappy with one's physical appearance is simply   26
a part of being a teen-ager, and that maturity can be the cure. Michael Seifert,
14, of Los Angeles, has a bump on his nose and a father who is a plastic surgeon. The son wanted surgery. The father refused on the grounds that Michael
is too young.

Lately, Michael has found a new girlfriend, who thinks the bump on his   27
nose gives him "character." He no longer wants to go under the knife.   ■

SYNTHESIZING

Synthesis is closely related to summary, and it demands many of the same skills.
The principal difference is that while summary involves identifying the major
points of a single work or passage, synthesis requires identifying related material in two or more works and tying them smoothly together. Synthesis is often
an extension of summary because writers may need to summarize various
sources before they can relate these sources to one another. Synthesis does not
necessarily require you to cover *all* the major points of the individual sources.
You may go through an entire article or book and identify only one point that
relates to another work you have read. And the relationships involved in your
synthesis may be of various kinds. For example, two different authors may have
made the same claim, or one might provide specific information that supports
a generalization made by the other. On the other hand, one author might provide information that makes another author's generalization seem inadequate
or even wrong.

When reading material that you may need to synthesize, always try to
ask yourself: "How does this material relate to whatever else I have already
read on this topic?" If you are unable to answer this question, consider a few
more specific questions: Does the second of two works offer support for the
first or does it reflect an entirely different thesis? If the two sources share a
similar position, do they arrive at a similar conclusion by entirely different
means or do they overlap at any points? Would it be easier to compare the two
works or to contrast them? This process of identifying similarities and differences is essentially what synthesis is all about.

When you have determined the points that link your various sources to
one another, you are ready to write a synthesis. To see how a synthesis can be
organized, let us consider an example. Suppose you have read several articles
on the subject of AIDS. The first article was by a scientist, the second by a
clergyman, the third by a gay activist, and the fourth by a government official.
You were struck by how differently these four writers responded to this epidemic. Although they all agreed that AIDS is a serious problem, each writer

advanced a different proposal for fighting this disease. To write a synthesis, you would probably begin with an introductory paragraph that includes a clear thesis statement. In this case, it might be: "Although there is widespread agreement that AIDS is a serious problem, there is no consensus about how this problem can be solved." Each of the following four paragraphs could then be devoted to a brief summary of one of the different points of view. A final paragraph might emphasize the relationship of the several sources either by reviewing the major points of disagreement among them or by emphasizing one or two points about which everyone agreed. An outline for this type of synthesis would be something like this:

PARAGRAPH ONE:	Introduction
PARAGRAPH TWO:	Summary of first writer
PARAGRAPH THREE:	Summary of second writer
PARAGRAPH FOUR:	Summary of third writer
PARAGRAPH FIVE:	Summary of fourth writer
PARAGRAPH SIX:	Conclusion

Any good outline allows for some flexibility. Depending on the material and what you want to say, your synthesis might have fewer than six paragraphs or it might involve more. For example, if two of your sources were especially long and complex, there is no reason why you couldn't devote two paragraphs to each of these sources even though you were able to summarize your other two sources within single paragraphs.

An alternative method for organizing a synthesis involves linking two or more writers within paragraphs that focus on specific issues or points. This type of organization is especially useful when you have detected a number of similarities that you want to emphasize. Suppose that you have read six essays about abortion. Three writers favored legalized abortion for much the same reasons; three writers opposing abortion also used similar arguments. Your assignment is to identify the most common arguments made by people who favor legalized abortion and those made by people who oppose it. Your outline for synthesizing this material might be organized like this:

PARAGRAPH ONE:	Introduction
PARAGRAPH TWO:	One argument in favor of abortion that was made by different writers
PARAGRAPH THREE:	A second argument in favor of abortion that was made by different writers
PARAGRAPH FOUR:	One argument against abortion that was made by different writers
PARAGRAPH FIVE:	A second argument against abortion that was made by different writers
PARAGRAPH SIX:	Conclusion

Suppose, during the course of your reading, you identified several other arguments both for and against legalized abortion, but you have decided not to include them within your synthesis because each point came up only within a single work and your assignment was to identify the most commonly made arguments on this subject. If you feel uneasy about ignoring these additional points, you can easily remind your audience in either your introduction or your conclusion that other arguments exist and you are focusing only on those most commonly put forward.

For an example of a synthesis written by a student, see the essay by Andrew Shimek at the end of the section on AIDS in the workplace (pp. 171–173).

AVOIDING PLAGIARISM

You are guilty of plagiarism if you take someone else's words or ideas without giving adequate acknowledgement. Plagiarism is one of the worst forms of dishonest writing, and you may be severely penalized for it even if you did not intend to do it.

The most obvious form of plagiarism is to submit someone else's paper as your own. No one does this accidentally. Another form of plagiarism is to copy long passages from a book or article and pretend that the words are your own. Once again, anyone doing this is almost certain to know that she or he is cheating.

But students sometimes plagiarize without intending to do so. The most common form of plagiarism is an inadequate paraphrase. Some students will read a passage in a book, change the wording, and then believe that they have transformed the material into their own work. *You must always remember that it is important to give credit to the* ideas *of others, as well as their words.* If you take most of the information another writer has provided and repeat it in essentially the same pattern, you are only a half-step away from copying the material word-for-word. Here is an example:

Original Source

Hawthorne's political ordeal, the death of his mother—and whatever guilt he may have harbored on either score—afforded him an understanding of the secret psychological springs of guilt. *The Scarlet Letter* is the book of a changed man. Its deeper insights have nothing to do with orthodox morality or religion—or the universal or allegorical applications of a moral. The greatness of the book is related to its sometimes fitful characterizations of human nature and the author's almost uncanny intuitions: his realization of the bond between psychological malaise and physical illness, the nearly perfect, if sinister, outlining of the psychological techniques Chillingsworth deployed against his victim.

Plagiarism

Nathaniel Hawthorne understood the psychological sources of guilt. His experience in politics and the death of his mother brought him deep insights that don't have anything to do with formal religion or morality. The greatness of *The Scarlet Letter* comes from its characters and the author's brilliant intuitions: Hawthorne's perception of the link between psychological and physical illness and his almost perfect description of the way Roger Chillingsworth persecuted his victim.

This student has simplified the original material, changing some of its wording. But he is clearly guilty of plagiarism. Pretending to offer his own analysis of *The Scarlet Letter,* he owes all of his ideas to another writer who is unacknowledged. Even the organization of the passage has been followed. This "paraphrase" would still be considered a plagiarism even if it ended with a reference to the original source (p. 307 of *Nathaniel Hawthorne in His Times,* by James R. Mellow). A reference or footnote would not reveal the full extent to which this student is indebted to his source.

Here is an acceptable version:

Paraphrase

As James R. Mellow has argued in *Nathaniel Hawthorne in His Times, The Scarlet Letter* reveals a profound understanding of guilt. It is a great novel because of its insight into human nature—not because of some moral about adultery. The most interesting character is probably Roger Chillingsworth because of the way he was able to make Rev. Dimmesdale suffer (307).

This student has not only made a greater effort to paraphrase the original material, but he has also introduced it with a reference to the writer he is drawing upon. The introductory reference to Mellow, coupled with the subsequent page reference, "brackets" the passage—showing us that Mellow deserves the credit for the ideas in between the two references. Additional bibliographical information about this source is provided by the list of works cited at the end of the paper. Turning to the student's bibliography we find:

Mellow, James. *Nathaniel Hawthorne in His Times.* Boston: Houghton, 1980.

One final caution: It is possible to subconsciously remember a piece of someone else's phrasing and inadvertently repeat it. You would be guilty of plagiarism if the words in question embody a critically important idea or reflect a distinctive style or turn of phrase. When you revise your draft, look for such unintended quotations; if you use them, show who deserves the credit for them, and *remember to put quoted material within quotation marks.*

DOCUMENTING YOUR SOURCES

"Documenting your sources" means revealing the source of information you report. You must provide documentation for:

- Any direct quotation,
- Any idea that has come from someone else's work, and
- Any fact or statistic that is not widely known.

The traditional way to document a source is to footnote it. Strictly speaking, a "footnote" appears at the foot of the page, and an "endnote" appears at the end of the paper. But "footnote" has become a generic term covering both forms. Most writers prefer to keep their notes on a separate page (an easier method than remembering to save adequate space for notes at the bottom of each page). The precise form of such notes varies, depending on the style manual being followed. Here is how a documentary footnote would look according to the style guidelines of the Modern Language Association (MLA):

A. Bibliographic Form

> Manchester, William. American Caesar: Douglas MacArthur 1880-1964. Boston: Little, 1978.

B. Note Form

> [1]William Manchester, American Caesar: Douglas MacArthur 1880-1964 (Boston: Little, 1978) 65.

The indentation is reversed, the author's name is not inverted, and the publishing data are included within parentheses. Also, the author is separated from the title by a comma rather than a period. A subsequent reference to the same work would follow a shortened form:

> [5]Manchester 182.

If more than one work by this same author is cited, then a shortened form of the title would also be included:

> [7]Manchester, Caesar 228.

Documentary footnotes require what many authorities now regard as unnecessary repetition, because the author's full name and the publishing data are already included in the bibliography. Many readers object to being obliged to turn frequently to another page if they want to check the notes. Some writers still use notes for documentation purposes. But most important style guides now urge writers to provide their documentation parenthetically within the work itself, reserving numbered notes for additional explanation or discussion that is important but cannot be included within the actual text without a loss of focus. Notes used for providing additional information are called *content notes*. The essays by Stephanie Riger (225–241) and Marilyn Arnold (425–429) include content notes, as do other essays in Part 3.

The form of your documentation will vary, depending on the subject of your paper and the requirements of your instructor. Students in the humanities are usually asked to follow the form of the Modern Language Association (MLA) or that recommended by *The Chicago Manual of Style*. Students in the social sciences are often expected to follow the format of the American Psychological Association (APA). Students in the natural sciences are usually required to use either a parenthetical system resembling that of the APA or a system that involves numbering their sources. Make sure that you understand the requirements of your instructor, and remember that you can consult a specific manual in your field if you run into problems. Here is a list of manuals that can be found in many college libraries:

> American Institute of Physics. Publication Board. *Style Manual for Guidance in the Preparation of Papers*. 3rd ed. New York: American Inst. of Physics, 1978.
>
> American Chemical Society. *American Chemical Society Style Guide and Handbook*. Washington: American Chemical Soc., 1985.
>
> American Mathematical Society. *A Manual for Authors of Mathematical Papers*. 7th ed. Providence: American Mathematical Soc., 1980.
>
> American Psychological Association. *Publication Manual of the American Psychological Association*. 4th ed. Washington: American Psychological Assn., 1994.
>
> *The Chicago Manual of Style*. 14th ed. Chicago: University of Chicago Press, 1993.
>
> Council of Biology Editors. Style Manual Committee. *CBE Style Manual: A Guide for Authors, Editors, and Publishers in the Biological Sciences*. 5th ed. Bethesda: Council of Biology Editors, 1983.
>
> Gibaldi, Joseph. *MLA Handbook for Writers of Research Papers*. 4th ed. New York: Modern Language Assn., 1995.
>
> Harvard Law Review Association. *The Bluebook: A Uniform System of Citation*. 15th ed. Cambridge: Harvard Law Review Assn., 1991.

A detailed discussion of all of these styles is beyond the range of this chapter, but the following pages provide model entries for the most frequently used styles.

PARENTHETICAL DOCUMENTATION: THE MLA AUTHOR/WORK STYLE

Since 1984, the Modern Language Association has recommended that parenthetical documentation take the place of endnote or footnote citations. In MLA form, the author's name is followed by a page reference. It is not necessary to repeat within the parentheses information that is already provided within the text. If you are used to using footnotes for documentation, this format may seem a little strange at first, but it has the great merit of being easy to use and easy to understand. (Remember that additional information on these sources will be provided in a separate bibliography.)

A. A Work by a Single Author

Henry James often identified wickedness with sexual duplicity (Kazin 227).

or

Alfred Kazin has argued that Henry James identified wickedness with sexual duplicity (227).

There is no punctuation between the author's name and the page reference when both are cited parenthetically. Note also that the abbreviation "p." or "pp." is not used before the page reference.

B. A Work with More Than One Author

Cleanth Brooks and Robert Penn Warren have argued that "indirection is an essential part of the method of poetry" (573).

or

Although this sonnet may seem obscure, its meaning becomes clearer when we realize "indirection is an essential part of the method of poetry" (Brooks and Warren 573).

Note that when a sentence ends with a quotation, the parenthetical reference comes before the final punctuation mark. Note also that the ampersand (&) is not used in MLA style. When referring to a work by more than three authors, you should follow the guidelines for bibliographic entries and list only the first author's name followed by "et al." (Latin for *et alii*, "and others").

These works "derive from a profound disillusionment with modern life" (Baym et al. 910).

C. A Work with a Corporate Author

When a corporate author has a long name, you should include it within the text rather than within parentheses. For example:

The Council on Environmental Quality has reported that there is growing evidence of ground water contamination throughout the United States (81).

rather than

There is growing evidence of ground water contamination throughout the United States (Council on Environmental Quality 81).

Although both of these forms are technically correct, the first is preferred because it is easier to read. Long parenthetical references are unnecessarily intrusive, interrupting the flow of ideas.

D. A Work with More Than One Volume

When you wish to cite a specific part of a multivolume work, include the volume number between the author and the page reference:

As Jacques Barzun has argued, "The only hope of true culture is to make classifications broad and criticism particular" (2: 340).

Note that the volume number is given in an arabic numeral, and a space separates the colon and the page reference. The abbreviation "vol." is not used unless you wish to cite the entire volume: (Barzun, vol. 2).

E. More Than One Work by the Same Author

If you cite more than one work by the same author, you need to make your references distinct. You can do so by putting a comma after the author's name and then adding a shortened form of the title: (Hardy, *Mayor* 179). But your paper will be easier to read if you include either the author or the title directly in the text:

Twain's late work reflects a low opinion of human nature. But when Satan complains that all men are cowards (<u>Stranger</u> 184), he is only echoing Col. Sherburn's speech in <u>Huckleberry Finn</u> (123-24).

F. A Quotation within a Cited Work

If you want to use a quotation that you have discovered in another book, your reference must show that you acquired this material secondhand and that you have not consulted the original source. Use the abbreviation "qtd. in" (for "quoted in") to make the distinction between the author of the passage being quoted and the author of the work in which you found this passage:

In 1835 Thomas Macaulay declared the British to be "the acknowledged leaders of the human race" (qtd. in Davis 231).

G. A Quotation of Poetry

Identify line numbers when you quote poetry, but do not use the abbreviations "l." or "ll." These abbreviations can easily be confused with numbers. Write "line" or "lines" in your first citation of poetry; subsequent citations should include only the line numbers. Quotations of three lines or less should be included directly into the text of your paper. Separate the lines with a slash (/), leaving an extra space both before and after the slash:

> Yeats returned to this theme in "The Second Coming": "The best lack all conviction, while the worst / Are full of passionate intensity" (7-8).

Each line of longer quotations should begin on a new line, indented ten spaces from the margin.

PARENTHETICAL DOCUMENTATION: THE APA AUTHOR/YEAR STYLE

The American Psychological Association requires that in-text documentation identifies the author of the work being referred to and the year in which this work was published. This information should be provided parenthetically, although it is not necessary to repeat any information that has already been provided directly in the sentence.

A. One Work by a Single Author

> It has been argued that fathers can play an important role in the treatment of eating disorders (Byrne, 1987).

or

> Byrne (1987) argued that fathers can play an important role in the treatment of eating disorders.

or

> In 1987 Katherine Byrne argued that fathers can play an important role in the treatment of eating disorders.

If the reference is to a specific chapter or page, that information should also be included. For example:

> (Byrne, 1987, p. 93)
> (Byrne, 1987, chap. 6)

Note that the abbreviations for page and chapter emphasize the distinction between the year of publication and the part of the work being referred to.

B. A Work with Two or More Authors

If a work has two authors, you should mention the names of both authors every time a reference is made to this work:

A recent study of industry (Bell & Freeman, 1991) argued that . . . .

or

More recently, Bell and Walker (1994) have argued that . . . .

Note that the ampersand (&) is used only within parentheses.

Scientific papers often have multiple authors because of the amount of research involved. In the first reference to a work with five or fewer authors, you should identify each of the authors:

Hodges, McKnew, Cytryn, Stern, and Kline (1982) have shown . . . .

Subsequent references to the same work should use an abbreviated form:

This method was also used in an earlier study (Hodges et al., 1982).

If a work has six authors or more, this abbreviated form should be used even in the first reference. If confusion is possible because you refer to more than one work by the first author, list as many coauthors as necessary to distinguish between the two works.

C. A Work with a Corporate Author

When a work has a corporate author, your first reference should include the full name of the corporation, committee, agency, or institution involved. For example:

(United States Fish and Wildlife Service [USFWS], 1994)

Subsequent references to the same source can be abbreviated:

(USFWS, 1994)

D. A Reference to More Than One Work

When the same citation refers to two or more sources, the works should be listed alphabetically according to the first author's name and separated with semicolons:

(Pepler & Rubin, 1982; Schesinger, 1982; Young, 1984)

If you are referring to more than one work by the same author(s), list the works in the order in which they were published.

The validity of this type of testing is now well established (Collins, 1988, 1994).

If you refer to more than one work by the same author published in the same year, distinguish individual works by identifying them as "a," "b," "c," etc.:

These findings have been questioned by Scheiber (1994a, 1994b).

ORGANIZING A BIBLIOGRAPHY

Documenting your sources parenthetically or with notes allows you to reveal exactly which parts of your paper are supported by or owed to the works you have consulted. A bibliography, which is a list of the sources consulted, is also essential so that readers can evaluate your research and possibly draw on your sources for work of their own.

Works Cited in MLA Style

In an MLA style bibliography, the works cited are arranged in alphabetical order determined by the author's last name. MLA style requires that the author's first name be given. Every important word in the titles of books, articles, and journals is capitalized. The titles of books, journals, and newspapers are all underlined (italicized). The titles of articles, stories, and poems appear within quotation marks. Second and subsequent lines are indented one-half inch (or by five spaces). Here are some examples:

A. *A Book with One Author*

Mukherjee, Bharati. The Holder of the World. New York: Knopf, 1993.

Although it is important to give the author's full name, the book's full title, and the place of publication, you should use a shortened form of the publisher's name (Alfred A. Knopf, in this case) by citing one key term.

B. *A Book with Two or Three Authors*

Gilbert, Sandra M., and Susan Gubar. The Madwoman in the Attic: The Woman Writer and the Nineteenth-Century Literary Imagination. New Haven: Yale UP, 1979.

Note that the subtitle is included, set off from the main title by a colon. The second author's name is not inverted, and abbreviations are used for "University Press" to provide a shortened form of the publisher's name. For books with three authors, put commas after the names of the first two authors; separate the second two authors with a comma followed by "and."

C. *An Edited Book*

Baldick, Chris, ed. Oxford Book of Gothic Tales. New York: Oxford UP, 1992.

D. *A Book with More Than Three Authors or Editors*

Clark, Donald, et al., eds. English Literature. New York: Macmillan, 1960.

Give the name of the first author or editor only and add the abbreviation "et al."

E. *Edition after the First*

Carruth, Gorton. The Encyclopedia of American Facts and Dates. 8th ed. New York: Harper, 1987.

F. *A Work in an Anthology*

O'Brien, Patricia. "Michael Foucault's History of Culture." The New Cultural History. Ed. Lynn Hunt. Berkeley: U of California P, 1989. 25-46.

Note that a period comes after the title of the selection but before the second quotation marks. A period is also used to separate the date of publication from the pages between which the selection can be found. No abbreviation is used before the page reference.

G. *A Translated Book*

Eco, Umberto. The Aesthetics of Thomas Aquinas. Trans. Hugh Bredin. Cambridge: Harvard UP, 1988.

H. *A Work in More Than One Volume*

Leckie, Robert. The Wars of America. 2 vols. New York: Harper, 1992.

I. *An Introduction, Preface, Foreword, or Afterword*

Dove, Rita. Foreword. Jonah's Gourd Vine. By Zora Neale Hurston. New York: Harper, 1990. vii-xv.

J. An Article in an Encyclopedia

Hunt, Roberta M. "Child Welfare." Encyclopedia Americana. 1985 ed.

For citing material from well-known encyclopedias, give the author's name first, then the article title. If material is arranged alphabetically within the source, which is usually the case, there is no need to include volume and page numbers. You should give the full title of the encyclopedia, the edition if it is stated, and the year of publication (e.g., 11th ed. 1994). When no edition number is stated, identify the edition by the year of publication (e.g., 1994 ed.). If the author of the article is identified only by initials, look elsewhere within the encyclopedia for a list identifying the names these initials stand for. If the article is unsigned, give the title first. (Note: This same form can be used for other reference books, such as dictionaries and the various editions of *Who's Who*.)

K. A Government Publication

United States. Bureau of the Census, State and Metropolitan Data Book 1986.
     Washington: GPO. 1986.

For many government publications, the author is unknown. When this is the case, the agency that issued the publication should be listed as the author. State the name of the government (e.g., "United States." "Florida," "United Nations") followed by a period. Then give the name of the agency that issued the work, using abbreviations only if you can do so clearly (e.g., "Bureau of the Census," "National Institute on Drug Abuse," "Dept. of Labor") followed by a period. The underlined title of the work comes next, followed by another period. Then give the place of publication, publisher, and date. Most federal publications are printed in Washington by the Government Printing Office (GPO), but you should be alert for exceptions. (Note: Treat pamphlets just as you would a book.)

L. A Journal Article with One Author

Swann, Karen. "The Sublime and the Vulgar." College English 52 (1990): 7-20.

The volume number comes after the journal title without any intervening punctuation. The year of publication is included within parentheses after the volume number. A colon separates the year of publication and the page reference. Leave one space after the volume number and one space after the colon.

M. A Journal Article Paginated Anew in Each Issue

Rosen, Michael J. "Is There a Midwestern Literature?" The Iowa Review 20.3
  (1990): 94-102.

In this case, the issue number is included immediately after the volume number, and the two are separated by a period without any intervening space.

N. An Article from a Magazine Published Monthly

Renfrew, Colin. "World Linguistic Diversity." Scientific American Jan. 1994:
  116-123.

Instead of citing the volume number, give the month and year of the issue. Abbreviate the month when it has more than four letters. (May, June, and July are spelled out.)

O. An Article from a Magazine Issued Weekly

Wilkinson, Alec. "The Confession." New Yorker 4 Oct. 1993: 162-171.

The form is the same as for an article in a magazine that is issued monthly, but you add the day immediately before the month. Note that a hyphen between page numbers indicates consecutive pages. When an article is printed on nonconsecutive pages—beginning on page 34, for example, and continuing on page 78—give only the first page number and a plus sign: 34+.

P. An Article from a Daily Newspaper

Robinson, Karen. "The Line to Privacy Is Unlisted." Milwaukee Journal 26 Mar.
  1985, sunrise ed., sec. 2: 2.

If more than one edition is available on the date in question, specify the edition immediately after the date. If the city of publication is not part of the newspaper's name, identify the city in brackets after the newspaper title. Because newspapers often consist of separate sections, you should cite the section number if each section has separate pagination. If a newspaper consists of only one section, or if the pagination is continuous from one section to the next, then you do not need to include the section number. If separately paginated sections are identified by letters, omit the section reference (sec.) but include the letter of the section with the page number (e.g., 7B or D19). If the article is unsigned, begin the citation with the title of the article; alphabetize the article under its title, passing over small words like "a" and "the."

Q. *An Editorial*

Wicker, Tom. "The Key to Unity." Editorial. <u>New York Times</u> 30 Jan. 1991, natl.
ed.: A15.

Editorials are identified as such between the title of the article and
the title of the newspaper or magazine.

R. *An Interview*

Nelson, Veronica. Personal interview. 16 Aug. 1994.

If you interview someone, alphabetize the interview under the name
of the person interviewed.

References in APA Style

In APA style, the reference list is arranged alphabetically, the order being determined by the author's last name. The date of publication is emphasized by
placing it within parentheses immediately after the author's name. Unlike
MLA style, in which each entry begins flush with the left margin, APA style
calls for beginning each entry with a paragraph indent (which means leaving
five spaces blank). Additional lines are then flush with the left margin. (Exception: A hanging indent is used whan a work is typeset for publication. For
an example of a reference list with hanging indents, see pp. 237-41.)

A. *Book with One Author*

Choate, P. (1990). <u>Agents of influence</u>. New York: Knopf.

Note that the author's first name is indicated only by an initial. Capital letters are used only for the first word of the title and the first
word of the subtitle if there is one. (But when a proper name appears
within a title, it retains the capitalization it would normally receive.
For example: *A history of ideas in Brazil.*) The name of the publisher,
Alfred A. Knopf, is given in shortened form. A period comes after
the parentheses surrounding the date of publication, and also after the
title and publisher.

B. *Book with Two or More Authors*

Youcha, C., & Seixas, J. (1989). <u>Drugs, alcohol, and your children: How to
keep your family substance-free</u>. New York: Crown.

An ampersand is used to separate the names of two authors. When
there are three or more authors, separate their names with commas
and put an ampersand immediately before the last author's name.

C. Edited Book

> Preston, J. (Ed.) (1992). <u>A member of the family: Gay men write about their families</u>. New York: Dutton.

The abbreviation for editor is "Ed."; it should be included within parentheses between the name of the editor and the date of publication. The abbreviation for editors is "Eds." Give the names of all editors, no matter how many there are.

D. Article or Chapter in an Edited Book

> Howard, A. (1992). Work and family crossroads spanning careers. In S. Zedeck (Ed.), <u>Work, families, and organizations</u> (pp. 70-137). San Francisco: Jossey.

Do not invert the editor's name when it is not in the author's position. Do not put the title of the article or chapter in quotation marks. Use a comma to separate the editor from the title of the edited book. The pages between which the material can be found appear within parentheses immediately after the book title. Use "p." for page and "pp." for pages.

E. Translated Book

> Beauvoir, S. de. (1972). <u>The coming of age</u> (P. O'Brien, Trans.). New York: Putnam's. (Original work published 1970)

Within parentheses immediately after the book title, give the translator's name followed by a comma and the abbreviation "Trans." If the original work was published earlier, include this information at the end.

F. Revised Edition of a Book

> Hopkins, B. R. (1993). <u>A legal guide to starting and managing a nonprofit organization</u> (2nd ed.). New York: Wiley.

The edition is identified immediately after the title. Note that edition is abbreviated "ed." and should not be confused with "Ed." for editor.

G. Book with a Corporate Author

> American Medical Association. (1982). <u>Family medical guide</u>. New York: Random.

H. Multivolume Book

Jones, E. (1953-57). The life and work of Sigmund Freud (Vol. 2). New York: Basic.

The volume number is included within parentheses immediately after the title. When a multivolume book is published over a number of years, list the years between which it was published.

I. Journal Article with One Author

Farber, N. (1990). The significance of race and class in marital decisions among unmarried adolescent mothers. Social Problems, 37, 51-63.

Do not use quotation marks around the article title. Capitalize all important words in the journal title and underline. Put a comma after the journal title and then give the volume and page numbers. Abbreviations are not used for "volume" and "page." To distinguish between the numbers, underline the volume number and put a comma between it and the page numbers.

J. Journal Article with More than One Author

Korner, A., Zeanah, C. H., Linden, J., Berkowitz, R., Kraemer, H., & Agras, W. S. (1985). The relations between neonatal and later activity and temperament. Child Development, 56, 38-52.

K. Journal Article Paginated Anew in Each Issue

Major, B. (1993). Gender, entitlement, and the distribution of family labor. Journal of Social Issues, 49(3), 141-159.

When each issue of a journal begins with page 1, you need to include the issue number in parentheses immediately after the underlined volume number.

L. Article from a Magazine Issued Monthly

Gould, S. J. (1994, February). In the mind of the beholder. Natural History, 103, 14-23.

Within parentheses immediately after the author, include the month of issue after the year of publication. Follow the same form for an article in a magazine issued on a specific day, but add the day after the month:

Hazen, R. M. (1991, February 25). Why my kids hate science. Newsweek, 117, 7.

M. *Article from a Newspaper*

> Winslow, R. (1991, January 29). Medical costs soar, defying firms' cures. Wall Street Journal, p. B1.

Place the exact date of issue within parentheses immediately after the author. After the newspaper title, specify the page number(s). Use the abbreviation p. or pp. before the page number.

N. *Government Document*

> National Institute of Alcohol Abuse and Alcoholism. (1980). Facts about alcohol and alcoholism (DHHS Publication No. ADM 80-31). Washington, DC: U.S. Government Printing Office.

List the agency that produced the document as the author if no author is identified. Within parentheses immediately after the document title, give the publication number (assigned to the document by the government); it can usually be found on or near the title page and should not be confused with the call number that a library may have assigned to the document.

O. *Work with No Author*

> A breath of fresh air. (1991, April 29). Time, 137, 49.

Put the title in the author's position and alphabetize the work under the first important word in the title. Follow the form for the type of publication in question (in this case, a magazine published weekly). Use a short version of the title for the parenthetical citation in the text: ("Breath," 1991). If the author is designated as Anonymous, write Anonymous and alphabetize according to that word. Use the following for the parenthetical citation in the text: (Anonymous, 1995).

Numbered Systems

In a numbered system, the bibliography may be arranged in alphabetical order (determined by the authors' last names) or in the order in which the works are cited within the paper itself. Once this sequence is established, the items are assigned numbers in consecutive order beginning with 1, and these numbers are used as citations within the paper. There are many variations on the particular form of the bibliographical entries; authors of scientific papers should adopt the style recommended by the journal for which they are writing. But here are examples of two frequently used forms:

A. Biology

1. Avila, V. L. Biology: A Human Endeavor. Chula Vista: Bookmark, 1992.
2. Batistatou, A.; Green, L. Internucleosomal DNA cleavage and neurona; cell survival death. The Journal of Cell Biology. 22: 523-532; 1993.

Note that neither book nor journal titles are underlined. Quotation marks are not used for article titles. The names of multiple authors are separated with a semicolon rather than an ampersand. The year of publication appears at the end of the citation, and it is preceded by a semicolon.

B. Chemistry

(1) Rea, W. J. Chemical Sensitivity; Lewis: New York, 1992.
(2) Cargill, R. W. Chem. Soc. Rev. 1993, 22, pp. 135-141.

Note that book publishers appear before the city of publication. Journal titles are abbreviated, and article titles are not included. Lines after the first are not indented.

Although the precise form of the bibliography will vary from discipline to discipline, certain features remain constant when a numbered system is used:

- Whenever the same source is cited, the same number is cited.
- Numbers appear on the same line as the text, and they are usually either underlined or italicized so that they can be distinct from other numbers in the text.

With these two points in mind, you should not confuse a numbered system of references with the use of numbered footnotes. When footnotes are used, numbers appear in consecutive order, each number is used only once, and numbers are raised above the line. When a numbered system of references is used, the same number appears whenever the source assigned that number is cited within the text, and the numbers will not necessarily be consecutive.

A Numbered Reference

There are approximately 125,000 children at risk of developing Huntington's disease (4).

or

There are approximately 125,000 children at risk of developing Huntington's disease (4, p. 22).

A Footnote

There are approximately 125,000 children at risk of developing Huntington's disease.[4]

For an example of a numbered system in use, consult an issue of *Science,* a journal that can be found in most libraries.

A CHECKLIST FOR DOCUMENTATION

Whether you document your sources by using footnotes or one of the recommended systems for parenthetical references, you should honor the following principles:

1. Remember to document any direct quotation, any idea that has come from someone else's work, and any fact or statistic that is not widely known.
2. Be sure to enclose all quotations in quotation marks.
3. Make sure that paraphrases are in your own words but still accurately reflect the content of the original material.
4. Remember that every source cited in a reference should have a corresponding entry in the bibliography.
5. Be consistent. Don't shift from the author/year system to the author/work system in the middle of your paper.
6. Try to vary the introductions you use for quotations and paraphrases and make sure that the material in question has been incorporated smoothly into your text. Read your first draft aloud to be better able to judge its readability.
7. When you mention authorities by name, try to identify who they are so that your audience can evaluate the source. (For example, "According to Nadine Strossen, president of the American Civil Liberties Union, recent congressional legislation violates. . . .") Do not insult the intelligence of your audience by identifying well-known figures.
8. If in doubt about whether to document a source, you would probably be wise to go ahead and document it. But be careful not to over-document your paper. A paper that is composed of one reference after another usually lacks synthesis and interpretation.

PART 3

SOURCES FOR ARGUMENT

GUN CONTROL:
TRIGGERING A NATIONAL CONTROVERSY

ELIZABETH J. SWASEY

NRA WOMAN'S VOICE

Although the debate over gun control often seems dominated by men, women have a vital concern in the outcome of this debate. The following essay was first published in a 1993 issue of *The American Rifleman,* which is published by the National Rifle Association—a powerful lobby against gun control. As you read it, consider whether Swasey speaks for women and whether she is directing her argument to an audience of women.

One of America's most powerful politicians said on the May 2 edition of   1
"Meet the Press:" "'. . . to prevent you from getting weapons you need to
defend yourself' is a very difficult case to make morally."

It sure is.   2

Just ask Suzanna Gratia.   3

It was Suzanna's desire to obey Texas law that caused her to experience   4
hell on earth and made her an instant orphan. On Oct. 16, 1991, Suzanna

dutifully left her handgun in the trunk of her car while she joined her parents for lunch at Luby's cafeteria in Killeen, Tex. Minutes later, a madman entered and slaughtered 22 people—including Suzanna's parents. Today, Suzanna will tell you how, lying face-down on the floor, she reached for her purse . . . for a gun to stop the killing, a gun that wasn't there—thanks to Texas' law against concealed carry.

But that powerful politician wasn't talking about Suzanna. He was talk-   5
ing about the Muslims in Bosnia-Herzegovina.

If this politician supports the right of citizens in a country half a world   6
away to defend themselves, surely he supports the right of American women like Suzanna to do the same, right? Wrong.

This politician is Vice President Al Gore who, as a U.S. senator, voted   7
against the instant criminal background check while voting for a ban on certain semi-automatics.

No one doubts that following the breakup of Yugoslavia, the horror has   8
been unspeakable—including horrors perpetrated against women. The January 4 cover of *Newsweek* featured "A Pattern of Rape, War Crimes in Bosnia." The cover story said 30,000-50,000 Muslim women have been raped in Bosnia. But twice that number of women—106,593 to be exact—were raped in America in 1991 alone.

The fact is, there's a war going on in America, too. Every day, Ameri-   9
cans face an enemy that is very real: criminals. In his State of the Union address, President Clinton railed against "violent crime which terrorizes our people and which tears our communities apart."

The war in America is the war against crime. Unfortunately, the good   10
guys aren't taking any prisoners.

We didn't even take Mark Steven Hughes. After bludgeoning 10-month-   11
old James Pompa to death, Mark Steven Hughes pled guilty to "injury to a child" in Texas and received a 10-year sentence. With "good time" jail credit, Hughes became eligible for parole six months before he was even sentenced.

Why aren't we taking any prisoners? Simple. Politicians prevent us   12
from doing so by voting against building more prison space. They say "it's too expensive."

But according to National Institute of Justice, it's actually 17 times   13
cheaper to keep criminals in jail: keeping a criminal in jail for one year costs some $25,000, whereas releasing him early results in an average of 187–287 crimes a year committed by that one criminal, at a cost to society of $430,000. This figure doesn't include the cost of human suffering.

There is a war going on. And until we start taking prisoners to local jails   14
and state and federal prisons and keeping them there—citizens like Suzanna will likely come face-to-face with criminals like Mark Steven Hughes.

What happens then? In states without concealed carry laws, the answer   15
depends on where the attack takes place.

Most state legislators support the citizen's right to use a firearm to defend   16
him or herself at home, yet some oppose concealed carry legislation. This makes sense only if you believe the right of self-defense depends on where the victim is attacked: if inside the home then self-defense applies, if outside then it does not.

Why shouldn't our right to defend ourselves in the manner we choose   17
extend into places outside the home, where women are even more vulnerable?
Those opposing concealed carry answer "because it poses a threat to public
safety." But like the argument about building prisons, this too fails in the face
of facts.

Florida enacted a concealed carry law in 1987. Before the law, Florida's   18
homicide rate was 11.7 per 100,000. By 1991, it dropped 20% to 9.4 per
100,000. This compares with a 14% increase in the national average over the
same period. (All figures: FBI Uniform Crime Reports.)

Clearly, allowing law-abiding citizens to carry concealed firearms poses   19
no threat to public safety. VP Gore must know this; like Florida, his home
state of Tennessee allows licensed citizens to carry concealed firearms.

And right now, honest citizens in Missouri, North Carolina and Texas   20
are asking their state legislatures for the ability to defend themselves against
violent criminal attack regardless of where that attack takes place. They're
calling for passage of concealed carry laws in their states.

We can only hope our elected officials, both on the federal and state   21
level, apply the same standard to honest citizens on American soil as they do to
Muslims in Bosnia.

After all, there's a war going on in America, too. ■   22

Questions for Meaning

1. Why does Swasey believe that American citizens should be allowed to
   carry concealed weapons?
2. How does Swasey support her claim that, in the war against crime, "the
   good guys aren't taking any prisoners"?
3. Why do legislators who believe in the right to self-defense nevertheless
   object to citizens' carrying concealed weapons?
4. Vocabulary: perpetrated (8), bludgeoning (11), vulnerable (17).

Questions about Strategy

1. Swasey does not immediately identify the politician she quotes in her
   opening paragraph. What does she gain by temporarily withholding this
   information?
2. Consider the brevity of paragraphs 2 and 3, each of which consists of a
   single sentence. How does this paragraphing influence the way you read
   these sentences?
3. How effective is the analogy Swasey makes between violence in Bosnia-
   Herzegovina and violence in the United States? Could an opponent use
   this analogy to argue against laws permitting citizens to carry concealed
   weapons?
4. Is the information provided about Mark Steven Hughes relevant to
   Swasey's argument? Why is it included?

JONATHAN ALTER

THERE'S A WAR ON AT HOME

A staff writer for *Time* magazine, Jonathan Alter first published this article in September 1993, shortly after Israelis and Palestinians signed an agreement in Washington to pursue further peace talks. During that fall, a national debate on health care was also unfolding. As you read this article, note how Alter links gun control to other issues that were on the minds of readers.

In the eyes of the world, America is becoming Chicago. As a native of that city, I've been annoyed for years to hear in foreign locales, "Chicago? Ahh! [fingers pointed like a gun] Al Capone. Bang! Bang!" Now the entire country is splattered with the same bloody cliché. The Chicagofication of America isn't likely to dampen the desire of tourists to come to the United States. Many visitors even make a point of venturing into tough areas just so they can brag back home that they survived. But the fact remains that people around the world think that our gun culture is insane, and they're right. Why should we settle for peace in the Middle East without peace in the Middle West?

Those wise Norwegians (plus Germans, British and others) actually have a role to play in bringing American politicians to the bargaining table, too. I could get shot by an enraged travel agent for saying this, but I favor economic sanctions against the United States in the form of travel advisories. Threatening the $70 billion foreign tourism industry has a way of concentrating the mind. It might begin to attract the attention of NRA-addled legislators who can't seem to get it through their heads that laws allowing people to sell semi-automatic weapons out of the trunks of their cars are not—how to put this delicately?—*helpful.*

Should guns themselves really be blamed along with the criminals? As a matter of fact, yes. You can't stab someone from a passing car. Unfortunately, with 200 million firearms already out there, the Brady bill won't make much difference. That's why Sen. Daniel Patrick Moynihan is pushing bullet control. Because there's only a four-year supply of ammunition in existence, banning certain kinds of ammo rarely used for hunting could eventually make it harder to stand on top of a building and spray bullets. (It's not as if people need more than a few rounds to defend themselves.) Moynihan also has a bill to tax ammunition at 1,000 percent. This could have been one of the sin taxes that Bill Clinton used to raise a bit of money for health care, but the president flinched.

The paradox of the American gun culture is that it is undermining the very values it was meant to protect. Remember Franklin Roosevelt's famous Four Freedoms? These were what we ostensibly fought World War II over. One of them was "freedom from fear." That battle has been lost. As crime grows arithmetically, fear grows geometrically. Even outside major cities, ours is now a land of real freedom only during daylight and in certain

1

2

3

4

neighborhoods. We've reached a point in recent years where otherwise optimistic, spontaneous people believe they must constantly peer over their shoulders as if they were being pursued by the secret police in some old communist regime.

This routinized fear is now so much a part of American life that we've   5
begun to take it for granted. We instinctively avoid large sections of cities, using mental maps in our heads that are unavailable to tourists. In my case, it was a stay in Japan that jolted me into recognizing how much freedom I'd lost at home. Japan is crowded and culturally stifling, but it's possible to walk in a park in Tokyo at midnight without the slightest trepidation, just as it was here as recently as the 1950s. This freedom felt strange to me, as if a state of fear about physical safety is normal. And it is. Barricading oneself at home all night is now natural; wandering around freely and alone—once the quintessential American experience—is foolhardy. Roads like Route 66 once symbolized freedom; they now symbolize danger. Even a time-honored cultural tradition like flipping the bird to some idiot driver is now in jeopardy. Instead of just screaming back, he might blow your head off.

Imagine you're offered the choice of a vacation in Belfast, Northern Ireland, or Wichita, Kansas, two cities with populations of roughly 300,000. So   6
far this year, 19 people have been killed in Belfast, about average. In Wichita, the murder toll has reached 41, which isn't even particularly high on a per capita basis for an American city. In Belfast they kill each other over religious principle. In Wichita they kill each other over drugs, insults or, in the case of an innocent motorist earlier this month, in the cross-fire.

Back in the 1870s, Wyatt Earp was called into Wichita because that   7
rowdy cattle town was experiencing about one homicide a year, which the residents considered intolerable. Earp made sure that guns were checked at toll stations on the outskirts of town or confiscated. So much for the real Wild West. The idea that our murder rate is so high because of our legendary "frontier mentality" is grossly oversimplified. Canada expanded across a huge frontier. Australia was colonized by convicts. People like to kill each other there, too. The main difference is that they lack the means to do so with ease—the gun. In 1990, for instance, 10 people were killed in Australia by handguns, and 68 in Canada. In the United States, according to Handgun Control Inc., the figure was 10,567.

Fortunately, the American political climate is beginning to change. Jim   8
Florio in New Jersey and Mary Sue Terry in Virginia are finally going after the NRA in their campaigns for governor.* Clinton, who challenged the NRA in Arkansas, supports tighter licensing of gun dealers and a ban on certain assault weapons. If he's willing to raise his voice and make an issue out of guns and ammo—turn the NRA into the Sister Souljah of the 1996 campaign—he could prove he has some backbone after all, and rally exactly the committed constituency he now lacks. Obviously that won't end violence. But over time, a sane gun policy might just ease the fear a bit, and reduce the body count in America's long and bloody war at home.   ■

*Both of these candidates were subsequently defeated at the polls.

Questions for Meaning

1. What does Alter mean by the "Chicagofication of America"? In what sense is he invoking a "bloody cliché"?
2. Why might bullet control be a necessary supplement or alternative to gun control?
3. According to Alter, "As crime grows arithmetically, fear grows geometrically." What does he mean by this? Which type of growth is the largest?
4. Vocabulary: locales (1), sanctions (2), addled (2), trepidation (5), quintessential (5), constituency (8).

Questions about Strategy

1. How does Alter respond to opponents who argue that guns should not be blamed for the rate of violent crime in the United States?
2. Where does Alter compare the United States to other countries? How similar is the United States to the countries he cites?
3. Why does Alter use Wichita as a representative American city? How would the essay change if he used a larger city such as New York, Los Angeles, or Miami?

JAMES D. WRIGHT

IN THE HEAT OF THE MOMENT

James D. Wright is a nationally recognized authority on gun control and other social issues. Favrot Professor of Human Relations at Tulane University, he is the author of *Under the Gun: Weapons, Crime, and Violence in America; Address Unknown: The Homeless in America* (1989); and, with Peter Rossi, *Armed and Considered Dangerous: Felons and Their Firearms* (1986). He first published the following article in a 1990 issue of *Reason*, a journal that promotes libertarian views.

Bob and Jim are good drinking buddies. After a night at their favorite bar,   1
they head back to Jim's trailer for some whiskey. Jim begins praising his new
girlfriend. Bob questions her fidelity and claims that he has slept with her.
Seized by uncontrollable rage, Jim grabs a loaded .44 from the kitchen drawer
and ends the conversation with a bang.

This is the sort of scenario that most people probably imagine when they   2
hear that the majority of murders involve individuals who knew each other
before the crime. Based on this impression, gun-control advocates argue that
most homicides do not involve murderous intent. Rather, they are committed

in the heat of the moment, in disputes or altercations among loved ones or close associates that escalate into rage—disputes that turn fatal not so much because anyone intended to kill but because, in that lamentable fit of anger, a gun was at hand. And if that is really how most murders happen, it follows that if fewer guns were "at hand," fewer murders would be committed.

But the data on relationships between homicide victims and their killers   3
tell a different story. The conclusion in favor of gun control simply does not follow from the evidence.

FBI figures for 1987 and 1988 reveal that murders by strangers—for ex-   4
ample, in the course of a robbery—are rare. They account for only about one in eight homicides (12.6 percent). But this does not imply that the remaining seven in every eight homicides involve loved ones slaying one another. After all, very few people love everyone they meet. Just how close is the relationship between victim and killer in the typical murder?

In many cases—nearly a third of the total—the authorities simply cannot de-   5
termine the relationship. Next to "unknown," the largest relationship cate-
gory is "acquaintance," accounting for approximately one additional third of the murders. You might think that "acquaintance" refers to fairly close associates, but the FBI tallies neighbors, friends, boyfriends, girlfriends, and all types of relatives in their own separate categories. If there were any degree of intimacy of closeness between acquaintances, the FBI would almost certainly clas-
sify the homicide under another heading. In this context, "acquaintance" means only that the victim and killer had some idea of each other's identities before the murder.

All categories of relatives combined account for about one in six mur-   6
ders (15.9 percent on average). About half of these are slayings of spouses by spouses. Friends and neighbors add an average of 9.8 percent to the annual homicide total. Altogether, then, relatives, friends, and neighbors commit only about a quarter (25.7 percent) of murders. So it's not true that "most" murders involve persons who share some degree of intimacy or closeness. Most murders—some three-quarters of them—are committed by casual acquaintances (30.2 percent), perfect strangers (12.8 percent), or persons un-
known (31.2 percent).

Gun-control advocates, however, can easily convey the opposite im-   7
pression of these data. By simply omitting the unknown relationships from the calculation and including casual acquaintances within the category of intimates, they can make it seem as if every murder other than those committed by perfect strangers involves intimates. But given what the category of acquaintance specifically omits, this would be an irresponsible misrepre-
sentation.

That most murder victims know their killers prior to the crime is   8
scarcely a surprise. That people know one another is not in itself evidence that they like one another. Ordinarily, the only people a murderer would have good reasons to kill would be people he or she knows. Indeed, slayings in the course of some other felony are the only obvious exception; random killings

are understandably quite rare. So contrary to the common assumption, some degree of prior acquaintance between victim and offender definitely does not rule out murderous intent.

Cases of family members slaying one another figure prominently in the   9
gun-control debate but represent fewer than one-sixth of all murders. Studies of family homicide have shown that most of these families (about 85 percent of them) have had previous domestic quarrels serious enough to bring police to the residence; in nearly half the cases, the police had been called to the residence five or more times before the killing occurred. Indeed, most of the families in which such homicides occur have histories of abuse and violence going back years or even decades. These slayings are generally not isolated outbursts of rage between normally placid and loving couples. They are, instead, the culminating episodes in long, violent, abusive family relations.

At least some family homicides probably do result from the stereotypical   10
"moment of rage." Others result from a thoroughly willful intention to kill. Knowing only that victim and killer are related by blood or marriage does not in itself tell us which explanation is correct for a given homicide.

Consider the bizarre case of Theron and Leila Morris, a Florida couple   11
recently accused of killing their son, Christopher. Police say the Morrises were plotting with their son to murder his ex-wife for her insurance money. Then the conspirators learned that the ex-wife's insurance policy had lapsed, so there was nothing to be gained in killing her. Evidently annoyed by this turn of events, the Morrises then allegedly plotted between themselves to kill Christopher, in order to collect on *his* insurance policy, which was still in force and worth twice what his ex-wife's policy was worth. The Associated Press reported that the parents were also angry with Morris because he had "sold them bogus cocaine for $1,000 that they had intended to resell."

Morris's killing will appear in the FBI's 1990 Uniform Crime Report   12
tabulation as a family homicide; having been slain by his own parents, he will be included in the category "son." What, then, will we know about the circumstances of his death, given that he was the child of his killers? Nothing at all.

How many murders are committed in a moment of rage, brought to   13
fruition largely because a gun was available, and how many result from an unambiguous intention to kill? The fact is, nobody knows the answer to this question. An adequate answer would require getting inside the heads of murderers as they contemplate and commit their crimes.

Clearly, though, the assumption that heat-of-the-moment murders far   14
outnumber willful murders cannot be justified by evidence on prior victim–offender relationships. Such information does not support conclusions about homicidal motives or about the number of slayings that might be prevented if fewer guns were available. ■

Questions for Meaning

1. According to Wright, why do advocates of gun control believe that reducing the number of guns in circulation would reduce the number of murders committed?
2. Why does Wright believe that gun control is unlikely to reduce the murder rate?
3. According to the categories used by the FBI, what does it mean to be the "acquaintance" of a murder victim?
4. Vocabulary: fidelity (1), altercations (2), placid (9), tabulation (12), fruition (13).

Questions about Strategy

1. Wright begins his argument with a fictional example that does not represent what his research has revealed. What is the advantage of this strategy?
2. Where does Wright show that he is aware of arguments supporting gun control? Does he make any concessions?
3. Wright devotes two paragraphs to the story of Theron, Leila, and Christopher Morris. What is this example meant to establish?

ROGER KOOPMAN

SECOND DEFENSE

After graduating from the University of Idaho in 1973, Roger Koopman served as a congressional press secretary and administrative assistant before becoming a public relations specialist for the National Rifle Association's Institute for Legislative Action. He left the NRA in 1980 to pursue a business career in western Montana. A regular political columnist for the *Bozeman Daily Chronicle*, he has published articles in many national magazines. "Second Defense" was first published in 1990 by *Outdoor Life.*

Last year was a rough one for the right to keep and bear arms. Fueled by the   1
school-yard tragedy in Stockton, California, the Second Amendment's organized enemies have made great strides. Yet the erosion of our rights cannot be blamed on mere circumstance; the fault rests squarely in the laps of gun owners themselves, who for years have been employing every possible argument to defend their constitutional rights except the constitutional one.

   In reality, we couldn't have played into the gun controllers hands more if   2
they had written the script! Consider, for example, our response to the current

hysteria over so-called "assault rifles." We have argued, ad nauseam, that people should be "allowed the right" to own these firearms (whatever they are)
because of the "legitimate uses" (whatever that means) for such guns, uses that
include hunting, target practice, collecting, competitive shooting and self-
defense. The predictable result? Whenever gun owners seem to be outnum-
bered by non-gun owners in a particular area, the legislatures and city councils
have gone right ahead and banned these guns anyway, regardless of whether
there are "legitimate uses" for them or not.

That's politics, and the process is, to say the least, a two-edged sword that   3
groups such as the National Rifle Association have lived by—and, at times,
died by. Certainly no one would suggest that the battles the NRA fights
shouldn't be fought. But the Constitution of the United States transcends politics, and its wisdom and truth are not dependent upon the nightly opinion
polls on CNN News. The Constitution's Second Amendment does not speak
in terms of "legitimate" and "illegitimate" uses for privately owned firearms.
Rather, it proclaims, in simple and emphatic words, that a "free State" is secure only if the peoples' right to "keep and bear Arms" remains inviolate.

The gun control issue, then, is never a question of what the government   4
"allows" us to own. The Constitution states that government has *no authority*
over the firearms ownership of the people. The people, not the government,
possess an absolute right in the area of gun ownership. If you or I want to own
an AR-15 or any other gun, it is none of the government's business *why* we
want it, and certainly none of its business to presume that we may be up to no
good. In a free society, the salient question is *never* whether the government
can trust the people, but always whether the people can trust their government. The history of the Second Amendment makes this point ever so clear.
You could spend a lifetime studying the writings of the Founding Fathers and
would never find among any of them the kinds of sentiments expressed by our
20th century gun controllers—sentiments that reflect a profound distrust for a
free people. You would not find a single person among all of the founders of
our nation who was worried about firearms in the hands of the citizenry. The
very idea is preposterous.

What you *will* find is that there was a very widespread concern over   5
firearms in the hands of the government, especially in the form of a federal
"standing army." As great scholars of human history, our forefathers knew full
well the threat to liberty posed by governments that developed a monopoly of
force over the people. Thus, they authored the Second Amendment, guaran-
teeing that an armed citizenry (spoken of as the "militia") would always hold
sway over the central government and would be a constant check against governmental excesses.

As with so many constitutional principles in this century, the essence of   6
the Second Amendment has been turned upside down by an anti-gun establishment that reveres big government and distrusts the people. Make no mistake about it. What these folks stand for is a total reversal of our
constitutional system, where rights and powers become vested *not* in the people, but in the government. They promote an alien, Old World mentality

that turns the citizenry against itself by convincing us that we should "trust" the government and distrust our neighbor. Understood in this way, the issue becomes a lot larger than our opportunity to shoot a deer or plink a can. The issue is not guns; the issue is freedom, and it involves not just gun owners, but everyone—especially our children.

It's vitally important that we not allow the gun control lobby and its   7
friends in the national media to paint us into a corner and narrowly define our position as "pro-gun." We are "pro-constitution" and "pro-freedom." And for goodness' sake, let's not fall into the trap of debating among ourselves what types of guns are "needed" and what guns can be outlawed; what gun-related freedoms are "necessary" and what ones we can afford to lose. Freedom is indivisible. Once we accept the notion that government has the right to deny *any* of our firearms rights, we have thrown in the towel and torn apart our Constitution.

If we are going to start winning these battles and regaining ground al-   8
ready lost, we must start framing the so-called "gun issues" in constitutional terms, and show how *every* citizen has a stake in the outcome. Even in states such as Montana, where I reside, the gun control lobby can carry the day by dividing and conquering the general populace with convincing, if thoroughly unconstitutional arguments. I am reminded of a proposal in the last legislative session that would have returned to Montana citizens at least a measure of their *rights* to carry firearms in a concealed fashion—something that the law enforcement community has always enjoyed the undisputed "right" to do. Following a heavy lobbying effort against the bill by some (not all) of these law enforcement people, legislators who should have known better were convinced to vote the measure down. Yet by doing so, they were essentially saying that law enforcement personnel (an arm of local and state government) possess firearms rights that the citizenry at large could be denied. The problem, of course, was that few, if any, of the legislators were made to look at the issue in constitutional terms.

In recent years, the battle lines on gun control have gradually shifted. De-   9
fenders of the Second Amendment are now fighting not only the Liberal Left, but an increasing number of persons claiming to speak for the law enforcement community—our traditional ally! This is cause for real concern, not only strategically, but philosophically. Should current trends toward the polarization of law enforcement with the armed citizen continue, it raises an ominous specter: Are we moving toward a society that will be dominated by law and order "professionals" who reign supreme over a disarmed and once free people?

The advice of Larry Pratt, executive director of Gun Owners of Amer-   10
ica, is well worth repeating. Pratt warns that it is the natural tendency of government to concentrate power by "reserving for itself the monopoly of fire power." He also believes that sport shooting is a pleasant derivative of underlying constitutional principles, but it is not the reason the Founders wrote the Second Amendment. It was their deep concern over the power of government, with its standing military, that made them seek to guarantee for all time the right of every citizen to be armed.

The issue, indeed, is freedom. You will not find a single government in   11
the world today that would be able to enslave its people *if* those people enjoyed
the unrestricted right to private gun ownership. It couldn't be done. China, on
the other hand, tells us a very different story. It is not so much that an armed
citizenry could have fought off the tanks in Tianamen Square* as it is that an
armed citizenry would have seen to it that the tanks were never there in the
first place. The point is no less valid for this place we call America—the land
of the free.   ■

Questions for Meaning

1. Would Koopman accept any government restraints on the ownership of
   guns?
2. According to Koopman, why was the Second Amendment written into
   the Constitution?
3. In paragraph 7, Koopman claims "Freedom is indivisible." What does
   he mean by this?
4. Why did Koopman favor legislation in Montana that would have made
   it legal for citizens to carry concealed weapons?
5. Vocabulary: ad nauseam (2), transcends (3), salient (4), vested (6), polarization (9).

Questions about Strategy

1. Koopman begins his argument by claiming that opponents of gun control have ignored the constitutional argument that the Second Amendment protects the right to "keep and bear Arms." Is this claim
   convincing?
2. Consider how Koopman quotes the Second Amendment in paragraph
   3. Why doesn't he quote the entire Amendment?
3. How fairly does Koopman characterize advocates of gun control?
4. Why does Koopman emphasize children at the end of paragraph 6?
   What is he implying here?
5. Koopman claims that opponents of gun control should describe themselves as "pro-constitution" or "pro-freedom" rather than "pro-gun."
   What is the difference? Has attention to language of this sort helped to
   shape the debate over any other public issues?

*A public space in the heart of Beijing that was the site of a large political protest which was
violently suppressed by the Chinese government in 1989.

WILLIAM R. TONSO

WHITE MAN'S LAW

A professor of sociology at the University of Evansville, William R. Tonso is the author of *Gun and Society: Existential Roots of the American Attachment to Firearms* (1982) and *The Gun Culture and Its Enemies* (1989). Drawing on the work of a number of other scholars, he argues that the demand for gun control is the result of prejudice against minorities and the poor. The following essay provides an example of his views. It was first published in 1985.

Chances are that you've never heard of General Laney. He hasn't had a brilliant military career, at least as far as I know. In fact, I'm not certain that he's even served in the military. General, you see, isn't Laney's rank. General is Laney's first name. General Laney does, however, have a claim to fame, unrecognized though it may be. 1

Detroit resident General Laney is the founder and prime mover behind a little-publicized organization known as the National Black Sportsman's Association, often referred to as "the black gun lobby." Laney pulls no punches when asked his opinion of gun control: "Gun control is really race control. People who embrace gun control are really racists in nature. All gun laws have been enacted to control certain classes of people, mainly black people, but the same laws used to control blacks are being used to disarm white people as well." 2

Laney is not the first to make this observation. Indeed, allied with sportsmen in vocal opposition to gun controls in the 1960s were the militant Black Panthers. Panther Minister of Information Eldridge Cleaver noted in 1968: "Some very interesting laws are being passed. They don't name me; they don't say, take the guns away from the niggers. They say that people will no longer be allowed to have (guns). They don't pass these rules and these regulations specifically for black people, they have to pass them in a way that will take in everybody." 3

Some white liberals have said essentially the same thing. Investigative reporter Robert Sherrill, himself no lover of guns, concluded in his book *The Saturday Night Special* that the object of the Gun Control Act of 1968 was black control rather than race control. According to Sherrill, Congress was so panicked by the ghetto riots of 1967 and 1968 that it passed the act to "shut off weapons access to blacks, and since they (Congress) probably associated cheap guns with ghetto blacks and thought cheapness was peculiarly the characteristic of imported military surplus and the mail-order traffic, they decided to cut off these sources while leaving over-the-counter purchases open to the affluent." Congressional motivation may have been more complex than Sherrill suggests, but keeping blacks from acquiring guns was certainly a large part of that motivation. . . . 4

There is little doubt that the earliest gun controls in the United States were blatantly racist and elitist in their intent. San Francisco civil-liberties 5

attorney Don B. Kates, Jr., an opponent of gun prohibitions with impeccable
liberal credentials (he has been a clerk for radical lawyer William Kunstler, a
civil-rights activist in the South, and an Office of Economic Opportunity
lawyer), describes early gun control efforts in his book *Restricting Handguns:
The Liberal Skeptics Speak Out*. As Kates documents, prohibitions against the
sale of cheap handguns originated in the post-Civil War South. Small pistols
selling for as little as 50 or 60 cents became available in the 1870s and '80s, and
since they could be afforded by recently emancipated blacks and poor whites
(whom agrarian agitators of the time were encouraging to ally for economic
and political purposes), these guns constituted a significant threat to a southern
establishment interested in maintaining the traditional class structure.

Consequently, Kates notes, in 1870 Tennessee banned "selling all but 'the   6
Army and Navy model' handgun, i.e., the most expensive one, which was beyond the means of most blacks and laboring people." In 1881, Arkansas enacted
an almost identical ban on the sale of cheap revolvers, while in 1902, South
Carolina banned the sale of handguns to all but "sheriffs and their special
deputies—i.e., company goons and the KKK." In 1893 and 1907, respectively,
Alabama and Texas attempted to put handguns out of the reach of blacks and
poor whites through "extremely heavy business and/or transactional taxes" on
the sale of such weapons. In the other Deep South states, slavery-era bans on
arms possession by blacks continued to be enforced by hook or by crook.

The cheap revolvers of the late 19th and early 20th centuries were re-   7
ferred to as "Suicide Specials," the "Saturday Night Special" label not becoming widespread until reformers and politicians took up the gun control cause
during the 1960s. The source of this recent concern about cheap revolvers, as
their new label suggests, has much in common with the concerns of the gun-
law initiators of the post-Civil War South. As B. Bruce-Briggs has written in
the *Public Interest,* "It is difficult to escape the conclusion that the 'Saturday
Night Special' is emphasized because it is cheap and is being sold to a particular class of people. . . ."

Those who argue that the concern about cheap handguns is justified be-   8
cause these guns are used in most crimes should take note of *Under the Gun:
Weapons, Crime, and Violence in America,* by sociologists James D. Wright, Peter
H. Rossi, and Kathleen Daly. The authors, who undertook an exhaustive, fed-
erally funded, critical review of gun issue research, found *no conclusive proof that
cheap handguns are used in crime more often than expensive handguns.* (Interestingly, the makers of quality arms, trying to stifle competition, have sometimes
supported bans on cheap handguns and on the importation of cheap military
surplus weapons. Kates observes that the Gun Control Act of 1968, which
banned mail-order gun sales and the importation of military surplus firearms,
"was something domestic manufacturers had been impotently urging for
decades.") But the evidence leads to one conclusion that cheap handguns are
considered threatening primarily because minorities and poor whites can afford them.

Attempts to regulate the possession of firearms began in the northern   9
states during the early part of the 20th century, and although these regulations

had a different focus from those that had been concocted in the South, they were no less racist and elitist in effect or intent. Rather than trying to keep handguns out of the price range that blacks and the poor could afford, New York's trend-setting Sullivan Law, enacted in 1911, required a police permit for legal possession of a handgun. This law made it possible for the police to screen applicants for permits to possess handguns, and while such a requirement may seem reasonable, it can be and has been abused.

Members of groups not in favor with the political establishment or the   10
police are automatically suspect and can easily be denied permits. For instance, when the Sullivan Law was enacted, southern and eastern European immigrants were considered racially inferior and religiously and ideologically suspect. (Many were Catholics or Jews, and a disproportionate number were anarchists or socialists.) Professor L. Kennett, coauthor of the authoritative history *The Gun in America,* has noted that the measure was designed to "strike hardest at the foreign-born element," particularly Italians. Southern and eastern European immigrants found it almost impossible to obtain gun permits.

Over the years, application of the Sullivan Law has become increasingly   11
elitist as the police seldom grant handgun permits to any but the wealthy or the politically influential. A beautiful example of this hypocritical elitism is the fact that while the *New York Times* often editorializes against the private possession of handguns, the publisher of that newspaper, Arthur Ochs Sulzberger, has a hard-to-get permit to own and carry a handgun. Another such permit is held by the husband of Dr. Joyce Brothers, the pop psychologist who has claimed that firearms ownership is indicative of male sexual inadequacy.

Gun-control efforts through the centuries have been propelled by racist   12
and elitist sentiments. Even though European aristocrats were members of a weapons-loving warrior caste, they did their best to keep the gun from becoming a weapon of war. It was certainly all right to kill with civilized weapons such as the sword, the battle ax, or the lance; these were weapons that the armored knights were trained to use and which gave them a tremendous advantage over commoners who didn't have the knights' training or possess their expensive weapons and armor. But guns, by virtue of being able to pierce armor, democratized warfare and made common soldiers more than a match for the armored and aristocratic knights, thereby threatening the existence of the feudal aristocracy.

As early as 1541, England enacted a law that limited legal possession of   13
handguns and crossbows (weapons that were considered criminally dangerous) to those with incomes exceeding 100 pounds a year, though long-gun possession wasn't restricted—except for Catholics, a potentially rebellious minority after the English Reformation. Catholics couldn't legally keep militia-like weapons in their homes, as other Englishmen were encouraged to do, but they could legally possess defensive weapons—except, as Bill of Rights authority Joyce Lee Malcolm has noted in her essay "The Right to Keep and Bear Arms: The Common Law Tradition," during times "of extreme religious tension."

According to Malcolm, when William and Mary★ came to the English   14
throne, they were presented with a list of rights, one of which was aimed at
staving off any future attempt at arms confiscation—"all Protestant citizens
had a right to keep arms for their defence." England then remained free of
restrictive gun legislation until 1920 when, even though the crime rate was
very low, concern about the rebellious Irish and various political radicals ushered in today's draconian gun laws. (Colin Greenwood, former superintendent
of the West Yorkshire Metropolitan Police, has discovered in his research at
Cambridge University that the English gun crime rate is significantly *higher*
now than it was before that nation's strict gun laws were enacted.)

Alas, the European aristocracy wasn't able to control gun use, and at least   15
in part, the spread of effective firearms helped to bring down aristocracy and
feudalism. By contrast, in 17th-century Japan the ruling Tokugawa Shogunate
was able to establish a rigidly stratified society that deemphasized the development of guns and restricted arms possession to a warrior aristocracy, the *samurai*. When Commodore Perry† "reopened" Japan to the rest of the world in the
middle of the 19th century, few Japanese were familiar with guns (the sword
was the most honored weapon of the samurai) and the most common guns
were primitive matchlocks similar to those introduced to Japan by the Portuguese in the middle of the 16th century. As post-Perry Japan modernized
and acquired a modern military, it also quickly developed modern weaponry.
But a citizenry without a gun-owning tradition was easily kept in place in a
collectivist society where individuals were more susceptible to formal and informal social controls than are westerners.

The preceding are just samples of the political uses to which gun controls   16
have been put throughout the world. Nazi Germany, the Soviet Union, and
South Africa are modern examples of repressive governments that use gun
control as a means of social control. Raymond G. Kessler, a lawyer-sociologist
who has provided some of the most sociologically sophisticated insights into
the gun control issue, suggests in a *Law and Policy Quarterly* article that attempts to regulate the civilian possession of firearms have five political functions. They "(1) increase citizen reliance on government and tolerance of
increased police powers and abuse; (2) help prevent opposition to government;
(3) facilitate repressive action by government and its allies; (4) lessen the pressure for major or radical reform; and (5) can be selectively enforced against
those perceived to be a threat to government."

Of course, while many gun control proponents might acknowledge   17
that such measures have been used in the ways Kessler lists, they would deny
that the controls that they support are either racist or elitist, since they would
apply to everybody and are aimed at reducing violence for everybody. Yet

★William III (1650–1702) and his wife Mary I, the protestant daughter of James II, came to
power in 1689 after a period of civil unrest.
†Matthew Calbraith Perry (1784–1858), an American Naval officer, negotiated an 1854
treaty that permitted American ships to use two Japanese ports.

the controls that they advocate are in fact racist and classist in *effect,* and only the naive or the dishonest can deny their elitist *intent.*

Kessler has also written that while liberals are likely to sympathize with   18
the poor and minorities responsible for much of this nation's violent crime, when they are victimized themselves, "or when they hear of an especially heinous crime, liberals, like most people, feel anger and hostility toward the offender. The discomfort of having incompatible feelings can be alleviated by transferring the anger away from the offender to an inanimate object—the weapon."

A perfect example of this transference is provided by Pete Shields, the   19
chairman of the lobbying group Handgun Control Inc., whose son was tragically murdered with a handgun by one of San Francisco's Zebra killers—blacks who were killing whites at random in the early 1970s. This killing was carried out by a black man who was after whites—his own skin color and that of his victim were important to the killer—but in his grief, the white liberal father couldn't blame the criminal for this racist crime. So the gun was the culprit. The upshot is that we now have Handgun Control Inc., with its emphasis on the *weapon* used to commit a crime rather than the criminal. Yet blacks and minorities, who would be prevented from defending themselves, are likely to be harmed most by legislation proposed by Handgun Control Inc., the National Coalition to Ban Handguns, and other proponents of strict handgun controls.

Since the illegal possession of a handgun (or of any gun) is a crime that   20
doesn't produce a victim and is unlikely to be reported to the police, handgun permit requirements or outright handgun prohibitions aren't easily enforced. And as civil liberties attorney Kates has observed, when laws are difficult to enforce, "enforcement becomes progressively more haphazard until at last the laws are used only against those who are unpopular with the police." Of course minorities, especially minorities who don't "know their place," aren't likely to be popular with the police, and these very minorities, in the face of police indifference or perhaps even antagonism, may be the most inclined to look to guns for protection—guns that they can't acquire legally and that place them in jeopardy if possessed illegally. While the intent of such laws may not be racist, their effect most certainly is.

Today's gun-control battle, like those of days gone by, largely breaks   21
down along class lines. Though there are exceptions to the rule, the most dedicated and vociferous proponents of strict gun controls are urban, upper-middle-class or aspiring upper-middle-class, pro-big-government liberals, many of whom are part of the New Class (establishment intellectuals and the media), and most of whom know little or nothing about guns and the wide range of legitimate uses to which they are regularly put. Many of these elitists make no secret of their disdain for gun-owners. For instance, Gov. Mario Cuomo of New York recently dismissed those who are opposed to the Empire State's mandatory seat-belt law as "NRA hunters who drink beer, don't vote, and lie to their wives about where they were all weekend."

On the other hand, the most dedicated opponents of gun control are often   22
rural- or small-town-oriented, working- or middle-class men and women, few

of whom possess the means to publicize their views, but many of whom know a great deal about the safe and lawful uses of guns. To these Americans, guns mean freedom, security, and wholesome recreation. The battle over gun controls, therefore, has come about as affluent America has attempted to impose its anti-gun prejudices on a working-class America that is comfortable with guns (including handguns), seldom misuses them (most gun crime is urban), and sees them as protection against criminal threats and government oppression.

How right you are, General Laney. "All guns laws have been enacted to   23
control certain classes of people. . . ." ■

Questions for Meaning

1. Why does Tonso object to New York State's Sullivan Law?
2. What led England to adopt gun control in the 1920s?
3. According to this essay, what are the political motives that lead to gun control?
4. What does Tonso mean by "transference" in paragraph 19?
5. What is wrong with a law that is selectively enforced?
6. Vocabulary: impeccable (5), emancipated (5), agrarian (5), impotently (8), authoritative (10), collectivist (15), vociferous (21).

Questions about Strategy

1. Why do you think Tonso chose to begin this essay with a reference to General Laney when he realized that his audience was probably unfamiliar with this man?
2. Consider Tonso's use of sources in this essay. How well are they incorporated into Tonso's own argument? Which is the most effective?
3. Why does Tonso discuss both English and Japanese history?
4. How does Tonso characterize his opponents? Does he treat them fairly? What is the quotation from Mario Cuomo meant to illustrate?

JOSH SUGARMANN

THE NRA IS RIGHT

Most of the debate over gun control has focused on whether there's a need to restrict handgun ownership. In the following essay, first published in 1987, Josh Sugarmann argues on behalf of banning handguns altogether. A freelance writer living in New York, Sugarmann was communications director of the National Coalition to Ban handguns from 1984 to 1986.

One tenet of the National Rifle Association's faith has always been that handgun controls do little to stop criminals from obtaining handguns. For once, the NRA is right and America's leading handgun control organization is wrong. Criminals don't buy handguns in gun stores. That's why they're criminals. But it isn't criminals who are killing most of the 20,000 to 22,000 people who die from handguns each year. We are.   1

This is an ugly truth for a country that thinks of handgun violence as a "crime" issue and believes that it's somehow possible to separate "good" handguns (those in our hands for self-defense) from "bad" handguns (those in the hands of criminals).   2

Contrary to popular perception, the most prevalent form of handgun death in America isn't murder but suicide. An additional 1,000 fatalities are accidents. And of the 9,000 handgun deaths classified as murders, most are not caused by predatory strangers. Handgun violence is usually the result of people being angry, drunk, careless, or depressed—who just happen to have a handgun around. In all, fewer than 10 percent of handgun deaths are felony-related.   3

Though handgun availability is not a crime issue, it does represent a major public health threat. Handguns are the number one weapon for both murder and suicide and are second only to auto accidents as the leading cause of death due to injury. Of course there are other ways of committing suicide or crimes of passion. But no means is more lethal, effective, or handy. That's why the NRA is ultimately wrong. As several public health organizations have noted, the best way to curb a public health problem is through prevention—in this case, the banning of all handguns from civilian hands.   4

The Enemy Is Us

For most who attempt suicide, the will to die lasts only briefly. Only one out of every ten people attempting suicide is going to kill himself no matter what. The success or failure of an attempt depends primarily on the lethality of the means. Pills, razor blades, and gas aren't guaranteed killers, and they take time. Handguns, however, lend themselves well to spontaneity. Consider that although women try to kill themselves four times as often as men, men succeed three to four times as often. For one reason: women use pills or less lethal means; men use handguns. This balance is shifting, however, as more women   5 own or have access to handguns. Between 1970 and 1978 the suicide rate for young women rose 50 percent, primarily due to increased use of handguns.

Of course, there is no way to lock society's cupboard and prevent every distraught soul from injuring him or herself. Still, there are ways we can promote public safety without becoming a nation of nannies. England, for instance, curbed suicide by replacing its most common means of committing suicide—coal stove gas—with less toxic natural gas. Fifteen years after the switch, studies found that suicide rates had dropped and remained low, even though the number of suicide *attempts* had increased. "High suicide rates seem to occur where highly lethal suicidal methods are not only available but also where they are culturally acceptable," writes Dr. Robert Markush of the University of Alabama, who has studied the use of handguns in suicide.

6

Most murders aren't crime-related, but are the result of arguments between friends and among families. In 1985, 59 percent of all murders were committed by people known to the victim. Only 15 percent were committed by strangers, and only 18 percent were the result of felonious activity. As the FBI admits every year in its *Uniform Crime Reports,* "murder is a societal problem over which law enforcement has little or no control." The FBI doesn't publish separate statistics on who's killing whom with handguns, but it is assumed that what is true of all murders is true of handgun murders.

7

Controlling the Vector

Recognizing that eliminating a disease requires prevention, not treatment, health professionals have been in the forefront of those calling for a national ban on handguns. In 1981, the Surgeon General's Select Panel for the Promotion of Child Health traced the "epidemic of deaths and injuries among children and youth" to handguns, and called for "nothing short of a total ban." It is estimated that on average, one child dies from handgun wounds each day. Between 1961 and 1981, according to the American Association of Suicidology, the suicide rate for 15- to 24-year-olds increased 150 percent. The report linked the rise in murders and suicides among the young to the increased use of firearms—primarily handguns. In a 1985 report, the Surgeon General's Workshop on Violence and Public Health recommended "a complete and universal ban on the sale, manufacture, importation, and possession of handguns (except for authorized police and military personnel)."

8

Not surprisingly, the American Public Health Association, the American Association of Suicidology, and the American Psychiatric Association, are three of the 31 national organizations that are members of National Coalition to Ban Handguns (NCBH).

9

Comparing the relationship between handguns and violence to mosquitos and malaria, Stephen P. Teret, co-director of the Johns Hopkins Injury Prevention Center, says, "As public health professionals, if we are faced with a disease that is carried by some type of vehicle/vector like a mosquito, our initial response would be to control the vector. There's no reason why if the vehicle/vector is a handgun, we should not be interested in controlling the handgun."

10

The NRA refers to handgun suicides, accidental killings, and murders by   11
acquaintances as "the price of freedom." It believes that handguns right
enough wrongs, stop enough crimes, and kill enough criminals to justify these
deaths. But even the NRA has admitted that there is no "adequate measure
that more lives are saved by arms in good hands than are lost by arms in evil
hands." Again, the NRA is right.

A 1985 NCBH study found that a handgun is 118 times more likely to   12
be used in a suicide, murder, or fatal accident than to kill a criminal. Between 1981 and 1983, nearly 69,000 Americans lost their lives to handguns.
During that same period there were only 583 justifiable homicides reported
to the FBI, in which someone used a handgun to kill a stranger—a burglar,
rapist, or other criminal. In 1982, 19 states reported to the FBI that not once
did a private citizen use a handgun to kill a criminal. Five states reported that
more than 130 citizens were murdered with handguns for each time a handgun was justifiably used to kill a criminal. In no state did the number of
self-defense homicides approach the murder toll. Last year, a study published
in the *New England Journal of Medicine* analyzing gun use in the home over a
six-year period in the Seattle, Washington area, found that for every time a
firearm was used to kill an intruder in self-defense, 198 lives ended in murders, suicides, or accidents. Handguns were used in more than 70 percent of
those deaths.

Although handguns are rarely used to kill criminals, an obvious question   13
remains: How often are they used merely to wound or scare away intruders?
No reliable statistics are available, but most police officials agree that in a
criminal confrontation on the street, the handgun-toting civilian is far more
likely to be killed or lose his handgun to a criminal than successfully use the
weapon in self-defense. "Beyond any doubt, thousands more lives are lost every year because of the proliferation of handguns than are saved," says Joseph
McNamara, chief of police of San Jose, who has also been police chief in Kansas City, a beat cop in Harlem, and is the author of a book on defense against
violent crime. Moreover, most burglaries occur when homes are vacant, so the
handgun in the drawer is no deterrent. (It would also probably be the first
item stolen.)

Faced with facts like these, anti-control advocates often turn to the argu-   14
ment of last resort: the Second Amendment. But the historic, 1981 Morton
Grove, Illinois, ban on handgun sale and possession exploded that rationale. In
1983, the U.S. Supreme Court let stand a lower court ruling that stated,
"Because the possession of handguns is not part of the right to keep and bear
arms, [the Morton Grove ordinance] does not violate the Second Amendment."

Criminal Equivocation

Unfortunately, powerful as the NRA is, it has received additional help from   15
the leading handgun control group. Handgun Control Inc. (HCI) has helped
the handgun lobby by setting up the perfect strawman for the NRA to shoot
down. "Keep handguns out of the wrong hands," HCI says. "By making
it more difficult for criminals, drug addicts, etc., to get handguns, we can

reduce handgun violence," it promises. Like those in the NRA, HCI chairman Nelson T. "Pete" Shields "firmly believe(s) in the right of law-abiding citizens to possess handguns . . . for legitimate purposes."

In its attempt to paint handgun violence solely as a crime issue, HCI goes   16
so far as to sometimes ignore the weapon's non-crime death tally. In its most recent poster comparing the handgun murder toll in the U.S. with that of nations with strict handgun laws, HCI states: "In 1983, handguns killed 35 people in Japan, 8 in Great Britain, 27 in Switzerland, 6 in Canada, 7 in Sweden, 10 in Australia, and 9,014 in the United States." Handguns *killed* a lot more than that in the United States. About 13,000 suicides and accidents more.

HCI endorses a ban only on short-barrelled handguns (the preferred   17
weapon of criminals). It advocates mandatory safety training, a waiting period during which a background check can be run on a purchaser, and a license to carry a handgun, with mandatory sentencing for violators. It also endorses mandatory sentencing for the use of a handgun in a crime. According to HCI communications director Barbara Lautman, together these measures would "attack pretty much the heart of the problem."

HCI appears to have arrived at its crime focus by taking polls. In his   18
1981 book, *Guns Don't Die—People Do,* Shields points out that the majority of Americans don't favor a ban on handguns. "What they do want, however, is a set of strict laws to control the easy access to handguns by the criminal and the violence prone—*as long as those controls don't jeopardize the perceived right of law-abiding citizens to buy and own handguns for self defense* [italics his]." Shields admits "this is not based on any naive hope that criminals will obey such laws. Rather, it is based on the willingness of the rest of us to be responsible and accountable citizens, and the knowledge that to the degree we are, we make it more difficult for the criminal to get a handgun." This wasn't always HCI's stand. Founded in 1974 as the National Council to Control Handguns, HCI originally called a ban on private handgun possession the "most effective" solution to reducing violent crime rapidly and was at one time a member of NCBH. Michael Beard, president of NCBH, maintains the HCI's focus on crime "started with a public relations concern. Some people in the movement felt Americans were worried about crime, and that was one way to approach the problem. That's the problem when you use public opinion polls to tell you what your position's going to be. And I think a lot of the handgun control movement has looked at whatever's hot at the time and tried to latch onto that, rather than sticking to the basic message that there is a relationship between the availability of handguns and the handgun violence in our society. . . . Ultimately, nothing short of taking the product off the market is really going to have an effect on the problem."

HCI's cops and robbers emphasis has been endlessly frustrating to many   19
in the anti-handgun movement. HCI would offer handgun control as a solution to crime, and the NRA would effectively rebut their arguments with the commonsensical observation that criminals are not likely to obey such laws. I can't help but think that HCI's refusal to abandon the crime argument has harmed the longterm progress of the movement.

Saturated Dresser Drawers

In a nation with 40 million handguns—where anyone who wants one can get   20
one—it's time to face a chilling fact. We're way past the point where registration, licensing, safety training, waiting periods, or mandatory sentencing are
going to have much effect. Each of these measures may save some lives or help
catch a few criminals, but none—by itself or taken together—will stop the
vast majority of handgun suicides or murders. A "controlled" handgun kills
just as effectively as an "uncontrolled" one.

Most control recommendations merely perpetuate the myth that with   21
proper care a handgun can be as safe as any other. Nothing could be further
from the truth. A handgun is not a blender.

Those advocating a step-by-step process insist that a ban would be too   22
radical and therefore unacceptable to Congress and the public. A hardcore 40
percent of the American public has always endorsed banning handguns. Many
will also undoubtedly argue that any control measure—no matter how ill-
conceived or ineffective—would be a good first step. But after more than a
decade, the other foot hasn't followed.

In other areas of firearms control there has been increasing recognition   23
that bans are the most effective solution. The only two federal measures passed
since the Gun Control Act of 1968 have been bans. In each case, the reasoning
was simple: the harm done by these objects outweighed any possible benefit
they brought to society. In 1986, Congress banned certain types of armor-
piercing "cop-killer" bullets. There was also a silver lining to last year's NRA–
McClure-Volkmer handgun "decontrol" bill, which weakened the already lax
Gun Control Act of 1968, making it legal, for instance, for people to transport
unloaded "not readily accessible" handguns interstate. A last-minute amendment added by pro-control forces banned the future production and sale of
machine guns for civilian use.

Unfortunately, no law has addressed the major public health problem.   24
Few suicides, accidental killings, or acquaintance murders are the result of
cop-killer bullets or machine guns.

Outlawing handguns would in no way be a panacea. Even if handgun   25
production stopped tomorrow, millions would remain in the dresser drawers
of America's bedrooms—and many of them would probably stay there. Contrary to NRA fantasies, black-booted fascists would not be kicking down
doors searching for handguns. Moreover, the absolute last segment of society
to be affected by any measure would be criminals. The black market that has
fed off the legal sale of handguns would continue for a long while. But by
ending new handgun production, the availability of illegal handguns can only
decrease.

Of course, someone who truly wants to kill himself can find another   26
way. A handgun ban would not affect millions of rifles and shotguns. But experience shows that no weapon provides the combination of lethality and convenience that a handgun does. Handguns represent only 30 percent of all guns
out there but are responsible for 90 percent of firearms misuse. Most people

who commit suicide with a firearm use a handgun. At minimum, a handgun ban would prevent the escalation of killings in segments of society that have not yet been saturated by handgun manufacturers. Further increases in suicides among women, for instance, might be curtailed.

But the final solution lies in changing the way handguns and handgun   27 violence are viewed by society. Public health campaigns have changed the way Americans look at cigarette smoking and drunk driving and can do the same for handguns.

For the past 12 years, many in the handgun control movement have con-   28 fined their debate to what the public supposedly wants and expects to hear— not to reality. The handgun must be seen for what it is, not what we'd like it to be.   ■

Questions for Meaning

1. Why does Sugarmann believe that banning handguns would reduce the number of deaths that occur each year in the United States?
2. What causes of handgun violence are identified by Sugarmann?
3. What does Sugarmann mean by "strawman" in paragraph 15?
4. How does Sugarmann's position differ from the policy of Handgun Control Inc.?
5. Why is it that men kill themselves more often than women do even though women attempt suicide more frequently?
6. Vocabulary: tenet (1), prevalent (3), predatory (3), nannies (6), rationale (14), fascists (25), curtailed (26).

Questions about Strategy

1. Consider the title of this essay. Why do you think Sugarmann chose it?
2. Does Sugarmann make any concessions to opponents of gun control?
3. Why does Sugarmann link gun control with public health campaigns?
4. Sugarmann devotes five paragraphs to attacking an organization that is working to control handguns, an organization with which he might have forged an alliance. Was this wise? Did he have any choice?

Franklin E. Zimring

FIREARMS, VIOLENCE, AND PUBLIC POLICY

Franklin E. Zimring first published this article in the November 1991 issue of *Scientific American*, a journal that publishes fairly long and data-filled articles for readers who respect serious research. Professor of law at the Earl Warren Legal Institute of the University of California, Berkeley, Zimring directed research on firearms for the National Commission on the Causes and Prevention of Violence. With Gordon Hawkins, he is the author of *The Citizen's Guide to Gun Control* (1987), and *Deterrence: The Legal Threat in Crime Control* (1976).

Even though the U.S. has many more gun-control laws than any other nation, Americans are more likely to be victims of gun-related violence. We have no hope of greatly improving this situation as long as we continue to construct gun-control policy on a weak foundation of facts.   1

Since the 1960s some social and behavioral scientists have been investigating how violence is related to firearms. But their conclusions have largely been ignored. Neither supporters nor opponents of gun-control laws have felt any great need to cite facts. Strong emotions have kept the conflicting parties at each other's throats.   2

Recent congressional debates on gun control have also relied on undocumented assertions. The 1991 Brady bill aims to reduce the violence associated with guns by making handgun purchases subject to waiting periods and police notification.★ The congressional debate over these issues is no more informed than it was during the deliberations that led to the Gun Control Act of 1968. A distaste for facts is also evident in the emphasis Americans have placed on research: much more money is spent on newspaper advertisements about gun control than on research about firearms and violence.   3

During the past three decades, investigators have learned about the relation between guns and the death rate from violent crime, accidents and suicides. They recorded the kinds of firearms used in these situations, and they measured how gun-control laws have influenced crime and the ownership of guns.   4

The accumulating evidence provides reasons for discomfort on both sides of the political struggle. Ample data confirm that as guns become more available, people are more likely to die during violent crimes—a connection that opponents of gun control have tried to deny. Research also shows that many laws do not significantly diminish the number of guns used in violence, although many advocates of gun control have assumed they would.   5

Lawmakers have agreed to many measures that try to keep guns out of the hands of criminals. But these regulations have not brought violence down   6

★After several years of debate, the Brady Bill was approved by Congress in 1993.

to a level that most Americans can tolerate. At the same time, we have not confronted the controversial issue of reducing the 35 million handguns that play the greatest role in violence caused by firearms.

The Federal Bureau of Investigation reports that in 1990 criminals in the   7
U.S. committed more than 1.8 million acts of homicide, robbery, forcible rape and serious assault. More than 28 percent of these violent crimes involved firearms. And, most notably, guns were the cause of death in 64 percent of the 23,000 homicides. Although the statistics portray the magnitude of gun-related violence, they provide no information about why or how the flow of firearms should be regulated.

The issue of gun control hinges on whether the death rate from violence   8
would subside if people were forced to abandon firearms and choose other weapons such as knives. As Philip J. Cook and Daniel Nagin of Duke University once asked, "Does the weapon matter?"

The answer is not obvious. In 1958 Marvin E. Wolfgang of the Univer-   9
sity of Pennsylvania claimed that the choice of weapon did not make much difference in criminal homicide. He argued that if guns were unavailable, assailants would wield other deadly weapons to achieve their goal. His analysis assumed that most people who commit criminal homicide have a single-minded and unconditional intention to kill.

A decade after Wolfgang's work, I found evidence that the weapon used is   10
important in determining whether a violent assault will lead to death. I reviewed Chicago police records of more than 16,000 violent assaults, both fatal and nonfatal, to determine the outcomes of attacks with guns and knives, the two weapons most commonly used in criminal homicide. The study showed that most attackers seemed to stop short of ensuring the victim's death. In eight out of 10 assaults with guns, the attacker shot the victim only once. Attackers also inflicted one wound in seven out of 10 cases in which the victim died.

In general, fatality seemed to be an almost accidental outcome of a large   11
number of assaults committed with guns or knives. The Chicago study indicated that most nonfatal attacks, like most homicides, resulted in wounds to vital parts of the body. According to the study, homicide and serious assaults involved the same kinds of motives (mostly spontaneous arguments), and they occurred in the same places at the same times.

One important difference among assaults was the weapon used: an assault   12
with a gun was five times more likely to result in a fatality than an assault with a knife. And assaults with guns to all vital body areas—head, neck, shoulders, chest and abdomen—were many times more likely to kill than attacks to the same locations with knives. In 1990 more than 23 percent of the one million serious assaults involved guns, whereas knives played a role in 20 percent of assaults.

Do attackers who carry guns simply have more lethal intentions than as-   13
sailants who use knives? The Chicago data indicated otherwise: compared with assaults with guns, attacks with knives were more likely to result in multiple wounds, and they were equally likely to damage a part of the body where

death can result. The five-to-one difference in death rate thus seems to stem from the greater dangerousness of the firearm as a weapon, what is known as an instrumentality effect.

If such instrumentality effects are large, a shift from guns to knives   14
would cause a drop in the homicide rate even if the total rate of violent assault did not change. Other studies have corroborated the presence of large instrumentality effects in urban violence.

When Hans Zeisel of the University of Chicago and other sociologists   15
compared assaults in cities that had different mixes of guns and knifes, they found a difference in death rate between the two kinds of assaults. Zeisel, who examined New York and Houston, wrote, "If the level of gun attacks in Houston were reduced from 42 percent to New York's level of 24 percent, 322 gun attacks would have been knife attacks. At present, these 322 gun attacks resulted in 63 fatalities. . . . If they were knife attacks, roughly 12 fatalities would result—a reduction from 20 deaths per 100 attacks to four per 100."

Although all guns are deadly, some types of firearms are more harmful than   16
others because they are more likely to be used in crime and violence. In the U.S., handguns—small, concealable weapons that can be fired with one hand—account for one third of the 120 to 150 million firearms estimated to be owned by civilians. Handguns are used in more than 75 percent of firearm-related homicides and more than 80 percent of firearm-related robberies. On

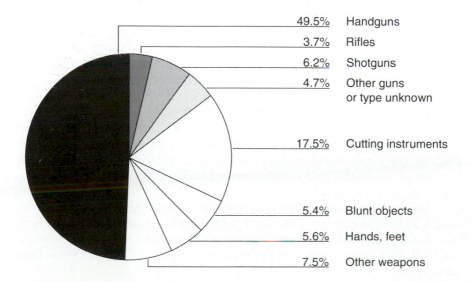

49.5%	Handguns
3.7%	Rifles
6.2%	Shotguns
4.7%	Other guns or type unknown
17.5%	Cutting instruments
5.4%	Blunt objects
5.6%	Hands, feet
7.5%	Other weapons

Source: FBI Uniform Crime Reports

FIGURE I
Weapons used in homicide in 1990

the average, rifles and shotguns are seven times less likely than handguns to be used in criminal violence. In states and cities that have made special efforts to restrict handguns, the major problem is still illegal handguns rather than long guns. (No one has recorded how many crimes are committed with what are called military assault weapons. These semiautomatic rifles and handguns require a separate trigger pull for each bullet discharged but can fire many rounds of ammunition quickly.)

To determine whether the type of gun influences the outcome of violent   17
assaults, my colleagues and I conducted a follow-up study in Chicago in 1972. Not surprisingly, we found that a large-caliber gun was twice as likely to kill as a small-caliber gun in cases in which the guns inflicted the same number of wounds to the same part of the body. This statistic indicated that mortality from criminal violence is strongly correlated with the dangerousness of the weapon, not just the attacker's intent.

Some sociologists have criticized the conclusion that the motivations be-   18
hind most homicides are ambiguous. They argue that the similarity between fatal and nonfatal assaults might be superficial. Furthermore, they maintain that attackers who wield guns may have substantially different intentions from criminals who use knives. But so far no evidence derived from data on assault has been presented that argues against instrumentality effects in homicide.

The role of weapons is largely unknown in another kind of assault,   19
forcible rape. More than 100,000 cases are reported to the police every year, and roughly 8,000 of them involve firearms. Although a change in firearm use could prevent many rapes at gunpoint, most rapists use personal force or other means. No studies have yet determined the different rates of death from forcible rape involving different types of weapons.

A central issue in the gun-control debate is robbery. Each year the FBI tallies   20
more than 500,000 robberies and 3,000 deaths of robbery victims. (This type of crime produces by far the most killings of strangers.)

In 1990 criminals carried firearms in 37 percent of 640,000 robberies   21
reported to the police. Criminals do not rely heavily on firearms for robberies of vulnerable individuals on the street. But they often carry guns to rob stores. My colleagues and I found that in Chicago firearms are involved in two thirds of robberies of commercial establishments but fewer than two fifths of street robberies.

Because robberies need involve only the threat of injury, it cannot be as-   22
sumed that the choice of weapon in a robbery will influence the outcome in the same way as the choice in assaults does. Only in recent years have investigators published special reports on the influence of guns on the death rate from robbery.

The National Crime Survey reports that crime victims are less likely to   23
resist robbers who carry guns than those who wield other weapons. Apparently, a firearm makes the threat of force by a robber conspicuously credible. The risk of any victim injury is therefore lower when a robber has a gun instead of, say, a knife.

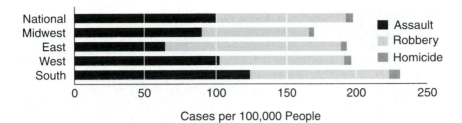

Cases per 100,000 People

Source: FBI Uniform Crime Reports

FIGURE 2
Crimes with guns by region in 1990

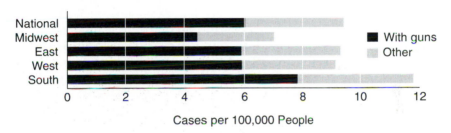

Cases per 100,000 People

Source: FBI Uniform Crime Reports

FIGURE 3
Homicides by region in 1990

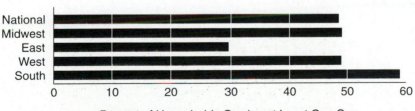

Percent of Households Owning at Least One Gun

Source: Gallup Poll

FIGURE 4
Households with guns by region in 1991

	National	Midwest	East	West	South
Handgun	47%	33%	48%	54%	52%
Shotgun	51%	56%	53%	36%	55%
Rifle	50%	46%	59%	52%	49%

Source: Gallup Poll

FIGURE 5

Type of firearm in households with guns in 1991

But in cases where robberies result in injuries, guns are far more deadly   24
than other weapons. James Zuehl and I at the University of Chicago found
that the death rate is three times higher for robberies at gunpoint than for robberies with knives, the next most dangerous robbery weapon. Cook has found
that in areas where gun ownership is unusually prevalent, death rates from
robbery are high. [See Figure 6.]

These findings independently confirm the instrumentality effects found   25
in assaults because robbers presumably do not select their weapons with the
intent of injuring their victim. Robberies with firearms, like assaults with
guns, contribute greatly to the crime-related death rate, independent of the
motivations of the criminal.

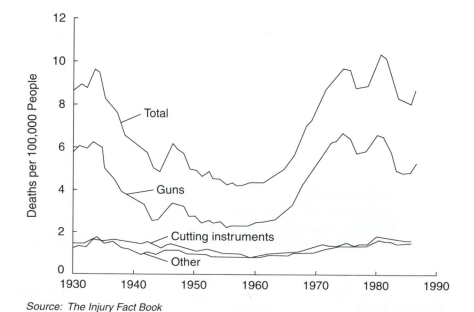

Source: The Injury Fact Book

FIGURE 6

Death rates from homicide by year and method

One question not yet answered is how much the availability of guns in- 26
fluences the rate of robberies. Presumably, when guns are widely available,
robberies become easier to commit and increase in frequency. Yet in one study
of U.S. cities, Cook did not find a correlation between gun availability and
total robbery rate. No one has yet investigated the more specific comparison of
commercial robbery rates.

Very few scholars have studied how firearms are related to two impor- 27
tant forms of noncriminal violence: suicide and accidents. In the U.S. death by
self-inflicted gunshot wounds accounts for over half the more than 30,000 suicides committed every year. Firearms are no more effective a means of suicide
than are such methods as hanging or jumping. But when firearms are not at
hand, people most frequently attempt suicide by drug overdoses. If guns were
not available to people with suicidal intentions, how many attempts might be
redirected to less lethal means and how many lives would be saved? This question deserves far more attention that it has received.

Accidents involving firearms claim about 2,000 lives every year in the 28
U.S., a much lower death rate than that for homicides or suicides. About 60
percent of accidental fatalities occur in or around the home. The population
groups that have the highest fatality rates from accidents are male children and
adolescents, who are generally inexperienced in using guns and are often
tempted to play with them. Clearly, if young people did not have access to
guns, the death rate would drop.

Two other findings about the misuse of firearms have some significance 29
when considering strategies of firearm control. First, the percentage of gun-
related crimes in an area is related to the proportion of owners of firearms in
that area. In 1969 the Task Force on Firearms demonstrated that if a city ranks
high in gun use for one kind of crime, such as aggravated assault, the use of
guns tends to be high for other types of crime, such as robbery. Cook has also
found that high rates of gun use in suicide are positively correlated with rates
of gun use in violent crime. As more firearms are available to the civilian population, more guns are also available for misuse.

Second, in the 1970s the Federal Bureau of Alcohol, Tobacco and 30
Firearms conducted studies of handguns confiscated on city streets. The bureau showed that handguns are most likely to be misused in the first few years
after the weapons are introduced to the civilian market. In four U.S. cities
studied by the bureau, handguns three years old or younger constituted half of
those confiscated on the streets but less than a quarter of the total number
owned by civilians. Consequently, handguns play their greatest role in street
crime when they are a few years old, even though they often function for
many years.

All gun-control measures seek to reduce the influence of the use of firearms in 31
crimes and violence. The ideal gun-control measure would prevent all crime
and violence involving guns without interfering with their legitimate use in
contemporary life. More realistically, regulations should reduce the problems
caused by illegitimate uses as much as possible while minimizing the restraints

on legitimate uses of guns. To achieve this goal, lawmakers have proposed many different types of regulations. [See Figure 7.] The laws are usually based on one of three strategies: prohibiting high-risk uses of firearms, keeping guns out of the hands of high-risk users or banning high-risk firearms.

Regulations that prohibit high-risk uses of firearms include "place and manner" prohibitions and extra penalties for unlawful use. Most gun laws in the U.S. seek to regulate the place and manner in which firearms may be used. They prohibit such high-risk uses as carrying firearms in a motor vehicle or discharging a firearm in populated areas or concealing weapons on one's person. Place-and-manner laws attempt to deter high-risk behavior with guns, and they rely on the police to intervene before violence occurs. These laws prevent violence only to the extent that the police can discover and arrest persons who violate such laws. How much violence is deterred because guns are not carried is not known. But the rate of gun-related violence would almost certainly increase if carrying loaded weapons became widespread.   32

High-risk behavior with guns can also be discouraged by instituting particularly stiff penalties for criminals who use firearms. Such laws attempt to deter the would-be robber or attacker from using a gun during a crime. More than half of the states have passed such laws. This approach is popular with gun owners because the penalties concern only gun-related crime and place no restrictions on firearm ownership.   33

Extra-penalty laws are limited, however, in their potential to curb firearm violence. To reduce the number of crimes involving guns, such laws would have to discourage persons who would not be deterred by the already severe penalties for robbery and assault. Can the threat of additional punishment succeed? A robber might be deterred from using a gun if the penalty for robbery with a gun were several times greater than that of robbery without a gun. But punishment for robbery is already severe, at least as set forth in the statutes. In addition, a robber who carries a gun should not be punished so harshly that the additional penalty he risks if he injures or kills his victim is relatively small. It seems unlikely, therefore, that such laws have much more potential to deter gun use in robberies.   34

The issue of additional deterrence is also complicated for the crime of assault with a gun because the person who attacks someone with a gun is already risking the maximum punishment if the victim dies. A series of studies—the most notable by Colin Loftin and his associates at the University of Maryland—find that at best extra-punishment laws reduce gun-related crime by a small amount.   35

Extra punishment and place-and-manner regulation do have a role in comprehensive firearm control. But they cannot be used as the primary controls in a system that aspires to influence the death rate from violence substantially.   36

Laws attempting to discourage high-risk use of firearms can be more effective when they are combined with selective ownership prohibitions. This second gun-control strategy seeks to deny high-risk users access to firearms. Usually   37

Strategy	Cost and Inconvenience	Effect on Legitimate Uses of Guns	Potential Number of Lives Saved	Problems
Stop Dangerous Uses				
Extra punishment for crimes committed with guns and laws that regulate the proper use of guns	Minor	Minor	Few	Weak threat, no logistical barrier to prevent gun misuse
Stop Dangerous Users				
Laws that prohibit convicted felons from buying guns	Minor	Minor	Few	Ineffective against those willing to lie about criminal record
Gun licenses for those who are not convicted felons and gun registration	Some	Some	Some	Difficult to monitor tens of millions of guns
Reduce Supply of Firearms				
Restrictions on ownership of exotic firearms	Minor	Minor	Some	Little control over guns obtained illegally
Restrictions on ownership of handguns	Major	Major	Many	Costly, interferes with legitimate uses, little control over guns obtained illegally

FIGURE 7
Strategies for gun control

the law considers high-risk users to include convicted felons, minors, adjudicated mental incompetents, drug addicts and fugitives from justice. The theory is that high-risk users should not be allowed to own firearms, because the societal damage they cause through violence outweighs the social value of their interests in using guns legitimately.

The federal government and nearly every state prohibit some type of high-risk ownership. But many of these laws do not make a person prove his eligibility to own a gun before obtaining one. The ownership ban is supposed to be effective because the ineligible person will be subject to criminal penalties if caught possessing a firearm. Although such a law will not keep guns out of the hands of high-risk users who lie about their status, it is hoped high-risk users will be deterred by the threat of criminal punishment.   38

The ownership bans represent some improvement over simply passing stiffer penalties for gun-related crimes because the law attempts to separate the potential criminal from his gun before he commits a crime with it. And if such laws could reduce the number of gun owners by excluding the people subject to the prohibition, they would indeed reduce violence.   39

But it is no easy matter to keep guns away from a group of "bad guys" while allowing a larger group of "good guys" to own millions of them. Furthermore, bans are not very effective when the purchaser does not have to prove his eligibility as a gun purchaser. For instance, a convicted felon, who is prohibited from acquiring a gun under federal law, can easily obtain one if he is willing to lie about his record.   40

To prevent high-risk groups from freely obtaining firearms, many state and local governments now attempt to identify ineligible gun buyers before they acquire weapons. The screening system included in the Brady bill permits the police to determine whether a prospective gun purchaser has a criminal record. If the check turns up nothing, or even if it is not done, the purchaser can obtain the gun.   41

Screening systems are more effective than simple bans because screening prevents some high-risk users from obtaining guns even if they are willing to break the law. But because the screening systems mean additional costs and delays to all who wish to buy firearms, gun-owner groups usually oppose screening.   42

Screening systems and ownership prohibitions have a limited effect on homicides because most are committed by people who were not previously convicted of a felony and therefore who can purchase a gun legally. Still, screening systems are helpful to the extent that they keep firearms away from convicted felons and minors.   43

Many systems of owner screening suffer from another limitation. They affect only the purchase of weapons from commercial retailers. The measures do not apply to transactions between private citizens, who are continually selling and passing on some 35 million handguns. Prospective criminals can easily steal or purchase these guns.   44

To prevent the transfer of guns from private citizens to ineligible users, a few states require owners of firearms to register their weapons. In such   45 schemes, owners must give information identifying each firearm they own. Gun accountability works like car registration, whereas owner screening is analogous to driver's licenses. But owner licensing schemes will have a limited impact on violence because they leave a large arsenal of firearms to which potential criminals have easy access.

The dangers of widespread access to firearms can be alleviated, in part, by reg-   46
ulating guns that are particularly dangerous. Laws that limit the supply of high-risk weapons can complement the strategy of decreasing high-risk uses and users. Supply-reduction laws strive to make the most dangerous guns so scarce that potential criminals cannot obtain them easily. The laws are justified on the grounds that the harm caused by owning and using these particularly dangerous firearms is greater than the benefit, even in the noncriminal population. [See Figure 7.]

Supply-reduction laws usually deny citizens the opportunity to own a   47
high-risk firearm unless they prove a special need for the weapon or belong to an exempt group, such as the military or the police. The idea behind supply reduction is that gun-related violence will decrease significantly only if the firearms most often used in violence are not available to most people.

The first weapons singled out for high-risk classification were machine   48
guns and sawed-off shotguns as specified in the National Firearms Act of 1934. More than three decades later federal law put special restrictions on destructive devices of military origin and forbade the importation of handguns that were classified as unsuitable for sporting purposes. Several current proposals are designed to prohibit civilian ownership of military assault weapons.

Some state and local governments also single out the handgun as a high-   49
risk firearm and require special licenses to purchase handguns. The system in New York City is the most prominent example of this approach. City residents must demonstrate a special need for a handgun, whereas in permissive licensing systems only high-risk users are disqualified. Gun-control supporters frequently advocate restricting the supply of handguns on a nationwide basis.

But a decrease in handguns will reduce firearm violence only if other   50
guns are not substituted. It has been difficult so far to determine what effect restrictive licensing has had. Cities and states that have such licensing schemes have found that long guns are not replacing handguns as crime weapons. But one reason for this lack of substitution is that the laws have failed, so far, to reduce the supply of handguns significantly.

It is all too easy to move guns across state and city borders from areas   51
where guns are easily available to places where firearm supplies are regulated. Law enforcement agencies in Massachusetts and New York City have shown that, in jurisdictions that have tight controls, more than 80 percent of guns confiscated by police were originally acquired out of state. Current federal law is trying to inhibit the flow of firearms between states, but the problem remains substantial.

In most northeastern cities with restrictive handgun laws, the use of guns   52
in violent crime is lower than that in other U.S. cities. In Washington, D.C.,

the Federal Bureau of Alcohol, Tobacco and Firearms strictly enforced federal laws for nine months in 1976, and it reported success in reducing the flow of firearms. But the effort was not sustained. Washington currently experiences high rates of gun-related violence despite a restrictive handgun law.

Analysts do not have sufficient information to make predictions about   53
the impact of gun control in the U.S. Some have compared the U.S. with such countries as England, France, Germany and Holland. They have discovered that nations with much lower rates of firearm ownership have lower rates of crimes involving guns. But these Western nations also have much lower rates of violent crimes that do not involve firearms.

Indeed, it is the very high rate of violence in the U.S. that makes the   54
costs of gun use so large. The U.S. has both a "crime problem" and a "gun problem," and each exacerbates the other. No Western nation has ever instituted strict controls under conditions similar to those in the U.S.

Although most citizens support such measures as owner screening, public   55
opinion is sharply divided on laws that would restrict the ownership of handguns to persons with special needs. If the U.S. does not reduce handguns and current trends continue, it faces the prospect that the number of handguns in circulation will grow from 35 million to more than 50 million within 50 years. A national program limiting the availability of handguns would cost many billions of dollars and meet much resistance from citizens. These costs would likely be greatest in the early years of the program. The benefits of supply reduction would emerge slowly because efforts to diminish the availability of handguns would probably have a cumulative impact over time.

At the heart of the debate over handgun restrictions is a disagreement   56
about the character of American life in the 21st century. Roughly half of Americans believe that strict handgun control is not worth the hardship of changing policy in the U.S. They assume that the weapons can remain a part of American life for the indefinite future. But just as many Americans see the removal of the current stockpile of handguns as a necessary down payment on the American future. They regard free availability of handguns as a severe threat to urban life. American policy on handgun control will ultimately depend on which of these attitudes prevails. ■

Questions for Meaning

1. Does Zimring favor any forms of gun control?
2. What does Zimring mean by "instrumentality effect"?
3. What are the three principal approaches to regulating the use of guns?
4. Why does Zimring believe that the number of homicides will not significantly decline as the result of screening gun purchasers to check for prior felonies?

5. Why does Zimring believe that gun control in the United States is unlikely to have the same impact as gun control in other countries such as France and Holland?
6. Vocabulary: subside (8), corroborated (14), correlated (17), prospective (41), complement (46), exacerbates (54).

Questions about Strategy

1. What is Zimring's rationale for providing the information he reports in this article? What is his purpose?
2. "The answer is not obvious," states Zimring at the beginning of paragraph 9. At what points does the author indicate that his data do not lead to certain conclusions? What is the effect of these cautions?
3. How were you affected by the use of the first person in paragraphs 10 and 17? If Zimring had not cited his own findings, would his article have been more convincing or less convincing? Why?

ONE STUDENT'S ASSIGNMENT

Summarize William Tonso's "White Man's Law" in 500 words or less. Be sure to include the most important points made in Tonso's article and to accurately convey its thesis. Be careful not to let your own opinions interfere with your summary of Tonso's views.

A Summary of William Tonso's "White Man's Law"
Sara Jenkins

History shows that governments have repeatedly sought to restrict gun ownership to social elites. In 1541, the English government restricted handgun ownership to people who earned more than one hundred pounds a year (which was a great deal of money at the time). European aristocrats were concerned about guns because these weapons threatened the established social order. The rulers might have horses and fancy armor, but bullets could pierce right through armor.

A similar pattern can be found in American history. Gun control was initially favored by those in power. Cheap guns could be purchased by poor people, and the ruling class was afraid of what could happen if too many poor people had guns.

The first gun control laws were passed in the south soon after the Civil War. Tennessee, Arkansas, South Carolina, Alabama, and Texas all sought

1

2

3

to restrict gun ownership by allowing only for the legal purchase of expensive guns or by putting heavy taxes on the sale of handguns. As a result, poor whites and blacks could not afford to own handguns legally. Some southern states even banned black people from owning any kind of gun.

In the north, gun control was inspired by similar thinking. In 1911, New   4
York passed the Sullivan Law, which required would-be gun owners to get a police permit. Although this law may not have been designed specifically to keep African-Americans from owning guns, it did have the effect of granting the police the power of giving permits only when they wanted. Minorities—especially immigrants from countries that were not popular at the time—were discriminated against. Today, most permits in New York go to the rich and influential.

More recent gun control laws have also been inspired by fear of minori-   5
ties. The Gun Control Act of 1968 was passed only one year after riots broke out in big cities because of conditions in the ghettos. And since then much attention has been given to the "Saturday Night Special"—the sort of cheap gun that poor people are most likely able to afford. "Saturday Night Specials" are blamed for crime, but research shows that they are not used in crimes any more often than expensive guns are used. So once again, government seems to want to keep poor people unarmed—even if they need guns to defend themselves.

Liberals who are in favor of gun control probably don't understand the   6
history of gun control. They may also be blaming guns because they are unwilling to blame the criminals who misuse guns. Unfortunately, the debate over gun control continues to show divisions along class lines. Many advocates of gun control have security and power. Many opponents do not.

SUGGESTIONS FOR WRITING

1. Swasey and Alter both claim that the criminal use of guns has created the equivalent of war within the United States, but they reach different conclusions about how government should respond to this war. If you agree that "there's a war on at home," write a paper explaining how you think this war can be ended.
2. If you have ever used a gun, or lived in a house where a gun was present, write an argument on gun control that begins with an account of your own experience.
3. Regardless of your own opinion of gun control, which essay in this section is the most persuasive? Write an essay in defense of this writer, evaluating the techniques she or he used.
4. Write an essay explaining why advocates of gun control are especially concerned about handguns.

5. Write an argument for or against taxing bullets.
6. Write an argument on behalf of the right to own a rifle or shotgun.
7. Drawing on the argument by Roger Koopman and at least one other source that you discover on your own, write a paper defining the extent to which the Second Amendment guarantees a right to bear arms.
8. Tonso takes the position that gun control is racist. Write a paper arguing that it is racist *not* to control guns.
9. Write a summary of the article by Franklin E. Zimring.
10. Synthesize the arguments for and against gun control.

COLLABORATIVE PROJECT

Both Sugarmann and Zimring argue that guns are more lethal than other weapons. Form a writing team from your class and investigate violence in your city or county. Sources to consider include the police department, the sheriff's office, the district attorney's office, the coroner's office, the health department, and indexes to local newspapers. Divide research and writing responsibilities among teammates but use the entire team to compose the paper in which you report your findings.

AIDS IN THE WORKPLACE:
HOW SHOULD BUSINESS RESPOND?

WILLIAM F. BANTA

A LEGAL PERSPECTIVE

As increasing numbers of Americans of working age become infected with the AIDS virus, more and more businesses will need to decide how to respond to this crisis. Whether influenced by economic, moral, or personal concerns, such businesses will need to operate within the law. The following article is excerpted from the introduction to *AIDS in the Workplace: Legal Questions and Practical Answers* (1993). It raises some of the many concerns employers should consider as they prepare to respond to AIDS. William F. Banta is an attorney recognized for his knowledge in this area.

1   I was in the office of the human resources manager of a hospital client of our law firm, reviewing employment records pertaining to a civil rights charge she described as frivolous, when the hospital administrator abruptly pushed the door open. Another, more demanding issue had emerged that very morning which consumed the remainder of that day and a portion of the evening: a female registered nurse (RN) assigned to the emergency room had just informed the director of nursing that she was HIV positive.

2   The arrest of the RN's husband for selling illegal drugs the previous week had fed the rumor mill: "Did you hear that Charlene's husband was caught red-handed selling dope? He's no good and never has been." "Have you noticed how much weight he's lost recently? He looks god-awful. I'll bet he's gotten AIDS from shooting up all those drugs. Maybe he's infected Charlene." "Did you see the photographs of Charlene's husband in the newspaper last week? Boy, did he look bad. Either he's in withdrawal or he's got AIDS. I sure hope Charlene hasn't been sleeping with him." "Did you notice that scab on Charlene's right hand? She cut herself last week while treating a patient. I'd hate to have her blood get on me." "Charlene has

been looking a little peaked lately. Maybe her jerk of a husband infected her with HIV."

The director of nursing had just spoken privately with Charlene, men- 3
tioning the rumors and asking pointedly whether Charlene was concerned
about her HIV status. Charlene immediately broke into tears, sobbing that her
husband had been diagnosed with AIDS six months earlier, and that her test
for the HIV antibodies, conducted immediately after her husband's diagnosis,
was positive. She reminded the director of nursing that she had three children,
explained that her husband lacked insurance and was incurring substantial
medical bills, and begged not to fired.

The director of nursing sent her home for the remainder of the shift, 4
with pay, and reported the matter to the hospital administrator, who now
posed a series of questions to me: Should Charlene be removed from her job as
an emergency room RN; if so, what action should be taken and how should it
be explained? What obligations, if any, does the hospital have to identify the
patients treated by Charlene during the last year, and to notify them of her
positive HIV status? Does the hospital have a legal duty to disclose her condition to fellow employees, or does the law protect Charlene's privacy and prohibit disclosure to other personnel? What should the hospital do if some of
Charlene's fellow employees refused to perform their duties when she was in
their area or walked off the job? And if Charlene continues to work at the
hospital, does the hospital have a duty to disclose her positive HIV status to
patients with whom she comes in contact?

The questions were endless, easy answers elusive. As the discussion con- 5
tinued, the civil rights case seemed simple compared to the multiple and complex issues raised by a single employee carrying an infectious, fatal virus.

Charlene was an excellent worker with long seniority, had never been 6
disciplined, had always been in excellent health, and had an almost perfect attendance record. The director of nursing captured the humane perspective of
the problem when she spoke sympathetically about Charlene's personal situation: her mother was dead, her father had remarried and lived in another state;
her husband was being treated for AIDS-related illness in another hospital, and
if his health improved he faced a criminal trial and a probable jail term; medical and legal bills were accumulating; her children, aged two, ten, and fourteen, needed care and comfort; and she now feared that her job—her only
source of income—was in jeopardy. The nursing director wanted to visit
Charlene that evening, to express care and concern, and to assure her that she
could continue in her job.

The hospital administrator was worried about talk in the community; he 7
was afraid that his hospital would be labeled "the AIDS hospital," and that bad
publicity would cause a drop in admissions. He also expressed concern about
lawsuits against the hospital filed by patients Charlene had treated in the emergency room. He suggested placing Charlene on paid leave of absence for a
month "to cool things off" and then offering her a clerical job at a lower rate
of pay in which she would have no contact with the blood or body tissue of
patients or fellow employees. With this approach, he argued, disclosure of her

condition to others would be unnecessary, her privacy would be protected, talk in the community would "die down," and both Charlene and the hospital would be better off.

The human resources director, discerning the difficulty of replacing an experienced RN in the emergency room, first argued that Charlene could be reinstructed on the "universal precautions" prescribed by the federal Centers for Disease Control (CDC), and then given double gloves and special gear to wear while continuing to work in the emergency room. Then, remembering that some emergency room personnel had already expressed concern about working with Charlene, the director proposed that Charlene switch jobs with an RN assigned to a patient ward. Away from the emergency room Charlene would rarely come into contact with bleeding patients, and therefore would pose less of a threat. She saw no reason to inform employees about Charlene's condition, counseled secrecy, and concluded that any employees who refused to work with her should be fired.   8

I supplied the legal perspective, explaining that involuntary removal of Charlene from her position would probably violate state and federal laws protecting the handicapped, and that disclosing her HIV condition, without her informed, written consent, to patients and fellow employees could invade her right to privacy and breach the hospital's duty of confidentiality. I also emphasized, however, that if the risk of transmitting the virus from Charlene to patients during the performance of her duties was greater than remote, then leaving her in the emergency room position could constitute negligence. I suggested medical evaluation of the degree of risk Charlene posed, based, in part, on the latest findings of the CDC. Such a report would determine how to respond to the problems of possible disclosure of Charlene's HIV status to patients and fellow employees. I endorsed the idea of a transfer on the condition that it be voluntary, suggested medical evaluation of Charlene and counseling for her and her family at hospital expense, and advised that any employees refusing to work with her simply be sent home without mention of discharge.   9

As we attempted to resolve these issues over the next week, our discussions were hampered by a lack of written policy and no precedents to follow. While the hospital had a general infectious disease policy, it was unclear how it would apply to HIV situations. Realizing that decisions concerning Charlene would create precedents that would influence future, related issues, the administrator met with the medical director and key members of the board of directors several times during the ensuing days. Finally, Charlene voluntarily and gratefully accepted a transfer to a ward position, at the same rate of pay and without loss of any benefits. The medical director met with all personnel in the emergency room, to explain the latest findings issued by the CDC on transmitting the virus and to demonstrate the protective gear they were supposed to wear while working. With the written consent of Charlene, fellow employees in her ward were informed of her HIV status and urged to treat her empathetically. After review of the medical records of patients treated by Charlene during the past year, and a lengthy interview with her about any   10 potential exposures, we decided not to inform any patients of her HIV condition. No lawsuits were ever filed against the hospital by Charlene's former patients. The hospital drafted and implemented a written AIDS policy.

This story of an actual situation presents, in capsule form, many of the 11 legal issues, practical concerns, individual attitudes, and real-life tragedies of AIDS in the workplace. It raises a number of difficult questions about how an employer should proceed in these circumstances. It illustrates the medical, legal, and personnel aspects of the issues. It also spotlights a critical omission on the part of many employers: the failure to develop an AIDS policy that will facilitate the handling of AIDS-related issues that are likely to arise.

A survey of corporate executives found that they ranked AIDS as the 12 third most important problem facing our country today (behind the federal deficit and drug abuse), but that over 50 percent of the companies where they were employed had no AIDS policy. In other human resources areas, managers have relied upon carefully crafted and well-implemented written policies to guide them through personnel problems and crises and to promote consistency. Inconsistent treatment of similarly situated employees is evidence of improper conduct in the eyes of judges and arbitrators; uniform application of written policies, however, reduces the risk of costly legal challenge.

Since its discovery in 1981, AIDS has become of paramount interest to 13 the American public. Realizing that AIDS has all the ingredients of a long-running soap opera—sex, drugs, and death—the media maintain a steady barrage of stories on the fatal syndrome and its impact on people. Medical, legal, and personnel associations and periodicals debate the issues. Legislatures, courts, and businesses are presented with novel situations. The following list of news stories indicates the pervasiveness of AIDS and the kinds of problems it is creating in our society:

- An Oakland HIV-positive man was arrested for assault with a deadly weapon after vowing to infect all the women he could through sex before he dies, and for throwing blood from a self-inflicted wound on another man.

- A judge sentenced a man to sexual abstinence for having sex with his girlfriend after learning that he had the HIV virus.

- A woman's application for life insurance was rejected because of a positive test for HIV. Later, she and her husband arranged for separate tests, which were negative. After being sued by the couple for emotional distress, the insurance company explained that its earlier report of a positive test result was "a clerical error."

- A man with AIDS killed a store clerk with a knife during a robbery. Arrested with her blood and the knife on him, he confessed. At the trial his attorney presented evidence that he was suffering from dementia caused by AIDS and argued that he lacked the necessary legal intent to kill. The jury acquitted him of first degree murder but found him guilty of second degree murder.

- The president of the National Hockey League sent a letter to all teams recommending voluntary and confidential HIV testing for all personnel because a young woman who died of AIDS-related causes had informed her doctor that she had sex with more than fifty professional hockey players.

- A toy manufacturer distributed a new game called "Bacteria Panic" in which the player left holding a card marked "AIDS" is the loser. The game was quickly recalled following complaints that it was insensitive.

- The National Commission on AIDS reported that our prison system provides inadequate medical treatment for inmates with HIV infection and subjects them to unnecessary indignities that offend their basic human rights.

- A new Mississippi law requires all convicted sex offenders to be tested for HIV and mandates that positive results be reported to the victim, the victim's spouse, and the spouse of the person convicted of the sex offense.

- College clinics experienced a sudden surge in student testing for HIV following Magic Johnson's revelation that he has the HIV virus.

- *Ebony* magazine included a letter from "C. J. of Dallas" who claims she contracted HIV from a man and is now attempting to infect others by picking up men in bars and having sex with them.

- Concerned about their own safety, medical associations lobbied for and in some states obtained laws that allow physicians to test patients for HIV without the patient's consent in certain circumstances.

- Upon being diagnosed with AIDS, a teacher was reassigned from the classroom to the school office where he is supposed to write applications for grants. His lawyer, however, secured an injunction returning him to teaching duties which the court rules do not present a significant risk of harm to students.

As the number of people infected increases with the passage of time, fewer and fewer employers will remain untouched by the AIDS crisis. A job applicant who unknowingly contracted the virus from a sexual partner is hired. An employee who successfully completed a drug rehabilitation program more than a year ago begins displaying the symptoms of symptomatic HIV disease (at times referred to as AIDS-related complex). Another employee becomes extremely ill with a form of cancer that is connected to AIDS; eventually it is discovered that a blood transfusion he received after surgery seven years earlier was the means of transmission.   14

Questions that will be presented to these employers are many and varied. An employee, like Charlene, may test positive for HIV antibodies but be quite healthy—and as capable of performing job duties as ever—for many, many years. Some people exposed to the virus have developed AIDS within two years, while others continue to be AIDS-free eight years after exposure.   15

Administration of AZT, DDI and DDC has been found to slow down the course of AIDS and to impede many of the illnesses that accompany it. Hence, an employee like Charlene who recently became infected may be able to perform all the duties of her or his job for many years, without impairment of any type. Thereafter, the employee may develop symptomatic HIV disease which could or could not affect her or his ability to perform work. Moreover, even an employee with full-blown AIDS may have long periods of relative health during which she or he could carry out all or some of their job duties. Each person with AIDS (PWA) has a different illness history. In an early stage of the disease, which could consume several years, a person with AIDS (PWA) might be physically capable of performing all job duties as usual, while in the late stages of illness the PWA could be entirely incapacitated for a long period of time. Between the early and late stages, there can be months and even years of widely fluctuating degrees of ability to perform work. One employee with AIDS can perform all essential duties but not some of the incidental ones. Another cannot do one physically demanding duty classified as essential but requests a reasonable accommodation so he can continue in his job. Still another claims that he can continue to perform all his duties but that he requires a special schedule because he becomes extremely tired and cannot work more than five hours per day. Complicating the issue even further is the significant percentage of AIDS patients who suffer deterioration of mental facilities at some point. Occasionally, this deterioration begins early and progresses quickly. But many PWAs remain as mentally alert as ever through the final stage of their illness. Hence, an employee with AIDS could be physically but not mentally qualified or vice versa to perform the duties of the job in question. There is no simple answer to questions involving what to do with a job applicant or an employee with an AIDS condition. Neither is there an established formula to apply for every case. While written policies can be extremely helpful, as I suggested above, the facts and circumstances of the physical and mental condition of every applicant and employee and the specific qualifications of the job in question must be thoroughly analyzed before reaching conclusions.

   In preparing to draft or revise an AIDS policy, employers should pose 16 and analyze numerous questions. Should it conduct its own tests of employees, like Charlene, who are rumored to be HIV positive? Should the employer offer or demand a thorough physical examination by the employer's doctor at the employer's expense? Suppose the employee refuses to be tested and declines the medical examination? May an employer, such as a restaurant, hotel, or hospital, take into account the anticipated loss of business if it permits an employee with AIDS to continue on its payroll? If the employee does not lose pay, benefits, or seniority, could he or she be involuntarily transferred to another non-public job or placed on leave of absence? Suppose fellow employees refuse to work with a person who is HIV infectious: could they be threatened with termination or, in the event of repeated refusals, discharged? Suppose a job applicant or employee confides to a manager that he or she is HIV positive, but emphasizes that the communication is confidential and none of his family, friends, or fellow employees is to know. Does the employer have a legal obligation to notify a spouse? Children? Employees who work with him or her? Patients or customers? If any disclosures are made, is the employer vulnerable to claims of invasion of privacy and breach of confidentiality?

Managers desiring to approach AIDS-related questions in the workplace   17
with sound judgment, sensitivity, and an awareness of legal precedent are frequently confused by a myriad of state and federal laws, lack of past precedent, and conflicting advice from doctors, lawyers, and fellow managers.

Aside from questions of hiring, transferring, promoting, placing on leave   18
of absence, and terminating persons with AIDS conditions, managers are concerned about the cost of caring for the several million people who will suffer from AIDS in the years to come. Who will pick up the tab for treating them? The lifetime cost of caring for PWAs is estimated to be approximately $80,000 per patient. As the number of AIDS patients skyrockets, so will the cost for their care. Approximately $100 billion dollars was expended in treating AIDS patients from 1986 through 1991. Employers attempting to contain rising insurance premiums may be tempted to exclude AIDS-related illnesses from coverage in return for lower premiums. Hospitals may refuse admission of PWAs who do not have insurance. As these types of situations develop, governmental regulations and new statutes will probably be used to achieve social objectives, including protection of PWAs from being discriminatorily deprived of insurance benefits and medical treatment. ■

Questions for Meaning

1. Why did Charlene's superiors consider transferring her to a clerical job at lower pay?
2. Under what circumstances would a hospital to able to transfer an HIV-positive nurse against her will?
3. What personal information about Charlene influenced the director of nursing? Was this information relevant to deciding how the hospital should respond to this case?
4. Why is it important for employers to treat workers in similar situations equally?
5. What do you think Banta means in paragraph 15 when he uses the phrase "reasonable accommodation"?
6. Vocabulary: elusive (5), jeopardy (6), empathetically (10), paramount (13), injunction (13), impairment (15), myriad (17).

Questions about Strategy

1. Banta devotes all of his second paragraph to gossip. What is the purpose of this paragraph?
2. Most American workers do not come into contact with other people's blood. How useful then is Charlene's story as an example of AIDS in the workplace?

3. Paragraphs 4 and 16 consist largely of questions. What can a writer gain by raising so many questions? Once they have been asked, would you expect them to be answered?
4. Consider the list of news stories included in paragraph 13. Is it appropriate for this context or should Banta have limited himself to providing examples of AIDS in the workplace?

BARBARA PRESLEY NOBLE

ABSTRACT TOLERANCE

Is there a difference between how people feel about the rights of HIV-positive workers in the abstract and how they feel when told that one of their own coworkers is HIV-positive? The following article provides recent information in response to this question. Barbara Presley Noble writes about business issues for the New York Times, which first published "Abstract Tolerance" in November 1993.

When the National Leadership Coalition on AIDS asked working Americans how their employers would treat a person who is H.I.V.-positive, 78 percent said he or she would be treated like any other person with a serious disability or illness. Even more—80 percent—said someone who is H.I.V.-positive should be treated like any other employee.   1

But when the coalition asked those polled at their co-workers would feel comfortable working near someone who is H.I.V.-positive, two-thirds predicted they would not, and a quarter said they should not feel comfortable. A third said the person would be dismissed or put on disability at the first sign of illness, and a quarter said he or she should be dismissed or put on disability.   2

How to explain the apparent conflict between the first response and the latter two? People knew what they were supposed to believe, but the coalition wanted to know what they really believed. Asking about co-workers allowed respondents to put socially unacceptable thoughts in someone else's head.   3

"They could project it onto someone else," said Patrick May, communications director for the coalition, a Washington-based group that advises business and labor on AIDS-related issues. "It's probably closer to how people themselves feel, not just because of homophobia but because of death and mortality and being in the close presence of a dying person."   4

Therein lies the raison d'être of the coalition . . . . Well into the second decade of AIDS, free-floating anxiety and misinformation are epidemic among millions of Americans not at high risk for H.I.V. infection. And though the coalition has been thumping this tub since 1987, when it was founded, the rhythm keeps changing as awareness grows and the disease spreads to unfamiliar terrain. "Issues that urbanites dealt with seven or eight years ago are just reaching Wisconsin or small-town Florida or Topeka," Mr. May said. Efforts   5 to teach Americans about AIDS through the workplace got a boost in late September when President Clinton announced an education initiative for Federal workers. . . .

Corporate America received a mixed report card from one gay rights or-   6
ganization on the basis of its quality-of-work-life survey, released at a gay and lesbian employment conference last month. The National Gay and Lesbian Task Force Policy Institute got only 98 completed surveys from the Fortune 1,000 companies included in the study and 145 outright refusals. Of the 98, three-quarters indicated they have nondiscrimination policies that include sexual orientation.

Here are other findings from the participating companies.

- Five companies offer domestic-partner benefits to same-sex partners of employees.
- Half include sexual orientation issues in diversity training programs.
- Three-quarters recognize gay and lesbian employee groups.
- More than two-thirds offer some type of support for people with H.I.V. or AIDS, including AIDS education programs.

The task force expects to repeat the survey annually. [See Figures 1–3.]

Although more people die from other causes...
Leading causes of death in 1992, as a percentage of total deaths

Cause	Percentage
Heart disease	33.1%
Cancer	23.9
Strokes	6.6
Emphysema and other lung diseases	4.2
Accidents	4.0
Pneumonia and influenza	3.5
Diabetes	2.3
Human immunodeficiency virus infection	**1.5**
Suicide	1.4

FIGURE 1
Employee attitudes about AIDS

...AIDS generates the most concern.
Health concerns cited by working Americans
in a recent survey by the National Leadership
Coalition on AIDS.

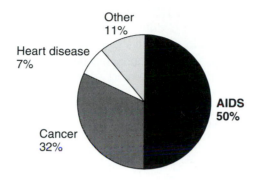

Other
11%

Heart disease
7%

AIDS
50%

Cancer
32%

FIGURE 2

(a)   Working Americans were asked how H.I.V.-positive
people **would** and **should** be treated at work.

Treated like any employee   Dismissed or put on disability
with a serious illness.   at the first sign of illness.

 78%   32%
89   24

(b)   Working Americans were asked if co-workers **would**
and **should** feel uncomfortable working with someone
who is H.I.V.-positive.

 67%
26

(c)   Employees who **did** receive AIDS education at work
and those who feel their employers **should** offer AIDS
education.

 28%
75

*Sources: National Center for Health Statistics, National Leadership
Coalition on AIDS*

FIGURE 3

Questions for Meaning

1. What accounts for the different responses recorded in paragraphs 1 and 2?
2. What is the purpose of the National Leadership Coalition on AIDS?
3. How has awareness of AIDS changed since 1987?
4. According to paragraph 6, only 98 out of 1,000 companies responded to the survey described in this article, and 145 companies refused outright. Why do you think so many companies decided not to respond?
5. Vocabulary: respondents (3), project (4), raison d'être (5), terrain (5).

Questions about Strategy

1. How useful are the illustrations accompanying this article?
2. How credible a source is Patrick May? Should Noble have drawn on any other sources?
3. Noble ends her article with by reporting, "The task force expects to repeat the survey annually." Why do you think the task force plans to do this, and why do you think Noble gives this information prominence?

SHELIA BRANTS

COPING WITH AIDS

Shelia Brants is the cofounder and president of a company in Georgia that wholesales and distributes microcomputers and peripherals. In the following essay, first published in 1991, she tells how her company was affected when one her most valuable employees contracted AIDS. As you read it, consider whether you agree with the decisions Brants made when trying to respond wisely to an unexpected crisis.

On a spring day in 1987, I found out my credit manager had AIDS. He sat in   1
my office sobbing and said he had just been told that his test for the virus had come back positive—contrary to a report he had received the day before. Someone had telephoned to say that the laboratory had made a mistake. It must have been quite a conversation: "Oops, remember that fatal disease we called you about yesterday? Looks as if you've got it after all. Sorry for the mix-up." I tried to console him. I also suggested he take the rest of the week off. He needed time to absorb the news and so, for that matter, did I.

    I had plenty to think about, including more than 40 other employees, a   2
partner, and dozens of customers and suppliers, not to mention myself and my family. Steven Fowler was not just any employee. He was one of the people I depended on most at a time when my company was almost doubling in size.

Beyond that, he was a close friend. He'd been to my house and played with my children. We'd gone to the beach together. He was in Key West when I took my kids there on vacation, and he came over to visit us. What did I know about AIDS? What did any of us know back then? Maybe we'd all been exposed and were going to die. That really was my first reaction: fear.

Not that I was totally shocked. Steven and I had often talked about his   3
risk of getting AIDS. I had known he was gay ever since his job interview, about five years earlier. He had ridden in on a motorcycle, wearing lizard-skin cowboy boots. In the course of the interview, he told me he was gay. I didn't care. At the time, I was working for another company and needed help booking and tracking orders. Steven was an outgoing guy with a lot of personality. He could take control of a conversation without offending anyone. I hired him on the spot. When I left, a couple of years later, to start my own business, he was the second or third person I brought on board.

He started out in sales, but he could do almost anything. I found that if   4
I gave him a job, I didn't have to think about it again. When you're growing fast, people like that are invaluable because you never have enough help or enough time. So I just kept giving Steven more and more to do. He started handling credit in 1986. By early 1987 we were getting ready to move from 9,000 to 30,000 square feet of office space. Steven did all the floor plans and the office layouts for the new building. He coordinated the efforts of two designers. He worked with all the contractors. Meanwhile he was running the credit department so smoothly we hardly knew it was there.

I relied on him in so many ways. I often used him to vent my frustra-   5
tions, and he never took it personally or got intimidated. He knew I needed an outlet. And he was always doing something to make us laugh. Once he entered, and won, a newspaper contest for having the most kissable bald head in the United States. Around the office he was everybody's friend. Whenever a new employee was hired, Steven would serve as the welcoming committee, taking the person out to lunch, offering tips on what to do and what not to do. He made a few people uncomfortable, but in general he was very well liked.

None of that counted for much, however, in the face of a disease like   6
AIDS. When the word got out, people were panic-stricken. My partner wanted to fire Steven. "This will ruin our business," my partner said when I told him the news. After I settled him down, I did a little research. I talked to Steven's doctor, my own physician, and the Centers for Disease Control (CDC) in Atlanta, and they all assured me we weren't at risk. Nevertheless, my partner and I kept going back and forth for a week, discussing what we should do.

It was worse with the employees. People wouldn't drink out of the water   7
fountain. They inspected the bathroom before using it. I was constantly trying to calm them down. I talked to each of them, one-on-one. I called their husbands or wives. I offered to pay for them to see their own physicians. I gave them pamphlets from the CDC. Sometimes I'd telephone the CDC with the employee in the room, and we'd get the answers right there. It all helped, but

the fear didn't go away. Every time I managed to calm one person's fears, somebody else would show up with a new need.

I remember in particular one girl who worked in the same office as   8
Steven. She came in to see me after she heard you could get AIDS by having infected blood splashed into an open wound. "I didn't get a wink of sleep last night," she said. "I kept thinking, What would happen if I were sitting there at my desk with a scratch on my hand, and Steven got cut and began bleeding profusely? I could get AIDS, couldn't I?"

I was speechless. I really didn't know how to respond. I thought to my-   9
self. Yes, honey, and what would happen if Steven were sitting there with a hard-on and you accidentally fell into his lap? Finally, I said, "Tell me some-thing. In all the years you've worked here, how many times were people bleed-ing profusely while you sat nearby with an open crack in your skin? I mean, forget about AIDS. How often have you been exposed to the blood of other employees?" I guess that more or less satisfied her, because she didn't raise the matter again.

I suppose I should have been more tolerant, but I couldn't help feeling   10
overwhelmed. By then the news had gotten down to the customers, and I was hearing from them as well. One of them would call up and start screaming, "Can it be communicated over the telephone? I'm not getting it through the phone, am I?" What exactly do you say to a hysterical customer who's afraid of getting AIDS over the phone? I was angry at people for overreacting, yet I couldn't get *too* angry, because I knew how they felt. It was such a new disease that you couldn't just tell them, "That's the dumbest thing I've ever heard." You had to say, "Now, now, don't worry." You had to work it through. You had to try to talk them into doing reasonable things—consulting a physician, say, or calling the CDC.

I suppose someone might ask, Why didn't I just send Steven home? Why   11
didn't I pay him to get out of my hair? He would have been willing. His atti-tude was, I'll do whatever you want. The truth is, we needed him. He was really that important to the company. I didn't think we could afford *not* to have him there if he was well enough to work.

So Steven stayed. And I kept talking. I must have spent two months doing   12
nothing but dealing with people's fears. After a while, things began to settle down. Then, toward the end of August, Steven started feeling very tired and having trouble with his breathing. We decided to set up a modem in his apart-ment, so he could work at home and rest whenever he wanted. He continued to do his job, but he was clearly quite sick. Finally, the doctors made their diagnosis: he had tuberculosis.

Once again, I had a totally panic-stricken crew. To make matters worse,   13
it turned out that Steven had a highly contagious form of TB. People were wor-ried not only that they might get it, but that they might infect their children. One girl dragged me to her doctor, who was very reassuring. He explained that people with normal immune systems weren't likely to catch Steven's TB no matter how contagious it was. Just to be safe, he gave us both tests, which later

came back negative. That put my mind at ease, which was important. If I could ease my own mind, I could handle everybody else's anxieties. Back at the company, I started another round of one-on-one talks with people. I told each of them what the doctor had said and suggested they all get TB tests at my expense. A lot of them did.

We got over the TB scare, and a new mood settled in. It was as if people thought, Well, if I didn't get TB, I'm sure as hell not going to get AIDS. So let's leave this hysteria behind and focus on the fact that we're losing a friend.   14

And Steven was pretty dramatically ill by that time, although I might have been the last to see it. I did a lot of denying right up to the end. He'd always been a bit of a hypochondriac. I told myself nothing was going to happen anytime soon; he was going through a rough period; he could live five years, seven years, maybe longer. I really couldn't face the idea that he was about to die, and I became angry whenever he brought it up. One evening he called me at home. "I can't make it," he said. "I just know I can't make it." We got into a big fight. I said: "Steven, stop talking like that. You're being a baby. You've got to fight this thing. You'll get over it."   15

It was the last conversation I ever had with him. The next day someone called and told me Steven had been admitted to the hospital. When I got there, he was in a coma. The doctor said he would probably die before morning. I stayed the whole night, and he was still alive when I left for work.   16

He hung on for a week. There was a group of about 16 people from the company who stayed with him day and night. They were the ones who had worked with him the longest. They went to the hospital in shifts, three or four at a time, and I think they would have quit if I'd told them they couldn't go. The nurses said there had never been an AIDS patient in the history of St. Joseph's Hospital with so many people keeping watch. It just goes to show that they really, really loved him, although they were really afraid of him, too. But they'd had a pretty good education about AIDS, and they felt all right about going into his room, holding his hand, and talking to him.   17

The last days were devastating to watch. He shrank down to nothing. He was six feet tall, and I'd guess he weighed 100 pounds at the end. I'd visit him after work, but I don't think he knew I was there. His mother was pretty distraught because he looked so bad. She asked me to go in and talk to him—to tell him, "Please just let go and die." I talked to him for a long time—not that he heard me. He hung on for another day or two. The following Sunday I got a call in the middle of the night, saying he'd died.   18

His mother decided to bury him in North Carolina, where he came from. She asked me if I would give the eulogy. She said Steven used to talk about me a lot, and she thought he would have liked me to say a few words. Of course, I said I would.   19

A huge number of people from the company went up to North Carolina for the ceremony. We got a lot of emotion out that day. A friend of Steven's sang "Ave Maria," in a voice so incredibly beautiful that everybody was reduced to tears. By the time I stood to give my eulogy, I was pretty choked up, but I got through it. I talked about Steven and how unfair it seemed that he   20 had died so young. He had led such a worthwhile life. He had so many friends. Sure, his lifestyle was different, but so what? He was a good person. Anyway, I said it without crying, or at least without bawling. The place was full. Afterward a lot of people came up and told me the things we all knew about Steven—what an unusual and interesting person he was. It was really great. It was really beautiful.

But the mourning didn't end with the ceremony. There were 15 or 20 people at the company who had been around since the early days, and who had worked with Steven during good times and bad. His death had a very unsettling effect on them and, because they were key employees, on the company as well. There was a lot of grief. I think the whole company grieved, although each person handled it in a different way. Some people seemed to get sick more often. Some people didn't come back to work for a while. Some people were angry all the time. A fair number of people left.   21

Looking back, I don't think they left so much because of the company, but rather because they needed a change. We all needed a change. It was as if we had had a death in the family. We'd been together for five years, and we'd grown very close, and then one of us had died young, and it didn't make any sense. An experience like that changes you. It forces you to look at your life differently. You begin to question your values and your priorities, your sense of right and wrong. You realize you don't have everything under nearly as much control as you thought, so you're forced to sit up and take a fresh look at the whole picture. It was a life-altering time for each of us and for the company as a whole.   22

After Steven died the business began to encounter problems. Within six months our accounts receivable went downhill, and I lost control of my credit department, which created all kinds of other headaches. Eventually we wound up in Chapter 11, from which we're just now emerging. I'm convinced we wouldn't have had a lot of the problems if Steven had been around. Even my partner came to see that. He told me later, "God, I really wish I'd been more appreciative of Steven and all he did for the company when he was alive."   23

We dedicated our new building—the one for which he'd done all the planning and coordinating—to Steven. We put up a bronze plaque in his memory. It's a reminder, not just of him but of the experience we all went through. For all the trauma, I think we came away from it with a pretty good feeling about ourselves. It would have been easy to give in to fear, but we didn't. Today each of us can look in the mirror and say, "I did what was right, and I was a real human being, even though there were risks."   24

I still think about that, and I still think about Steven. He was an unusual person and a great guy. Sometimes I really, really miss him a lot. ■   25

Questions for Meaning

1. What steps did Brants take when she first learned that Steven had AIDS? Why were these steps necessary?
2. What misconceptions about AIDS emerged once Steven's condition became known to others at work?
3. In paragraph 20, Brants states Steven's "lifestyle was different." How do you read this line? What do you think the author means by "lifestyle" in this context?
4. What did Brants learn from her experience with Steven?

Questions about Strategy

1. Consider the quotation in paragraph 1, a reconstruction of what Brants imagines Steven heard over the telephone. How would you describe the tone of this line? Is it appropriate for the context?
2. At the beginning of paragraph 10, Brants reflects, "I suppose I should have been more tolerant, ..." Where else does she indicate that her responses to this crisis were less than ideal? What does she achieve through these admissions?
3. How would this essay change if Brants had ended it after paragraph 20? Why do you think she chose to continue the story beyond this point?
4. At the conclusion of this essay, Brants observes, "Today each of us can look in the mirror and say. 'I did what was right, and I was a real human being, even though there were risks.'" Is this an appropriate conclusion? Are you convinced by the information that precedes this claim?

CAROL POGASH

A NURSE'S STORY

After a widely publicized case in which a Florida dentist infected his patients with HIV, many people expressed concern about whether HIV-positive medical person-nel should be legally required to disclose their HIV status. A closely related con-cern—especially for those who work in hospitals—is how employers should respond to HIV-positive personnel who became infected in the line of duty. The following article tells the story of a nurse who became infected while recapping a needle used to supply medication for an AIDS patient. Carol Pogash is the author of As Real As It Gets: The Life of a Hospital at the Center of the AIDS Epidemic (1992), from which "A Nurse's Story" is an excerpt.

Over two-thirds of companies with more than 2,500 employees and nearly   1
1 in 10 small companies have had an employee with HIV infection or AIDS.
But perhaps no workers are more at risk than the health-care employees who
come into daily contact with HIV-positive patients. The federal Centers for
Disease Control (CDC) has found 31 health-care workers who contracted the
disease on the job, and experts estimate that the real numbers are much higher.
Some health-care workers don't know—or don't want to know—they're infected, or they don't want to report it for fear of being stigmatized or dismissed. Now Congress has required that by the end of this month all states
adopt guidelines for health-care workers to prevent AIDS transmission. In a
report issued late last summer, the National Commission on AIDS, which advises the President and Congress, recommended against mandatory testing of
these workers and said that those who are infected should not be required to
tell their patients. The Commission's report made the point that the chance of
a doctor or other health-care worker transmitting HIV to a patient is "almost
nonexistent" if proper sanitary procedures are followed. By contrast, those exposed to patients' blood in surgery, emergency treatment or routine procedures such as changing an IV are much likelier to become infected.

One of those who did, a young San Francisco nurse, contracted the virus   2
five years ago. Her case, known as *Jane Doe* v. *The City and County of San Francisco,* laid the foundation for the fight to secure medical benefits without sacrificing privacy. Her story raises troubling questions about how to deal with
AIDS in the workplace. And as the disease continues to spread—between one
and two million Americans are now HIV-positive, and women are the fastest-
growing patient group—there are questions that no one can ignore.

On her first day at San Francisco General Hospital in 1987, the CDC issued a   3
worrisome report. Three more health-care workers had been infected with
HIV on the job, making a total of nine. "How long before my mother calls?"
the young nurse joked to co-workers. At 24, she felt invulnerable. Contracting

AIDS seemed as likely as being struck by an oncoming car; she didn't think about either one very often.

She had wanted to be a nurse since high school. Having excelled at math and science, she considered medical school but rejected what she saw as grinding competition. Nursing seemed a more direct way to help people.   4

Her first job was at an affluent private hospital in New York, where too much time was spent inching tissue boxes closer to bedsides. One of her supervisors sensed that she had a different calling. "Nursing is more than a job for you," the older woman observed. And it was true. She still cared long after everyone else had given up trying. When most city residents had become immune to downtown beggars, she would make eye contact and plunk money in a needy hand. Every week she pitched in at a soup kitchen. She moved to San Francisco to work at the General, a sprawling, 350-bed county hospital jammed with the poor and the disenfranchised. Here, at this hospital of last resort, many patients were desperately sick, and an estimated one-fourth of them were HIV-positive.   5

It pleased her to work with AIDS patients, whom others considered pariahs, and she enlisted in an ongoing study of HIV and health-care workers. ("My part for medical science," she joked.) Dr. Julie Louise Gerberding of the University of California at San Francisco, the study's director, drew three tubes of her blood and treated them. The results were negative.   6

Then, early on a summer morning at the end of a 12-hour shift, the young nurse made the kind of mistake that less experienced nurses often make. An AIDS patient's medicine had run out, and his blood was backing up into his IV tube. The nurse removed the tubing. She wasn't supposed to recap the needle; hospital policy declared such moves too risky. For nurses, "needlesticks" are a standard occupational hazard, made deadly by AIDS. Jostle a finger an eighth of an inch and you could inject yourself.   7

She was supposed to weave through the hospital room carrying the awkward pole, bag and unsheathed needle, like a player on an obstacle course, heading for the bathroom. There, she was to toss the needle into a special, narrow-necked "sharps" disposal box. It would have made more sense for the box to be stationed on the wall by the patient's bed, but the hospital contended that the more hidden the box was, the less likely it was that drug addicts or curious children would wander in and try to fish out discarded needles.   8

The procedure just seemed too cumbersome. Instead, the nurse placed her left, ungloved hand on the back of the IV bag to steady it and tried to insert the needle safely in the rubber port with her right hand. Her hand slipped. The needle pierced the bag, puncturing her left index finger. A deep stick. Following procedure, she squeezed her finger, bleeding it out. She scrubbed her hand and notified the charge nurse. "Oh," said the sympathetic supervisor, "it's always hardest the first time."   9

The next day the nurse returned to work. Five days later she came down with a flulike illness and a fever that came and went for four weeks. She suspected she had mononucleosis. Hearing about the young nurse's condition, a worried Gerberding asked her to be tested again for AIDS.   10

Seven weeks after the needlestick, her doorbell rang on a Saturday morn-   11
ing. The nurse threw open the window and looked down at the sidewalk.
Standing there was the head nurse. Part of her knew immediately why the
woman had come. Then her boss came into the apartment and spoke the
words.

She was HIV-positive.   12

At first, she failed to respond. Her innocence was shattered. "Thanks,"   13
she kiddingly remarked. "You just took 50 years off my life." She was only 25.

The stigma that the diagnosis carries was as severe then as it is today.   14
Despite the fact that the First Lady and Princess Diana have been photographed hugging AIDS babies, despite the startling public pronouncements
of a smiling Magic Johnson and a saddened Arthur Ashe and the wearing of red
ribbons by politicians and stars, the stigma remains. Partly it derives from ignorance and partly from just plain fear of the gruesome disease. If people found
out about the nurse, she might lose her insurance, her job, her friends and her
apartment. Others had.

That day and the next, the young nurse walked all over San Francisco.   15
Everything seemed distorted, out of focus. She felt awful, yet she still had all
her limbs. She could still walk, after all. "I can dance!" she thought. "I can
dance." And for four days she played hooky by day and danced with her
boyfriend every night.

Then she went back to work. She decided she would tell the smallest pos-   16
sible number of people about her condition. To officialdom, she would call
herself Jane Doe. That's what the hospital began to call her after a meeting was
held and the staff was told what had happened.

Three weeks later Jane Doe flew back East to tell her parents. It was, she   17
said, the hardest thing she had ever had to do. They were devastated, but they
didn't blame her for choosing to work at the General, for knowingly working
with AIDS patients. Her mother, the designated worrier of the family, cried
but was rational. "This," she said, "is what happens in life."

All along, Jane Doe assumed that her employer, the liberal city of San   18
Francisco, would take care of her. She never doubted that the medical expenses
she incurred would be paid for by the municipality. And she was sure that,
with the exception of a few individuals, no one needed to know her true identity. She didn't think about getting a lawyer to guide her through the red tape
until friends urged her to do so. And when her pro bono attorney, Patricia
Hastings, contacted the city retirement system, which handles workers' compensation claims, she didn't expect any problems, either.

Hastings was informed, however, that she couldn't speak for someone   19
the city wasn't sure she really represented; Jane Doe would have to declare
who she was and be investigated like any other applicant—despite the fact
that a leak might provoke discrimination, even panic. Despite the fact that
Gerberding would vouch for her and testify that her clear before-and-after
blood-tests results made an ironclad case for occupational infection. As the
nurse's medical visits and costs grew, she sought therapy for the anxiety related to her diagnosis.

For nearly two years she and her lawyer battled the bureaucrats, and for   20
nearly two years she paid her enormous medical bills-over $4,000—with no
reimbursement. She continued to work full-time and was not physically ill,
but, depressed by the delays and a breakup with her boyfriend, she started
spending spare hours just lying in bed in the dark.

Frustrated and frightened for Jane Doe, a good friend wrote to Randy   21
Shilts, the *San Francisco Chronicle* reporter who had written the best-selling
AIDS book *And the Band Played On.* The newspaper looked into the case and
ran a series of hard-hitting pieces that told of Jane Doe's dilemma.

Only then did the logjam begin to break. Sympathetic physicians at the   22
General offered her a $10,000 loan to help defray costs, but she declined the
kind offer. Her union held a press conference at which several members threatened to stop performing risky procedures unless her case was settled. Finally,
when she was scheduled for a deposition, she went to the city attorney's office—but not alone: With her was a crowd of nurses and demonstrators from
ACT UP, the activist AIDS organization, all wearing Jane Doe name tags.
The crowd, with TV cameras recording, lambasted the city attorney. Shielded
by her anonymity, the real Jane Doe got to confront the lawyer, attacking him
for his arrogance and refusal to accept the information she provided. After 20
months of bureaucratic nightmares, she found it exhilarating.

Within days the city succumbed, promising that no more than four offi-   23
cials would ever know her identity. "It is kind of a sobering joy," she said,
"like when a war ends and you count the casualties."

Of course, for Jane Doe, the war was hardly over. Nothing her friends or   24
coworkers or lawyer did could alter the unalterable. She was still HIV-positive.

And the war wasn't over for those who would come after Jane Doe. Al-   25
though San Francisco now offers the same confidentiality provisions to any
city health-care worker who contracts the virus on the job, such provisions are
rare in other cities. And in most states, insurance companies are still free to
cancel the policies of HIV-positive clients or any clients with severe (read: expensive) illnesses.

Only one dentist, David Acer of Stuart, Fla., is known to have infected   26
patients. He infected Kimberly Bergalis and four others. After the Acer incident, studies of more than 15,000 patients who were cared for by 32 HIV-
positive health-care workers revealed not a single case of transmission.

The National Commission on AIDS report, in recommending against   27
mandatory testing of health-care workers, indicated that 360 surgeons, 5,000
other doctors, 1,200 dentists and 35,000 other health-care workers are currently infected with the virus in the United States. The commission said that
forcing those workers out of the medical system would be harmful to society,
pointing out that many of them treat other AIDS patients. The commission
concluded: "The 'cure' for the risk of H.I.V. transmission in the health care
setting must not be more damaging than the risk to public health."

There are a few safeguards to protect health-care workers from their pa-   28
tients. At San Francisco General, Dr. Lorraine Day, the former chief of ortho-
pedic surgery—a discipline awash in blood—reacted to the news of Jane Doe's

infection by testing her patients before performing nonemergency surgery. The majority of the hospital's nurses and doctors attacked her for her action, believing that her next step would be to deny patients care (a charge she has always refuted). Day has since left the General. Today nurses and doctors there are exhorted to be a lot more careful about needles and blood splashes than they were in 1987. Only recently did the hospital move the red sharps boxes closer to the bedsides, and it is now experimenting with newer, safer needles.

Jane Doe continues to work full-time. She looks and feels healthy, gob- 29 bles vitamins, exercises—she's learning ethnic dancing. She also feels great sorrow and rage. In Utica, N.Y., a nurse recently won a $5.4 million suit after being stuck with a contaminated needle in a struggle with an HIV-positive patient, a prisoner. Another nurse at the General and two others at a nearby hospital have contracted HIV on the job.

But they never had to fight for anonymity or payments from workers' 30 compensation. They say that Jane Doe battled the establishment for them. ∎

Questions for Meaning

1. How did "Jane Doe" become infected with HIV? Were hospital procedures to blame?
2. Why did this nurse choose to keep her real name from city officials?
3. Why was the city of San Francisco reluctant to provide benefits for "Jane Doe"? How was this reluctance overcome?
4. Why did the National Commission on AIDS recommend against mandatory testing of nurses, doctors, and other health-care workers?
5. Vocabulary: pariahs (6), stigma (14), pro bono (18), deposition (22), lambasted (22).

Questions about Strategy

1. How does Pogash establish a rationale for reporting this story?
2. How does Pogash establish an identity for "Jane Doe" without revealing her real name?
3. Although she is clearly sympathetic to HIV-positive health-care workers who wish to maintain their privacy and to go on working, Pogash also reports the story of a Florida dentist who infected his patients. What is the function of paragraph 26?
4. What does Pogash achieve by reporting information about Dr. Lorraine Day?

MIREYA NAVARRO

AS H.I.V. PATIENTS STAY AT WORK, PROBLEMS, AND SOLUTIONS, EMERGE

Mireya Navarro is a reporter for the *New York Times,* which published the follow-ing article on November 23, 1992. Note that the title of the article provides a clear indication of what the article reports—a convention readers welcome when they scan a newspaper to decide which articles to read. As you read this piece, try to imagine how you would feel if your were HIV-positive and still going to work. Consider, in particular, why people who have been exposed to the AIDS virus may be anxious to hold on to their jobs.

Jason Worth, a Housing Court judge in Brooklyn who is infected with H.I.V., comes to work only one day a week because of fatigue and because he wants to avoid the risk of exposure to diseases like tuberculosis from the dozens of peo-ple who come through his courtroom every day.   1

But the 42-year-old judge recently asked state court officials to allow him to use a telephone equipped with a television screen so he could handle settlement conferences from home. Working, he says, is as crucial to staying alive as any precaution he can take to protect his health.   2

"I believe that in order to survive one has to have goals," he said. "My goal is to be a judge with my medical condition."   3

As more people live longer and stay healthier because of advances in the treatment of the AIDS virus, many, like Judge Worth, are trying to hold on to jobs. Some work despite symptoms of illness because they have no choice—they need the income or the health-insurance benefits. But many others work as long as they can for the vitality, camaraderie and sense of self-worth a job can provide.   4

What these workers are finding in the work place varies greatly. Some companies have issued policies stating that AIDS will be treated like any other life-threatening disease and have accommodated employees with H.I.V. with flexible work schedules and other measures. At other companies, the response is to dismiss the worker, although most states have laws prohibiting dismissing employees simply because they have AIDS.   5

Illness Often Hidden

As a result, many people with H.I.V. believe they must hide their infection if they want to work. Many worry about being discriminated against or written off and losing, if not their jobs, at least promotions. Many do not disclose their condition until they really must, such as when they have to explain frequent absences.   6

Some show up for work even while sick. Others do not file claims for   7
H.I.V.-related treatments to hide their condition from employees or out of
fear of being dropped from health plans.

"I don't want to feel ostracized on the job," said a 49-year-old clothing   8
salesman in Manhattan who has kept his status secret for four years.

He tells fellow employees he is taking vitamins when he takes AIDS   9
medication, and he uses his lunch hour for doctor's appointments.

"I don't want to be deprived of duties or responsibilities until the time I   10
have to relinquish them," he said.

AIDS is a personal issue shrouded in secrecy even for some advocates for   11
people with H.I.V. Thomas B. Stoddard, 44, former executive director of the
Lambda Legal Defense and Education Fund, a public-interest law firm that
handles H.I.V.-related litigation, said he revealed his H.I.V. status to only
three close assistants. He kept his staff in the dark even when he decided to
leave last January because he found his job too draining.

"I didn't want to be a victim," he said. "I would have been treated dif-   12
ferently."

For their part, employers who encounter a worker with H.I.V. for the   13
first time usually grapple with questions like: "Will customers be driven
away? Will insurance rates go up? Will the worker's productivity suffer?
How will others in the work place react? Can the privacy of the worker be
maintained?

There may also be technical questions. In Judge Worth's case, for in-   14
stance, court officials are now weighing whether the telephone arrangement he
is proposing would satisfy the legal rights of litigants to be physically present
before the court.

On a more personal level, AIDS can redefine working relationships in   15
painful ways. Gary E. Banas, director for administration for the northeastern
district of the Federal Comptroller of the Currency in New York City, said he
was torn between compassion and professional duty when he dealt with two
subordinates in the advanced stages of the disease.

Mr. Banas reassigned both workers to lesser duties when their perform-   16
ances declined. One of the workers objected. Mr. Banas said the man, who has
since died, was a supervisor and staff morale had sunk as co-workers needed to
cover for him.

But realizing that he had to put the agency first was not an easy choice,   17
Mr. Banas said.

"I had a lot of sleepless nights over it," said the 44-year-old manager. "I   18
was able to deal with it because I recognized that I had other employees I was
responsible for."

Conditions Are Changing

Business groups say that most private or public employers have not prepared   19
for the fears, risks and disruptions AIDS can cause, but that is changing. One

reason is a new Federal law to be phased in through 1994, the Americans with Disabilities Act, which prohibits discrimination against disabled workers, including people disabled by AIDS, and will require employers with more than 15 workers to make "reasonable accommodations" for them.

Another reason is that AIDS mostly affects the working-age population: 76 percent of the 242,146 AIDS cases reported as of last September in the United States were in the 25-to-44 age group.   20

Fear of transmission is still a worry for co-workers even this far into the AIDS epidemic, employers say. In settings where most Americans work, like offices, some reactions indicate a lack of basic knowledge about how infection with the virus occurs.   21

"Can I catch AIDS from the telephone? Can I catch it from the bathroom?" said Celia Ussak, director of personnel for the Metro-North Commuter Railroad. "They still ask those questions."   22

Next year, Ms. Ussak said, Metro-North plans to start a companywide AIDS-education program. Other companies have offered or required similar training for employees, business groups say.   23

Employers Respond

In addition, many employers have already responded to the needs and impairments of infected workers.   24

A marketing-project manager with Pacific Bell in San Francisco said he revealed his H.I.V. infection to his company four years ago when fatigue and other symptoms forced him to take time off for hospitalizations. He said the company offered not only flexible hours—he works at home one day a week—but support groups where he could meet with other H.I.V.-positive employees.   25

The 43-year-old manager said that several times over the years he has had to explain to a new boss that he has H.I.V.   26

Two bosses cried, he said. But in recent years, he said, the exchanges have acquired the semblance of normalcy.   27

"They're used to it," he said. "There are a lot of employees with the condition."   28

Judging from complaints to civil-rights watchdogs and AIDS organizations, however, workers with H.I.V. sometimes are simply dismissed. In New York State, allegations of employment-related discrimination accounted for 90 of 161 complaints filed by people with H.I.V. with New York City's Human Rights Commission and the State Division of Human Rights last year.   29

One man appealed to the state agency last November when a supermarket in Rockland County laid him off from his job as a baker. A few months earlier, he said, he had confided to a co-worker that he had tested positive for H.I.V.   30

He said he did not suspect discrimination until another co-worker asked him one day if it was true he had AIDS.   31

"It clicked," the 34-year-old man, who has no symptoms of illness, said.   32
"I knew right then that everybody knew."

He settled the case for $7,500 and now works as a cook for a food-service   33
company that knows about his infection, he said.

Benefits Costs Cited

But civil-rights groups say that, increasingly, employment-related discrimina-   34
tion against people with H.I.V. is based not on fear but on cost. Business leaders say some companies have faced higher health-insurance premiums or have
had policies canceled because of H.I.V.-related claims by their employees.

Mark Scherzer, a health-benefits consultant in New York City, said he   35
knew of at least five recent instances in New York and New Jersey in which
self-insured union health plans have capped benefits for people with H.I.V. at
$5,000, $25,000, or in one case, $100,000. In a similar case in Texas, a self-
insured plan capped an employee's benefits after he began filing claims for
treatment of AIDS-related conditions. The United States Supreme Court refused this month to hear an appeal of lower court decisions upholding the cap.

Such efforts often stem from a perception that AIDS is more expensive   36
than other types of major illnesses, but health economists say there is no evidence that this is the case.

New treatments and improved survival have undoubtedly raised costs,   37
experts say. Officials from Empire Blue Cross and Blue Shield, the largest private payer of AIDS claims in the country, say the average lifetime cost of a
person with H.I.V. has risen to about $200,000 today from $60,000 in 1986.

But at the same time, others note, preventive drugs have cut down on   38
hospitalizations.

"Some of our employees on these drugs are doing better than some peo-   39
ple who have cancer or severe heart conditions," said Carl Pope, benefits director for Time Inc., which has about 6,000 employees.

Whether to work or to devote time to other endeavors is an overriding   40
question for people with H.I.V., according to psychotherapists and other professionals who work with this population. Many, they say, ponder questions
like whether job pressures could be harmful to their health or whether they
could set realistic career goals.

Special Problems for Women

The burden is often heavier for women, many of whom are less well paid than   41
men and have children they must support.

"You stress-yourself more out," said a 35-year-old sales clerk from the   42
Bronx who is the mother of a 13-year-old boy. "You have to worry about a
baby sitter. If my skin breaks out, I can't say some things around him. I have
to be careful I don't make him nervous about my condition."

Women are also more likely to keep their infection secret because they   43
feel they would be judged more harshly than men, counselors say.

But for many people with AIDS, work can also become a means to prove   44
that they can still lead productive lives. It also offers solace, and an escape.

"I don't think I could stay home and just worry about the virus," the   45
sales clerk said.   ■

Questions for Meaning

1. Aside from financial considerations, what other motives do HIV–positive workers have for wishing to remain employed?
2. What worries employers of HIV–positive workers?
3. What factors are causing employers to address the needs of HIV–positive workers?
4. Vocabulary: camaraderie (4), litigants (14), accommodations (19), impairments (24).

Questions about Strategy

1. Navarro opens her article with information about a judge. She subsequently reports information about several other cases. Why do you think she chose to emphasize Judge Worth by putting his story in such a prominent position?
2. Consider the type of work done by the various HIV–positive individuals cited in this story. How representative are they of the work force as a whole?
3. How successful is Navarro in reporting concerns of both employers and employees? Is her reporting fair or biased?

GERALYN MCCLURE FRANKLIN, ALICIA BRINEY GRESHAM, AND GWEN F. FONTENOT

CURRENT PRACTICES AND CRITICAL ISSUES

"Current Practices and Critical Issues" was first published in 1992 by the *Journal of Small Business Management*. The excerpt reprinted here focusses on how small businesses are responding to the AIDS epidemic and provides the sort of detailed information that its original audience would expect from an article in a professional journal. It is included here so that you can see how writing in a journal differs from writing in a magazine in general circulation. As you read it, consider how the authors have tried to sound objective and professional.

Although the majority of AIDS-afflicted individuals are of working age, most   1
businesses have yet to confront the disease with comprehensive human resource policies. In fact, national surveys reveal that less than 11 percent of
American companies have developed policies addressing AIDS in the workplace. Synopses of surveys and findings on this topic follow.

- An American Management Association (AMA) survey (of readers of its journal, *Personnel,* and 400 other human resource managers in the United States) queried companies about what they were doing about AIDS in the workplace. Of the 124 responding organizations, only 4 percent had developed a formal policy pertaining to AIDS, and only 15 percent had implemented AIDS education programs (Levine 1986).

- A Society for Human Resource Management (formerly the American Society for Personnel Administration) survey of its membership found only 3 percent had a written policy for dealing with employees with AIDS (Myers and Myers 1987).

- A U.S. Bureau of National Affairs survey of 238 organizations found that 2 percent had AIDS policies (Myers and Myers 1987).

- A survey by Alexander and Alexander Consulting Group, Inc., found that 8.3 percent of 2,000 firms in a nationwide survey had written policies on AIDS. Ten percent reported that one or more of their employees had been afflicted with AIDS (Fritz 1988).

- The Executive Committee, a San Diego-based company that organizes meetings and support groups for chief executive officers, reported that only 10.6 percent of its member companies had developed policies and 12 percent had provided education about AIDS (Clark 1989).

- A recent Rutsohn and Law (1991) survey examined how small businesses in the southeastern United States are responding to AIDS in the workplace. Findings indicate that 98 percent do not have a written AIDS policy, and 95 percent do not operate AIDS education programs.

The research in the area of business response to AIDS is entirely descriptive. However, these surveys failed to address an important issue: does business size influence the development of AIDS policy and education programs? The purpose of the study presented below was to address that issue in an exploratory and descriptive manner.   2

Sample Methodology

The study sample was drawn from the membership of the Houston Human Resource Management Association (HHRMA). The association was chosen because it is comprised of human resource generalists and specialists that represent 381 diverse companies in Houston, Texas, one of the largest metropolitan areas in the United States. Furthermore, according to the October 1990 *HIV/ AIDS Surveillance* (U.S. CDC 1990), Houston follows only three other metropolitan areas (New York City, San Francisco, and Los Angeles) in total AIDS cases reported to date (4,481).[1]   3

The definition of "small businesses" used by the U.S. Small Business Administration (SBA), 500 or fewer employees was used to operationalize large versus small businesses for this study (U.S. SBA 1989). Thirty-nine percent of the member companies have fewer than 500 employees, and 59 percent have more than 500 employees (2 percent did not respond).   4

Questionnaires were mailed to a representative of each of the 381 companies. The questionnaire requested four different kinds of information: (1) a description of the organization's AIDS policy (if any); (2) the structure of the AIDS education program; (3) the methods of handling AIDS-related problems in the workplace; and (4) demographic information.   5

The response rate from the mailing was 36 percent: 43.8 percent are small businesses, while 56.2 are large businesses. Within the group of small businesses, 28.5 percent have fewer than 250 employees, and 15.3 percent have between 251 and 500 employees. Of the large businesses responding, 18.2 percent have between 501 and 1,000 employees; 5.1 percent have between 1,001 and 1,500 employees; 13.1 percent have between 1,501 and 2,500 employees; and 19.7 percent have more than 2,500 employees.   6

The responding companies represented a broad range of businesses, including 69 service organizations, 50 manufacturers, 9 retailers, 6 wholesalers, and 3 government organizations. The sample represented the HHRMA well,   7

---

[1]In addition, HHRMA endorsement of the study indicates that AIDS is a recognized problem by human resource managers in Houston. Therefore, businesses in the sample are likely to be actively seeking solutions to AIDS-related problems and willing to provide researchers with information.

and there was no significant difference between the sample group and the HHRMA membership in either size or types of businesses (*p* value <.05). Therefore, a nonresponse bias based on these two characteristics does not exist.

Research Findings

The responses of large and small businesses in the sample were tabulated and compared to see how the two groups are dealing with AIDS in the workplace. Thirty-three percent of the large businesses and 16.7 percent of the small businesses reported having a written policy covering employees with AIDS. The resulting chi-square statistic was 5.09 (*p* value = .0785). Although the *p* value does not meet the generally accepted .05 significance level criteria, it does indicate strong evidence of the association between business size and the presence of a written AIDS policy.   8

As for AIDS education programs, 35.1 percent of the large businesses reported having one, and 24.0 percent indicated plans to implement one in the future. Of the small businesses, 11.7 percent had an AIDS education program, and 26.4 percent indicated they had plans to implement such a program in the future. These findings indicate that large businesses are conducting more AIDS education programs than are small businesses (chi-square 10,307, *p* value <.01). See Table 1 for a breakdown of methods used to educate employees about AIDS.   9

Comparison with Rutsohn and Law Study

Rutsohn and Law's survey of AIDS in the workplace examined many of the same variables identified in this study. Together the two surveys increase our knowledge about this important issue. Table 2 contrasts the responses of the   10

TABLE 1
Types of AIDS Education Programs

	Small Businesses		Large Businesses	
Education Program	*Number*	*Percent*	*Number*	*Percent*
Brochures	21	35.0	38	49.4
Training Films	7	11.7	18	23.4
Question/Answer Sessions	6	10.0	14	18.2
Outside Consultants	5	8.3	6	7.8
Seminars	4	6.7	14	18.2
Company Publications	2	3.3	16	20.8
Other Responses	4	6.7	10	13.0

Note: Percentages do not add to 100 since businesses could indicate the use of more than one education program.

TABLE 2
A Comparison of Survey Findings

Statement	Rutsohn and Law (percent)	Franklin, Gresham, and Fontenot (percent)
Do not have a written AIDS policy	98.0	81.7
Are not aware of an employee having the AIDS virus	1.0	11.7
AIDS education program not currently offered	95.0	86.7
Do not plan to offer education program in the future	82.0	53.3
How the business would deal with an AIDS-infected employee:		
No change in job assignment	NA	38.3
Dismiss	9.2	0.0
Provide support	66.3	13.3
Educate employees	60.2	16.7
Isolate the employee(s)	20.4	0.0
Health plan covers AIDS	27.0	90.0
Not sure if health plan covers AIDS	65.0	6.7

Note: NA means there was no equivalent response.

small businesses surveyed for both studies. For comparison purposes, only percentages are shown, and only variables common to both surveys are included.

Several methodological differences between the two studies should be noted. First, Rutsohn and Law (1991) examined small businesses in the southeastern United States, while the current study surveyed businesses of all sizes in Houston, Texas. Second, the response rates differed (20 percent for Rutsohn and Law and 36 percent for this survey). 11

The questionnaire content of the two surveys also differed, with the current study examining more closely the issue of health plan coverage and dollar limits of the coverage. The current study found that 35 percent of the small businesses stated that their health plan specified a dollar limit for the coverage of AIDS. The limits were as follows: $250,000 (20 percent); $500,000 (20 percent); $1,000,000 (50 percent); and $2,000,000 (5 percent). 12

The current study also presents a comparison of the reactions from both large and small businesses. Results indicate that many more large businesses (45.5 percent) than small businesses (11.67) have had to deal with AIDS-infected employees in the workplace. Therefore, small businesses learn a great deal about handling the AIDS problem from larger businesses. 13

Implications

The findings of this survey indicate that large businesses are taking a more proactive approach to developing AIDS policies and education programs than are small businesses. In fact, a majority of small businesses have not yet begun 14 to address AIDS-related issues. Since no business is immune from the AIDS epidemic—and just one case of AIDS could have a particularly devastating financial effect on a small business—small firms should protect themselves by developing comprehensive AIDS policies and education programs. The remainder of this article will focus on a strategy small employers can use to avoid AIDS-related problems.

The Ten-Point AIDS Strategy for Small Businesses

A strategy to cope with AIDS in the workplace should ideally be developed   15 before the first case is diagnosed. Rutsohn and Law (1991) outlined six recommendations for small business owners-managers: (1) stay well-informed, (2) formulate and practice company policies, (3) enter into frank discussions and negotiations with the company's health insurance carrier, (4) provide employees with opportunities to attend company-sponsored AIDS education seminars, (5) explore the option of joining a multi-employer trust for insurance coverage, and (6) stay abreast of legislation in the company's home state. The following 10-point plan, developed prior to the publication of Rutsohn and Law's article, includes many of the same recommendations; however, additional strategies and pragmatic details on how to implement the plan in the workplace are included.

Point 1: Form a Task Force of Key Personnel

This task force will develop the organization's AIDS policy and guide the   16 AIDS education program. The group should include the small business owner-manager and representatives from the human resource, medical, safety, and labor relations arenas, if possible. In smaller businesses, the task force can include employees who are interested in the issue and willing to participate. Members of the task force should be knowledgeable about and have good access to up-to-date medical, social, and legal information about AIDS. To obtain this knowledge, consultation with local health officials and lawyers is recommended.

Point 2: Review the Company Benefits Package

The company's employee health insurance should be reviewed to ensure that it   17 provides broad-spectrum coverage for *all* catastrophic illnesses, including AIDS. While some insurance companies are treating AIDS as they would any other major catastrophic disease, other insurance companies are limiting coverage due to the tremendous treatment costs involved. Since courts have ruled both ways concerning the rights of insurance companies to limit coverage for AIDS victims, it is imperative to stay abreast of the legal issues.

Rutsohn and Law (1991) make several worthwhile suggestions about   18 benefits options. First, they suggest that organizations obtain in writing insurance companies' policies on covering treatment and disability costs incurred by AIDS-afflicted employees. Thereafter, businesses should shop around for the most effective coverage. They also suggest that small employers explore the possibility of joining a multi-employer trust (MET) for insurance coverage.[2]

Point 3: Understand the Legal Responsibilities of the Business and of Employees

The courts have determined that AIDS is a workplace issue and that employ-   19
ers' responsibilities extend to both infected and non-infected employees. Thus, infected employees are protected against discrimination, and non-infected employees have the right to a safe workplace. AIDS also is considered a handicap under both federal and state laws that prohibit discrimination against the handicapped. In addition, AIDS victims have a right to medical coverage and long-term disability benefits. Therefore, adverse employment decisions about an AIDS-afflicted employee should only be made if the employee has become incapable of acceptable job performance.

Point 4: Develop a Written AIDS Policy

The written AIDS policy should present factual information on the disease   20
and indicate that those afflicted will be treated the same as employees with *any* life-threatening, catastrophic disease. It also should state that employees with AIDS-related conditions will be viewed as having a disability, that discrimination will not be tolerated, and that provisions will be made to reasonably accommodate AIDS-afflicted employees. The policy should also indicate that medical information will remain confidential and that all policies, including sick leave and other benefits, will be applied uniformly.

Point 5: Train Personnel as AIDS Resource Specialists or Enlist Outside Specialists to Provide Education Programs

Local health officials, representatives of the American Red Cross, and other   21
resource providers are often available to provide education programs or train in-house specialists to serve as the primary presenters. The latter is preferable because employees tend to trust people they know.

Point 6: Formal Introduction of the Topic

A regular employee communication vehicle, such as the company newsletter   22
or a bulletin board, can be used to familiarize employees with the AIDS issue. Employers may consider sending each employee a letter about the upcoming employee seminar.

Point 7: Educate Managerial and Supervisory Employees

Managerial and supervisory employees play an important role in every organi-   23
zation; therefore, they should be educated first. Employees can then rely on managers and supervisors for guidance and information. A "For Managers/

---

[2]METs are voluntary associations of organizations that join together to spread risk. Since smaller, self-insured firms face the greatest financial risks from AIDS, METs may be a viable alternative.

Supervisors Only AIDS Education Seminar" should focus on the medical, social, and legal issues involved with the disease. In addition, managerial/supervisory employees must be properly prepared to handle confidential information.

Point 8: Educate the General Workforce

An easy-to-follow program is recommended for educating the general work-   24
force. If in-house presenters have been properly trained, outside experts need
not serve as the primary presenters. . . .

After welcoming the employees and thanking them for taking the time   25
to learn the facts about this deadly disease, company policies regarding AIDS
and/or catastrophic illnesses should be discussed. It should be stressed that
AIDS is not transmitted by casual contact, particularly the type of contact that
occurs in the workplace. The seminar should inform employees about the disease and answer their questions, but care should be taken not to pass judgment
on anyone or intrude into personal matters.

Showing of a videotape on the basic facts about AIDS is recommended,   26
and the viewing should be followed by group discussion period.[3] Employees
should be encouraged to ask questions, as well as to write questions down.
These written questions are then collected and raised by the discussion leader.
This procedure ensures that no employee will be directly linked to a specific
question and creates a more open environment.

Although the primary presenters should, if possible, be in-house special-   27
ists, local medical and legal experts should also be present to answer frequently asked medical and legal questions about AIDS. If their presence is not
possible, the in-house specialists should be completely prepared to answer
such questions.

At the conclusion of the program, general information brochures and a   28
seminar evaluation form should be distributed to all employees; in-house resource specialists should be introduced; employees should be informed that the
company will provide them with updated information as it becomes available;
and local community resources should be discussed. Finally, employees should
be asked to share what they have learned with family and friends.

Point 9: Keep Employees Informed about the Disease

Information about AIDS changes almost daily; therefore, the organization   29
must stay abreast of new developments and disseminate up-to-date information as it becomes available. Continual education is the best weapon for combating employee fears about AIDS.

Point 10: Evaluate the Program for Overall Effectiveness

This evaluation process should begin by asking whether the task force members   30
have sufficient knowledge about all aspects of the disease and its ramifica-

---

[3]A variety of videotapes can be used for AIDS education seminars. For additional information, contact local health officials, the American Red Cross, or other resource providers.

tions—and the ability to effectively communicate that knowledge. Managers' and supervisors' understanding of employees' concerns, as well as the importance of confidentiality, should be carefully assessed.[4] In addition, the evaluation should examine whether the general workforce understands the important facts about AIDS and related company policies. Do they know how AIDS is (and is not) transmitted, and do they understand the in-house AIDS-related policies and procedures? If employees can correctly answer these crucial questions, the program can be considered successful.

Conclusion

Many small employers may believe that developing AIDS policies and education programs would be costly and difficult. Yet dealing responsibly, effectively, and proactively with AIDS will, in the long run, benefit both owner-managers and their employees. Armed with intelligent and reasoned application of AIDS policies and comprehensive education programs, small businesses will be well-prepared to cope effectively with AIDS in the workplace.   31

References*

Americans with Disabilities Act of 1990, Pub. L. No. 101-336, Section 101, et seq.

Barnes, Deborah M. (1987), "New Questions About AIDS Test Accuracy," *Science* 238 (November), 884–885.

Choi, Keewhan (1986), "Assembling the AIDS Puzzle: Epidemiology," in *AIDS: Facts and Issues,* ed. Victor Gong and Norman Rudnick, New Brunswick, N.J.: Rutgers University Press, 15.

Clark, Cheryl (1989), "AIDS Impact Now Being Felt by Many Firms," *San Diego Union* (October 5), E5.

Consolidated Omnibus Budget Reconciliation Act of 1986, Pub. L. No. 99-272, Section 10001, et seq.

"Corporate Policy on AIDS" (1988), *Small Business Report* 13 (April), 42–45.

Employee Retirement Income Security Act of 1974, 29 U.S.C., Section 10001, et seq.

Franklin, Geralyn McClure, and Robert K. Robinson (1987), "AIDS and the Law," *Personnel Administrator* 33 (April), 118–121.

Friedland, Gerald, and Robert Klein (1987), "Transmission of the Human Immunodeficiency Virus," *New England Journal of Medicine* 317 (October 29), 1125.

Fritz, Norma R. (1988), "Writing the Rules on AIDS," *Personnel* 67 (August), 12–14.

Frumkin, Lyn Robert, and John Martin Leonard (1987), *Questions and Answers on AIDS,* Oradell, N.J.: Medical Economics Books, 5.

Gallo, Robert C., and Luc Montagnier (1988), "The AIDS Epidemic," in *The Science of AIDS: Readings from Scientific American Magazine,* ed. Jonathan Piel, New York, N.Y.: W. H. Freeman, 1.

---

[4]To date, only medical personnel are required to report the names of persons with AIDS to state health departments. Other legislation does not obligate an employer to disclose to co-workers or any other party that an employee is infected with the AIDS virus.

*This reference list covers the entire article from which this excerpt was taken. It follows a documentation style favored by the journal in which it was published. It is similar to APA style but has several differences.

Gong, Victor (1986), "Facts and Fallacies: An AIDS Overview," in *AIDS: Facts and Issues,* ed. Victor Gong and Norman Rudnick, New Brunswick, N.J.: Rutgers University Press, 11.

Israel, David, and Debra Scott (1990), "AIDS-Related Insurance Ceilings Are Risky," *HR Administrator* 36 (November), 85–86.

Leonard, Arthur S. (1985). "Employment Discrimination Against Persons with AIDS," *University of Dayton Law Review* 10, 681–703.

Levine, Hermine Zagat (1986), "AIDS in the Work Place," *Personnel* 65 (March), 56–64.

McGann v. H & H Music Company, No. H-89-1995 (S.1) Tex. June 27, 1990 appeal docketed, No. 90-2672 (5th Cir. 7/27/90).

Mitchell, P. (1986), "Employment Discrimination and AIDS: Is AIDS a Handicap Under Section 504 of the Vocational Rehabilitation Act?" *University of Florida Law Review* 38, 649–671.

Myers, Phyllis Schiller, and Donald W. Myers (1987), "AIDS: Tackling a Tough Problem Through Policy," *Personnel Administrator* 32 (April), 95.

Naglieri, Thomas J. (1987), "Coping with AIDS on the Job," *Risk Management* 34 (June), 36–40.

Nichols, Eve K. (1989), *Mobilizing Against AIDS,* Cambridge, Mass. Harvard University Press, 291–295.

Nussbaum, David (1988), "Group Insurance and AIDS," *Best's Review* (April), 26, 28, 116–118.

Occupational Safety and Health Act of 1970, 29 U.S.C., Section 5, et seq.

Osborn, June E. (1986), "The AIDS Epidemic: An Overview of the Science," *Issues in Science and Technology* 3 (Winter), 40–45.

Pollick, Michael (1987), "Preparing for the Worst," *Nation's Business* (October), 28, 30, 32.

Ritter, David B., and Ronald Turner (1987), "AIDS: Employer Concerns and Options," *Labor Law Journal* 38 (February), 67–83.

Rutsohn, Philip, and Donald Law (1991), "Acquired Immune Deficiency Syndrome: A Small Business Dilemma," *Journal of Small Business Management* 29 (January), 62–71.

Singer, Ira D. (1987), "AIDS in the Workplace," *Nation's Business* (August), 36–39.

U.S. Centers for Disease Control (1981), "Pneumocystis Pneumonia—Los Angeles," *Morbidity and Mortality Weekly Report* 30, 250–252.

———. (1983), "Acquired Immune Deficiency Syndrome (AIDS) Update—United States," *Morbidity and Mortality Weekly Report* 32, 310.

———. (1985a), "Provisional Public Health Service Inter-Agency Recommendations for Screening Donated Blood and Plasma for Antibody to the Virus Causing Acquired Immunodeficiency Syndrome," *Morbidity and Mortality Weekly Report* 34, 1.

———. (1985b), "Revision of Case Definition of Acquired Immunodeficiency Syndrome for National Reporting—United States," *Morbidity and Mortality Weekly Report* 34, 373–375.

———. (1987a), "Prevention of HIV Transmission in Health-Care Settings," *Morbidity and Mortality Weekly Report* 36 (August 14 Sup.), 2S.

———. (1987b), "Revision of the CDC Surveillance Case Definition for Acquired Immunodeficiency Syndrome," *Morbidity and Mortality Weekly Report* 36 (August 14 Sup.), 1S.

———. (1990), *HIV/AIDS Surveillance* (October), Atlanta, Ga.: U.S. Centers for Disease Control, 6–7.

U. S. Small Business Administration (1989), *The State of Small Business: A Report of the President,* Washington, D.C.: U.S. Government Printing Office, 18.

U.S. Vocational Rehabilitation Act of 1973, 29 U.S.C. Section 701, et seq. ■

Questions for Meaning

1. In paragraph 2, the authors note that previous research is "entirely descriptive" but that their article would be both "exploratory and descriptive." What is the difference?
2. The research cited in this article shows that large businesses have been more responsive to AIDS than small businesses have been. What factors do you think might account for this difference?
3. When do the authors believe employers can penalize HIV–positive workers?
4. Why do the authors recommend continual education about AIDS rather than relying on a single workshop or seminar?
5. Vocabulary: demographic (5), methodological (11), proactive (14), pragmatic (15), implement (15), imperative (17), disseminate (29).

Questions about Strategy

1. What do the authors achieve by opening their article with synopses of previous studies? Why do they mark each study with a black dot?
2. Why do the authors find it necessary to distinguish their work from the work of Rutsohn and Law? How effective are they in establishing the legitimacy of their own findings?
3. What do the tables contribute to the article?
4. After discussing both large and small businesses, the authors conclude their article with ten recommendations for small businesses. How do they justify narrowing their focus?

RHONDA WEST AND ART DURITY

DOES MY COMPANY NEED TO WORRY ABOUT AIDS?

It's always easy to reassure ourselves that the problems we read about are some-one else's problems—not our own. As the title of their article suggests, Rhonda West and Art Durity wanted their original readers to consider how AIDS in the workplace affects their own companies. West developed the AIDS program at Southwestern Bell Corporation; Durity is a former editor of *Personnel,* which published this article in April 1991.

There are many reasons for a company to have a comprehensive AIDS program   1
that includes a written policy, supervisor training and employee education.

For many, the moral reason is enough: People are dying, and corporate   2
America is in a position to do something about it.

Every 54 seconds another person in the United States is infected with the   3
AIDS virus; 3,000 diagnosis are reported every month. By 1994, those num-bers will triple. It is the leading cause of death in men between 24 and 35 years old, and it is the third leading cause of death in women of childbearing age. As workers, they are at the height of their productive years, building the econ-omy, making contributions to society and paying taxes.

The law of probability suggests that AIDS will enter your workplace   4
soon, if it hasn't already. The moral argument suggests that because you are in a position to save the lives of your employees by developing something as sim-ple as an AIDS education program, you are obligated to do so.

But morals have rarely been the stock and trade of the corporate world.   5
So consider the following two business reasons. If unaddressed, each will have a severe impact on the bottom line in a way that won't please your CEO, the board of directors or your stockholders.

Keep AIDS Out of Court

First, a well-documented AIDS policy is a company's first line of defense   6
against a discrimination lawsuit.

By most analyses, AIDS is a protected handicap under the current Amer-   7
icans with Disabilities Acts. It clearly will be protected under the revised ADA that will go into effect in 1992. Therefore, companies cannot legally exempt people with AIDS—or even those perceived to have AIDS—from a potential or current labor pool. Considering that the vast majority of people with AIDS are in their prime, wage-earning years, the odds favor that a manager in your company will face some kind of employment decision that revolves around AIDS. To keep that decision out of court, managers must be aware that they and the company they represent have a legal responsibility to act equitably.

A documented AIDS policy is the most simple and cost-effective means   8
to reduce a company's potential liability. It tells managers how they should act
regarding AIDS issues, and it lets employees know what they can expect from
the company. Such a policy should be effective before AIDS enters your workplace if you are to avoid privacy complications. Communicate it regularly to
employees in the same manner as EEO policies.

You can't rely on managers doing the "right thing" just because they un-   9
derstand that AIDS is not casually transmitted. The American Civil Liberties
Union has found that even people who know the facts about AIDS transmission sometimes prevent people from keeping jobs, finding housing or securing
insurance coverage and medical care. And AIDS bias is growing fast. The
number of AIDS discrimination cases increased from fewer than 400 in 1984
to 92,548 in 1988, and 37 percent of those were employment related.

Keep AIDS-Related Healthcare Costs Down

Second, community involvement is the first line of defense against catastrophic   10
healthcare costs associated with AIDS.

Life is precious, and enormous sums are paid to protect it. When it comes   11
to "socially acceptable" chronic diseases, such as lung cancer, business gener-
ously supports campaigns against them—by sponsoring in-house medical programs, public service ads on television and radio, health-education programs
in schools, research and alternative patient care. Such strong support of alternative, nonprofit healthcare systems serves to control costs in two ways. By
educating people, it serves to prevent future contraction of disease. And, by
underwriting alternative care programs, it increases the supply of care and
forces down the price for all forms of care.

Unfortunately, no such support system exists for the AIDS epidemic,   12
which is one of the most socially stigmatized epidemics ever. In corporate giving programs, prejudice against homosexuals and drug addicts still challenges
the validity of the population with AIDS, despite the rising number of fathers,
mothers, sons and daughters who have it. And so business and private funding
is virtually non-existent for the many public education, research and alternative care projects that address AIDS.

Lack of funding certainly isn't for lack of programs that could put it to   13
good use. Not only are AIDS activists effectively fighting discrimination, they
are mobilizing to create their own cost-effective healthcare system. Virtually
every major city has an AIDS organization that provides some kind of case
management—either through volunteers or through paid professionals who
know the systems in their areas—and all serve members of the corporate community.

The problem for these organizations is funding. The tragic result is the   14
absence of an adequate system to ensure that preventative measures are in place
and that care is available at a reasonable price. They need your help. They need
your money and management expertise. And they need your *moral* support to
help them overcome the prejudice still imbedded at other companies.

Remember: Hundreds of thousands of people will develop AIDS in the   15
next decade. Many will work for you, or will be related to someone who does,
which means that they are covered by your corporate health insurance plan.
And so business, in one form or another, will bear the catastrophic costs unless
it acts now.   ■

Questions about Meaning

1. If the statistics in paragraph 3 are accurate, how many people will be
   infected with the AIDS virus each week?
2. Why do statistics indicate that increasing numbers of business managers
   will need to make decisions about workers with AIDS?
3. Why have corporate giving programs been more supportive of programs involving diseases such as cancer than programs addressing AIDS?
4. Vocabulary: documented (8), underwriting (11), stigmatized (12), virtually (12), imbedded (14).

Questions about Strategy

1. After recognizing that there is a moral reason for comprehensive AIDS
   programs, the authors subsequently focus on business reasons. What
   does this focus reveal about their sense of audience? Do you think this
   strategy is appropriate?
2. Consider the use of the second person in paragraphs 5, 7, and 14–15.
   What management level do the authors seem to have in mind? Does the
   use of the second person limit the number of readers who will find this
   article relevant?
3. Do what extent to the authors play on fear in this article? What anxieties
   do they raise, and where do they do so? Do the authors appeal to any
   other emotions?

ONE STUDENT'S ASSIGNMENT

Read all the articles on AIDS in *The Informed Argument.* As you move from one article to another, be alert for ideas that connect with ideas you have already noted. Draw these ideas together in an essay of approximately 750 words. Focus on *one* of the following questions: "What are the principal concerns of employees who learn that a coworker is HIV-positive?" *Or,* "How can employers respond effectively to AIDS in the workplace?" Because all of your sources are from this book, you do not need to include a list of works cited at the end of your essay, but you should use MLA style parenthetical documentation to show the source of each idea.

AIDS at Work: A Synthesis of Managerial Concerns
Andrew Shimek

With the AIDS epidemic growing at alarming rates, AIDS in the work-   1
place becomes an increasingly urgent issue. More and more companies are
faced with employees who are HIV-positive. "Over two-thirds of companies
with more than 2,500 employees, and nearly one in 10 small companies,
have had an employee with HIV infection or AIDS" (Pogash 148). Unfortunately, managers are often in a quandary, not knowing how to respond to
this trend.

Research shows that there is currently too little being done by busi-   2
nesses to deal with AIDS in the workplace. Franklin, Gresham, and
Fontenot note that "national surveys reveal that less than 11 percent of
American companies have developed policies addressing AIDS in the
workplace" (158). Banta claims that this is a "critical omission on the part
of many employers" (135). These statistics alone convey the critical need
for businesses to have a written policy dealing with AIDS.

Moreover, the legal ramifications a company could face are also very   3
serious. Navarro notes that the Americans with Disabilities Act (ADA),
which protects people with disabilities including people with AIDS (PWA),
could pose a threat to companies that are not dealing with AIDS in the
workplace (154–55). Such companies may face major lawsuits. West and
Durity affirm this notion, claiming that "a well-documented AIDS policy is a
company's first line of defense against a discrimination lawsuit" (168). The
ADA also protects employees that are dropped from group health plans because they have contracted AIDS. While this legislation ensures that "AIDS
victims have a right to medical coverage," the ADA does not apply to employers that are self-insured (Franklin, Gresham, and Fontenot 163). Mark
Scherzer, a health benefits consultant in New York City notes that he
"knew of at least five recent instances in New York and New Jersey in

which self-insured union health plans have capped benefits for people with HIV" (Navarro 156). Banta concurs, noting that regardless of present legislation, the reality exists: "Employers attempting to contain rising insurance premiums may be tempted to exclude AIDS-related illnesses from coverage" (138). Because of this, Franklin et al. stress how important it is for companies to "stay abreast of legislation" (162).

In addition to the need for a written policy concerning AIDS and the need   4 to stay well-informed, managers are faced with the responsibility of educating the work force about AIDS. This task is necessary because many people are still misinformed about the disease. Navarro, Brants, and Noble's articles all reveal anxieties in the workplace concerning AIDS. For example, two of the articles noted a concern of contracting AIDS over the telephone. These sentiments alone reveal a general need for education in the workplace. Noble reports a study that states only 28 percent of employers receive AIDS education at work but 75 percent feel that they should receive this (141). Franklin and her coauthors affirm the need for education and recommend that educational programs should stress that "AIDS is not transmitted by casual contact, particularly the type of contact that occurs in the workplace" (164). Brants's situation alone shows that an education program would have made her relationship with her employees much less stressful because she would not have been "constantly trying to calm them down" (143).

The manager is faced not only with dealing with the work force but also   5 with the individual with AIDS. A written policy is a starting point for this. But Banta notes that while such policies can be very beneficial "the facts and circumstances of the physical and mental condition of every applicant and employee and the specific qualifications of the job in question must be thoroughly analyzed before reaching conclusions" (137). Banta explores the complexity of the situation deriving a number of questions that employers must ask when dealing with a PWA. A question often discussed is: "If any disclosures are made, is the employer vulnerable to claims of invasion of privacy and breach of confidentiality?" (138). Pogash deals specifically with this question as she describes Jane Doe's struggle to maintain her privacy regarding her HIV-positive status. This case is a useful precedent for an AIDS policy regarding privacy. Others may feel a sense of indebtedness to Jane Doe, realizing that she "battled the establishment for them" (152).

In addition to addressing the privacy issue, managers are required by   6 the ADA to provide PWA with "reasonable accommodations" in the workplace. Franklin and her coauthors emphasize the importance of this, and Banta deals specifically with the issue of reasonably accommodating the employee. Banta's article depicts a nurse, Charlene, in the emergency room contracting AIDS and subsequently discusses various courses of action that her employers considered. Banta notes that "involuntary removal of Charlene from her position would probably violate state and federal laws" (000). Unfortunately, the hospital is also at risk leaving Charlene in the emergency room where she may pose a risk to others and this may constitute negligence. Finding themselves in a double bind situation, the hospital decides its best course of action is to offer Charlene a comparable job in another ward and hope she will agree. This case shows the delicate balance an employer must be conscious of when accommodating the employee, yet also ensuring the safety of others.

While the need to address AIDS in the workplace may seem increasingly evident, it is not as clear what is the best course of action to take, when setting policy. This is due in part to the lack of sufficient legal precedents, and only time can bring these precedents. For the present it seems clear that the discussion of forming policies for dealing with AIDS in the workplace is still very much open-ended. As the disease spreads, additional precedents will emerge and these precedents will have to be followed closely by managers.

SUGGESTIONS FOR WRITING

1. Banta, Brants, and Pogash all focus on specific cases of AIDS in the workplace. Choose one of these cases and write an evaluation of how well management responded to an HIV-positive worker.
2. As Pogash points out, a national commission argued against requiring HIV-positive health-care workers to inform patients of their condition. If you believe such disclosure should be required, write an argument advancing your view.
3. Mireya Navarro reports the case of a baker who was fired because he was HIV-positive but who subsequently found a job with a food service company that knows of his condition. Write an argument for or against the employment of HIV-positive workers in a particular segment of the food industry.
4. If you believe that modern technology enables people to work efficiently at home, write an argument for or against providing HIV-positive workers with that option.
5. If you know someone who is HIV-positive and willing to discuss the disease, interview that person and report on how his or her employment has been affected.
6. Check the yellow pages in your telephone directory, and look for an AIDS office, a gay or lesbian community organization, or a local office of the Red Cross. Interview officials from two organizations with different agendas and then compare or contrast their views.
7. If a company in your area has a written AIDS policy, obtain a copy. Read it carefully and then write an evaluation of it.

8. Research how another country is responding to AIDS in the workplace and compare your findings to what you have learned from the articles in this section.

COLLABORATIVE PROJECT

Form a writing group and invent a company for which you are the board of directors. Write a brief description of your firm; then draft an AIDS policy for your employees.

SECTION 3

SEXUAL HARASSMENT: DEFINING THE BOUNDARIES

SHARON BEGLEY

CLIPPING CUPID'S WINGS

Although sexual harassment can take many forms, it is especially disturbing when it occurs in professional relationships in which one individual has more power than the other. On college campuses, harassment can take the form of faculty propositioning their students—students who may be graded by the same person who is asking them out. In response to growing concerns about sexual harassment, colleges have been formulating policies to distinguish what kind of behavior is unacceptable. As Sharon Begley reports in "Clipping Cupid's Wings," some colleges are considering a complete ban on faculty–student dating. Begley is a staff writer for *Newsweek*, which first published this piece in 1993.

When "Steve" ran into his foreign-language instructor last April at a café near   1
the University of California, Berkeley, where he was a junior, she asked him
"to go out sometime." He declined—and later received the second lowest
grade in the class, "a grade I didn't deserve," he says. "I don't think that's a
coincidence."

   Was this sexual harassment going unpunished? Or another crazed P.C.er   2
seeing evil in every innocent gesture? Colleges aren't waiting for nasty Hill/
Thomas-type hearings★ to sort out the predatory from the friendly. Although
the idea that it's dumb to bed someone you teach is implicit in sexual-
harassment codes, more and more schools are flat-out prohibiting faculty from
dating students in their classes. Harvard, Tufts and the Universities of Iowa
and Pennsylvania, among others, have banned such dating. Amherst College
requires faculty who venture into sexual relationships with students to remove
themselves from any supervisory role over them. Last week the University of
Virginia faculty senate prepared to vote on what would have been the most

★When Clarence Thomas was nominated for the Supreme Court, his confirmation hearings
in 1991 focused on claims from Anita Hill that she had been sexually harassed by him.

far-reaching ban: a prohibition on sexual relationships and "amorous over-tures" between students and *any* faculty member.

Coerced Consent

But in a heated two-hour session, UVA's blanket prohibition never came to a   3
vote; proponents, sensing defeat, instead offered a narrower ban on instructors
dating students they teach or supervise. That passed 31 to 4. But the debate
over where to draw the line on campus romances is still resounding in dorms
from Cambridge to Palo Alto. It's fueled by the growing belief that many campus relationships deemed "consensual" are not—that (usually female) students
get pressured into bed with (usually male) faculty or graduate teaching assistants. Professors' power to determine their students' future, through grades and
recommendations, "makes 'consensual' a suspect notion," argued UVA's history professor and director of women's studies Ann Lane. UVA received more
than 100 student complaints last year about romantic feelers from faculty; most
believed that spurning the advances would jeopardize their grades.

Even if both student and teacher freely choose romance, others can be   4
adversely affected. A grad student living with an assistant professor may get
invited to department parties, making other students jealous. Such romances
also call into question the objectivity of the grading system. At Harvard, most
of the dozen or so complaints received each year about student–instructor affairs come from suspicious undergraduates in the same class as the teacher's
love interest. "It would take a Solomon to be entirely fair when you've become romantic with a person you're trying to evaluate," says UVA engineer
Thomas Hutchinson.

UVA's attempt to clip Cupid's wings failed because it prohibited ro-   5
mances even between faculty and students who have no academic relationship.
Many students were outraged over an infringement on their cherished right to
date whomever they please. "During four years at UVA, a student will take
classes with just 2 percent of the faculty," says student-council president
Matthew Cooper. "[Banning all relationships] denies our autonomy as adults."
Stanford University is about to accept that argument: its proposed sexual-
harassment policy will not prohibit consensual affairs, but warns of "special
risks involved in any sexual or romantic relationship between individuals in
inherently unequal positions." (Not all such romances end in disaster. UVA
president John T. Casteen 3rd is married to a grad student he met when he was
a professor at Berkeley in the early 1970s; he won't say whether or not he oversaw her work.) Absolutists, though, reject exceptions for people in different
departments. A music student who has an affair with a physics prof may later
switch majors and find herself sitting in front of his lectern.

Policing Bedrooms

Are blanket prohibitions constitutional? The right to free association is not   6
absolute; a "compelling state interest" can limit it, and some scholars argue that

keeping a college free of the problems caused by student–faculty romances is one such interest. Policing a prohibition is another matter. Says Hutchinson, "To regulate the moral behavior of 18,000 people puts an unbearable load on the administration." UVA will enforce its ban only if a grievance is brought; Tufts doesn't police bedrooms and no one's been reported for breaking the ban. Few of the prohibitions carry an explicit penalty.

In a 1988 survey of 800 faculty at a West Coast university, 25 percent of   7 those questioned admitted bedding students, most more than once. Few students actually ask to be protected from lascivious faculty, but surely those who do ought to have some recourse. For schools, the arguments boil down to practacalities. Sexual harassment can require a subjective determination, but a ban on dating draws an unambiguous line. "People have to learn to be decent to each other," says associate provost Samuel Jay Keyser of the Massachusetts Institute of Technology. "No policies, no matter how good or complete, can achieve that." ■

Questions for Meaning

1. Why are colleges prohibiting faculty from dating students?
2. How might other students be affected when a professor dates one of her own students?
3. Consider the quote by Thomas Hutchinson in paragraph 4. To what biblical scene is Hutchinson alluding?
4. Why are some opponents of faculty–student dating unwilling to make an exception for people working and studying in different departments?
5. Vocabulary: predatory (2), resounding (3), autonomy (5), lascivious (7).

Questions about Strategy

1. Although women are more frequently harassed then men, according to paragraph 3, Begley opens with an example of a man who was allegedly accosted by one of his instructors. How seriously do you take this example? Does it matter that the student's real name has been withheld?
2. Why bother to report that the president of the University of Virginia refused to comment on whether he oversaw his wife's work when she was still a student? How are you influenced when you are told that someone declined to answer a reporter's question?
3. Consider the quotation which with this news story concludes. Why do you think the author decided to give Samuel Jay Keyser the last word? How would the article change if it concluded with the quotation from Ann Lane that now appears in paragraph 3?

COURTNEY LEATHERMAN

THE DEBATE OVER FACULTY-STUDENT DATING

In 1993, two weeks after *Newsweek* published the preceding article by Sharon Begley, *The Chronicle of Higher Education* published the following article by staff writer Courtney Leatherman. *The Chronicle of Higher Education* is a weekly newspaper read principally by college administrators and faculty. As you read "The Debate over Faculty–Student Dating," consider how objective Leatherman is in her reporting.

Greg Marsden's marriage to one of his undergraduate gymnasts a decade ago was the stuff of storybook romances.   1

Local and national news organizations fawned over the couple in the 1980s when Mr. Marsden coached his then-fiancée, Megan McCunniff, and the rest of the University of Utah's women's gymnastics team to the national championships. They had begun dating when he was 31 and she was 19.   2

"Most looked at it like a fairy tale," says Ms. Marsden now, after 10 years of marriage. "The public ate it up."   3

That was then. Now, it's not clear the media or the public would take such a starry-eyed view.   4

Context of Sexual Harassment

Utah and many other colleges across the country are now debating policies— often within the context of sexual harassment—to prohibit professors from dating their students. Within those debates are questions about whether professors are breaching professional ethics or colleges are legislating love.   5

Mr. Marsden, who says he fell in love, doesn't generally condone faculty–student relationships and believes colleges are right to discourage them. But he worries that his relationship would today be perceived as scandalous or "ugly." He worked hard to keep it from being seen that way—consulting everyone from Utah's athletics director to Ms. McCunniff's parents before the first date.   6

Nonetheless, many administrators and professors say the more tainted view of liaisons between professors and students has grown out of the awareness that few of these relationships share the Marsdens' happily-ever-after ending. In fact, many of the campuses say the relationships often end with a student's feeling victimized or a department torn apart. Those are the cases that prompted colleges to develop policies to protect the parties involved in the relationships, as well as other students and professors—and the colleges themselves.   7

For years, colleges have quietly wrestled with how far to go in limiting such relationships. The University of Iowa is regarded as the first to prohibit professors from dating students whom they teach or supervise. Other campuses have strongly discouraged such relationships, but stopped short of prohibiting them.   8

Debate at Virginia

The issue attracted national attention recently after a faculty committee at the   9
University of Virginia proposed a complete ban on dating between professors
and undergraduates, whether or not the two were linked academically (*The
Chronicle,* April 14). Ultimately the faculty approved a modified policy similar
to Iowa's.

But debate over the issue continues on many campuses, including the   10
University of South Carolina and California State University at Chico, where
faculty governing bodies recently adopted policies to deter faculty–student relationships. Some professors are disappointed by the debate. They assumed that
overt policies weren't needed for such ethical issues.

Some professors and students believe universities have gone too far. Col-   11
leges are trying either to police passions or to revive *in loco parentis,* the critics
argue. Others say universities are doing their job by preventing potential harassment and definite conflicts of interest. And some call the policies a necessary evil.

"As a living, breathing, often lonely human being, I disapprove of the   12
policy," says John Robert Gardner, a graduate teaching assistant at Iowa's
school of religion. "But as a teacher who hopes to survive and wants the freedom to challenge the academic establishment, I have no choice but to abide
surgically by it," he adds.

Mr. Gardner, who also is president of the university's Student Assembly,   13
has never dated his students, though he's had offers. Mr. Gardner says Iowa's
policy has led to a certain paranoia among his colleagues. Even meeting a student to talk about class over coffee or a beer is suspect, he says.

Professors on the Chico campus took steps to make sure such platonic   14
encounters wouldn't be questionable under their policy. It prohibits "sexual
relationships."

But even innocent beginnings can blossom into love affairs. That's what   15
happened with a 35-year-old linguistics professor teaching at Iowa for a year
and an undergraduate in his graduate-level class. "When I first met her I made
a mental promise to myself that this was not appropriate and I was not going to
get involved," says the professor, who now teaches at the University of South
Carolina.

Warning from Chairman

But casual racquetball games with the 20-year-old junior soon evolved into a   16
romantic relationship, which the two unsuccessfully attempted to keep secret.
They kept dating even after he was warned by the head of the department to
end the affair. He doesn't believe the relationship affected his teaching or
grading.

The student, however, admits that it affected *her* performance.   17

She is now his wife. She earned a B in her husband's class, but says, "My   18
performance went downhill." She adds: "Every time I sat down to do my

homework for that class I was faced with the fact that he would be reading it and that he would judge me based on my performance in that class."

The woman is now a graduate student in music at South Carolina. She   19
didn't want to be identified further, because when her current professors learned how she had met her husband, they appeared to disapprove. The faculty at South Carolina just adopted a policy to prohibit such relationships.

Both she and her husband support such policies—in theory. But, as he   20
says, "I think it's ultimately unenforceable, unless people start to enforce draconian class segregation, where you're not allowed to socialize, or go for coffee, or go out for drinks, or students and professors are only allowed to meet in groups of four."

The point of the policy is not to legislate love or prevent friendships, says   21
Judith P. Aikin, dean of the College of Liberal Arts at Iowa. "But once the emotional involvement is there, the solution should be to get the two out of the teacher–student relationship," she says.

That's what Iowa's policy requires. The professor must choose—the rela-   22
tionship or the professional responsibility. Ms. Aikin says she had about 10 cases of consensual relationships to deal with in this academic year but believes that others were dealt with at the departmental level. She and others believe that most cases involve graduate students' dating professors or undergraduates.

"Reactionary"

A 26-year-old graduate student at the University of Virginia waited until the   23
end of the course he was teaching last fall before he began dating a 20 year-old-student from the class. But he wasn't kept in line by one of the policies, which he calls "reactionary." "I felt an ethical and moral obligation not to do it," he says. He did, however, date her the following semester, when he was a teaching assistant without grading responsibilities in her class.

Ms. Aikin believes Iowa's policy is enforceable, but she calls total bans   24
like the one Virginia had proposed "ridiculous."

Bernice R. Sandler, senior associate for the Center for Women Policy   25
Studies, isn't so sure. "There's a piece of me that wants an incest taboo in the classroom," says Ms. Sandler, who consults with colleges on sexual-harassment issues.

Mostly she wonders, What's in it for the professor? Ms. Sandler believes   26
it's sex, not marriage, that most professors are looking for. Even when a student consents to such relationships, Ms. Sandler argues, a professor has so much power over a student that it's not really consent. Students often wind up exploited, and those cases rarely make headlines, she says.

Protecting Junior Professors

Catherine Ringen, the head of Iowa's linguistics department, says professors   27
are more sensitive to the problems surrounding romantic relationships with students because of the policy. But she wonders whether it should be stronger.

Consensual relationships often damage departments even when the two people involved aren't directly linked academically, she says.

Iowa requires couples in a department to agree to "leave the relationship at home." To protect junior professors, Iowa now prohibits a professor who is involved with a teaching assistant from having a role in any employment decisions affecting that student's professors for six years.   28

But what about love? Isn't it likely that some professors working closely with students in small college towns may fall in love?   29

Ms. Ringen isn't swayed. You could make the same argument for gynecologists and the patients who come for office visits, she says. "But no one suggests that that's where doctors should go shopping for their dates." ■   30

Questions for Meaning

1. Leatherman refers to the idea *in loco parentis* in paragraph 11. What does this mean?
2. How can a student's class performance be jeopardized if she or he is romantically involved with the instructor teaching the class?
3. One of the sources cited in this article links faculty–student dating to incest. What is the connection?
4. According to this article, what kind of students are most frequently involved in consensual relationships with faculty?
5. Vocabulary: tainted (7), liaisons (7), overt (10), abide (12), platonic (14), reactionary (23).

Questions about Strategy

1. Consider the example with which this article opens. What points does it emphasize? How did the story of the Marsden courtship and marriage influence you?
2. How effective is the analogy in paragraph 30 between teachers and gynecologists?
3. Is Leatherman reporting information in this article or using information to be persuasive? Consider the sources she quotes. Do they represent a range of opinion or reveal a consensus of some sort?

JACK HITT, JOAN BLYTHE, JOHN BOSWELL, LEON BOTSTEIN, AND WILLIAM KERRIGAN

NEW RULES ABOUT SEX ON CAMPUS

The following discussion was sponsored by *Harper's* magazine in 1993 as "an attempt to lend a shrill debate a more. . . collegial air." Jack Hitt is a contributing editor of *Harper's*. Joan Blythe is an associate professor of English at the University of Kentucky. John Boswell is the A. Whitney Griswold Professor of History at Yale University. Leon Botstein is president of Bard College and music director for the American Symphony Orchestra. William Kerrigan is a professor of English at the University of Massachusetts where he is also director of the Program on Psychoanalytic Studies. Moderated by Hitt, the discussion took place in a restaurant on the campus of Columbia University. The results were published in *Harper's*. As you read, consider whether this discussion succeeds in making the debate over sexual harassment on campus less "shrill."

I. Why Now?

JACK HITT: Students returning to campuses around the country this fall will   1
be resuming a conversation I cannot imagine unfolding ten or twenty years
ago—a debate about whether formal bans should be adopted on some or all
student–professor sexual relationships. How did we get here?

JOHN BOSWELL: These bans are very much a result of the rootlessness that is   2
prevalent among the students arriving on campus. In times of social disruption, people tend to rely on institutions and laws to replace more private
and traditional mechanisms for maintaining order. This shift is backed up
by the widespread belief that American eighteen-year-olds should not be
tainted with sexuality. But these are not children we are talking about. In
fact, they are at a point in their lives when they are really exploring their
erotic feelings.

JOAN BLYTHE: One supposition is that freshmen are naive eighteen-year-olds   3
who need protecting. Another is that the university experience can be reduced to a business deal: students pay money, hear lectures, get diplomas,
and are provided a secure place in an increasingly troubled economy. An
experience that was once one of transformation is now more commonly
thought of as a *transaction*—a predictable product for money paid.

WILLIAM KERRIGAN: It's the consumer approach to education. It says: Yes, I   4
want higher education. But I want a warranty that nothing formative, vital,
or transformative will happen to me. In particular, should one of my teachers initiate a sexual moment of sufficient power to upset me, I reserve the
right to destroy his career.

LEON BOTSTEIN: Let's give the supporters of a ban their due. There *is* a power   5
differential in the relationship between a student and his or her teacher.
And a sexual relationship between a teacher and a student is, in fact, at odds

with the task of teaching. Before we start nailing our opponents as puritans, hypocrites, or idiots, let's realize that we're dealing in murky definitions that could cause problems in the conduct of teacher–student relationships.

KERRIGAN: This debate forces those, like myself, who abhor the notion of a   6
ban to say things that used to go without saying. Prudery is a great offense against life. Without a sex act, none of us would be here. And whenever civilization sets out a law against a sexual practice or expression, it invariably produces a desire to break that law. That's the way eroticism works.

HITT: Then wouldn't a ban be good? Wouldn't legislation create new and exciting taboos?   7

KERRIGAN: There already is a connection between student–faculty sex and   8
what Freud called the supreme taboo—the incest taboo. Teachers are like parents—*in loco parentis*—but because we're not parents there is no obvious sexual revulsion that prevents relations with students. What we're creating with these bans are not taboos but punishments.

BOTSTEIN: It's important to grasp that the context in which this student–   9
teacher issue is couched is a political debate in the United States that is, in general, an impoverished one. People are reluctant to really debate political issues. Sexuality has become a substitute for politics. There's been an erosion of the political interchange. Look at the presidential election. We're more interested in Clinton's sex life than his politics. Sexuality has *become* America's politics, and the university is a victim of the dissolution between matters private and public.

KERRIGAN: I happen to think that the debate over this issue *is* a real political   10
discussion. Alcibiades in Athens, Nero in Rome*—such issues have always been part of the political debate, just as sexuality has always been a part of education. The university is not a sex-free environment. Nor is the classroom.

BLYTHE: The political debate today, on campus and off, is about identity. And   11
sexual identity—which includes whom you have relationships with and under what terms—is among the most fundamental of issues being debated.

II. The Education of a Virgin

HITT: To hear those supporting a ban on student–professor relationships, you'd   12
think there were suddenly hundreds of teachers on every campus who are sleeping with their students. But this isn't the case. What kind of phenomenon are we talking about here?

KERRIGAN: I have been the subject of advances from male and female students   13
for twenty-five years. I've had them come at me right and left. I've had people take their clothes off in my office. And there is a particular kind of student I have responded to. I am not defending Don Juanism, you know,

---

*Alcibiades (c. 405–404 B.C.) was an Athenian general and politician; Nero (37–68 A.D.) was a Roman Emperor. Their political authority was damaged by their reputations for personal extravagance.

sex for grades and so forth. But there is a kind of student I've come across in my career who was working through something that only a professor could help her with. I'm talking about a female student who, for one reason or another, has unnaturally prolonged her virginity. Maybe there's a strong father, maybe there's a religious background. And if she loses that virginity with a man who is not a teacher, she's going to marry that man, boom. And I don't think the marriage is going to be very good.

There have been times when this virginity has been presented to me as   14
something that I, not quite another man, half an authority figure, can handle—a thing whose preciousness I realize. These relationships, like all relationships, are hard to describe, and certainly difficult to defend in today's environment. Like all human relationships, they are flawed and sometimes tragic. There usually is this initial idealism—the teacher presents ideas in a beautiful form, and so there is this element of seduction in pedagogy. And then things come down to earth, and there often follows disappointment and, on the part of the student, anger. But still, these relationships exist between adults and can be quite beautiful and genuinely transforming. It's very powerful sexually and psychologically; and because of that power, one can touch a student in a positive way. So if you want to oppose the imposition of this ban, I say, let's get honest and describe positive instances of sex between students and faculty.

BOTSTEIN: What comes to my mind is, one, a sense of relief that you're not on   15
the faculty at my college. And two, I'm not certain anyone wants to make a virtue of a private act.

BOSWELL: But what these bans do is conflate the public and private realms.   16
Should we allow the public to interfere in what is essentially a private issue?

BOTSTEIN: I agree, there should be no bans. I am against them. But I share the   17
implicit *ideology* of the bans. What I disagree with is their political entrance into the public arena.

KERRIGAN: I *do* disagree with their ideology. Sometimes these affairs last a   18
week, and they're gone. Sometimes a semester or two. Sometimes they grow into things of great constancy, such as, I may as well reveal, my own marriage. Are you saying you want a generation in which no marriages or affairs result from student–teacher relationships?

BOTSTEIN: I favor a voluntary system, something on the order of a Hippo-   19
cratic oath. You internalize enough of what people expect so that intelligent, responsible people can make judgments and discriminations by circumstance and event.

BOSWELL: I agree. There are already harassment procedures at most schools.   20

BLYTHE: And students are glad of that, but they think the bans are ludicrous.   21
I asked my sophomore Western Lit survey class and my Milton seminar about this ban. One girl said, "I'd see how many professors I could screw that week." For others it was an idea they had never entertained and suddenly they were saying, "Hmm, my professor . . . ". It's like medieval penitential manuals. In confessing parishioners, priests were warned

against bringing up sins not yet committed by asking questions like, Did you give your neighbor's husband a blow job? Maybe she just hadn't thought of it yet.

BOSWELL: I don't think the problem is putting sex with professors in the stu-   22
dents' minds. Like William, I have students absolutely throw themselves at me. I had this incredibly attractive jock come to my office when eighty students were applying for fifteen seats in a class. So I had them all turn in a written statement signed only by their last name. I didn't even want to know their gender. So he came to my office after hours wearing nothing but a pair of gym shorts. Not even shoes. I looked him up and down. And he said, "Professor Boswell, is there something else I can do to get into your class?" And I said, "No, I think you've done all you decently can."

BLYTHE: Did he get in?   23

BOSWELL: No. But had I given in to temptation, imagine the complications   24
and necessary subterfuges I would have invited. I think self-restraint is the way to avoid being unfair.

BOTSTEIN: The most important element of a university is honesty. What I   25
don't like about an overt ban is that it forces people to lie. When you make legislation that can't be enforced in human communities, you undermine the law. And on the campus, this distorts the fundamental integrity of the university, which is self-regulation and respect for truth. Instead of admit-ting that something went wrong, the student acts as we do on the outside. We lie—and hire lawyers to get us off. We deny—and put our hope in an adversarial proceeding in which the best defense wins. Our stand at the academy should be different. It ought to be about proof and truth and a sensible notion of fact and fiction. What we're teaching these young people with these adjudications is that those who admit they were drunk or they did something wrong and deal with it openly are *fools*.

III. Who's Fighting the Fight?

HITT: Why does this ban seem largely to concern young women and their   26
virtue? I thought that traditionally the great fear was of homosexual student–teacher relations.

BOSWELL: It is true that the ban is being promoted by feminists, but the homo-   27
sexual subtext is there. In fact, in a society that did not have this horror of young boys being seduced, I doubt you would see the kind of support you do for the kind of ban we're talking about. Many, many Americans fear homosexuality. People out there are paranoid about gay men coming on to their sons.

BLYTHE: On campuses, where the battle is being waged, homosexuality is not   28
the central issue, because the people proposing these bans are heterosexual and this debate is really about *their* private lives. About what they fear in themselves, their own relationships and their own desire. The people who voice these concerns are precisely those who desire the eighteen-year-old.

These codes have to do with protecting the most privileged of American students. This is not a debate burning at the community-college level. Those pushing for a ban are people who fear real life, especially the protean power of lust. College for them is about *isolation* from the real world, not an introduction to it.

KERRIGAN: This is a case where the left and the right are in bed together.   29

BOTSTEIN: That's right, although "left" and "right" aren't great words. The   30
alliance focuses on the power relationship between men and women in the academy. The majority of faculty members are male, and this ban uses the paradigm of male faculty and female student to reveal the abuse of male-dominated—

KERRIGAN: The "paradigm" is a generation of academic feminists who push   31
this legislation because in an era when a leer constitutes rape, they believe they are powerful enough to punish womanizing male colleagues.

BOSWELL: Why are they so disturbed? Is this simply one of the few areas they   32
can regulate?

BOTSTEIN: Well, I do think there's a history here. To give the other side some   33
due, a fair amount of data shows a long tradition of abuse. Graduate students may be the worst-treated creatures, reduced to servility, and if sexuality's a part, then—

BLYTHE: It also may be the most pleasant part of graduate school.   34

BOTSTEIN: Well, you're assuming something about the quality of the sexual   35
exchange that I don't want to comment on. But let's not be unfair. I've had enough encounters with parents who are not bizarre or crazy, and they are concerned.

BLYTHE: What age students are you talking about?   36

BOTSTEIN: Between eighteen and twenty-one.   37

BLYTHE: Most students at eighteen know more about sex than their own   38
parents.

KERRIGAN: Exactly. Who are these women? Are they all like Anita Hill, who,   39
you'll remember, testified that she had to check into a hospital with stomach ailments after hearing from Clarence Thomas an account of a Long Dong Silver movie?

BOTSTEIN: Don't trivialize the critic, please.   40

HITT: Is there some larger agenda or motive behind these bans?   41

BLYTHE: Yes. The force that is pushing for these bans is abetted by an adminis-   42
tration whose agenda includes castration of the humanities.

BOTSTEIN: That's absurd. The administrators haven't sought out this problem.   43
If anything, they've ducked it. They've run for the hills, fearful of litigation, suits seeking financial damages, and so on. They have simply been forced into this arena, kicking and screaming, by a divisive faculty debate.

BLYTHE: It's a simple fact that these romances are most often found in the hu-   44
manities. Since the administration is biased against any unprofitable part of the university—especially those that can't attract fat research grants—it's not coincidence that administrators have chosen to jump on this issue.

KERRIGAN: But in the faculty, who's behind this? By and large, feminists.   45

BOTSTEIN: They may be people who have a real concern about victimization.   46
They may be authentic puritans; still, I respect such people.

BLYTHE: Except they're *not* puritans. They think non-marital sex is fine, as   47
long as they can control it.

BOTSTEIN: Now, wait. Let's get straight what the proponents of the ban are   48
arguing. They're not arguing the absence of sexuality.

BLYTHE: They are arguing the abdication of responsibility by an individual for   49
her or his own actions.

BOTSTEIN: No, they're not. They are suggesting that in the relationship of stu-   50
dent and teacher, restraint be exercised.

IV. The Obligations of Intercourse

BOTSTEIN: Do we share some residual partial allegiance to the idea that pas-   51
sion and reason are in some sense at odds?

BLYTHE: No.   52

KERRIGAN: No, sir.   53

BOTSTEIN: I assumed as much. I think part of the ban rests on the assumption   54
that there's something dispassionate about the conduct of reason that passion
interrupts. It's an eighteenth-century construct of the human personality.

BOSWELL: The relationship is not antipodal, but it is complicated.   55

KERRIGAN: The problem with the reason/passion division is the assumption   56
that reason recognizes complexity and ambiguity and that passion is this an-
imalistic thing that merely takes possession. Now, I know Norman Mailer★
is very out of fashion today, but one thing he taught me when I was twenty
years old is that good sex is fabulously complicated, in the way that a great
poem is complicated. This is not a matter of mindless passion versus complex philosophy.

BOTSTEIN: Let me say this: I think sexual relations trigger a set of ethical obli-   57
gations.

BLYTHE: Ethical obligations?   58

BOTSTEIN: Ethical obligations.   59

KERRIGAN: *Ethical* obligations?   60

BOTSTEIN: Allow me to approach it this way. I am partisan, out of obligation,   61
to my parents, my spouse, my children, and other members of my family in
a way that overrides fairness. I will stop at nothing to advance them. If I am
a judge in a violin competition and my grandmother enters, my opinion
would be slanted toward her from the start, no matter what. That's why
judges disqualify themselves. Now, I happen to think that when, as a
teacher, you go beyond flirtation with a student, you trigger a set of ethical

★Norman Mailer (b. 1923) is an American writer known for his controversial views. His
books include *The Naked and the Dead* (1948) and *The Prisoner of Sex* (1971).

obligations that override the desire to be fair. I happen to think, as well, that the process of teaching is a process of the adjudication of fairness. So my conclusion is that when you are having sexual relations with one of your students, you are in this sense being unfair to the others.

BOSWELL: A way to solve that problem is disclosure. A colleague of mine who 62 married his graduate student and continues to write her recommendations should begin his letters, "My wife . . ."

BLYTHE: I totally disagree. No judgment is purely musical or purely literary— 63 purely objective as to merit. It's always subjective.

BOSWELL: You don't think people should aspire to be fair? 64

BLYTHE: I think people should aspire to be great. I would hope if your grand- 65 mother were the best violinist out there, you would give her the award.

BOTSTEIN: What if my grandmother were not the best violinist? 66

BLYTHE: Then you *wouldn't* give her the award. See how it works? 67

KERRIGAN: What's tiresome about what you've been saying, Leon, is the as- 68 sumption that we have this Kantian moral sense, a system of absolutes that we must either abide by or recede into corruption. You assume that when you sleep with someone, you gain these obligations that override other intellectual perceptions. I wouldn't describe it that way. If you're asked to compare your beloved's talent to that of three others in a contest, you'll get disillusioned pretty quickly. In the end, you may be in the best position of all to make the judgment or write a letter of recommendation.

V. Secular Pentecostalism

HITT: How is the campus changing? People in their late thirties and forties say 69 that for them, college was a time to try on new identities, be fitted with a radical idea or two, and experiment in many ways. Nowadays, this line of thinking goes, college is about upwardly adjusting one's résumé.

BOTSTEIN: Nostalgia. In the twenty-two years I've been involved with col- 70 leges, there hasn't been any appreciable change in idealism. It's the fraudulent nostalgia of aging people who look back on their college youth and say, "When I went to college . . . ." Nonsense, wrong.

What *has* changed is the sense of informality in the American university. 71 What's been lost is the sense of comfort people had with an informal relationship between students and faculty. And this involves taking a drink, smoking, and all forms of informality that might result in an accusation of "I have been victimized." So you restrict your behavior until it's "beyond reproach," and what you've lost—

KERRIGAN: Are the rough edges of human beings. 72

BOTSTEIN: Remember *Chariots of Fire?* It may have been a bit romanticized, 73 but it showed an Oxford common room where professors offered undergraduates sherry. That's against the law today. Not possible. Forbidden. A certain sensibility has driven out conviviality.

BLYTHE: Where I'm from, we call it Pentecostalism—a desire to have the 74 truth set in stone, Moses-style. This sensibility yearns for sound doctrine that doesn't change, is expressed in absolutes, and against which is set a tasty array of penalties. Pentecostalism has an element of the fascist to it.

BOTSTEIN: I agree.   75

BLYTHE: Pentecostalism is pyramidal, hierarchical, and looks to a father figure   76
to tell us what to do. It has no sense of history. Pentecostalism shuns ambiguity and distrusts any statement that can't be fashioned into a simple certainty. On the most practical level, take course evaluations: Once upon a time, students were asked, "What did you get out of this course?" Today they are asked, on a standardized sheet, "How effective is the instructor?" with the options—"Excellent?" "Good?" "Average?" "Below Average?" "Poor?"—in bubbles to be blackened in with a No. 2 lead pencil.

BOTSTEIN: In my experience, a recurrent complaint among students is that   77
they had hoped for more informality with professors. Instead, campus life seems more impersonal, "cut and dried," if you will.

HITT: Is the loss of informality a matter of a new and increasingly heteroge-   78
neous population showing up on campus? In a way, American colleges have promoted diversity as a theory for generations, but only recently has true diversity finally arrived on campus. Maybe it has everyone nervous.

BOTSTEIN: I don't think it's that much more diverse.   79

BOSWELL: Maybe not. But the expression of that diversity is different. Calvin   80
Trillin's new book, *Remembering Denny,* is about how his generation repressed many of their differences to present a kind of homogeneity, which was achieved then at the price of many people pretending to be someone they were not. Today, that's no longer the case.

BOTSTEIN: This shift turns the idea of the traditional university inside out. In   81
the Middle Ages, the university sought to be a place that was immune from the severity of civil jurisdiction. There was to be a spirit of liberty and self-regulation—hence fraternities and other such developments. Now the rules the universities promulgate are more ferocious than those found in civil society. Consider the category of date rape.

KERRIGAN: Or offensive speech. The standards are comically higher.   82

HITT: Couldn't it be that these kids are begging for rules? Given the campus's   83
diversity—or the heightened expression of differences—could one assume that these kids are anxious and confused about what the common code of behavior is? So they cry out for rules, look to their smart professors for help, but find instead a bunch of liberals who get the willies around "rules."

BOSWELL: You're right, but our reply is, and rightly so, "Tough. We can't   84
make life simple for you. You must think for yourselves." Getting across this message has always been the university's ultimate mission.

BLYTHE: And look at what gets preserved by such rules—a desiccated sexual-   85
ity. Narrow and pinched, it assumes that sex is merely an act of physical engineering, some kind of biological insertion. Sexuality is not a simple act but the very air we breathe. People can have orgasms sitting in a class listening to a good lecturer. Why are we defining sexuality so narrowly? It's a university. The air is alive with sexuality without anyone touching. When these proponents of a student–professor sex ban talk about sexuality, they

mean only something harmful. They are not talking about desire, about
eros. Education is a kind of desire, the desire to learn. You cannot rein it in
with the blunt instrument of a policy manual.

VI. The Lyricism of a Pat on the Ass

HITT: Couldn't all this confusion on campus be an argument—a kind of con-   86
versation—among disparate groups as they struggle to create a new etiquette, a new common culture with simple table manners and dating rituals
for a complex mosaic of people?

BLYTHE: And the only common language among these groups is sexuality. It's   87
the only common language we have.

HITT: Then it makes sense that sexuality is the arena where such a conversa-   88
tion would take place, no?

BLYTHE: Precisely. Everyone's got a sexuality, and everyone's most fundamen-   89
tal identity is tied up with it. It's your history, your first history, and the
most interesting history. Each of us is a series of transformations related to
sexuality, whether it's ex-wives, boyfriends, girlfriends, husbands, or
charged glands in the library.

BOTSTEIN: That seems to be the least interesting history to me, frankly.   90

BLYTHE: We no longer have a religious common ground, a shared cultural   91
background.

HITT: Therefore, sexuality is the common crucible in which a new etiquette   92
for a more diverse culture is forged. Maybe the only thing we have in common, at long last, are our genitals.

BOTSTEIN: I'm getting very depressed.   93

KERRIGAN: You know, I recently had a serious philosophical debate with a   94
graduate student. Tell me, which is the truer expression of desire for a male
toward a female: writing her a sonnet or patting her on the ass?

BOTSTEIN: It depends on whether the person can write.   95

HITT: And, therefore, does it also depend on the quality of the ass?   96

BOTSTEIN: Actually, for me it would be a really committed performance in   97
music, without words. That would be the highest expression in this higher
range of discussion of sexuality. That's as close as I can get to the creative
power.

KERRIGAN: I ask the question because it reveals something about etiquette. A   98
pat on the ass in, say, a redneck bar is not decried as rape but fits into a
friendly culture that allows a man or a woman to say, "I like you. I want to
touch you." A pat on the ass nowadays is an interesting problem. One pat
and you're a lout; more than one, and you are Bob Packwood, hauled to the
stockades, buried in lawsuits.

BOTSTEIN: I find it all offensive. Call me a puritan. I think a pat on the ass is   99
offensive.

KERRIGAN: Really? There's something wrong about a hand and an ass coming   100
into contact?

BOTSTEIN: Without consent. There's the issue of consent.   101

KERRIGAN: *Without* consent. Imagine it.   102

BOTSTEIN: Without consent, it's offensive. I am not in favor of it.   103

BOSWELL: Baseball players can get away with this. But if you just did it to a   104
strange man on the subway, he'd punch you in the nose, and I think you'd
deserve it.

HITT: I guess I have trouble, too, William. A pat on the ass at the first meet- 105
ing? I don't know.

KERRIGAN: Fifth or sixth encounter?   106

HITT: Well, okay, probably.   107

KERRIGAN: See, following the track of this conversation, you wind up mak-   108
ing any pass at a woman into something offensive. Now, flirtation is a matter of etiquette, etc. But it's a wretched culture indeed that can't make
room for flirtation—some way for one soul to tell another, "I want to
touch you."

BOSWELL: Both of you may be right, in that Leon says that etiquette should be   109
observed because it is convention and William is saying that convention can
be changed with consideration for human feeling. And yet, William, even
though we can change the way we eat, that doesn't mean we can ask people
to throw food on the floor and have them gobble it down there.

VII. A Nostalgia for the Stockade

BOTSTEIN: It's interesting. I would argue that students through the 1960s ac- 110
cepted the idea that higher education was about trying on the clothes of
adulthood, so they eagerly accepted responsibility for their actions. If they
got involved with someone, if they got drunk, if they hurt someone, they
sought to take responsibility. Today's students believe they are not responsible; quite the opposite, they feel they are *owed* something—an entitlement
to a reward from distress. And when they are hurt, they are more prone to
call themselves "victims." Life, as the theologians have taught us for a long
time, is inherently victimizing. So when something goes wrong, a student
feels empowered to distribute the blame elsewhere. Let's say a relationship
between a student and professor goes sour, for whatever reason.

KERRIGAN: It's bound to.   111

BOTSTEIN: Rather than say, "This is my life, I take responsibility," the reac- 112
tion today is, "I have suffered, I wish to be entitled to some reparation."
And where the puritan character really comes out is in the desire for punishment, a public flogging of a presumed wrongdoer. The ban proponents
believe that punishment has a psychic benefit. They want to put the mal-
efactor in stockades and force him to feel the heat of public humiliation. So
the final message of higher education becomes not, as John said, "Life is
tough, unfair, tricky, difficult, complex; ergo, learn to take responsibility
and live with it," but "All problems in your life can be reduced to the task
of exacting redress."

BOSWELL: People don't have the attitude "Well, it's rotten, let's make it bet- 113
ter," but "I've suffered, so give me my fifteen minutes of fame."

BOTSTEIN: Or "I feel guilty about my participation in what went wrong. I   114
wish to displace my guilt by focusing on somebody who did it to me." It's
a disavowal of responsibility.

BLYTHE: We've spoken about the ill effect these bans have on students. But we   115
forget ourselves, the teachers. Education is also a transformation of us by
our students, allowing us to learn and be changed by the encounter of a
classroom. This ban is a prophylactic to that kind of fertility as well. It
erects a barrier because it presents me, the teacher, as rapacious, predatory,
and dangerous even before I walk into the classroom.

BOTSTEIN: But does it take a consummation of the sexual dimension to be   116
transformed?

BLYTHE: Of course not. But in setting up a law, you have immediately cast   117
me as a potential raptor. You are emphasizing my role not as educator but
as assailant. You define me in negative terms, stripping me of my ability to
teach.

BOTSTEIN: This is interesting. You're saying that by writing the law, you are   118
instantly identified as a potential predator?

BLYTHE: Yes. This discussion turns on one of the seven deadly sins—lust,   119
specifically between a professor and a student. According to Dante, it was
the least dangerous sin, closest to heaven and farthest from the pit of hell. If
we mean to ban medieval sins on the campus, we should reconsider sloth.
We hardly know what the word means anymore. Laziness, people say. But
sloth was far more invidious. It represented a kind of passivity that infected
the soul so that the sinner was crippled by a *refusal of joy*.

As professors, we all have in our minds an ancient ideal of education, a   120
joyful road of learning. This higher education deals with many of the horrors visited upon us as women and men, but then strives to reach beauty
and pronounce a more positive celebration of learning. The ban on student–
teacher relations is, finally, a broad attempt to poison the first adult experience for many young people—a complex, intimate, at times dangerous
relationship with a grown-up who's not mom or dad. The ban's proponents
refuse to recognize the broad spectrum of sexuality inherent on a campus;
they would impose on all of us a withered sexuality that, like Milton's Satan
in Paradise, is undelighted amid all delights.   ■

Questions for Meaning

1. According to John Boswell, what social factors explain demands for colleges to prohibit faculty–student dating?
2. On what grounds does William Kerrigan defend his sexual relations
   with students?
3. According to Joan Blythe, how might bans on faculty–student dating
   actually encourage such dating?
4. To what extent is the debate over faculty–student dating determined by
   social class and sexual orientation?

5. What does Blythe mean by "Pentecostalism"?
6. According to Botstein, how have students and campus life changed in recent years?
7. Vocabulary: prudery (6), conflate (16), internalize (19), penitential (21), subterfuges (24), adversarial (25), adjudications (25), protean (28), abetted (42), antipodal (55), partisan (61), conviviality (73), desiccated (85).

Questions about Strategy

1. Instead of drawing on the sources quoted here for a feature article, *Harper's* chose to publish the dialogue that occurred among them. What advantage is there to encountering ideas in this form? Is there any disadvantage?
2. Do any of these individuals sound more credible than others? If so, what led you to take some views more seriously than others?
3. Was it a good decision to exclude students from this conversation? How would the dialogue change if students had a voice within it?
4. Is it significant that this dialogue includes only one woman among four men? What is Blythe's role in this dialogue?

CAROL SIMPSON STERN

AVOIDING BAD POLICIES

Chairman of the performance studies department at Northwestern University, Carol Simpson Stern is a former president of the American Association of University Professors (AAUP). When she published the following article in *The Chronicle of Higher Education* in 1993, she emphasized that the opinions expressed within it are her own and not that of her university. As you read, consider why she would have found it necessary to make that distinction.

College administrators recently have been working aggressively to develop   1
guidelines for dealing with sexual harassment to insure a non-discriminatory, non-hostile educational environment. The new guidelines and codes are, in part, a response to evidence of a disturbing amount of sexual harassment on campuses. Colleges' concerns have intensified in the aftermath of the Supreme Court's ruling last year in *Franklin v. Gwinett County Public Schools,* which allows victims of intentional sexual harassment to sue for damages under Title IX of the Education Amendments of 1972.

The heightened consciousness of harassment is all to the good, but we   2
must be careful not to write bad policies or rely unduly on detailed regulations

authorizing sanctions against individuals as the means to cure our ills. Some recent campus guidelines reach beyond conduct in their efforts to protect women from harassment, putting at risk academic freedom and rights to privacy. For example, the wording of some codes designed to bar unwelcome sexist remarks could cause trouble for a faculty member who lectures on theories of racial or sexual inferiority.

The academic freedom to teach is chilled when professors are afraid to discuss topics related to sexuality lest they be accused of sexist attitudes or verbally seductive behavior. Freedom of inquiry and the right to discuss any ideas, no matter how hateful, are essential conditions of academic freedom. Probably the best way to end this society's sexism is not to stifle its expression but to stimulate discussion about it, answering bad speech with more speech.   3

I believe, as does the American Association of University Professors, that universities do not need separate codes or mechanisms to handle complaints of sexual harassment. Most institutions already have statements on ethics and on the responsibilities of faculty and staff members: adding specific statements about sexual harassment to already existing documents and procedures often is all that is needed. (If institutions do not have policy statements on unprofessional conduct that state that intimidation and harassment are inconsistent with academic freedom, whether the behavior is based on sex, race, religious, or political grounds, then they should develop such a statement.)   4

Besides their policies concerning ethics and professional behavior, institutions have grievance procedures and appeal bodies to judge allegations of misconduct. If administrators turned to these mechanisms rather than devising a new set of rules, often lamentably deficient in due process, we would be better off.   5

Sexual harassment is best addressed in the context of an institution's educational mission. When faculty and staff members are involved, harassment should be viewed as a question of professional ethics and responsibility. Meaningful discussion of these problems by faculty and staff members is long overdue.   6

Faculty members and other college employees of both sexes need to examine our cultural messages about sexuality and the status of women. They need to discuss what constitutes harassment, since people can hold vastly differing opinions about what that term means. Without wider faculty and staff involvement, it is unlikely that the actions of the courts alone or the promulgation of more guidelines proscribing conduct and verbal acts will bring the changes we need.   7

Let us look at some of the problems arising as a result of recent regulations.   8

The phrases "verbal and physical conduct of a sexual nature" and "hostile or offensive work environment," which are used in the Equal Employment Opportunity Commission's definition of sexual harassment, are dangerously vague and over-broad. Many academic policies have followed this language   9 without considering the pitfalls. It is all too obvious, for example, that such language has the potential to chill artistic expression. Many incidents already have been reported on campuses in which students or institutions have censored artistic expression, removing artworks or banning alleged pornography, in the name of protecting students from a "hostile" environment.

Institutions should restrict their definition of sexual harassment to conduct. The emphasis on verbal harassment that is present in most policies chills speech. It is true that it is often difficult to determine when someone has crossed the line between speech and conduct—when speech becomes conduct. However, recent court decisions striking down some university speech codes have demonstrated the dangers of attempting to proscribe speech, even of the most provocative kind. 10

Many of the outrageous incidents reported on campuses could have been handled under regulations that did not require college officials to punish speech. Ugly, sexually harassing statements often arise in situations where a faculty member or student is under the influence of either drink or drugs. This kind of conduct is already susceptible to discipline under existing standards of professional behavior or under regulations governing student life. Faculty members under the influence of drugs or drink can be punished without reaching to the content of their speech. Harassment, whether sexual, political, or personal, is a form of misconduct and should be treated as such. 11

Educators also should not encourage the idea that the mere fact that someone "feels" harassed means that they have *been* harassed. Such fuzzy thought stifles effective teaching. Some students have interpreted discussion of homosexuality as a kind of "cruising" behavior or a discussion of the erotic as a Don Juan behavior, in each case concluding that it constituted harassment. If teachers have to worry about whether a vulnerable student might misinterpret a discussion of race or sexuality, their speech will be chilled and they will be likely to lose perspective, treating students not as equals but as children. 12

It also is very important to differentiate between physical contact and sexual contact when determining whether conduct is wrongful harassment. This is particularly important in fine-arts disciplines such as dance, voice, and theater, in which the body is the instrument. It may be impossible for faculty members to teach certain techniques without touching their students. Teachers of voice often press on a student's diaphragm in order to demonstrate diaphragmatic breathing: a teacher of dance may place the student's leg or body in a particular position, to give the student the bodily feel of the correct alignment. Acting teachers and directors may touch performers as they move them about the stage to get the proper visual image. 13

Most of us are aware of how easily certain kinds of behavior can be misconstrued as harassment, with dire consequences for the accused. Some cases that have resulted in the dismissal of faculty members have been built upon such "wrongful" behaviors as hugging a student in a recital hall after a performance when other teachers and students are also offering congratulatory 14 hugs: touching a student in the midriff area during a vocal lesson: being too familiar when directing an acting scene.

Contrary to what many books on harassment say, it is important to un-   15
derstand the intention behind an act in order to determine whether it is appropriate or inappropriate. Recent studies on harassment contend that we need not inquire into the intention behind an act, but this has very dangerous implications. If a faculty member hugs a student who is weeping about a grade and the gesture is meant to be comforting, not harassing, surely the teacher's motive matters to an interpretation of the act.

Another worry stemming from the zeal for regulation is the adverse im-   16
pact that sexual-harassment codes may be having upon homosexuals. Although empirical studies have suggested that only 5 percent of sexual-harassment cases involve homosexuals, gay-rights activists and other faculty members and administrators believe that homosexual professors accused of harassment are dismissed or asked to resign far more often than male harassers in heterosexual encounters.

Homosexuals are far less able than women to get a fair hearing from   17
their peers or in court. Homophobia, like sexism, is deeply rooted in our society. Many members of gay and lesbian academic caucuses are skeptical that gay faculty members accused of harassment can get a fair hearing in the current climate.

Yet another set of difficulties arises when campuses adopt codes that ex-   18
tend the reach of sexual harassment to include consensual romantic or sexual relationships between faculty members and students. These codes either warn professors that they will be held accountable if a complaint arises or they explicitly ban such relationships. Such policies imply that it is not possible to have a consensual relationship within a context of unequal power.

Faculty members at several universities have rejected attempts to bar   19
consensual romantic relationships between faculty members and students, arguing that such relationships are private and that barring them is overly intrusive and may violate people's rights of association and of privacy. Some feminists balk at the idea that consenting woman students should be barred from entering into romantic or sexual relationships with their professors.

However, romantic relationships between faculty members and students   20
have been known to lead to some of the worst abuses of students. A professor who is sexually involved with a student is not sufficiently disinterested to be able to make fair judgments about grades, assistantships, and academic or financial awards. When the romantic attachment goes awry, the student often feels that she or he has been treated unfairly and may leave the discipline or the institution.

Faculty members need to hold themselves to a high professional standard   21
and avoid such intimacy, not because of Puritan ideas about sexuality or because their student consensual partner is subordinate to them in power, but because the relationship poses a professional conflict of interest, making it difficult, if not impossible, to carry out their role as educators.

Whatever kind of policy or code a campus decides to use, given the very pri-   22
vate nature of sexual harassment, it is essential that the due-process rights of
both the complainant and the faculty or staff member be protected when a
complaint is made. Sometimes these cases are managed in total disregard of
due process and fairness; complainants may be provided with an advocate
while the accused faculty member is denied either an academic adviser or
legal counsel.

Charges of sexual harassment are frequently cloaked in secrecy; many ac-   23
cusers are promised confidentiality. Cases may be handled quietly in a dean's
or provost's office, resulting in a forced resignation or dismissal. The accused
fear publicity and tend to distrust the peer-review system. Some cases are
taken up by faculty unions and heard by arbitrators, but, in too many instances, dismissals come swiftly and silently. Whether they are deserved is
never tested.

Colleges and universities face many difficulties in trying to balance the   24
need to rid higher education of sexual harassment while preserving the fundamental mission of the academy—to educate and do research. Most faculty
members have been slow to take these issues seriously, but administrators cannot carry on this task alone. It is time to encourage robust discussion of sexual
harassment so that broadly representative campus groups can formulate effective rules and procedures to root out the behaviors that most reasonable persons—women and men—would agree are inappropriate.   ■

Questions for Meaning

1. What is the significance of the Supreme Court decision in *Franklin v. Gwinett County Public Schools?*
2. According to Stern, why are special codes for sexual harassment unnec-essary at most colleges and universities?
3. What does "academic freedom" mean, and how can badly written codes have a detrimental effect on it?
4. Why does Stern believe that homosexual faculty might be victimized by sexual-harassment codes?
5. To what extent is "intention" relevant in determining whether physical contact is equivalent to sexual contact?
6. Vocabulary: lamentably (5), promulgation (7), proscribing (7), dire (14), disinterested (20).

Questions about Strategy

1. In paragraph 4, Stern reveals that her position is supported by the American Association of University Professors, but she reports this in-formation within a nonrestrictive phrase. What does she achieve by subordinating this information rather than highlighting it?

2. Where in her argument does Stern reveal that she is concerned about students who have been abused? Where does she express concern for the rights of faculty? How successfully does she balance these concerns?
3. Stern opens and concludes her essay with a call for open discussion. Judging from the tone of this piece, would you trust her to moderate such a discussion?
4. Would your response to this argument differ if you were told that it had been written by a man?

MARY CRYSTAL CAGE

GAY BASHING ON CAMPUS

Much of the discussion of sexual harassment focuses on women being harassed by heterosexual men. As Mary Crystal Cage points out in the following article, there is another form of sexual harassment on campus today. Gay and lesbian students are being harassed by students and faculty who fear or hate homosexuality. Cage is a staff writer for *The Chronicle of Higher Education,* which published this article in 1993. It was originally published under the newspaper heading "Openly Gay Students Face Harassment and Physical Assaults on Some Campuses."

Libby Smith knows what it is like to be a victim of gay bashing. First, there   1
were the harassing telephone calls to her home. Then, one evening last March as she went to get her book bag out of a locker at the University of Wisconsin at Eau Claire, she was attacked by two men.

They called her a dyke, kicked and punched her in the stomach, and ran   2
after they heard a loud *pop* when her shoulder dislocated. They were never apprehended.

The university responded by having a teach-in. Students passed out hun-   3
dreds of buttons that said "Respect Differences." But Ms. Smith, who is now a junior, was neither Eau Claire's first victim of gay bashing in 1992, nor the last.

Says Sharon Knopp, faculty adviser to the gay-student association at Eau   4
Claire: "Since the group has become so public, there is a certain amount of risk. I think the incidents were a backlash to the growing visibility. This community is used to its gays' staying in the closet."

The tense climate for gay students is not unique to Eau Claire. Across   5
the country, openly gay students are facing a backlash from fellow students who maintain that homosexuality is legally or morally wrong.

A survey of 213,000 incoming freshmen last fall by the Higher Educa-   6
tion Research Institute at the University of California at Los Angeles found that about 38 per cent of all students surveyed, and 49 per cent of the men, said they believed there should be laws prohibiting homosexuality.

Seniors generally are more accepting than freshmen, the UCLA re-   7
searchers found. Even so, a substantial block of seniors also say homosexuality
is wrong. In a follow-up study on 1987 freshmen, "The American College
Student, 1991," the UCLA researchers reported that in 1987, 60 per cent of
the male freshmen had said there should be laws prohibiting homosexuality.
Four years later, only 33 per cent of them still supported such laws.

Financing Blocked

Most students keep their views on homosexuality to themselves. On more and   8
more campuses, however, students who oppose gay rights are becoming vocal,
demonstrating their opposition by blocking student-government financing,
harassing campus gay-rights activists, and—in some cases—physically assaulting students whose sexual orientation they do not accept. In the past year:

- The Student Government Association at the University of Alabama
  cut the appropriation for the Alabama Gay/Lesbian Alliance by one-
  third—leaving an amount equal to the alliance's 1991-92 telephone
  bill. The money was restored by the university's Student Life Committee.

- *The Stanford Daily* reported that a student who was thought to be gay
  by residents of his dorm had been harassed. On several occasions, his
  belongings—including his shoes and research materials—were thrown
  from a third-story balcony of his men-only dormitory.

- Harassing telephone calls have become almost routine for the officers
  of the Lesbian, Gay, Bisexual Alliance at the University of Oregon,
  who recently asked the university to expel a student who was arrested
  in connection with a gay-bashing incident.

- A student at Eastern Washington University has filed a complaint
  with the Associated Students' court challenging a decision by the Student Union Board of Control to give office space to the campus Gay-
  Lesbian Alliance.

Students who oppose gay rights offer a variety of reasons for their stand.   9
Student-government leaders at the University of Alabama, for example, cited
an opinion by the state's Attorney General that public buildings and money
could not be used to support a group that promotes sodomy. Sodomy is a
crime in Alabama.

Students at Ohio Northern University cited the Bible in a campaign to   10
persuade student-government officers to vote against giving recognition to a
gay-student group.

David Helsley, president of Sigma Theta Epsilon at Ohio Northern, says: 11
"We don't believe a group like this is appropriate for a United Methodist-
affiliated college. I think a majority of the students share our reservations
about homosexuality."

Ultimately, the fraternity's view prevailed. The Student Senate last   12
month rejected the gay group's request for recognition by a vote of 15 to 9.

Fighting "Rumor and Innuendo"

Derrick B. Strobl, vice-president of the Ohio Northern Student Senate, is a   13
member of the Gay, Lesbian, Bisexual Alliance. He says that education is the
key to improving the campus climate for gay students.

"Most students here are from rural Ohio. About the only information   14
they have on the issue is from rumor, innuendo, and people like Pat Robertson," he says.

Although Mr. Helsley says he and his fraternity brothers opposed recog-   15
nizing the gay alliance because of their religious convictions, Mr. Strobl doubts
that the student body as a whole opposed recognition because of moral or religious concerns. "That vote was about prejudice. You couldn't convince me
that this is really a religious issue," he says. "If they told students that they had
to stop smoking, drinking, and having premarital sex, they would have been
laughed off the campus."

Even amid what some gay-rights leaders fear is a backlash on campuses,   16
administrators at many institutions are trying to improve the climate for gay
students. A handful of institutions, including Stanford University and the Universities of Oregon and Pennsylvania, have assigned student-affairs personnel
specifically to work with them.

Troy Gilbert, who coordinates programs for gay students at Stanford,   17
says the university has made great strides in improving services for them. But,
he says, some areas still need to be addressed—among them, housing. "We've
had self-proclaimed heterosexual students who said they didn't want to share a
room with a gay student," he says.

At Cornell University, gay students and their supporters are fighting for   18
the establishment of a Gay/Lesbian, Bisexual Living-Learning Unit. In December the Cornell Student Assembly proposed setting aside a dormitory floor
that would have rooms for about 50 gay students.

"Major Concerns" at Cornell

The plan will not become a reality unless the university administration ap-   19
proves. Frank H. T. Rhodes, president of Cornell, says he has several concerns
about the plan, including the suggestion from its backers that university approval would "assist in celebrating and promoting gay, lesbian, and bisexual
awareness."

In a letter to the president of the Student Assembly, Mr. Rhodes said: 20
"There are major concerns with the university 'promoting' any particular belief, preference, conviction or life-style." Furthermore, he is concerned that
establishing a gay dormitory would "provide a target for antagonism."

Rather than reject the idea outright, Mr. Rhodes asked student leaders to   21
reconsider the issues he outlined and to seek more student opinions. In response, the Student Assembly held a public forum and conducted a poll, the
results of which are due to be released this week.

Joseph L. Barrios, the lesbian/gay/bisexual representative in Cornell's   22
Student Assembly, is optimistic about the outcome. But he says that gay students are concerned about the president's response, for several reasons. For one
thing, he says, "They're concerned that it calls for allowing a majority of the
students to make a decision about housing for a minority group."

In addition, he says that when theme houses were established for black   23
students and others, "the administration didn't turn to students and say let's
have more discussion about it. They simply instituted it."

As for the president's concerns about violence, Mr. Barrios says: "That   24
is a reality that gay students face every day. Visibility is essential to our enterprise."

Trying to Avoid Political Stance

On some campuses, such as the University of Idaho, many of the gay students   25
remain in the closet. The Gay, Lesbian, and Bisexual Association, for example,
did not challenge a newly elected student-government president who ousted a
fellow officer he thought was gay. The officer had supported financing for the
gay association.

"Our group didn't respond because we didn't want to become political.   26
We're here to provide information to students about coming out," says Eric,
the association's president.

Eric, who asked that his last name not be published, says: "The campus is   27
slowly becoming more accepting. We're starting to go around and speak to
student clubs and the residence advisers." But Eric and other members of the
club are still afraid of how others—particularly their current and future employers—will respond to their homosexuality.

"I don't think there's that much more fear about being out here than   28
there would be at a Vanderbilt or a Purdue," says Betty Thomas, the association's faculty adviser. "Gay bashing is on the increase, and the economy is certainly not in the shape it was in 1983. If it is a flourishing economy, you don't
worry as much about being fired if you come out of the closet."

Jackie Balzer, coordinator of education and support services for gay stu-   29
dents at the University of Oregon, says the climate for gay students on her
campus is mixed. "Although I think there's increased acceptance, there are still
those out there who do not accept it," she says.

To a certain extent, the situation in Oregon is unique. Last year the Or-   30
egon Citizens Alliance led a campaign to amend the state constitution to prohibit public agencies—including colleges and universities—from using state
tax dollars "to promote, encourage, or facilitate homosexuality, pedophilia,
sadism, or masochism."

"An Atmosphere of Hate"

Although the measure was defeated, 43 per cent of Oregon's voters backed it.   31
Says Ms. Balzer: "The OCA has created an atmosphere of hate. Incidents of
violence are up. More and more of our students are being fed myths."

In such a political environment, say Oregon officials, trying to improve   32
the campus climate for gay students at the university is a challenge.

"This is a group that people will hate without knowing them," says   33
Gerald F. Moseley, vice-provost for academic planning and student services at
the University of Oregon. "We want to address it immediately. But it will take
time."

Even before the anti-gay measure was placed on the ballot, gay students   34
at the University of Oregon were harassed. In 1989 two student-government
candidates, one of whom was gay, received death threats.

In response, the university president, Myles Brand, established a commit-   35
tee in 1989 on gay concerns. The committee surveyed students, as well as faculty and staff members, about the campus climate for gay people. "Most of us
thought the campus was a safe place," Mr. Moseley says. "But the people who
were affected didn't think so."

Of the 105 gay, lesbian, or bisexual students who responded to the sur-   36
vey, 61 per cent said that anti-gay harassment on the campus was prevalent
enough that they feared for their safety, and 54 per cent said they had been
harassed or threatened.

In the two years since that report was released, says Troy Shields, co-   37
director of the Lesbian Gay Bisexual Alliance, "There has been a lot of effort
to improve the climate for gay students." Ms. Balzer's position was created, a
speakers bureau on gay issues was established, and now self-defense training is
being provided for gay students.

President's Support Is Key

Mr. Brand says that improving the campus climate for gay students should not   38
be viewed as a problem: "It's an issue of creating a campus community that is
tolerant. I think it's important to be very public and clear."

Lee Morris, president of the Alabama Gay Lesbian Alliance, says that   39
having the support of the university president is the key to creating a positive
campus climate. "The administration is without doubt uncompromising in its
commitment to diversity," he says. "I can't guarantee that someone who is gay
won't be called 'faggot' or 'dyke' or something like that, but we do have a very
strong administrative framework to deal with an incident like that."

Last year, for instance, a teaching assistant used a homophobic example   40
in an economics class and within 36 hours was called into the dean's office,
Mr. Morris reports. In another case, he says, a gay student was being harassed
by callers. The university put a monitoring device on his telephone and
traced the call. The caller was "disciplined just short of expulsion," Mr.
Morris says.

More than that, he says, the alliance, which is about 12 years old, is part   41
of the university's student-governance structure. Mr. Morris serves on the
president's advisory council, the student center's planning board, and the
Council of Presidents, which is temporarily serving as the university's student
government.

"That's really what Alabama has done that is so unique. Instead of leav-   42
ing gays and lesbians outside the door, we're part of the structure," he says.
"That's really how the tolerance and acceptance process begins."   ∎

Questions for Meaning

1. What factors explain harassment of gay and lesbian students?
2. According to paragraph 7, "Seniors generally are more accepting than
   freshmen . . . ." What could account for the difference in attitude?
3. Is there any reason to believe that men and women view homosexuality
   differently?
4. What are the arguments for and against establishing gay or lesbian dormitories?
5. How can greater tolerance and acceptance be fostered on campus?

Questions about Strategy

1. Cage opens her article with an example of harassment directed against a
   woman. Is this example effective? Would you respond the same to the
   example if the student were male?
2. Paragraph 8 is devoted to a series of examples. What does the author
   achieve by listing four different incidents?
3. Consider the reasoning in paragraph 15. How convincing is Strobl's response to opposition based on religious convictions?
4. Consider the language of the amendment proposed by the Oregon Citizens Alliance (quoted in paragraph 30). How do you think gay or lesbian citizens would respond to it? What does Cage accomplish by using
   this quotation?

PETER HELLMAN

CRYING RAPE: THE POLITICS OF
DATE RAPE ON CAMPUS

Rape is more than "harassment." It is a crime of violence. But as colleges respond to growing concern over sexual harassment, they must also consider how to respond to rape on campus. Cases of "date rape"—or rape that occurs between two people who have gone out together to do something socially—trouble both the victims and the institutions that want to design policies that will help prevent violence and define how violators will be treated. In "Crying Rape," first published in 1993 by *New York* magazine, Peter Hellman examines how Columbia University has responded to "a major campus issue of the nineties." As you read it, consider how fair-minded the author seems to be.

Olivia, a Columbia College senior with an Orthodox Jewish upbringing, re-   1
members that as her classmate David date-raped her in her dorm room on a
Sabbath evening, she looked up at him and felt "like a piece of meat hung on
a hook in a stall." After strolling back to her dorm following a campus religious service, they'd been necking on her bed—but Olivia, a virgin, had no
inkling that David would do what he did. His knitted skullcap remained on
his head, fixed by a bobby pin, the whole time. Olivia washed the blood-
stained bed sheets the next day and never reported the rape. A year and a half
later, she is still obsessive about what happened that evening.[1]

In February 1992, four months after Olivia's date rape, Columbia Uni-   2
versity joined dozens of other colleges across the country by establishing a
rape-crisis center—a facility where victims can find safety, sympathy, and re-
ferrals from peer counselors. It's just because of cases like Olivia's, its advocates
claim, that the center is needed—to augment services provided by the respected rape-crisis center of St. Luke's-Roosevelt Hospital, now 15 years old,
which is right across the street. On campus, psychologists and doctors at the
student-health service also stand ready to treat victims of sexual assault. Still,
to call the new Rape Crisis Center redundant would be missing the point.
Sexual assault—mainly date rape and acquaintance rape—is a major campus
issue of the nineties.

But there are growing questions about how real the campus rape threat is and   3
how much of the controversy is fueled not so much by psychosexual concerns
as by political ones. Camille Paglia, the warrior-polemicist who feasts on orthodox feminism, says the whole issue has, incorrectly, "swelled into a
catastrophic, cosmic event, like an asteroid threatening the earth in a fifties
science-fiction film." Even a sophisticated urban university like Columbia can

---

[1]The names in this incident have been changed. [Hellman's note]

get swept away. In a master's thesis that became a *Playboy* article, Stephanie Gutmann, who graduated from Columbia's Graduate School of Journalism in 1990, described the campus dating atmosphere as "Salem Revisited"—albeit with students accused of rape instead of witchcraft. Still, Judy Yu, a Barnard student, wrote in the *Columbia Daily Spectator* last year, "We are raped on this campus every day," and Andrew Stettner, a Columbia College sophomore, says, "Rape and sexual assault are a primary problem on this campus." A Columbia creative-writing professor says, "My students reveal cases of date rape in their assignments all the time—things they're afraid to report to deans or doctors."

Is the problem really that pervasive? Or is a genuine case of date rape like Olivia's the exception rather than the rule? Last October, Barnard College released crime statistics showing not one rape reported by its 2,200 students during the previous year. Columbia, with its 19,300 students, reported two rape claims in the same period—neither of which, upon investigation, proved sustainable. Both cases, according to campus security chief Dominick Moro, involved drinking. In one, the victim reported she had been only "pushed to her bed" by her date. In the other, two women accompanied several men students back to a fraternity house after a night of bar-hopping. The woman who brought the charge claimed she'd repelled her would-be attacker by pretending that she was about to vomit. 4

On an urban campus with its fair share of violent crime at the gates, the lack of a single prosecutable rape in a year seemed like a cause for celebration. But many declared themselves outraged. It was just one more example, they said, of the social, psychological, and legal factors that make rape one of the most underreported crimes. 5

The best-known report on the subject of campus rape, the *Ms.*-magazine "Project on Campus Sexual Assault," published in 1985, includes responses from 6,159 men and women from around the country who answered a questionnaire. Among the striking findings: that more than one in four college-aged women had been the victim of rape or attempted rape. Forty-two percent of the victims told no one. Seventy-three percent of the men and 55 percent of the women had used alcohol or drugs prior to the assault. It's a grim picture that the survey presents—perhaps grimmer than need be. The central finding of the study—that one in four students is a victim of rape or attempted rape—is problematic, according to Dr. Richard Gelles, a University of Rhode Island sociologist. "Seventy-three percent of the respondents who were classified [by the researchers] as having been raped based on their answers to the questionnaire," says Gelles, "didn't classify themselves as victims of rape." He compares the "ambiguity" in the situation to the spanking of a child. When does that act become abuse? That ambiguity could explain one of the more curious findings of the study . . . that 42 percent of the "victims" said they had sex with their attacker again. 6

Columbia isn't alone in its dearth of reported rapes. Crime reports from 2,400 campuses across the country, newly mandated by a federal law called the Student Right-to-Know and Campus Security Act of 1990, show fewer than 7

1,000 rapes for the year reported—less than half a rape per campus. Specialists who work in the field argue that the figures are low because no crime is harder to summon the courage to report.

"It can set you up to be re-victimized," says Dr. Rachel Efron, a sexual-assault specialist with Columbia's counseling service as well as adviser to the Rape Crisis Center. "It leaves you open to all the old myths about rape—that you encouraged it, that you dressed provocatively, that somehow you must have lured the guy on. Often when people report sexual assault, they feel dirty and humiliated." According to a report by the National Victim Center, in the population at large, 84 percent of rapes go unreported.   8

At Columbia, the debate over sexual assault has engulfed the Rape Crisis Center itself. A new campus group calling itself the Rape Crisis Center Coalition, ostensibly created to push for more staff and longer hours at the Rape Crisis Center, found itself instead at unexpected odds with the center's staff, which did not wish to be politicized. The center has also been beset by staff turnover. Both its supervisor and assistant supervisor quit at the beginning of the fall term.   9

The campus sex wars are sure to intensify next month when the militant feminist group Take Back the Night, chapters of which now seem nearly as common at colleges as football teams, conducts its sixth annual march and all-night speak-out. Last year, more than 600 chanting women marched from the campus to fraternity row along Riverside Park. Then, joined by male supporters who had been forbidden to march with them, they gathered in front of an open microphone on the Barnard lawn, where, one after another, women told their personnel stories of sexual assault.   10

While the public disclosure of personal suffering may be cathartic for the speakers, to the unconverted it can seem more like an exercise in "can you top this" victimhood. At last year's speak-out, according to a report in the *Manhattan Spirit,* a lively local newspaper, one woman told in "a desperate, hollow voice" how, since the age of 11, "I counted the times I had a penis in me that I haven't wanted and I had to stop at 594." The question arises, How did she keep such a precise count? Told of this case, sex researcher Dr. Pepper Schwartz, a sociologist who is president of the National Society for the Scientific Study of Sex, scoffed, "What was she, a professional?"   11

It's not that Schwartz is unsympathetic to the deep and enduring damage that sexual assault can do. She just feels that "it infantilizes a woman to say she doesn't know her own mind. If you're murmuring, 'Oh, I don't think so,' that's a gray area," Schwartz explains. "But you don't get to call it rape when you did something you didn't really want to do but didn't protest it. The next step is that psychologists help them to create identities around these situations. It becomes 'Hi, I'm a survivor.'" Christina Sommers, currently writing an irreverent account of feminism, accuses the date-rape militants of "criminalizing collegial male lust." "I can't understand how feminism has led us down this path—this hysteria around intimacy," she says. "I object to redefining date rape to include behavior that most people don't think of as rape."   12

No testimony can be questioned amidst the high solemnity of the Take   13
Back the Night talkathon—even when a speaker seems to get carried away.
This proved to be the case at Princeton's 1991 Take Back the Night rally, according to Ruth Shalit's account in the libertarian magazine *Reason,* when a
senior told a crowd of 600 her "deepest, darkest secret" of how a "very drunk"
student had dragged her back to his room after a party and raped her while "he
shouted the most degrading obscenities imaginable." He also boasted that "my
father buys me cheap girls like you to use up and throw away." Afterward, as
she told it, he smashed her head against his metal bed frame until she lost consciousness. Then, like a grunting Ivy League caveman, he slung his victim
over his shoulder and carried her back to her dorm, "where he dropped me at
the bottom of my entryway."

After her recitation at Take Back the Night, the woman repeated the aw-   14
ful tale in an op-ed piece in the college newspaper, the *Princetonian.* Mingled
with victimhood, now, was a note of smug celebrityhood: "If you don't know
how to react next time you see me, give me a hug and tell me I'm very brave.
Because I, like the other campus rape victims at Take Back the Night, am very
brave and need your support." But holes in the woman's story quickly became
evident. Contrary to her claim, she had filed no complaint against the accused—whose name she'd whispered about campus. At the end of the
semester, in a startling about-face, the woman wrote another op-ed piece, this
one admitting that her story about had been a hoax. "I have, in fact," she said,
"never met this person or spoken to him."

The Barnard campus in November 1991 had its own version of colle-   15
giate "Rapegate." In this episode, a male guest of a Barnard student at Plimp-
ton Hall claimed he had been sodomized by a Columbia student who'd entered
the dormitory elevator with him. Instead of going up, they'd gone down to
the basement, where the crime had allegedly occurred. There was an immediate student protest, and the protesters, rather than venting their anger on the
supposed assailant, put the blame on "security," even though both men had
been properly checked into the dorm. "Now I'm f---ing pissed off, pissed off
at security," Andrew Ingall, a Columbia college senior and a member of the
campus Lesbian Bisexual and Gay Coalition (LBGC), told the campus newspaper, the *Spectator.* Furthermore, Ingall said, campus cops were "living in the
dark ages," from which "they need to wake up and change." (An off-duty
contract security guard had, in fact, raped a Columbia student in 1990.)

Ingall also co-signed a letter of outrage to the *Spectator* from the LBGC   16
that took pains to point out that the sodomizer's "sexual orientation is unknown" and that one "should not assume that he was homosexual, as most
male rapes are committed by heterosexual men." That let the LBGC's own
members off the hook. But there was silence when, a few days later, the
"victim" dropped all charges and admitted that the act of sodomy had been
consensual.

That admission was derided by a group of Take Back the Night members   17
at their regular Wednesday-night meeting, a few weeks ago. "He had to back
down because the other guy had more lawyers," said one of the women at the

meeting. Some members of Take Back the Night insist that nobody should ever back down from a claim of sexual assault—even if confused circumstances become clarified after a few days, "It's extremely dangerous to do that," said one member, a Barnard senior, "because it's so easy." Another woman said, "Women are always doubted, so they mustn't back down."

In the past, women who said no to sex, particularly a weak no, were of-   18 ten presumed to really mean yes. It was sometimes an element of seduction. Now militants make it clear that "yes means yes, and no means no." But aren't there occasions when two people slide into sex without a yes or a no? Is it right to add the "no"—and with it an accusation of rape—days, weeks, or some- times years later?

"If a woman says she's been sexually assaulted," the women of Take Back   19 the Night say, "then she has been."

What if drinking has muddled things?   20

"If a woman has been drinking, then she cannot give consent to having   21 sex," said a member of Take Back the Night. Which means, de facto, she can claim to have been raped.

"Anyway, we don't talk here about objective, legalistic rape."   22

To prove rape, Susan Estrich writes in her book *Real Rape,* women once   23 had to convince a judge and jury that they'd submitted to sex only after putting up "utmost resistance." Take Back the Night has now turned the ta- bles. Without "objective, legalistic" standards, a man has little chance of prov- ing he isn't a rapist. In a guerrilla technique pioneered at Brown University a few years ago and now used at other schools, including Columbia, the names of male students accused of being rapists are "stickered" or scrawled on cam- pus walls. No defense is possible, because the accusers never reveal themselves.

Plans for Columbia's Rape Crisis Center took shape in the summer of 1991. Its   24 founding mothers were Margie Metsch, the Sexual Assault Awareness Pro- grams coordinator at the health service, and Jane Bennett, an associate professor at Barnard's women's-studies program. The university, despite a reactionary reputation (remember its plan to cut a gym into Morningside Park?), was more than willing. "One of the important things about this center is its name," ex- plains Fred Catapano of the university administration. "The word *rape* was rarely heard on this campus. As an institution, we decided purposely to use it." And so that is its name, even though a bare minimum of the users of the center have been raped.

The center is located on the fifth floor of Butler Library—the univer-   25 sity's scholarly heart. It is divided into one large room, furnished sparsely with a desk and an old sofa, and two small interview rooms. Modeled on pioneering centers at the University of Michigan and Harvard, this one is staffed entirely by volunteer peer counselors, who are currently on hand from six to ten o'clock every evening except Mondays. Students also administer the center. That pleases Dr. Richard Carlson, director of health services. "I like student- run services," he says.

But Carlson wasn't pleased, during the Rape Crisis Center's first 26 semester of operation, that Margie Metsch was spending nearly all her time there instead of at the health-service job she'd been hired to do. "She was exhausted all the time," remembers Carlson. But not because the center was particularly busy. Unpublished figures, supplied by Carlson, show that during its first semester of operation, 79 people visited the center. Of those only about 10 percent, according to Carlson, were brought on by a recent case of sexual assault. Most concerned sexual assault in the past, including childhood incest and sexual molestation.

Last September, Metsch abruptly took a new job in the city school system. Jane Bennett, the center's assistant supervisor, who had always been on 27 hand in Metsch's absence, has apparently left the country. In the stead, Carlson hired Rachel Efron, who advises the center on a number of matters. Ten hours a week of her time is allotted to the training and supervision of peer counselors at the Rape Crisis Center. But that wasn't enough of a commitment from the university in the eyes of a group of campus activists, who formed the Rape Crisis Coalition last fall to demand "24-hour service and two full-time paid staff members" at the center. The coalition's rallying cry was "We need it forever. The university owes us."

As it happened, the peer counselors at the center decided they didn't need 28 or want the attentions of the coalition. That was partly because, as one counselor said, "We don't want people to think we're in a shambles and not come if they need us." But the main problem was that the peer counselors didn't want to see others politicize their work. As they wrote in a collective letter to the *Spectator,* "Feminist activism was necessary for the creation of the Rape Crisis Center, but the center cannot be a place for just feminists because rape is an issue for all women." Olivia, now a Columbia graduate student, also dismissed the coalition, saying, "I don't want what happened to me reduced to some kind of feminist ideology or a slogan on a signboard."

The dimensions of the rift between the two groups became apparent one 29 fall night as the coalition met to plan a rally on behalf of the Rape Crisis Center. Quietly but firmly, the lone peer counselor on hand told the coalition members that the Rape Crisis Center staff would not take part in the rally. Cindy Suchomel, a recent Barnard graduate who was chairwoman of the meeting, fought back tears.

"Why have I been working day and night on this event if you're not with 30 us?" she asked. "Why didn't you show up at our meetings until now?"

The coalition pushed ahead with plans for the rally, enlisting at least 30 31 campus organizations. But when the rally was finally held last November on the steps of Low Library, glaringly absent was anyone from the rally's "honoree," the Rape Crisis Center. And attendance was sparse. Few in the lunchtime crowd bothered to stop, causing a speaker named Kim Worobec, representing Take Back the Night, to lash out at them. "I am furious at all these people who are passing us by. They may know survivors; they may be survivors," she said.

Last month, Worobéc, on behalf of Take Back the Night, placed a large   32
blank book with marbleized covers in the library of Barnard's Center for Research on Women. It's meant to be a communal diary of sexual assault in
which students can write anonymously. So far, it remains blank.

The word *survivor* is normally invoked to identify people who make it   33
out of death camps like Auschwitz or who get through disasters like airplane
crashes, shipwrecks, fires, or volcanic eruptions. But on campus, *survivor,*
rather than *victim,* now denotes anyone claiming to have been sexually assaulted, even if the experience fell short of rape. The word *victim* is frowned
upon, since it does not convey the sense that the survivor of date rape might
well have been killed. For those who have so far escaped being survivors,
members of the coalition, at one of their winter meetings, used the term
"potential survivors."

While most survivors and potential survivors are women, men who have rela-   34
tionships with the survivor are now identified as "co-survivors." As defined
by Kathleen Kapila, a staff social worker at St. Luke's, a co-survivor is one who
is the boyfriend, or perhaps the sibling, of the survivor. Since the co-survivor
experiences feelings of helplessness and rage, just like the survivor's, he also can
be expected to need counseling, as Kapila explained at a seminar on co-
survivorship she gave in February. It featured an exercise in which members of
the audience each took a partner they didn't know. Kapila instructed each pair
to take turns telling a story of personal victimhood while the listener said
nothing. Unexpectedly, a few people seemed to have trouble thinking of an
appropriate example of being a victim.

Amidst the politicized furor over rape on campus, it's easy to lose sight of   35
the damage done by the reality of sexual assault. "The world is never the same
for the survivor," says Dr. Efron, the sexual-assault specialist. "She's especially
vulnerable because she's left home and is out there in the world for the first
time. And then this happens. It's so devastating, so traumatizing. How do you
ever trust anyone ever again? If somebody can stick his penis in you that way,
then he could do anything. If a person feels violated by being burglarized
when they're not even home, imagine what the impact of sexual violation
must feel like." Almost wistfully, she says, "If only we had good egalitarian
attitudes about sexuality. But in this culture, the subject is all f---ed up."

On a recent Saturday night, a shift of three peer counselors sat in the Rape   36
Crisis Center—one a backup to the other two. Because of the atmosphere the
rape controversy has generated, it was not hard to imagine that elsewhere on
campus, traditional romantic courtship rites of decades past had now been replaced by wary maneuverings more suited to opponents in a chess match. Out
in the dorms and fraternity houses, maybe even in remote corners of the stacks
in Butler Library, date rape could be one touch away, but here at the center, all
was peaceful, hour after hour. Nobody called; nobody came. As if in a fire-
house, the three women sat alertly and waited for disaster to strike. It was easy
to forget these were the fading hours of the eve of Valentine's Day. ■

Questions for Meaning

1. Why did Columbia create its Rape Crisis Center even though another center already existed across the street?
2. On what grounds has the statistic "one in four students is a victim of rape or attempted rape" been questioned?
3. Consider the incident reported in paragraph 15. Why do you think students blamed "security" rather than the assailant?
4. Why did the Rape Crisis Center staff refuse to participate in a rally organized on its behalf?
5. What is the distinction between "survivor" and "victim" in the rhetoric of rape?
6. Vocabulary: redundant (2), pervasive (4), dearth (7), beset (9), cathartic (11), infantilizes (12), ideology (28).

Questions about Strategy

1. At the beginning of this article, Hellman reports a specific example of date rape, but he changes the names of the students involved. Was this a good decision? What would be the probable consequences of revealing true identities in this case?
2. Consider the example in paragraph 11. Is it presented fairly?
3. In paragraph 14, Hellman describes how an example of date rape was proven to be fraudulent. Why is it useful to have an example like this? Is there any risk in using it?
4. Why does Hellman put the last sentence in paragraph 15 within parentheses?
5. Consider the conclusion of this article. Why does Hellman end with a reference to Valentine's Day?

ANNE B. FISHER

SEXUAL HARASSMENT: WHAT TO DO?

Sexual harassment is by no means confined to college campuses. The following article focuses on sexual harassment in the workplace. How should businesses respond?
Anne B. Fisher explores this and other questions in the following 1993 article from
Fortune magazine, a well-respected monthly business magazine. As you read, note
what Fisher reports about the law and how it is changing.

Tailhook. New rules on college campuses against romances between professors   1
and students. A controversial book that purports to tell the real story of Anita
Hill and Clarence Thomas. And of course that staple of late-night-TV jokes,
Senator Bob Packwood.* In the shift and glimmer of the media kaleidoscope,
sexual harassment is a constant glinting shard.

Yet no headline-making subject in recent memory has stirred so much   2
confusion. No doubt you've read your company's policy statement and, from
just under its surface, you feel the legal eagles' gimlet stare. But what does sexual harassment really mean? Managers of both sexes are sifting through the
past and fretting about next week. Was it all right to say I liked her dress? Is it
okay to ask him out to lunch to talk about that project? Should I just stop
touching anybody, even if it's only a congratulatory pat on the back? For that
big client meeting in Houston, wouldn't it be less risky to fly out with Frank
than with Francine? Or, for female managers, vice versa?

If you think you've got reason to worry, you probably don't; the ones   3
who do are usually unaware they have a problem. But right in your own organization, maybe even in your own department, your hallway, your pod,
somebody may be so befuddled and self-destructive as to miss the point entirely. Sexual harassment is not really about sex. It's about power—more to the
point, the abuse of power.

Imagine it this way. Suppose one of your most senior and valued people   4
has a little problem. Great producer, terrific salesperson, meets every goal, ex-
ceeds every guideline, but, well, there's this one glitch: He steals things. Every
time he leaves an office he takes something with him—a pen, a coffee mug, a
book, some change that was lying around. He's been at it a long time, can't
seem to help it and, anyway, he's a good guy, a *great* guy. You're his boss. What
are you going to do when he walks off with somebody's $3,000 notebook
computer? That's grand larceny, and the victim is hopping mad.

For more and more managers these days, the analogy fits. Let's suppose   5
the fellow isn't stealing material things but rather chipping away at the human dignity and professional self-respect of other people. Can't seem to resist

---

*Senator Bob Packwood of Oregon was accused of sexually harassing many of the women
who worked in his office. He was widely criticized by his colleagues.

patting fannies and whispering innuendoes. Told a subordinate he'd like to negotiate her raise at the local No-Tell Motel. Cornered a female colleague and
loudly compared her physical attributes with those of the current Playmate of
the Month. All the time he's producing great stuff. But the whispering behind
his back is getting louder; the troops are murmuring about calling the lawyers
and human resources people. What do you do with this guy? (Alas, despite a
much publicized $1 million jury award in May to a male plaintiff harassed by
his female boss in Los Angeles, harassers are, in nine cases out of ten, guys.)

Talk to him, of course. If that doesn't work, and odds are it won't, turn   6
him in to the human resources person in charge of these matters. And do it
pronto. Otherwise you could be liable along with your employer. Unsolicited,
unwelcome, and downright extortionate sexual demands are as illegal as stealing computers. So are purposeful and repeated efforts to intimidate colleagues
by transforming the office into a remake of *Animal House*—what the law calls
"hostile environment" harassment. He who steals my briefcase, to paraphrase
Shakespeare, steals trash. But the loss of someone's dignity, productivity, and
eagerness to come to work in the morning is a theft not only from the person
robbed of it, but from the company too.

Sexual harassment is not a compliment on anyone's wardrobe or a   7
friendly pat on the shoulder. It is not the occasional tasteless remark or careless
quip. It is not even asking someone for a date the second time, when she's already said no once. To stand up in court, a harassment charge must rest on
either a persistent and calculated pattern of antisocial behavior or a single quid
pro quo—"You'll never get anywhere in this company unless you sleep with
me"—that is so egregious as to leave no room for misinterpretation.

The courts have recognized sexual harassment as an offense under Title   8
VII since 1977. But the number of complaints filed with the Equal Employment Opportunity Commission has nearly doubled in the past five years, to
10,532 in 1992. It's debatable whether that rise occurred because instances of
harassment increased or whether events like the Hill–Thomas hearings encouraged people who had long remained silent to speak up. The EEOC
doesn't keep a record of how many cases end up in litigation; many are settled
on the courthouse steps. One thing is certain. The consequences for corporations are costly.

Research by Freada Klein Associates, a workplace-diversity consulting firm in   9
Cambridge, Massachusetts, shows that 90 percent of Fortune 500 companies
have dealt with sexual harassment complaints. More than a third have been
sued at least once, and about a quarter have been sued over and over again.
Klein estimates that the problem costs the average large corporation $6.7 mil-
lion a year.

Bettina Plevan, an attorney at Proskauer Rose Goetz & Mendelsohn in   10
New York City, specializes in defending companies against sexual harassment
lawsuits. She says employers spend an average of $200,000 on each complaint
that is investigated in-house and found to be valid, whether or not it ever gets
to court. Richard Hafets, a labor lawyer at Piper & Marbury in Baltimore,

believes sexual harassment could be tomorrow's asbestos, costing American business $1 billion in fees and damages in the next five years.

But the costs of sexual harassment go well beyond anything that can be   11
measured on a profit-and-loss statement. Women, often still treated like inter-lopers in the office, say they feel vulnerable to the myriad subtle—and not so subtle—sexual power trips some men use to keep them in their place. At an Aetna Life & Casualty golfing party last September, four executives vented their resentment of female managers' presence at what had traditionally been an all-male event. Their mildest offense—and the only one we're halfway willing to describe in a magazine your kids might see—was calling women executives "sluts." In response Aetna demoted two of the men and asked the two others to resign.

Jeannine Sandstrom, a senior vice president of the executive recruiting   12
firm Lee Hecht Harrison in Dallas, knows of instances where harassers were caught because they sent X-rated messages to their victims via voice mail or E-mail. Marvels Sandstrom: "How self-destructive do you have to be to do something like this, knowing how easy it is to trace?"

In most cases harassment is more subtle—and far more difficult to prove.   13
As agonizing as it may be, women have an obligation to speak up and tell someone who is hounding them to stop it. Although federal law defines sexual harassment as "unwelcome" behavior, the courts say it doesn't count as such unless the offender knows it's unwelcome. Yet a 1991 study by two professors at the University of St. Thomas in St. Paul, Minnesota, revealed that, among women in a nationwide survey who said they had been victims of sexual ha-rassment, only 34 percent told the harasser to knock it off; just 2 percent filed a formal complaint.

With the economy in its current shaky state, many women may be too   14
fearful of losing their jobs to speak up. Or they may be reluctant to be seen as whiners, either by their peers or by the people above them. But if a woman wants to file a grievance, it's important to be able to prove that she told the perpetrator to back off. Some experts suggest tape-recording the conversation or sending a registered letter (return receipt requested) detailing the offending behavior and declaring it not OK. This helps in any follow-up by human re-sources or legal staff, even in cases where witnesses or other direct proof of the harassment are available.

As for men, the majority of whom wouldn't dream of harassing anybody, they   15
are terrified of being falsely accused—with some reason. "What I'm seeing lately is that companies are overreacting, and accusers are believed on the basis of very little evidence or none at all," says Ellen Wagner, an attorney and au-thor who specializes in labor law. "And the ultimate punishment, termination, is a first resort rather than a last one."

Consider the case of Louis Kestenbaum. From 1977 to 1984, Kesten-   16
baum was vice president in charge of guest operations at a secluded ranch and spa that Pennzoil operated in northern New Mexico. In January 1984, some-one wrote an anonymous letter to Pennzoil's top management accusing

Kestenbaum of sexual harassment and other misdeeds. Kestenbaum denied the allegations but was fired anyway. He sued Pennzoil and won $500,000 in damages for wrongful discharge. The reason? Pennzoil's in-house investigator admitted in court that she had relied on rumor and innuendo in compiling the sexual-harassment report that got Kestenbaum the ax. "No attempt was made to evaluate the credibility of the persons interviewed," wrote the judge.

Both sexes sometimes feel they're stumbling around in a minefield, lost 17 in enemy territory without a helicopter. What makes the terrain so treacherous is that people have an inconvenient way of seeing the same behavior quite differently. Margaret Regan is a Towers Perrin partner who has conducted a senior-management training program called Respect at Work for dozens of corporations. She points out that some of what might look like sexual harassment is in reality an innocent error arising from past experience. "My favorite example is when we ask a group of men and women, "How many times is it all right to ask someone out after they've said no once?" says Regan. "In one class I led, one of the men said, 'Ten.' The women were appalled. They said, '*Ten times?* No way! Twice is enough!'"

It turned out, when he got a chance to explain his answer, that the of- 18 fending fellow had to ask 10 or 12 times before the girl of his dreams agreed to go to the senior prom with him in 1959. It worked out fine: They've been married for 32 years. "Naturally ten times seemed reasonable to him," says Regan. "So much of what people think about these things comes from stuff they grew up with—and just never had any reason to question."

Consultants who design sexual harassment workshops, and managers 19 who have attended them, agree on one thing: The best training gives participants a chance to talk to each other, instead of just listening to a lecture or watching a film. In classes where men and women are asked to compare their impressions of the same hypothetical situation, real revelations can occur.

Perhaps not surprisingly, Aetna has stepped up its training program since 20 the infamous golfing incident last fall. Anthony Guerriero, 34, a pension consultant at the company, took the course in January. He says, "The guys in the class were absolutely not resistant to it, not at all. In fact, it's a relief to have someone spell out exactly what sexual harassment is. The men in my session were all saying, 'It's about time.'"

Male managers aren't the only ones who benefit from the classes. 21 Women are sometimes startled to find how widely their perceptions differ from those of other women. Janet Kalas, 45, director of Medicare administration at Aetna, has 300 people reporting to her. "What startled me about the training was how tolerant I am," she says. In one group-discussion exercise, the instructor described an imaginary scenario in which a male and a female colleague, both married to others, are out of town on business. Late in the evening, they're still working on a client presentation for the next morning, and they decide to finish it in the female manager's hotel room. Recalls Kalas, "My reaction was, Well, that's practical. What's the big deal? But other people, men and women both, were saying, 'My gosh, don't do that, it's like an *invitation* to this guy.' I was surprised."

Towers Perrin recently queried executives at 600 major U.S. companies   22
and found that about half planned to increase the amount of sexual harassment
training they give managers and employees. A dozen or so big corporations
have already built shining reputations among consultants and researchers for
the quality, creativity, and overall earnestness of their training programs.
Among them: Du Pont, Federal Express, General Mills, Levi-Strauss, Merck,
and Syntex. But will they talk about what they're doing? Not a chance.
"Nobody likes to acknowledge that this problem even exists," says Robert
Steed, who runs a consulting firm in Westchester County, New York, that
specializes in sexual-harassment training. "It makes people queasy. So their
view is, the less said the better." Adds a public relations manager at a Fortune
500 company: "The general feeling is, what if we get written up somewhere as
having this terrific training program—and then we get sued a week later? In
other words, no comment."

For a company's policy to do any good, much less be taken seriously in a   23
courtroom, employees have to understand it. Barbara Spyridon Pope, the
Navy assistant secretary who almost single-handedly exposed the Tailhook
scandal, recently established a consulting firm in Washington, D.C., to advise
corporate clients on how to communicate their sexual-harassment guidelines
to the troops. Her surveys show that 60 percent to 90 percent of U.S. workers
know there is a policy but haven't the foggiest what it says. "Having a policy is
fine, but by itself it isn't enough," says Pope. "The Navy had a policy too."

Sitting people down to discuss their differences on this issue is more than a   24
therapeutic parlor game. Case law over the past decade has established that a
company with a well-defined anti-sexual-harassment stance can escape liability for hostile-environment harassment. No wonder, then, that you keep getting all those policy memos and invitations to sign up for workshops. But to
prevail in court, companies must also have clear procedures for handling complaints when they arise. Typically, employers choose an impartial ombudsperson, usually in the human resources department, to hear and investigate
charges before the lawyers get into the act. If the complaint seems legitimate,
the company must then take what the judge in a pivotal 1986 case, *Hunter* v.
Allis-Chalmers, called "immediate and appropriate action." Depending on the
circumstances, this might range from transferring the harassed or the harasser
to a different department, to docking the harasser a couple of weeks' pay, to
firing the guilty party outright.

This fall the Supreme Court will hear *Harris* v. *Forklift Systems,* its first   25
sexual harassment case since 1986. The suit was filed by Teresa Harris, who
left her job at a Nashville truck-leasing company after months of crude remarks and propositions from the firm's president. The matter was dismissed by
a federal judge in Tennessee and ended up in federal appeals court in Cincinnati, where the dismissal was upheld. Reason: Ms. Harris had not proven that
she was psychologically damaged by her boss's behavior.

If psychological damage becomes the new standard in harassment cases,   26
which is what the high court has agreed to decide, plaintiffs will have a far

harder time winning. Says Anne Clark, an attorney for the National Organization of Women: "You shouldn't have to suffer a nervous breakdown before you can make a claim." Lawyers who represent companies reply that a decision in favor of the psychological-damage standard would cut down on frivolous suits. To which working women are apt to say: "Frivolous? Nobody in her right mind would have her name dragged through the dirt over a frivolous charge!"

27   No matter how the court rules, managers and employees would do well to keep their own responsibilities in mind. For actual or potential harassers that means: Watch it, buster. For women, it means: Speak up. For their bosses, the best advice is: Get help. Says Susan Crawford, a partner at Holtzmann Wise & Shepard in Palo Alto, California: "I've found that managers too often are reluctant to refer a complaint to human resources. Instead they try to handle it themselves. But bosses need to see that this is a complicated issue with a lot of pitfalls, and it is not a sign of failure on their part to say, 'Hey, I need help with this. I'm not the expert here.'" The people in your company who really know where all the pitfalls are—and who will try to be fair to everybody—are not in your department. They are probably upstairs somewhere. Call them.

28   For all the seriousness of the issue, it would be a great pity if men and women got to the point of giving up on workplace friendships altogether—a point some men say privately they've already reached. Remember Rob, Buddy, and Sally on the old *Dick Van Dyke Show?* Okay, it was way back in the supposedly benighted early Sixties, but those three were a great professional team, and they were pals. For men and women in corporate America, there could be far worse role models. It will be a sad day, if it ever comes, when people are too nervous to ask a pal out for a drink.   ■

Questions for Meaning

1. According to Fisher, what is sexual harassment ultimately about?
2. What is the quotation from Shakespeare paraphrased in paragraph 6?
3. If a woman is being harassed by a man, why is it important that she make it clear to him that she finds his behavior objectionable?
4. What kind of training is most likely to help men and women avoid harassment in the workplace?
5. Why is it advantageous for companies to have clearly defined harassment policies?
6. Vocabulary: gimlet (2), innuendoes (5), extortionate (6), quip (7), egregious (7), interlopers (11), myriad (11), infamous (20), ombudsperson (24), pivotal (24), benighted (28).

Questions about Strategy

1. Consider the analogy in paragraph 4. Fisher states that it works for many managers. Does it work for you?
2. What is the implication of the statistics quoted in paragraph 13?
3. How reputable are the sources cited in this article?
4. How appropriate is the allusion in paragraph 28? Who is most likely to understand it? What does this allusion reveal about Fisher's sense of audience?

ELLEN FRANKEL PAUL

BARED BUTTOCKS AND FEDERAL CASES

What kinds of legal protection can people expect from behavior they find offensive? According to Ellen Frankel Paul, "A distinction must be restored between morally offensive behavior and behavior that causes serious harm." As you read her article, note the distinction that she makes. Paul teaches political science at Bowling Green State University. Her books include *Property Rights and Eminent Domain* (1987) and *Equality and Gender: The Comparable Worth Debate* (1988). The following article was first published in *Society* in 1991.

Women in American society are victims of sexual harassment in alarming pro-   1
portions. Sexual harassment is an inevitable corollary to class exploitation; as capitalists exploit workers, so do males in positions of authority exploit their female subordinates. Male professors, supervisors, and apartment managers in ever increasing numbers take advantage of the financial dependence and vulnerability of women to extract sexual concessions.

These are the assertions that commonly begin discussions of sexual ha-   2
rassment. For reasons that will be adumbrated below, dissent from the prevailing view is long overdue. Three recent episodes will serve to frame this disagreement.

Valerie Craig, an employee of Y & Y Snacks, Inc., joined several co-   3
workers and her supervisor for drinks after work one day in July of 1978. Her supervisor drove her home and proposed that they become more intimately acquainted. She refused his invitation for sexual relations, whereupon he said that he would "get even" with her. Ten days after the incident she was fired from her job. She soon filed a complaint of sexual harassment with the Equal Employment Opportunity Commission (EEOC), and the case wound its way through the courts. Craig prevailed, the company was held liable for damages, and she received back pay, reinstatement, and an order prohibiting Y & Y from taking reprisals against her in the future.

Carol Zabowicz, one of only two female forklift operators in a West   4
Bend Co. warehouse, charged that her co-workers over a four-year period
from 1978–1982 sexually harassed her by such acts as: asking her whether she
was wearing a bra; two of the men exposing their buttocks between ten and
twenty times; a male co-worker grabbing his crotch and making obscene suggestions or growling; subjecting her to offensive and abusive language; and exhibiting obscene drawings with her initials on them. Zabowicz began to show
symptoms of physical and psychological stress, necessitating several medical
leaves, and she filed a sexual harassment complaint with the EEOC. The district court judge remarked that "the sustained, malicious, and brutal harassment meted out . . . was more than merely unreasonable; it was malevolent
and outrageous." The company knew of the harassment and took corrective
action only after the employee filed a complaint with the EEOC. The company, was, therefore, held liable, and Zabowicz was awarded back pay for the
period of her medical absence, and a judgment that her rights were violated
under the Civil Rights Act of 1964.

On September 17, 1990, Lisa Olson, a sports reporter for *The Boston*   5
Herald, charged five football players of the just-defeated New England Patriots
with sexual harassment with making sexually suggestive and offensive remarks
to her when she entered their locker room to conduct a post-game interview.
The incident amounted to nothing short of "mind rape," according to Olson.
After vociferous lamentations in the media, the National Football League
fined the team and its players $25,000 each. The National Organization of
Women called for a boycott of Remington electric shavers because the owner
of the company, Victor Kiam, also owns the Patriots and allegedly displayed
insufficient sensitivity at the time when the episode occurred.

All these incidents are indisputably disturbing. In an ideal world—one   6
needless to say far different from the one that we inhabit or are ever likely to
inhabit—women would not be subjected to such treatment in the course of
their work. Women, and men as well, would be accorded respect by co-workers
and supervisors, their feelings would be taken into account, and their dignity
would be left intact. For women to expect reverential treatment in the workplace is utopian, yet they should not have to tolerate outrageous, offensive sexual overtures and threats as they go about earning a living.

One question that needs to be pondered is: What kinds of undesired sex-   7
ual behavior women should be protected against by law? That is, what kind of
actions are deemed so outrageous and violate a woman's rights to such extent
that the law should intervene, and what actions should be considered inconve-
niences of life, to be morally condemned but not adjudicated? A subsidiary
question concerns the type of legal remedy appropriate for the wrongs that do
require redress. Before directly addressing these questions, it might be useful to
diffuse some of the hyperbole adhering to the sexual harassment issue.

Surveys are one source of this hyperbole. If their results are accepted at   8
face value, they lead to the conclusion that women are disproportionately victims of legions of sexual harassers. A poll by the Albuquerque *Tribune* found
that nearly 80 percent of the respondents reported that they or someone they

knew had been victims of sexual harassment. The Merit Systems Protection Board determined that 42 percent of the women (and 14 percent of men) working for the federal government had experienced some form of unwanted sexual attention between 1985 and 1987, with unwanted "sexual teasing" identified as the most prevalent form. A Defense Department survey found that 64 percent of women in the military (and 17 percent of the men) suffered "uninvited and unwanted sexual attention" within the previous year. The United Methodist Church established that 77 percent of its clergywomen experienced incidents of sexual harassment, with 41 percent of these naming a pastor or colleague as the perpetrator, and 31 percent mentioning church social functions as the setting.

A few caveats concerning polls in general, and these sorts of polls in particular, are worth considering. Pollsters looking for a particular social ill tend to find it, usually in gargantuan proportions. (What fate would lie in store for a pollster who concluded that child abuse, or wife beating, or mistreatment of the elderly had dwindled to the point of negligibility!) Sexual harassment is a notoriously ill-defined and almost infinitely expandable concept, including everything from rape to unwelcome neck massaging, discomfiture upon witnessing sexual overtures directed at others, yelling at and blowing smoke in the ears of female subordinates, and displays of pornographic pictures in the workplace. Defining sexual harassment, as the United Methodists did, as "any sexually related behavior that is unwelcome, offensive or which fails to respect the rights of others," the concept is broad enough to include everything from "unsolicited suggestive looks or leers [or] pressures for dates" to "actual sexual assaults or rapes." Categorizing everything from rape to "looks" as sexual harassment makes us all victims, a state of affairs satisfying to radical feminists, but not very useful for distinguishing serious injuries from the merely trivial.

Yet, even if the surveys exaggerate the extent of sexual harassment, however defined, what they do reflect is a great deal of tension between the sexes. As women in ever increasing numbers entered the workplace in the last two decades, as the women's movement challenged alleged male hegemony and exploitation with ever greater intemperance, and as women entered previously all-male preserves from the board rooms to the coal pits, it is lamentable, but should not be surprising, that this tension sometimes takes sexual form. Not that sexual harassment on the job, in the university, and in other settings is a trivial or insignificant matter, but a sense of proportion needs to be restored and, even more importantly, distinctions need to be made. In other words, sexual harassment must be de-ideologized. Statements that paint nearly all women as victims and all men and their patriarchal, capitalist system as perpetrators, are ideological fantasy. Ideology blurs the distinction between being injured—being a genuine victim—and merely being offended. An example is this statement by Catharine A. MacKinnon, a law professor and feminist activist:

> Sexual harassment perpetuates the interlocked structure by which women have been kept sexually in thrall to men and at the bottom of the labor market. Two forces of American society converge: men's control over women's sexuality and

capital's control over employees' work lives. Women historically have been required to exchange sexual services for material survival, in one form or another. Prostitution and marriage as well as sexual harassment in different ways institutionalize this arrangement.

Such hyperbole needs to be diffused and distinctions need to be drawn. Rape, a nonconsensual invasion of a person's body, is a crime clear and simple. It is a violation of the right to the physical integrity of the body (the right to life, as John Locke or Thomas Jefferson would have put it). Criminal law should and does prohibit rape. Whether it is useful to call rape "sexual harassment" is doubtful, for it makes the latter concept overly broad while trivializing the former.   11

Intimidation in the workplace of the kind that befell Valerie Craig—that is, extortion of sexual favors by a supervisor from a subordinate by threatening to penalize, fire, or fail to reward—is what the courts term *quid pro quo*★ sexual harassment. Since the mid-1970s, the federal courts have treated this type of sexual harassment as a form of sex discrimination in employment proscribed under Title VII of the Civil Rights Act of 1964. A plaintiff who prevails against an employer may receive such equitable remedies as reinstatement and back pay, and the court can order the company to prepare and disseminate a policy against sexual harassment. Current law places principal liability on the company, not the harassing supervisor, even when higher management is unaware of the harassment and, thus, cannot take any steps to prevent it.   12

Quid pro quo sexual harassment is morally objectionable and analogous to extortion: The harasser extorts property (i.e., use of the woman's body) through the leverage of fear for her job. The victim of such behavior should have legal recourse, but serious reservations can be held about rectifying these injustices through the blunt instrument of Title VII: In egregious cases the victim is left less than whole (for back pay will not compensate her for ancillary losses), and no prospects for punitive damages are offered to deter would-be harassers. Even more distressing about Title VII is the fact that the primary target of litigation is not the actual harasser, but rather the employer. This places a double burden on a company. The employer is swindled by the supervisor because he spent his time pursuing sexual gratification and thereby impairing the efficiency of the workplace by mismanaging his subordinates, and the employer must endure lengthy and expensive litigation, pay damages, and suffer loss to its reputation. It would be fairer to both the company and the victim to treat sexual harassment as a tort—that is, as a private wrong or injury for which the court can assess damages. Employers should be held vicariously liable only when they know of an employee's behavior and do not try to redress it.   13

As for the workplace harassment endured by Carol Zabowicz—the bared buttocks, obscene portraits, etc.—that too should be legally redressable. Presently, such incidents also fall under the umbrella of Title VII, and are termed hostile environment sexual harassment, a category accepted later than   14

★Latin for "one thing in return for another."

quid pro quo and with some judicial reluctance. The main problem with this category is that it has proven too elastic: cases have reached the courts based on everything from off-color jokes to unwanted, persistent sexual advances by co-workers. A new tort of sexual harassment would handle these cases better. Only instances above a certain threshold of egregiousness or outrageousness would be actionable. In other words, the behavior that the plaintiff found offensive would also have to be offensive to the proverbial "reasonable man" of the tort law. That is, the behavior would have to be objectively injurious rather than merely subjectively offensive. The defendant would be the actual harasser not the company, unless it knew about the problem and failed to act. Victims of scatological jokes, leers, unwanted offers of dates, and other sexual annoyances would no longer have their day in court.

A distinction must be restored between morally offensive behavior and   15
behavior that causes serious harm. Only the latter should fall under the jurisdiction of criminal or tort law. Do we really want legislators and judges delving into our most intimate private lives, deciding when a look is a leer, and when a leer is a Civil Rights Act offense? Do we really want courts deciding, as one recently did, whether a school principal's disparaging remarks about a female school district administrator was sexual harassment and, hence, a breach of Title VII, or merely the act of a spurned and vengeful lover? Do we want judges settling disputes such as the one that arose at a car dealership after a female employee turned down a male co-worker's offer of a date and his colleagues retaliated by calling her offensive names and embarrassing her in front of customers? Or another case in which a female shipyard worker complained of an "offensive working environment" because of the prevalence of pornographic material on the docks? Do we want the state to prevent or compensate us for any behavior that someone might find offensive? Should people have a legally enforceable right not to be offended by others? At some point, the price for such protection is the loss of both liberty and privacy rights.

Workplaces are breeding grounds of envy, personal grudges, infatuation,   16
and jilted loves, and beneath a fairly high threshold of outrageousness, these travails should be either suffered in silence, complained of to higher management, or left behind as one seeks other employment. No one, female or male, can expect to enjoy a working environment that is perfectly stress-free, or to be treated always and by everyone with kindness and respect. To the extent that sympathetic judges have encouraged women to seek monetary compensation for slights and annoyances, they have not done them a great service. Women need to develop a thick skin in order to survive and prosper in the workforce. It is patronizing to think that they need to be recompensed by male judges for seeing a few pornographic pictures on a wall. By their efforts to extend sexual harassment charges to even the most trivial behavior, the radical feminists send a message that women are not resilient enough to ignore the run-of-the-mill, churlish provocation from male co-workers. It is difficult to imagine a suit by a longshoreman complaining of mental stress due to the display of nude male centerfolds by female co-workers. Women cannot expect to have it both ways: equality where convenient, but special dispensations when

the going gets rough. Equality has its price and that price may include unwelcome sexual advances, irritating and even intimidating sexual jests, and lewd and obnoxious colleagues.

Egregious acts—sexual harassment per se—must be legally redressable.   17
Lesser but not trivial offenses, whether at the workplace or in other more social settings, should be considered moral lapses for which the offending party receives opprobrium, disciplinary warnings, or penalties, depending on the setting and the severity. Trivial offenses, dirty jokes, sexual overtures, and sexual innuendoes do make many women feel intensely discomfited, but, unless they become outrageous through persistence or content, these too should be taken as part of life's annoyances. The perpetrators should be either endured, ignored, rebuked, or avoided, as circumstances and personal inclination dictate. Whether Lisa Olson's experience in the locker room of the Boston Patriots falls into the second or third category is debatable. The media circus triggered by the incident was certainly out of proportion to the event.

As the presence of women on road gangs, construction crews, and oil   18
rigs becomes a fact of life, the animosities and tensions of this transition period are likely to abate gradually. Meanwhile, women should "lighten up," and even dispense a few risqué barbs of their own, a sure way of taking the fun out of it for offensive male bores.   ■

Questions for Meaning

1. Explain the analogy in paragraph 1. What parallel can be drawn between sexual harassment and "class exploitation"?
2. Which of the cases discussed in paragraphs 3 through 5 are clearly illegal in Paul's view?
3. Why is Paul skeptical of statistics gathered by pollsters?
4. According to Paul, why has sexual harassment in the workplace become evident?
5. Why does Paul question prosecuting sexual harassment cases under Title VII of the Civil Rights Act of 1964?
6. On what grounds does Paul argue that women should be prepared to accept a degree of inappropriate behavior in the workplace?
7. Vocabulary: corollary (1), adumbrated (2), malevolent (4), vociferous (5), hyperbole (8), hegemony (10), patriarchal (10), proscribed (12), extortion (13), egregious (13), scatological (14), churlish (16), opprobrium (17).

Questions about Strategy

1. Paul opens her argument with the views she challenges. What is the advantage of this strategy?
2. Does Paul treat sexual harassment lightly, or does she recognize that women have cause for concern?

3. Consider paragraphs 8 and 9. How effectively does Paul challenge statistics showing a high rate of sexual harassment?

4. In paragraph 15, Paul asks, "Do we want the state to prevent or compensate us for any behavior that someone might find offensive?" What answer does she expect to this question? Has she brought you to the point where you are prepared to give it?

STEPHANIE RIGER

GENDER DILEMMAS IN SEXUAL HARASSMENT POLICIES AND PROCEDURES

Discussion of sexual harassment often reveals that men and women have a different understanding of what kind of behavior constitutes harassment. Recognizing these differences may be essential in designing policies and programs to prevent the problem from occurring. The nature of these differences is the focus of the following article by Stephanie Riger, Professor of Psychology and Women's Studies at the University of Illinois, Chicago. With Margaret T. Gordon, she coauthored *The Female Fear* (1988). "Gender Dilemmas in Sexual Harassment Policies and Procedures" was first published by *American Psychologist* in 1991. You will find that Riger draws upon an extensive body of scholarship and uses APA style documentation to identify her sources.

Many organizations have established policies and procedures to deal with sexual harassment, yet few complaints are reported. Some have suggested that the lack of complaints is due to the absence of a problem, or the timidity or fearfulness of victims. This article proposes that the reasons for the lack of use of sexual harassment grievance procedures lie not in the victims, but rather in the procedures themselves. Women perceive sexual harassment differently than men do, and their orientation to dispute-resolution processes is likely to differ as well. The way that policies define harassment and the nature of dispute resolution procedures may better fit male than female perspectives. This gender bias is likely to discourage women from reporting complaints.

Sexual harassment—unwanted sexually oriented behavior in a work context—   1
is the most recent form of victimization of women to be redefined as a social rather than a personal problem, following rape and wife abuse. A sizeable proportion of women surveyed in a wide variety of work settings reported being subject to unwanted sexual attention, sexual comments or jokes, offensive touching, or attempts to coerce compliance with or punish rejection of sexual advances. In 1980 the U.S. Merit Systems Protection Board (1981) conducted the first comprehensive national survey of sexual harassment among federal

employees: About 4 out of 10 of the 10,648 women surveyed reported having been the target of sexual harassment during the previous 24 months. A recent update of this survey found that the frequency of harassment in 1988 was identical to that reported earlier: 42% of all women surveyed in 1988 reported that they had experienced some form of unwanted and uninvited sexual attention compared to exactly the same percentage of women in 1980 (U.S. Merit Systems Protection Board, 1988).

Women ranging from blue-collar workers (LaFontaine & Tredeau, 1986;   2
Maypole & Skaine, 1982) to lawyers (Burleigh & Goldberg, 1989) to airline personnel (Littler-Bishop, Seidler-Feller, & Opaluch, 1982) have reported considerable amounts of sexual harassment in surveys. Among a random sample of private sector workers in the Los Angeles area, more than one half of the women surveyed by telephone reported experiencing at least one incident that they considered sexual harassment during their working lives (Gutek, 1985). Some estimate that up to about one third of women in educational institutions have experienced some form of harassment (Kenig & Ryan, 1986). Indeed, Garvey (1986) stated that "Unwanted sexual attention may be the single most widespread occupational hazard in the workplace today" (p. 75).

It is a hazard faced much more frequently by women than men. About   3
40% of the women in the original U.S. Merit Systems Protection Board survey reported having experienced sexual harassment, compared with only 15% of the men (U.S. Merit Systems Protection Board, 1981). Among working people surveyed in Los Angeles, women were nine times more likely than men to report having quit a job because of sexual harassment, five times more likely to have transferred, and three times more likely to have lost a job (Konrad & Gutek, 1986). Women with low power and status, whether due to lower age, being single or divorced, or being in a marginal position in the organization, are more likely to be harassed (Fain & Anderton, 1987; LaFontaine & Tredeau, 1986; Robinson & Reid, 1985).

Sex differences in the frequency of harassment also prevail in educational   4
environments (Fitzgerald et al., 1988). A mailed survey of more than 900 women and men at the University of Rhode Island asked about a wide range of behavior, including the frequency of respondents' experience of sexual insult, defined as an "uninvited sexually suggestive, obscene or offensive remark, stare, or gesture" (Lott, Reilly, & Howard, 1982, p. 309). Of the female respondents, 40% reported being sexually insulted occasionally or often while on campus, compared with 17% of the men. Both men and women reported that women are rarely the source of such insults. Similar differences were found in a survey of social workers, with 2½ times as many women as men reporting harassment (Maypole, 1986).

Despite the high rates found in surveys of sexual harassment of women,   5
few complaints are pursued through official grievance procedures. Dzeich and Weiner (1984) concluded, after reviewing survey findings, that 20% to 30% of female college students experience sexual harassment. Yet academic institutions averaged only 4.3 complaints each during the 1982–1983 academic year (Robertson, Dyer, & Campbell, 1988), a period roughly consecutive with the

surveys cited by Dzeich and Weiner. In another study conducted at a university in 1984, of 38 women who reported harassment, only 1 reported the behavior to the offender's supervisor and 2 reported the behavior to an adviser, another professor, or employer (Reilly, Lott, & Gallogly, 1986). Similar findings have been reported on other college campuses (Adams, Kottke, & Padgitt, 1983; Benson & Thompson, 1982; Brandenburg, 1982; Cammaert, 1985; Meek & Lynch, 1983; Schneider, 1987).

Low numbers of complaints appear in other work settings as well. In a   6
survey of federal workers, only about 11% of victims reported the harassment to a higher authority; and only 2.5% used formal complaint channels (Livingston, 1982). Similarly, female social workers reacted to harassment by avoiding or delaying the conflict or attempting to defuse the situation rather than by adopting any form of recourse such as filing a grievance (Maypole, 1986). The number of complaints alleging sexual harassment filed with the Equal Employment Opportunity Commission in Washington, DC, has declined since 1984, despite an increase in the number of women in the workforce during that time (Morgenson, 1989), and surveys that suggest that the rate of sexual harassment has remained relatively stable (U.S. Merit Systems Protection Board, 1981, 1988).

It is the contention of this article that the low rate of utilization of   7
grievance procedures is due to gender bias in sexual harassment policies that discourages their use by women. Policies are written in gender-neutral language and are intended to apply equally to men and women. However, these policies are experienced differently by women than men because of gender differences in perceptions of harassment and orientation toward conflict. Although victims of all forms of discrimination are reluctant to pursue grievances (Bumiller, 1987), women, who are most likely to be the victims of sexual harassment, are especially disinclined to pursue sexual harassment grievances for at least two reasons. First, the interpretation in policies of what constitutes harassment may not reflect women's viewpoints, and their complaints may not be seen as valid. Second, the procedures in some policies that are designed to resolve disputes may be inimical to women because they are not compatible with the way that many women view conflict resolution. Gender bias in policies, rather than an absence of harassment or lack of assertiveness on the part of victims, produces low numbers of complaints.

Gender Bias in the Definition of Sexual Harassment

The first way that gender bias affects sexual harassment policies stems from   8
differences between men and women in the interpretation of the definition of harassment. Those writing sexual harassment policies for organizations typically look to the courts for the distinction between illegal sexual harassment and permissible (although perhaps unwanted) social interaction (see Cohen, 1987, for a discussion of this distinction in legal cases). The definition of harassment in policies typically is that provided by the U.S. Equal Employment Opportunity Commission (1980) guidelines:

Unwelcome sexual advances, requests for sexual favors, and other verbal or physical conduct of a sexual nature constitute sexual harassment when (1) submission to such conduct is made either explicitly or implicitly a term or condition of an individual's employment, (2) submission to or rejection of such conduct by an individual is used as the basis for employment decisions affecting such individual, or (3) such conduct has the purpose or effect of unreasonably interfering with an individual's work performance or creating an intimidating, hostile, or offensive working environment. (p. 74677)

The first two parts of the definition refer to a quid pro quo relationship involving people in positions of unequal status, as superior status is usually necessary to have control over another's employment. In such cases bribes, threats, or punishments are used. Incidents of this type need happen only once to fall under the definition of sexual harassment. However, courts have required that incidents falling into the third category, "an intimidating, hostile, or offensive working environment," must be repeated in order to establish that such an environment exists (Terpstra & Baker, 1988); these incidents must be both pervasive and so severe that they affect the victim's psychological well-being (Trager, 1988). Harassment of this type can come from peers or even subordinates as well as superiors.

In all three of these categories, harassment is judged on the basis of conduct and its effects on the recipient, not the intentions of the harasser. Thus, two typical defenses given by accused harassers—"I was just being friendly," or "I touch everyone, I'm that kind of person"—do not hold up in court. Yet behavior may have an intimidating or offensive effect on some people but be inoffensive or even welcome to others. In deciding whose standards should be used, the courts employ what is called the *reasonable person rule,* asking whether a reasonable person would be offended by the conduct in question. The dilemma in applying this to sexual harassment is that a reasonable woman and a reasonable man are likely to differ in the judgements of what is offensive.   9

Definitions of sexual harassment are socially constructed, varying not only with characteristics of the perceiver but also those of the situational context and actors involved. Behavior is more likely to be labelled harassment when it done by someone with greater power than the victim (Gutek, Morasch, & Cohen, 1983; Kenig & Ryan, 1986; Lester et al., 1986; Popovich, Licata, Nokovich, Martelli, & Zoloty, 1987); when it involves physical advances accompanied by threats of punishment for noncompliance (Rossi & Weber-Burdin, 1983); when the response to it is negative (T. S. Jones, Remland, & Brunner, 1987); when the behavior reflects persistent negative intentions toward a woman (Pryor & Day, 1988); the more inappropriate it is for the actor's social role (Pryor, 1985); and the more flagrant and frequent the harasser's actions (Thomann & Wiener, 1987). Among women, professionals are more likely than those in secretarial–clerical positions to report the more subtle behaviors as harassment (McIntyre & Renick, 1982).   10

The variable that most consistently predicts variation in people's definition of sexual harassment is the sex of the rater. Men label fewer behaviors at   11 work as sexual harassment (Kenig & Ryan, 1986; Konrad & Gutek, 1986; Lester et al., 1986; Powell, 1986; Rossi & Weber-Burdin, 1983). Men tend to find sexual overtures from women at work to be flattering, whereas women find similar approaches from men to be insulting (Gutek, 1985). Both men and women agree that certain blatant behaviors, such as sexual assault or sexual bribery, constitute harassment, but women are more likely to see as harassment more subtle behavior such as sexual teasing or looks or gestures (Adams et al., 1983; Collins & Blodgett, 1981; Kenig & Ryan, 1986; U.S. Merit Systems Protection Board, 1981). Even when they do identify behavior as harassment, men are more likely to think that women will be flattered by it (Kirk, 1988). Men are also more likely than women to blame women for being sexually harassed (Jensen & Gutek, 1982; Kenig & Ryan, 1986).

These gender differences make it difficult to apply the reasonable person   12
rule. Linenberger (1983) proposed 10 factors that permit an "objective" assessment of whether behavior constitutes sexual harassment, regardless of the perception of the victim and the intent of the perpetrator. These factors range from the severity of the conduct to the number and frequency of encounters, and the relationship of the parties involved. For example, behavior is less likely to be categorized as harassment if it is seen as a response to provocation from the victim. But is an objective rating of provocation possible? When gender differences are as clear-cut and persistent as they are in the perception of what behavior constitutes sexual harassment, the question is not one of objectivity, but rather of which sex's definition of the situation will prevail. Becker (1967) asserted that there is a "hierarchy of credibility" in organizations, and that credibility and the right to be heard are differently distributed: "In any system of ranked groups, participants take it as given that members of the highest group have the right to define the way things really are" (p. 241). Because men typically have more power in organizations (Kanter, 1977), Becker's analysis suggests that in most situations the male definition of harassment is likely to predominate. As MacKinnon (1987) put it, "objectivity—the nonsituated, universal standpoint, whether claimed or aspired to—is a denial of the existence or potency of sex inequality that tacitly participates in constructing reality from the dominant point of view," (p. 136). "The law sees and treats women the way men see and treat women" (p. 140). This means that men's judgments about what behavior constitutes harassment, and who is to blame, are likely to prevail. Linenberger's 10 factors thus may not be an objective measure, but rather a codification of the male perspective on harassment. This is likely to discourage women who want to bring complaints about more subtle forms of harassment.

Sex Differences in the Attribution of Harassment

Attribution theory provides an explanation for the wider range of behaviors   13
that women define as harassment and for men's tendency to find women at fault (Kenig & Ryan, 1986; Pryor, 1985; Pryor & Day, 1988). Attribution theory suggests that people tend to see their own behaviors as situationally

determined, whereas they attribute the behaviors of others to personality characteristics or other internal causes (E. E. Jones & Nisbett, 1971). Those who see sexual harassment through the eyes of the actor are likely to be male. As actors are wont to do, they will attribute their behaviors to situational causes, including the "provocations" of the women involved. They will then not perceive their own behaviors as harassment. In fact, those who take the perspective of the victim do see specific behaviors as more harassing than those who take the perspective of the actor (Pryor & Day, 1988). Women are more likely to view harassment through the eyes of the victim; therefore they will label more behaviors as harassment because they attribute them to men's disposition or personality traits. Another possibility is that men, as potential harassers, want to avoid blame in the future, and so shift the blame to women (Jensen & Gutek, 1982) and restrict the range of behaviors that they define as harassment (Kenig & Ryan, 1986). Whatever the cause, a reasonable man and a reasonable women are likely to differ in their judgments of whether a particular behavior constitutes sexual harassment.

Men tend to misinterpret women's friendliness as an indication of sexual   14 interest (Abbey, 1982; Abbey & Melby, 1986; Saal, Johnson, & Weber, 1989; Shotland & Craig, 1988). Acting on this misperception may result in behavior that is harassing to women. Tangri, Burt, and Johnson (1982) stated that "Some sexual harassment may indeed be clumsy or insensitive expressions of attraction, while some is the classic abuse of organizational power" (p. 52). Gender differences in attributional processes help explain the first type of harassment, partially accounting for the overwhelming preponderance of sexual harassment incidents that involve a male offender and a female victim.

Gender Bias in Grievance Procedures

Typically, procedures for resolving disputes about sexual harassment are writ-   15 ten in gender-neutral terms so that they may apply to both women and men. However, men and women may react quite differently to the same procedures.

Analyzing this problem requires looking at specific policies and proce-   16 dures. Educational institutions will serve as the context for this discussion for three reasons. First, they are the most frequent site of surveys about the problem, and the pervasive nature of harassment on campuses has been well documented (Dzeich & Weiner, 1984). Second, although sexual harassment is harmful to women in all occupations, it can be particularly devastating to those in educational institutions, in which the goal of the organization is to nurture and promote development. The violation of relationships based on trust, such as those between faculty and students, can leave long-lasting and deep wounds, yet many surveys find that those in positions of authority in educational settings are often the source of the problem (Benson & Thomson, 1982; Fitzgerald et al., 1988; Glaser & Thorpe, 1986; Kenig & Ryan, 1986; Maihoff & Forrest, 1983; Metha & Nigg, 1983; Robinson & Reid, 1985; K. R. Wilson & Kraus, 1983). Third, educational institutions have been leaders in the development of sexual harassment policies, in part because of concern about litigation. In *Alexander v. Yale University* (1977) the court decided that sexual harassment constitutes a form of sex discrimination that denies equal access to educational opportunities, and falls under Title IX of the Educational Amendments of 1972. The Office of Civil Rights in the U.S. Department of Education now requires institutions that receive Title IX funds to maintain grievance procedures to resolve complaints involving sexual discrimination or harassment (M. Wilson, 1988). Consequently, academic institutions may have had more experience than other work settings in developing procedures to combat this problem. A survey of U.S. institutions of higher learning conducted in 1984 (Robertson et al., 1988) found that 66% of all responding institutions had sexual harassment policies, and 46% had grievance procedures specifically designed to deal with sexual harassment complaints, with large public schools more likely to have them than small private ones. These percentages have unquestionably increased in recent years, given the government funding regulations. Although the discussion here is focused on educational contexts, the problems identified in sexual harassment policies exist in other work settings as well.

Many educational institutions, following guidelines put forward by the   17
American Council on Education (1986) and the American Association of University Professors (1983), have established policies that prohibit sexual harassment and create grievance procedures. Some use a formal board or hearing, and others use informal mechanisms that protect confidentiality and seek to resolve the complaint rather than punish the offender (see, e.g., Brandenburg, 1982; Meek & Lynch, 1983). Still others use both types of procedures. The type of procedure specified by the policy may have a great impact on victims' willingness to report complaints.

Comparison of Informal and Formal Grievance Procedures

Informal attempts to resolve disputes differ from formal procedures in impor-   18
tant ways (see Table 1; for a general discussion of dispute resolution systems, see Brett, Goldberg, & Ury, 1990). First, their goal is to solve a problem, rather than to judge the harasser's guilt or innocence. The assumptions underlying these processes are that both parties in a dispute perceive a problem (although they may define that problem differently); that both share a common interest in solving that problem; and that together they can negotiate an agreement that will be satisfactory to everyone involved. Typically, the goal of informal processes is to end the harassment of the complainant rather than judge (and punish, if appropriate) the offender. The focus is on what will happen in the future between the disputing parties, rather than on what has happened in the past. Often policies do not specify the format of informal problem solving, but accept a wide variety of strategies of reconciliation. For example, a complainant might write a letter to the offender (Rowe, 1981), or someone might talk to the offender on the complainant's behalf. The offender and victim might participate in mediation, in which a third party helps them negotiate an agreement. Many policies accept a wide array of strategies as good-faith attempts to solve the problem informally.

TABLE 1
A Comparison of Formal and Informal Grievance Procedures

Elements	Procedures	
	Informal	Formal
Purpose	Problem solving or reconciliation	Judge guilt or innocence
Time Focus	What will happen in the future	What happened in the past
Format	Usually unspecified	Usually specified
Completion	When complainant is satisfied	When hearing board decides
Control	Complainant	Hearing board
Compliance	Voluntary	Punishment is binding

In contrast, formal procedures generally require a written complaint [19] and have a specified procedure for handling cases, usually by bringing the complaint to a group officially designated to hear the case, such as a hearing board. The informal process typically ends when the complainant is satisfied (or decides to drop the complaint); the formal procedure ends when the hearing board decides on the guilt or innocence of the alleged harasser. Thus, control over the outcome usually rests with the complainant in the case of informal mechanisms, and with the official governance body in the case of a hearing. Compliance with a decision is usually voluntary in informal procedures, whereas the decision in a formal procedure is binding unless appealed to a higher authority. Formal procedures are adversarial in nature, with the complainant and defendant competing to see whose position will prevail.

A typical case might proceed as follows: A student with a complaint [20] writes a letter to the harasser (an informal procedure). If not satisfied with the response, she submits a written complaint to the sexual harassment hearing board, which then hears both sides of the case, reviews available evidence, and decides on the guilt or innocence of the accused (a formal procedure). If the accused is found guilty, the appropriate officer of the institution decides on punishment.

Gender Differences in Orientation to Conflict

Women and men may differ in their reactions to dispute resolution procedures [21] for at least two reasons. First, women typically have less power than men in organizations (Kanter, 1977). Using a grievance procedure, such as appearing before a hearing board, may be inimical because of the possibility of retaliation for a complaint. Miller (1976) suggested that differences in status and power affect the way that people handle conflict:

> As soon as a group attains dominance it tends inevitably to produce a situation of conflict and . . . it also, simultaneously, seeks to suppress conflict.

> Moreover, subordinates who accept the dominant's conception of them as passive and malleable do not openly engage in conflict. Conflict . . . is forced underground. (p. 127)

This may explain why some women do not report complaints at all. 22 When they do complain, however, their relative lack of power or their values may predispose women to prefer informal rather than formal procedures. Beliefs about the appropriate way to handle disputes vary among social groups (Merry & Silbey, 1984). Gilligan's (1982) distinction between an orientation toward rights and justice compared with an emphasis on responsibilities to others and caring is likely to be reflected in people's preferences for ways of handling disputes (Kolb & Coolidge, 1988). Neither of these orientations is exclusive to one sex, but according to Gilligan, women are more likely to emphasize caring. Women's orientation to caring may be due to their subordinate status (Miller, 1976). Empirical support for Gilligan's theories is inconclusive (see, e.g., Mednick, 1989, for a summary of criticisms). Yet the fact that most victims of sexual harassment state that they simply want an end to the offending behavior rather than punishment of the offender (Robertson et al., 1988) suggests a "caring" rather than "justice" perspective (or possibly, a fear of reprisals).

In the context of dispute resolution, an emphasis on responsibilities and 23 caring is compatible with the goals of informal procedures to restore harmony or at least peaceful coexistence among the parties involved, whereas that of justice is compatible with formal procedures that attempt to judge guilt or innocence of the offender. Thus women may prefer to use informal procedures to resolve conflicts, and indeed most cases in educational institutions are handled through informal mechanisms (Robertson et al., 1988). Policies that do not include an informal dispute resolution option are likely to discourage many women from bringing complaints.

Problems with Informal Dispute-Resolution Procedures

Although women may prefer informal mechanisms, they are problematic for 24 several reasons (Rifkin, 1984). Because they do not result in punishment, offenders suffer few negative consequences of their actions and may not be deterred from harassing again. In institutions of higher learning, the most common form of punishment reported is a verbal warning by a supervisor, which is given only "sometimes" (Robertson et al., 1988). Dismissal and litigation are almost never used. It seems likely, then, that sexual harassment may be viewed by potential harassers as low-risk behavior, and that victims see few incentives for bringing official complaints.

The confidentiality usually required by informal procedures prevents 25 other victims from knowing that a complaint has been lodged against a multiple offender. If a woman knows that another woman is bringing a complaint against a particular man who has harassed both of them, then she might be more willing to complain also. The secrecy surrounding informal complaint processes precludes this information from becoming public and makes it more difficult to identify repeat offenders. Also, complaints settled informally may not be included in reports of the frequency of sexual harassment claims, making these statistics underestimate the scope of the problem. Yet confidentiality is needed to protect the rights of the accused and may be preferred by those bringing complaints.

These problems in informal procedures could discourage male as well as   26 female victims from bringing complaints. Most problematic for women, however, is the assumption in informal procedures that the complainant and accused have equal power in the process of resolving the dispute. This assumption is likely to put women at a disadvantage. Parties involved in sexual harassment disputes may not be equal either in the sense of formal position within the organization (e.g., student versus faculty) or status (e.g., female versus male students), and position and status characteristics that reflect levels of power do not disappear simply because they are irrelevant to the informal process. External status characteristics that indicate macrolevel social stratification (e.g., sex and age) help explain the patterns of distribution of sexual harassment in the workplace (Fain & Anderton, 1987). It seems likely that these external statuses will influence the interpersonal dynamics within a dispute-resolution procedure as well. Because women are typically lower than men in both formal and informal status and power in organizations, they will have less power in the dispute resolution process.

When the accused has more power than the complainant (e.g., a male   27 faculty member accused by a female student), the complainant is more vulnerable to retaliation. Complainants may be reluctant to use grievance procedures because they fear retaliation should the charge be made public. For example, students may fear that a faculty member will punish them for bringing a complaint by lowering their grades or withholding recommendations. The person appointed to act as a guide to the informal resolution process is usually expected to act as a neutral third party rather than advocate for the complainant, and may hold little formal power over faculty: "Relatively few institutions have persons empowered to be (nonlegal) advocates for the complainants; a student bringing a complaint has little assurance of stopping the harassment and avoiding retaliation" (Robertson et al., 1988, p. 801). The victim then is left without an advocate to face an opponent whose formal position, age, and experience with verbal argument is often considerably beyond her own. The more vulnerable a woman's position is in her organization, the more likely it is that she will be harassed (Robinson & Reid, 1985); therefore sexual harassment, like rape, involves dynamics of power and domination as well as sexuality. The lack of an advocate for the complainant who might equalize power between the disputing parties is particularly troubling. However, if an advocate is provided for the complainant in an informal process, fairness and due process require that the defendant have an advocate as well. The dilemma is that this seems likely to transform an informal, problem-solving process into a formal, adversarial one.

Other Obstacles to Reporting Complaints

Belief That Sexual Harassment of Women Is Normative

Because of differences in perception of behavior, men and women involved in   28
a sexual harassment case are likely to have sharply divergent interpretations of
that case, particularly when a hostile environment claim is involved. To
women, the behavior in question is offensive, and they are likely to see themselves as victims of male actions. The requirement that an attempt be made to
mediate the dispute or solve it through informal processes may violate their
perception of the situation and of themselves as victims of a crime. By comparison, a victim of a mugging is not required to solve the problem with the
mugger through mediation (B. Sandler, personal communication, 1988). To
many men, the behavior is not offensive, but normative. In their eyes, no
crime has been committed, and there is no problem to be solved.

Some women may also consider sexual harassment to be normative.   29
Women may believe that these sorts of behaviors are simply routine, a commonplace part of everyday life, and thus not something that can be challenged.
Younger women—who are more likely to be victims (Fain & Anderton, 1987;
LaFontaine & Tredeau, 1986; McIntyre & Renick, 1982)—are more tolerant
of harassment than are older women (Lott et al., 1982; Reilly et al., 1986).
Indeed, Lott et al. concluded that "younger women in particular have accepted
the idea that prowling men are a 'fact of life'" (p. 318). This attitude might
prevent women from labeling a negative experience as harassment. Surveys
that ask women about sexual harassment and about the frequency of experiencing specific sexually harassing behaviors find discrepancies in responses to
these questions (Fitzgerald et al., 1988). Women report higher rates when
asked if they have been the target of specific harassing behaviors than when
asked a general question about whether they have been harassed. Women are
also more willing to report negative reactions to offensive behaviors than they
are to label those behaviors as sexual harassment (Brewer, 1982).

Normative beliefs may deter some male victims of harassment from re-   30
porting complaints also, because men are expected to welcome sexual advances
if those advances are from women.

Negative Outcomes for Victims Who Bring Complaints

The outcome of grievance procedures does not appear to provide much satis-   31
faction to victims who bring complaints. In academic settings, despite considerable publicity given to a few isolated cases in which tenured faculty have
been fired, punishments are rarely inflicted on harassers, and the punishments
that are given are mild, such as verbal warnings (Robertson et al., 1988).
Among federal workers, 33% of those who used formal grievance procedures
to protest sexual harassment found that it "made things worse" (Livingston,
1982). More than 65% of the cases of formal charges of sexual harassment filed
with the Illinois Department of Human Rights involved job discharge of the
complainant (Terpstra & Cook, 1985). Less than one third of those cases resulted in a favorable settlement for the complainant, and those who received

financial compensation got an average settlement of $3,234 (Terpstra & Baker, 1988). Similar findings in California were reported by Coles (1986), with the average cash settlement there of $973, representing approximately one month's pay. Although a few legal cases have resulted in large settlements (Garvey, 1986), these studies suggest that typical settlements are low. Formal actions may take years to complete, and in legal suits the victim usually must hire legal counsel at considerable expense (Livingston, 1982). These small settlements seem unlikely to compensate victims for the emotional stress, notoriety, and financial costs involved in filing a public complaint. Given the consistency with which victimization falls more often to women than men, it is ironic that one of the largest settlements awarded to an individual in a sexual harassment case ($196,500 in damages) was made to a man who brought suit against his female supervisor (Brewer & Berk, 1982), perhaps because sexually aggression by a woman is seen as especially egregious.

Emotional Consequences of Harassment

In academic settings, harassment can adversely affect students' learning, and therefore their academic standing. It can deprive them of educational and ca-reer opportunities because they wish to avoid threatening situations. Students who have been harassed report that they consequently avoid taking a class from or working with a particular faculty member, change their major, or leave a threatening situation (Adams et al., 1983; Lott et al., 1982). Lowered self-esteem follows the conclusion that rewards, such as a high grade, may have been based on sexual attraction rather than one's abilities (McCormack, 1985). Decreased feelings of competence and confidence and increased feelings of anger, frustration, depression, and anxiety all can result from harassment (Cammaert, 1985; Crull, 1982; Hamilton, Alagna, King, & Lloyd, 1987; Liv-ingston, 1982; Schneider, 1987). The psychological stress produced by harass-ment is compounded when women are fired or quit their jobs in fear or frustration (Coles, 1986).

Meek and Lynch (1983) proposed that victims of harassment typically go through several stages of reaction, at first questioning the offender's true inten-tions and then blaming themselves for the offender's behavior. Women with traditional sex-role beliefs are more likely to blame themselves for being ha-rassed (Jensen & Gutek, 1982). Victims then worry about being believed by others and about possible retaliation if they take formal steps to protest the behavior. A victim may be too frightened or confused to assert herself or pun-ish the offender. Psychologists who work with victims of harassment would do well to recognize that not only victims' emotional reactions but also the nature of the grievance process as discussed in this article may discourage women from bringing formal complaints.

Prevention of Sexual Harassment

Some writers have argued that sexual harassment does not occur with great frequency, or if it once was a problem, it has been eliminated in recent years.

Indeed, Morgenson (1989), writing in the business publication *Forbes,* suggested that the whole issue had been drummed up by professional sexual harassment counselors in order to sell their services. Yet the studies cited in this article have documented that sexual harassment is a widespread problem with serious consequences.

Feminists and union activists have succeeded in gaining recognition of   35 sexual harassment as a form of sex discrimination (MacKinnon, 1979). The law now views sexual harassment not as the idiosyncratic actions of a few inconsiderate males but as part of a pattern of behaviors that reflect the imbalance of power between women and men in society. Women in various occupations and educational settings have sought legal redress for actions of supervisors or coworkers, and sexual harassment has become the focus of numerous organizational policies and grievance procedures (Brewer & Berk, 1982).

Well-publicized policies that use an inclusive definition of sexual harass-   36 ment, include an informal dispute resolution option, provide an advocate for the victim (if desired), and permit multiple offenders to be identified seem likely to be the most effective way of addressing claims of sexual harassment. However, even these modifications will not eliminate all of the problems in policies. The severity of the consequences of harassment for the victim, coupled with the problematic nature of grievance procedures and the mildness of punishments for offenders, makes retribution less effective than prevention of sexual harassment. Organizational leaders should not assume that their job is completed when they have established a sexual harassment policy. Extensive efforts at prevention need to be mounted at the individual, situational, and organizational level.

In prevention efforts aimed at the individual, education about harass-   37 ment should be provided (e.g., Beauvais, 1986). In particular, policymakers and others need to learn to "think like a woman" to define which behaviors constitute harassment and recognize that these behaviors are unacceptable. Understanding that many women find offensive more subtle forms of behavior such as sexual jokes or comments may help reduce the kinds of interactions that create a hostile environment. Educating personnel about the punishments involved for offensive behavior also may have a deterring effect.

However, education alone is not sufficient. Sexual harassment is the prod-   38 uct not only of individual attitudes and beliefs, but also of organizational practices. Dzeich and Weiner (1984, pp. 39–58) described aspects of educational institutions that facilitate sexual harassment, including the autonomy afforded the faculty, the diffusion of authority that permits lack of accountability, and the shortage of women in positions of authority. Researchers are beginning to identify the practices in other work settings that facilitate or support sexual harassment, and suggest that sexual harassment may be part of a pattern of unprofessional and disrespectful attitudes and behaviors that characterizes some workplaces (Gutek, 1985).

Perhaps the most important factor in reducing sexual harassment is an or-   39 ganizational culture that promotes equal opportunities for women. There is a strong negative relationship between the level of perceived equal employment opportunity for women in a company and the level of harassment reported (LaFontaine & Tredeau, 1986): Workplaces low in perceived equality are the site of more frequent incidents of harassment. This finding suggests that sexual harassment both reflects and reinforces the underlying sexual inequality that produces a sex-segregated and sex-stratified occupational structure (Hoffman, 1986). The implementation of sexual harassment policies demonstrates the seriousness of those in authority; the language of the policies provides some measure of clarity about the types of behavior that are not acceptable; and grievance procedures may provide relief and legitimacy to those with complaints (Schneider, 1987). But neither policies nor procedures do much to weaken the structural roots of gender inequalities in organizations.

Reforms intended to ameliorate women's position sometimes have un-   40
intended negative consequences (see Kirp, Yudof, & Franks, 1986). The presence of sexual harassment policies and the absence of formal complaints might promote the illusion that this problem has been solved. Assessment of whether organizational policies and practices promote or hinder equality for women is required to insure that this belief does not prevail. A long-range strategy for organizational reform in academia would thus attack the chilly climate for women in classrooms and laboratories (Project on the Status and Education of Women, 1982), the inferior quality of athletic programs for women, differential treatment of women applicants, the acceptance of the masculine as normative, and a knowledge base uninfluenced by women's values or experience (Fuehrer & Schilling, 1985). In other work settings, such a long-range approach would attack both sex-segregation of occupations and sex-stratification within authority hierarchies. Sexual harassment grievance procedures alone are not sufficient to insure that sexual harassment will be eliminated. An end to this problem requires gender equity within organizations.

References

Abbey, A. (1982). Sex differences in attributions for friendly behavior. Do males misperceive females' friendliness? *Journal of Personality and Social Psychology, 42*, 830–838.

Abbey, A., & Melby, C. (1986). The effects of nonverbal cues on gender differences in perceptions of sexual intent. *Sex Roles, 15*, 283–298.

Adams, J. W., Kottke, J. L., & Padgitt, J. S. (1983). Sexual harassment of university students. *Journal of College Student Personnel, 23*, 484–490.

Alexander et al. v. Yale University, 459 F. Supp. 1 (D. Conn. 1977), affirmed 631 F.2d 178 (2nd Cir. 1980).

American Association of University Professors. (1983). Sexual harassment: Suggested policy and procedures for handling complaints. *Academe, 69*, 15a–16a.

American Council on Education. (1986). *Sexual harassment on campus: Suggestions for reviewing campus policy and educational programs.* Washington, DC: Author.

Beauvais, K. (1986). Workshops to combat sexual harassment: A case study of changing attitudes. *Signs: Journal of Women in Culture and Society, 12*, 130–145.

Becker, H. S. (1967). Whose side are we on? *Social Problems, 14*, 239–247.

Benson, D. J., & Thomson, G. (1982). Sexual harassment on a university campus: The confluence of authority relations, sexual interest and gender stratification. *Social Problems, 29*, 236–251.

Brandenburg, J. B. (1982). Sexual harassment in the university: Guidelines for establishing a grievance procedure. *Signs: Journal of Women in Culture and Society, 8*, 320–336.

Brett, J. M., Goldberg, S. B., & Ury, W. L. (1990). Designing systems for resolving disputes in organizations. *American Psychologist, 45*, 162–170.

Brewer, M. (1982). Further beyond nine to five: An integration and future directions. *Journal of Social Issues, 38*, 149–157.

Brewer, M. B., & Berk, R. A. (1982). Beyond nine to five: Introduction. *Journal of Social Issues, 38*, 1–4.

Bumiller, K. (1987). Victims in the shadow of the law: A critique of the model of legal protection. *Signs: Journal of Women in Culture and Society, 12*, 421–439.

Burleigh, N., & Goldberg, S. (1989). Breaking the silence: Sexual harassment in law firms. *ABA Journal, 75*, 46–52.

Cammaert, L. P. (1985). How widespread is sexual harassment on campus? *International Journal of Women's Studies, 8*, 388–397.

Cohen, C. F. (1987, November). Legal dilemmas in sexual harassment cases, *Labor Law Journal*, 681–689.

Coles, F. S. (1986). Forced to quit: Sexual harassment complaints and agency response. *Sex Roles, 14*, 81–95.

Collins, E. G. C., & Blodgett, T. B. (1981). Some see it . . . some won't. *Harvard Business Review, 59*, 76–95.

Crull, P. (1982). The stress effects of sexual harassment on the job. *American Journal of Orthopsychiatry, 52*, 539–543.

Dziech, B., & Weiner, L. (1984). *The lecherous professor.* Boston: Beacon Press.

Fain, T. C., & Anderton, D. L. (1987). Sexual harassment: Organizational context and diffuse status. *Sex Roles, 5/6*, 291–311.

Fitzgerald, L. R., Schullman, S. L., Bailey, N., Richards, M., Swecker, J., Gold, Y., Ormerod, M., & Weitzman, L. (1988). The incidence and dimensions of sexual harassment in academia and the workplace. *Journal of Vocational Behavior, 32*, 152–175.

Fuehrer, A., & Schilling, K. M. (1985). The values of academe: Sexism as a natural consequence. *Journal of Social Issues, 41*, 29–42.

Garvey, M. S. (1986). The high cost of sexual harassment suits. *Labor Relations, 65*, 75–79.

Gilligan, C. (1982). *In a different voice: Psychological theory and women's development.* Cambridge, MA: Harvard University Press.

Glaser, R. D., & Thorpe, J. S. (1986). Unethical intimacy: A survey of sexual contact and advances between psychology educators and female graduate students. *American Psychologist, 41*, 43–51.

Gutek, B. A. (1985). *Sex and the workplace.* San Francisco: Jossey-Bass.

Gutek, B. A., Morasch, B., & Cohen, A. G. (1983). Interpreting social-sexual behavior in a work setting. *Journal of Vocational Behavior, 22*, 30–48.

Hamilton, J. A., Alagna, S. W., King, L. S., & Lloyd, C. (1987). The emotional consequences of gender-based abuse in the workplace: New counseling programs for sex discrimination. *Women and Therapy; 6*, 155–182.

Hoffman, F. L. (1986). Sexual harassment in academia: Feminist theory and institutional practice. *Harvard Educational Review, 56*(2), 107–121.

Jensen, I. W., & Gutek, B. A. (1982). Attributions and assignment of responsibility in sexual harassment. *Journal of Social Issues, 38*, 121–136.

Jones, E. E., & Nisbett, R. E. (1971). *The actor and the observer: Divergent perceptions of the causes of behavior.* Morristown, N.J.: General Learning Press.

Jones, T. S., Remland, M. S., & Brunner, C. C. (1987). Effects of employment relationship, response of recipient and sex of rater on perceptions of sexual harassment. *Perceptual and Motor Skills, 65*, 55–63.

Kanter, R. M. (1977). *Men and women of the corporation.* New York: Basic Books.

Kenig, S., & Ryan, J. (1986). Sex differences in levels of tolerance and attribution of blame for sexual harassment on a university campus. *Sex Roles, 15*, 535–549.

Kirk, D. (1988, August). *Gender differences in the perception of sexual harassment.* Paper presented at the Academy of Management National Meeting, Anaheim, CA.

Kirp, D. L., Yudof, M. G., & Franks, M. S. (1986). *Gender justice.* Chicago: University of Chicago Press.

Kolb, D. M., & Coolidge, G. G. (1988). *Her place at the table: A consideration of gender issues in negotiation* (Working paper series 88-5). Harvard Law School, Program on Negotiation.

Konrad, A. M., & Gutek, B. A. (1986). Impact of work experiences on attitudes toward sexual harassment. *Administrative Science Quarterly; 31*, 422–438.

LaFontaine, E., & Tredeau, L. (1986). The frequency, sources, and correlates of sexual harassment among women in traditional male occupations. *Sex Roles, 15*, 433–442.

Lester, D., Banta, B., Barton, J., Elian, N., Mackiewicz, L., & Winkelried, J. (1986). Judgments about sexual harassment: Effects of the power of the harasser. *Perceptual and Motor Skills, 63*, 990.

Linenberger, P. (1983, April). What behavior constitutes sexual harassment? *Labor Law Journal*, 238–247.

Littler-Bishop, S., Seidler-Feller, D., & Opaluch, R. E. (1982). Sexual harassment in the workplace as a function of initiator's status: The case of airline personnel. *Journal of Social Issues, 38*, 137–148.

Livingston, J. A. (1982). Responses to sexual harassment on the job: Legal, organizational, and individual actions. *Journal of Social Issues, 38*(4), 5–22.

Lott, B., Reilly, M. E., & Howard, D. R. (1982). Sexual assault and harassment: A campus community case study. *Signs: Journal of Women in Culture and Society, 8*, 296–319.

MacKinnon, C. A. (1979). *Sexual harassment of working women: A case of sex discrimination.* New Haven, CT: Yale University Press.

MacKinnon, C. A. (1987). Feminism, Marxism, method and the state: Toward feminist jurisprudence. In S. Harding (Ed.), *Feminism and methodology: Social science issues.* Bloomington: Indiana University Press.

Maihoff, N., & Forrest, L. (1983). Sexual harassment in higher education: As assessment study. *Journal of the National Association for Women Deans, Administrators, and Counselors, 46*, 3–8.

Maypole, D. E. (1986). Sexual harassment of social workers at work: Injustice within? *Social Work, 31*, 29–34.

Maypole, D. E., & Skaine, R. (1982). Sexual harassment of blue-collar workers. *Journal of sociology and social welfare, 9*, 682–695.

McCormack, A. (1985). The sexual harassment of students by teachers: The case of students in science. *Sex Roles, 13*, 21–32.

McIntyre, D. I., & Renick, J. C. (1982). Protecting public employees and employers from sexual harassment. *Public Personnel Management Journal, 11*, 282–292.

Mednick, M. T. (1989). On the politics of psychological constructs: Stop the bandwagon, I want to get off. *American Psychologist, 44*, 1118–1123.

Meek, P. M., & Lynch, A. Q. (1983). Establishing an informal grievance procedure for cases of sexual harassment of students. *Journal of the National Association for Women Deans, Administrators, & Counselors, 46*, 30–33.

Merry, S. E., & Silbey, S. S. (1984). What do plaintiffs want? Reexamining the concept of dispute. *Justice System Journal, 9*, 151–178.

Metha, J., & Nigg, A. (1983). Sexual harassment on campus: An institutional response. *Journal of the National Association for Women Deans, Administrators, & Counselors, 46,* 9–15.

Miller, J. B. (1976). *Toward a new psychology of women.* Boston: Beacon Press.

Morgenson, G. (1989, May). Watch that leer, stifle that joke. *Forbes,* 69–72.

Popovich, P. M., Licata, B. J., Nokovich, D., Martelli, T., & Zoloty, S. (1987). Assessing the incidence and perceptions of sexual harassment behaviors among American undergraduates. *Journal of Psychology, 120,* 387–396.

Powell, G. N. (1986). Effects of sex role identity and sex on definitions of sexual harassment. *Sex Roles, 14,* 9–19.

Project on the Status and Education of Women. (1982). The campus climate: A chilly one for women? Washington, DC: Association of American Colleges.

Pryor, J. B. (1985). The lay person's understanding of sexual harassment. *Sex Roles, 13,* 273–286.

Pryor, J. B., & Day, J. D. (1988). Interpretations of sexual harassment: An attributional analysis. *Sex Roles, 18,* 405–417.

Reilly, M. E., Lott, B., & Gallogly, S. (1986). Sexual harassment of university students. *Sex Roles, 15,* 333–358.

Rifkin, J. (1984). Mediation from a feminist perspective: Promise and problems. *Mediation, 2,* 21–31.

Robertson, C., Dyer, C. E., & Campbell, D. (1988). Campus harassment: Sexual harassment policies and procedures at institutions of higher learning. *Signs: Journal of Women in Culture and Society, 13,* 792–812.

Robinson, W. L., & Reid, P. T. (1985). Sexual intimacy in psychology revisited. *Professional Psychology: Research and Practice, 16,* 512–520.

Rossi, P. H., & Weber-Burdin, E. (1983). Sexual harassment on the campus. *Social Science Research, 12,* 131–158.

Rowe, M. P. (1981, May-June). Dealing with sexual harassment. *Harvard Business Review,* 42–46.

Saal, F. E., Johnson, C. B., & Weber, N. (1989). Friendly or sexy? It may depend on whom you ask. *Psychology of Women Quarterly, 13,* 263–276.

Schneider, B. E. (1987). Graduate women, sexual harassment, and university policy. *Journal of Higher Education, 58,* 46–65.

Shotland, R. L., & Craig, J. M. (1988). Can men and women differentiate between friendly and sexually interested behavior? *Social Psychology Quarterly, 51,* 66–73.

Tangri, S. S., Burt, M. R., & Johnson, L. B. (1982). Sexual harassment at work: Three explanatory models. *Journal of Social Issues, 38,* 33–54.

Terpstra, D. E., & Baker, D. D. (1988). Outcomes of sexual harassment charges. *Academy of Management Journal, 31,* 185–194.

Terpstra, D. E., & Cook, S. E. (1985). Complainant characteristics and reported behaviors and consequences associated with formal sexual harassment charges. *Personnel Psychology, 38,* 559–574.

Thomann, D. A., & Wiener, R. L. (1987). Physical and psychological causality as determinants of culpability in sexual harassment cases. *Sex Roles, 17,* 573–591.

Trager, T. B. (1988). Legal considerations in drafting sexual harassment policies. In J. Van Tol (Ed.), *Sexual harassment on campus: A legal compendium* (pp. 181–190). Washington, DC: National Association of College and University Attorneys.

U.S. Equal Employment Opportunity Commission. (1980, November 10). Final amendment to guidelines on discrimination because of sex under Title VII of the Civil Rights Act of 1964, as amended. 29 CFR Part 1604. *Federal Register, 45,* 74675–74677.

U.S. Merit Systems Protection Board. (1981). *Sexual harassment in the federal workplace: Is it a problem?* Washington, DC: U.S. Government Printing Office.

U.S. Merit Systems Protection Board. (1988). *Sexual harassment in the federal government: An update.* Washington, DC: U.S. Government Printing Office.

Wilson, K. R., & Krause, L. A. (1983). Sexual harassment in the university. *Journal of College Student Personnel, 24,* 219–224.

Wilson, M. (1988). Sexual harassment and the law. *The community psychologist, 21,* 16–17. ■

Questions for Meaning

1. How does Riger define "sexual harassment"?
2. Why are women more likely than men to be victims of sexual harassment?
3. Why are women reluctant to report incidents of sexual harassment?
4. What is meant by "the reasonable person rule"? Why does Riger find this rule problematic?
5. How do formal and informal grievance procedures differ? What are the disadvantages of an informal procedure?
6. According to Riger, what may be the best way of preventing sexual harassment?
7. Vocabulary: prevail (4), respondents (4), pervasive (8), noncompliance (10), nonsituated (12), wont (13), inimical (21), stratification (26), normative (28), idiosyncratic (35), ameliorate (40).

Questions about Strategy

1. As called for by the *Publication Manual of the American Psychological Association,* Riger prefaces her article with an abstract. What is the advantage in doing so? Is there any risk?
2. How would you describe the tone of this article? Is it appropriate for the topic and audience?
3. How does Riger justify her decision to focus on educational institutions?
4. Riger first states her thesis at the beginning of paragraph 7. What does she achieve by reserving her thesis until this point? How would the article change if Riger decided to include her thesis in the opening paragraph?
5. Riger draws on a large number of sources. How effectively has she drawn on them? When you encounter a reference list such as Riger's, how do you respond as a reader?

ONE STUDENT'S ASSIGNMENT

Write an argument for or against an official policy banning faculty from dating students. Include material from at least two sources in *The Informed Argument*. If you wish, you may also draw on other reading that you have done so long as you are careful to cite all sources. Use MLA documentation. Understand, however, that your paper should show evidence of your own thinking. Draw on written sources to help support what you have to say, but do not allow these sources to dominate your paper.

Risk Taking

Erik Miles

From orientation to graduation, universities promote individual growth   1
both in and beyond the classroom. They encourage us to be involved in campus life and sensitive to race, gender, and other political issues in the hope that we will become good citizens and not simply competent professionals.

In addition to encouraging students to grow into full adulthood, universi-   2
ties can also treat students like children. We are cautioned about STDs, AIDS, eating disorders, and chemical abuse. But some universities have gone beyond cautioning their students and have taken on the responsibility of protecting their students from risk. One way in which some universities have attempted this is through proposing bans which categorically prohibit romantic relationships between their students and their faculty (Begley 175–76). This is a difficult responsibility to fulfill, because those who assume the responsibility of protection have an obligation to accurately present the risks. If the real risks are not portrayed honestly, individuals are left vulnerable.

A startling example of inaccurately portraying harmful effects surrounded   3
the release of "Reefer Madness." It was a "scare movie," exaggerating the harmful effects of marijuana. While attempting to dissuade the use of marijuana, it instead "became a cult film for jeering potheads in the '60's and early '70's. And in turn . . . helped foster the [idea that] cocaine itself is safe" (Martz 55).

The effects of not accurately presenting the risks of a harmful situation   4
were again demonstrated in campaigns against hard drug use in the late 1980s. Advertising strategies that stated "Drugs kill" have unintentionally left users wide open to addiction. Because the campaign portrayed death as the risk of using drugs, and death was not the automatic effect of drug use, users were able to ignore the more likely danger in using the drug: addiction. Moreover, their natural vulnerability toward addiction was heightened by the feeling that they were "beating the odds" every time they used

drugs and did not die. Bans against romantic relationships between professors and students possess the same potential to obscure the real risks and
to possibly encourage illicit behavior.

When one attempts to dissuade someone from engaging in harmful be-   5
havior, one assumes someone does not understand the risks involved. To
do this, one must demonstrate the risks, and it is tempting to focus on the
most dramatic ones. But the most dramatic risk is not necessarily the most
dangerous risk. In the case of the antidrug advertisers, the dramatic risk
was death. The dangerous risk was addiction. In the case of dating bans,
the dramatic risk is the consequence of getting caught. The dangerous risk
is emotional pain.

Universities assume that their students and faculty do not understand   6
the potential for exploitation and emotional and psychological harm involved
in developing romantic relationships. It is simpler to threaten professional, legal, or academic consequences for such behavior, thereby creating artificial
risks as consequences of this behavior rather than address the real risks.

If these bans cannot physically prevent student–faculty relationships,   7
what is their intent? If the intent of the bans is to prevent students and faculty from emotional and psychological suffering, the bans do not fulfill their
purpose. Administrations cannot prevent individuals from suffering emotional pain. Although policies can define unacceptable behavior, they have
no jurisdiction over feelings.

Instead, by threatening litigation, dismissal, and monetary restitution,   8
policies prohibiting relationships deceive students into believing that what
is really at risk is something for which they can receive compensation. The
introduction of artificial punishments (litigation, etc.), which are not inherently related to the acts they wish to prevent (student faculty dating), allows individuals to persist in their natural tendency to abstract the
consequences of their behavior and deny what is truly at stake.

Not understanding what is truly at stake leaves one vulnerable to the   9
risks that the bans do not address. The universities' bans give individuals a
false sense of understanding of, and thus a false sense of control over, the
situation. In the case of drug use, the user needs only to avoid death to
feel in control of the drug. In the case of a student and a professor involved
in a relationship at a university that has a ban on dating, all the couple
needs to do to feel in control of the situation is avoid being "found out" by
the university.

Students and faculty are naive in the belief that they have control over   10
the situation. It is not the universities' bans that make these relationships
illicit, and it is not the universities' prohibitions that make these relationships
wrong. It is the extreme power differential, which some have suggested is in-
cestuous in nature (Leatherman 180), that makes these relationships illicit

and potentially harmful. The potential for damage inherent in these relationships goes beyond broken hearts. Because they have a dynamic similar to
that between a therapist and a client, they have the potential to be emotionally and psychologically devastating. This does not make all professors
sexually predatory. While students are not simply unsuspecting Red Rid-
inghoods at the mercy of lustful Wolves, these relationships by their nature
have the potential to be exploitive.

Undoubtedly, these bans are intended to assist students and faculty in   11
making choices about their relationships. But instead, the bans obscure
the real choice to be made. If this is true, then the bans neither physically
prevent student–faculty relationships, nor do they honestly portray them in
such a way that individuals can make decisions about whether to enter into
them. Unable to accomplish its primary intention, such a ban would be useless. And by creating potential for greater harm, such a ban would be unethical and therefore should not be instated.

Works Cited

Begley, Sharon. "Clipping Cupid's Wings." The Informed Argument. Ed. Robert K.
    Miller. Fort Worth: Harcourt, 1995. 175–77.
Leatherman, Courtney. "The Debate over Faculty–Student Dating." The Informed
    Argument. Ed. Robert K. Miller. Fort Worth: Harcourt, 1995. 178–81.
Martz, Larry. "A Dirty Drug Secret: Hyping Instant Addiction doesn't help." Drugs,
    Society, and Behavior 92/93. Ed. Erich Goode. Guilford: Dushkin, 1993. 55–56.

SUGGESTIONS FOR WRITING

1. Research the problem of date rape and write an essay explaining how
   people can reduce the risk of becoming a victim.
2. In "Crying Rape," Peter Hellman presents a negative picture of "the
   politics of date rape." Respond to his views in an argument in favor of
   establishing rape crisis centers.
3. Respond to the opinions expressed in "New Rules about Sex on Campus," in an argument for or against the establishment of policies that
   restrict faculty–student dating.
4. How should college administrators respond to the harassment of gay
   and lesbian students? Drawing on the article by Mary Crystal Cage,
   write a policy statement appropriate for your school.
5. Write an argument for or against creating gay and lesbian dormitories.

6. Draw on your knowledge of your own gender and write an essay explaining what you think "the other sex" most needs to understand about sexual harassment.
7. Does your school have a policy against sexual harassment? If so, obtain a copy of it and write an evaluation of it.
8. Drawing on the articles by Anne B. Fisher and Ellen Frankel Paul, write a grievance procedure for sexual harassment in the workplace.
9. Read the Supreme Court opinions in *Hunter v. Allis-Chambers* or *Harris v. Forklift Systems*. Write a summary of the majority view and another of the minority view.
10. Write a summary of the article by Stephanie Riger.

COLLABORATIVE PROJECT

Write a code defining acceptable behavior when initiating a relationship. Indicate also what kind of behavior is unacceptable. Be sure to consider the views of people of different gender and different sexual orientation.

SECTION 4

IMMIGRATION:
WHO GETS TO BECOME AN AMERICAN?

EMMA LAZARUS

THE NEW COLOSSUS

Emma Lazarus (1849–1887) was a Russian-born poet who settled in New York. Her works include *Admetus and Other Poems* (1871), *Alide* (1874), *Songs of the Semite* (1882), and *By the Waters of Babylon* (1887). But of all her works, none is so famous as her sonnet to the Statue of Liberty. Now carved on the statue's pedestal, the poem was first published in 1883. As you read it, note the pattern with which lines are rhymed.

Not like the brazen giant of Greek fame,   1
With conquering limbs astride from land to land;
Here at our sea-washed, sunset gates shall stand
A mighty woman with a torch, whose flame
Is the imprisoned lightning, and her name   5
Mother of Exiles. From her beacon-hand
Glows world-wide welcome; her mild eyes command
The air-bridged harbor that twin cities frame.
"Keep, ancient lands, your storied pomp!" cries she
With silent lips. "Give me your tired, your poor,   10
Your huddled masses yearning to breathe free,
The wretched refuse of your teeming shore.
Send these, the homeless, tempest-tost to me,
I lift my lamp beside the golden door!"

Questions for Meaning

1. Lazarus calls her poem "The New Colossus" and begins by contrasting the Statue of Liberty with "the brazen giant of Greek fame." To what is she alluding?

246

2. Although the Statue of Liberty is on the American east coast, Lazarus associates it with "sunset gates." From what point of view would New York be associated with the setting sun rather than the rising sun?
3. In the final line, Lazarus makes "golden door" a metaphor for New York harbor. In what sense then can arrival in America be seen as reaching a "golden door"?
4. Vocabulary: astride (line 2), beacon (line 6), pomp (line 9), teeming (line 12).

Questions about Strategy

1. Lazarus composed her poem as a sonnet: a fourteen-line poem expressing a complete thought written with a fixed number of stressed and unstressed syllables in each line and divided into an octave (eight lines) and a sextet (six lines). In this form, the end of the first line rhymes with the end of the fourth, fifth and eighth line; the second line rhymes with the third, sixth, and seventh; and, in the sextet, two new sounds are introduced, with every other line rhyming. Does her use of this poetic form contribute to the argument made by the poem?
2. In line 6, Lazarus renames the Statue of Liberty. The statue's actual name is "Liberty Enlightening the World." Lazarus calls it "Mother of Exiles." How do these names differ, and how does the change reveal the poet's purpose in this poem?

MICHAEL KINSLEY

GATECRASHERS

Responding to growing concerns about immigration, Michael Kinsley published the following editorial on December 28, 1992. A Harvard-educated attorney who is cohost of CNN Crossfire, Kinsley is senior editor of *The New Republic,* a magazine that usually reflects liberal political opinions.

A new Census Bureau report predicts that there will be 383 million Americans   1
in the year 2050. That's 128 million more than there are now, and 83 million more than the bureau was predicting just four years ago, when it appeared that the U.S. population would peak and stabilize at around 300 million.

   Part of the startling upward revision reflects an unexpected increase in   2
the birthrate. But most of it is due to an increase in immigration. The Census Bureau expects an average of 880,000 new arrivals a year, legal and illegal. By 2050 a fifth of the American population will be folks who arrived here after

1991 and their children. Almost half the population (47 percent) will be "minority"—black, Asian, Hispanic, Native American—compared with just a quarter today.

Immigration has not been much of a political issue lately. In fact a 1990   3
law increasing the annual legal quota by 40 percent passed almost unnoticed. And there's been little fuss over the total failure of the hotly contested 1986 immigration reform—which for the first time made it a crime to employ illegal aliens—to achieve its purpose of reducing illegal immigration.

But the politics of immigration may be heating up. And the political col-   4
oration of anti-immigrant sentiment may be changing too. Despite the traditional association of the Democratic Party with immigrant groups, what little opposition there has been to immigration in recent years has come vaguely from the left. Some environmentalists believe that immigrants contribute to overpopulation and strain the nation's natural resources. And some blacks (and white sympathizers) worry that immigrants are stealing opportunities from America's oldest and still most down-trodden minority.

What's new, though, is the re-emergence of anti-immigrant sentiment   5
on the right. Here it takes the traditional form of concern about the nation's ethnic character. This fits in with other social concerns about matters like multiculturalism and even gay rights: a sense that some classic and comfortable image of America is being changed before our eyes.

Presidential candidate Pat Buchanan sometimes included immigration in   6
his riffs on this general theme. And the *National Review* (edited by an immigrant—although only from Britain) ran a long cover story (by another immigrant from Britain) condemning immigration as a liberal elitist plot and predicting an America of "ethnic strife . . . dual loyalties . . . collapsing like the Tower of Babel" if the foreign hordes aren't kept out. ("Tired? Poor? Huddled? Tempest-Tossed?" asked the witty cover. "Try Australia.") Free market capitalism itself, the author suggests at one point, may depend on the continued predominance of Anglo-Saxon stock.*

There have been Americans who feared that our country is "running out   7
of room" since the frontier closed off more than a century ago. Although 128 million extra people in the next six decades sounds like an awful lot, that is no greater than the population increase over the past six decades. (And it's a much smaller proportional increase.) Only environmentalist zealots could believe that America would be better off if our population were still only 125 million—even accepting the complacent assumption that everyone reading this column would be one of the lucky 125 million.

There is no answer to the argument that "at some point" the country   8
becomes too crowded, but there's no particular reason to believe we're at that point yet. Germany, with less than a third of America's population in a far smaller area, is currently accepting new arrivals in almost the same volume.

Germany may not seem the happiest example for my side of the immigra-   9
tion argument. There, immigration is straining the social fabric and producing

*An excerpt from this article appears on pages 272–276.

riots and violence by neo-Nazi punks. Not to defend such xenophobic outrages, but Germany is different from the United States. Like most countries in the world (Israel, to pick a sensitive example), its sense of nationhood has a large ethnic component. This is neither good nor evil; it's just a fact. Although any civilized nation should be prepared to take in refugees from oppression, the "otherness" of foreigners will always be more vivid elsewhere than in America. In other countries, concern about diluting the nation's ethnic stock even has a certain validity.

Such concerns have no validity in America. In fact, they are un–American.   10
If applied in earlier times, when they were raised with equal passion, they would have excluded the ancestors of many who make the ethnic/cultural preservation argument today. The anti-immigration literature seems to regard this point as some kind of cheap shot. But I cannot see why.

On the economic effects of immigration, there are studies to suit every   11
taste. Immigrants take jobs from poor Americans; or they go on welfare and bloat the tax bill; or both; or neither. Basic economic logic suggests that even when a new arrival "takes" a job, the money he earns and spends will in turn create a job or so. The more the merrier is a tenet of capitalism dating back to Adam Smith, and nothing I've seen disproves it.

The propaganda from FAIR (Federation for American Immigration Re-   12
form, the liberal anti-immigration lobby) on these issues is unpersuasive because it tends to "prove too much," as the lawyers say. With a straight face, FAIR compares immigration to slavery and child labor, as if the trouble with these practices were the burden they placed on rival sources of labor. In one recent broadside FAIR's executive director, Dan Stein, suggests that America should have curtailed immigration after the Civil War in order to increase economic opportunities for ex-slaves. Whether this would actually have benefited blacks or not, it might have spared us Dan Stein.

The emerging case for curtailing immigration has many byways. There's   13
the argument that we need "time to digest" the immigrant wave of the past couple of decades, just as previous waves were followed by periods of low immigration. There's the argument that today's ethnic assertiveness and social welfare apparatus mean that the machinery of assimilation no longer works to turn immigrants into middle-class Americans. There's the undeniable fact that instant communication and cheap transportation have eroded the natural restraints of distance and ignorance on the demand for places in America.

There are counterarguments to all these points, and others. And counter-   14
counterarguments. No one can know the effect of future large-scale immigration on our country. It has always been beneficial in the past, but that's no guarantee it will be so in the future. The previous tenant of this column, the late Richard Strout believed passionately that America's achievement of a liberal welfare state depended on levels of both affluence and social cohesion that were threatened by large-scale immigration.

Immigration is a subject, I suspect, of which very few opinions are   15
changed because of arguments or statistics. It's almost a matter of faith. Your views of immigration depend on your sense of what makes America America.

For some it's endless open spaces. For some it's a demographic image frozen in time. For some that stuff on the Statue of Liberty still plucks a chord. All these visions of America have a large component of fantasy. But I know which fantasy I prefer. ■

Questions for Meaning

1. How is the American population likely to change in the next half-century?
2. Kinsley claims that concern about "the nation's ethnic stock" is less pressing in the United States than in other countries. Why does he believe this?
3. According to Kinsley, how is the debate over immigration changing?
4. In paragraph 12, Kinsley introduces the idea that an argument can be unpersuasive if it proves too much. How could this be?
5. Vocabulary: riffs (6), elitist (6), complacent (7), xenophobic (9), curtailed (12), assimilation (13).

Questions about Strategy

1. Kinsley opens his argument by emphasizing that the U.S. population is increasing and that recent Census Bureau reports were apparently inaccurate. How does this opening contribute to the argument that follows?
2. In paragraph 5, Kinsley associates immigration with such controversial issues as multiculturalism and gay rights. Is the association appropriate?
3. At the beginning of paragraph 9, Kinsley concedes, "Germany may not seem the happiest example for my side of the immigration argument." If Germany is *not* a good example, should he have used it?
4. Consider the use of "fantasy" in paragraph 15, especially in the last sentence. Does it leave Kinsley open to counterargument?

GARY S. BECKER

ILLEGAL IMMIGRATION: HOW TO TURN THE TIDE

The winner of the 1992 Nobel prize in economics, Gary S. Becker teaches at the University of Chicago. He is also a Fellow of the Hoover Institution at Stanford University. Drawing on his knowledge of economics, Becker has written on the costs of current immigration policies. He first published the following article in *Business Week* in 1993.

The uproar over White House nominees for Attorney General who had em-   1
ployed illegal aliens has focused attention once again on unlawful entry of workers from poor countries. This is a perplexing issue not only for the U.S. but also for France, Germany, Italy, Japan, and other prosperous, democratic countries. I believe such immigration can be effectively discouraged by sizably increasing the number of legal immigrants and at the same time punishing more severely the illegal entrants or those who hire them.

Given the yawning gap between the incomes of rich and poor countries,   2
the issue will not simply go away—as long as it remains so easy to enter prosperous countries illegally or on tourist visas. Workers are attracted to rich countries because the jobs available there are much better-paying than anything they can find in their homelands. And that's true even though they are usually employed as low-paid, unskilled labor in restaurants, households, agriculture, or, in a few cases, manufacturing industry.

Since illegal aliens mainly take jobs shunned by native workers, some   3
economists oppose punishing them. Instead, they advocate what amounts to "benign neglect"—especially if the immigrants are not eligible for tax-supported benefits. But democracies find it politically impossible to deny them health care, education for their children, and other benefits paid for by the taxpayer. And when the number of illegals in a country gets large, political pressure often mounts to grant them amnesty, as happened in the 1980s in the U.S. I am troubled, too, by the morality of a policy that encourages violations of the law by employers and illegal immigrants, while entry is denied to millions who stoically wait their turn for the right to enter legally.

Seldom Penalized

This is why democratic countries must take stronger steps than simply shipping   4
illegal entrants who get caught back to where they came from. Entry cannot be reduced without effective punishment of either illegal aliens or their companies. Employers will not stop hiring illegal aliens on their own, because they do not believe they are doing anything wrong. The 1986 U.S. Immigration Control & Reform Act includes penalties for companies that hire illegal aliens, but households and very small businesses have seldom been penalized. Even though

domestic help is believed to account for a considerable fraction of all off-the-books workers, Zoë Baird's household appears to be the first one fined.

The reasons I have given for greater restrictions on illegal entrants should   5
be distinguished from erroneous claims that they take jobs from native work-ers or that they are often exploited. Research has found that the employment prospects of native workers are only slightly reduced when immigrants enter a local labor market. And although some illegal workers are afraid to complain about bad treatment—because they may be deported—there isn't room for ex-tensive exploitation in the highly competitive labor markets where most ille-gals find jobs. For example, those households and small companies that do not pay Social Security and unemployment compensation taxes for illegal em-ployees are forced by the competition for labor to pay higher wages than if these taxes were paid. In a study of apprehended illegal workers, economist Barry R. Chiswick of the University of Illinois at Chicago found that their average pay was in fact well above the minimum wage.

Same Asylum

I am not advocating the erection of a wall against immigration. Instead a more   6
generous immigration policy should go hand in hand with greater punishment of illegal entrants, including fines and possibly jail terms. Greater legal immi-gration is not only desirable in its own right but would also reduce the number who seek to enter illegally. Not surprisingly, illegal entry generally expands when a country contracts the number of immigrants accepted.

France, Germany, and other countries are mistaken if they believe that   7
they can reduce their immigration problem by cutting back on the right to political asylum or other legal means of entry. When legal immigration is cur-tailed, the number who sneak in or seek work after entering on a tourist visa will expand—unless a country is willing to punish effectively either the illegal entrants or the households and small companies that hire them.

I suggested in an earlier column that the most rational approach would be   8
to sell the right to immigrate, but a less radical method of improving present policy and combating illegal immigration would be to allow a larger number of skilled and young people to enter legally. To prevent immigrants from taking advantage of government handouts, however, they should not be eligible for welfare, food stamps, government-financed health care, or certain other bene-fits until they become naturalized citizens. Politicians on both sides of the de-bate might well support this requirement, because it would not permanently exclude legal immigrants from taxpayer-financed benefits. Meanwhile, it would give them an incentive to become citizens as soon as they could. ■

Questions for Meaning

1. What is Becker's thesis and where does he state it?
2. On what grounds is U.S. immigration policy morally questionable? Is it questionable on any other grounds?
3. According to Becker, what happens when legal immigration is restricted?
4. Does Becker make any distinction between the rights of immigrants and the rights of citizens?
5. Vocabulary: shunned (3), benign (3), stoically (3), erroneous (5), compensation (5).

Questions about Strategy

1. Becker opens his argument by referring to a controversy in the news. (President Clinton had nominated Zoë Baird for Attorney General. During her confirmation hearing, Baird admitted hiring illegal aliens for whom she did not pay Social Security taxes.) How would this strategy have benefited Becker in 1993? Has he now lost this benefit?
2. Does Becker make any concessions that are likely to appeal to readers who are opposed to immigration?
3. In his concluding paragraph, Becker refers to an earlier article in which he advocated a different approach to immigration. What does he achieve by making this reference? Is there any risk to this strategy?

JACLYN FIERMAN

IS IMMIGRATION HURTING THE U.S.?

As the title of her article suggests, Jaclyn Fierman focuses on a basic question in debates over immigration policy. Advocates of immigration believe that immigrants make valuable contributions to the American economy. Opponents believe they contribute to unemployment and high costs for social services. As you read the following article, first published in *Fortune* in 1993, note how Fierman answers the question she poses in her title.

A record nine million people immigrated to the U.S. in the 1980s, roughly equal to the number of tempest-tossed citizens now out of work and yearning to rejoin the labor market. This coincidence has not been lost on low-skilled Americans, who are competing for fewer jobs at lower wages. But even many among the well-educated and highly paid have begun to wonder whether Lady Liberty should dim her beacon. As Cornell University labor economist Vernon Briggs puts it, "Why allow even one unskilled worker into this country when we have so many of our own?"   1

Fully 61% of respondents polled in June by the *New York Times* and CBS News said the nation's open-armed immigration policy should be curtailed. Congress is now considering several bills to stem a separate tide—the growing number of people seeking political asylum. Last year over 100,000 of these poured in; many disappeared permanently into the crowd after receiving temporary working papers and a date for a formal hearing. Immigration has also captured the attention of President Clinton, who says he plans to make the issue "a priority."   2

Such concern is global. In Europe, rising immigration at a time of record unemployment is expanding the ranks of right-wing parties and sparking ugly urban riots. Germany, which long boasted the Old World's most open borders, stopped hearing most new pleas for political asylum as of July 1.   3

While things aren't nearly so bad in the U.S., recent events are fanning public anxiety. Islamic fundamentalists, some residing in the U.S. illegally, were among the suspects arrested in connection with the World Trade Center bombing and a later plot to blow up New York tunnels and buildings. The wreck along New York City's coastline of a boat loaded with nearly 300 illegal Chinese immigrants turned a spotlight on the booming Asian black market that smuggles foreigners (for hefty fees) into the U.S.   4

What should be done? Obviously Washington can and must improve its efforts to keep out the truly dangerous. And while it's impossible to eliminate illegal immigration, the government also ought to ensure that the number of incoming illegals—perhaps as many as 300,000 annually in recent years—at least doesn't move higher and even begins to abate. Beyond that, however, U.S. immigration policy is basically sound and humane. There's no economic   5 case for trimming back the current target of roughly 700,000 authorized immigrants a year, some 500,000 of whom are members of families being reunited. If anything, the U.S. should welcome *more* newcomers from especially desirable groups—namely, the gifted, the ambitious, and the rich.

How many more? In 1935 economist Bernhard Ostrolenk, a Polish immigrant, rejected the idea that new arrivals competed with Americans for a finite number of jobs: "The number is not fixed by some occult power, but increases with industrial activity."   6

Prescribing slightly higher legal immigration will inflame hotheads convinced that such a policy would damage the U.S. economy. But it's based on cold facts. The Urban Institute estimates that about 74% of adult male immigrants hold jobs, vs. 72% of the general male population. Even illegals with limited education have acquitted themselves well. In 1986 the U.S. granted amnesty to three million illegal aliens, about two-thirds of whom were Mexican. Today, says economist Demetrios Papademetriou, chief immigration expert in the Bush Administration, virtually all the adults are earning more than the minimum wage.   7

This relative paucity of freeloaders and deadbeats means that rookie Americans, as a group, more than pay their way. George Borjas, an economics professor at the University of California at San Diego, calculates that the nation's 20 million immigrants currently receive about $1.1 billion more in cash welfare payments each year than they pay into the welfare system through taxes. But by working and spending on things like food, rent, and clothing, they also contribute $5 billion annually to the economy. Net gain for the U.S.: almost $4 billion a year.   8

What about high unemployment among America's troubled urban underclass? Can't much of that be pinned on record levels of immigration? No, says Wade Henderson, director of the Washington, D.C., office of the National Association for the Advancement of Colored People: "You can't blame immigrants for the problems of the black poor." Their plight, he says, mainly arises from failures in domestic social policy rather than from immigration policy.   9

That's not to say that wrenching displacement never occurs. Janitors in Los Angeles and hotel workers in Washington, D.C., to select two instances, were once predominantly black Americans and are now mainly immigrants. But experts agree that in most cases new arrivals replace and compete for low-skilled jobs with other immigrants, not with Americans. The garment industry is a prime example: Men and women from Latin America, the Caribbean, and the Far East sit at machines once operated by Italians and Jews. "The garment district has always been a stepping stone for immigrants, especially those who speak no English," says Thomas Glubiak of New York State's Department of Labor.   10

Compelling evidence even shows that immigrants boost overall employment on balance. In a study of the 400 largest U.S. counties, María Enchautegui, an economist at the Urban Institute, found that for every   11

100-person increase in the population of adult immigrants, the number of new jobs rose by 46. By contrast, for every 100 new native-born Americans, the number of jobs rose by just 25.

Toy Town in Los Angeles demonstrates how immigrants can raise em-   12
ployment, revitalize neighborhoods, even expand global trade. Smack in the middle of L.A.'s version of the Bowery, some 300 wholesalers sell over $1 billion a year of low-tech toys made in the Far East—blocks, guns, jump ropes, soldiers, dolls. The merchants were largely born in Taiwan, Hong Kong, and Vietnam, and arrived in the U.S. almost penniless. But the business required little English, and warehouse space in the area was cheap. Today Toy Town employs 2,000 people. Its entrepreneurs sell not only to toy outlets in the U.S., but also to those in Mexico, Canada, and Eastern Europe.

Among the most successful is Charles Woo, 41, born in Hong Kong   13
and partially paralyzed by a childhood bout with polio. In 1969 he came to the U.S. to study physics at UCLA. Ten years later, on the verge of receiving his doctorate, he quit school to start ABC Toys with his brother, Shu. "We know what American kids want," he says. Five years ago he started a second wholesale company, Mega Toys, whose 15 employees sell $15 million of goods a year.

Though immigration's long-term benefits are compelling, the short-   14
term adjustment costs can be high, particularly since the task of absorbing one million people a year is not evenly distributed across the country. It falls hardest on six cities: Los Angeles, New York, Chicago, Houston, Washington, and Miami. While illegals don't qualify for, say, food stamps or welfare payments, every youngster living in the U.S. is entitled by law to an education, regardless of the family's immigration status. Likewise, public hospitals, despite acute overcrowding and underfunding, must be blind when responding to medical emergencies.

Record inflows of refugees, immigrants, and illegals have forced the   15
overburdened to go begging. California Governor Pete Wilson has asked Washington for $1.45 billion to cover immigrant expenses. New York has asked the federal government to take custody of the 3,000 illegal aliens crowding state jails at a cost of $65 million a year.

Others who have a right to feel shortchanged are the country's unskilled   16
laborers. During the Eighties the gap between what they pocketed, on average, and what college graduates earned grew from 26% to 55%. This widening wage differential is mainly caused by rising competition from low-paid foreign workers who stay *at home*—and who are taking away market share in industries the U.S. once dominated. Still, Harvard economist Richard Freeman attributes about one-third of the gap to the fact that the ranks of willing but poorly educated workers were swelled by immigrants. However, the only surefire way to help displaced blue-collar Americans, he says, is through better education and training, not through immigration policy.

Even so, don't make the mistake of assuming that every last newcomer   17
entering the country is short on book learning. Fully 25% of the arrivals in the Eighties had college degrees, according to the Urban Institute. The new

American is someone around 26 years old, as likely to be male as female. He or she is an urban creature, apt to settle in an ethnic enclave along a public transportation line, and similar to the people *Harper's* magazine described in 1914: "America's attraction is not to the good or the bad, to the saint or to the sinner, but to the young, the aggressive, the restless, the ambitious."

What has changed is the skin color, culture, and language of immigrants. In the Fifties, 53% of them came from Europe and just 6% from Asia. During the Eighties only 11% were European; most of the rest were evenly split between Asians and Latinos. Asians settled mainly in California; Latinos spread out.

Behind the geographic flip-flop was a sweeping immigration reform in the mid-Sixties that redressed a long history of racist policy. Despite a sterling record—the U.S. currently admits more legal immigrants than all other potential host nations combined—the country has always been of two minds about coping with hordes of newcomers. Almost every poll every published on the subject, and there have been dozens since the 1930s, shows that a majority of Americans—predominantly descendants of immigrants—favor further limits on immigration. Says Rita Simon, author of *The Ambivalent Welcome,* a new book on the subject: "It is something of a miracle that over 50 million immigrants gained entry to the U.S. between 1880 and 1990."

Swept up in the spirit of the civil rights movement, however, the U.S. in 1965 started to do away with quotas that favored white Europeans and made family reunification the pillar of its new policy. (Before, family ties carried less weight in decisions to grant entry.) In poured children, parents, spouses, and siblings from all parts of the world.

In 1990, Congress took another stab at immigration reform, this time with a more focused economic eye. The government nearly tripled to 140,000 the number of visas distributed on the basis of skills. Here's the breakdown. Skilled workers and their families get roughly 120,000 visas; the unskilled, 10,000. Another 10,000 visas are reserved for people willing to invest $1 million in the U.S. Even among the half a million visas handed out to unite families, don't assume the bulk go to unskilled workers. Most families are a mix. Tagging along behind Papa, who has a sixth-grade education, might be his son the rocket scientist.

When Washington revisits immigration policy, what talents should it favor? One of the most urgently needed might not strike some as a "skill." In the alphabet soup of categories, unskilled visas—classified EW, jokingly referred to as the Eternally Waiting group—include those for child care workers and home health aides. "The wait is 16 years, time enough for that person to care for the next generation," says Theodore Ruthizer, a New York immigration attorney. Ruthizer argues compellingly that foreign-born nannies and other caretakers ought to be able to work lawfully while they wait for their papers—a limbo that should be limited to three years. Washington might consider reclassifying these much-in-demand people as skilled workers. Any conscientious parent would agree with that designation.

The road for artists who uplift our spirits can be as tortuous as the one   23
the unskilled must travel. German cinematographer Michael Ballhaus, 57, is
valued in Hollywood for his ability to "shoot a $10 million movie on a $5
million budget," as he puts it. His credits include hits like Martin Scorsese's
Goodfellas and Mike Nichols's *Working Girl*. But despite investing three years
and $20,000 for immigration lawyers, Ballhaus was repeatedly denied a green
card in the category reserved for gifted artists on grounds that his talents were
technical, not artistic. In 1987 he—and 1.4 million others—entered the immigration sweepstakes, a quirky component of U.S. immigration law that now
selects 40,000 winners a year. Ballhaus won his green card; Hollywood won
too.

America's ambivalence about welcoming the talented, the tired, and the   24
poor even extends to the rich. The 1990 reform made a modest effort to
change that, allocating 10,000 visas a year to foreigners willing to set up shop
in the U.S. with at least a $1 million investment (or $500,000 in depressed
areas) and hire ten Americans to work at the business. So far only 725 people
have sought permanent residence by this route. By the end of May the Immigration and Naturalization Service had approved 296 applications and rejected
140, and was still weighing the rest.

One who knocked on this door is Taiwan's Tomi Huang, 46. Huang started   25
a tour bus company in California in 1991. Huang bought four buses for
$300,000 each and employs the requisite ten people, plus one. She rents out the
buses—complete with drivers who speak Spanish, English, or Chinese—to
travel agents who in turn book foreign clients to Disneyland, Las Vegas, and
other West Coast attractions. Huang, whose family owns a taxi company in
Taiwan and "half a mountainside" with fruit trees, says she started the business
after taking a bus tour herself. "It looked like fun, and I figured I could do it,"
she says. "You don't need a college degree to do an honest day's work."

Why have so few entrepreneurs applied for the new program? For one   26
thing, the approval process is arduous and risky. Prospective Americans must
first make the investment plunge and then wait two years before the federal
government will even consider issuing a permanent visa. The approval process
itself can take up to a year. "If the business fails before you get your final papers, you could get deported," says Howard Hom, a Los Angeles immigration
lawyer. Many entrepreneurs and investors with money to spare have bypassed
the U.S. and headed for Canada. Little wonder. The red tape there is minimal,
and the investment threshold can be as low as $250,000. Result: Canada has
attracted some $3 billion in new investment since 1986, far more than the U.S.
is on track to achieve.

Other than stealing a page from Canada, what else should Washington   27
do? Approving a few additional impact grants to help cities that host the
poorest of arrivals might make sense. But footing local bills entirely is not the
answer, since these communities ultimately benefit from immigrants' economic activism. Instead, Washington ought to consider doubling what it spends
on English-language programs for children and adults, to about $1 billion.

Learning their adopted land's tongue, most immigrants agree, is the hardest challenge they face and the biggest barrier to getting a foot on the job ladder—and then climbing it.

Supporting efforts like the North American Free Trade Agreement 28 should also help bolster Third World economies and stem the tide of impoverished, unskilled workers seeking opportunity in the U.S. Certainly NAFTA seems a far better bet than trying to police 7,582 miles of border with fewer than 4,000 patrolmen. Economist Sherman Robinson of the University of California at Berkeley estimates that each percentage point increase in the value of Mexico's capital stock—the new buildings, businesses, and factories that a NAFTA-spurred investment boom would give rise to—would be enough stimulus to keep 25,000 of its citizens at home.

Finally, if Bill Clinton is really hankering for an exciting new way to 29 shake up U.S. immigration policy and boost job creation, here's a terrific idea from Nobel Prize-winning economist Gary Becker: Sell visas. Fix the price at perhaps $50,000 or some level sufficient to attract those seriously seeking opportunity, not a free ride. Lack of wealth or skills should not exclude prospective Americans. Let the poor come on a federal loan that they would have to pay back over time or face deportation. "This would ensure we would get only the ambitious," says Becker. What better population screen could the U.S. ask for? ■

Questions for Meaning

1. What does Fierman think of current immigration policy? Does she recommend any changes?
2. Is there any evidence to suggest that immigrants are contributing to the American economy?
3. Does immigration increase unemployment?
4. What effect are immigrants having on American cities?
5. How have immigrants changed in recent years?
6. Vocabulary: fundamentalists (4), abate (5), occult (6), paucity (8), acute (14), redressed (19), ambivalence (24), arduous (26).

Questions about Strategy

1. Consider the reference, in paragraph 1, to "tempest-tossed citizens" who are "yearning to rejoin the labor market." Do you detect an allusion in this language? What is its effect?
2. What does Fierman achieve through her use of numbers in paragraph 21?
3. Where does Fierman link her discussion of immigration to news that was current when she wrote? Why do you think she made these references?

4. Why does Fierman draw attention to the program that offers visas for foreigners prepared to invest a million dollars in the United States?
5. Fierman concludes by endorsing a recommendation by Gary Becker, the author of another article in this section. Is this a fitting conclusion for her article?

MICHAEL MANDELL, CHRISTOPHER FARRELL, AMY BORRUS, RUSSELL MITCHELL, AND IRENE RECIO

THE PRICE OF OPEN ARMS

To what account are aliens straining budgets and producing intolerance? To what extent do traditional American values require that aliens be treated well when they reside here? These are among the questions addressed in the following article by a team of writers for *Business Week,* which published "The Price of Open Arms" in June 1993. Michael Mandell and Christopher Farrell are based in New York, Amy Borrus in Washington, Russell Mitchell in San Francisco, and Irene Recio in Miami. As you read their article, note how reports from different locations have been drawn together.

On June 6, in the dead of night, a tramp steamer ran aground off a New York City beach with nearly 300 illegal Chinese immigrants on board. The week before, a freighter slipped into San Francisco and disgorged 250 Chinese aliens at an unused pier near the Golden Gate Bridge. Last winter, as the dust settled around the bomb-scarred World Trade Center in New York, one fact was clear: Uncountable Middle Easterners enter the U.S. illegally—then disappear.

More than 1 million immigrants from all over the world are settling in America every year—and some 200,000 of them are coming in with neither an invitation nor approval to stay. That's partly because the U.S., unlike other industrialized countries, seeks to keep an open door for those looking for better opportunities or trying to escape brutalities. The U.S. economy, after all, was largely built by immigrants. Across the U.S., countless hotels, garment factories, and restaurants still depend on their labor—both skilled and unskilled.

"Emergency"

But is America's dedication to the ideals of the Statue of Liberty and the portals of Ellis Island outdated? The nation now faces the largest immigrant wave in its history. And across the country, economists, politicians, and some just plain folks are worried that the American economy and its culture are on the verge of being swamped. A major factor behind their fears: Immigrants, legal and not, are posing huge costs on the system, even while local

governments struggle to cope with high unemployment and strained budgets. "I definitely don't believe the last one in should pull up the gangplank,"
says Douglas J. Besharov, a resident scholar at the American Enterprise Institute for Public Policy Research and the son of immigrants. "But that doesn't
mean we shouldn't have an orderly policy for deciding who comes and who
doesn't."

Those who risk life and limb and a lifetime's savings to come to the U.S.   4
aren't much interested in policy. Take "Mei Yok," a 32-year-old Malaysian
woman who has worked illegally in Manhattan's garment trade for more than
two years. Employers have taken her wages, then threatened her with violence
or deportment, she says. But the payoff is sweet. "If you take one dollar back
to Malaysia, it is double the value," she says. "You work here to earn U.S.
dollars so you can greatly improve your living standard in Malaysia. I can buy
a house in Malaysia even though I can't buy one here."

Economic opportunity has long been an inducement for immigration to   5
the U.S. What has stepped up the flow is shifting politics: As capitalism
spreads to less developed countries and former communist nations, it is shaking
people loose from their traditional roots and allowing them to leave in order to
seek better opportunities abroad. That has produced a new surge of illegal immigrants from China and Russia. "People will give up all their worldly pos-
sessions to get here," says Seattle immigration lawyer Dan P. Damlov. "My
clients tell me, 'I would rather live in an American jail than go back to the rice
fields of China.'"

These new migrants are also driven by the well-founded hope of achiev-   6
ing legal refugee status in America. Since 1980, the U.S. has welcomed more
than 1.2 million refugees, mainly from communist countries. The same legacy
of the cold war now gives special preference, first to Cubans and Vietnamese,
and now to Russians and Chinese. "We have a migration emergency," says
one Administration Official. "We're being inundated with more refugees and
those who might not be."

Taxpayer Burden

The price of the emergency? In Los Angeles County, the average cost of   7
providing health, welfare, and other noneducation services to each illegal immigrant is about $440 a year—about 40% more than the cost for the rest of the
population.

Then there's schooling. Education represents the best way to integrate   8
immigrants and their children into American society: But the flood of newcomers is putting enormous stresses on already taxed school systems. Public
schools in Dade County were overwhelmed in the last school year by some
75,000 non-English-speaking immigrant children, many illegal. That meant
an $80 million bill for special programs in Spanish and Creole. "We can't turn
away kids because of their parents' problems, so we take many that are illegally
here," said Henry Fraind, chief spokesperson at the Dade County Public
School System. "And the American taxpayer pays."

The taxpayer is also bearing the burden of other costs. The percentage of   9
immigrants on welfare in California rose from about 8.6 percent in 1980 to
10.4 percent in 1990, according to George Borjas, an economist at the University of California at San Diego. And at least 25 percent of the jail population
in Southern California, and perhaps much more, consists of illegal aliens, according to Kenneth J. Elwood, an assistant director of the INS in Los Angeles.

"Scut Work"

In response, California recently passed a law that cuts Medi-Cal payments to   10
hospitals giving many kinds of nonemergency care to illegals. That's supposed
to save the state and the feds $90 million. But local governments complain that
they'll have to pick up the tab, and it could actually cost more money as illegals
try to get nonemergency care by going to emergency rooms. The law is unfair,
says Dr. Larry A. Bedard, who sits on the hospital board in affluent Marin,
where taxpayer groups have organized to stem government spending on illegals. "We want them to clean our houses, rake our leaves, take care of our
children, do the scut work of life," Bedard says of the illegals. "But if they get
sick, we don't want to take care of them."

Indeed, most immigrants, legal and illegal, are highly productive work-   11
ers. That's why they came to the U.S. and why they're in such demand in
some parts of the country. "I was praying some of them would wash up on the
shores of Gore Creek," which runs through Vail, Colo., says Jim H. Osterfoss,
owner of the Roost Lodge in Vail, talking about the Chinese boat people who
tried to land in New York. Facing a shortage of housekeepers, he already has
permission from the INS to bring in two foreign housekeepers this year—but
he says he could use an additional eight such workers.

It's also true that illegal aliens actually pay a sizable amount of taxes. The   12
problem: Most of the costs, such as schooling and education, show up at the
local level, while most of the tax revenue goes to the federal and state governments. Take Los Angeles County, which recently estimated that illegal immigrants paid $904 million in taxes and fees to all levels of government in
1991–92. The county and other local governments, however, received no
more than $127 million of that, about 14 percent—far less than the costs of
services to illegal immigrants.

Hot Button

With a weak economy forcing local governments to tighten budgets, it's little   13
surprise that anti-immigration sentiment is on the rise in California. In last
week's Los Angeles mayoral election, won by Republican Richard Riordan,
opponent Michael Woo "turned himself into a mild version of Pat Buchanan
on immigration issues," says Mark Petracca, professor of political science at the
University of California at Irvine. In the earlier primary, a third candidate had
called for the immediate deportation of city gang members who were undocumented aliens. And illegal immigration may replace abortion as the hot-
button issue in California's next gubernatorial race two years from now.

The same qualms are driving immigration policy at the federal level. The   14
White House, alarmed at the growing number of illegal Chinese and other
immigrants who are slipping into the U.S., this winter directed the National
Security Council to try to curb the flow without trampling on the rights of
bona fide political refugees. As a result, the Coast Guard has stepped up
surveillance of offshore vessels, and the INS now routinely detains Chinese
illegals while their requests for asylum are pending. In the past, they were usually released on their own recognizance.

But no one expects anything like a major overhaul of refugee or immigra-   15
tion policies. For starters, President Clinton still hasn't appointed a new INS
commissioner. The whole issue is politically explosive. And advocacy groups
fiercely resist any curbs on due process—let alone numbers—of immigrants.

Indeed, at a time when the new French government is talking about a   16
"zero-immigration" policy and Germany has scaled back the right of asylum,
there are no signs of such a movement in the U.S. Thirty-year-old Leila, an
illegal immigrant from Honduras, knows that. She came to Miami on May 16
with a job lined up as a maid for a wealthy family here. "I've seen that in this
country you can work for money to buy things and lead a better life," she says.
To people such as Leila, America's door remains wide open.   ■

Questions for Meaning

1. How is American immigration policy different from the immigration
   policies of other industrialized countries?
2. Why are immigrants willing to work even when victimized by their
   employers?
3. What economic and political changes are changing the nature of American immigration?
4. According to this article, why are the taxes paid by immigrants not necessarily paying for the services they receive?
5. Vocabulary: portals (3), deportment (4), inducement (5), legacy (6), inundated (6), qualms (14), bona fide (14)

Questions about Strategy

1. What is the purpose of paragraph 1? How do the three examples it includes affect you?
2. Consider the quotation from Larry A. Bedard in paragraph 10. What
   do the authors achieve by locating this quotation at the end of the paragraph?
3. To what extent do the authors recognize that there is more than one
   side to the controversy over immigration?
4. How diverse are the people quoted in this article? Are the quotations
   well chosen?

WESTON KOSOVA

THE INS MESS

Weston Kosova is an associate editor at Washington's *City Paper.* He was formerly a reporter and researcher for *The New Republic,* which published "The INS Mess" in 1992. You will find references to the Bush Administration, which was still in power when Kosova wrote. But do not assume this material is dated. The Immigration and Naturalization Service (INS) continues to be a large government bureaucracy that has difficulty meeting the many demands made of it. As you read, imagine that you are seeking to immigrate legally to the United States.

"No, no, I do not know what is the number of the form. It is the one for a person who has a family to bring to the country. Do you have that one? The one for relatives? . . . No. I tell you. I do not know the number of the form."   1

It was early afternoon on a Wednesday in December, and the line at the United States Immigration and Naturalization Service's regional office in Northern Virginia was backed up to the door. A fortyish man at the head of the line, a Pakistani, had been pleading his case for nearly five minutes to an agitated clerk, who shifted on her stool behind the high counter.   2

"Sir, like I told you, you've got to give me more to go on than that," the clerk said. "You see how many forms I've got sitting back here? I need the *number.*" She called the next person in line.   3

Despite her insistence, the clerk did know which form the man wanted: after the line dissipated, I walked up to the same window and, in flawless Midwestern, asked for "the form you need to bring a family member here from another country to live." Without so much as a question she reached back to the stack of papers behind her and handed over INS I-130, Petition for Alien Relative—the most commonly requested of INS forms.   4

Incidents like this are familiar to anyone who has encountered the Immigration and Naturalization Service. Mention the INS to a recent immigrant or someone trying to get a green card or work permit and you will see eyes roll. Xenophobic paper pushers are just a small part of the problem. Every immigrant has his own tales of lost forms, ill-trained inspectors, usurious fees, arbitrarily enforced rules, and notoriously sluggish bureaucracy.   5

In November 1990 the General Accounting Office issued a scathing, 177-page report on the INS that laid bare the Justice Department agency's negligence. "Over the past decade weak management systems and inconsistent leadership have allowed serious problems to go unresolved," the GAO charged. The report revealed how INS employees rigged their work schedules, allowing them to take home as much as $20,000 a year in overtime pay. It described an INS office in Los Angeles that deposited the thousands of dollars in fees it took in each day by mailing the cash to the bank.   6

The GAO scolding was issued a year after Raymond Momboisse, a senior INS attorney, quit after penning a twenty-two-page internal memo in   7 which he described the agency as "totally disorganized." Among other things, Momboisse revealed that the INS regularly shifted funds from office to office to cover nearly $40 million in overspending, and that it deliberately overhired border patrol guards as a way to pressure Congress for more money.

Momboisse's memo came on the heels of yet another investigation of the INS that had been ordered by then Attorney General Richard Thornburgh. This inspection foreshadowed many of the abuses that the GAO would detail in its report a year later. Thornburgh discovered that the INS had lost 23,059 certificates of citizenship with "an estimated street value ranging from $11 million to $115 million." The Justice Department also charged that INS "data reported for applications received, applicants interviewed, and fees collected were inaccurate and unreliable at all organizational levels."

Shortly after the Justice Department audit, INS director Alan C. Nelson was forced to resign. In his place, President Bush appointed Gene McNary, a St. Louis County executive (and county chairman of Bush's 1988 presidential campaign). At a press conference the day after his confirmation, McNary pledged to clean up the agency and overhaul its management. "I intend to see that it is brought under control and that it is centralized," he said. In the months that followed, McNary pored over the Justice Department report and the Momboisse memo. He ordered the INS's four regional managers to review the offices under their jurisdictions. He acquainted himself with the workings of the vast, 16,000-employee, $1 billion agency.

Yet now, more than two years later, McNary and his crew haven't even begun to reform the INS. McNary came up with a few nutty, ill-fated proposals—requiring all Americans and residents over age 16 to carry national worker-identification cards, offering Nicaraguan refugees cash "loans" to leave the country—but nothing resembling the plan he promised would bring the agency "under control."

Even if McNary were to set about gauging the immigration service's various management sores, however, the frustrations immigrants face wouldn't ease. Immigrants are treated shabbily by the INS not only because the agency is careless and inept, but because, despite its name, "immigration" and "naturalization" are not really its first concerns; the INS is far more interested in tracking down and expelling illegal aliens.

"The internal mentality of the INS continues to be one of [law] enforcement, while at the same time the INS tries to maintain a p.r. image of providing public services and immigration benefits," says Ignatius Bau of the San Francisco-based Coalition for Immigration Reform. Among immigration lawyers like Bau, this is commonly referred to as the "cop mentality," an attitude that is borne out in McNary's own assessment of his agency's purpose. In a *Washington Post* profile, McNary said that his top five priorities are: to "gain control of the southern border; increase efforts to deport criminal aliens; put into effect new regulations on granting asylum; enforce sanctions against employers who hire illegal aliens; and update the data processing system." In other words, he considers the INS to be at least four-fifths a police agency.

As a result, the agency's enforcement details are watched closely by top   13
management. The INS maintains twenty-four-hour armed patrols along every
open yard of the U.S. border. Under the 1986 Federal Immigration Reform
and Control Act, businesses that hire illegal aliens now risk draconian fines.
Swift deportation awaits those nabbed without proper papers. Last year the
INS rounded up and expelled nearly 1 million illegals.

In contrast to its concerted enforcement effort, the INS only grudgingly ad-   14
ministers the other, more mundane half of its responsibility. Since navigating
incoming legal immigrants through the labyrinth of immigration laws is of
comparatively little concern to agency brass, they don't bother to keep a close
watch on how immigration benefits are handled. Instead, INS regional offices
around the country are granted virtually a free hand in deciding for themselves
how and to whom they should give out green cards, visas, and work permits.
Predictably, the result is chaos. In his parting memo, Momboisse compared the
INS to "a feudal state with each region, district, and sector acting independently to give its own interpretation to the law."

For example, the city of Chevy Chase sits on the border between Wash-   15
ington, D.C., and Maryland, and is divided by Western Avenue. One side of
Western Avenue is considered Chevy Chase, D.C., and falls under the control
of the INS regional office in Arlington, Virginia. The other side is considered
Chevy Chase, Maryland, and falls under the jurisdiction of the INS office in
Baltimore.

Suppose, for instance, that you are a non-American who married a U.S.   16
citizen, which makes you automatically eligible for permanent residence status.
If your spouse lives in Chevy Chase, Maryland, you must travel to Baltimore,
file the proper documents, and wait nine to twelve months (or longer, depending on the time of year) for an interview from an INS inspector before you will
be granted permanent residence papers. During that time, you cannot leave the
country for any reason or else you lose your eligibility to return. If, however,
your spouse lives across Western Avenue in Chevy Chase, D.C., you will be
interviewed by an INS inspector in Arlington the same day that you file your
papers. In Baltimore you cannot submit papers without attaching a copy of a
birth certificate. In Arlington they don't even ask to see a birth certificate.

Each regional office also decides how many applications it will process a   17
day. The Arlington office typically hands out numbers to the first 125 people
in line when it opens in the morning, and turns everyone else away. Lines usually start forming for the next day soon after the office closes in the evening.
Other offices compound the problem by accepting applications only two or
three days a week. Still others are open during business hours every day and
take all comers.

And the rules vary not only from office to office, but often from inspec-   18
tor to inspector within the same office. One recent immigrant from the
Philippines told me that after waiting in line from two in the morning until
noon to file naturalization papers, he was finally seen by an inspector. "The
lady told me that my application was no good," he said. "She told me that I

needed to show her my birth certificate, but I didn't have it." The inspector informed him that he would have to come back with his birth certificate before he could file his papers. So the following week he once again waited in line for nearly ten hours. This time he brought his birth certificate and presented it to the inspector—a different one from the week before. "She said I don't need it," he says. "She didn't look at it, even."

Some immigrants especially those whose English is poor, have taken to hiring   19
lawyers to accompany them to their meetings with INS inspectors, precisely to avoid this sort of frustration. But many immigrants can't afford the immigration service's prohibitive filing fees, let alone attorney's fees. Every INS form has a fee, and every fee must be paid up front. Except under very limited circumstances, there are no waivers of fees for people who cannot afford to pay. And fees are not refunded, even if the application is rejected.

Coming to America isn't cheap. Filing an application with the INS for   20
naturalization costs $90. Becoming a permanent resident runs $120. Requesting permission to bring a foreign relative runs $75. For a work permit, add $50 more. Add to that fees for fingerprinting and photographs that are required for many applications, and in some cases the total for the application alone can top $500 to $600, says Bau, and sometimes reaches into the thousands.

Last year the INS attempted to charge Salvadoran refugees fees totaling   21
$380 when they applied for temporary resident status under a special amnesty program. A family of five or more was subject to $1,435 in fees. But under pressure from immigration groups and Joe Moakley, a Democratic representative from Massachusetts, the INS scaled back the fees to $75 per person, $225 for a family of three or more. In order to remain in the country, however, Salvadorans must renew their status every six months, at a cost of $60 per person. And, true to form, the INS refused to pay refunds to those refugees who paid the original $380.

For those who can afford the filing fees, there is still the matter of figuring out   22
which combination of forms is required. There are dozens of combinations governing every possible circumstance under which a person could immigrate.

"How do you immigrate to the United States? A very good question,"   23
says INS spokesman Duke Austin. "Very difficult to answer. . . . I mean, we're talking hundreds of pages of legislation." Indeed, immigration laws are needlessly, often mindlessly, complex. Every few years, in a fit of immigration "reform," Congress trowels a new layer of benefits and restrictions on top of existing legislation, making it more difficult both for immigrants trying to figure out if they qualify to enter the country and for the INS. "I've been working at it for fifteen years," admits Austin, "and there are things that even I don't understand about the law."

For example, under the law there are three broad categories of people   24
who are allowed to immigrate: 1) family members of U.S. citizens or legal permanent residents; 2) people found eligible to work in the United States; and 3) political refugees. A would-be immigrant who doesn't fall into one of these

three categories can't immigrate. But even immigrants who do appear to meet the requirements still may not be allowed to enter.

Take the first category. The INS claims that keeping families together is   25 a primary concern, so immediate family members of American citizens or permanent legal residents are eligible for visas without waiting. However, what you consider to be your immediate family and what the immigration laws consider it to be are probably very different. The INS, for instance, does not count brothers or sisters as immediate family. It does not recognize a child either, if he or she is married or over 21. Neither does it consider a husband or wife immediate family if, as INS documents put it, "you were not both physically present at the marriage ceremony, and the marriage was not consummated." The INS considers these family members "restricted."

The distinction is important. While an unlimited number of "immed-   26 iate" family members are allowed to immigrate each year, "restricted" family are subject to quotas and long waits. Under new immigration laws that went into effect last October, a total of approximately 25,000 restricted family members from each country will be allowed to immigrate this year (up from 20,000 previously). When their eight-digit visa number comes up, they can enter the country. But from many countries thousands more than the limit apply each year, resulting in huge backlogs. For most countries, the wait for restricted relatives now stands at about three years. From Mexico, the wait is nine years. The Philippines tops the list with 12.5 years.

Equally quirky rules apply to immigrants who come to the United States   27 to work. Not everyone is eligible. Immigrant workers must fall under one of the agency's three work "preference" classes. "First Preference" workers, according to the INS, are "aliens with extraordinary ability in the arts, sciences, education, business, or athletics which has been demonstrated by sustained national or international acclaim, or outstanding professors or researchers or certain multinational executives and managers." "Second Preference" workers are essentially the same as First Preference workers but not as famous. "Third Preference" workers are skilled and unskilled laborers, such as fruit pickers, who perform usually low-paying, menial jobs that employers can't find enough Americans to do.

But an immigrant who meets the INS's requirements might still be pre-   28 vented from immigrating. Suppose that a catering company in New York has its eye on a famed Turkish ice sculptor and wants to hire her full time. She would be eligible to enter the United States under the "extraordinary ability" category, right? Probably not. Because as defined by the immigration laws, extraordinary skills aren't skills that are extraordinary in themselves, but those that no other person in the United States possesses. This means that before a company may bring a foreign citizen here to work, it must prove that it has searched for an American to do the job and failed, usually by posting notices and advertising in newspapers. And the United States already has its share of ice sculptors, many of whom doubtless are unemployed. Even if the ice sculptor is found eligible to immigrate, that still isn't a guarantee she'll get in, since the INS puts a yearly cap of 40,000 on immigrant workers (with the exception

of Third Preference workers, who are admitted only when shortages of laborers arise).

Similarly, immigrants applying for green cards as political refugees may be re-   29
jected even if technically they are eligible under the law. According to INS
Form I-589, Request for Asylum in the United States, "The burden of proof
is upon you to establish that you have a well-founded fear of persecution on
account of your race, religion, nationality, membership in a particular social
group, or political opinion." The INS defines persecution as "to pursue; to
harass in a manner designed to injure, grieve, or afflict; to oppress; specifically, to cause or put to death because of belief."

     Sounds fair enough, but that isn't the definition that the government ac-   30
tually applies in deciding who is granted political refugee status. If it were,
President Bush wouldn't be summarily turning away the latest wave of Haitian
boat refugees, many of whom would qualify. Rather, political refugee status is
largely granted not on the basis of persecution itself, but on the basis of which
country is doing the persecuting. A 1987 GAO study revealed that the government was far more likely to grant political asylum to refugees from countries
hostile to the United States than those from friendly countries. Thus, the administration granted asylum to scores of refugees from Afghanistan during the
1980s and to refugees who escaped from Cuba in a helicopter last year, but
refused thousands from El Salvador and Guatemala.

There are still further immigration restrictions. Under the law, not even an   31
extraordinarily skilled, politically persecuted husband of an American citizen
can immigrate to the United States if he is or was at any time in the previous
ten years a member of the Communist Party. Under federal law, this prohibition is supposed to be illegal. In 1987 Congress passed legislation reforming
the 1952 McCarren–Walter Act, which barred Communists from entering the
United States. The new law prohibits the government from shunning people
who hold political beliefs that, for an American citizen, would be legal. But
that hasn't stopped the INS from requiring immigration applicants to "list
your present and past membership in or affiliation with every organization,
association, fund, foundation, party, club, society, or similar group in the
United States or any other place," including "location, dates of membership,
and the nature of the organization." Write down "Communist Party" and you
won't get in. The INS also maintains a "lookout list" of people from various
countries who, because of their political beliefs, would be rejected out of hand
if they attempted to immigrate. The list, which dates back to 1904, contains
more than 350,000 names; 250,000 of them were added after 1980.

     Otherwise qualified applicants are also prohibited from immigrating if   32
they are infected with what the government terms a "highly communicable
disease" and thereby pose a health risk to Americans. The administration's
definition of this term, however, is strangely selective. As Donald Goldman, a
member of the National Commission on AIDS, points out, "Tuberculosis isn't
included on the government's list of infectious diseases. Neither is bubonic

plague." In practice, the term "highly communicable disease" has become a euphemism for AIDS. The administration claims that HIV and AIDS carriers are barred because the government cannot afford health care for infected indigent immigrants. This is a specious argument. After all, the government doesn't stop terminal cancer patients at the border.

There is one way under the new immigration laws that a lucky few can   33
circumvent all these nitpicky regulations and enter the country whether they're eligible to or not. For the first time, the INS is holding a lottery this year that will grant green cards to a total of 40,000 people. For four days last October, applicants were allowed to mail in as many entry forms as they wanted. There were only three restrictions. Applicants couldn't be Communists. They couldn't be "highly communicable." And they couldn't be from Mexico. Or the Philippines. Or China. Or from any country other than thirty-three mostly white, mostly European nations chosen to participate. It is probably no coincidence that many of the excluded countries are the same non-white nations on which the United States had severe immigration restrictions before country-by-country quotas were abolished in 1965. And it is certainly not a coincidence that fully 40 percent of the 40,000 lottery winners have to be from Ireland. Edward Kennedy, who sits on the Senate's Immigration and Refugee Affairs Subcommittee, wrote the requirement into the bill.

Immigration law is excessively complex because Congress has no incentive to   34
make it more simple. From the standpoint of Capitol Hill, there's no percentage in immigration. The people affected by the immigration laws aren't citizens, and noncitizens don't vote. Yet it wouldn't require a midnight session of Congress to reform the laws enough so that immigrating to America would become a less harrowing experience:

Split the agency in two. Even in the face of the INS's elaborate defense   35
machinery, the number of people attempting to sneak into the United States these days isn't dwindling. While the estimated number of illegal immigrants declined between 1986 and 1988, a December INS newsletter reports that in the past two years, the numbers have once again hit pre-1986 levels. The number of illegal aliens in this country is now about 4.5 million.

Granted, controlling the borders is an impossible task. But in its zeal to   36
catch every illegal, the INS regards everyone on the other side with suspicion. To the service, a legal immigrant is merely an illegal alien with papers. The logical way to ease the agency's internal conflict is to form two agencies: a true Immigration and Naturalization Service, concerned with assisting eligible applicants, and an Identification and Expulsion Service to police the borders and remove illegals.

Get rid of the forms. The INS could easily get by with one or two well-   37
designed application forms. Current forms are endlessly redundant, requiring the same information line after line. The only purpose multiple forms serve is to justify the agency's fees—which wouldn't be needed if there weren't so many forms.

Gut the immigration laws. Start by tossing out the lookout list, ending re-   38
strictions on AIDS carriers, and getting rid of all others you can't explain in
one breath.

Reforming the INS not only would benefit legal immigrants, it would   39
also bring closer to truth a chapter in American mythology. The agency that
ushered millions of eager immigrants through the gates of Ellis Island and into
the promised land has been transformed into an impenetrable army of cops and
bureaucrats. The INS should at least try to live up to the "give us your poor"
refrain.

Meanwhile, America's huddled masses can find the agency's new face   40
reflected on TV. Recently, ABC bumped its long-running sitcom "Perfect
Strangers," about a wide-eyed island immigrant who comes to America to live
with his cousin. Taking over the same time slot is "Billy," a sitcom about a
Scottish college professor whose visa runs out. In "Perfect Strangers," the
foreign cousin finds family, adventure, and a beautiful American bride. In
"Billy," the professor marries a student to avoid being deported by the INS. ■

Questions for Meaning

1. According to Kosova, what is the primary concern of the United States
   Immigration and Naturalization Service?
2. How expensive is it to be a legal immigrant to this country? Can you
   imagine other expenses besides those stated in this article?
3. What categories of people are allowed to immigrate legally?
4. How does immigration law define "immediate family"?
5. Does INS policy and procedure reveal any evidence of racism?
6. Vocabulary: dissipated (4), usurious (5), scathing (6), draconian (13),
   mundane (14), labyrinth (14), euphemism (32), specious (32).

Questions about Strategy

1. Consider the story with which this article begins. What does it illustrate? Why does Kosova point out that INS I-130 is "the most commonly requested of INS forms"?
2. In paragraph 16, Kosova asks readers to imagine that they are applying
   for permanent resident status. Why does he use the second person in this
   paragraph?
3. In paragraph 31, Kosova points out that 250,000 out of 350,000 names
   on a list dating back to 1904 were added after 1980. What is he implying here?
4. The article concludes with three specific recommendations for reform.
   Has Kosova prepared the way for them? Do these proposals seem reasonable to you by the time you get to them?
5. What is Kosova suggesting when he uses his conclusion to briefly contrast two television shows?

PETER BRIMELOW

A NATION OF IMMIGRANTS

Born and educated in Great Britain, Peter Brimelow now lives and works in the United States. His books include *The Patriot Game: Canada and the Canadian Question Revisited* (1986) and *The Wall Street Game* (1988). "A Nation of Immigrants" is an editor's title for the following short excerpt from a long, controversial article on immigration that Brimelow published in *National Review* in 1992. Founded by William F. Buckley Jr., *National Review* is a monthly magazine that reflects politically conservative opinions.

Everyone has seen a speeded-up film of the cloudscape. What appears to the naked eye to be a panorama of almost immobile grandeur writhes into wild life. Vast patterns of soaring, swooping movement are suddenly discernible. Great towering cumulo-nimbus formations boil up out of nowhere, dominating the sky in a way that would be terrifying if it were not, in real life, so gradual that we are barely aware that anything is going on. 1

This is a perfect metaphor for the development of the American nation. American, of course, is exceptional. What is exceptional about it, however, is not the way in which it was created, but the speed. 2

"We are a nation of immigrants." No discussion of U.S. immigration policy gets far without someone making this helpful remark. As an immigrant myself, I always pause respectfully. You never know. Maybe this is what they're taught to chant in schools nowadays, a sort of multicultural Pledge of Allegiance. 3

But it secretly amuses me. Do they really think other nations sprouted up out of the ground? ("Autochthonous" is the classical Greek word.) The truth is that *all* nations are nations of immigrants. But the process is usually so slow and historic that people overlook it. They mistake for mountains what are merely clouds. 4

This is obvious in the case of the British Isles, from which the largest single proportion of Americans are still derived. You can see it in the place-names. Within a few miles of my parents' home in the north of England, the names are Roman (Chester, derived from the Latin for camp), Saxon (anything ending in -*ton,* town, like Oxton), Viking (-*by,* farm, like Irby), and Norman French (Delamere). At times, these successive waves of peoples were clearly living cheek by jowl. Thus among these place-names is Wallesey, Anglo-Saxon for "Island of the Welsh"—Welsh being derived from the word used by low-German speakers for foreigners wherever they met them, from Wallonia to Wallachia. This corner of the English coast continued as home to some of the pre-Roman Celtic stock, not all of whom were driven west into Wales proper as was once supposed. 5

The English language that America speaks today (or at least spoke until the post-1965 fashion for bilingual education) reflects the fact that the peoples 6 of Britain merged, eventually; their separate contributions can still be traced in it. Every nation in Europe went through the same process. Even the famously homogeneous Japanese show the signs of ethnically distinct waves of prehistoric immigration.

But merging takes time. After the Norman Conquest in 1066, it was nearly three hundred years before the invaders were assimilated to the point where court proceedings in London were again heard in English. And it was nearly nine centuries before there was any further large-scale immigration into the British Isles—the Caribbean and Asian influx after World War II.   7

Except in America. Here the process of merging has been uniquely rapid. Thus about 7 million Germans have immigrated to the U.S. since the beginning of the nineteenth century. Their influence has been profound—to my British eye it accounts for the odd American habit of getting up in the morning and starting work. About 50 million Americans told the 1980 Census that they were wholly or partly of German descent. But only 1.6 million spoke German in their homes.   8

So all nations are made up of immigrants. But what is a nation—the end-product of all this merging? This brings us into a territory where words are weapons, exactly as George Orwell pointed out years ago. "Nation"—as suggested by its Latin root *nascere,* to be born—intrinsically implies a link by blood. A nation is an extended family. The merging process through which all nations pass is not merely cultural, but to a considerable extent biological, through intermarriage.   9

Liberal commentators, for various reasons, find this deeply distressing. They regularly denounce appeals to common ethnicity as "nativism" or "tribalism." Ironically, when I studied African history in college, my politically correct tutor deprecated any reference to "tribes." These small, primitive, and incoherent groupings should, he said, be dignified as "nations." Which suggests a useful definition: tribalism/nativism is nationalism of which liberals disapprove.   10

American political debate on this point is hampered by a peculiar difficulty. American editors are convinced that the term "state" will confuse readers unless reserved exclusively for the component parts of the United States—New York, California, etc. So when talking about sovereign political structures, where the British would use "state," the Germans *"Staat,"* and the French *"l'état,"* journalists here are compelled to use the word "nation." Thus in the late 1980s it was common to see references to "the nation of Yugoslavia," when Yugoslavia's problem was precisely that it was not a nation at all, but a state that contained several different small but fierce nations—Croats, Serbs, etc. (In my constructive way, I've been trying to introduce, as an alternative to "state," the word "polity"—defined by Webster as "a politically organized unit." But it's quite hopeless. Editors always confuse it with "policy.")   11

This definitional difficulty explains one of the regular entertainments of U.S. politics: uproar because someone has unguardedly described America as a   12

"Christian nation." Of course, in the sense that the vast majority of Americans are Christians, this is nothing less than the plain truth. It is not in the least incompatible with a secular *state* (polity).

But the difficulty over the N-word has a more serious consequence: it   13
means that American commentators are losing sight of the concept of the "nation-state"—a sovereign structure that is the political expression of a specific ethno-cultural group. Yet the nation-state was one of the crucial inventions of the modern age. Mass literacy, education, and mobility put a premium on the unifying effect of cultural and ethnic homogeneity. None of the great pre-modern multinational empires have survived. (The Brussels bureaucracy may be trying to create another, but it has a long way to go.)*

This is why Ben Wattenberg is able to get away with talking about a   14
"Universal Nation." On its face, this is a contradiction in terms. It's possible, as Wattenberg variously implies, that he means the diverse immigrant groups will eventually intermarry, producing what he calls, quoting the English poet John Masefield a "wondrous race." Or that they will at least be assimilated by American culture, which, while globally dominant, is hardly "universal." But meanwhile there are hard questions. What language is this "universal nation" going to speak? How is it going to avoid ethnic strife? dual loyalties? collapsing like the Tower of Babel? Wattenberg is not asked to reconcile these questions, although he is not unaware of them, because in American political discourse the ideal of an American nation-state is in eclipse.

Ironically, the same weaknesses were apparent in the rather similar con-   15
cept of "cultural pluralism" invented by Horace M. Kallen at the height of the last great immigration debate, before the Quota Acts of the 1920s. Kallen, like many of today's pro-immigration enthusiasts, reacted unconstionally against the cause for "Americanization" that the 1880-to-1920 immigrant wave provoked. He argued that any unitary American nationality had already been dissipated by immigration (sound familiar?). Instead, he said the U.S. had become merely a political state (polity) containing a number of different nationalities.

Kallen left the practical implications of this vision "woefully undevel-   16
oped" (in the words of the *Harvard Encyclopedia of American Ethnic Groups*). It eventually evolved into a vague approval of tolerance, which was basically how Americans had always treated immigrant groups anyway—an extension, not coincidentally, of how the English built the British nation.

But in one respect, Kallenism is very much alive: he argued that authen-   17
tic Americanism was what he called "the American Idea." This amounted to an almost religious idealization of "democracy," which again was left undeveloped but which appeared to have as much to do with non-discrimination and equal protection under the law as with elections. Today, a messianic concern for global "democracy" is being suggested to conservatives as an appropriate objective for U.S. foreign policy.

---

*Brussels is the site of the European Community, which governs the Common Market among other responsibilities.

And Kallenism underlies the second helpful remark that someone always 18
makes in any discussion of U.S. immigration policy: *"America isn't a nation like
the other nations—it's an idea."*

Once more, this American exceptionalism is really more a matter of de- 19
gree than of kind. Many other nations have some sort of ideational reinforce-
ment. Quite often it is religious, such as Poland's Roman Catholicism;
sometimes cultural, such as France's ineffable Frenchness. And occasionally it
is political. Thus—again not coincidentally—the English used to talk about
what might be described as the "English Idea": English liberties, their rights as
Englishmen, and so on. Americans used to know immediately what this
meant. As Jesse Chickering wrote in 1848 of his diverse fellow-Americans:
"English laws and institutions, adapted to the circumstances of the country,
have been adopted here . . . The tendency of things is to mold the whole
into one people, whose leading characteristics are English, formed on American soil."

What is unusual in the present debate, however, is that Americans are 20
now being urged to abandon the bonds of a common ethnicity and instead to
trust entirely to ideology to hold together their state (polity). This is an extraordinary experiment, like suddenly replacing all the blood in a patient's
body. History suggests little reason to suppose it will succeed. Christendom
and Islam have long ago been sundered by national quarrels. More recently, the
much-touted "Soviet Man," the creation of much tougher ideologists using
much rougher methods than anything yet seen in the U.S., has turned out to
be a Russian, Ukrainian, or Kazakh after all.

Which is why Shakespeare has King Henry V say, before the battle of 21
Agincourt, not "we defenders of international law and the dynastic principle as
it applies to my right to inherit the throne of France," but

We few, we happy few, we band of brothers.

However, although intellectuals may have decided that America is not a nation
but an idea, the news has not reached the American people—especially that
significant minority who sternly tell the Census Bureau their ethnicity is
"American." (They seem mostly to be of British origin, many generations
back.) And it would have been considered absurd throughout most of American history.

John Jay in *The Federalist Papers* wrote that Americans were "one united 22
people, a people descended from the same ancestors, speaking the same language, professing the same religion, attached to the same principles of government, very similar in their manners and customs." Some hundred years later,
Theodore Roosevelt in his *Winning of the West* traced the "perfectly continuous history" of the Anglo-Saxons from King Alfred to George Washington.
He presented the settling of the lands beyond the Alleghenies as "the crowning
and greatest achievement" of "the spread of the English-speaking peoples,"
which—though personally a liberal on racial matters—he saw in explicit

276   PART 3 / SOURCES FOR ARGUMENT

terms: "it is of incalculable importance that America, Australia, and Siberia should pass out of the hands of their red, black, and yellow aboriginal owners, and become the heritage of the dominant world races."

Roosevelt himself was an example of ethnicities merging to produce this   23
new nation. He thanked God—he teased his friend Rudyard Kipling—that there was "not a drop of British blood" in him. But that did not stop him from identifying with Anglo-Saxons or from becoming a passionate advocate of an assimilationist Americanism, which crossed ethnic lines and was ultimately to cross racial lines.

And it is important to note that, at the height of the last great immigra-   24
tion wave, Kallen and his allies totally failed to persuade Americans that they were no longer a nation. Quite the contrary: once convinced that their nation-hood was threatened by continued massive immigration, Americans changed the public policies that made it possible. While the national-origins quotas were being legislated, President Calvin Coolidge put it unflinchingly: "America must be kept American."

Everyone knew what he meant. ■   25

Questions for Meaning

1. Why does Brimelow question the value of asserting that the United States is a nation of immigrants?
2. How does Brimelow distinguish between "nation" and "state"? Why does he believe that the distinction is important?
3. According to Brimelow, how has the debate over immigration changed? Why is he concerned about this change?
4. In paragraph 21, Brimelow alludes to the Battle of Agincourt. When was this battle fought? Who won? And why was this outcome signifi-cant?
5. Vocabulary: writhes (1), discernible (1), homogeneous (6), deprecated (10), sundered (20), incalculable (22).

Questions for Strategy

1. How effective is the comparison Brimelow makes between a speeded-up film of clouds and the development of American history?
2. How would you describe the tone of this article? Can you point to specific lines that support your view?
3. Consider paragraphs 22 and 23. Has Brimelow strengthened his case by appealing to American figures of historical importance? Has he left himself open to counterargument?
4. Brimelow concludes by stating that "everyone" knew what it meant to be American back in the 1920s. What is Brimelow implying here? How does this implication affect you?

TED CONOVER

THE UNITED STATES OF ASYLUM

One of the most troubling aspects of American immigration is how our nation responds to refugees who are seeking asylum from persecution and even from death. What does it mean to be a victim of persecution? To what extent should refugees from tyranny be welcomed in the United States? Is everyone who asks for asylum necessarily the victim of persecution? These are among the questions addressed in the following article by Ted Conover, first published in the *New York Times Magazine* in 1993. Conover is a freelance writer and the author of *Rolling Nowhere* (1985) and *Coyotes: A Journey Through the Secret World of America's Illegal Aliens* (1987). To investigate the lives of illegal aliens, Conover learned to speak Spanish fluently and disguised himself as an alien.

Dong Yishen looks a lot better in person than in his lawyer's photo of him. The picture, taken the night of his arrival in Queens on the Golden Venture, shows him wearing a thin, ragged blazer and dark turtleneck, his hair still plastered down from the Atlantic Ocean. Now, in the crisp blue uniform of the Salisbury Interim Correctional Facility in Pennsylvania, he looks composed, if a bit nervous.   1

Fellow prisoners in the visitor's room of the medium-security jail stare as he bows to me and my interpreter. They are in for crimes ranging from burglary to drug offenses. But Dong is a different kind of prisoner—accused not of any crime but of "an administrative violation" of United States immigration rules. Technically, he and the other 60 Chinese held at the jail are free to leave—but only for China. And Dong, who is 34, does not want to go back to China.   2

"In the countryside, if you are a farmer and your first child is a girl the Government won't argue too much if you have a second child after five years. But my second one was also a girl. In China we really want to have a son."   3

Dong and his wife kept trying. To hide from the Government, they had their third child in a distant village. It was the long-awaited son. For the first few years, he was raised in the house of childless friends. "But then I admitted that this was my own son—he is now 6 years old." As a result, says Dong, the authorities, whom he barely eluded, destroyed his furniture and knocked down his house.   4

Like four other Golden Venture survivors I interviewed, Dong is sharp on the details of his persecution but vague about the smugglers. The trip was arranged for him "by friends." He claims he doesn't know exactly how much they paid up front or how much he has to pay off.   5

One reason for his reticence may be the presence of Chinese "enforcers" in the jail—the Immigration and Naturalization Service suspects that several were on board, and presumes they are mixed in among those imprisoned. He   6 will say that during a horrific storm near the Cape of Good Hope the boat, battered by 50-foot waves for seven or eight hours, nearly sank.

Though his life has been completely sedentary since he left China's Fujian   7
Province six months ago, he has strong arms, farmer's arms. As we stand up to say goodbye, we shake hands, and Dong will not release his grip. He is shaking my hand with both of his and speaking at me instead of to the interpreter.

"The life I had was not good," he says. "I was so poor. . . . If I'm not   8
allowed to stay, I will have to commit suicide."

It is hard to come face to face with someone in such straits and not feel   9
sympathy. And yet who is to know if he is telling the truth? There is only his word. Dong came here with high hopes. President George Bush, in fact, specifically encouraged this kind of flight in the wake of the 1989 Tiananmen Square killings and pressure from the antiabortion lobby. Dong had reason to think he might qualify for the formal status called political asylum—refuge from political persecution.

But China has nearly 1.2 billion people, more than a fifth of the planet's   10
total; 500 million are of childbearing age. "Is the United States prepared to let them all in?" asks Ling-Chi Wang, associate professor of Asian-American studies at the University of California at Berkeley. More broadly, in terms of the asylum debate, does Dong's flight from birth control really qualify as polit-ical persecution? And if so, is political asylum an idea that we as a country can still stand behind?

Skyrocketing asylum applications and the abuse of the system by nefarious fig-   11
ures have brought asylum into the news. Sheik Omar Abdel-Rahman, whose followers are accused of bombing the World Trade Center, has applied for asy-lum in order to prevent his removal to Egypt. Mir Aimal Kansi, the Pakistani suspected of killing two C.I.A. employees outside their headquarters with an AK-47 early this year, had purchased his weapon using documents obtained with his official work authorization, supplied by the Government to most asy-lum applicants.

Asylum is much in the news because the average citizen lumps it together   12
with all forms of immigration, and in these recession-plagued times, the pen-dulum is making a swing toward intolerance of immigrants. It is one more component of the fear that we've "lost control of our borders."

In contrast to many European countries, however, asylum here adds only   13
a sliver to overall numbers of immigrants. A hundred thousand people applied for asylum in the last fiscal year (the approval rate is about 30 percent), com-pared with almost a million who immigrated legally in other Government programs (see Figure 1).

Notwithstanding recent bad press, asylum, at least in its conception, is a   14
beautiful idea. The notion of granting protection to those fleeing persecution gained strength after World War II from the widespread agreement that what had happened to the Jews would never be allowed to happen again to anybody, anywhere. Countries that signed the United Nations 1951 Convention Relat-ing to Refugees, and its 1967 Protocol, agreed to protect those who met the

Asylum's Sliver

Selected immigration statistics,
fiscal year ending Sept. 30, 1992

TOTAL LEGAL IMMIGRATION: 973,977

Immigrants admitted under family-reunification
rules: 448,607
Immigrants admitted under highly-skilled-worker
preferences: 116,198

REFUGEES ADMITTED: 132,173

Applicants granted asylum: 4,019
Asylum applications received: 103,000
Asylum applications expected, fiscal year '93:
130,000
Asylum backlog: 300,000
Average annual growth in illegal population:
300,000

*The annual cost of adjudicating 132,000 asylum claims—the immigration
service's projection for next year—is $32 million, while the State
Department's cost this year to bring in 122,000 refugees from areas strategic
to our interests—presently Vietnam and the former Soviet Union—is $205
million, plus some $381 million in resettlement assistance administered by the
Department of Health and Human Services.*

SOURCES: IMMIGRATION AND NATURALIZATION SERVICE AND STATE DEPARTMENT

Figure 1

documents' definition of a refugee: a person with "a well-founded fear of
being persecuted for reasons of race, religion, nationality, membership of a
particular social group or political opinion." Asylum is offered to refugees
who make it to a "safe country" on their own. In the United States, it is administered by the Immigration and Naturalization Service. (The State Department has a separate program that brings over groups of refugees from
selected countries.)

World War II also created a world divided into East and West, and asy-   15
lum, conceived of as ideology-free, soon became an instrument of cold-war
politics. Until the collapse of the Soviet Union, asylum was a weapon used to
"embarrass our enemies," says Arthur C. Helton, director of the Refugee

Project for the Lawyers Committee for Human Rights. Asylees, as they're
called—whether ballet dancers, physicists or fighter pilots—were testimony to
the superiority of our system."

The "clear anti-Communist ideology . . . favored only those who ap-   16
peared to share it," wrote Gil Loescher and John A. Scanlan in their book
Calculated Kindness: Refugees and America's Half-Open Door, 1945-Present.
"Cubans were the principal beneficiary of this double standard. The Haitians
were the principal losers." Eastern Europeans fleeing Communist regimes
were practically all approved for asylum; victims of violence in Central American countries that had the support of the United States Government were
routinely denied.

Now that the cold war is no more, replaced by what might be called the   17
new world disorder, what is going to be acceptable as an evil to flee from?

Fidel Castro may no longer be on the list, as a Cuban airline captain has   18
discovered, after he diverted his plane to Miami last December and, along
with all but 5 of the 53 people on board, requested political asylum. Instead of
granting his request, Federal law-enforcement officials, with Cuba's help, are
pursuing criminal charges against the airline captain. This change may reflect
not only the thaw in relations with Cuba but also a growing suspicion that
asylum applicants, rather than fleeing persecution, are simply seeking entry to
the developed world.

Accustomed to measuring dissent from Communism, officials who pre-   19
side over asylum cases are suddenly faced with a bewildering variety of persecution claims. A homosexual escaping from death squads in Brazil . . . a
woman from Africa who does not want to undergo the cruel, potentially crip-
pling procedure called clitoridectomy . . . a Peruvian who has aroused the
wrath of the Shinning Path . . . a Guatemalan union worker threatened
with death for organizing against the Government . . . a Christian Sudanese
fleeing from Islamic fundamentalists. Many of the world's people, rather than
suffer in silence, would prefer to live somewhere else. Like here.

Since millions fear for their lives in many lands, political asylum now   20
raises a much larger immigration question: How many asylees can America
take in? And which ones?

People who arrive at Kennedy International Airport without proper papers   21
and apply for asylum are often released, pending their hearings, because of a
lack of space at the Wackenhut detention facility, a bleak converted warehouse
run by a private company for the immigration service, in Queens, near the
airport. Occasionally someone will arrive when one of the 125 beds is empty.
Such was the luck of Luis.

Wackenhut, a building intended for goods, not people, has no outdoor   22
exercise yard and practically no windows. Luis, a welder from Peru, has lived
10 months under artificial light, leaving the facility only once, for a hearing in
Manhattan. His appeal of an immigration judge's ruling against him was recently turned down.

"I've changed a lot here," says Luis. (His last name is withheld to protect 23 him from persecution should he be returned to Peru.) "I had a big fear of speaking openly, but now less. I want the authorities here to pay attention. The injustice gives me courage. I worry that our cries for justice are being silenced."

Once he begins to talk there is no holding him back. I have seen the 24 slums of Lima and know the place where Luis lives. To see a man like him— bursting with life and moral outrage—come out of that environment is astonishing enough. But to see him in this country and yet not in this country, penned with a block of metal and concrete, fills me with despair.

Luis's story begins in one of the sprawling poor communities known as 25 *pueblos jóvenes* (young towns) on the outskirts of Lima. There he became a leader in a civic group that tried to secure services like electricity and water for the city's half-million people. The group's efforts to help the poor have been recognized by the Pope and the United Nations, but its continuing success has attracted the unwanted attention of Sendero Luminoso, or Shining Path, Peru's violent Maoist guerrilla movement.

"They began to infiltrate our assemblies. We noticed that the ideas being 26 suggested were the ideas of terrorists—that we start an armed struggle. They talked of Communism. But we had never spoken of armed struggle. Our only weapons are work and truth and the faith we have. Seeing that we wouldn't help, the Shining Path started putting on more pressure. Their fliers said that anyone who didn't support the armed struggle was a traitor and would die. But we held firm."

The Shining Path's campaign of intimidation escalated in the late 1980's 27 with the execution of various directors of the group. "One guy they took to a central park and machine-gunned in front of his family. Another time they threw dynamite into a house and many innocents died. They blow up banks, schools and hospitals. There were 2,000 of us leaders when it began. Many were killed or had to flee. Some of us kept fighting."

Luis says he has "always had the courage to face the bad." But the Shin- 28 ing Path learned that he opposed them from his work counseling teen-agers involved with drugs. Soon messages began to be left at his house, telling him to resign his leadership position. His father, in another part of Peru, was also threatened. In a third note delivered to his home, they said they would kill him. Luis, his wife and three children moved to a safe house.

Fearful for his life and for his family, Luis secured a plane ticket, passport 29 and false visa from his associates. But in February his application for asylum in the United States was denied by a judge who, noting that Luis had claimed persecution on account of "political opinion," cited a State Department memo on Peru that stated Sendero Luminoso's "choice of victims does not appear to be the result of their personal political views. Rather, the Sendero uses force to intimidate and recruit, to coerce financial support, and to retaliate against those inside and outside the Government who are perceived as opposing its goals or undermining its support."

In other words, the Shining Path singled him out for his position, not for   30
his views. But the State Department memo also contradicts itself. If Sendero
retaliates against those "who are perceived as opposing its goals," isn't it sin-
gling them out for their views? Luis's lawyer appealed, and recently the Board
of Immigration Appeals turned him down. Luis's lawyer is appealing again.

Meanwhile, Luis waits in Wackenhut. "I have the hope to return to   31
Peru, to continue my work someday, but I can't right now. I came here to
escape death."

I exit Wackenhut, and re-enter my privileged position as a citizen of one of the   32
world's prosperous countries, one troubled much less with political ideology,
these days, than with the question, mainly, of how much do we share? Are
these people our brothers and sisters? And if not, what do we owe a stranger?

"The growth of a global economy has emphasized rather than reduced   33
inequality between nations," says a new report by the United Nations Population Fund, and the number of migrants worldwide is at least 100 million. This
migration, away from trouble and poverty and toward peacefulness and opportunity, "could become the human crisis of our age," says the report.

This is not to imply that a hundred million people are packing their bags   34
for America. Gregg A. Beyer, director of asylum for the Immigration and Naturalization Service, uses the example of Latin America to illustrate that most
people would probably rather stay home. "From settled countries like Chile
and Bolivia, we get very few applications," he notes (60 and 93, respectively,
in the past 10 months). "It is the countries in turmoil—like Peru and Colom-
bia—that produce the greatest number" (2,529 and 998, respectively). Beyer's
program handles 90 percent of the country's asylum cases—those who apply
on their own: the rest—those who are apprehended—fall within the purview
of the immigration court.

Still, the numbers are rising rapidly, and if the asylum apparatus is a re-   35
flection of the way Americans think about it, it is a subject we find difficult to
think about at all. From 1968 to 1975 the United States averaged only 200
applications per year. The startling rise in applications since—130,000 are expected this year—has until recently been met with bureaucratic paralysis. A
ballyhooed asylum corps of 150 specially trained officers (Germany has 3,000;
Sweden, 800) inherited a backlog of 114,000 cases the day they started work in
1991. There is now a backlog of 300,000 cases.

Those awaiting adjudication are not deportable and, in most cases, are   36
given a work authorization. This means that the backlog itself now attracts
spurious claims. Apply for asylum in the United States, it is known, and you
can pretty much plan to stay. Depending on where you enter the byzantine
process, if you are denied, up to four appeals are possible. Some cases have
been pending for 12 years.

But with rising sentiment against immigration and given the notoriety   37
of the recent asylum cases, reform is on the horizon. "We cannot and will not
surrender our border to those who wish to exploit our history of compassion

and justice," said President Clinton at a White House ceremony in July announcing a package of immigration reforms.

"Expedited exclusion," which deals with asylum, provides for adjudication within a few days for those arriving at airports without documents and for boat people like Dong Yishen. As the term indicates, the emphasis is on moving people out quickly.   38

In addition, the President has instructed the Immigration and Naturalization Service to come up with, by the end of this month, new procedures to streamline its unwieldy bureaucracy and to curb its worst abuses. According to Gregg Beyer, these could include a time limit on applying for asylum (there presently is none), a withholding of work authorization from all but those who are granted asylum, and enforcement of the idea of "country of first asylum." Under this last restriction, foreigners who have passed through a country that has a procedure for providing asylum will be returned to that country, if possible.   39

These reforms—introduced recently in the Senate by Edward M. Kennedy and in the House by Jack Brooks, Democrat from Texas—appear to enjoy broad bipartisan support. But they also have their critics. Warren R. Leiden, executive director of the American Immigration Lawyers Association, notes that if Clinton's "expedited exclusion" becomes law, it will be practically impossible for an airport asylum-seeker to be represented by an attorney, since it takes time to find lawyers, who may need more than a week to prepare their cases. The attorney can make a difference: a 1987 General Accounting Office study noted that applicants with attorneys were three times more likely to succeed in proceedings before an immigration judge.   40

Lucas Guttentag, director of the Immigrants' Rights Project of the American Civil Liberties Union, worries that the new hurdles will result in bona fide applicants being summarily returned. "Experience has shown that persons who were found by the I.N.S. not to have a credible fear initially were later granted asylum under a full hearing," he says. Equally troubling, he adds, is "the absence of judicial review and the attempt to strip the courts of any power to oversee the entire process, because it attempts to insulate the I.N.S. from any independent judicial oversight." On many occasions, courts have found the enforcement-minded immigration service to have abridged immigrant rights.   41

Doubtless one goal of the Clinton reform effort is to send a signal to citizens who fear America has lost control of the borders and to foreign nationals hoping the same thing. But even if the President succeeds in curbing the worst asylum abuses—like the ease in claiming asylum at Kennedy Airport and allowing Chinese claiming persecution under the one-child policy to enter—he will not have touched the underlying shortcomings in the system.   42

Those applying for asylum upon arriving at an airport or who get caught trying to get in on a boat account for only about 10 percent of the total number of asylum applicants. The rest, who apply once they are in the country (having entered legally on a visa, for example, or illegally across the border)   43 will not be affected by the changes. The backlog continues to grow. And the number of asylum officers remains woefully inadequate.

A Congressional staff member who helped frame the Refugee Act of 44 1980, which gave a real-life commitment to America's symbolic support of refugee protection, recalls that the country was then receiving a little more than 2,000 asylum applications a year. "Let's double it," he said, making a worst-case projection; and Congress foresaw some 5,000 annually. Instead, 26,000 were received the first year.

Unless more money and thought are given this problem, the increase in 45 world refugee numbers will guarantee that America continues its historic pattern of unpreparedness.

In the basement offices of Central American Legal Assistance in Williams- 46 burg, Brooklyn, I meet Vicente Osorio, his wife, Maria, and their 8-month-old daughter. Of the 300,000 people in the asylum backlog, 145,000 are from either Guatemala or El Salvador—a result of the exodus from those countries in the 1980's and lawsuits that forced the Immigration and Naturalization Service to rehear their cases.

Osorio is a short, round man of strong opinions. A street cleaner, he was 47 on the executive board of a municipal workers' union when it got into a dispute with the Guatemalan Government. After the union called a strike that the Government termed illegal, 72 union members were selectively fired, including Osorio. In response, the union began a long campaign, in the news media and on the streets, to win support for their cause. As the campaign geared up, union members began getting killed or abducted.

"José Mercedes Sotz was beaten, and three months later, as he and his 48 child walked to a bus stop, his child, 3 years old, was shot and paralyzed," he says. "Other leaders were killed. Some were kidnapped. Others fled. My friend Rufino Reyes, may he rest in peace, died fighting. He was working on a union case at the administration building and he won. Two blocks away from there, after leaving, he was stabbed." (In Osorio's asylum application there are documents from Amnesty International and Americas Watch attesting to this violence.)

Osorio started receiving threats. A man in the office of the municipal 49 government said Osorio should stop his organizing or he would get "disappeared." Written death threats followed, delivered to his home. "I didn't want to leave my wife a widow. Though we were people of bravery and strength, we would only be martyrs if we stayed." The Osorios fled Guatemala, leaving the children with their grandmother. Vicente and Maria Osorio's fourth child, the 8-month-old, was born in the United States.

The Osorios' initial application for asylum was denied, as was their first 50 appeal. According to immigration officials, "the fundamental nature" of Vicente Osorio's dispute with the Guatemalan Government was economic, concerning wages and the reinstatement of workers. "The possible existence of a generalized 'political' motive underlying the Government's action is inadequate to establish that the respondent fears persecution on account of political opinion."

The Osorios' lawyer is appealing to a Federal Court of Appeals. 51

Exactly what constitutes political persecution? 52

Sometimes it's hard to tell. Sadruddin Aga Khan, the former United 53 Nations High Commissioner for Refugees, wrote recently in *The International Herald Tribune* that the identity of refugees has become blurred. Many are "victims of complex socioeconomic and political crises. . . . They may not be pushed out at the end of a rifle or with the threat of execution looming over them, but population pressure, regional conflicts, environmental degradation and absence of work opportunities combine to encourage if not force them to leave."

In San Francisco in July, probably for the first time in the United States, 54 an immigration judge granted asylum to a homosexual Brazilian fleeing "antigay death squad gangs, who are often joined by the police in their massacres of gays." France recently recognized genital mutilation as a form of persecution in the asylum case of a woman from West Africa. Should these claims be accepted?

Such new directions, says Dan Stein, executive director of the Federation 55 for American Immigration Reform, represent "a backdoor immigration program for people who are displeased and dispossessed, of which there are billions." "When you get into these gray areas where people are fleeing a status"— i.e., a sexual preference—"or a cultural, or an economic repression, you are dealing with the kind of generalized dissatisfaction that our refugee and asylum laws cannot handle, and it's impractical to think they ever could," he says.

The A.C.L.U.'s Guttentag says Stein "betrays an appalling ignorance" of 56 both the facts and the law and the international standards regarding refugee protection. "The Tenorio decision, if he's read it, reflects a very careful analysis of the actual facts in Brazil, the kinds of threats and attacks to which this person and gay persons in Brazil are actually subjected," says Guttentag. "It was not a person fleeing because of their status. It was a person fleeing because of the discrimination and persecution and the physical threats that that person has specifically suffered."

Though immigration law is based upon benchmark standards like the 57 "well-founded fear of persecution" (echoing language in the United Nations Convention) and guided by the occasional Supreme Court ruling, most precedents are set by the Board of Immigration Appeals, in Falls Church, Va. Some lawyers complain that many of the board's decisions are subjective and increasingly restrictive. "They are defining persecution out of existence," says Anne Pilsbury of Central American Legal Assistance. "'Persecution' is not an easily definable term," wrote Loescher and Scanlan, "and always derives some of its meaning from the political perspectives of those employing it."

Western Europe has always accepted asylum-seekers in far greater num- 58 bers than the United States, but even there the doors are closing. There was a moment following World War II when the world decided that asylum was the right thing to do. It is still the right thing to do. But in the world of the 1990's, Americans are being forced to rethink the implications of that promise.

At William Ochan's hearing before an immigration judge in Newark, things   59
have suddenly taken a bad turn. Ochan, 29, is a Christian from southern Sudan. The radical Islamic Government of northern Sudan, says Africa Watch, has for nine years waged "a war in the south of extreme brutality" to turn the Sudan into an Islamic state "by whatever means necessary." "The policy has resulted in the suppression of all forms of civil society, the arrest, detention and torture of dissidents, and the relocation and deprivation of hundreds of thousands of people."

One of the displaced, according to his own testimony, is William Ochan.   60

He became a refugee, he says, the year he was born; his parents, fearing   61
oppression by Muslims, fled with their children to Uganda. After a truce, he returned to the Sudan at age 11 to live with his grandfather, a pastor and headmaster. While his brother joined the Sudanese People's Liberation Army, the armed Christian guerrilla resistance, William Ochan opted for peaceful resistance. Still, the demonstrations he led landed him in jail in Juba, where during his interrogation soldiers hung him by cords tied to his fingers. His left middle finger was mangled as a result. He shows it to the judge, who describes it for the record. She seems moved by his testimony.

Ochan's application is also supported by a dean's-list record at two New   62
Jersey colleges (he supported himself with two full-time jobs while studying), active participation in church, an Op-Ed piece he wrote on the Sudan's crisis that was published in *The Los Angeles Times*. His lawyer has even brought a video of Ochan being interviewed by Charles Kuralt.

But now the Immigration and Naturalization Service lawyer represent-   63
ing the Government has found a serious discrepancy in his story. It turns out that Ochan was first interviewed five years ago, after sneaking in on a boat from Turkey and while living in a Newark homeless shelter. At the time, she points out, he submitted a written asylum request that mentioned nothing about his finger and in which he claimed to have escaped from the infamous Cobra Prison in Khartoum during a celebrated jail break. She submits this statement as Exhibit 7.

Ochan confers with his lawyer, who is upset because she is unaware of   64
the earlier statement. He says that, over the course of five years, he forgot. Today, in any event, he admits that he has never been to Khartoum. He made that up, he says, because at his initial interview the immigration officials were openly hostile. They seemed not to have heard of the Sudan, and they asked if he was fleeing Communism, which has hardly been a factor there for two decades.

"I put in Khartoum because it is more famous than Juba," he explains. "I   65
needed to impress them somehow." As for the finger, he says he didn't mention it in the written statement because he had already discussed it during the interview.

But the judge is concerned. Consistency is crucial in asylum hearings   66
because of the frequent paucity of other evidence to support a claim of persecution. She had hoped to issue an oral decision from the bench today, she says,
but "credibility is now such an obvious issue. Exhibit 7 has opened up a can
of worms."

I have got to know Ochan over the past few weeks, most recently at a   67
demonstration he organized at the United Nations, on July 31, to publicize the
persecution of Christians in the war in the Sudan, and I sympathize with him
as we walk to the elevator.

"When will they give me back my life?" he asks. "I am like their pris-   68
oner."

At the same time, I doubt I will ever know him well. Asylum-seekers,   69
most of them so alone in the world and so at risk, have many secrets. I wonder
with him, as I wondered with Dong, whether I appear as just another representative of The System, another person to impress. In his shoes, what would I
do? All I can feel sure of is that he has gone through hell and would make a
good neighbor. Unlike many of the millions who immigrate unofficially, he
wants to be a part of the system; he craves legitimacy; he would cherish citizenship. The decision the judge will make, her balancing of sympathy and
hardheadedness, will be in microcosm the decision that America and the rest
of the developed world must make. ■

Questions for Meaning

1. What makes a request for asylum different from other requests to immi-
    grate?
2. How many applicants for asylum is the United States now receiving?
    How significant is this number in terms of the total number of immi-
    gration applications?
3. Who is a "refugee," and what promises have been made to refugees by
    the United Nations?
4. Does Conover provide any evidence of political violence in countries
    that refugees are fleeing?
5. What effect has the growth of a global economy had on the movement
    of people from one country to another?
6. Vocabulary: composed (1), eluded (4), sedentary (7), nefarious (11), ad-
    judication (36), byzantine (36), bipartisan (40), dissidents (59), micro-
    cosm (69).

Questions about Strategy

1. Why do you think Conover takes the trouble to report that Dong
    Yishen is imprisoned with men charged with crimes such as burglary
    and drug use?

2. To what extent does Conover evoke sympathy for immigrants seeking asylum? Can you point to specific lines where you felt sympathetic?
3. Consider the questions posed in paragraph 32. Based on the information reported in this article, how do you think Conover expects readers to answer this question?
4. Conover describes the cases of individuals from China, Peru, Guatemala, and the Sudan. Why do you think he chose cases from these countries?
5. To what extent has Conover recognized the complexity of the problem he discussed in this article?

ONE STUDENT'S ASSIGNMENT

Drawing on at least two of the sources in *The Informed Argument*, write an argument for or against encouraging additional immigration to the United States. Focus your essay on the economic consequences of immigration, and make any recommendations for change you think advisable. Use MLA style documentation, but you do not need to include a Works Cited List for this assignment if you use sources only from *The Informed Argument*.

The Economics of Immigration

Christopher J. Lovrien

America has long been called a nation of immigrants. It has been said   1
so many times that it has become a cliché. Yet the fact remains, the United
States' 200-year rise from newborn to superpower was made possible
largely because of the skills and ambitions of immigrants. People such as
the Kennedys and the Rockefellers helped lead their new country to world
prominence. Immigrants have long brought a vitality to this nation and that
is why we should continue to encourage legal immigration.

However, more and more Americans seem to want immigration to be re-   2
stricted. Some have gone so far as to call for a total freeze on immigration
for a period of time. As the economy took a downturn in the early 1990s
and unemployment rose, some cried out that immigrants were taking jobs
from low-skilled Americans. While this may be true in the short term, in the
long run immigrants positively affect the economy. More immigrants means
not only more workers but also more consumers. In economic terms, this
means an increase in demand and the creation of more jobs. Economists
will tell you that the number of jobs in an economy is not finite. Also,
research shows that native workers' employment opportunities are only
slightly reduced when immigrants enter a local labor market (Becker 252).

Another concern about the influx of immigrants is that they place an ex-   3
tra burden on the welfare system. This concern is understandable and I
share it. Many of the immigrants who seek refuge come having fled their
country with very little in the way of economic security. But it might be appropriate to look at welfare to immigrants as an investment. By helping
these newcomers out in the beginning, we will enable them to become contributing members of American society. In fact George Borjas, an economics professor at the University of California at San Diego, calculates that
even though immigrants receive more welfare than they pay in taxes, they
actually add $4 billion to the economy by paying for things like food, rent,
and clothing (Fierman 255). Quite simply, most immigrants are not leech-
ing off the system. In fact, the Urban Institute reports that 74 percent of
adult male immigrants are employed, versus 72 percent of the general male
population (Fierman 255).

So what should the U.S. policy on immigration be? We should be con-   4
scious that immigration can be a tremendous tool for improving this country. By allowing, and even seeking out skilled immigrants to enter the
United States, we can direct immigration to help strengthen our country. In
a sense, we could select immigrants to fit our needs. These people would
find it easier to acquire work and could be immediate contributors to American economic health.

The first step is for the government to ensure it is aware of who is enter-   5
ing the country. To do this, illegal immigration needs to be curbed. We can,
of course, increase the number of border patrol officers and erect barriers,
both of which amount to throwing money at the problem and may or may
not be effective. But the best way to decrease illegal immigration may be to
increase legal immigration. Currently, the government allows about
700,000 immigrants to legally enter the country per year. It is estimated
that another 300,000 enter illegally. Statistics show that, when legal immigration is cut, illegal immigration generally increases. Increasing the quota
of legal immigrants could decrease the number entering illegally (Becker
252). We might have the same number of people entering the country, but
we would be in better control of who they are. More legal immigrants would
mean we could allow more people with special skills and education to enter
the country.

Another means to decreasing illegal immigrants is through measures   6
such as NAFTA. A large percentage of illegal immigrants are Mexicans who
cross the border to escape poverty. NAFTA should work to bring the wages
in Mexico and the United States closer together. It will also raise the
standard of living in Mexico. This would decrease the incentive for Mexicans to sneak into the United States. In fact, University of California at
Berkeley economist Sherman Robinson "estimates that each percentage

point increase in the value of Mexico's capital stock . . . would be enough
stimulus to keep 25,000 of its citizens at home" (Fierman 259).

Looking at the history of opposition to immigration, I see some interesting   7
trends. There seems to always have been those who felt that certain immigrants were going to ruin the country. When the Germans began immigrating
to America, some "ethnic" Americans said they would cause the breakdown
of America. In fact, the country became stronger. When the potato famine
drove a wave of Irish immigrants to America, some Americans (including
some of the new German-Americans) said they would ruin the country. They
were wrong. The country became stronger and the Irish-Americans eventually flourished despite prejudice. With history as a precedent, why is there
any reason to believe that this new wave of immigrants will be anything but
good for America? Unless it is because this new wave is largely non-white. I
certainly hope the value of these immigrants is not being judged on the basis
of skin color. People like Peter Brimelow who say that large-scale immigration will cause America to lose its culture, fail to realize that American culture has been immensely enriched by other ethnic cultures.

Why are immigrants to America often able to do so well in their new coun-   8
try and add so much to it? In no small part, it's because of their character.
Immigrants must be ambitious to leave their native country. Think what a decision that must be. These are people willing to leave everything they know,
and search for a better life for themselves. They bring this ambition and desire to America. Contrary to what we are led to believe, they are not just the
poor and the outcasts of the world. Many are well educated. According to the
Urban Institute, 25 percent of the immigrants arriving in the 1980s had college degrees (Fierman 256). By increasing legal immigration and selecting
skilled people, we can make that ratio even higher.

None of what I have suggested means we should restrict immigration   9
only to those who are affluent. We currently accept those who have been
politically and economically oppressed. We should continue to do so. For
underneath the shackles of poverty might exist an incredible entrepreneur.

America has had a long history of talented immigrants. The next great   10
physicist might very well be arriving in New York or San Francisco right
now, and whether she is European, Asian, or African, I hope we are bright
enough not to send her away.

SUGGESTIONS FOR WRITING

1. Is the United States "a nation of immigrants"? Does our country have
   a special responsibility to accept "huddled masses yearning to breathe
   free"? Write an essay focused on how traditional American values—as
   you define them—should determine our immigration policy.

2. Kinsley draws attention to neo-Nazi violence directed against immigrants to Germany. Look for articles published within the last few years on this topic and report your findings.
3. Locate the earlier column to which Becker refers at the end of his article. Compare his recommendation in that column with the position he takes in "Illegal Immigration: How to Turn the Tide." Then argue on behalf of the position you prefer.
4. Becker, Fierman, and Mandell et al. all focus on the economic consequences of immigration. Drawing on these sources, write an argument for or against the belief that immigration causes harm to the American economy.
5. Write an essay comparing U.S. and Canadian immigration laws.
6. Write an argument for or against increasing the number of legal immigrants from Mexico.
7. How should the American government respond when illegal immigrants arrive safely in America after a dangerous voyage? Should these aliens be returned to the country from which they fled? Or should they be allowed to remain within the United States?
8. Drawing on the articles by Kosova and Conover, write an argument recommending a specific change in procedures followed by the U.S. Immigration and Naturalization Service.
9. Is U.S. immigration policy racist? Write an essay attempting to answer this question. Draw on information provided by Brimelow and Conover.
10. Write an essay defining the meaning of *asylum* and the extent to which the United States should accept foreigners seeking asylum. Draw on Conover and at least one other source that you have discovered on your own.

COLLABORATIVE PROJECT

Interview immigrants living in your own community as well as any local officials who have responsibility for immigrants. Evaluate how fairly new arrivals are being treated in your area. Then write a report that identifies anything you discover that is positive and suggests any changes that you believe are necessary.

SECTION 5

CULTURE AND CURRICULUM: WHAT SHOULD STUDENTS BE TAUGHT?

WILLIAM CELIS, 3RD

SHAKEN TO THE CORE

Although the history of American education reveals long-standing debates about what students should know, recent years have seen increasing controversy about what courses should be required of college students outside of their major. In the following article, first published by the *New York Times* in 1993, William Celis, 3rd summarizes one of the major conflicts over the "core curriculum," or courses required of all students.

Ever since Stanford University overhauled its curriculum in 1988 from a rigid core of courses dealing with Western civilization to one that includes few required courses and a larger, more varied menu of subjects on women and minorities from which students can choose, life hasn't been the same at the nation's colleges and universities.

College core curriculums, those courses that supposedly represent the core of learning that each institution wants to instill in its graduates, are undergoing a reformation. The process is leaving the intellectual underpinnings of some institutions teetering and others firmly set upon a new educational path.

The major battle in this revolution pits those who believe the core should be based on the Western canon against those who support a broader, multicultural base rich in the voices of women, minorities and foreign cultures. But an examination of curriculum revisions nationwide indicates that while this struggle draws the passion and attention, it is a lesser issue whose heat masks the main question: whether a particular American college or university needs a core curriculum, and if so, what purpose it should serve.

It is a challenge that few institutions are consciously undertaking. But whether by design or default, a clear trend in core curriculums is emerging: American colleges and universities are moving away from an emphasis on content—requiring all students to take specific courses in which they will study the same texts—and toward an emphasis on intellectual processes: requiring students to sample certain subjects, within which they can take any courses as long as they are taught to think critically and analytically.

According to a survey by the American Council on Education, an associ- 5
ation of 1,700 public and private colleges and universities, the percentage of its members that maintained core curriculums in the spring of 1992 was 80 percent, down from 82 percent in 1987. But Clifton Conrad, a professor of higher education at the University of Wisconsin at Madison, said the slight drop over the last five years masks great turmoil among colleges. "Literally hundreds of them are revising their curriculums," Professor Conrad said.

O. T. Hargrave, associate dean for student academic affairs at Southern 6
Methodist University in Dallas, which revised its curriculum this academic year, agrees that "There is across the country a lot of revision going on." At S.M.U., Mr. Hargrave said, curriculum revisions "focus more on teaching critical analysis rather than making sure we have covered all the basic contents."

However, according to Professor Conrad, who has been following the 7
core curriculum debate closely: "People think it's just an issue about whose voices we hear, but it's much more profound. There are some essential questions we should be asking."

Students of higher education reform say many institutions are avoiding 8
the task. Most, they say, are distracted by the debate over Western versus multicultural curriculums because it is an emotional one, defined by issues of race and gender. Among faculty members, too, there is some resistance to change because "the university is the most conservative of all our social institutions," said Professor Conrad.

"And, frankly," he added, "anytime anyone has certain control or privi- 9
leges they are unwilling to give up their power."

There are questions of cost, too: New materials often must be purchased 10
and new professors hired to teach the new courses.

As a result, revised curriculums often are politicized by the fights over 11
Western versus non-Western thought and the relative importance of each department or subject, and without any obvious educational focus, critics say. Indeed, many students earn bachelor's degrees without knowledge of "basic landmarks of history and thought," wrote Lynne V. Cheney, chairman of the National Endowment for the Humanities, in a 1989 report, "50 Hours." The report urged institutions of higher learning to revise curriculums so that undergraduates study a more cohesive, focused curriculum, including Western thought, math, science and social science.

The endowment backed its complaints with evidence: 25 percent of 700 12
college seniors surveyed in 1989, for example, did not know that Columbus landed in the Western Hemisphere before 1500, according to a Gallup poll released with the endowment's study. And most students surveyed could not identify Magna Carta. "Many American colleges and universities fail to provide enough structure in curriculums," the Endowment report concluded.

Some students concur, saying they feel as if they are in a supermarket making   13
disparate selections that find them at the checkout counter without the
makings of a complete, intellectually nutritious meal and graduating without
a sense of what they know. Other students have avoided institutions with
cafeteria-style curriculums.

When Jeff A. Zanarini graduated from high school in Omaha, Neb.,   14
three years ago, for example, he visited Stanford. He was turned off, he said,
by the smorgasbord approach to curriculum. "Universities like Stanford have
really gone too far," said Mr. Zanarini, now a junior with a double major in
economics and French at Southern Methodist University, whose curriculum is
largely based on the Western canon and requires students to take one multicultural course. "Every student expects some non-Western course; I feel I'm getting the right dose at S.M.U."

For administrators and faculty who may feel less sure, the Association of   15
American Colleges last month released a 127-page book, *Core Curriculum and
Cultural Pluralism: A Guide for Campus Planners* by Betty Schmitz, director of
the Curriculum Transformation Project at the University of Washington.

Meanwhile, to fill the vacuum that has resulted from the battle over core   16
curriculums, individual schools and departments in which students major are
producing increasingly structured curriculum requirements of their own. The
purpose of these requirements—to equip graduates for the job market—stands
in marked contrast to the purpose of their progenitors.

Columbia University instituted the grandfather of core curriculums in   17
1919, a year after the end of World War I. Columbia took war issues as a
model for an innovative course called "Contemporary Civilization." The idea
won faculty support by promising to provide students with a common background of ideas and by spanning compartmentalized disciplines. But the course
also had an ideological mission: "Contemporary Civilization" would inoculate
young people against Bolshevism and other subversive doctrines. One dean
said it would produce students "who shall be safe for democracy."

That purpose rarely obtains on today's college campuses. Rather, new   18
core curriculums, where instituted, must be geared to a world that has experienced an information explosion, the globalization of national economies and a
radically changing job market.

There are many ways to design core curriculums that will achieve these   19
new ends. At some institutions, the debate comes down to using the Western
canon or a multicultural curriculum as stepping stones to critical thinking.
Western core advocates and universities that embrace the "Great Books"—
disparagingly referred to by some as works by Dead White European Males, or
DWEM—argue that certain universal truths speak to all generations of students. This is a Western culture, they say, and all students should understand
its underpinnings.

Supporters of multicultural curriculums say they recognize that knowl-   20
edge is neither finite nor static. This nation, they maintain, is a multicultural
society whose constituents bring strength and vigor to college studies. Core
curriculums should include these new voices, proponents say, and new ways to
teach students how to approach learning and thinking.

At other institutions the debate seems to be between structuralists, who   21
advocate a rigid set of courses required of all students, and advocates of choice,
who see little merit in all students studying the same materials. At St. John's
College in Annapolis, Md., for instance, the curriculum is based on the Western core, with no apologies. "We are supplying students with the common and
the universal root of their present conditions," said Eva T. H. Brann, dean of
the college. And works by Asian or African-American women writers are
"not central to the tradition."

"They say everyone should read the same thing," said Henry Rosovsky,   22
the architect of Harvard University's core curriculum, disparaging the structuralists as politically motivated. "Our curriculum offers choice."

Harvard's core was revamped in 1978, well before Stanford triggered the   23
current debate, but because of Harvard's stature it remains a lightning rod in
the curriculum wars. The Harvard core, say critics, is too broad and poorly
focused. "It is not a core," said William J. Bennett, the United States Secretary
of Education from 1985 to 1988 and now a fellow at the Hudson Institute, a
conservative research institution. Mr. Bennett derisively called Harvard's curriculum "core light," and added: "The Harvard core is essentially a group of
professorial idiosyncrasies elevated to the status of a seeming coherent core."

Not so, responds Mr. Rosovsky, who chronicled some of the debate in his   24
book *The University: An Owner's Manual* (Norton, 1990). Harvard students
must take 16 courses across a spectrum of 10 academic areas including historical
studies, literature and arts, social analysis, science and moral reasoning.

Within these areas, students are offered so many choices that they could   25
graduate without ever taking a course in Western civilization. "Can one—as
has often been asked—graduate from Harvard without reading Shakespeare?"
Mr. Rosovsky writes. "Yes, but one cannot get a degree without reading literary classics in a critical and analytical way under the guidance of a specialist."

"At Harvard, We Have Chosen One Way"

"There is no one way to define an educated person," Mr. Rosovsky added in   26
an interview. "The requirements are aimed at broadening someone's intellectual perspective. At Harvard, we have chosen one way. I am not saying it is the
only way."

Scholars at the University of California at Berkeley agree. "Knowledge   27
comes in a lot of different ways, and the strength of a larger university is its
ability to offer intellectual diversity," said Arnold L. Lieman, chairman of the
psychology department.

At Berkeley, for instance, the 14 colleges and schools that constitute the   28
university design their own curriculums and maintain their own requirements. Two courses are required of all students: "American Cultures" and basic English. Besides those, students fill their plates with a dizzying array of
requirements for their majors.

There have been few cries of protest from students on campus, many of   29
whom say they welcome the choice. "U.C. Berkeley offers enough in terms
of selection," said Nick Perimuter, a junior from Huntington Beach, Calif.,

majoring in environmental science. Mr. Perimuter said he didn't feel cheated by the lack of other required courses because "what they are training us to do is go out and find the information, because it's already there, and analyze it."

Unlike many other universities, Boise State University in Idaho is asking   30
hard questions about curriculum. The faculty is considering revisions that take a more measured approach, one that balances the Western canon with non-Western courses and that teaches all courses in a way that helps students think and analyze information in different ways. "A core curriculum should reflect certain common experiences or knowledge that most undergraduates should be exposed to," said Daryl E. Jones, interim executive vice president. "It is one of the things that binds us all together."

Currently, Boise State maintains a 51-credit core curriculum, which re-   31
quires students to take six credits of English composition and pass a writing exam, and 12 credits each of required courses in three areas: arts and humanities, social sciences, and natural science and mathematics. They are also required to take nine more elective credits in those three areas.

But as Boise State ponders revisions, "the key issue is how that relates to   32
other cultures and other experiences and fits in the overall education of a student," Mr. Jones said. "We haven't resolved all the issues ourselves."   ∎

Questions for Meaning

1. According to Celis, what is the principal debate about the curriculum? What question underlies this debate?
2. What is the current trend in American higher education?
3. What motivated Columbia University to adopt a core curriculum? What is motivating core curriculums emerging today?
4. On what grounds is it possible to argue for a core curriculum based on Western civilization?
5. Vocabulary: canon (3), cohesive (11), disparate (13), progenitors (16), finite (20).

Questions about Strategy

1. Consider the colleges and universities cited in this article. How representative are they of American higher education?
2. Does Celis adequately consider the views of students?
3. What is the purpose of citing a report from the National Endowment for the Humanities? How do you respond to the information in paragraph 12?
4. Why does Celis conclude with a paragraph that emphasizes unresolved questions?

JAWANZA KUNJUFU AND KIMBERLY R. VANN

THE IMPORTANCE OF AN AFROCENTRIC, MULTICULTURAL CURRICULUM

Believing that schools have the responsibility to increase understanding of diverse cultures, Jawanza Kunjufu and Kimberly R. Vann published the following argument in *Phi Delta Kappan* in 1993. Kunjufu is the author of *The Conspiracy to Destroy Black Boys* (1990) and the executive producer of *Up Against the Wall.* Vann is a freelance writer.

Was America discovered by Columbus, or was it invaded? Is Thanksgiving a day to give thanks or a day of sadness for Native Americans? Why should African-Americans celebrate the Fourth of July? The answers to these questions are apt to vary if you ask Native Americans, African-Americans, and white Americans. 1

Native Americans were already living on this continent when Columbus arrived. In *They Came Before Columbus,* noted scholar Ivan Van Sertima reports that Africans may have traveled to America as early as 800 B.C.—more than 2,000 years before Columbus. To many Americans, Thanksgiving is a holiday of appreciation for family, health, and other good fortunes. To Native Americans, Thanksgiving is a day of mourning because the kindness their ancestors bestowed on the Pilgrims was ultimately rewarded with the loss of their lands and the near-extinction of their people. The Fourth of July is a holiday that commemorates America's freedom from British domination. When America's first Independence Day was celebrated in 1776, African-Americans were not independent; they were not even citizens; they were slaves. 2

These issues clearly illustrate the need for an Afrocentric, multicultural curriculum. Whether the subject is history, science, or literature, the experiences of all cultures involved must be equally recognized and legitimized. Such a curriculum would embrace the perspectives of many cultures. When historical or contemporary issues were examined, the viewpoints of African-Americans, Native Americans, and other ethnic groups would be considered equally. This form of education is not anti-American or antiwhite; it seeks to provide balance in an unbalanced education system. An Afrocentric, multicultural curriculum is not exclusive; it is inclusive. 3

Everyone is now taught about the great civilizations of Rome and Greece, but how many people learn about the mighty empires of Ethiopia and Ghana? Thomas Edison is credited with inventing the light bulb and the phonograph, yet how much do students learn about Benjamin Banneker, one of America's first black intellectuals, who invented and built a wooden clock that kept accurate time for many years and who was instrumental in designing the blueprints for the nation's capital? *Julius Caesar* and *A Tale of Two Cities* are required reading in literature classes across America. Are students also required 4 to read *Miseducation of the Negro,* by Carter Woodson, or *Introduction to Black Studies,* by Maulana Karenga?

A strictly Eurocentric perspective will not properly prepare students for   5
a successful future in a multicultural world. We must have a curriculum that
teaches African-American history and culture—and the histories and cultures
of other ethnic groups as well—on a continual basis and not just during the
shortest month of the year. Yet African-American and other students are
taught from a Eurocentric frame of reference. In textbooks, African-American
history begins with American slavery, instead of with the genesis of civilization in Africa. Therefore, African-Americans are considered as descendants
only of slaves, not of kings and queens. Perhaps one page of a textbook discusses the civil rights movement; perhaps one paragraph summarizes the life
and works of Dr. Martin Luther King, Jr.

White and African-American students read volumes about the achieve-   6
ments of Americans of European descent in academics, in medicine, in business, in politics, and so on. Heroic figures range from Aristotle to Thomas
Jefferson to Jonas Salk. White students see themselves as descendants of superior achievers.

Schools are powerful institutions. They teach, socialize, and indoctrinate.   7
They can dispel myths or perpetuate them. If you have been constantly taught
that your ancestors were well-educated, cultured innovators, how would you
feel about the descendants of slaves? If you have been taught that your ancestors
were illiterate, impoverished sharecroppers, how would you feel about yourself? Because students internalize what they are taught, schools have a profound effect on the confidence and self-esteem of children. An Afrocentric,
multicultural curriculum is a major step toward addressing these vital issues.

African American Images, the Chicago-based publisher, has developed   8
Self-Esteem Through Culture Leads to Academic Excellence, a curriculum package
that uses history lessons to instill knowledge and self-esteem. We also salute
Atlanta's Infusion Conference, the authors of Portland's *African-American Base-
line Essays,* and the public school system in Oakland, California, for rewriting
sections of their social studies curriculum.

All students would benefit from an Afrocentric, multicultural curricu-   9
lum. White students would learn that all cultures have made outstanding contributions throughout the world by means of innovation, creativity, hard
work, and suffering. African-American students would finally inherit a legacy
of excellence and develop confidence, knowing that they too are capable of
achieving greatness. Our society today is multicultural. We must, therefore,
foster a greater awareness, appreciation, and acknowledgment of the achievements of the many instead of the few.   ■

Questions for Meaning

1. Why do the authors believe that a European-based curriculum is undesirable?
2. What do the authors mean by an "Afrocentric, multicultural curriculum"?
3. What is the objection to beginning African-American history with the study of slavery?
4. According to this argument, why would all students benefit from an Afrocentric, multicultural curriculum?
5. Vocabulary: instrumental (4), dispel (7), internalize (7), legacy (9), foster (9).

Questions about Strategy

1. Kunjufu and Vann begin their article with three questions. How appropriate are these questions as an introduction to the argument that follows?
2. Where do the authors attempt to reassure readers who have misgivings about multiculturalism?
3. Consider the books cited in paragraph 4. How appropriate are these examples?
4. What do the authors achieve by offering praise in paragraph 8?

HUGH B. PRICE

MULTICULTURALISM: MYTHS AND REALITIES

Hugh B. Price is vice president of the Rockefeller Foundation, one of the country's most prestigious sources of funding for research. Trying to clarify the debate over multiculturalism and reduce misunderstanding of its purpose, Price published the following article in a 1992 issue of *Phi Delta Kappan*. As you read it, note how Price draws on his own experience as an African American who attended segregated schools.

Academe is in high dudgeon these days over multiculturalism—what it means   1
and what are its appropriate curricular manifestations. It's a fascinating debate and in many respects an exasperating one, especially with regard to K–12 education. It is being carried out on the ideological extremes, but the issues are seldom discussed from the perspective of students and teachers inside the classroom. Usually the argument centers on whether Western culture and history should dominate instruction. Are school curricula sufficiently sensitive to

multicultural perspectives? Are Afrocentrism and other "centrisms" appropriate responses to perceived insensitivity on the part of curriculum designers?

These questions, which are the ones we hear most often, raise an intriguing set of subsidiary issues that are seldom discussed in depth but that may actually lie at the core of the debate. Is there even such a thing as objective history? Should schools attempt to instill self-esteem? And what metaphor most appropriately characterizes what America actually is and what it ought to be—a melting pot or a mosaic? 2

But first, a warning. I am neither a scholar nor an educator, neither a participant in the debate over multiculturalism nor an ideologue. I am only a captivated and sometimes puzzled observer of the furor, who happens also to be a colored/black/Negro/Afro/African-American. I have borne each of these labels during my nearly five decades on this earth. I wonder what new label awaits me this decade. 3

Now, the issue of history. Many scholars and educators are up in arms over demands that school curricula be revised and over the denunciation of Western civilization courses as instruments of cultural imperialism. And, for that matter, many are upset over the rejection of the so-called canon (or list of essential books) as an instrumentality of the entrenched power structure. Advocates of the ascendancy of Western values argue that there is a disinterested Western cultural tradition that is rooted in a commitment to rational inquiry, that is governed by rigorous standards of evidence, and that has, over the centuries, converged on the truth. Yet minorities and women argue that history texts have not gone nearly far enough in portraying their cultures and contributions. They say the texts are rife with glaring omissions, cultural stereotypes, and misrepresentations of their histories. 4

These accusations ring true. I, for one, was an adult before I learned that Pushkin, the celebrated Russian poet, and Alexandre Dumas, the noted French author, were black. No one in secondary school or college taught me those salient facts. Why was there no mention in the standard literary anthologies? 5

This pattern of denial helps explain the deep-rooted suspicions among minorities and women about the accuracy of history as taught in the schools. And these suspicions have been both the driving force behind the Afrocentrist movement, which has spawned a new body of scholarship by black authors on the African-American cultural heritage, and the impetus for much of the other pressure for multicultural education in this country. There is emerging research that suggests that ancient Egypt was to a large extent a black African society. According to Asa Hilliard of Georgia State University, school curricula should teach that Africa is the birthplace of mankind and thus of the arts, the sciences, mathematics, and the great philosophies. 6

Some scholars take issue with that assertion, of course. They contend that many of the purported contributions of the Egyptians are inflated and that some claims are downright false. And they contend that Hilliard's view of history has not been confirmed by recognized scholars from major universities. 7

Rather than foam at the mouth, as the protagonists on both sides of the issue are prone to do, why not find out whether these exciting and provocative 8 assertions are well-founded? Defenders of traditional Western content argue that history must meet the highest standards of accuracy and integrity as an intellectual discipline based on commonly accepted standards of evidence. They contend that revision of history occurs not as a result of political imposition, but because better history corrects and improves on previous research and teachings. Is this really so?

I grew up in Washington, D.C., and am old enough to have attended segre-   9
gated schools and to have witnessed the onset of integration. In the early Fifties we learned one version of the Civil War—the Southern version. Yet there was another, Northern version of the war that we weren't taught. Those contrasting versions of the Civil War were clearly products of conscious decisions by historians to codify, of textbook publishers to disseminate, and of schoolteachers to teach one as opposed to the other.

Are historians entirely objective when they write about the past? An ar-   10
ticle in the *Chronicle of Higher Education* suggests that history isn't the exacting, disinterested discipline that it is reputed to be.[1] Ever since the 19th century, mainstream historians have argued that historical interpretation is an objective, unbiased, and accurate reflection of the past. But that belief is now being shattered by the fragmentation of historical research and by emerging theories that knowledge is indeed subjective. According to Peter Novick, author of *That Noble Dream: The Objectivity Question and the American Historical Profession,* "What has come under attack among historians is not the commitment to amassing evidence, but the notion that there is one right version of history, a single truth about the past." Novick continues, "There is a distinction between upholding singular factualities, like saying I am wearing a red tie, and larger questions of synthesis."[2]

J. H. Hexter, professor emeritus of history at Washington University,   11
distinguishes between writing history with a capital *H* and writing history with a small *h*. The former deals with what Hexter characterizes as major trends, large movements, deep-running tides, and portentous rumbles. It's impossible, he says, to write capital *H* history objectively. However, according to Hexter, many historians believe they can answer the small *h* questions objectively, using accepted standards of evidentiary accuracy.[3]

But even small *h* history can befuddle historians on occasion. An inter-   12
esting article appeared in the *New York Times* not long ago that illuminated the perils faced by historians. The article was headlined "Vienna Takes Aim at Myths About Mozart." Supposedly Mozart died of poisoning while working on a requiem mass that was commissioned by a "gray-cloaked stranger." The article went on: "Too poor to buy even a proper coffin, his wife supposedly buried the composer in an unmarked pauper's grave with four other bodies." Viennese historians now have second thoughts. Contemporary researchers have concluded, according to the article, that Mozart probably died of the effects of a bloodletting administered to counter acute rheumatic fever. And he almost certainly knew that the requiem that he was working on the night of his death had been commissioned not by a stranger, but by a count.[4]

What's the moral of that revelation? Perhaps historians who attack Afro-   13
centrists should be humbler in their accusations. At the same time, Afrocen-
trists might be more cautious in their claims. And everyone should be more
temperate in their tones.

The formulation of history is an evolutionary process of discovery, argu-   14
mentation, interpretation, and codification. The cycle repeats itself over the
years as investigators dig ever deeper for evidence and synthesis. Why is it even
necessary to present all history as settled truth? When there is sharp disagreement, why not couch the issue as an unsettled question in the quest for truth?
Why not pose the contrasting positions to students as propositions to be studied—in effect, as an exercise in inquiry-based learning? Instead of asking students to absorb history, challenge them to "do" history. Teach them how to
ferret out primary sources, weigh evidence, critique arguments, and formulate
their own views. This learning process would be a prelude to the kinds of
judgments they will be called on to make as adults.

Next, the nettlesome issue of self-esteem. Advocates of multicultural and   15
"centrist" curricula argue that, if students do not feel good about themselves,
they will not fare well in school. They say that students do better academically
when they see people like themselves represented in the curriculum. In some
communities, parent groups have even gone so far as to sue on behalf of multicultural education. The parents claim that, as the result of glaring omissions in
the curriculum, their children's sense of self-worth has suffered. The lack of
multicultural curricula, they contend, has contributed to such problems as student disengagement and high dropout rates.

Proponents of this view have come under withering criticism. Their op-   16
ponents say that the role of those who formulate curricula is critical analysis,
accuracy, and objectivity—not making students feel better about themselves.
Teaching self-esteem is not the province of schools. Russell Baker, the *New
York Times* columnist, questions the notion that education has a duty to affect
people's feelings in a positive way. What's depressing about the arguments over
"centrism," in his view, is the indifference to the idea that education entails
training people to think clearly.[5]

Is it really the case that instilling self-esteem has no place in school and is   17
of dubious educational value? I take issue with that assertion, based on personal experience if not personal research. When I was growing up in segregated Washington, I attended B. K. Bruce Elementary School. Although most
of our curriculum was standard mainstream stuff, elements of an Afrocentric
curriculum were included. We were taught that Benjamin Banneker had laid
out the street system in Washington, D.C.; that Ralph Bunche helped bring
peace to the Middle East in the late Forties; that Charles Drew discovered
blood plasma and saved the lives of many American soldiers in World War II;
and, yes, that Jackie Robinson had integrated major league baseball.

In other words, we learned that blacks had made seminal contributions   18
to mainstream society. We learned that we belonged intellectually as well as
constitutionally and that we were of value to mainstream society, whether
others thought so or not. Moreover, our families maintained close ties with

Howard University, which was considered a citadel of learning with a distinguished faculty and student body.

Thus, even though we were reared in a segregated society, we were brimful of pride in our people and in our contributions to all mankind. There was never any doubt in my young mind about my self-worth or my capacity to succeed in school and beyond. Nor were there any doubts in the minds of my parents and other relatives. It's impossible to overstate the impact of this mindset on our confidence, our capacity, and our determination to succeed in school.

In my commonsense view, there is an unequivocal connection between self-esteem and success in life. Just imagine the handicaps that burden a child from a chronically poor family that is shut off from the mainstream—a family in which the parents harbor little hope for themselves, much less for their children. Imagine the odds against the child who lacks self-esteem and receives scant support from home.

We may argue that instilling self-esteem is no business of the schools, but we are deluding ourselves if we think there isn't a link between self-esteem and achievement—or that the close nexus between mainstream schools and well-functioning, intact families hasn't promoted the self-esteem of mainstream children all along. If schools are to succeed for millions of at-risk children who lack adequate support at home and in the community, then educators simply must fill this void in the children's lives.

As James Comer of Yale argues, schools must learn to respond flexibly and creatively to students' needs. When he was a youngster, three of Comer's neighborhood friends fell by the wayside. Comer succeeded largely because his parents, unlike those of his buddies, imparted the social skills and the self-confidence that enabled him to take advantage of educational opportunities.[6] These days there is a vast gulf between home and school. The lack of support for children makes such a difference that educators have to try to bridge that gulf.

What's more, Jeffrey Howard, a social psychologist who heads the Efficacy Institute in Boston, uses "attribution theory" to explain the inner governing mechanisms and external signals that influence whether or not students believe they can achieve. If students have confidence in their ability, then success or failure in school and in life is largely a function of effort. Whether children achieve is contingent on whether they possess self-esteem and confidence in their ability—and on whether their teachers share that confidence in them.[7]

I don't mean to suggest by citing Comer and Howard that they necessarily subscribe to Afrocentrism—or other "centrisms"—as appropriate curricular strategies. Or even that they believe Afrocentrism will instill self-esteem in minority students. I don't know how they feel about these propositions. But I do mean to suggest that their views lend credence to the argument that self-esteem and academic achievement go hand in hand. Thus, if we care about the academic development of children and if we acknowledge the reality that many at-risk children come from families and communities that don't instill the forms of self-esteem that foster school performance, then educators who teach such children must tackle self-esteem too.

The issue for me is not whether to boost students' self-esteem, but how   25
and toward what end. It does students no favor to build self-esteem on a specious historical foundation or to use history to insulate or alienate them from
others. Rather, the fundamental purpose should be to ensure that young people achieve the necessary intellectual and social development to function confidently and effectively as adults in a highly competitive world.

Finally, I come to the issue of "melting pot" versus "mosaic." Which is the   26
myth and which is the reality? America has been called a great melting pot for
races and ethnic groups that are constantly dissolving and re-forming. It is said
that most people who have emigrated to the U.S. over the years have arrived
expecting to become Americans. Their goals were deliverance from a harsh
past and assimilation into a hopeful future.

The trouble is that the melting pot works only at the margins and only in   27
some aspects of life. It seldom works socially and has succeeded in education
and the labor market only under duress. It took decades of political, judicial,
and legislative pressure to include some, and only some, minorities and women
in the melting pot.

In my view, mounting economic hardship may well lie at the heart of the   28
rising ethnic tensions that have increasingly called the melting pot metaphor
into question. Note the coincidence between the erosion of earnings among
working-class people—white, black, and Latino—and the rise in strident multiculturalism. The social compact in America between our society and its
working people—white and minority alike—is gradually dissolving. Once
upon a time, whether or not you were a capable student, if you played by the
rules, worked hard, and were willing to sweat, America would reward you
with a readily available, reasonably well-paying job that enabled you to be the
head of your household, to support your family, to buy a car and a home, to
educate your children, and to take an occasional vacation.

This simply is no longer so. Those manufacturing jobs that once pro-   29
vided dignity and decent wages for high school graduates and dropouts alike
are vanishing. All are victims of a new world industrial order that is redis-
tributing manufacturing jobs and redefining the economic role of our communities. It is true that the service industries have sopped up some of these
workers, but in such jobs they earn much less than the factory workers of old.
Families whose primary breadwinners lack high school degrees earned 30 percent less in 1987 (adjusted for inflation) than they did in 1973.[8]

Essentially, the income of "haves" has risen steadily while that of "have-   30
nots" has declined alarmingly. According to Richard Freeman, a labor economist at Harvard University, "Young working people, particularly men,
particularly non-college-graduate men, have taken a terrible beating in the job
market over the last twenty years." Adds Arnold Packer, executive director of
the Labor Department's Commission on Wages and Education, "A kid used to
be able to drop out of school and get a job with his old man at General Motors. Now the old man is lucky if he can keep his job and his kid has to start
somewhere else at the minimum wage."[9] To compound the problem, the

Army doesn't even want dropouts anymore. Young people must pass the General Education Development exam or possess a high school diploma to get into the Army.

Millions of Americans, a disproportionate number of them minorities, are going backward, losing hope, finding it increasingly difficult to share in the American dream. How can we expect them to accept, much less treasure, Western history and values if they're incessantly under economic siege? Why, under the circumstances, are we surprised that people seek solace and security among their own and adopt an increasingly insular view of the world? Try looking at the world through their prism and wonder how long it would take before paranoia, defeatism, or even defiance would set in.

What then is the role of the schools in this emerging world? Irreversible demographic trends will force public institutions to respond in new ways. Schools have traditionally served to mainstream students, divesting them of the language and culture of their countries of origin. But the reality also is that schools, with their testing systems, have long performed a sorting rather than a developmental function—which is to say, they have selected out some students for advanced opportunities and shunted most others aside to the armed forces, the factories, or the farm. This sorting function has affected young people, I hasten to add, of all races.

To compete successfully in the world economy, America must revamp the way it develops *all* of its human talent. The economy needs the productivity of highly skilled workers, regardless of complexion or cultural background. Schools have to equip young people to function successfully and harmoniously in a truly new world.

And what is that new world? Let me cite an anecdote shared by Beverly White, superintendent of schools in rural, predominantly black Lee County, Arkansas. She told me that Sanyo, the Japanese appliance manufacturer, has opened a plant in Lee County. The local schools have no choice but to embrace multiculturalism and global education because Lee County's children will soon enter the world of work—many of them at Sanyo's plant. What's more, the adults of Lee County and the Japanese managers who reside there must learn to live with "others"—namely, each other. Ideology aside, multiculturalism is a matter of good citizenship and of survival for Lee County.

Charles Krauthammer, writing in the *Washington Post,* has expressed concern that we are witnessing the rise of tribalism, of balkanization, and of multiculturalism. He lumped all these forces together. We see, he lamented, tribes surfacing within nations within empires. In his view, this worrisome trend should be a warning to America, which alone among multiethnic countries in the world has managed to assimilate its citizenry into a common nationality. According to Krauthammer, we risk squandering this great achievement.[10]

Interestingly enough, several pioneering scholars in the field of multiculturalism are also worried about the soaring decibel level of the debate. According to Henry Louis Gates, "routinized righteous indignation is being substituted for rigorous criticism." He says society simply won't survive without the values of tolerance. Perhaps, Gates suggests, we should think of

American culture as a conversation among different voices, even if it is a conversation that some were able to join only recently.[11]

In 1991 Nicholas Lemann, author of *The Promised Land,* wrote in the   37
New York Times Magazine of the families stranded for generations in Robert
Taylor Homes, a massive public housing project in Chicago. Where there once
were poor people and others in the neighborhood, there are now only poor
people.[12] A week after Lemann's article appeared, Harvard University political
economist Robert Reich, also writing in the *New York Times Magazine,* be-
moaned the growing isolation of America's elite, who are curled up in their
comfortable economic enclaves, unwilling to support those in need outside.
This secession of the fortunate fifth has been encouraged by the "newest fed-
eralism," which is shifting increased responsibility to state and local governments. In Reich's view, the political challenge ahead is to reaffirm that
America remains a society whose citizens have a binding obligation to one another, who honor the mutual obligations of the social compact.[13]

I wonder, frankly, how we can in clear conscience bewail the phenomena   38
of tribalization and multiculturalism when we do so little to eliminate the
economic and educational disparities that fuel them. The appropriate antidote
for cultural insularity is a culture of inclusiveness that infuses every facet of
our society. The blame for balkanization rests more with those who have the
power to include but won't than with those outside who are barred entry.

In fact, economic inclusion may well be the more original, enduring, and   39
compelling characteristic of this country. I'm no historian, but I submit it is
the opportunity to breathe politically and advance economically—not a desire
to assimilate—that has lured millions of immigrants to our shores for centuries
and that continues to draw them to this day.

That is the transcendent American attribute that defines our society, that   40
bonds us together, and that sets our nation noticeably apart from others. Were
those who ardently preach American values truly to practice them, then perhaps our collective anxiety about the growing intolerance and insularity in
America would, shall we say, melt away.

1. Karen J. Winkler, "Challenging Traditional Views, Some Historians Say Their Scholarship
   May Not Be Truly Objective," *Chronicle of Higher Education,* 16 January 1991, p. A-4.
2. Ibid.
3. Ibid.
4. "Vienna Takes Aim at Myths About Mozart," *New York Times,* 16 January 1991, p. A-5.
5. Russell Baker, "School as Spin Control," *New York Times,* 30 October 1990, p. A-25.
6. James P. Comer, *Maggie's American Dream: The Life and Times of a Black Family* (New
   York: NAL-Dutton, 1988).
7. Jeffrey Howard and Ray Hammond, "Rumors of Inferiority: The Hidden Obstacles to
   Black Success," *New Republic,* 9 September 1985, p. 17.
8. Lawrence Mishel and David M. Frankel, *The State of Working America: 1990-91 Edition*
   (Armonk, N.Y.: M. E. Sharpe, 1991), p. 199.
9. Peter T. Kilborn, "Youths Lacking Special Skills Find Jobs Leading Nowhere," *New York
   Times,* 27 November 1990, p. A-1.

10. Charles Krauthammer, "The Tribalization of America," *Washington Post,* 6 August 1990, p. A-11.
11. Karen J. Winkler, "Proponents of 'Multicultural' Humanities Research Call for a Critical Look at Its Achievements," *Chronicle of Higher Education,* 28 November 1990, p. A-5.
12. Nicolas Lemann, "Four Generations in the Projects," *New York Times Magazine,* 13 January 1991, p. 17.
13. Robert B. Reich, "Secession of the Successful," *New York Times Magazine,* 20 January 1991, p. 16. ■

Questions for Meaning

1. According to Price, why are minorities and women suspicious about history as it is traditionally taught?
2. How are historians reconsidering the nature of their discipline?
3. What is the difference between *History* and *history?*
4. Why does Price believe that fostering self-esteem is a legitimate mission for schools?
5. What is the difference between a "mosaic" and a "melting pot" view of America?
6. Vocabulary: dudgeon (1), subsidiary (2), imperialism (4), ascendancy (4), salient (5), impetus (6), imposition (8), codification (14), nettlesome (15), seminal (18), contingent (23), credence (24), duress (27), demographic (32), transcendent (40).

Questions about Strategy

1. In paragraph 3, Price advises readers that he is "neither a scholar nor an educator, neither a participant in the debate over multiculturalism nor an ideologue." What is the purpose of this disclaimer? How did if affect you?
2. Where does Price summarize conflicting views about the curriculum? What does he achieve by doing so?
3. How effectively does Price incorporate personal experience into his argument?
4. What is Price illustrating by his discussion of Mozart's death in paragraph 12?
5. On what basic values has Price built his argument? Are these values likely to appeal to a diverse audience?

RONALD TAKAKI

AN EDUCATED AND CULTURALLY LITERATE PERSON MUST STUDY AMERICA'S MULTICULTURAL REALITY

Professor of Ethnic Studies at the University of California at Berkeley, Ronald Takaki is the author of *Strangers from a Different Shore: A History of Asian Americans* (1989), *Iron Cages: Race and Culture in Nineteenth-Century America* (1990), and *A Different Mirror: A History of Multicultural America* (1993). He first published the following article in the *Chronicle of Higher Education* in 1989.

In Palolo Valley, Hawaii, where I lived as a child, my neighbors were Japanese, Chinese, Portuguese, Filipino, and Hawaiian. I heard voices with different accents and I heard different languages. I played with children of different colors. Why, I wondered, were families representing such an array of nationalities living together in one little valley? My teachers and textbooks did not explain our diversity.   1

After graduation from high school, I attended a college on the mainland where students and even professors would ask me how long I had been in America and where I had learned to speak English. "In this country," I would reply. "I was born in America, and my family has been here for three generations."   2

Today, some twenty years later, Asian and also Afro-Americans, Chicano/ Latino, and Native-American students continue to find themselves perceived as strangers on college campuses. Moreover, they are encountering a new campus racism. The targets of ugly racial slurs and violence, they have begun to ask critical questions about why knowledge of their histories and communities is excluded from the curriculum. White students are also realizing the need to understand the cultural diversity of American society.   3

In response, colleges and universities across the country, from Brown to Berkeley, are currently considering requiring students to take courses designed to help them understand diverse cultures.   4

The debate is taking place within a general context framed by academic pundits like Allan Bloom and E. D. Hirsch.★ Both of them are asking: What is an educated, a culturally literate person?   5

I think Bloom is right when he says: "There are some things one must know about if one is to be educated. . . . The university should try to have a vision of what an educated person is." I also agree with Hirsch when he   6

★Educators Allan Bloom and E. D. Hirsch achieved national prominence during the 1980s by arguing that American colleges were failing to produce culturally literate citizens. Bloom is best known for *The Closing of the American Mind* (1987); Hirsch for *The Philosophy of Composition* (1981) and *Cultural Literacy: What Every American Needs to Know* (1987).

insists that there is a body of cultural information that "every American needs to know."

But the question is: What should be the content of education and what does cultural literacy mean? The traditional curriculum reflects what Howard Swearer, former president of Brown University, has described as a "certain provincialism," an overly Eurocentric perspective. Concerned about this problem, a Brown University visiting committee recommended that the faculty consider requiring students to take an ethnic-studies course before they graduate. "The contemporary definition of an educated person," the committee said, "must include at least minimal awareness of multicultural reality." 7

This view now is widely shared. Says Donna Shalala, chancellor of the University of Wisconsin at Madison: "Every student needs to know much more about the origins and history of the particular cultures which, as Americans, we will encounter during our lives." 8

This need is especially felt in California, where racial minorities will constitute a majority of the population by 2000, and where a faculty committee at the University of California at Berkeley has proposed an "American-cultures requirement" to give students a deeper understanding of our nation's racial and cultural diversity. Faculty opposition is based mainly on a disdain for all requirements on principle, an unwillingness to add another requirement, an insistence on the centrality of Western civilization, and a fear that the history of European immigrant groups would be left out of the proposed course. 9

In fact, however, there are requirements everywhere in the curriculum (for reading and composition, the major, a foreign language, breadth of knowledge, etc.). The American-cultures requirement would not be an additional course, for students would be permitted to use the course to satisfy one of their social-sciences or humanities requirements. Western civilization will continue to dominate the curriculum, and the proposed requirement would place the experiences of racial minorities within the broad context of American society. Faculty support for some kind of mandatory course is considerable, and a vote on the issue is scheduled this spring. 10

But the question often asked is: What would be the focus and content of such multicultural courses? Actually there is a wide range of possibilities. For many years I have been teaching a course on "Racial Inequality in America: a Comparative Historical Perspective." Who we are in this society and how we are perceived and treated have been conditioned by America's racial and ethnic diversity. My approach is captured in the phrase "from different shores." By "shores," I intend a double meaning. One is the shores that immigrants left to go to America—those in Europe, Africa, Latin America, and Asia. The second is the different and often conflicting shores or perspectives from which scholars have viewed the experiences of racial and ethnic groups. 11

In my course, students read Thomas Sowell's *Ethnic America: A History* along with my *Iron Cages: Race and Culture in 19th-Century America*. Readings also include Winthrop Jordan on the colonial origins of racism, John Higham on nativism, Mario Barrera on Chicanos, and William J. Wilson on the black underclass. By critically examining the different "shores," students are able to 12 address complex comparative questions: How have the experiences of racial minorities such as blacks and Asians been similar to, and different from, one another? Is "race" the same as "ethnicity?" How have race relations been shaped by economic developments, as well as by culture? What impact have these forces had on moral values about how people should think and behave, beliefs about human nature and society, and images of the past as well as the future?

Other courses could examine racial diversity in relation to gender, im-   13
migration, urbanization, technology, or the labor market. Courses could also study specific topics such as Hollywood's racial images, ethnic music and art, novels by writers of color, the civil rights movement, or the Pacific Rim. Regardless of theme or topic, all of the courses should address the major theoretical issues concerning race and should focus on Afro-Americans, Asians, Chicanos/Latinos, and Native Americans.

Who would teach these courses? Responsibility could be located solely in   14
ethnic-studies programs. But this would reduce them to service-course programs and also render even more remote the possibility of diversifying the traditional curriculum. The sheer logistics of meeting the demand generated by an institutionwide requirement would be overwhelming for any single department.

Clearly, faculty members in the social sciences and humanities will have   15
to be involved. There also are dangers in this approach, however. The diffusion of ethnic studies throughout the traditional disciplines could undermine the coherence and identity of ethnic studies as a field of teaching and scholarship. It could also lead to area-studies courses on Africa or Asia disguised as ethnic studies, to revised but essentially intact Western-civilization courses with a few "non-Western" readings tacked on, or to amorphous and bland "American studies" courses taught by instructors with little or no training in multicultural studies. Such courses, though well-intentioned, could result in the unwitting perpetuation of certain racial stereotypes and even to the transformation of texts by writers and scholars of color into "mistexts." This would only reproduce multicultural illiteracy.

But broad faculty participation in such a requirement can work if there is   16
a sharply written statement of purpose, as well as clear criteria for courses on the racial and cultural diversity of American society. We also need interdisciplinary institutes to offer intellectual settings where faculty members from different fields can collaborate on new courses and where ethnic-studies scholars can share their expertise. More importantly, we need to develop and strengthen ethnic-studies programs and departments as academic foundations for this new multicultural curriculum. Such bases should bring together a critical mass of faculty members committed to, and trained in ethnic studies, and should help to preserve the alternative perspectives provided by this scholarly field.

In addition, research must generate knowledge for the new courses, and   17
new faculty members must be trained for ethnic-studies teaching and scholarship. Berkeley already has a doctoral program in ethnic studies, but other

graduate schools must also help prepare the next generation of faculty members. Universities will experience a tremendous turnover in teachers due to retirements, and this is a particularly urgent time to educate future scholars, especially from minority groups, for a multicultural curriculum.

The need to open the American mind to greater cultural diversity will   18
not go away. We can resist it by ignoring the changing ethnic composition of our student bodies and the larger society, or we can realize how it offers colleges and universities a timely and exciting opportunity to revitalize the social sciences and humanities, giving both a new sense of purpose and a more inclusive definition of knowledge.

If concerted efforts are made, someday students of different racial back-   19
grounds will be able to learn about one another in an informed and systematic way and will not graduate from our institutions of higher learning ignorant about how places like Palolo Valley fit into American society.   ■

Questions for Meaning

1. Consider the questions, in paragraph 2, that Takaki was often asked when he was a college student. What do they reveal?
2. According to Takaki, why did faculty at his school oppose a required course in American cultures?
3. In paragraph 12, Takaki asks, "Is 'race' the same as 'ethnicity'"? How would you answer this question?
4. Who should teach multicultural courses? What risks does Takaki see in giving responsibility for such courses to a single department? Why is he concerned about locating such courses within traditional academic disciplines?
5. Vocabulary: pundits (5), provincialism (7), logistics (14), amorphous (15), criteria (16).

Questions about Strategy

1. Takaki opens his essay by drawing on personal experience from twenty years ago. Is it relevant to the question at hand?
2. Why does Takaki choose Brown and Berkeley as examples of "colleges and universities across the country"?
3. Why does Takaki draw particular attention to educational needs in California?
4. What is the function of paragraph 6?
5. Consider paragraphs 12 and 13. Why does Takaki offer both a description of his own course and a list of other possibilities?

CHRISTINE E. SLEETER

WHAT IS MULTICULTURAL EDUCATION?

Professor of Teacher Education at the University of Wisconsin at Parkside, Christine E. Sleeter is the coauthor of *Making Choices for Multicultural Education* (1988) and the editor of *Empowerment Through Multicultural Education* (1990). The following 1992 article was published by Sleeter in *Kappa Delta Pi Record*. As its title suggests, the article describes several different approaches to multicultural education.

Three teachers are sitting in a graduate course discussing their teaching. All three say they are actively involved in multicultural education, but as their discussion evolves, all three describe it differently. The first teacher says she has taught in an inner-city school for years and has learned to adapt her teaching successfully to the students; most of the students in her class score above the national average on standardized tests. The second teacher, rather surprised at that conception of multicultural education, says she has developed a series of intense units about the history of four different oppressed groups in the United States and has organized much of her instruction around these units.   1

The third teacher argues that the other teachers do not understand multicultural education. He has reconstructed his teaching in such a way that students analyze various social justice issues across different subject areas through the perspectives of diverse American sociocultural groups. He has also challenged tracking and ability grouping in his school.   2

Which of these conceptions of multicultural education is "correct"? All of them are, and they illustrate a few of the many conceptions of multicultural education teachers ascribe to in today's classrooms. In this article I will briefly outline five different "correct" approaches to multicultural education that many teachers use and educational theorists discuss.   3

To respond to American diversity more effectively, all five approaches involve a substantial reworking of the existing education program. However, each approach defines "effective education" differently and makes different assumptions about how it is achieved. These approaches to multicultural education have been developed in much more detail by me and Carl Grant elsewhere (Sleeter and Grant 1989; 1988).   4

First, let me briefly point out what these approaches have in common that makes them "multicultural education." First, each attempts to improve how schools address diversity in the United States, acknowledging that racism, sexism, and other forms of discrimination still exist and are perpetuated through "business as usual." Simply teaching a diverse class of students does not, in and of itself, constitute multicultural education. Teaching a White supremacist curriculum and maintaining relatively low expectations for minority student learning, for example, reproduces inequalities rather than confronts them. Second, each approach addresses only diversity in the United States.   5

Some may also include international diversity, but do not equate American diversity with immigrants or international education. Some multicultural educators focus mainly on race and ethnicity, and some focus mainly on gender. My discussion will include race, ethnicity, social class, gender, and disability.

The *Teaching the Exceptional and Culturally Different Approach* to multicultural education aims to help students of color, low-income students, and/or special education students to achieve, assimilate, and "make it" in society as it currently exists. This approach assumes that the United States and Western culture provide abundant opportunities to citizens and show leadership in cultural development. It recognizes that students who are not achieving and succeeding may require bridges between their backgrounds and the schools to make the curriculum more "user friendly." Teachers who actually work with this approach have very high expectations for academic achievement. They believe the traditional academic curriculum is sound for all students, but that different students require different teaching approaches to connect successfully with it. Bridges may consist of instructional strategies that build on students' learning styles, culturally relevant materials, use of students' native language to teach academic content and Standard English, or compensatory programs that try to bring students up to grade-level. This approach does not advocate changing the emphasis or content of disciplines of study, only "marketing" them more effectively to a wider diversity of students.

Much research addresses how some teaching strategies either hinder or help the achievement of students who are members of groups that historically have not achieved well in schools. For example, research in anthropology and psychology documents a relationship between culture and cognitive style, suggesting that if teachers match their teaching strategies with students' learning styles, students will learn better (Shade 1989). Much work in bilingual education follows this model, providing considerable guidance for the development of school programs that build students' first language, teach new academic content and skills through the first language, and teach English as a second language (Crawford 1989; Trueba 1989).

Many teachers who are new to multicultural education are attracted to this approach. They are concerned about low achievement among students and believe that if students get a "boost" from the school (many regard this boost as making up for deficiencies at home) or are actually taught aspects of Western culture their parents are unable to teach, the students—regardless of their background—will be able to go on in life and achieve what they want.

One can distinguish educators who favor this approach in two ways. First, the changes they advocate in schooling are mainly or solely for members of a particular group, such as students from the inner city, bilingual students, mainstreamed special-education students, and immigrant students. If asked about parallel changes in the education of members of dominant groups, they either view few changes as needed or are not interested in expending energy trying to change the education of dominant group members. Second, advocates generally support much of the dominant discourse about the United States—that it is a free country with limitless opportunity, that its history is one of progress, and that only a few changes are needed to extend the American Dream to everyone.

The *Human Relations Approach* attempts to foster positive interpersonal relationships among members of diverse groups in the classroom and to strengthen each student's self-concept. Teachers who are attracted to this approach are concerned primarily with how students feel about and treat each other. The Human Relations curriculum includes lessons about stereotyping, individual differences and similarities, and contributions to society made by groups of which students are members; lessons and special events are supplemental to the main curriculum. Cooperative learning is used for the purpose of promoting student-student relationships. Much of what many schools do in the name of multicultural education is actually in reality Human Relations, such as ethnic fairs or special celebrations to feature a particular group—*Cinco de Mayo,* Asian/Pacific American Heritage Week, Black History Month, Women's History Month, etc. Usually the main purpose of such celebrations is affective—to attempt to deconstruct stereotypes students may have of each other and to help them feel good about contributions members of such groups have made.

The Human Relations Approach seems to fit particularly well with EuroAmericans' conception of their own ethnicity. Today ethnicity for Euro-Americans is acknowledged voluntarily, is connected with family history, and is acted upon mainly in the form of festivals and food (Alba 1990).

Like those who favor the Teaching the Exceptional and Culturally Different Approach, teachers who are attracted to the Human Relations approach generally regard American society at large as fair and open. They view disharmony among students (such as racial name-calling or social segregation on the playground) to be a result of misunderstanding and untrue stereotypes. They believe that providing positive information about groups as well as contact experiences will eliminate sources of such disharmony.

The next three approaches to multicultural education offer much stronger critiques of American society than do the first two. Educators who are sympathetic to the next three approaches usually have experienced and/or studied inequality in the United States sufficiently to appreciate the degree to which it is embedded in social institutions and perceive a need for far-reaching changes in education.

"Single-Group Studies" is an umbrella term for units or courses of study that focus on particular groups, such as ethnic studies, labor studies, women's studies, or disability studies. The *Single-Group Studies Approach* seeks to raise consciousness about a group by teaching its history, culture, and contributions, as well as how that group has worked with or been oppressed by the dominant group in society. Single-Group Studies courses were created during the 1960s and 1970s as alternatives to the main curriculum of the university or school, which is strongly based on the experience of White men.

Although textbooks today may appear to be multicultural, careful analysis finds them to be still White and male-dominant and to treat other groups

10

11

12

13

14

15

in a very fragmented fashion (Sleeter and Grant 1991). For example, examine several current textbooks to see how well they help answer the following questions: What historical and contemporary factors account for the persistent poverty of Mexican Americans? Why do full-time working women still earn only about 70 percent of what men earn, even with the same level of education? To what degree is wealth concentrated in a small number of hands in the United States? What insights does traditional and contemporary Native American literature give about how life should be lived? Why do persons with disabilities tend to see themselves as an oppressed minority rather than a group with a particular medical condition?

Often teachers attempt well-meaning lessons and units about other   16
groups, but without realizing it, they replicate distortions, inaccuracies, or what one writer has termed "fantasies of the master race" (Churchill 1992). This happen when we ourselves have not studied another group in much depth, nor talked much with members of that group regarding the group's history or experiences. For example, I have observed units during Women's History Month that suggest sexism has been eliminated, and young girls today can simply go forth and do whatever they wish, the only remaining barrier being their own aspirations.

Most teachers have not studied an oppressed group in enough depth to   17
realize the degree to which disciplinary knowledge is being reconstructed in Single-Group Studies departments in higher education.

Since the late 1960s, scholars working in university departments of eth-   18
nic studies, women's studies, and labor studies have unearthed and synthesized an enormous amount of information about particular groups of study. In addition, scholars have begun to reconceptualize fields of study based on the experiences and perspectives of previously marginalized groups. For example, Afrocentric scholars, placing people of African rather than European descent at the center of inquiry, have reconceptualized and restructured fields such as history, communication, art, and philosophy. Latino theorists question the traditional definition of "American culture" as meaning culture created within the boundaries of the United States. According to Lauter:

> One might argue that, for example, the virtual exclusion of early Spanish and French exploration texts, or of black and Indian sermons and autobiographies from received definition of "American literature" served the important ideological role of maintaining boundaries between what was truly "American," "ours," and what was "other," marginal (1991).

Schools controlled by African Americans and Native Americans are pro-   19
ducing excellent K-12 materials in the Afrocentric curricula and Native American curricula. Further, university libraries are housing rapidly growing collections of fascinating, vibrant work. It may be initially daunting to come to terms with how little one may know about other groups and the degree to which other groups' perspectives challenge much of what one may take for

granted about the broader American society. However, there is plenty of material available to educate one's self and a fair amount available to use to educate one's students.

The *Multicultural Approach* to education reconstructs the entire educa-   20
tion process to promote equality and cultural pluralism. Content in the curriculum is reorganized around the perspectives and knowledge of diverse
American racial and ethnic groups (oppressed groups as well as EuroAmericans), both sexes, disability groups, and diverse social classes. A multicultural
poetry unit usually features a wider variety of language use, lived experience, and perspective than does a monocultural unit, making it rich and fostering critical thinking.

The Multicultural Approach also reconstructs other processes in educa-   21
tion that traditionally have not promoted high achievement for all students.
Under this approach, tracking and ability grouping would be greatly reduced
or eliminated because they are viewed as institutionalizing differential achievement and learning opportunity, which contradicts the ideal of equality. The
Multicultural Approach advocates staffing schools with a diverse teaching
force and breaking up traditional role designations (such as men teaching math
and technical education or women working as secretaries and foreign-language
teachers). It builds on students' learning styles, adapts to their skill level, and
involves students actively in thinking and analyzing life situations. It encourages native language maintenance for students whose first language is not English and multilingual acquisition for all students.

Often teachers who are new to multicultural education confuse the   22
Human Relations Approach with the Multicultural Approach, since both
involve integrating diverse groups into the curriculum. They are quite different, however. The Multicultural Approach transforms everything in the
entire school program to reflect diversity and uphold equality. The school
program becomes quite rich and dynamic although not harmonious. For
example, in a multicultural classroom, students would become used to considering different perspectives as "right;" they would discuss and debate different viewpoints and consider whether diversity actually means "anything
goes." This approach deliberately fosters equal academic achievement across
groups; achievement does not take a back seat to interpersonal relationships.
Further, in the Multicultural Approach the entire curriculum is rewritten to
be multicultural, drawing on content developed through Single-Group
Studies; the Human Relations Approach adds on lessons without rewriting
the curriculum.

The *Education that is Multicultural and Social Reconstructionist Approach*   23
builds on the previous approaches, especially Single-Group Studies and the
Multicultural Approach, teaching students to analyze inequality and oppression in society and helping them develop skills for social action. The main
raison d'etre★ for multicultural education is that, while Americans espouse

★Justification (from the French for "reason to be").

ideals of democracy, justice, and equality, the social system does not work—and has never worked—that way for large segments of the population. For example, the average EuroAmerican in the 1990s has greater access to a wide range of resources, such as access to jobs, decent housing, good education, and health care, than does the average American of color. Single-Group Studies focuses on a particular group, examining why this is the case historically as well as today, and exploring the creative and intellectual work of a group despite oppression. The Multicultural Approach offers a synthesis of Single-Group Studies, but one that is not overtly political.

24 The Social Reconstructionist approach begins with contemporary social-justice issues that cut across diverse groups, using disciplinary knowledge to examine them and create ways of affecting change. For example, a theme that appears in literature, art, and other creative works of oppressed groups is criticism of oppressive social structures and cultural representations. This is not generally a theme in the creative work of dominant groups, and educators who are members of dominant groups often mute or eliminate such criticism in constructing curriculum; it would, however, be a theme salient to Education that is Multicultural and Social Reconstructionist.

25 For example, a history course could begin with the following problem. Americans today as well as historically have proclaimed the United States stands for equality, justice, and liberty for all. Yet, one can amass abundant data illustrating great inequalities, lack of justice, and restricted liberties in the United States.

26 Historically, how have different groups defined "equality," "justice," and "liberty," and how have the different definitions been acted out and contested? Using these questions as a basis for analysis, one could then structure a fascinating examination of United States history that would connect with questions Americans today are asking.

27 In the Social Reconstructionist Approach, students are encouraged to learn to take action on issues. On the basis of studying an issue such as religious freedom, for example, some members of a class may decide to organize a letter-writing campaign to congressional representatives on behalf of Native American religious freedom.

28 Ultimately, I regard this last approach as the one most in keeping with American ideals of equality and democracy. But the approach takes democracy and equality very seriously, not accepting the platitudes with which we all were raised. As such, it is challenging and uncomfortable for many people. The approach also takes a good deal of work to master, since it builds on the information base of Single-Group Studies and Teaching the Exceptional and Culturally Different. There are texts available to help teachers get started (Nieto 1992; Schniedewind and Davidson 1983; Sleeter 1991; Sleeter and Grant 1989 and 1988).

29 In the long run, I do not believe our school system, or our social institutions more broadly, will survive without radical reconstruction. While our own diversity grows, so also does the frustration of people who experience continued blocked access to the "American Dream." Some argue that

multicultural education is divisive. To me, multicultural education means listening to and taking seriously what diverse Americans are saying about themselves and the conditions of their lives, then acting on what we learn, to build a better system for us all. Failure to do so is divisive.

References

Alba, Richard D. *Ethnic Identity: The Transformation of White America.* New Haven, Conn.: Yale University Press, 1990.

Churchill, Ward. *Fantasies of the Master Race: Literature, Cinema and the Colonization of American Indians.* Monroe, Me.: Common Courage Press, 1992.

Crawford, Jack. *Bilingual Education: History, Politics, Theory and Practice.* Trenton, N.J.: Crane Publishing Co., 1989.

Grant, Carl A., and Christine E. Sleeter. *Turning on Learning.* Columbus, Oh.: Merrill, 1989.

Lauter, Paul. *Canons and Contexts.* New York: Oxford University Press, 1991.

Nieto, Sonia. *Affirming Diversity.* New York: Longman, 1992.

Schniedewind, Nancy, and Ellen Davidson. *Open Minds to Equality.* Englewood Cliffs, N.J.: Prentice-Hall, 1983.

Shade, Barbara J. R. *Culture, Style, and the Educative Process.* Springfield, IL: Charles C. Thomas, 1989.

Sleeter, Christine E., ed. *Empowerment Through Multicultural Education.* Albany, N.Y.: SUNY Press, 1991.

Sleeter, Christine E., and Carl A. Grant. "An Analysis of Multicultural Education in the United States," *Harvard Educational Review,* 57 (4), 421–444.

Sleeter, Christine E., and Carl A. Grant. *Making Choices for Multicultural Education.* Columbus, Oh.: Merrill, 1988.

Sleeter, Christine E., and Carl A. Grant. "Race, Class, Gender, and Disability in Current Textbooks." *The Politics of the Textbook.* Michael W. Apple and Linda K. Christian-Smith, eds. New York: Routledge, 1991, 78–110.

Trueba, Henry T. *Raising Silent Voices: Educating the Linguistic Minorities for the 21st Century.* New York: Newbury House, 1989. ■

Questions for Meaning

1. What do different approaches to multicultural education have in common?
2. What does Sleeter mean by "bridges," and what is their purpose?
3. Why do some educators adopt pedagogies designed to teach "the exceptional and culturally different"? On what grounds is this approach questionable?
4. What is necessary to succeed in teaching "single-group studies"?
5. How does the "human relations" approach differ from the "multicultural" approach?
6. Vocabulary: perpetuated (5), stereotyping (10), embedded (13), marginalized (18), daunting (19), pluralism (20), salient (24), platitudes (28).

Questions about Strategy

1. Sleeter opens her article with an emphasis on description. Does she confine herself to describing approaches to multicultural education or does she advocate one or more of these approaches?
2. On what basic principle does Sleeter justify the need for multicultural education?
3. Where does Sleeter advise readers of potential problems in multicultural classrooms? Why does she do this?
4. How does Sleeter respond to the argument that multicultural education is divisive?

THOMAS SOWELL

MULTICULTURAL INSTRUCTION

Educated at Harvard, Columbia, and the University of Chicago, Thomas Sowell taught at Rutgers, Brandeis, and UCLA before joining the Hoover Institution at Stanford. His books include *The Economics and Politics of Race* (1983), *Civil Rights: Rhetoric or Reality* (1985), *Choosing a College* (1989), *Preferential Policies* (1990), and *Inside American Education* (1992). He first published the following article in a 1993 issue of *The American Spectator,* a monthly periodical that advances politically conservative positions.

Most of the arguments for so-called "multicultural" education are so flimsy, inconsistent, and downright silly that it is hard to imagine that they would have been taken seriously if they were not backed up by shrill rhetoric, character assassination, and the implied or open threat of organized disruption and violence on campus.   1

Let us examine the multiculturalists' questions, one by one.   2

• *Why do we study Western civilization, to the neglect of other civilizations?*

Why is that question asked in English, rather than in some non-Western   3
language? Because English is what we speak. Why do we concern ourselves with the Earth, which is an infinitesimal part of the known universe? Because that is where we live. If we want to understand the cultural and institutional world in which we carry on our daily lives, we need to understand the underlying rationale and the historical evolution of the way of life we have been born into.

None of this has anything to do with whether English is a better language than some other languages. English is in fact more inconsistent and less   4
melodic than French, for example. But we speak English for the same practical

reasons that cause people in China to speak Chinese. Attempts to turn this into an invidious comparisons issue miss the fundamental point that (1) languages exist to serve practical purposes and (2) they serve those purposes better, the more people in the same society speak the same language.

Why don't we study other civilizations equally? The most obvious answer is the 24-hour day and the limited number of days we spend in college. It is stretching things very thin to try to cover Western civilization in two semesters. Throw in a couple of other civilizations and you are just kidding yourself that you are educating anybody, when all that you are really doing is teaching them to accept superficiality. Those whose real agenda is propaganda are of course untroubled by such considerations.

Any suggestion that any aspect of Western civilization has been admirable, or better in any way than the corresponding aspect of any other civilization, will of course be loudly denounced as showing bias instead of being "non-judgmental." However, the one thing that no civilization has ever been is non-judgmental. Much of the advancement of the human race has occurred because people made the judgment that some things were not simply different from others, but better. Often this judgment was followed by abandoning one cultural feature and using the other instead.

We use Arabic numerals today, instead of Roman numerals, even though our civilization derived from Rome, and the Arabs themselves got these numerals from India. Arabic numerals (or Indian numerals) have displaced other numbering systems around the world because they are better—not just different. Paper, printing, and books are today essential aspects of Western civilization, but all three came out of China—and they have displaced parchment, scrolls, and other forms of preserving writings all around the world. Books are not just different, they are better—not just in my opinion, or in the opinion of Western civilization, but in the practice of people around the world who have had an opportunity to make the comparison. Firearms have likewise displaced bows and arrows wherever the two have come into competition.

Many of those who talk "non-judgmental" rhetoric out of one side of their mouths are quick to condemn the evils of "our society" out of the other side. Worse, they condemn American society or Western civilization for sins that are the curse of the human race all across the planet. Indeed, they condemn the West for sins that are worse in many non-Western societies.

Perhaps the classic case is slavery. The widespread revulsion which this hideous institution inspires today was largely confined to Western civilization a century ago, and a century before that was largely confined to a portion of British society. No one seems interested in the epic story of how this curse that covered the globe and endured for thousands of years was finally gotten rid of. It was gotten rid of by the West—not only in Western societies but in other societies conquered, controlled, or pressured by the West.

The resistance put up by Africans, Asians, and Arabs was monumental in defense of slavery, and lasted for more than a century. Only the overwhelming military power of the West enabled it to prevail on this issue, and only the moral outrage of Western peoples kept their governments' feet to the fire politically to maintain the pressure against slavery around the world. Of course, this is not the kind of story that appeals to the multiculturalists. If it had been the other way around—if Asian or African imperialists had stamped out slavery in Europe—it would still be celebrated, in story and song, on campuses across America.

• *Why are the traditional classics of Western civilization written by dead white males?*

Take it a step at a time. They are written by dead people for two reasons: First, there are more dead people than living people. Second, a classic is not something that is hot at the moment but something that survives the test of time. There may be things written today that will survive to become classics, but we won't be here when that happens. The things we know as classics were almost by definition written by dead people.   11

Why were they white? Do we ask why the great classics of China were written by people who were Chinese? If we found that the great classics of China were written by Swedes, wouldn't we wonder what the hell was going on?   12

Should there be any mystery as to why they were written by males? Is anyone so utterly ignorant of history that they do not know that females had more than enough other work to keep them busy for most of the history of the human race? Maybe men should have shared some of that work. But history is what happened, not what we wish had happened. If most of the people who were educated were male—as they have been throughout history, and even are today in some societies—then most of the people who leave the kind of written material left by educated people will be men. You don't get great mathematical discoveries from people who were never taught algebra.   13

Much the same reasoning applies to other groups considered to be (1) oppressed and (2) "under-represented" among those whose historic achievements and contributions are recognized. But how can a people's achievements be unaffected by their oppression? One of the many reasons to be against oppression is that it keeps people from achieving all that they could have achieved if they had been treated more decently. To proclaim oppression and still expect to find the oppressed equally represented among those with historic achievements and contributions is almost a contradiction in terms.   14

The past is many things, but one thing it is, is irrevocable. A past to your liking is not an entitlement.   15

• *Don't we need multiculturalism to get people to understand each other and get along with each other?*

Since this is an empirical question, you would expect people to seek an empirical answer, yet most of those who talk this way seem content to treat the matter as axiomatic. But is there any evidence that colleges that have gone whole hog into multiculturalism have better relations among the various groups on campus? Or is it precisely on such campuses that separatism and hostility are worse than on campuses that have not gone in for the multicultural craze?   16

You want to see multiculturalism in action? Look at Yugoslavia, at   17
Lebanon, at Sri Lanka, at Northern Ireland, at Azerbaijan, or wherever else
group "identity" has been hyped. There is no point in the multiculturalists
saying that this is not what they have in mind. You might as well open the
floodgates and then say that you don't mean for people to drown. Once you
have opened the floodgates, you can't tell the water where to go.

• *How are we to be part of the global economy, or engage in all sorts of other interna-*
tional activities, without being multicultural?

Ask the Japanese. They are one of the most insular and self-complacent   18
peoples on Earth today. Yet they dominate international markets, international finance, international scientific and technological advances, and send
armies of tourists around the world. This is not a defense of insularity or of the
Japanese. It is simply a plain statement of fact that contradicts one of the many
lofty and arbitrary dogmas of multiculturalism.   ■

Questions for Meaning

1. Why does Sowell believe that the study of slavery ultimately reflects
   well on the West?
2. How does Sowell justify curriculums that emphasize the study of works
   by writers who are no longer living?
3. How does Sowell account for curriculums dominated by works written
   by men?
4. On what grounds does Sowell oppose oppression? How does oppression of marginalized groups account for their status in the standard
   curriculum?
5. Vocabulary: revulsion (9), irrevocable (15), empirical (16), axiomatic
   (16), insular (18).

Questions about Strategy

1. Consider the opening paragraph. To whom is this paragraph most likely
   to appeal? Is it a good strategy to open an argument with a paragraph
   like this?
2. Does Sowell make any attempt to recognize the achievements of non-
   Western cultures?
3. How does Sowell respond to the argument that different civilizations
   should be studied in school?
4. Consider the countries cited in paragraph 17. Why does Sowell choose
   these countries as examples? Are they representative of "multiculturalism in action"?
5. Most of Sowell's argument is framed as a response to points made by
   advocates of multiculturalism. How effective is it to structure an argument this way?

DINESH D'SOUZA

THE VISIGOTHS IN TWEED

A critic of what he perceives as the left wing in American education, Dinesh D'Souza is the author of *Illiberal Education: The Politics of Race and Sex on Campus* (1991), which argues that American higher education is dominated by radicals. Born in India, D'Souza was educated at Dartmouth, Yale, and Princeton. He published the following 1991 article in *Forbes,* a widely read business magazine.

"I am a male wasp who attended and succeeded at Choate (preparatory) School, Yale College, Yale Law School, and Princeton Graduate School. Slowly but surely, however, my life-long habit of looking, listening, feeling, and thinking as honestly as possible has led me to see that white, male-dominated, western European culture is the most destructive phenomenon in the known history of the planet.   1

"[This Western culture] is deeply hateful of life and committed to death; therefore, it is moving rapidly toward the destruction of itself and most other life forms on earth. And truly it deserves to die. . . . We have to face our own individual and collective responsibility for what is happening—our greed, brutality, indifference, militarism, racism, sexism, blindness. . . . Meanwhile, everything we have put into motion continues to endanger us more every day."   2

This bizarre outpouring, so reminiscent of the "confessions" from victims of Stalin's show trials,★ appeared in a letter to *Mother Jones* magazine and was written by a graduate of some of our finest schools. But the truth is that the speaker's anguish came not from any balanced assessment but as a consequence of exposure to the propaganda of the new barbarians who have captured the humanities, law, and social science departments of so many of our universities. It should come as no surprise that many sensitive young Americans reject the system that has nurtured them. At Duke University, according to the *Wall Street Journal,* professor Frank Lentricchia in his English course shows the movie *The Godfather* to teach his students that organized crime is "a metaphor for American business as usual."   3

Yes, a student can still get an excellent education—among the best in the world—in computer technology and the hard sciences at American universities. But liberal arts students, including those attending Ivy League schools, are very likely to be exposed to an attempted brainwashing that deprecates Western learning and exalts a neo-Marxist ideology promoted in the name of multiculturalism. Even students who choose hard sciences must often take required courses in the humanities, where they are almost certain to be inundated with an anti-Western, anticapitalist view of the world.   4

★During the 1930s, Joseph Stalin conducted a massive purge of the Soviet elite. After being tortured, intellectuals, army officers, and government officials read prepared statements at staged trials before being put to death or imprisoned in concentration camps.

Each year American society invests $160 billion in higher education,   5
more per student than any nation in the world except Denmark. A full 45
percent of this money comes from the federal, state, and local governments.
No one can say we are starving higher education. But what are we getting for
our money, at least so far as the liberal arts are concerned?

A fair question? It might seem so, but in university circles it is considered   6
impolite because it presumes that higher education must be accountable to the
society that supports it. Many academics think of universities as intellectual
enclaves, insulated from the vulgar capitalism of the larger culture.

Yet, since the academics constantly ask for more money, it seems hardly   7
unreasonable to ask what they are doing with it. Honest answers are rarely
forthcoming. The general public sometimes gets a whiff of what is going on—
as when Stanford alters its core curriculum in the classics of Western civilization—but it knows very little of the systematic and comprehensive change
sweeping higher education.

An academic and cultural revolution has overtaken most of our 3,535   8
colleges and universities. It's a revolution to which most Americans have paid
little attention. It is a revolution imposed upon the students by a university
elite, not one voted upon or even discussed by the society at large. It amounts,
according to University of Wisconsin—Madison Chancellor Donna Shalala,
to "a basic transformation of American higher education in the name of multiculturalism and diversity."

The central thrust of this "basic transformation" involves replacing tra-   9
ditional core curricula—consisting of the great works of Western culture—
with curricula flavored by minority, female, and Third World authors.

Here's a sample of the viewpoint represented by the new curriculum.   10
Becky Thompson, a sociology and women's studies professor, in a teaching
manual distributed by the American Sociological Association, writes: "I begin
my course with the basic feminist principle that in a racist, classist, and sexist
society we have all swallowed oppressive ways of being, whether intentionally
or not. Specifically, this means that it is not open to debate whether a white
student is racist or a male student is sexist. He/she simply is."

Professors at several colleges who have resisted these regnant dogmas   11
about race and gender have found themselves the object of denunciation and
even university sanctions. Donald Kagan, dean of Yale College, says: "I was a
student during the days of Joseph McCarthy, and there is less freedom now
than there was then."*

As in the McCarthy period, a particular group of activists has cowed the   12
authorities and bent them to its will. After activists forcibly occupied his office, President Lattie Coor of the University of Vermont explained how he
came to sign a sixteen-point agreement establishing, among other things, minority faculty hiring quotas. "When it became clear that the minority students
with whom I had been discussing these issues wished to pursue negotiations *in*

---

*Senator Joseph McCarthy (1908–1957) achieved great influence during the early 1950s by
charging that important figures in government, the military, and the arts were communists.

the context of occupied offices . . . I agreed to enter negotiations." As frequently happens in such cases, Coor's "negotiations" ended in a rapid capitulation by the university authorities.

At Harvard, historian Stephan Thernstrom was harangued by student   13
activists and accused of insensitivity and bigotry. What was his crime? His course included a reading from the journals of slave owners, and his textbook gave a reasonable definition of affirmative action as "preferential treatment" for minorities. At the University of Michigan, renowned demographer Reynolds Farley was assailed in the college press for criticizing the excesses of Marcus Garvey and Malcolm X★; yet the administration did not publicly come to his defense.

University leaders argue that the revolution suggested by these examples   14
is necessary because young Americans must be taught to live in and govern a multiracial and multicultural society. Immigration from Asia and Latin America, combined with relatively high minority birth rates, is changing the complexion of America. Consequently, in the words of University of Michigan President James Duderstadt, universities must "create a model of how a more diverse and pluralistic community can work for our society."

No controversy, of course, about benign goals such as pluralism or diver-   15
sity, but there is plenty of controversy about how these goals are being pursued. Although there is no longer a Western core curriculum at Mount Holyoke or Dartmouth, students at those schools must take a course in non-Western or Third World culture. Berkeley and the University of Wisconsin now insist that every undergraduate enroll in ethnic studies, making this virtually the only compulsory course at those schools.

If American students were truly exposed to the richest elements of other   16
cultures, this could be a broadening and useful experience. A study of Chinese philosophers such as Confucius or Mencius would enrich students' understanding of how different peoples order their lives, thus giving a greater sense of purpose to their own. Most likely, a taste of Indian poetry such as Rabindranath Tagore's *Gitanjali* would increase the interest of materially minded young people in the domain of the spirit. An introduction to Middle Eastern history would prepare the leaders of tomorrow to deal with the mounting challenge of Islamic culture. It would profit students to study the rise of capitalism in the Far East.

But the claims of the academic multiculturalists are largely phony. They   17
pay little attention to the Asian or Latin American classics. Rather, the non-Western or multicultural curriculum reflects a different agenda. At Stanford, for example, Homer, Plato, Dante, Machiavelli, and Locke are increasingly scarce. But often their replacements are not non-Western classics. Instead the students are offered exotic topics such as popular religion and healing in Peru, Rastafarian poetry, and Andean music.

★Marcus Garvey (1887–1940) was a prominent African-American leader who worked for world unity among blacks. Malcolm X (1925–1965) was one of the most important advocates for African-Americans during the 1960s.

What do students learn about the world from the books they are re-   18
quired to read under the new multicultural rubric? At Stanford one of the
non-Western works assigned is *I, Rigoberta Menchú,* subtitled "An Indian
Woman in Guatemala."

The book is hardly a non-Western classic. Published in 1983, *I, Rigoberta*   19
Menchú is the story of a young woman who is said to be a representative voice
of the indigenous peasantry. Representative of Guatemalan Indian culture? In
fact, Rigoberta met the Venezuelan feminist to whom she narrates this story at
a socialist conference in Paris, where, presumably, very few of the Third
World's poor travel. Moreover, Rigoberta's political consciousness includes the
adoption of such politically correct causes as feminism, homosexual rights, socialism, and Marxism. By the middle of the book she is discoursing on
"bourgeois youths" and "Molotov cocktails," not the usual terminology of Indian peasants. One chapter is titled "Rigoberta Renounces Marriage and
Motherhood," a norm that her tribe could not have adopted and survived.

If Rigoberta does not represent the convictions and aspirations of   20
Guatemalan peasants, what is the source of her importance and appeal? The
answer is that Rigoberta seems to provide independent Third World corroboration for Western left-wing passions and prejudices. She is a mouthpiece for a
sophisticated neo-Marxist critique of Western society, all the more powerful
because it seems to issue not from some embittered American academic but
from a Third World native. For professors nourished on the political activism
of the late 1960s and early 1970s, texts such as *I, Rigoberta Menchú* offer a welcome opportunity to attack capitalism and Western society in general in the
name of teaching students about the developing world.

We learn in the introduction of *I, Rigoberta Menchú* that Rigoberta is a   21
quadruple victim. As a person of color, she has suffered racism. As a woman,
she has endured sexism. She lives in South America, which is—of course—a
victim of North American colonialism. She is also an Indian, victimized by
Latino culture within Latin America.

One of the most widely used textbooks in so-called multicultural courses   22
is *Multi-Cultural Literacy,* published by Graywolf Press in St. Paul, Minnesota.
The book ignores the *The Tale of Genji,* the Upanishads and Vedas, the Koran
and Islamic commentaries. It also ignores such brilliant contemporary authors
as Jorge Luis Borges, V.S. Naipaul, Octavio Paz, Naguib Mahfonz, and Wole
Soyinka. Instead it offers thirteen essays of protest, including Michele Wallace's
autobiographical "Invisibility Blues" and Paula Gunn Allen's "Who Is Your
Mother? The Red Roots of White Feminism."

One student I spoke with at Duke University said he would not study   23
Paradise Lost because John Milton was a Eurocentric white male sexist. At the
University of Michigan, a young black woman who had converted to Islam
refused to believe that the prophet Muhammad owned slaves and practiced
polygamy. She said she had taken courses on cultural diversity and the courses
hadn't taught her that.

One of the highlights of this debate on the American campus was a pas-   24
sionate statement delivered a few years ago by Stanford undergraduate

William King, president of the Black Student Union, who argued the benefits of the new multicultural curriculum before the faculty senate of the university. Under the old system, he said, "I was never taught . . . the fact that Socrates, Herodotus, Pythagoras, and Solon★ studied in Egypt and acknowledged that much of their knowledge of astronomy, geometry, medicine, and building came from the African civilization in and around Egypt. [I was never taught] that the Hippocratic oath acknowledges the Greeks' 'father of medicine,' Imhotep, a black Egyptian pharaoh whom they called Aesculapius. . . . I was never informed when it was found that the 'very dark and wooly haired' Moors in Spain preserved, expanded, and reintroduced the classical knowledge that the Greeks had collected, which led to the 'renaissance.' . . . I read the Bible without knowing Saint Augustine looked black like me, that the Ten Commandments were almost direct copies from the 147 Negative Confessions of Egyptian initiates. . . . I didn't learn Toussaint L'Ouverture's defeat of Napoleon in Haiti directly influenced the French Revolution, or that the Iroquois Indians in America had a representative democracy which served as a model for the American system."

This statement drew wild applause and was widely quoted. The only   25
trouble is that much of it is untrue. There is no evidence that Socrates, Pythagoras, Herodotus, and Solon studied in Egypt, although Herodotus may have traveled there. Saint Augustine was born in North Africa, but his skin color is unknown, and in any case he could not have been mentioned in the Bible; he was born over 350 years after Christ. Viewing King's speech at my request, Bernard Lewis, an expert on Islamic and Middle Eastern culture at Princeton, described it as "a few scraps of truth amidst a great deal of nonsense."

Why does multicultural education, in practice, gravitate toward such   26
myths and half-truths? To find out why, it is necessary to explore the complex web of connections that the academic revolution generates among admissions policies, life on campus, and the curriculum.

American universities typically begin with the premise that in a demo-   27
cratic and increasingly diverse society the composition of their classes should reflect the ethnic distribution of the general population. Many schools officially seek "proportional representation," in which the percentage of applicants admitted from various racial groups roughly approximates the ratio of those groups in society at large.

Thus universities routinely admit black, Hispanic, and American Indian   28
candidates over better-qualified white and Asian American applicants. As a result of zealously pursued affirmative action programs, many selective colleges

★Socrates (469–399 B.C.) was one of the most important theorists in the development of Western philosophy. Herodotus (484?–425? B.C.) was the first great historian in the West; Pythagoras (582?–507? B.C.) was an important Greek philosopher and mathematician best remembered today for the theorem that the square of the length of the hypotenuse of a right triangle equals the sum of the squares of the lengths of the other two sides; Solon (639?–559? B.C.) was an Athenian statesman and reformer who helped establish the fundamental principles of democracy.

admit minority students who find it extremely difficult to meet demanding academic standards and to compete with the rest of the class. This fact is reflected in the dropout rates of blacks and Hispanics, which are more than 50 percent higher than those of whites and Asians. At Berkeley a study of students admitted on a preferential basis between 1978 and 1982 concluded that nearly 70 percent failed to graduate within five years.

For affirmative action students who stay on campus, a common strategy   29
of dealing with the pressures of university life is to enroll in a distinctive minority organization. Among such organizations at Cornell University are Lesbian, Gay & Bisexual Coalition; La Asociacion Latina; National Society of Black Engineers; Society of Minority Hoteliers; Black Students United; and Simba Washanga.

Although the university brochures at Cornell and elsewhere continue to   30
praise integration and close interaction among students from different backgrounds, the policies practiced at these schools actually encourage segregation. Stanford, for example, has "ethnic theme houses" such as the African house called Ujaama. And President Donald Kennedy has said that one of his educational objectives is to "support and strengthen ethnic theme houses." Such houses make it easier for some minority students to feel comfortable but help to create a kind of academic apartheid.

The University of Pennsylvania has funded a black yearbook, even   31
though only 6 percent of the student body is black and all other groups appeared in the general yearbook. Vassar, Dartmouth, and the University of Illinois have allowed separate graduation activities and ceremonies for minority students. California State University at Sacramento has just established an official "college within a college" for blacks.

Overt racism is relatively rare at most campuses, yet minorities are told   32
that bigotry operates in subtle forms such as baleful looks, uncorrected stereotypes, and "institutional racism"—defined as the underrepresentation of blacks and Hispanics among university trustees, administrators, and faculty.

Other groups such as feminists and homosexuals typically get into the   33
game, claiming their own varieties of victim status. As Harvard political scientist Harvey Mansfield bluntly puts it, "White students must admit their guilt so that minority students do not have to admit their incapacity."

Even though universities regularly accede to the political demands of vic-   34
tim groups, their appeasement gestures do not help black and Hispanic students get a genuine liberal arts education. They do the opposite, giving the apologists of the new academic orthodoxy a convenient excuse when students admitted on a preferential basis fail to meet academic standards. At this point student activists and administrators often blame the curriculum. They argue that it reflects a "white male perspective" that systematically depreciates the views and achievements of other cultures, minorities, women, and homosexuals.

With this argument, many minority students can now explain why they   35
had such a hard time with Milton in the English department, Publius in political science, and Heisenberg in physics. Those men reflected white male aesthetics, philosophy, and science. Obviously, nonwhite students would fare

much better if the university created more black or Latino or Third World courses, the argument goes. This epiphany leads to a spate of demands: Abolish the Western classics, establish new departments such as Afro–American Studies and Women's Studies, hire minority faculty to offer distinctive black and Hispanic "perspectives."

Multicultural or non-Western education on campus frequently glamor- 36 izes Third World cultures and omits inconvenient facts about them. In fact, several non-Western cultures are caste-based or tribal, and often disregard norms of racial equality. In many of them feminism is virtually nonexistent, as indicated by such practices as dowries, widow-burning, and genital mutilation; and homosexuality is sometimes regarded as a crime or mental disorder requiring punishment. These nasty aspects of the non-Western cultures are rarely mentioned in the new courses. Indeed, Bernard Lewis of Princeton argues that while slavery and the subjugation of women have been practiced by all known civilizations, the West at least has an active and effective movement for the abolition of such evils.

Who is behind this academic revolution, this contrived multiculturalism? 37 The new curriculum directly serves the purposes of a newly ascendant generation of young professors, weaned in the protest culture of the late 1960s and early 1970s. In a frank comment, Jay Parini, who teaches English at Middlebury College, writes, "After the Vietnam War, a lot of us didn't just crawl back into our library cubicles. We stepped into academic positions. . . . Now we have tenure, and the work of reshaping the university has begun in earnest."

The goal that Parini and others like him pursue is the transformation of 38 the college classroom from a place of learning to a laboratory of indoctrination for social change. Not long ago most colleges required that students learn the basics of the physical sciences and mathematics, the rudiments of economics and finance, and the fundamental principles of American history and government. Studies by the National Endowment for the Humanities show that this coherence has disappeared from the curriculum. As a result, most universities are now graduating students who are scientifically and culturally impoverished, if not illiterate.

At the University of Pennsylvania, Houston Baker, one of the most 39 prominent black academics in the country, denounces reading and writing as oppressive technologies and celebrates such examples of oral culture as the rap group N.W.A. (Niggers With Attitude). One of the group's songs is about the desirability of killing policemen. Alison Jaggar, who teaches women's studies at the University of Colorado, denounces the traditional nuclear family as a "cornerstone of women's oppression" and anticipates scientific advances enabling men to carry fetuses in their bodies so that child-bearing responsibilities can be shared between the sexes. Duke professor Eve Sedgwick's scholarship is devoted to unmasking what she terms the heterosexual bias in Western culture, a project that she pursues through papers such as "Jane Austen and the Masturbating Girl" and "How To Bring Your Kids Up Gay."

Confronted by racial tension and Balkanization on campus, university 40 leaders usually announce that, because of a resurgence of bigotry, "more needs to be done." They press for redoubled preferential recruitment of minority students and faculty, funding for a new Third World or Afro-American center, mandatory sensitivity education for whites, and so on. The more the university leaders give in to the demands of minority activists, the more they encourage the very racism they are supposed to be fighting. Surveys indicate that most young people today hold fairly liberal attitudes toward race, evident in their strong support for the civil rights agenda and for interracial dating. However, these liberal attitudes are sorely tried by the demands of the new orthodoxy: many undergraduates are beginning to rebel against what they perceive as a culture of preferential treatment and double standards actively fostered by university policies.

Can there be a successful rolling back of this revolution, or at least of its excesses? One piece of good news is that blatant forms of racial preference are having an increasingly tough time in the courts, and this has implications for university admissions policies. The Department of Education is more vigilant than it used to be in investigating charges of discrimination against whites and Asian Americans. With help from Washington director Morton Halperin, the American Civil Liberties Union has taken a strong stand against campus censorship. Popular magazines such as *Newsweek* and *New York* have poked fun at "politically correct" speech. At Tufts University, undergraduates embarrassed the administration into backing down on censorship by putting up taped boundaries designating areas of the university to be "free speech zones," "limited speech zones," and "Twilight Zones."   41

    Even some scholars on the political left are now speaking out against such dogmatism and excess. Eugene Genovese, a Marxist historian and one of the nation's most respected scholars of slavery, argues that "too often we find that education has given way to indoctrination. Good scholars are intimidated into silence, and the only diversity that obtains is a diversity of radical positions." More and more professors from across the political spectrum are resisting the politicization and lowering of standards. At Duke, for example, sixty professors, led by political scientist James David Barber, a liberal Democrat, have repudiated the extremism of the victims' revolution. To that end they have joined the National Association of Scholars, a Princeton, New Jersey–based group devoted to fairness, excellence, and rational debate in universities.   42

    But these scholars need help. Resistance on campus to the academic revolution is outgunned and sorely needs outside reinforcements. Parents, alumni, corporations, foundations, and state legislators are generally not aware that they can be very effective in promoting reform. The best way to encourage reform is to communicate in no uncertain terms to university leadership and, if necessary, to use financial incentives to assure your voice is heard. University leaders do their best to keep outsiders from meddling or even finding out what exactly is going on behind the tall gates, but there is little doubt that they would pay keen attention to the views of the donors on whom they depend. By threatening to suspend donations if universities continue harmful policies, friends of liberal learning can do a lot. In the case of state-funded schools,   43 citizens and parents can pressure elected representatives to ask questions and demand more accountability from the taxpayer-supported academics.

The illiberal revolution can be reversed only if the people who foot the   44 bills stop being passive observers. Don't just write a check to your alma mater; that's an abrogation of responsibility. Keep abreast of what is going on and don't be afraid to raise your voice and even to close your wallet in protest. Our Western, free-market culture need not provide the rope to hang itself. ■

Questions for Meaning

1. Who were the Visigoths? What does D'Souza mean by Visigoths in tweed?
2. Why does D'Souza believe that the general public deserves a voice in determining college curriculums?
3. Why does D'Souza believe that universities are fostering a "contrived multiculturalism" rather than a curriculum that is truly multicultural?
4. What connection does D'Souza make between social activism in the 1960s and current interest in multicultural education?
5. What does D'Souza mean when he refers, in paragraph 40, to "Balkanization on campus"?
6. Vocabulary: indifference (2), enclaves (6), regnant (11), capitulation (12), harangued (13), pluralistic (14), indigenous (19), corroboration (20), polygamy (23), zealously (28), epiphany (35).

Questions about Strategy

1. D'Souza devotes the first two paragraphs of his argument to quoting someone with a view very different from his own. What does he achieve by this strategy?
2. In paragraph 11, D'Souza incorporates an allusion to Joseph McCarthy. What is his reason for doing so?
3. Where does D'Souza respond to arguments made by advocates of multi-culturalism? Does he make any concessions?
4. In paragraphs 18 through 21, D'Souza discusses a book by Rigoberta Menchú. Why does he devote so much space to this example? Was it a wise decision?
5. According to D'Souza, "universities routinely admit black, Hispanic, and American Indian candidates over better-qualified white and Asian American applicants." How well does he support this claim?
6. Toward what kind of audience is this argument directed?
7. Paragraphs 19, 29, 33, and 35 include references to homosexuality. Do they strengthen D'Souza's argument or do they seem homophobic?

IRVING HOWE

THE VALUE OF THE CANON

The author of numerous books on literature, politics, and ethnicity, Irving Howe has been a productive scholar for more than forty years. He has taught many courses in American literature and published works on Ralph Waldo Emerson, Sherwood Anderson, and William Faulkner. He is also known for *World of Our Fathers: The Journey of the East European Jews to America and the Life They Found and Made* (1989). His *Selected Writings: 1950–1990* were published in 1990. Drawing on his experience as a college professor, Howe published the following article in *The New Republic* in 1991.

Of all the disputes agitating the American campus, the one that seems to me   1
especially significance is that over "the canon." What should be taught in the
humanities and social sciences, especially in introductory courses? What is the
place of the classics? How shall we respond to those professors who attack
"Eurocentrism" and advocate "multiculturalism"? This is not the sort of tedious quarrel that now and then flutters through the academy; it involves matters of public urgency. I propose to see this dispute, at first, through a narrow,
even sectarian lens, with the hope that you will come to accept my reasons for
doing so.

Here, roughly, are the lines of division. On one side stand (too often,   2
fall) the cultural "traditionalists," who may range politically across the entire
spectrum. Opposing them is a heterogeneous grouping of mostly younger
teachers, many of them veterans of the 1960s, which includes feminists, black
activists, Marxists, deconstructionists, and various mixtures of these.

At some colleges and universities traditional survey courses of world and   3
English literature, as also of social thought, have been scrapped or diluted. At
others they are in peril. At still others they will be. What replaces them is
sometimes a mere option of electives, sometimes "multicultural" courses introducing material from Third World cultures and thinning out an already
thin sampling of Western writings, and sometimes courses geared especially
to issues of class, race, and gender. Given the notorious lethargy of academic
decision-making, there has probably been more clamor than change; but if
there's enough clamor, there will be change.

University administrators, timorous by inclination, are seldom firm in   4
behalf of principles regarding education. Subjected to enough pressure, many
of them will buckle under. So will a good number of professors who vaguely
subscribe to "the humanist tradition" but are not famously courageous in its
defense. Academic liberalism has notable virtues, but combativeness is not often one of them. In the academy, whichever group goes on the offensive gains
an advantage. Some of those who are now attacking "traditionalist" humanities and social science courses do so out of sincere persuasion; some, from a
political agenda (what was at first solemnly and now is half-ironically called

p.c.—politically correct); and some from an all-too-human readiness to follow the academic fashion that, for the moment, is "in."

Can we find a neutral term to designate the antitraditionalists? I can't   5
think of a satisfactory one, so I propose an unsatisfactory one: let's agree to call them the insurgents, though in fact they have won quite a few victories. In the academy these professors are often called "the left" or "the cultural left," and that is how many of them see themselves. But this is a comic misunderstanding, occasionally based on ignorance. In behalf of both their self-awareness and a decent clarity of debate, I want to show that in fact the socialist and Marxist traditions have been close to traditionalist views of culture. Not that the left hasn't had its share of ranters (I exclude Stalinists and hooligans) who, in the name of "the revolution," were intent upon jettisoning the culture of the past; but generally such types have been a mere marginal affliction treated with disdain.

Let me cite three major figures. Here is Georg Lukacs, the most influen-   6
tial Marxist critic of the twentieth century:

> Those who do not know Marxism may be surprised at the respect for *the classical heritage of mankind* which one finds in the really great representatives of that doctrine. [Emphasis added.]

Here is Leon Trotsky,* arguing in 1924 against a group of Soviet writers   7
who felt that as the builders of "a new society" they could dismiss the "reactionary culture" of the past:

> If I say that the importance of *The Divine Comedy* lies in the fact that it gives me an understanding of the state of mind of certain classes in a certain epoch, this means that I transform it into a *mere historical document*. . . . How is it thinkable that there should be not a historical but a *directly aesthetic relationship* between us and a medieval Italian book? This is explained by the fact that in class society, in spite of its changeability, there are certain common features. Works of art developed in a medieval Italian city can affect us too. What does this require? . . . That these feelings and moods shall have received such broad, intense, powerful expression as to have raised them above the limitations of the life of those days. [Emphasis added.]

Trotsky's remarks could serve as a reply to those American professors of   8
literature who insist upon the omnipresence of ideology as it seeps into and perhaps saturates literary texts, and who scoff that only "formalists" believe that novels and poems have autonomous being and value. In arguing, as he did in his book *Literature and Revolution,* that art must be judged by "its own laws," Trotsky seems not at all p.c. Still less so is Antonio Gramsci, the Italian Marxist, whose austere opinions about education might make even our conservatives blanch:

*Leon Trotsky (1879–1940) was one of the leaders of the Bolshevik revolution in Russia. After Lenin's death, he lost influence and eventually his life in a power struggle with Stalin.

Latin and Greek were learnt through their grammar, mechanically, but the accusation of formalism and aridity is very unjust. . . . In education one is
dealing with children in whom one has to inculcate certain habits of diligence,
precision, poise (even physical poise), ability to concentrate on specific subjects, which cannot be acquired without the mechanical repetition of disciplined and methodical acts.

These are not the isolated ruminations of a few intellectuals; Lukacs,   9
Trotsky, and Gramsci speak with authority for a view of culture prevalent in
the various branches of the Marxist (and also, by the way, the non-Marxist)
left. And that view informed many movements of the left. There were the
Labor night schools in England bringing to industrial workers elements of the
English cultural past; there was the once-famous Rand School of New York
City; there were the reading circles that Jewish workers, in both Eastern Europe and American cities, formed to acquaint themselves with Tolstoy, Heine,
and Zola.★ And in Ignazio Silone's novel *Bread and Wine* we have a poignant
account of an underground cell in Rome during the Mussolini years that reads
literary works as a way of holding itself together.

My interest here is not to vindicate socialism or Marxism—that is an-   10
other matter. Nor is there anything sacrosanct about the opinions I have
quoted or their authors. But it is surely worth establishing that the claims of
many academic insurgents to be speaking from a left, let along a Marxist, point
of view are highly dubious. Very well, the more candid among them might
reply, so we're not of the left, at least we're not of the "Eurocentric" left. To
recognize that would at least help clear the atmosphere. More important, it
might shrink the attractiveness of these people in what is perhaps the only area
of American society where the label of "the left" retains some prestige.

What we are witnessing on the campus today is a strange mixture of   11
American populist sentiment and French critical theorizing as they come together in behalf of "changing the subject." The populism provides an underlying structure of feeling, and the theorizing provides a dash of intellectual
panache. The populism releases anti-elitist rhetoric, the theorizing releases
highly elitist language.

American populism, with its deep suspicion of the making of distinctions   12
of value, has found expression not only in native sages (Henry Ford: "History
is bunk") but also in the writings of a long line of intellectuals—indeed, it's
only intellectuals who can give full expression to anti-intellectualism. Such
sentiments have coursed through American literature, but only recently,
since the counterculture of the 1960s, have they found a prominent place in
the universities.

As for the French theorizing—metacritical, quasi-philosophical, and   13
at times of a stupefying verbal opacity—it has provided a buttress for the

★Leo Tolstoy (1828–1910) was a Russian novelist whose works include *War and Peace* (1863–
1869) and *Anna Karenina* (1875–1877); Heinrich Heine (1797–1856) is widely considered
one of the great German poets; Émile Zola (1840–1902) was an important French novelist
and social reformer best known today for *Nana* (1888) and *Germinal* (1885).

academic insurgents. We are living at a time when all the once-regnant world systems that have sustained (also distorted) Western intellectual life, from theologies to ideologies, are taken to be in severe collapse. This leads to a mood of skepticism, an agnosticism of judgment, sometimes a world-weary nihilism in which even the most conventional minds begin to question both distinctions of value and the value of distinctions. If you can find projections of racial, class, and gender bias in both a Western by Louis L'Amour and a classical Greek play, and if you have decided to reject the "elitism" said to be at the core of literary distinctions, then you might as well teach the Western as the Greek play. You can make the same political points, and more easily, in "studying" the Western. And, if you happen not to be well informed about Greek culture, it certainly makes things still easier.

I grew up with the conviction that what Georg Lukacs calls "the classical her-   14
itage of mankind" is a precious legacy. It came out of historical circumstances often appalling, filled with injustice and outrage. It was often, in consequence, alloyed with prejudice and flawed sympathies. Still, it was a heritage that had been salvaged from the nightmares, occasionally the glories, of history, and now we would make it "ours," we who came from poor and working-class families. This "heritage of mankind" (which also includes, of course, Romantic and modernist culture) had been denied to the masses of ordinary people, trained into the stupefaction of accepting, even celebrating, their cultural deprivations. One task of political consciousness was therefore to enable the masses to share in what had been salvaged from the past—the literature, art, music, thought—and thereby to reach an active relation with these. That is why many people, not just socialists but liberals, democrats, and those without political tags, kept struggling for universal education. It was not a given; it had to be won. Often, winning proved to be very hard.

　　Knowledge of the past, we felt, could humanize by promoting distance   15
from ourselves and our narrow habits, and this could promote critical thought. Even partly to grasp a significant experience or literary work of the past would require historical imagination, a sense of other times, which entailed moral imagination, a sense of other ways. It would create a kinship with those who had come before us, hoping and suffering as we have, seeking through language, sound, and color to leave behind something of enduring value.

By now we can recognize that there was a certain naïveté in this outlook. The   16
assumption of progress in education turned out to be as problematic as similar assumptions elsewhere in life. There was an underestimation of human recalcitrance and sloth. There was a failure to recognize what the twentieth century has taught us: that aesthetic sensibility by no means assures ethical value. There was little anticipation of the profitable industry of "mass culture," with its shallow kitsch and custom-made dreck. Nevertheless, insofar as we retain an attachment to the democratic idea, we must hold fast to an educational vision somewhat like the one I've sketched. Perhaps it is more an ideal to be approached than a goal to be achieved; no matter. I like the epigrammatic

exaggeration, if it is an exaggeration, of John Dewey's remark that "the aim of education is to enable individuals to continue their education."*

This vision of culture and education started, I suppose, at some point in   17
the late eighteenth century or the early nineteenth century. It was part of a great sweep of human aspiration drawing upon Western traditions from the Renaissance to the Enlightenment. It spoke in behalf of such liberal values as the autonomy of the self, tolerance for a plurality of opinions, the rights of oppressed national and racial groups, and soon, the claims of the women's movements. To be sure, these values were frequently violated—that has been true for every society in every phase of world history. But the criticism of such violations largely invoked the declared values themselves, and this remains true for all our contemporary insurgencies. Some may sneer at "Western hegemony," but knowingly or not, they do so in the vocabulary of Western values.

By invoking the "classical heritage of mankind" I don't propose anything   18
fixed and unalterable. Not at all. There are, say, seven or eight writers and a similar number of social thinkers who are of such preeminence that they must be placed at the very center of this heritage; but beyond that, plenty of room remains for disagreement. All traditions change, simply through survival. Some classics die. Who now reads Ariosto?† A loss, but losses form part of tradition too. And new arrivals keep being added to the roster of classics—it is not handed down from Mt. Sinai or the University of Chicago. It is composed and fought over by cultivated men and women. In a course providing students a mere sample of literature, there should be included some black and women writers who, because of inherited bias, have been omitted in the past. Yet I think we must give a central position to what Professor John Searle in a recent *New York Review of Books* article specifies as "a certain Western intellectual tradition that goes from, say, Socrates to Wittgenstein in philosophy, and from Homer to James Joyce in literature. . . . It is essential to the liberal education of young men and women in the United States that they should receive some exposure to at least some of the great works of this intellectual tradition."

Nor is it true that most of the great works of the past are bleakly retro-   19
grade in outlook—to suppose that is a sign of cultural illiteracy. Bring together in a course on social thought selections from Plato and Aristotle, Machiavelli and Rousseau, Hobbes and Locke, Nietzsche and Freud, Marx and Mill, Jefferson and Dewey, and you have a wide variety of opinions, often clashing with one another, sometimes elusive and surprising, always richly complex. These are some of the thinkers with whom to begin, if only later to deviate from. At least as critical in outlook are many of the great poets and novelists. Is there a more penetrating historian of selfhood than Wordsworth? A more scathing critic of society than the late Dickens? A mind more devoted to ethical seriousness than George Eliot? A sharper critic of the corrupting effects of money than Balzac or Melville?

---

*John Dewey (1859–1952) was an American philosopher and educator who defined basic assumptions about education that subsequently prevailed in our century.
†Ludovico Ariosto (1474–1533) was an important Italian poet, best known for *Orlando furioso.*

These writers don't necessarily endorse our current opinions and pi-   20
eties—why should they? We read them for what Robert Frost calls "counter-
speech," the power and brilliance of *other minds,* and if we can go "beyond"
them, it is only because they are behind us.

What is being invoked here is not a stuffy obeisance before dead texts   21
from a dead past, but rather a critical engagement with living texts from powerful minds still very much "active" in the present. And we should want our
students to read Shakespeare and Tolstoy, Jane Austen and Kafka, Emily Dickinson and Léopold Sénghor, not because they "support" one or another view
of social revolution, feminism, and black self-esteem. They don't, in many instances; and we don't read them for the sake of enlisting them in a cause of our
own. We should want students to read such writers so that they may learn to
enjoy the activity of mind, the pleasure of forms, the beauty of language—in
short, the arts in their own right.

By contrast, there is a recurrent clamor in the university for "relevance,"   22
a notion hard to resist (who wishes to be known as irrelevant?) but proceeding
from an impoverished view of political life, and too often ephemeral in its ex-
citements and transient in its impact. I recall seeing in the late 1960s large
stacks of Eldridge Cleaver's *Soul on Ice* in the Stanford University bookstore.
Hailed as supremely "relevant" and widely described as a work of genius, this
book has fallen into disuse in a mere two decades. Cleaver himself drifted off
into some sort of spiritualism, ceasing thereby to be "relevant." Where, then,
is *Soul on Ice* today? What lasting value did it impart?

American culture is notorious for its indifference to the past. It suffers   23
from the provincialism of the contemporary, veering wildly from fashion to
fashion, each touted by the media and then quickly dismissed. But the past is
the substance out of which the present has been formed, and to let it slip away
from us is to acquiesce in the thinness that characterizes so much of our culture. Serious education must assume, in part, an adversarial stance toward the
very society that sustains it—a democratic society makes the wager that it's
worth supporting a culture of criticism. But if that criticism loses touch with
the heritage of the past, it becomes weightless, a mere compendium of momentary complaints.

Several decades ago, when I began teaching, it could be assumed that en-   24
tering freshmen had read in high school at least one play by Shakespeare and
one novel by Dickens. That wasn't much, but it was something. These days,
with the disintegration of the high schools, such an assumption can seldom be
made. The really dedicated college teachers of literature feel that, given the
bazaar of elective courses an entering student encounters and the propaganda
in behalf of "relevance," there is likely to be only one opportunity to acquaint
students with a smattering—indeed, the merest fragment—of the great works
from the past. Such teachers take pleasure in watching the minds and sensibilities of young people opening up to a poem by Wordsworth, a story by
Chekhov, a novel by Ellison. They feel they have planted a seed of responsive-
ness that, with time and luck, might continue to grow. And if this is said to be
a missionary attitude, why should anyone quarrel with it?

Let me now mention some of the objections one hears in academic circles to   25
the views I have put down here, and then provide brief replies.

By requiring students to read what you call "classics" in introductory courses, you   26
impose upon them a certain worldview—and that is an elitist act.

In some rudimentary but not very consequential sense, all education en-   27
tails the "imposing" of values. There are people who say this is true even when
children are taught to read and write, since it assumes that reading and writing
are "good."

In its extreme version, this idea is not very interesting, since it is not   28
clear how the human race could survive if there were not some "imposition"
from one generation to the next. But in a more moderate version, it is an idea
that touches upon genuine problems.

Much depends on the character of the individual teacher, the spirit in   29
which he or she approaches a dialogue of Plato, an essay by Mill, a novel by
D. H. Lawrence. These can be, and have been, used to pummel an ideological line into the heads of students (who often show a notable capacity for
emptying them out again). Such pummeling is possible for all points of view
but seems most likely in behalf of totalitarian politics and authoritarian theologies, which dispose their adherents to fanaticism. On the other hand, the
texts I've mentioned, as well as many others, can be taught in a spirit of
openness, so that students are trained to read carefully, think independently,
and ask questions. Nor does this imply that the teacher hides his or her opinions. Being a teacher means having a certain authority, but the student
should be able to confront that authority freely and critically. This is what
we mean by liberal education—not that a teacher plumps for certain political
programs, but that the teaching is done in a "liberal" (open, undogmatic)
style.

I do not doubt that there are conservative and radical teachers who teach   30
in this "liberal" spirit. When I was a student at City College in the late 1930s,
I studied philosophy with a man who was either a member of the Communist
Party or was "cheating it out of dues." Far from being the propagandist of the
Party line, which Sidney Hook kept insisting was the necessary role of Communist teachers, this man was decent, humane, and tolerant. Freedom of
thought prevailed in his classroom. He had, you might say, a "liberal" character, and perhaps his commitment to teaching as a vocation was stronger than
his loyalty to the Party. Were such things not to happen now and then, universities would be intolerable.

If, then, a university proposes a few required courses so that ill-read   31
students may at least glance at what they do not know, that isn't (necessarily)
"elitist." Different teachers will approach the agreed-upon texts in different
ways, and that is as it should be. If a leftist student gets "stuck" with a conservative teacher, or a conservative student with a leftist teacher, that's part
of what education should be. The university is saying to its incoming students: "Here are some sources of wisdom and beauty that have survived the
centuries. In time you may choose to abandon them, but first learn something about them."

Your list of classics includes only dead, white males, all tied in to notions and val- 32
ues of Western hegemony. Doesn't this narrow excessively the horizons of education?

All depends on how far forward you go to compose your list of classics. 33
If you do not come closer to the present than the mid–eighteenth century,
then of course there will not be many, or even any, women in your roster. If
you go past the mid–eighteenth century to reach the present, it's not at all true
that only "dead, white males" are to be included. For example—and this
must hold for hundreds of other teachers also—I have taught and written
about Jane Austen, Emily Brontë, Charlotte Brontë, Elizabeth Gaskell,
George Eliot, Emily Dickinson, Edith Wharton, Katherine Anne Porter,
Doris Lessing, and Flannery O'Connor. I could easily add a comparable list of
black writers. Did this, in itself, make me a better teacher? I doubt it. Did it
make me a better person? We still lack modes of evaluation subtle enough to
say for sure.

The absence of women from the literature of earlier centuries is a result 34
of historical inequities that have only partly been remedied in recent years.
Virginia Woolf, in a brilliant passage in *A Room of One's Own,* approaches this
problem by imagining Judith, Shakespeare's sister, perhaps equally gifted but
prevented by the circumstances of her time from developing her gifts:

> Any woman born with a great gift in the sixteenth century would certainly
> have gone crazed, shot herself, or ended her days in some lonely cottage out-
> side the village, half witch, half wizard, feared and mocked at. . . . A highly
> gifted girl who had tried to use her gift for poetry would have been so
> thwarted and hindered by other people, so tortured and pulled asunder by her
> own contrary instincts, that she must have lost her health and sanity. . . .

The history that Virginia Woolf describes cannot be revoked. If we look 35
at the great works of literature and thought through the centuries until about
the mid–eighteenth century, we have to recognize that indeed they have been
overwhelmingly the achievements of men. The circumstances in which these
achievements occurred may be excoriated. The achievements remain precious.

To isolate a group of texts as the canon is to establish a hierarchy of bias, in behalf 36
of which there can be no certainty of judgment.

There is mischief or confusion in the frequent use of the term 37
"hierarchy" by the academic insurgents, a conflation of social and intellectual
uses. A social hierarchy may entail a (mal)distribution of income and power,
open to the usual criticisms; a literary "hierarchy" signifies a judgment, often
based on historical experience, that some works are of supreme or abiding
value, while others are of lesser value, and still others quite without value. To
prefer Elizabeth Bishop to Judith Krantz is not of the same order as sanction-
ing the inequality of wealth in the United States. To prefer Shakespeare to Sidney Sheldon is not of the same order as approving the hierarchy of the
nomenklatura★ in Communist dictatorships.

★The ruling elite.

As for the claim that there is no certainty of judgment, all tastes being   38
historically molded or individually subjective, I simply do not believe that the
people who make it live by it. This is an "egalitarianism" of valuation that
people of even moderate literacy know to be false and unworkable—the making of judgments, even if provisional and historically modulated, is inescapable
in the life of culture. And if we cannot make judgments or demonstrate the
grounds for our preferences, then we have no business teaching literature—we
might just as well be teaching advertising—and there is no reason to have departments of literature.

   The claim that there can be value-free teaching is a liberal deception or self-   39
deception; so too the claim that there can be texts untouched by social and political bias.
Politics or ideology is everywhere, and it's the better part of honesty to admit this.

   If you look hard (or foolishly) enough, you can find political and social   40
traces everywhere. But to see politics or ideology in all texts is to scrutinize
the riches of literature through a single lens. If you choose, you can read all or
almost all literary works through the single lens of religion. But what a sad
impoverishment of the imagination, and what a violation of our sense of reality, this represents. Politics may be "in" everything, but not everything is in
politics. A good social critic will know which texts are inviting to a given
approach and which it would be wise to leave to others.

   To see politics everywhere is to diminish the weight of politics. A serious   41
politics recognizes the limits of its reach; it deals with public affairs while leaving alone large spheres of existence: it seeks not to "totalize" its range of interest. Some serious thinkers believe that the ultimate aim of politics should be to
render itself superfluous. That may seem an unrealizable goal; meanwhile, a
good part of the struggle for freedom in recent decades has been to draw a line
beyond which politics must not tread. The same holds, more or less, for literary study and the teaching of literature.

   Wittingly or not, the traditional literary and intellectual canon was based on re-   42
ceived elitist ideologies, the values of Western imperialism, racism, sexism, etc., and the
teaching of the humanities was marked by corresponding biases. It is now necessary to
enlarge the canon so that voices from Africa, Asia, and Latin America can be heard.
This is especially important for minority students so that they may learn about their
origins and thereby gain in self-esteem.

   It is true that over the decades some university teaching has reflected in-   43
herited social biases—how, for better or worse, could it not? Most often this
was due to the fact that many teachers shared the common beliefs of American
society. But not all teachers! As long as those with critical views were allowed
to speak freely, the situation, if not ideal, was one that people holding minority
opinions and devoted to democratic norms had to accept.

   Yet the picture drawn by some academic insurgents—that most teachers,   44
until quite recently, were in the grip of the worst values of Western society—is
overdrawn. I can testify that some of my school and college teachers a few
decades ago, far from upholding Western imperialism or white supremacy,
were sharply critical of American society, in some instances from a boldly re-
formist outlook. They taught us to care about literature both for its own sake

and because, as they felt, it often helped confirm their worldviews. (And to love it even if it didn't confirm their worldviews.) One high school teacher introduced me to Hardy's *Jude the Obscure* as a novel showing how cruel society can be to rebels, and up to a point, she was right. At college, as a fervent anti-Stalinist Marxist, I wrote a thoughtless "class analysis" of Edmund Spenser's poetry for an English class, and the kindly instructor, whose politics were probably not very far from mine, suggested that there were more things in the world, especially as Spenser had seen it, than I could yet recognize. I mention these instances to suggest that there has always been a range of opinion among teachers, and if anything, the American academy has tilted more to the left than most other segments of our society. There were of course right-wing professors too: I remember an economics teacher we called "Steamboat" Fulton, the object of amiable ridicule among the students who nonetheless learned something from him.

Proposals to enlarge the curriculum to include non-Western writings—if made in good faith and not in behalf of an ideological campaign—are in principle to be respected. A course in ancient thought might well include a selection from Confucius; a course in the modern novel might well include a work by Tanizaki or García Márquez.   45

There are practical difficulties. Due to the erosion of requirements in many universities, those courses that survive are usually no more than a year or a semester in duration, so that there is danger of a diffusion to the point of incoherence. Such courses, if they are to have any value, must focus primarily on the intellectual and cultural traditions of Western society. That, like it or not, is where we come from and that is where we are. All of us who live in America are, to some extent, Western: it gets to us in our deepest and also our most trivial habits of thought and speech, in our sense of right and wrong, in our idealism and our cynicism.   46

As for the argument that minority students will gain in self-esteem through being exposed to writings by Africans and black Americans, it is hard to know. Might not entering minority students, some of them ill-prepared, gain a stronger sense of self-esteem by mastering the arts of writing and reading than by being told, as some are these days, that Plato and Aristotle plagiarized from an African source? Might not some black students feel as strong a sense of self-esteem by reading, say, Dostoyevsky and Malraux (which Ralph Ellison speaks of having done at a susceptible age) as by being confined to black writers? Is there not something grossly patronizing in the notion that while diverse literary studies are appropriate for middle-class white students, something else, racially determined, is required for the minorities? Richard Wright found sustenance in Dreiser, Ralph Ellison in Hemingway, Chinua Achebe in Eliot, Léopold Sénghor in the whole of French poetry. Are there not unknown young Wrights and Ellisons, Achebes and Senghors in our universities who might also want to find their way to an individually achieved sense of culture?   47

In any case, is the main function of the humanities directly to inculcate self-esteem? Do we really know how this can be done? And if done by   48

bounding the curriculum according to racial criteria, may that not perpetuate the very grounds for a lack of self-esteem? I do not know the answers to
these questions, but do the advocates of multiculturalism?

One serious objection to "multicultural studies" remains: that it tends to   49
segregate students into categories fixed by birth, upbringing, and obvious environment. Had my teachers tried to lead me toward certain writers because
they were Jewish, I would have balked—I wanted to find my own way to
Proust, Kafka, and Pirandello, writers who didn't need any racial credentials.
Perhaps things are different with students today—we ought not to be dog-
matic about these matters. But are there not shared norms of pride and independence among young people, whatever their race and color?

The jazz musician Wynton Marsalis testifies: "Everybody has two her-   50
itages, ethnic and human. The human aspects give art its real enduring
power. . . . The racial aspect, that's a crutch so you don't have to go out into
the world." David Bromwich raises an allied question: Should we wish "to
legitimize the belief that the mind of a student deserves to survive in exactly
the degree that it corresponds with one of the classes of socially constructed
group minds? If I were a student today I would find this assumption frightening. It is, in truth, more than a license for conformity. It is a four-year sentence
to conformity."

What you have been saying is pretty much the same as what conservatives say.   51
Doesn't that make you feel uncomfortable?

No, it doesn't. There are conservatives—and conservatives. Some, like   52
the editor of *The New Criterion,* are frantic ideologues with their own version
of p.c., the classics as safeguard for the status quo. This is no more attractive
than the current campus ideologizing. But there are also conservatives who
make the necessary discriminations between using culture, as many have tried
to use religion, as a kind of social therapy and seeing culture as a realm with its
own values and rewards.

Similar differences hold with regard to the teaching of past thinkers. In a   53
great figure like Edmund Burke you will find not only the persuasions of conservatism but also a critical spirit that does not readily lend itself to ideological
coarseness. Even those of us who disagree with him fundamentally can learn
from Burke the disciplines of argument and resources of language.

Let us suppose that in University X undergoing a curriculum debate   54
there is rough agreement about which books to teach between professors of the
democratic left and their conservative colleagues. Why should that trouble
us—or them? We agree on a given matter, perhaps for different reasons. Or
there may be a more or less shared belief in the idea of a liberal education. If
there is, so much the better. If the agreement is momentary, the differences
will emerge soon enough. ■

Questions for Meaning

1. In his opening paragraph, Howe expresses special concern for what is taught in introductory courses. Why would the content of such courses be considered particularly important in debates over the curriculum?
2. Why does Howe believe that university administrators and faculty cannot be depended on to defend "the value of the canon"?
3. Why does Howe prefer to speak of "insurgents" rather than "the cultural left"?
4. Why does Howe believe that the canon is a "precious legacy"?
5. What does Howe mean when he complains that American culture "suffers from the provincialism of the contemporary"?
6. What is the role of the teacher when helping students to understand canonical works?
7. Vocabulary: sectarian (1), lethargy (3), timorous (4), austere (8), vindicate (10), panache (11), nihilism (13), stupefaction (14), recalcitrance (16), kitsch (16), epigrammatic (16), hegemony (17), retrograde (19), ephemeral (22), patronizing (47).

Questions about Strategy

1. What does Howe achieve by quoting Lukacs, Trotsky, and Gramsci?
2. Consider Howe's use of *Soul on Ice* in paragraph 22. Is this book a good example to illustrate his point? Does it leave Howe open to counter-argument?
3. How fairly does Howe restate the arguments of his opponents? How effective are his responses?
4. Does Howe make any concessions?
5. Howe draws on personal experience in paragraphs 30, 44, and 49. To what extent does this help his argument? Would he have been able to use experience as effectively if he came from a culturally privileged background?
6. Throughout his argument, Howe makes allusions to writers and philosophers without identifying them. What do these allusions reveal about his sense of audience? How do they make you feel?

MICHELLE L. HUDSON

EPITOME OF REFORM

A reporter for the New York Times, *which first published the following article in 1993, Michelle L. Hudson focuses on the curriculum at a specific college to help readers understand how a core curriculum can function with apparent success. As you read her article, consider how the Earlham curriculum compares to that required at your school.*

When Earlham College gingerly began offering a two-semester sequence in   1
the humanities that centered on short takes of literature, its creators feared it
would overwhelm the average student.

"In 1954, when it was started, it was seen as something only the very   2
best students could do," said Paul A. Lacey, an English professor at Earlham, a
Quaker liberal arts college in Richmond, Ind. And for eight years they were
the only ones who did it. By 1962, Professor Lacey recalled, "all students were
taking the course."

"That was a reflection," he added, "of our sense that our students were   3
coming well enough prepared from high school that they all could take the
same course." A decade and a half later, in the 1977–78 school year, the humanities sequence was made a required set of core courses and expanded to
four semesters, demanding that students read longer, more complex works, including history texts.

Another decade and a half later, in the words of the academic dean and   4
provost, Len Clark, "The most distinctive thing about Earlham that has to do
with core curriculum is the humanities program."

Many educators consider it to be the epitome of how to update and re-   5
form a core curriculum. "They are not following in the path of other colleges
who have followed the same core curriculum for years," said Maria-Helena
Price, assistant director of programs for the Association of American Colleges
in Washington D.C., speaking of Earlham's program. "They are willing to review the curriculum so the curriculum remains alive. There are many schools
that have stuck with the same curricula regardless of the change in society. It's
one of the models for other institutions."

Earlham began to expand its core curriculum in the 1960's, an endeavor   6
that ran counter to the trend at many colleges, which were trimming rather
than expanding the number of required courses. Besides the humanities sequence it instituted a three-year emphasis on a foreign language as well as
work in the fine arts and in the natural and social sciences.

"We have an unusually large number of requirements compared with   7
other schools," Earlham's president, Richard Wood, asserted in an interview,
and the humanities program is the centerpiece.

All Earlham students take the four-course humanities sequence. The first   8
three courses are taken during the three terms of the freshman trimester year;
the final course may be taken at any other time.

The students examine a list of texts from a variety of different cultures   9
and periods, responding to them through papers and class discussions. Each
trimester is taught by different faculty members from several departments, using a reading list drawn up by a committee of humanities faculty members and
subject to approval by the entire faculty and the administration.

Some of this year's literary works include "Showa: The Japan of Hiro-   10
hito," by Carol Gluck; "The Iliad" of Homer, and "Their Eyes Were Watching God," by Zora Neale Hurston. "It is important that they not be restricted
to one culture, one gender or one kind of issue," Mr. Clark said.

While earning the 36 course credits necessary to graduate, Earlham's   11
1,100 undergraduates are also required to take two courses in social sciences,
one course in fine arts, two in religion and philosophy, four in natural science
and four sports–activities courses.

Earlham faculty members and administrators say the humanities pro-   12
gram provides students with instruction and practice in interpretation and argument, and introduces students to literature and history as modes for
understanding the human condition. The purpose, they say, is to teach students to read critically, interpret different literary works and write clearly.
The program is also designed to help students learn from each other by cri-
tiquing one another's work.

"We recognized that what we were doing in separate courses could bring   13
us together," Professor Lacey said. "The courses emphasize the process of
learning. They center on the idea that reading can improve writing and discussion skills and reading a variety of different works helps students understand
complex ideas."

Mr. Clark added: "We think it is important that students come to under-   14
stand how novels and poetry can help them to think deeply about what it
means to be human. We think significant works of history help deepen their
understanding of the kinds of challenges that face humans and how particular
human beings have dealt with those challenges. It helps them understand the
significance of the choices they make."

Students say they enjoy the humanities program. Kristen Overbeck, a   15
senior from Atlanta, said the first-year sequences were particularly valuable to
her. "Reading a lot of books and responding was a really good bridge for me
from high school to college, and it has been very valuable to me in my later
studies," said Miss Overbeck, an interdepartmental history and art history
major who plans to attend graduate school. "It helped me learn to think about
what I was reading and not just regurgitate information."

A Core of Basic Learning

Gina Reif, a senior who transferred to Earlham from a state school in Pennsyl-   16
vania in her sophomore year, said she regretted missing the first-year portion of

the humanities program. "It kind of bonds the first-year class together," Miss Reif said.

The rest of the curriculum at Earlham resembles that offered at other lib-   17
eral arts colleges and universities, although Earlham places more emphasis on foreign language than most other colleges do.

"Most colleges in the country have given up on language requirements   18
altogether," President Wood said. "Less than 8 percent of American under-graduate schools still have language requirements."   ■

Questions for Meaning

1. Why has Earlham College been praised for its core curriculum?
2. How many core courses are Earlham students required to take?
3. What is the rationale at Earlham for studying literature and history?
4. What common purpose is shared by Earlham faculty?
5. Vocabulary: gingerly (1), epitome (5), endeavor (6), sequence (8), inter-departmental (15).

Questions about Strategy

1. Hudson sketches the history of the Earlham curriculum since 1954. Was this necessary for the purpose of this article?
2. Consider the works cited in paragraph 10. What is Hudson illustrating by choosing these examples?
3. All of the individuals quoted in this article praise the Earlham curriculum. Should Hudson have included the views of students or faculty who have reservations about the curriculum?
4. How effective is the conclusion of this article?

ONE STUDENT'S ASSIGNMENT

Write an argument for retaining a Western emphasis in core courses or for making such courses multicultural. Because you are limited to a short essay of between three and four pages, you should focus your argument on a specific area of study such as literature, history, economics, or philosophy. Demonstrate that you are familiar with more than one side of the debate. Draw exclusively on sources in *The Informed Argument* and your own ideas. Use MLA style documentation.

The Great Conversation
Alicia Fedorczak

Plato or Angelou?? Wordsworth or Morrison?? In recent years, universi-   1
ties and colleges have debated the material necessary for a strong core

curriculum. Much of the battle centers around the selection of appropriate and necessary readings. On one side, many scholars seek to preserve a traditional Western canon, insisting that all students must know and understand the basic ideas of Western culture. Their opponents encourage a broader, multicultural curriculum that exposes students to the literature and thought of many overlooked minorities. Although both groups present some valid arguments, many scholars have forgotten the true purpose of literature and education. Effective education must prepare all students for success, not only as members of the work force, but most importantly as human beings. Universities must be committed to providing the best possible education, a difficult task that requires the voices of many cultures and backgrounds.

As new curriculums develop, educators must consider the changing   2
needs of today's students. Deteriorating nuclear families and rising racial tensions force institutions to define new objectives in the classroom. Today, preparing students for success becomes a challenging and complicated duty. Effective education must provoke thinking, encourage cooperation, raise self-esteem, and promote the understanding and acceptance of all cultures and people. As universities attempt to produce successful students, they must employ every available resource.

Literature serves as an essential tool in the process of modern educa-   3
tion. Literature itself is a reflection of the human spirit, a guide to understanding people and their societies. Like art or history, literature provides insight necessary for personal development and professional growth. One administrator insists that literature can help students "think deeply about what it means to be human . . ." (qtd. in Hudson 345). Certainly, literature teaches a highly individualized lesson to each reader, as students discover and apply a book's wisdom in their own lives. Yet, even the best scholars have not discovered a magical equation for genius. If literature has no universal meaning, how can it have universal significance? There is no single definition of a classic, and no possible way for any person to read every great book; even critics disagree over the importance of many contributions. Therefore, no single person can determine a canon of indispensable reading. Rather, universities should focus on effectively using literature to ensure the best possible education.

A broad range of literature provides students with the potential for   4
greater growth and learning. The importance of the Western canon remains, but must be supplemented with the voices of other cultures. Rather than limiting ideas, students should be exposed to a variety of viewpoints and then determine the valuable lessons of each. The integration of many authors provides strong role models, understanding of other cultures, and finally new perspectives. As one writer argues, "A strictly European perspective will not properly prepare students for a successful future in a

multicultural world" (Kunjufu and Vann 298). Students may only develop a world view by listening to many voices.

Promoting reform does not undermine the importance of Western ideas   5
and thought. By encouraging the expansion of the curriculum, scholars do not intend to belittle or reduce the importance of Western literature. The works of the traditional canon have survived time, defining a significant piece of American culture. As universities face reform, they must retain the wisdom of the past, remembering that "the past is the substance out of which the present has been formed" (Howe 337). Western literature should remain an important component of education, simply not the only compo-nent. The point of reform is not to encourage separation or "balkanization," but to achieve understanding. By recognizing the importance and achieve-ments of all groups, students may survive in a diverse society.

Universities must attempt to integrate both multicultural and Western   6
literature within a single core curriculum. When administrators concentrate on the goals of education, a balanced curriculum becomes feasible. Rather than focusing on the exact percentage of minority authors on a syllabus, educators must determine how to adequately introduce a variety of per-spectives. At present, scholars seem to be caught up in numbers and statistics, instead of honestly attempting to aid student success. Only a few of the best Western authors can be adequately covered in a short course, and two professors may even teach the same course with entirely different readings. By including multicultural voices, the Western sample becomes increasingly smaller. Yet, administrators should not worry about changing curriculums to include new voices. Education is not a question of numbers and quotas, but one of growth and development. Rather than placing blame and calling names, scholars must reform the process of edu-cation in an attempt to further student learning.

At times, literature has been described as a great conversation, a signif-   7
icant exchange of ideas. Every great piece of writing provokes response. Authors are forced to respond to the assumptions, thoughts, and ideas of the works that exist before them. By examining this great conversation, students unlock the knowledge that literature has to share. Rather than limiting education, universities should encourage the introduction of new ideas and perspectives. As one educator suggests, "we should think of American culture as a conversation among different voices, even if it is a conversation that some were able to join only recently" (Price 305). When universities learn to put education first, the debates will cease and the great conversation may resume.

SUGGESTIONS FOR WRITING

1. Synthesize the arguments on behalf of core courses in the humanities.
2. Drawing on Kunjufu and Vann, Price, and Sleeter, write an argument in defense of a multicultural curriculum.
3. Drawing on Sowell, D'Souza, and Howe, argue for a curriculum that emphasizes Western civilization.
4. Write an essay explaining how you benefited (or failed to benefit) from a required course that you probably would not have taken as an elective.
5. Consider the five views of multicultural education described by Sleeter. Do you have a sixth view? Argue on behalf of a model of your own design.
6. In your opinion, which author in this section seems the most reasonable, and which author seems the most biased? Contrast these authors by showing how they differ in terms of how respectful they are of opposing points of view.
7. What, in your view, is the purpose of higher education? Write an argument on behalf of that purpose.
8. Write an argument for or against studying a foreign language.
9. Write a defense of one course that you believe all students should take regardless of their major.
10. When planning a syllabus, how much attention should instructors give to the gender of the authors whose texts will be used? Does it matter to you whether you are reading a work by a man or by a woman? Write an argument for or against the consideration of gender as a factor in course design.

COLLABORATIVE PROJECT

Study the requirements at your school as described in your college catalog. Interview students and faculty to learn how much support these requirements have and to determine whether there is a desire for change.

SECTION 6

FREEDOM OF EXPRESSION: WHO GETS TO SAY WHAT?

CHARLES R. LAWRENCE III

ON RACIST SPEECH

The following article, first published by the *Chronicle of Higher Education* in 1989, is adapted from a speech the author gave to a conference of the American Civil Liberties Union. A nationally recognized authority on hate speech, Lawrence teaches law at Georgetown University. His most recent work is *Words That Wound: Critical Race Theory, Assaultive Speech, and the First Amendment* (1993), which he coauthored with Mari Matsuda, Richard Delgado, and Kimberlè Crenshaw.

I have spent the better part of my life as a dissenter. As a high school student, I   1
was threatened with suspension for my refusal to participate in a civil-defense
drill, and I have been a conspicuous consumer of my First Amendment liberties
ever since. There are very strong reasons for protecting even racist speech. Perhaps the most important of these is that such protection reinforces our society's
commitment to tolerance as a value, and that by protecting bad speech from
government regulation, we will be forced to combat it as a community.

But I also have a deeply felt apprehension about the resurgence of racial   2
violence and the corresponding rise in the incidence of verbal and symbolic assault and harassment to which blacks and other traditionally subjugated and excluded groups are subjected. I am troubled by the way the debate has been
framed in response to the recent surge of racist incidents on college and university campuses and in response to some universities' attempts to regulate harassing speech. The problem has been framed as one in which the liberty of free
speech is in conflict with the elimination of racism. I believe this has placed the
bigot on the moral high ground and fanned the rising flames of racism.

Above all, I am troubled that we have not listened to the real victims, that   3
we have shown so little understanding of their injury, and that we have abandoned those whose race, gender, or sexual preference continues to make them
second-class citizens. It seems to me a very sad irony that the first instinct of

civil libertarians has been to challenge even the smallest, most narrowly framed efforts by universities to provide black and other minority students with the protection the Constitution guarantees them.

The landmark case of *Brown v. Board of Education* is not a case that we   4
normally think of as a case about speech. But *Brown* can be broadly read as articulating the principle of equal citizenship. *Brown* held that segregated schools were inherently unequal because of the *message* that segregation conveyed—that black children were an untouchable caste, unfit to go to school with white children. If we understand the necessity of eliminating the system of signs and symbols that signal the inferiority of blacks, then we should hesitate before proclaiming that all racist speech that stops short of physical violence must be defended.

University officials who have formulated policies to respond to incidents   5
of racial harassment have been characterized in the press as "thought police," but such policies generally do nothing more than impose sanctions against intentional face-to-face insults. When racist speech takes the form of face-to-face insults, catcalls, or other assaultive speech aimed at an individual or small group of persons, it falls directly within the "fighting words" exception to First Amendment protection. The Supreme Court has held that words which "by their very utterance inflict injury or tend to incite an immediate breach of the peace" are not protected by the First Amendment.

If the purpose of the First Amendment is to foster the greatest amount of   6
speech, racial insults disserve that purpose. Assaultive racist speech functions as a preemptive strike. The invective is experienced as a blow, not as a proffered idea, and once the blow is struck, it is unlikely that a dialogue will follow. Racial insults are particularly undeserving of First Amendment protection because the perpetrator's intention is not to discover truth or initiate dialogue but to injure the victim. In most situations, members of minority groups realize that they are likely to lose if they respond to epithets by fighting and are forced to remain silent and submissive.

Courts have held that offensive speech may not be regulated in public   7
forums such as streets where the listener may avoid the speech by moving on, but the regulation of otherwise protected speech has been permitted when the speech invades the privacy of the unwilling listener's home or when the unwilling listener cannot avoid the speech. Racist posters, fliers, and graffiti in dormitories, bathrooms, and other common living spaces would seem to clearly fall within the reasoning of these cases. Minority students should not be required to remain in their rooms in order to avoid racial assault. Minimally, they should find a safe haven in their dorms and in all other common rooms that are a part of their daily routine.

I would also argue that the university's responsibility for ensuring that these   8
students receive an equal educational opportunity provides a compelling justification for regulations that ensure them safe passage in all common areas. A minority student should not have to risk becoming the target of racially assaulting speech every time he or she chooses to walk across campus. Regulating

vilifying speech that cannot be anticipated or avoided would not preclude announced speeches and rallies—situations that would give minority-group
members and their allies the chance to organize counterdemonstrations or
avoid the speech altogether.

The most commonly advanced argument against the regulation of racist   9
speech proceeds something like this: We recognize that minority groups suffer
pain and injury as the result of racist speech, but we must allow this hate mon-
gering for the benefit of society as a whole. Freedom of speech is the lifeblood
of our democratic system. It is especially important for minorities because often it is their only vehicle for rallying support for the redress of their
grievances. It will be impossible to formulate a prohibition so precise that it
will prevent the racist speech you want to suppress without catching in the
same net all kinds of speech that it would be unconscionable for a democratic
society to suppress.

Whenever we make such arguments, we are striking a balance on the one   10
hand between our concern for the continued free flow of ideas and the democratic process dependent on that flow, and, on the other, our desire to further
the cause of equality. There can be no meaningful discussion of how we
should reconcile our commitment to equality and our commitment to free
speech until it is acknowledged that there is real harm inflicted by racist speech
and that this harm is far from trivial.

To engage in a debate about the First Amendment and racist speech   11
without a full understanding of the nature and extent of that harm is to risk
making the First Amendment an instrument of domination rather than a vehicle of liberation. We have not all known the experience of victimization by
racist, misogynist, and homophobic speech, nor do we equally share the burden of the societal harm it inflicts. We are often quick to say that we have
heard the cry of the victims when we have not.

The *Brown* case is again instructive because it speaks directly to the psy-   12
chic injury inflicted by racist speech by noting that the symbolic message of
segregation affected "the hearts and minds" of negro children "in a way unlikely ever to be undone." Racial epithets and harassment often cause deep
emotional scarring and feelings of anxiety and fear that pervade every aspect
of a victim's life.

Brown also recognized that black children did not have an equal oppor-   13
tunity to learn and participate in the school community if they bore the additional burden of being subjected to the humiliation and psychic assault
contained in the message of segregation. University students bear an analogous
burden when they are forced to live and work in an environment where at any
moment they may be subjected to denigrating verbal harassment and assault.
The same injury was addressed by the Supreme Court when it held that sexual
harassment that creates a hostile or abusive work environment violates the
ban on sex discrimination in employment of Title VII of the Civil Rights
Act of 1964.

Carefully drafted university regulations would bar the use of words as   14
assault weapons and leave unregulated even the most heinous of ideas when

those ideas are presented at times and places and in manners that provide an opportunity for reasoned rebuttal or escape from immediate injury. The history of the development of the right to free speech has been one of carefully evaluating the importance of free expression and its effects on other important societal interests. We have drawn the line between protected and unprotected speech before without dire results. (Courts have, for example, exempted from the protection of the First Amendment obscene speech and speech that disseminates official secrets, that defames or libels another person, or that is used to form a conspiracy or monopoly.)

Blacks and other people of color are skeptical about the argument that   15
even the most injurious speech must remain unregulated because, in an unregulated marketplace of ideas, the best ones will rise to the top and gain acceptance. Our experience tells us quite the opposite. We have seen too many demagogues elected by appealing to America's racism. We have seen too many good liberal politicians shy away from the issues that might brand them as being too closely allied with us.

Whenever we decide that racist speech must be tolerated because of the   16
importance of maintaining societal tolerance for all unpopular speech, we are asking blacks and other subordinated groups to bear the burden for the good of all. We must be careful that the ease with which we strike the balance against the regulation of racist speech is in no way influenced by the fact that the cost will be borne by others. We must be certain that those who will pay that price are fairly represented in our deliberations and that they are heard.

At the core of the argument that we should resist all government regula-   17
tion of speech is the ideal that the best cure for bad speech is good, that ideas that affirm equality and the worth of all individuals will ultimately prevail. This is an empty ideal unless those of us who would fight racism are vigilant and unequivocal in that fight. We must look for ways to offer assistance and support to students whose speech and political participation are chilled in a climate of racial harassment.

Civil-rights lawyers might consider suing on behalf of blacks whose right   18
to an equal education is denied by a university's failure to ensure a non-discriminatory educational climate or conditions of employment. We must embark upon the development of a First Amendment jurisprudence grounded in the reality of our history and our contemporary experience. We must think hard about how best to launch legal attacks against the most indefensible forms of hate speech. Good lawyers can create exceptions and narrow interpretations that limit the harm of hate speech without opening the floodgates of censorship.

Everyone concerned with these issues must find ways to engage actively   19
in actions that resist and counter the racist ideas that we would have the First Amendment protect. If we fail in this, the victims of hate speech must rightly assume that we are on the oppressors' side. ■

Questions for Meaning

1. What does Lawrence mean by "verbal and symbolic assault"?
2. On what grounds does Lawrence claim that racist speech violates the spirit of the First Amendment?
3. What is the difference between hearing offensive speech in a public area and hearing it in one's home?
4. Why does Lawrence believe that blacks and other people of color need legal protection from injurious speech?
5. Does Lawrence make any specific recommendations in this argument?
6. Vocabulary: caste (4), preemptive (6), haven (7), preclude (8), unconscionable (9), misogynist (11), homophobic (11), denigrating (13), unequivocal (17).

Questions about Strategy

1. Why is it useful for Lawrence to establish that he is a "dissenter"?
2. Why does Lawrence cite *Brown v. Board of Education* even though he recognizes that it is "not a case that we normally think of as a case about speech"?
3. Where does Lawrence respond to the arguments of his opposition? Does he make any concessions?
4. In paragraphs 3 and 11, Lawrence links racist speech with speech that damages women and homosexuals. What does he gain by making this association?
5. Consider the use of "we" and "our" in paragraphs 15 and 18. What do these references reveal about Lawrence's sense of audience?

HENRY LOUIS GATES, JR.

LET THEM TALK

A distinguished scholar of African American studies, Henry Louis Gates has taught at Yale, Cornell, and Duke. Educated at Yale and Cambridge, Gates is currently a professor of English at Harvard, where he chairs the Afro-American Studies Department. His books include *Black Literature and Literary Theory* (1985), *Figures in Black* (1987), *In the House of Osubgo* (1989), and *Colored People* (1994). He is also editor of *The Schomburg Library of Nineteenth-Century Black Women Writers* (1988). The following article was first published by *The New Republic* in 1993.

I.

"As a thumbnail summary of the last two or three decades of speech issues in the Supreme Court," the great First Amendment scholar Harry Kalven Jr. wrote in 1965 in *The Negro and the First Amendment,* "we may come to see the Negro as winning back for us the freedoms the Communists seemed to have lost for us." Surveying the legal scene in the heyday of the civil rights era, Kalven was confident that civil rights and civil liberties were marching in unison; that their mutual expansion represented, for a nation in a time of tumult, an intertwined destiny. He might have been surprised had he lived to witness the shifting nature of their relations. Today the partnership named in the title of this classic book seems hopelessly in disrepair. Civil liberties are regarded by many as a chief obstacle to civil rights. To be sure, blacks are still on the front lines of First Amendment jurisprudence—but this time we soldier on the other side. The byword among many black activists and black intellectuals is no longer the political imperative to protect free speech; it is the moral imperative to suppress "hate speech."

Like such phrases as "pro-choice" and "pro-life," the phrase "hate speech" is ideology in spansule form. It is the term-of-art of a movement, most active on college campuses and in liberal municipalities, that has caused many civil rights activists to rethink their allegiance to the First Amendment, the very amendment that licensed the protests, the rallies, the organization and the agitation that galvanized the nation in a recent, bygone era. Addressing the concerns of a very different time, the hate speech movement has enlisted the energies of some of our most engaged and interesting legal scholars. The result has been the proliferation of campus speech codes as well as municipal statutes enhancing penalties for bias crimes.

No less important, however, is the opportunity that this movement has provided, for those outside it, to clarify and to rethink the meaning of their commitment to the freedom of expression. It is an opportunity, I must say, that we have miserably bungled. Content with soundbites and one-liners, our deliberations on the subject have had all the heft of a talk-show monologue. Free speech? You get what you pay for.

The irony that lurks behind this debate, of course, is that the First   4
Amendment may be the central article of faith in the civil religion of America,
if America has a civic religion. "It's a free country," we say, and shrug; and
what we usually mean is that you can say what you please. "Sticks and stones
can break my bones," we are taught to chant as children, "but words can never
hurt me." As Catharine MacKinnon writes with some asperity in *Only Words,*
her new book, Americans

> are taught this view by about the fourth grade, and continue to absorb it
> through osmosis from everything around them for the rest of their
> lives . . . to the point that those who embrace it think it is their own per-
> sonal faith, their own original view, and trot it out like something learned
> from their own personal lives every time a problem is denominated one of
> "speech," whether it really fits or not.

The strongest argument for regulating hate speech is the unreflective   5
stupidity of most of the arguments for the other side. I do not refer to the
debate as it has proceeded in the law reviews, where you find a quality of
caution, clarity and tentativeness that has made few inroads into the larger
public discourse; the law professors who offer the best analysis of public discourse exert very little influence on it. And this leaves us with a familiar
stalemate. On the one side are those who speak of "hate speech," a phrase
that alludes to the argument instead of making it; and to insist on probing
further is to admit that you "just don't get it." On the other side are those
who invoke the First Amendment like a mantra and seem immediately to fall
into a trance, so oblivious are they to further discussion and evidence. A
small number of anecdotes, about racism on campus or about P.C. inquisi-
tions on campus, are endlessly recycled, and a University of Pennsylvania undergraduate named Eden Jacobowitz, of "water buffalo" fame, becomes a
Dreyfus *de nos jours.* ★

There is also a practical reason to worry about the impoverishment of the   6
national discourse on free speech. If we keep losing the arguments, then we
may slowly lose the liberties that they were meant to defend. We may come to
think that the bad arguments are the only arguments, and when someone finally disabuses us of them, we may switch sides without ever considering the
better arguments for staying put. That is why, for all the pleasures of
demonology, the burgeoning literature urging the regulation of racist speech
has a serious claim on our attention.

Now Westview Press has conveniently collected the three most widely cited   7
and influential papers making the case for the regulation of racist speech. (The
collection also includes a provocative essay by Kimberlè Williams Crenshaw

---

★A Dreyfus of our time. Alfred Dreyfus (1859–1935) was a French army captain who was
courtmartialed for selling military secrets to the Germans. A victim of anti-Semitism, he was
sentenced to life imprisonment under horrible conditions. His case provokes great controversy. In 1906, Dreyfus was found innocent of all charges that had been brought against him.

about the conflicting allegiances posed by race and gender.) Gathered together for the first time, these essays—which originally appeared in law reviews over the past several years, and were circulated more widely through the samizdat of the photocopier—complement each other surprisingly well. Their proximity to each other casts light on their strengths and their weaknesses.

The authors of these proposals are "minority" law professors who teach   8
at mainstream institutions—Mari J. Matsuda and Charles R. Lawrence III at Georgetown and Richard Delgado at the University of Colorado. They write vigorous and accessible prose. They are, one can fairly say, the legal eagles of the crusade against racist hate speech. But they are also, as the subtitle of their collection suggests, the principal architects of critical race theory, which is one of the most widely discussed trends in the contemporary legal academy; and their jointly written introduction to the volume serves as the clearest manifesto that the movement has yet received.

Critical race theory, we learn, owes its "social origins" to a student boy-   9
cott of a Harvard Law School course in 1981. The course was called "Race, Racism and American Law," and the university failed to accede to student demands that it be taught by a person of color. Organizing an informal alternative course, students invited lawyers and law professors of color to lecture weekly on the topic. Crenshaw was one of the student organizers of the alternative course, Matsuda was one of its participants and Delgado and Lawrence were among its guest lecturers. And thus was formed the nucleus of "a small but growing group of scholars committed to finding new ways to think about and act in pursuit of racial justice."

The intellectual ancestry of the movement is more complicated, but its two   10
main progenitors are the brand of feminist theory associated with MacKinnon and the radical skepticism toward traditional black-letter pieties associated with critical legal studies. Almost invariably, the literature arguing for hate speech regulation cites MacKinnon as an authority and a model, and takes on one or more of the traditional legal distinctions (such as the distinction between "private" and "public") whose dismantling is a staple of critical legal studies. So it is no surprise that conservative pundits denounce these theorists of hate speech as faddish foes of freedom. In fact, one could more accurately describe their approach as neotraditional. And those conservatives who dream of turning the cultural clock back to the '50s should realize that the First Amendment law of those years is precisely what these supposedly faddish scholars wish to revive.

For the conventional lay defense of free speech absolutism, and its con-   11
comitant attack on those who would curtail free speech, suffers from a bad case of historical amnesia. Just as Samuel Johnson thought he could refute Bishop Berkeley★ just by kicking a stone, the armchair absolutists often think

★Samuel Johnson (1709–1784), the author of the first comprehensive English Dictionary, emphasizes the importance of common sense. George Berkeley (1685–1753), Bishop of Cloyne, was a philosopher who argues that matter does not exist independent of human perception.

that they can win the debate just by adducing the authority of the First
Amendment itself. The invocation is generally folded together with a vague
sort of historical argument. The First Amendment, we are told, has stood us in
good stead through more than two centuries; and our greatness as a society
may depend on it. The framers of the Constitution knew what they were doing, and (this is directed to those inclined to bog down in interpretative quib-
bles) in the end the First Amendment means what it says.

The only flaw of this uplifting and well-rehearsed argument is that it is   12
false. Indeed, the notion that the First Amendment has been a historical main-
stay of American liberty is an exemplary instance of invented tradition. To
begin with, the First Amendment was not conceived as a protection of the free
speech of citizens until 1931. Before then, the Court took the amendment at
its word: "*Congress* shall make no law. . . ." Congress could not; but states
and municipalities could do what they liked. And so it is no surprise that once
the Supreme Court recognized freedom of expression as a right held by citizens, the interpretation of its scope still remained quite narrow. This changed
after World War II, when the Warren Court gradually ushered in a more generous vision of civil liberties. So the expansive ethic that we call the First
Amendment, the eternal verity that people either celebrate or bemoan, is really only a few decades old.

But the hate speech movement is not content with rehearsing the weaknesses   13
in the absolutist position. It has also aligned itself with earlier traditions of
jurisprudence—here the movement's atavism is most obvious—by showing
that the sort of speech it wishes to restrict falls into two expressive categories
that the Supreme Court has previously held (and, the advocates of restrictions
argue, correctly held) to be undeserving of First Amendment protection. The
categories are those of "fighting words" and group defamation, as exemplified by cases decided in 1942 and 1952.

The doctrine of "fighting words" was promulgated by the Supreme   14
Court in *Chaplinsky v. New Hampshire* (1942), in which the Court held that
the Constitution did not protect "insulting or 'fighting' words—those that by
their very utterance inflict injury or tend to incite an immediate breach of the
peace." "Such utterances are no essential part of any exposition of ideas," Justice Murphy wrote for the majority, "and are of such slight social value as a
step to truth that any benefit that may be derived from them is clearly outweighed by the social interest in order and morality." Those who would regulate hate speech argue that racist abuse is a variety of, or "functionally
equivalent to," the sort of language that the *Chaplinsky* decision declared to be
unprotected; indeed, the carefully drafted speech code adopted by Stanford
University in 1990 explicitly extends only to "fighting words" or symbols,
thus wearing its claim to constitutionality on its face. If *Chaplinsky* can shoulder the legal and ethical burdens placed upon it, the regulationists have a powerful weapon on their side.

Can it? Probably not. To begin with, it is an open question whether   15
Chaplinsky remains, as they say, "good law." For the Supreme Court, in the

fifty years since *Chaplinsky,* has never once affirmed a conviction for uttering either "fighting words" or words that "by their very utterance inflict injury." Indeed, in part because of this functional desuetude, in part because of the supposed male bias of the "breach of the peace" prong (men being more likely than women to throw a punch), the editors of the *Harvard Law Review* recently issued a call for the doctrine's explicit interment. So much for the doctrine's judicial value.

The young scholars at the *Harvard Law Review* also note, with others,   16
that statutes prohibiting "fighting words" have had discriminatory effects. An apparently not atypical conviction, upheld by the Louisiana state court, was occasioned by the following exchange between a white police officer and the black mother of a young suspect. He: "Get your black ass in the goddamned car." She: "You goddamn motherfucking police—I am going to [the superintendent of police] about this." No prize for guessing who was convicted for "fighting words." As the legal scholar Kenneth Karst reports, "Statutes proscribing abusive words are applied to members of racial and political minorities more frequently than can be wholly explained by any special proclivity of those people to speak abusively." So much for the doctrine's political value.

Even if we finally reject the appeal to *Chaplinsky,* the hate speech move-   17
ment can still link itself to constitutional precedent through the alternative model of group defamation. Indeed, the defamation model is more central, more weighty, in these arguments. And note that these are alternatives, not just different ways of describing the same thing. The "fighting words" or "assaultive speech" paradigm compares racist expression to physical assault: at its simplest, it characterizes an act of aggression between two individuals, victim and victimizer. The defamation paradigm, by contrast, compares racist speech to libel, which is an assault on dignity or reputation. The harm is essentially social; to be defamed is to be defamed in the eyes of other people.

Here the guiding precedent is Justice Frankfurter's majority opinion in   18
the case of *Beauharnais v. Illinois* (1952), in which the Court upheld a conviction under an Illinois group libel ordinance. The ordinance was clumsily written, but it essentially prohibited public expression that "portrays depravity, criminality, unchastity or lack of virtue in a class of citizens of any race, color, creed or religion," thereby exposing them to "contempt, derision or obloquy." In Frankfurter's opinion: "If an utterance directed at an individual may be the object of criminal sanctions we cannot deny to a state power to punish the same utterance directed at a defined group," at least as long as the restriction related to the peace and well-being of the state.

Beauharnais v. Illinois has since fallen into judicial disrepute, having been   19
reversed in its particulars by subsequent cases like the celebrated *Sullivan v. New York Times.* Indeed, more widely cited than Justice Frankfurter's opinion is Justice Black's dissent: "If there be minority groups who hail this holding as their victory, they might consider the possible relevancy of this ancient remark: 'Another such victory and I am undone.'" And yet Frankfurter's claim for the congruence of individual libel and group libel is not implausible, and many critical race theorists argue for its resurrection. Thus MacKinnon urges

"the rather obvious reality that groups are made up of individuals." That is why "libel of groups multiplies rather than avoids the very same damage through reputation which the law of individual libel recognizes when done one at a time, as well as inflicting some of its own."

What is wrong with the basic claim, endorsed by judges and scholars   20 across the ideological spectrum, that group libel is just individual libel multiplied? Begin with the assumption that individual libel involves the publication of information about someone that is both damaging and false. Charles Lawrence III inadvertently directs us to the source of the problem. The racial epithet, he writes, "is invoked as an assault, not as a statement of fact that may be proven true or false." But that suggests that the evaluative judgments characteristic of racial invective do not lend themselves to factual verification—and this is where the comparison with individual libel breaks down. The same problem emerges when MacKinnon identifies pornography as an instance of group defamation whose message is (roughly) that it would be nice if women were available for sexual exploitation. A proposition of that form may be right or wrong, but it cannot be true or false. You cannot libel someone by saying, "I despise you"; but that is precisely the message common to most racial epithets. "Nigger," used in the vocative, is not usefully treated as group libel for the same reason that it is not usefully treated as individual libel.

II.

Critical race theory is strongest not when it seeks to establish a bridgehead   21 with constitutional precedent, but when it frontally contests what has recently emerged as a central aspect of Supreme Court First Amendment doctrine: the principle of content and viewpoint neutrality. That principle is meant to serve as a guide to how speech can permissibly be regulated, ensuring basic fairness by preventing the law from favoring one partisan interest over another. So, for example, a law forbidding the discussion of race would violate the principle of content-neutrality, which is held to be a bad thing; a law forbidding the advocacy of black supremacy would violate the principle of viewpoint-neutrality, which is held to be a worse thing. When the Minnesota Supreme Court affirmed the content-sensitive hate speech ordinance at issue in *RAV v. St. Paul,* it cited Mari J. Matsuda's work in reaching its conclusions. When Justice Scalia reversed and invalidated the ordinance on the grounds of viewpoint discrimination, he was implicitly writing against Matsuda's argument. These are not mere conflicts of academic vision; these are arguments with judicial consequences.

Matsuda's rejection of what she calls the "neutrality trap" is, to my mind,   22 the most powerful element of her argument. Rather than trying to fashion neutral laws to further our social objectives, why not put our cards on the table and acknowledge what we know? As an example of where the neutrality trap leads, Matsuda cites the anti-mask statutes that many states passed "in a barely disguised effort to limit Ku Klux Klan activities":

These statutes purportedly cover the wearing of masks in general, with no specific mention of the intent to control the Klan. Neutral reasons such as the need to prevent pickpockets from moving unidentified through crowds or the need to unmask burglars or bank robbers are proffered for such statutes. The result of forgetting—or pretending to forget—the real reason for anti-mask legislation is farcical. Masks are used in protest against terrorist regimes for reasons both of symbolism and personal safety. Iranian students wearing masks and opposing human rights violations by the Shah of Iran, for example, were prosecuted under a California anti-mask statute.

I call here for an end of such unknowing. We know why state legislatures—those quirkily populist institutions—have passed anti-mask statutes. It is more honest, and less cynically manipulative of legal doctrine to legislate openly against the worst forms of racist speech, allowing ourselves to know what we know.

What makes Matsuda's position particularly attractive is that she offers a pragmatic, pro–civil liberties argument for content-specificity: 23

The alternative to recognizing racist speech as qualitatively different because of its content is to continue to stretch existing First Amendment exceptions, such as the "fighting words" doctrine and the "content/conduct" distinction. This stretching ultimately weakens the First Amendment fabric, creating neutral holes that remove protection for many forms of speech. Setting aside the worst forms of racist speech for special treatment is a non-neutral, value-laden approach that will better preserve free speech.

At the very least, this approach would promise a quick solution to the abuse of "fighting words" ordinances. Consider Matsuda's own approach to legal sanctions for racist speech. By way of distinguishing "the worst, paradigm example of racist hate messages from other forms of racist and non-racist speech," she offers three identifying characteristics: 24

(1) The message is of racial inferiority.
(2) The message is directed against a historically oppressed group.
(3) The message is persecutory, hateful and degrading.

The third element, she says, is "related to the 'fighting words' idea"; and the first "is the primary identifier of racist speech"; but it is the second element that "attempts to further define racism by recognizing the connection of racism to power and subordination."

The second element is the one that most radically departs from the current requirement that law be neutral as to content and viewpoint. But it would seem to forestall some of the abuses to which earlier speech ordinances have been put, simply by requiring the victim of the penalized speech to be a member of a "historically oppressed group." Surely there is something refreshingly straightforward about the call for "an end to unknowing."   25

Is Matsuda on to something? Not quite. Ironically enough, what trips up   26
the content-specific approach is that it can never be content-specific enough.
Take a second look at Matsuda's three identifying characteristics of paradigm
hate speech. First, recall, that the message is of racial inferiority. Now, Matsuda is clear that she wants her definition to encompass, inter alia, anti-Semitic
and anti-Asian prejudice; but anti-Semitism (as the philosopher Laurence
Thomas, who is black and Jewish, observes) traditionally imputes to its object
not inferiority, but iniquity. Moreover, anti-Asian prejudice often more
closely resembles anti-Semitic prejudice than it does anti-black prejudice.
Surely anti-Asian prejudice that depicts Asians as menacingly superior, and
therefore as a threat to "us," is just as likely to arouse the sort of violence that
notoriously claimed the life of Vincent Chin ten years ago in Detroit.

More obviously, the test of membership in a "historically oppressed"   27
group is either too narrow (just blacks) or too broad (just about everybody).
Are poor Appalachians, a group I knew well from growing up in a West Virginia mill town, "historically oppressed" or "dominant group members"?
Once we adopt the "historically oppressed" proviso, I suspect, it is a matter of
time before a group of black women in Chicago are arraigned for calling a
policeman a "dumb Polak." Evidence that Poles are a historically oppressed
group in Chicago will be in plentiful supply; the policeman's grandmother will
offer poignant firsthand testimony to that.

III.

The critique of neutrality would affect not simply how we draft our ordi-   28
nances, but also how we conduct our litigation. One quickly moves from asking whether our statutes can or should be neutral to asking whether the
adjudication of these statutes can or should be neutral. Indeed, many legal
pragmatists, mainstream scholars and critical race theorists converge in their
affirmation of the balancing approach toward the First Amendment and their
corresponding skepticism toward what could be called the "Skokie school" of
jurisprudence. When the American Civil Liberties Union defended the right
of neo-Nazis to march in Skokie, a predominantly Jewish suburb of Chicago
where a number of Holocaust survivors lived, they wished to protect and to
fortify the constitutional right at issue. Indeed, they may have reasoned, if a
civil liberty can be tested and upheld in so odious an exercise of it, then the
precedent will strengthen it for all the less obnoxious cases where it may be
disputed in the future. Hard cases harden laws.

The strategy of the Skokie school relies on a number of presuppositions   29
that critical legal theorists and others regard as doubtful. Most importantly, it
is premised on the neutral operation of principle in judicial decisionmaking.
But what if judges really decided matters in an unprincipled and political way,
and invoked principles only by way of window dressing? In cases close-run
enough to require the Supreme Court to decide them, precedent and principle
are elastic enough, or complex enough, that justices can often decide either
way without brazenly contradicting themselves. And even if the justices want

to make principled decisions, it may turn out that the facts of the case—in the real-world cases that come before them—are too various and complicated ever to be overdetermined by the rule of precedent, *stare decisis*. In either event, it could turn out that defending neo-Nazis was just defending neo-Nazis.

Moreover, it may be that the sort of formal liberties vouchsafed by this process are not the sort of liberties that we need most. Perhaps we have been overly impressed by the frisson of defending bad people for good causes, when the good consequences are at best conjectural and the bad ones real and immediate. Perhaps, these critics conclude, it is time to give up the pursuit of abstract principles and instead defend victims against victimizers, achieving your results in the here-and-now, not in the sweet hereafter.   30

There is something to this position, but it is, like the position it is meant to rebuff, overstated. Nadine Strossen of the ACLU can show, for example, that the organization's winning First Amendment defense of the racist Father Terminiello in 1949 bore Fourteenth Amendment fruit when the ACLU was able to use the landmark *Terminiello* decision to defend the free speech rights of civil rights protesters in the '60s and '70s. Granted, this may not constitute proof, which is an elusive thing in historical argument, but such cases do provide good prima facie reason to think that the Skokie school has pragmatic justification, not just blind faith, on its side.   31

Another problem with the abandonment of principled adjudication is what it leaves in its wake: the case-by-case balancing of interests. My point is not that "normal" First Amendment jurisprudence can completely eschew balancing, then there is a difference between employing it in background or *in extremis* and employing it as the first and only approach. An unfettered regime of balancing admits too much to judicial inspection. What we miss when we dwell on the rarefied workings of high court decisionmaking is the way in which laws exert their effects lower down the legal food chain. It's been pointed out that when police arrest somebody for loitering or disorderly conduct, the experience of arrest—being hauled off to the station and fingerprinted before being released—often *is* the punishment. And "fighting words" ordinances have lent themselves to similar abuse. Anthony D'Amato, a law professor at Northwestern, makes a crucial and often overlooked point when he argues: "In some areas of law we do not want judges to decide cases at all—not justly or any other way. In these areas, the mere possibility of judicial decisionmaking exerts a chilling effect that can undermine what we want the law to achieve."   32

But what if that chilling effect is precisely what the law is designed for? After all, one person's chill is another person's civility. It is clear, in any event, that all manner of punitive speech regulations are meant to have effects far beyond the classic triad of deterrence, reform and retribution.   33

IV.

The main appeal of speech codes usually turns out to be expressive or symbolic rather than consequential. That is, their advocates do not depend on the claim   34 that a speech-code statute will spare certain groups some foreseeable amount of psychic trauma. They say, rather, that such a statute expresses a university's opposition to hate speech and bigotry; and more positively, that it symbolizes a commitment to tolerance, to the creation of an educational environment in which mutual colloquy and comity are preserved.

In this spirit Matsuda writes that "a legal response to racist speech is a *statement*   35 that victims of racism are valued members of our polity," and that "in a society that *expresses* its moral judgments through the law," the "absence of laws against racist speech is telling." In this same spirit Delgado suggests that a tort action for racist speech would have the effect of "*communicating* to the perpetrator and to society that such abuse will not be tolerated either by its victims or by the courts" (italics mine). And also in this spirit Thomas Grey, the Stanford law professor who helped draft the campus speech regulations there, counsels that "authorities make the most effective statement when they are honestly concerned to do something *beyond* making a statement," thus "putting their money where there mouth is." The punitive function of speech codes is thus enlisted to expressive means, as a means of bolstering the credibility of the anti-racist statement.

　　Still, once we have admitted that the regulation of racist speech is partly   36 or wholly a symbolic act, we must register the force of the other symbolic considerations that may come into play. Thus, even if you think that the notion of free speech contains logical inconsistencies, you need to register the symbolic force of its further abridgement. And it is this level of scrutiny that may tip the balance in the other direction. The controversy over flag-burning is a good illustration of the two-edged nature of symbolic arguments. Safeguarding the flag may symbolize something nice for some of us, but safeguarding our freedom to burn the flag symbolizes something nicer for others of us.

　　Note, too, that the expressivist position suffers from an uncomfortable   37 contradiction. A university administration that merely condemns hate speech, without mobilizing punitive sanctions, is held to have done little, to have offered "mere words." And yet this skepticism about the power of "mere words" comports oddly with the attempts to regulate "mere words" that, since they are spoken by those not in a position of authority, would seem to have even less symbolic force. Why is it "mere words" when a university only condemns racist speech, but not "mere words" that the student utters in the first place? Whose words are "only words"? Why are racists words deeds, but anti-racist words just lip service?

　　And is the verbal situation really as asymmetrical as it first appears?   38 Surely the rebuke "racist" also has the power to wound. One of the cases that arose under the University of Michigan speech code involved a group discussion at the beginning of a dentistry class, in which the teacher, a black woman, sought to "identify concerns of students." A student reported that he had heard, from his roommate, who was a minority, that minority students had a hard time in the class and were not treated fairly. In response, the outraged teacher lodged a complaint against the student for having accused her (as she perceived it) of racism. For this black woman, at least, even an indirect accusation of racism apparently had the brunt of racial stigmatization.

One other paradox fissures the hate speech movement. Because these scholars wish to show that substantial restrictions on racist speech are consistent with the Constitution, they must make the case that racist speech is sui generis among offensive or injurious utterances; otherwise the domain of unprotected speech would mushroom beyond the point of constitutional and political plausibility. "Words That Wound," the title of Delgado's pioneering essay, designates a category that includes racist speech but is scarcely exhausted by it. Nor could we maintain that racist insults, which tent to be generic, are necessarily more wounding than an insult tailor-made to hurt someone: being jeered at for your acne or your obesity may be far more hurtful than being jeered at for your race or your religion.

    Alert to this consideration, scholars like Matsuda, Lawrence and Delgado argue that racist speech is peculiarly deserving of curtailment precisely because it participates in (and is at least partly constitutive of) the larger structures of racism that are "hegemonic" in our society. "Black folks know that no racial incident is 'isolated' in the United States," writes Lawrence:

> That is what makes the incidents so horrible, so scary. It is the knowledge that they are not the isolated unpopular speech of a dissident few that makes them so frightening. These incidents are manifestations of a ubiquitous and deeply ingrained cultural belief system, an American way of life.

To this consideration Matsuda annexes the further argument that what distinguishes racist speech from other forms of unpopular speech is "the universal acceptance of the wrongness of the doctrine of racial supremacy." Unlike Marxist speech, say, racist speech is "universally condemned."

    At first blush, this is a surprising claim. After all, if racist speech really were universally rejected, ordinances against it would be an exercise in antiquarianism. And yet there is something in what Matsuda says: a shared assumption about the weight of the anti-racist consensus, a conviction that at least overt racists are an unpopular minority, that authority is likely to side with *us* against *them*. This hopeful conviction about the magnitude of racist expression in America provides the hidden and rather unexpected foundation for the hate speech movement. Why would you entrust authority with enlarged powers of regulating the speech of unpopular minorities, unless you were confident that the unpopular minorities would be racists, not blacks? Lawrence may know that racial incidents are never "isolated," but he must also believe them to be less than wholly systemic. You don't go to the teacher to complain about the school bully unless you know that the teacher is on your side.

The tacit confidence of critical race theory in the anti-racist consensus also enables its criticism of neutral principles. This becomes clear when one

39

40

41

42

considers the best arguments in favor of such principles. Thus David Coles, a law professor at Georgetown University, suggests that

> in a democratic society the only speech government is likely to succeed in regulating will be that of the politically marginalized. If an idea is sufficiently popular, a representative government will lack the political wherewithal to suppress it, irrespective of the First Amendment. But if an idea is unpopular, the only thing that may protect it from the majority is a strong constitutional norm of content-neutrality.

Reverse his assumptions about whose speech is marginalized and you stand the argument on its head. If blatantly racist speech is unpopular and stigmatized, a strong constitutional norm of content-neutrality may be its best hope for protection. For these critics, however, that is a damning argument *against* content-neutrality.

This, then, is the political ambiguity that haunts the new academic activism. "Our colleagues of color, struggling to carry the multiple burdens of token representative, role model and change agent in increasingly hostile environments, needed to know that the institutions in which they worked stood behind them," declare our critical race theorists in their joint manifesto. *Needed to know that the institutions in which they worked stood behind them:* I have difficulty imagining this sentiment expressed by activists in the '60s, who defined themselves in a proudly adversarial relation to authority and its institutions. Here is the crucial difference this time around. The contemporary aim is not to resist power, but to enlist power.

V.

"Critical race theory challenges ahistoricism and insists on a contextual/ historical analysis of the law." So states the manifesto, and it is not necessarily a bad principle. What it suggests to me, however, is that we get down to cases, and consider, as these theorists do not, the actual results of various regimes of hate speech regulation.

Surveying United Nations conventions urging the criminalization of racist speech, Matsuda bemoans the fact that the United States, out of First Amendment scruple, has declined fully to endorse such resolutions. By contrast, she commends to our attention nations such as Canada and the United Kingdom. Canada's appeal to the hate speech movement is obvious; after all, the new Canadian Bill of Rights has not been allowed (as Matsuda observes) to interfere with its national statutes governing hate propaganda. And Canada's Supreme Court has recently promulgated MacKinnon's statutory definition of pornography as the law of the land. What you don't hear from the hate speech theorists is that the first casualty of the MacKinnonite anti-obscenity ruling was a gay and lesbian bookshop in Toronto, which was raided by the police because of a lesbian magazine it carried. (Homosexual literature is a frequent target of Canada's restrictions on free expression.) Nor are they likely to mention that in June copies of *Black Looks: Race and Representation* by the well-known black feminist scholar Bell Hooks, a book widely assigned in women's studies courses, was confiscated by Canadian authorities as possible "hate literature." Is the Canadian system really a beacon of hope?

Even more perplexing, especially in the context of an insistence on challenging ahistoricism and attending to context, is the nomination of Britain as an exemplar of a more enlightened free speech jurisprudence. Does anyone believe that racism has subsided in Britain since the adoption of the 1965 Race Relations Act forbidding racial defamation? Or that the legal climate in that country is more conducive to searching political debate? Ask any British newspaperman about that. When Harry Evans, then editor of the London *Times,* famously proclaimed that the British press was, by comparison to ours, only "half-free," he was not exaggerating much. The result of Britain's judicial climate is to make the country a net importer of libel suits launched by tycoons who are displeased with their biographers. Everyone knows that a British libel suit is like a Reno divorce. It is rather a mordant irony that American progressives should propose Britain, and its underdeveloped protection of expression, as a model to emulate at a time when many progressives in Britain are agitating for a bill of rights and broad First Amendment-style protections. 46

And what of speech codes on American campuses? The record may surprise some advocates of regulations. "When the ACLU enters the debate by challenging the University of Michigan's efforts to provide a safe harbor for its Black, Latino and Asian students," Lawrence writes, "we should not be surprised that nonwhite students feel abandoned." In light of the actual record of enforcement, however, the situation might be viewed differently. During the year in which Michigan's speech code was enforced, more than twenty blacks were charged—by whites—with racist speech. As Strossen notes, not a single instance of white racist speech was punished, a fact that makes Lawrence's talk of a "safe harbor" seem more wishful than informed. 47

At Michigan, a full disciplinary hearing was conducted only in the case of a black social work student who was charged with saying, in a class discussion of research projects, that he believed homosexuality was an illness, and that he was developing a social work approach to move homosexuals toward heterosexuality. ("These charges will haunt me for the rest of my life," the student claimed in a court affidavit.) By my lights, this is a good example of how speech codes kill critique. I think that the student's views about homosexuality (which may or may not have been well-intentioned) are both widespread and unlikely to survive intellectual scrutiny. Regrettably, we have not yet achieved a public consensus in this country on the moral legitimacy (or, more precisely, the moral indifference) of homosexuality. Yet it may well be that a class on social work is not an inappropriate forum for a rational discussion of why the "disease" model of sexual difference has lost credibility among social scientists. (In a class on social work, this isn't P.C. brainwashing, this is education.) The trouble is, you cannot begin to conduct this conversation when you outlaw the expression of the view that you would criticize. 48

Critical race theorists are fond of the ideal of conversation. "This chapter   49
attempts to begin a conversation about the First Amendment," Matsuda writes
toward the end of her contribution. "Most important, we must continue this
discussion," Lawrence writes toward the end of his. It is too easy to lose sight
of the fact that the conversation to which they are devoted is aimed at limiting
conversation. If there are costs to speech, then there are costs also to curtailing
speech, often unpredictable ones.

Speech codes, to be sure, may be more narrowly and responsibly tailored,   50
and the Stanford rules—carefully drafted by scholars, like Thomas Grey, with
civil libertarian sympathies—have rightly been taken as a model of such careful delimitation. For rather than following the arguments against racist speech
to their natural conclusion, the Stanford rules prohibit only insulting expression that conveys "direct and visceral hatred or contempt" for people on the
basis of their sex, race, color, handicap, religion, sexual orientation or national
and ethnic origin, and that is "addressed directly to the individual or individuals whom it insults or stigmatizes."

Chances are, the Stanford rule won't do much harm. Chances are, too, it   51
won't do much good. As long as the eminently reasonable Grey is drafting and
enforcing the restrictions, I won't lose much sleep over it. Yet we must be
clear how inadequate the code is as a response to the powerful arguments that
were marshaled to support it. Contrast the following two statements addressed
to a black freshman at Stanford:

(A) LeVon, if you find yourself struggling in your classes here, you should realize it isn't your fault. It's simply that you're the beneficiary of a disruptive policy of affirmative action that places underqualified, underprepared and often
undertalented black students in demanding educational environments like this
one. The policy's egalitarian aims may be well-intentioned, but given the fact
that aptitude tests place African Americans almost a full standard deviation
below the mean, even controlling for socioeconomic disparities, they are also
profoundly misguided. The truth is, you probably don't belong here, and your
college experience will be a long downhill slide.

(B) Out of my face, jungle bunny.

Surely there is no doubt which is likely to be more "wounding" and alienating
to its intended audience. Under the Stanford speech regulations, however, the
first is protected speech, and the second may well not be: a result that makes a
mockery of the words-that-wound rationale.

If you really want to penalize such wounding words, it makes no sense to   52
single out gutter epithets—which, on many college campuses, are more likely
to stigmatize the speaker than their intended victim—and leave the far more
painful disquisition alone. In American society today, the real power commanded by racism is likely to vary inversely with the vulgarity with which it
is expressed. Black professionals soon learn that it is the socially disfran-
chised—the lower class, the homeless—who are most likely to hail them as
"niggers." The circles of power have long since switched to a vocabulary of

indirection. Unfortunately, those who pit the First Amendment against the Fourteenth Amendment invite us to worry more about speech codes than coded speech.

I suspect that many of those liberals who supported Stanford's restrictions   53
on abusive language did so because they thought it was the civil thing to do. Few imagined that, say, the graduation rates or GPAs of Stanford's blacks (or Asians, gays, and so on) are likely to rise significantly as a result. Few imagined, that is, that the restrictions would lead to substantive rights or minority empowerment. They just believed that gutter epithets violate the sort of civility that ought to prevail on campus. In spirit, then, the new regulations were little different from the rules about curfews, drinking or the after-hours presence of women in male dormitories that once governed America's campuses and preoccupied their disciplinary committees.

Not that rules about civility are without value. Lawrence charges that   54
civil libertarians who disagree with him about speech regulations may be "unconscious racists." I don't doubt this is so; I don't doubt that some of those who support speech codes are unconscious racists. What I doubt is whether the imputation of racism is the most effective way to advance the debate between civil rights and civil liberties.

VI.

"What is ultimately at stake in this debate is our vision for this society," write   55
the authors of *Words That Wound,* and they are right. In parsing the reasoning of the movement against hate speech, it is essential that we not miss the civic forest for the legal trees. Far beyond the wrangling over particular statutes and codes lies an encompassing vision of state and civil society. And its wellsprings are to be found not in legal scholarship or critical theory, but in the more powerful cultural currents identified with the "recovery movement."

At the vital center of the hate speech movement is the seductive vision of   56
the therapeutic state. This vision is presaged in the manifesto itself:

> Too often victims of hate speech find themselves without the words to articulate what they see, feel and know. In the absence of theory and analysis that give them a diagnosis and a name for the injury they have suffered, they internalize the injury done them and are rendered silent in the fact of continuing injury. Critical race theory names the injury and identifies its origins.

This sounds, of course, like a popular primer on how psychotherapy is supposed to work; with a few changes, the passage might be addressed to survivors of toxic parenting. Indeed, "alexathymia"—the inability to name and articulate one's feelings—is a faddish diagnosis in psychiatry these days. Nor is critical race theory's affinity with the booming recovery industry a matter of chance. These days the recovery movement is perhaps the principal source of resistance to the older and much-beleaguered American tradition of individualism.

"When the ideology is deconstructed and injury is named, subordinated   57
victims find their voices," the manifesto asserts. "They discover they are not
alone in their subordination. They are empowered." Here the recovery/
survivor-group paradigm leads to a puzzling contradiction. We are told that
victims of racist speech are cured—that is, empowered—when they learn they
are "not alone" in their subordination, but subordinated as a group. But elsewhere we are told that what makes racist speech peculiarly wounding is that it
conveys precisely the message that you are a member of a subordinated group.
How can the suggestion of group subordination be the poison *and* the antidote?

The therapeutic claims made for critical race theory cut against the hate   58
speech offensive in more important ways. For if we took these claims at face
value, critical race theory would not buttress speech regulations, it would ob-
viate the need for them. The problem about which Lawrence worries, that
racist speech "silenc[es] members of those groups who are its targets," would
naturally be addressed not through bureaucratic regulations, but through the
sort of deconstruction and critique that will enable victims, according to critical race theory, to "find their voices." And here lies another painful irony. All
this sounds very much like Justice Brandeis's hoary and much-scorned pre-
scription for redressing harmful speech: "more speech."

Scholars such as Delgado and Matsuda understandably emphasize the ad-   59
verse psychological effects of racial abuse. "Because they constantly hear racist
messages, minority children, not surprisingly, come to question their competence, intelligence and worth," Delgado writes. And he further notes that the
psychic injuries incurred by racist speech have additional costs down the road:
"The person who is timid, withdrawn, bitter, hypertense or psychotic will almost certainly fare poorly in employment settings." (As a member of the Harvard faculty, I would venture that there are exceptions to this rule.) But the
proposed therapeutic regime is no mere talking cure. Indeed, in the Republic
of Self-Esteem, we are invited to conceive of the lawsuit as therapy. "When
victimized by racist language," Delgado explains, "victims must be able to
threaten and institute legal action, thereby relieving the sense of helplessness
that leads to psychological harm."

A similar therapeutic function could be played by criminal proceedings,   60
in Matsuda's view. When the government does nothing about racist speech,
she argues, it actually causes a second injury. "The second injury is the pain of
knowing that the government provides no remedy and offers no recognition of
the dehumanizing experience that victims of hate propaganda are subjected
to." In fact, "The government's denial of personhood through its denial of legal recourse may even be more painful than the initial act of hatred." Of
course, what this grievance presupposes is that the state is there, *in loco parentis,*
to confer personhood in the first place. Finally, Matsuda must repair not to an
instrumental conception of the state, but to a conception of it as the "official
embodiment of the society we live in," which is rather remote and abstracted
from the realities of our heterogeneous populace, with its conflicting norms
and jostling values.

Psychotherapy cannot do the hard work of politics. Yet a similar thera-   61
peutic vision animates the more broad-gauged campus regulations such as
those adopted in the late 1980s at the University of Connecticut. These rules
sought to proscribe such behavior as, inter alia:

> Treating people differently solely because they are in some way different from
> the majority. . . .

> Imitating stereotypes in speech or mannerisms. . . .

> Attributing objections to any of the above actions to "hypersensitivity" of the
> targeted individual or group.

That last provision was especially cunning. It meant that even if you believed
that a complainant was overreacting to an innocuous remark, the attempt to
defend yourself in this way would serve only as proof of your guilt.

The rationale of the university's rules was made explicit in its general   62
prohibition on actions that undermined the "security or self-esteem" of persons or groups. (Would awarding low grades count?) Not surprisingly, the
university's expressed objective was to provide "a positive environment in
which everyone feels comfortable working or living." It was unclear whether
any provisions were to be made for those who did not feel "comfortable"
working or living under such restrictive regulations. In any event, they were
later dropped under threat of legal action.

It may be that widespread skepticism about the distinction between the   63
public and the private made it inevitable that the recovery movement would
translate into a politics; and that this politics would center on a vocabulary of
trauma and abuse, in which the verbal forms and the physical forms are seen as
equivalent. Perhaps it was inevitable that the citizen at the center of the political theory of the Enlightenment would be replaced by the infant at the center
of modern depth psychology and its popular therapeutic variants. The inner
child may hurt and grieve, as we have been advised. But may the inner child
also vote?

VII.

What cannot be sidestepped, finally, is the larger question, the political ques-   64
tion, of how we came to decide that our energies were best directed not at
strengthening our position in the field of public discourse, but at trying to
move its boundary posts. I detect two motivations.

In the academy, there has been increased attention to the formative   65
power of language in the construction of our social reality, to language as
"performative," as itself counting as action and constituting a "speech act."
These are phrases and ideas that are owed to ordinary language philosophy, of
the kind that the Oxford philosopher J. L. Austin developed in the middle of
the century, but now MacKinnon adds them to her argumentative arsenal in

her latest book. The notion of the speech act certainly acquires new force when the act in question is rape.

MacKinnon's emphasis on the realness, the act-like nature, of expression   66
receives an interesting twist in the attempt by some hate speech theorists to "textualize" the Fourteenth Amendment. If expression is act, then act must be expression. If the First Amendment is about speech, then so, too, is the Fourteenth Amendment. Following this reasoning, Lawrence has proposed in an influential reinterpretation of legal history that *Brown v. Board,* and, by analogy, all subsequent civil rights decisions and legislation, are in fact prohibitions on expressive behavior. In Lawrence's reading, they forbid not racism, but the expression of racism. In line with this argument, he tells us that "discriminatory conduct is not racist unless it also conveys the message of white supremacy," thus contributing to the social construction of racism.

This is a bold and unsettling claim, which commits Lawrence to the   67
view that in the case of discriminatory conduct, the only crime is to get caught. By this logic, racial redlining by bankers is not racist unless people find out about it. And the crusading district attorney who uncovers hidden evidence of those bankers' discrimination is not to be hailed as a friend of justice, after all: by bringing it to light, he was only activating the racist potential of those misdeeds. Should anti-discrimination policy be founded, then, on the principle of "don't ask, don't tell"?

Lawrence's analysis of segregation reaches the same surprising conclu-   68
sion: "The nonspeech elements are by-products of the main message rather than the message being simply a by-product of unlawful conduct." By this logic, poverty is not really about material deprivation; it is really about the message of class inequality. We might conclude, then, that the problem of economic inequality would most naturally be redressed by promulgating a self-affirmative lower-class identity along the lines of Poverty Is Beautiful. Words may not be cheap, but they are much less costly than AFDC and job training programs.

Something, let us agree, has gone very wrong. The pendulum has swung from   69
the absurd position that words don't matter to the equally absurd position that only words matter. Critical race theory, it appears, has fallen under the sway of a species of academic nominalism. Yes, speech is a species of action. Yes, there are some acts that only speech can perform. But there are some acts that speech alone cannot accomplish. You cannot heal the sick by pronouncing them well. You cannot lift up the poor by declaring them rich.

In their manifesto, the authors of *Words That Wound* identify their fight   70
as "a fight for a constitutional community where 'freedom' does not implicate a right to degrade and humiliate another human being." These are heady words. Like much sweepingly utopian rhetoric, however, they invite a regime so heavily policed as to be incompatible with democracy. Once we are forbidden verbally to degrade and to humiliate, will we retain the moral autonomy to elevate and to affirm?

In the end, the preference for the substantive liberties supposedly vouch-   71
safed by the Fourteenth Amendment over the formal ones enshrined in the

First Amendment rehearses the classic disjunction that Isaiah Berlin analyzed a generation ago in "Two Conceptions of Liberty," but without having learned from him. Berlin's words have aged little. "Negative" liberty, the simple freedom from external coercion, seemed to him

> a truer and more humane ideal than the goals of those who seek in the great, disciplined, authoritarian structures the ideal of "positive" self-mastery by classes, or peoples or the whole of mankind. It is truer, because it recognizes the fact that human goals are many, not all of them commensurable, and in perpetual rivalry with one another.

To suggest, as the critical race theorists do, that equality must precede liberty is simply to jettison the latter without securing the former. The First Amendment may not secure us substantive liberties, but neither will its abrogation.

It is not hard to explain the disenchantment among minority critics with such liberal mainstays as the "marketplace of ideas" and the ideal of public discourse. I take their disenchantment to be a part of a larger crisis of faith. The civil rights era witnessed the development of a national consensus—hammered out noisily, and against significant resistance—that racism, at least overt racism, was wrong. Amazingly enough, things like reason, argument and moral suasion did play a significant role in changing attitudes about "race relations." But what have they done for us lately? 72

For all his good sense, Harry Kalven Jr. was spectacularly wrong when he wrote: "One is tempted to say that it will be a sign that the Negro problem has basically been solved when the Negro begins to worry about group libel protection." Quite the contrary. The disillusionment with liberal ideology that is now rampant among many minority scholars and activists stems from the lack of progress in the struggle for racial equality over the past fifteen years. Liberalism's principle of formal equality seems to have led us so far, but no further. As Patricia J. Williams observes, it "put the vampire back in its coffin but it was no silver stake." 73

The problem may be that the continuing economic and material inequality between black America and white America, and the continuing immiseration of large segments of black America, cannot be erased simply through better racial attitudes. Poverty, white and black, can take on a life of its own, to the point that removing the conditions that caused it can do little to alleviate it. The '80s may have been the "Cosby Decade," but you wouldn't know it from the South Bronx. It has become clear, in other words, that the political economy of race and poverty can no longer be reduced to a mirror of what whites think of blacks. 74

In some ways the intellectuals have not caught up to this changing reality. Generals are not the only ones who are prone to fight the last war. Rather than responding to the grim new situation with new and subtler modes of socioeconomic analysis, we have finessed the gap between rhetoric and reality by forging new and subtler definitions of the word "racism." Hence a new model of 75 institutional racism is one that can operate in the absence of actual racists. By redefining our terms, we can always say of the economic gap between black and white America: the problem is still racism . . . and, by stipulation, it would be true. But the grip of this vocabulary has tended to foreclose the more sophisticated models of political economy that we so desperately need. I cannot otherwise explain why some of our brightest legal minds believe that substantive liberties can be vouchsafed and substantive inequities redressed by punishing rude remarks; or why their analysis of racism owes more to the totalizing theory of Catharine MacKinnon than to the work of scholar-investigators like Douglas Massey or William Julius Wilson or Gary Orfield—people who, whatever their differences, are attempting to discover how things work in the real world, never confusing the empirical with the merely anecdotal.

Critical race theory has served, then, as a labor-saving device. For if   76
racism can be fully textualized, if its real existence is in its articulation, then racial inequity can be prized free from the moss and soil of political economy. "Gender is sexual," MacKinnon wrote in *Toward a Feminist Theory of the State.* "Pornography constitutes the meaning of that sexuality." By extension, racist speech must prove to be the real content of racial subordination: banish it, and you banish subordination. The perverse result is a see-no-evil, hear-no-evil approach toward racial inequality. Unfortunately, even if hate did disappear, aggregative patterns of segregation and segmentation in housing and employment would not disappear. And conversely, in the absence of this material and economic gap, not many people would care about racist speech.

Beliefs that go untested and unchallenged cannot prosper. The critical   77
race theorists must be credited with helping to reinvigorate the debate about freedom of expression; the intelligence, the innovation and the thoughtfulness of their best work deserve a reasoned response, and not, as so often happens, demonization and dismissal. And yet, for all the passion and all the scholarship that the critical race theorists have expended upon the problem of hate speech, I cannot believe that it will capture their attention for very much longer. "It is strange how rapidly things change," wrote Kalven in 1965. "Just a little more than a decade ago we were all concerned with devising legal controls for the libeling of groups. . . . Ironically, once the victory was won, the momentum for such legal measures seemed to dissipate, and the problem has all but disappeared from view." It is strange how rapidly things change—and change back. But the results, I suspect, will be similar this time around. The advocates of speech restrictions will grow disenchanted not with their failures, but with their victories, and the movement will come to seem yet another curious byway in the long history of our racial desperation.

And yet the movement will not have been without its political costs. I   78
cannot put it better than Charles Lawrence himself, who writes: "I fear that by framing the debate as we have—as one in which the liberty of free speech is in conflict with the elimination of racism—we have advanced the cause of racial oppression and placed the bigot on the moral high ground, fanning the rising flames of racism." He does not intend it as such, but I read this passage as a harsh rebuke to the movement itself. As the critical race theory manifesto

acknowledges, "This debate has deeply divided the liberal civil rights/civil liberties community." And so it has. It has created hostility between old allies and fractured longtime coalitions. Was it worth it? Justice Black's words may return, like the sound of an unheeded tocsin, to haunt us: "Another such victory and I am undone."   ■

Questions for Meaning

1. According to Gates how has the relationship between civil liberties and civil rights changed over the past thirty years?
2. What does Gates mean by "hate speech" and "critical race theory"?
3. How did the courts interpret the First Amendment before 1931? How has the interpretation changed since then?
4. What are the two legal models put forward by proponents of laws banning hate speech?
5. What is the legal definition of libel? Why does Gates believe that libel laws are not applicable to racist or sexist speech?
6. What does Gates mean when he writes, in paragraph 77, "The advocates of speech restrictions will grow disenchanted not with their failures, but with their victories. . .."?
7. Vocabulary: byword (1), spansule (2), demonology (6), samizdat (7), progenitors (10), concomitant (11), jurisprudence (13), atavism (13), desuetude (15), proclivity (16), congruence (19), vouchsafed (30), frisson (30), prima facie (31), asymmetrical (38), scruple (45), nominalism (69), abrogation (71).

Questions about Strategy

1. How fairly does Gates treat the various scholars he questions in this article? Does he ever concede that their arguments may have merit?
2. Where does Gates refute arguments on behalf of speech restrictions? How convincing are his refutations?
3. In paragraphs 28 and 29, Gates discusses a case in which the ACLU defended the right of neo-Nazis to march through a town inhabited by survivors of the Holocaust. What is this example meant to illustrate?
4. Does Gates provide any specific examples to support his claim that attempts to restrict hate speech may actually hurt the minorities they were intended to protect?
5. Consider statements (A) and (B) in paragraph 51. How do they differ? Gates observes, "Surely there is no doubt which is likely to be more 'wounding' and alienating to its intended audience." Do you agree?

JOHN A. WILLIAMS

PRIOR RESTRAINTS

John A. Williams is the author of many novels. They include *The Angry Ones* (1960), *Night Song* (1961), *Sissie* (1963), *The Man Who Cried I Am* (1967), *Mothersill and the Foxes* (1976), and *The Berhama Account* (1985). He has also published nonfiction, including a 1970 biography of Richard Wright, *The Most Native of Sons*. A 1950 graduate of Syracuse University, Williams has taught at the University of California, Santa Barbara, Boston University, and Rutgers University. The following argument on censorship was first published by *The Nation* in 1988. It reflects Williams' own experience as a black writer who is concerned about how minorities are treated in the United States.

In *The Media Monopoly* Ben Bagdikian notes that "in 1981 there were forty-six   1
corporations that controlled most of the business in daily newspapers, magazines, television, books and motion pictures. Five years later the number had shrunk to twenty-nine." It is now 1988 and the shrinkage continues. In 1965 my editor at Little, Brown & Company, the late Harry Sions, told me that Time Inc.'s intended purchase of the company would make no difference in the quality of books Little, Brown produced. I didn't believe him, but I stayed with the house for a while anyway. We all know now that such takeovers have been bad news for writers. For one thing, they increase the importance of the dollar sign—always a mark of the censors.

But another element of censorship has emerged with the severe con-   2
tractions of the publishing industry, and it is one black and other minority writers (and some white writers) have grumbled about for years. A dozen years ago I said in an interview, "PEN★ is so concerned with foreign authors and their plight, but how about the plight of black authors here?" The quote appeared in the June 7, 1976, edition of *Publishers Weekly*. The then secretary of PEN called me to say that PEN could not be responsible for "faddishness" in publishing. The possibility that a genteel sort of censorship lay hidden in the folds of a concern about "faddishness" did not occur to him—as it has not occurred to others. I saw no reason to pursue the issue, as I knew he did not believe one existed. The case has been made more legitimate, I think, by Irving Louis Horowitz's article "Monopolization of Publishing and Crisis in Higher Education" (*Academe,* November/December 1987). Horowitz has suggested that "the new monopolization has a direct bearing on the ability of publishing to satisfy a fundamental constitutional guarantee: free speech." He continues, "A free speech environment is more subtly eroded by different notions of appropriate profit goals that obtain in large and small firms."

★An international organization of writers.

Even before the domestic conglomerates took them over, publishing houses had become reluctant to accept works by black authors, so we cannot realistically expect the foreign conglomerates to do any better. Quite possibly they will do worse, and the erosion of a free speech environment will continue.   3

Twenty years ago there were several black editors in publishing houses. (That they are no longer in place may indicate that publishers do not feel them capable of editing books written by white writers.) True, they were mainly advisers to the major decision-makers, but they were there, and as a result there was some enthusiasm for the publication of black writers. That time is past, and I do not see it returning in my lifetime. I am not happy to have to write this, but the facts do tend to speak for themselves.   4

During that same brief period, newspapers and magazines also hired minorities, but staffing to achieve a quota did not mean bigotry had died. Fifteen years ago, for example, *The New York Times* and the Associated Press were sued by minorities and women. Both settled out of court. More recently, last year, the New York *Daily News*, unwise enough to go to court in the face of ample evidence of discrimination against blacks, lost a suit to four black journalists who had charged it with discrimination. There is, of course, a clear, indisputable relationship between the media and the publishing industry.   5

It must be noticed, if rarely mentioned, that black reviewers and critics are seldom asked to comment on works by white authors in the major review media. This, too, is censorship. PEN has a "Freedom-to-Write" committee. No one, however, actually bars an author's freedom to write; it is the freedom to publish, to be heard or read, that is at stake in both democratic and totalitarian states; it is the freedom to be judged on literary, and not only on racial or political, grounds. The problem here, though, is that the term "literary" can be used to exclude, especially by people who approach a work with a particular kind of historical, political and racial baggage but deny to others the right to bear the same freight. No doubt, this has always been true. No doubt, those who control this system still believe that minority writers either know nothing about it or else are fearful of what they do know and of the way that knowledge must reflect upon the controllers.   6

In *How We Live* (1968) Penney C. and L. Rust Hills inadvertently revealed a contradiction concerning black writers that is still prevalent in publishing and in the media. They wrote: "It is not that Negroes are not writing or being published; but aside from Ellison and Baldwin, they have not yet produced the kind of writing that satisfies the complex contemporary literary tastes and sensibilities." In the book's appendix, however, they note: "The way students are now taught to read literature in our colleges and universities obscures from them what literature can tell us about ourselves and the way we live."   7

The clause "satisfies the complex contemporary literary tastes and sensibilities" expresses a curiously incomplete thought. No doubt to have added "of white readers" would have been too obvious a declaration, too clearly a suggestion of literary prior restraint, first cousin to censorship. The contradiction emerges again in the complaint that the way students are taught "obscures   8 from them what literature can tell us about ourselves." Since most black writers never make it into the textbooks that are used in colleges and universities, what white (and minority) students can learn about American life is limited.

The kind of censorship present in the publishing industry could not exist   9
without the support of critics, reviewers and academics. Addison Gayle Jr. characterizes academics as being in "control of the nation's cultural apparatus." They work together with "critics who, more often than not, peer out upon American society with a condescension usually reserved for idiots and half-wits." On the rare occasions when some academics do seek to widen the scope of literary study or when they describe its present limitations, they become anathema. *The Washington Post's* Jonathan Yardley early this year described such efforts as being the work of "young fascists." Twenty-odd years ago the label would have been "radical" or "militant." What has happened to harden the language about what is essentially, in the case of Afro-American writers, censorship?

Actually, what we are witnessing is a hardening of attitudes about who is   10
going to send along the word. Some of this was already present in the 1960s. Reviewing Gwendolyn Brooks's *Selected Poems* for the *New York Herald Tribune's Book Week* in October 1963, Louis Simpson wrote, "I am not sure it is possible for a Negro to write well without making us aware that he is a Negro." He continued, "On the other hand, if being a Negro is the only subject, the writing is not important." Simpson later apologized for this statement. The fact is that almost all white writers detail white life in their works. Fair enough—that is their experience. Black critics and reviewers in the main are not permitted to comment favorably or unfavorably on such depictions, though they surely hold vigorous opinions about them. There is no lack of white reviewers and critics, however, who can easily secure platforms from which they can create the impression that most of the writing done by black authors—writing from their experience—is really not very good and therefore warrants little consideration. Literary agents, most of whom are white, buttress this attitude with the general philosophy that black writers do not produce "commercial" work, do not make money and therefore do not make suitable clients. Some white writers find themselves tagged as uncommercial, and for that reason are also de facto censored.

Long before Simpson there was Robert Bone's *The Negro Novel in America,* in which protest was viewed as inimical to "art." The literature of protest   11
had been an honorable endeavor for writers for over a century. In the hands of black writers, however, critics saw it as tainted. And, most recently, in *The New York Times Magazine,* Saul Bellow is credited with this statement: "Who is the Tolstoy of the Zulus? The Proust of the Papuans? I'd be glad to read them." It will be noted that both groups are black. Bellow's questions prompt one to ask if, at the core of this statement, he is saying that black people have produced no literature worthy of his time. "Every intellectual," Ignazio Silone once declared, "is a revolutionary." He was wrong, especially regarding this nation, where they seem to be growing more and more conservative.

I began this piece by discussing the effect of conglomerate takeovers on   12
writing and on the right of free speech. I believe that censorship, intended or
not, exists in publishing and affects black writers disproportionately, and that
the publishing industry, in concert with the media and the academy, reinforces
that second level of censorship created by profit-taking considerations. Sometimes this all comes together in the awarding of literary prizes. But the awarding of prizes cannot be separated from racist attitudes.

Recently, the names of forty-eight black writers—myself included—   13
appeared on a statement in the press praising Toni Morrison and expressing
concern that she has not received national recognition. As it was published,
however, the statement was different from the one read to me over the phone.
I was told it would deal, generally, with some of the concerns I've written
about here. Literary awards were not mentioned. Everyone in or close to the
publishing industry has heard gossip about publishing, editorial and authorial
machinations at prize giving time. For example, I suppose that from now on,
any mention of Toni Morrison's Pulitzer Prize will include reference to that
letter, an inference of black literary maneuvering. Whenever "major" prizes
are awarded to black writers, they tend to validate the individual but not in
any way the body of Afro-American writing they cannot help but represent.
That may be why James Baldwin never got a major award. Neither did
Langston Hughes. Baldwin got publicity. Richard Wright and Chester Himes
got very little of either. They all seemed to be men of the people, speakers for
them. What is really under consideration here is power. Censorship is an exercise in power, however gently, however harshly it is exercised—and prizes can
only be seen as accounterments of that power. At the heart of the need to display such power is the ancient conflict, always denied but deadly persistent:
race and racism.   ■

Questions for Meaning

1. How could corporate takeovers lead to censorship as defined by
   Williams?
2. Why have black writers been discriminated against?
3. According to Williams, who controls American culture?
4. What are the two levels of censorship that concern Williams?
5. Vocabulary: genteel (2), condescension (9), anathema (9), de facto (10),
   tainted (11), accouterments (13).

Questions about Strategy

1. Williams discusses publishing in the 1960s and 1970s as well as in the
   1980s. What purpose is served by discussing publishing over a twenty-
   year period? Do you think publishing has changed in the 1990s?

2. Consider the quote from Saul Bellow in paragraph 11. What is
    Williams implying about Bellow?
3. In paragraph 8, Williams claims that "most black writers never make it
    into the textbooks that are used in colleges and universities." Judging
    from your own experience, does this seem like a reasonable claim?
4. Williams draws on his own experience in paragraphs 1, 2, and 13. Has
    he done so effectively?

JON WIENER

MURDERED INK

A professor of history at the University of California, Irvine, Jon Wiener is a contributing editor to *The Nation,* which first published "Murdered Ink" in 1993. As
you read it, consider each of the separate publishing stories it includes and think
about what these stories have in common.

When Robert Sam Anson's book-in-progress on the Walt Disney Company   1
was killed by Simon and Schuster this past March a year before its due date,
people in the publishing industry were stunned. Here was an established writer
with a hefty contract and a powerful editor. If Anson was vulnerable, who was
safe? Are more books being killed these days by publishers who are increasingly likely to be part of large conglomerates?

There are many ways to kill a book, as anyone who has worked in pub-   2
lishing knows. Manuscripts can be rejected at a number of points before their
final delivery. Less frequently, manuscripts that have been copy-edited and announced in the publisher's catalogue can be yanked almost literally from the
presses. Then there's the publishing industry's death-in-life, books that are
printed rather than published, sent out into the world with tiny press runs and
no advertising. (And of course, as André Schiffrin, director of The New Press,
reminds us, there are also the worthy books that don't get killed but are never
born because they are never signed up to begin with.)

Why are books killed? It depends on whom you listen to. Authors will   3
tell you that publishers were afraid of the unvarnished truth. Some editors
will tell you that the books in question just weren't very good. But there are
some cases that seem indisputably to involve fear in publishing companies that
are part of corporate conglomerates—particularly concern not to offend company higher-ups in the movie end of the business. ("It's the newest way to
measure dick size in Hollywood," Anson says: "Whether you have enough
power to kill a book.") And corporate publishers seem to be especially unwilling to take risks to defend their books when libel suits, even unfounded

ones, are threatened. In the next few pages I examine a number of books that were killed in one way or another—books by established authors that can't be dismissed as "just not very good." Together they tell us something about where the increasing conglomeratization of publishing is taking us all.

M-G-M doesn't care what kind of book you write about its founder Louis B. Mayer, but the Disney Company cares deeply what you say about Walt. For sixty years the company has maintained a vast army of P.R. people promoting Walt as a kindly, child-loving, patriotic embodiment of all the true American virtues. Today, the $4.7 billion company he founded works relentlessly to protect his magical name, the name of the land that is "the happiest place on earth." Publishers know the Disney people are skilled at playing hardball; Marc Eliot learned that quickly when he set out to write the first independently researched Disney biography.   4

Eliot's book, *Walt Disney: Hollywood's Dark Prince,* was signed by Bantam in 1989 and killed in 1991. Eliot had already published two significant nonfiction books—a well-researched bio of Phil Ochs, published by Anchor, and a solid exposé of the music biz, *Rockonomics*—when he agreed with Charles Michener, editor at large at Bantam, to write a Disney biography. Twenty-four hours after the deal was signed, Eliot recalls, he got a call from Robyn Tynan in Disney's public relations department, telling him that Disney executives had read his proposal and were not happy. Neither Eliot nor Michener knew how Disney got a copy of his proposal.   5

The power of multinationals and conglomerates like Disney over the book industry has been growing steadily in the past decade. The Walt Disney Company not only makes movies and runs the world's various Disneylands, it owns The Disney Channel and a TV station, it records music and publishes books, it buys books to make into movies that are shown on its cable channel and it licenses products, songs and stories to publishers. Half a dozen other multinational media conglomerates do more or less the same thing: Time Warner, Times Mirror, Rupert Murdoch's News Corporation, Hearst, Bertelsmann. Their growing power to control the written word is bad news for readers, and for writers.   6

When Eliot made it clear to the Disney people that he wasn't going to back down, he was told that in that case Disney would like to open its archives to him and work with him to make sure he got it right. Eliot felt victorious. Then he got another call from Tynan, telling him that the Disney legal department wanted to review his completed manuscript before publication—to enable him to correct any errors. He agreed, but said he'd have to have the final say in any dispute. He remembers her replying, "Of course."   7

In Tynan's next call, she told Eliot the legal department now said they had to have the final say. He said he couldn't give them editorial control. "Then she says, 'We're going to offer to license the book and make it a Walt Disney product. You can make all the money, but we want to make it official. And we will not only cooperate, we will let you talk to everyone and give you   8 photos.'" He refused. When he went to Burbank for his first appointment with the head of the Disney studio archives, a security guard and a representative from Tynan's office escorted him off the grounds.

Robyn Tynan told me she didn't remember much about her contact with   9
Eliot, and explained, "By doing a license, we can be sure that all the information is correct. When a publisher doesn't want to do that, we say, 'Then we can't help you out with the book.'"

Eliot decided to push ahead without cooperation from Disney, and got   10
the agreement of Michener at Bantam. "Marc had done a tremendous number of interviews with people who had worked with Disney over the years," Michener recalled, "many of them in their 70s, no longer dependent on Disney, who had never talked to anyone before. They had fascinating things to say. . . . I thought, this is going to be one of the great Hollywood bios, way beyond the usual showbiz book."

A year and a half later Michener left Bantam, telling Eliot, "Don't   11
worry, your book is safe." A few weeks later, his new editor asked to see what he had done. He sent her forty pages of notes about Disney's childhood, he says, and explained that he was still researching the rest, and that his understanding with Michener was that he would take three or four years to write the book.

"She read my notes," Eliot recalls, "and she canceled the contract. She   12
said this was not of publishable quality. I said, 'This is not the book, these are notes. I'm waiting for Disney's F.B.I. file and I have reason to believe there is explosive material there. I have other material no one has ever dared write about. I can connect Disney to organized crime.' I ran the gamut. But I couldn't convince her." That was the only time he ever talked to her.

Then Eliot discovered that Bantam and Disney had a lucrative contract   13
for Bantam to publish children's book versions of Disney movies sold in supermarkets: the eighteen-volume "Disney Library," available since 1983 at $2.95 a volume, plus a twelve-volume "Disney Choose Your Own Adventure" series published in 1985–87 at $4.95 a volume. Eliot concluded that "there was no way Bantam was going to allow a critical bio of Walt Disney to be published while they were doing business with the Disney Company."

Michener comments, "It does seem very odd and unseemly if they re-   14
jected this book just on the basis of notes. It's not done—not to give him a chance to turn in a hundred pages. It invites the suspicion that there might have been nonliterary reasons, like not wanting to rock the boat with Disney."

Gene Young was the Bantam editor who killed the book. She subse-   15
quently left publishing. Asked what happened, she said "I don't think I should talk about that book," and referred me to Stuart Applebaum at Bantam. Linda Grey was president of Bantam when the book was killed; today she is president and publisher of Ballantine Books at Random House. She was unavailable for comment; her assistant also suggested I call Applebaum. When I asked Applebaum, the spokesman for Bantam, whether a conflict of interest had led to the killing of Eliot's book, he said, "I vigorously and laughingly deny it on behalf of the company." He added, "You'd have a hard time finding a publisher

without some Disney-oriented licensed book product in some aspect of their publishing program." But that's precisely the problem: A muckraking book like Eliot's would have a hard time finding a major publisher who doesn't have a conflict of interest.

Eliot took the book to Birch Lane Press, an imprint of Carol Publishing   16
Group, a privately owned company. *Walt Disney: Hollywood's Dark Prince* has a July 1993 pub date. *Publisher's Weekly* just gave the book a rave: "Meticulously researched and replete with surprises, this is a major biography." The *Kirkus* review was also strong. A *New York Times* feature story on the book explained why it was objectionable to the Walt Disney Company: Eliot revealed that Walt worked for twenty-five years as an F.B.I. informant. National Public Radio reported that "the man who created Mickey Mouse was a rat"; on his public radio program, Harry Shearer sang, "When you snitch upon a star." A Disney spokesman denounced Eliot. In short, the book was getting the kind of high-profile news coverage any publisher would be thrilled to receive—unless the publisher was doing business with Disney.

Would Eliot write a new book for Bantam tomorrow? "Probably," he   17
answers. "In publishing the cards are stacked against writers so much that you have to be able to work with the field. Otherwise you blacklist yourself."

18

Christopher Byron also wrote a book that offended the powerful. In his case, he did not realize that the story he told involved the wife of the president of the conglomerate that owned his publisher. The book was published, but it was promoted so feebly that it amounted to killing it. Byron writes the business column for *New York* magazine and is the author of *The Fanciest Dive,* the highly praised book about Time Inc.'s *TV-Cable Week* fiasco. Simon and Schuster signed him up to write *Skin Tight: The Bizarre Story of Guess v. Jordache,* a book that tells a great story: the most vicious fight in the history of the garment industry, a twisted feud for control over Guess jeans between two rival families of immigrant Jews from the Middle East and North Africa. The three Nakash brothers of Jordache and the four Marciano brothers of Guess were terrific businessmen, but they hated each other. A simple civil lawsuit between them over a breach of contract escalated into rival grand jury investigations in Los Angeles and New York as each side went to U.S. Attorneys to stir up tax fraud investigations of the other. Eventually this culminated in Congressional hearings on corruption in the I.R.S.

Byron learned that the Nakash family's charges against the Marcianos   19
made use of information they got from the former wife of Georges Marciano, the founder of Guess jeans. Her name was Melinda; she had started out working at the Marciano retail boutique in Beverly Hills. She and Marciano divorced shortly after the birth of her son.

The Nakash lawyers obtained a declaration in which Melinda de-   20
scribed her husband and his brothers bringing home large amounts of cash and dividing it up—she described one occasion on which "I personally counted $25,000 in cash." The Nakashes presented this as their primary evidence that the Marcianos were taking kickbacks from suppliers, skimming

perhaps millions of dollars from the company. Melinda then dropped from the story and disappeared from view after the divorce proceeding. Byron never interviewed her; his reporting was based on her legal declaration.

Simon and Schuster's catalogue announced a "four-city author tour" for 21 *Skin Tight* and "national advertising, including *The Wall Street Journal.*" The jacket blurbs were sensational (Alan Dershowitz called the book "a great read" that proved that "the ends just don't justify the jeans") and the pre-publication reviews were strong. *Kirkus* praised *Skin Tight* as "a first-rate and stylish account . . . as engrossing as it is nauseating." *Publishers Weekly* called it an "evocative" book with "a cast worthy of a suspense novel." And there was talk of a big movie deal—so bound galleys were sent to Paramount Pictures, the studio affiliated with Simon and Schuster through their corporate parent, Paramount Communications.

Just as the presses were set to roll, Byron received a call from his editor, 22 Bob Bender, who told him that Paramount wanted all references to Melinda Marciano to come out of the book. When he asked why, he was told that Marciano's ex-wife had undergone the greatest makeover in the history of Beverly Hills and was now married to Stanley Jaffe, the president of Paramount Communications.

So Byron went to work revising the book, now in bound galleys. He couldn't 23 remove Melinda completely because she was key to half the story. But her name was deleted virtually everywhere in the book: In the index she is referred to as "Marciano, Mrs. Georges"; in the text she is called "the missus," "the woman," and "Mrs. Marciano." Her name appears only once in the book: the endnotes cite "Declaration of Melinda Marciano." Byron refused to cut that because he felt he had to provide complete documentation of his sources.

The book was then published—but just barely, Byron says, without any 24 of the fanfare that had been promised. Byron had heard the first printing was to be 35,000–40,000; now he found out the press run had been cut to 11,000. His publicity bookings were canceled, and the promised national advertising never appeared. Simon and Schuster apparently made no attempt to sell the paperback rights. After a 2,000-word review on the cover of the *Los Angeles Times* Sunday book section, the book sank without a trace. Byron was so disheartened he never talked to anyone at Simon and Schuster about what had happened; he told friends he was shattered by the experience.

When I called Simon and Schuster, the operator answered, "Paramount 25 Communications." When I asked Byron's editor, Bob Bender, what happened with *Skin Tight,* he said only "I don't want to get into that." There's no reason to think that Stanley Jaffe himself demanded that his new wife be taken out of a Simon and Schuster book—it could well have been other Paramount employees, who knew that their jobs included protecting the boss from embarrassment.

The most recent victim of corporate murder, Robert Sam Anson's book-in- 26 progress at Simon and Schuster, is tentatively titled *The Rules of the Magic.* It was killed by S&S in March, before the due date, before he handed in a word of it. Anson had written his last book, *War News: A Young Reporter in In-dochina,* for Simon and Schuster in 1989 with editor Alice Mayhew, with whom he had developed a close relationship. He submitted a long list of possible topics for his next book, and Mayhew settled on the Disney idea; Anson moved to California with his family and went to work. The deal, signed in May 1991, was for $400,000, with an advance of $160,000. Serious medical problems afflicting his daughter slowed him down, but Mayhew convinced him to keep working.

The contract provided for a payment of $40,000 on presentation of evidence that a major portion of the research was finished. Anson and his six assistants had completed 375 interviews, he says, so he submitted his evidence this past February. According to Peter Shepherd, Anson's agent, "Alice said, 'This is super, the check is on its way.'"   27

Then, Shepherd recalls, "All of a sudden she invited me over to Simon and Schuster. When I arrived, there she was with her boss Carolyn Reidy. They announced to me they were going to drop the book. They said, 'We think Anson has to talk to some people at Paramount.' I said, 'Oh?' They said, 'And we don't think the people at Paramount are going to want to talk to him. And we can't help him. And therefore we have to terminate the contract.'" Shepherd concludes, "It was one of the most peculiar experiences I've had in thirty-five years of publishing."   28

Why would "the people at Paramount" pose a problem for a book on Disney studios? Anson thinks the problem was Martin Davis, chairman of Paramount Communications, which owns Simon and Schuster. Davis is relevant to a book on Disney studios because Disney hired its two top executives, Michael Eisner and Jeffrey Katzenberg, away from Paramount, where they had worked under Davis.   29

"I told Alice that Marty Davis was going to get roughed up a bit," Anson said, "but she didn't know any specifics. Two weeks after that conversation she called and said, 'We're concerned about you getting to sources.' I said, 'Like who?' She said, 'Barry Diller.' She didn't ask about anybody else. I can only surmise that they didn't want me to talk to Barry Diller. Nobody knows Marty Davis better or has a better reason to dislike him. Davis can't stand bad publicity—he loathes it as a matter of principle. He was concerned about what other people would be telling about him. And there's a lot to tell."   30

Anson got a distinguished First Amendment litigator, Martin Garbus, to represent him, and filed a million-dollar breach of contract lawsuit against Simon and Schuster. Why did Garbus, who has represented Andrei Sakharov, Nelson Mandela and Vaclav Havel, take Anson's case? "There's a relationship between free speech issues and publishing issues," Garbus explains. "It's important to protect authors with rules and requirements that relate to the publication of books." Anson does something like 350 interviews and they say they're dissatisfied. I've never seen that happen. They could have waited to see the manuscript, but their reasons for turning it down were transparent.   31

"Alice Mayhew is basically a fine editor who has done controversial books," Garbus said. "It was inconceivable to her that she would be faced with this problem. She would have liked to see the book published. But she can't say   32 that." Anson commented, "Marty Davis did not expect the publishing company he owns would turn around and hire a writer for 400,000 bucks who was going to trash him."

The lawsuit, filed in mid-March charged that the decision to suppress the book's publication was "the result of outside pressure from S&S's parent company, Paramount Communications, Inc., other persons and/or entities opposed to the book's publication." Jerry Sherman, Paramount's senior vice president for corporate communications, told the press that Anson's claims were "absolutely absurd" and "sheer fabrication and nonsense." 33

The S&S denial met with widespread skepticism. "Anson is a serious guy, a hard-working journalist who has written several good books," said Robert Scheer of the *Los Angeles Times.* "He's a fast, productive writer. He's been researching the hell out of this book." Anson has a track record; his seven previous books include the 1987 *Best Intentions: The Education and Killing of Edmund Perry,* published by Random House, which got impressive reviews; he's also written for *The New York Times, The Washington Post, Harper's, The Atlantic, Time* and *Esquire.* 34

The Authors Guild filed an affidavit in the suit supporting Anson, expressing "extreme concern" about the role of Paramount Communications in killing the book. PEN issued a similar statement. The story has a happy ending, though: Simon and Schuster settled the suit; the amount Anson received is confidential, but, Garbus said, "We are very pleased." Pantheon picked up the book; publishing industry sources say Anson's deal with them is for $300,000. And Disney has told Anson the company will give him full cooperation. 35

Anson and Byron both ran into the same problem: The values of entertainment conglomerates have infected book publishing. If a magazine wants to run an article on a star, the reporter does not ask for an interview; instead the magazine contacts the star's publicist, who first negotiates the placement of the piece—on the cover, the lead piece, whatever. Then they negotiate who will write it. The press is regarded as the P.R. apparatus of the entertainment business, and it's good business to use whatever power or influence you have to get good P.R. The rise of conglomerate publishing brought Paramount, Disney, Time Warner and others to impose those values on the publishers they own. 36

Defenders of conglomerate publishers argue that their immense size is a virtue because it enables them to stand up to the most dangerous form of censorship—pressure from the government itself. Several significant cases suggest the weakness of that argument. Thomas Hauser wrote the book that was made into the 1982 Costa-Gavras film *Missing.* The paperback edition was killed by Avon Books, a Hearst subsidiary, when author, publisher and filmmaker were sued for libel. 37

Missing was one of the great political films of the eighties. Like Hauser's book, it told the true story of Charles Horman, killed in the U.S.-backed coup that overthrew Salvador Allende and Chilean democracy in 1973. Horman's father, a deeply conservative man, traveled to Chile to look for him and came to the conclusion that U.S. officials were involved in his disappearance and in the coup. After the film came out, a libel suit was filed by three State 38

Department officials, including Nixon's Ambassador to Chile in 1973, Nathaniel Davis, who sought $150 million in damages.

Hauser, a lawyer with a big firm who decided he's rather write, had   39
originally published his book in hardcover with Harcourt Brace Jovanovich in 1978 under the title *The Execution of Charles Horman*. Harcourt sold the paperback rights to Avon, which published first in 1980 under the original title; up to this point nobody sued. The paperback was republished in 1982 as a movie tie-in under the new title; the State Department officials sued in 1983, and Avon then took the book out of print. Attorney Richard Bellman, who represented Hauser, recalled that "Avon said, 'We know there's nothing wrong with the book, but we are afraid of the costs of litigation and it's simpler for us to take it out of print.'"

The lawsuits against the book were dismissed as frivolous, but Avon still   40
would not put the book back in print—they said they feared they might be sued again. Hauser asked his publishers to revert the rights to him so that he could find somebody else to publish it; they said no, the book had commercial value and they might want to publish it in the future to make some money from it. Hauser had to sue his publishers in 1985 to get the rights back.

On the eve of the trial, Hauser's publishers settled. Avon and Harcourt   41
reverted the rights to him and paid him a huge settlement, insisting on confidentiality regarding the amount. Finally a new paperback edition was published by Touchstone—a Simon and Schuster imprint—in 1988. In the meantime the book had been kept out of print for five years by the publisher, including the time the movie was in theaters and then shown on TV (despite the continuing libel suits against the movie, it was broadcast on cable TV and then on CBS in 1985), when it would have found its largest readership.

The State Department officials who sued never sought to stop distribu-   42
tion of the book, and no court ever ordered any such action. Nathaniel Davis retired from the Foreign Service and joined the faculty at Harvey Mudd College in California, where he is now a professor of humanities.

Peter Matthiessen also learned that publishers have trouble standing up to gov-   43
ernment officials—in his case, the officials he criticized in his magnificent book *In the Spirit of Crazy Horse*. Published by Viking in 1983, it provided a solidly documented account of the events that culminated in a 1975 gun battle on the Pine Ridge Reservation in South Dakota between F.B.I. agents and members of the American Indian Movement (AIM) that left two agents and one Indian dead. Matthiessen is one of America's most acclaimed writers; *The New York Times Book Review* called *In the Spirit of Crazy Horse* "one of those rare books that permanently change one's consciousness." In the trial following the shootout, Leonard Peltier, an Ojibwa-Sioux AIM activist, was convicted of murdering the agents; now 48, he is serving consecutive life sentences at the federal penitentiary in Leavenworth, Kansas. Matthiessen's book presented compelling evidence that Peltier is innocent.

Shortly after the book's publication, South Dakota's Governor, William   44
Janklow, filed a libel suit against Matthiessen and his publisher, Viking Press, seeking $24 million in damages, and an F.B.I. agent involved in the case filed a

second suit for $25 million. Viking responded to the lawsuits by destroying the copies of the book it had in its warehouse and taking it out of print for seven years. Matthiessen was "horrified and indignant" over the destruction of his books, his wife said in an interview. "I did not agree to the destruction of my books," Matthiessen himself told me. "I didn't know about it. I felt they never should have withdrawn the book in the first place. It seemed to me over-cautious. Martin Garbus, their lawyer, told me he didn't think Viking should have withdrawn the book until they had a judgment against them in court."

Garbus, asked in an interview to comment, said, "The publishers told   45
me they didn't destroy anything." Viking decided to delay publication of the paperback, he said, because under the law the paperback would have been a new edition and thus more vulnerable to the libel suit than the hardcover had been—since the publisher had been informed that facts reported in the hard-cover were in dispute.

The libel cases were finally thrown out of court in 1990, and Viking at   46
last reissued the book the following year. In the meantime, the strongest case for Peltier's innocence had been kept from the public for seven years.

In both the Hauser and Matthiessen cases, publishers pursued overly cau-   47
tious strategies in response to libel suits. Large publishers who can afford libel insurance might in principle be expected to defend their books more vigor-ously against baseless libel suits than small ones. Yet the companies seem to be motivated more by fear and greed than by a commitment to their readers, their writers or the First Amendment.

Books about organized crime also raise publishers' fears of libel suits—even the   48
biggest publishers, as two *Time* magazine writers discovered. *Connections: American Business and the Mob* by Roy Rowan and Sandy Smith, was killed in 1990 by Little, Brown & Company, at the time a subsidiary of Time Inc. *Time* had reported back in 1981 that Reagan's Secretary of Labor, Raymond Dono-van, was linked to organized crime through a New Jersey firm, Schiavone Construction, of which he had been an executive. The author of the piece was Sandy Smith, one of the country's top mob reporters. Schiavone sued *Time* for libel in 1983. Smith and Rowan then wrote their book on American business and the mob, which included several chapters on Donovan's alleged mob ties, the Schiavone libel suit and the cover-up by the F.B.I. of what Attorney Gen-eral Edwin Meese described as "the possibility of organized crime ties involv-ing Donovan." *Time* fought the libel suit for five years, and federal district courts dismissed it twice. Then, as the Time Warner merger loomed, *Time* re-versed course and paid Schiavone half a million dollars to settle the suit. Sandy Smith was outraged and *Time* execs knew it. Less than a year later, Little, Brown killed the book.

The Rowan-Smith book had been listed in the fall 1989 Little, Brown   49
catalogue as forthcoming that October. It reproduced the jacket and extolled the book's exposé of "the delicately balanced system of 'business arrangements' among criminals, politicians and business leaders in this country." The cata-logue also announced "national advertising and promotion/national author

publicity." Howard Kaminsky, formerly a top editor at Random House and currently C.E.O. of William Morrow, told Richard Clurman in regard to this case, "in twenty-three years of publishing, I have never known of a book that was copy edited, advertised in the catalogue, and then withdrawn. It's almost unheard of—and very strange, even suspicious." Between the catalogue and the killing came an unusual four-month legal review; of the book's twenty chapters, Rowan and Smith were questioned only about the four that dealt with the history that culminated in *Time*'s decision to settle with Schiavone.

Why Little, Brown killed the book one month before the Time Warner 50
merger is still hotly debated. "*Time* suddenly sold out," Sandy Smith told *The New York Times,* "as they cleared the decks to merge with Warner." *Time* may have wanted to reassure Warner that it would shy away from tough reporting about corporate ties to organized crime, including problems at Warner. That theory was put forward in the rarest of all publishing events, when two former board members of Time Inc. joined the authors in criticizing the decision to cancel the book and charged that the decision was made not by the publisher but by the parent company.

Little, Brown's chief executive, Kevin Dolan, and Roger Donald, editor 51
of the book, insisted that the decision to cancel the book had been theirs, based on a report from the company's attorney, John Taylor Williams, that the book "contains libelous material." Martin Garbus, who read the same manuscript later when it was submitted to another publisher, told me he saw no libel problems in the book.

When the authors threatened to sue Time Warner for $1.5 million for 52
breach of contract, the company settled, paying the two authors an amount reported by Clurman, a former Time Inc. executive, to be "under $500,000." The book never found another publisher. John Hawkins, the agent who represented the authors, explained that "Little, Brown sat and sat on it, and by the time we were able to take it elsewhere it wouldn't have appeared for another year; in the meantime some of the material had come out in other stories. Some publishers were interested, but at reduced levels of advance."

Roy Rowan today says, "I have very good relations with all the people at 53
Time Warner. I've spent my whole life at that place. These are my very good friends." But things have been different for Sandy Smith. He put his house in Maryland up for sale and moved to Montana. Reached at his new home in Seeley Lake, a tiny town near Glacier National Park, all he would say was, "I just don't want to get into it." Friends say the man who was regarded by many as the premier mob reporter in the country now spends his time hunting and fishing.

The Rowan–Smith book on connections between American business 54
and the mob was "one of those inside stories about how our society really works," Sydney Schanberg wrote. The killing of that book is another one of those stories.

The problem of conglomerate control of publishing was laid out a decade ago 55
by Ben Bagdikian in his book *The Media Monopoly,* published in 1983 by

Beacon Press. In a perfect illustration of the problem he was describing, while his book was being edited its publisher received a letter from Simon and Schuster demanding to see a copy of the manuscript before publication, as well as the right to delete anything the company considered defamatory to S&S; they threatened legal action if these demands were not granted. Bagdikian and Beacon of course refused, and took the story to the press. "That was a great boost for the book," said Bagdikian, now dean emeritus of the school of journalism at the University of California, Berkeley—"a powerful publisher trying to censor the book of a small publisher."

What Simon and Schuster wanted to delete was Bagdikian's report that 56 in 1979 the publisher had killed a book called *Corporate Murder* proposed by Mark Dowie, the investigative reporter who discovered that the Ford Motor Company had designed the Pinto car with gas tanks it knew to be dangerous, after having decided that it was cheaper to pay off heirs of those killed in accidents than to spend the few dollars per car that would have made them safer. Bagdikian reported that the editor of the book, Nan Talese, told the author that Simon and Schuster president Richard Snyder "was vehemently opposed to the manuscript because, among other reasons, he felt it made all corporations look bad."

In response to the storm of bad publicity, Simon and Schuster press re- 57 leases declared it was not true that *Corporate Murder* had been killed because of pressure from Gulf + Western (which changed its name to Paramount Communications in 1989). Bagdikian replied that he had never made such a charge. "The point in my book is quite the opposite," he said. "It is that without any pressure, it is natural and inevitable that important people in a media subsidiary will be conscious of who their owners are. I have never had any reason to believe that Mr. Snyder rejected the book for anything other than sincere personal judgments."

Bagdikian's argument seems irrefutable: "A corporation dependent on 58 public opinion and government policy can call upon its media subsidiaries to help in what the media are clearly able to do—influence public opinion and government policy. At the very least, the corporation can make sure that one subsidiary does no preventable harm to another." It was an unfortunate irony for Mark Dowie that his title—*Corporate Murder*—described his book's fate. Today Dowie continues to work as an investigative reporter . . . .

What explains the spate of books killed lately by conglomerate publishers? 59 "The publishing business doesn't have a very high return on your money—6 percent," says Erica Jong, past president of the Authors Guild, whose most recent book, *The Devil at Large,* is about Henry Miller. "If you were investing for maximum return, you wouldn't invest in a publishing house. The reason people invest in publishing houses is to control the word. As long as Robert Maxwell owned the *News* he was 'Cap'n Bob' and they were writing wonderful things about him. When he went over the edge of his ship, he was suddenly discovered to be a crook who had looted the pension fund."

E. L. Doctorow explained the situation when he testified on behalf of 60 PEN before the Senate Antitrust and Monopoly Subcommittee in 1980.

"Apart from the good motives or the honor or the seriousness of purpose of any particular publisher or editor," he said, "the concentration into fewer and fewer hands of the production and distribution of literary work is by its nature constricting to free speech and the effective exchange of ideas and the diversity of opinion." While journalism, television and the film industry have long since been dominated by a few giant corporations, book publishing until recently remained "a cottage industry . . . spread among many hands, the decision-making process dispersed into thousands of independent and unconnected hands." That is what has changed.

The media conglomerates call what they are doing "synergy"—getting   61
all the parts of the company to work together to promote a single product: the movie, the book tie-in, the soundtrack album, the magazine features, the TV show appearances, the cable broadcasts, the videocassette, the mass-market paperback. "You can call that synergy," Erica Jong says, "or you can call it fixing the press. We're looking at a cynical attempt to control information. That's all it is. It's a desperate situation." ■

Questions for Meaning

1. How can publishers "kill a book"?
2. Judging from the information reported in this article, why do publishers decide to kill books that are of sufficiently good quality to deserve publication?
3. What economic factors have led to the concentration of power in the publishing industry?
4. How are the publishing decisions discussed by Wiener related to concerns about freedom of expression? Are these publishers violating the First Amendment?
5. According to this article, why do people invest in publishing houses when they could be earning a higher rate of return by investing in other kinds of business?
6. Vocabulary: conglomerates (1), lucrative (13), muckraking (15), blacklist (17), kickbacks (20), fabrication (33), affidavit (35), defamatory (55), spate (59).

Questions about Strategy

1. Of the five books Wiener discusses in this article, two are about Walt Disney, and one of these books appears in the first sentence. Why do you think Wiener chose to give so much attention to the Disney organization?
2. Authors who feel that they have been mistreated by their publishers may be biased sources of information. How does Wiener demonstrate that he did not rely exclusively on such authors for his research?
3. Consider the order in which Wiener has arranged the books discussed in this article. Why do you think they appear in this order?

4. Why do you think Wiener chose to write this article? If what he reports about the publishing industry is true, do you think he could have damaged his career? What can you infer about *The Nation,* the magazine that first published "Murdered Ink"?

JANICE EIDUS

CHILLING TRENDS

Is censorship something that happens to people? Or can it also be something that people do to themselves? Writer Janice Eidus explores both of these questions in the following essay, first published by *ANQ* in 1992. Originally titled *American Notes and Queries,* and published by the University of Kentucky, *ANQ* features short articles such as the one featured here. It was originally published under the title "Censorship from Without, Censorship from Within: Chilling Trends."

A dark cloud hovers over artistic expression in the United States today. A   1
reactionary, moralistic, conservatism is in the air, reflected by intolerance, fear, and scapegoating: established artistic institutions such as the National Endowment for the Arts are attacked on so-called "moral" grounds; books are banned from our libraries and schools, including the fairy tale, "Snow White"; important experimental venues for the arts are drained of financial resources, such as New York City's La Mama Theater; our government and our publishing institutions offer no strong, concerted, activist defense for Salmon Rushdie.

The United States economy is in terrible shape and all areas of the book   2
world have been hit hard, creating economic censorship, which goes hand in hand with "moralistic" censorship. Commercial and independent publishers alike are folding, and those that survive are cutting back their literary lists. Bookstores, too, are folding, and those that remain (chains and independents) are cutting back their orders and keeping the books they do order on their shelves for no longer than a few weeks (virtually no time at all, particularly for serious fiction, which has a very difficult time getting reviewed, and which rarely is accompanied by a major advertising campaign). Libraries, too, are closing branches, and those that remain are cutting back their hours and drastically cutting back their orders for books. In the midst of all this, the creators of the books—the authors—are having an increasingly difficult time finding publishers, and even those writers that do are earning so little money from advances and royalties that very few serious authors can survive (even minimally) on their writing efforts. As a result, in order to survive, writers have less and less time to devote to their writing.

And worst of all, it seems to me, is the *self*-censorship that politically   3
fostered moral and economic censorship can create among writers. It has become all too common these days for writers to plan to submit timid, bland,
"least offensive" stories (and, in some cases, to write such stories hurriedly) to
the N.E.A., in hopes of getting a grant, and to magazines and publishers, in
hopes of appearing in print. These stories, in other words, are stories without
any sexual scenes, stories that raise no issues of class, or race, or gender politics,
stories that are devoid of stylistic innovation, stories that do no more than fearfully celebrate and reinforce the status quo. I have sat among groups of writers
as they help one another to figure out—in cynical, defeated tones—which is
their least offensive work, work that will, therefore, have the greatest chance
of being rewarded.

This self-censorship is the trend that I fear most of all. We as working   4
writers—and as citizens—must *not* lapse into this timidity and mediocrity,
this passivity and accommodation. We must *not* become our own censors, we
must not give in. We must not become weak, and cynical, and terrified. We
must stand by each other, and find ways to publish ourselves, and one another;
we must continue to take risks; we must continue to challenge ourselves artistically, intellectually, and politically. Sinclair Lewis showed us that it *can* happen here; the McCarthy hearings and the lives ruined by those hearings are
proof that it *has* happened here; and the trends I am witnessing today make me
fear that it *will* happen here—again.   ■

Questions for Meaning

1. What does Eidus mean by "economic censorship"?
2. Why does Eidus find "*self*-censorship" especially objectionable?
3. Eidus alludes to Salmon Rushdie, Sinclair Lewis, and the McCarthy
   hearings. How do these references relate to concerns over freedom of
   expression?
4. Vocabulary: reactionary (1), scapegoating (1), virtually (2), devoid (3),
   innovation (3), accommodation (4).

Questions about Strategy

1. Although Eidus is concerned about writers, she locates her concern
   within the broader context of "artistic expression." What does paragraph 1 contribute to the essay as a whole?
2. In paragraph 3, Eidus notes with disappointment that writers she knows
   are now evaluating their work to discover which is their "least offensive." What assumption is she making about a writer's responsibilities?
   Do you agree with this assumption?
3. Consider the frequent use of "we" in paragraph 4. Why do you think
   Eidus chose to use this word so often in her conclusion?

GARRY WILLS

IN PRAISE OF CENSURE

A graduate of St. Louis University who received his Ph.D. from Yale in 1961, Garry Wills is widely recognized as a writer who applies the critical techniques of a scholar to the discussion of political and religious issues. For *Inventing America* (1978), he won the National Book Critics Circle Award in 1979. His other books include *Nixon Agonistes* (1970), *Bare Ruined Choirs* (1972), *Confessions of a Conservative* (1979), *Reagan's America* (1987) and *Under God: Religion and American Politics* (1990). He also contributes to numerous periodicals, including the *New York Review of Books, Harper's,* and *Time,* which published the following essay in 1989.

Rarely have the denouncers of censorship been so eager to start practicing it.   1
When a sense of moral disorientation overcomes a society, people from the least expected quarters begin to ask, "Is nothing sacred?" Feminists join reactionaries to denounce pornography as demeaning to women. Rock musician Frank Zappa declares that when Tipper Gore, the wife of Senator Albert Gore from Tennessee, asked music companies to label sexually explicit material, she launched an illegal "conspiracy to extort." A *Penthouse* editorialist says that housewife Terry Rakolta, who asked sponsors to withdraw support from a sitcom called *Married . . . With Children,* is "yelling fire in a crowded theater," a formula that says her speech is not protected by the First Amendment.

But the most interesting movement to limit speech is directed at defama-   2
tory utterances against blacks, homosexuals, Jews, women or other stigmatizable groups. It took no Terry Rakolta of the left to bring about the instant firing of Jimmy the Greek and Al Campanis from sports jobs when they made racially denigrating comments. Social pressure worked far more quickly on them than on *Married . . . With Children,* which is still on the air.

The rules being considered on college campuses to punish students for   3
making racist and other defamatory remarks go beyond social and commercial pressure to actual legal muzzling. The right-wing *Dartmouth Review* and its imitators have understandably infuriated liberals, who are beginning to take action against them and the racist expressions they have encouraged. The American Civil Liberties Union considered this movement important enough to make it the principal topic at its biennial meeting last month in Madison, Wisconsin. Ironically, the regents of the University of Wisconsin had passed their own rules against defamation just before the ACLU members convened on the university's campus. Nadine Strossen, of New York University School of Law, who was defending the ACLU's traditional position on free speech, said of Wisconsin's new rules, "You can tell how bad they are by the fact that the regents had to make an amendment at the last minute exempting classroom discussion! What is surprising is that Donna Shalala [chancellor of the university] went along with it." So did constitutional lawyers on the faculty.

If a similar code were drawn up with right-wing imperatives in mind—   4
one banning unpatriotic, irreligious or sexually explicit expressions on
campus—the people framing Wisconsin-type rules would revert to their liber-
atarian pasts. In this competition to suppress, is regard for freedom of expression just a matter of whose ox is getting gored at the moment? Does the left
just get nervous about the Christian cross when Klansmen burn it, while the
right will react only when Madonna flirts crucifixes between her thighs?

The cries of "un-American" are as genuine and as frequent on either   5
side. Everyone is protecting the country. Zappa accuses Gore of undermining
the moral fiber of America with the "sexual neuroses of these vigilant ladies."
He argues that she threatens our freedoms with "connubial insider trading"
because her husband is a Senator. Apparently her marital status should deprive
her of speaking privileges in public—an argument Westbrook Pegler used to
make against Eleanor Roosevelt.★ *Penthouse* says Rakolta is taking us down the
path toward fascism. It attacks her for living in a rich suburb—the old "radical
chic" argument that rich people cannot support moral causes.

There is a basic distinction that cuts through this free-for-all over free-   6
dom. It is the distinction, too often neglected, between censorship and censure
(the free expression of moral disapproval). What the campuses are trying to do
(at least those with state money) is use the force of government to contain
freedom of speech. What Donald Wildman, the free-lance moralist from Tu-
pelo, Miss., does when he gets Pepsi to cancel its Madonna ad is censure the ad
by calling for a boycott. Advocating boycotts is a form of speech protected by
the First Amendment. As Nat Hentoff, journalistic custodian of the First
Amendment, says, "I would hate to see boycotts outlawed. Think what that
would do to Cesar Chavez." Or, for that matter, to Ralph Nader.† If one dis-
approves of a social practice, whether it is racist speech or unjust hiring in lettuce fields, one is free to denounce that and to call on others to express their
disapproval. Otherwise there would be no form of persuasive speech except
passing a law. This would make the law coterminous with morality.

Equating morality with legality is in effect what people do when they   7
claim that anything tolerated by law must, in the name of freedom, be approved by citizens in all their dealings with one another. As Zappa says,
"Masturbation is not illegal. If it is not illegal to do it, why should it be illegal to sing about it?" He thinks this proves that Gore, who is not trying to
make raunch in rock illegal, cannot even ask distributors to label it. Anything goes, as long as it's legal. The odd consequence of this argument would
be a drastic narrowing of the freedom of speech. One could not call into
question anything that was not against the law—including, for instance,
racist speech.

★Journalist Westbrook Pegler (1894–1969) frequently criticized First Lady Eleanor Roosevelt
(1884–1962) for speaking on behalf of social reform.

†When Cesar Chavez organized farm workers to secure better wages and living conditions,
concerned citizens refused to buy lettuce grown with non-union labor. Ralph Nader is a
consumer advocate who has drawn attention to unsafe products and questionable business
procedures.

A false ideal of tolerance has not only outlawed censorship but discour-   8
aged censoriousness (another word for censure). Most civilizations have expressed their moral values by mobilization of social opprobrium. That, rather
than specific legislation, is what changed the treatment of minorities in films
and TV over recent years. One can now draw opprobrious attention by gay
bashing, as the Beastie Boys rock group found when their distributor told
them to cut out remarks about "fags" for business reasons. Or by anti-
Semitism, as the just disbanded rap group Public Enemy has discovered.

It is said that only the narrow-minded are intolerant or opprobrious.   9
Most of those who limited the distribution of Martin Scorsese's movie *The
Last Temptation of Christ* had not even seen the movie. So do we guarantee
freedom of speech only for the broad-minded or the better educated? Can
one speak only after studying whatever one has reason, from one's beliefs, to
denounce? Then most of us would be doing a great deal less speaking than we
do. If one has never seen any snuff movies, is that a bar to criticizing them?

Others argue that asking people not to buy lettuce is different from ask-   10
ing them not to buy a rocker's artistic expression. Ideas (carefully disguised)
lurk somewhere in the lyrics. All the more reason to keep criticism of them
free. If ideas are too important to suppress, they are also too important to ignore. The whole point of free speech is not to make ideas exempt from criticism but to expose them to it.

One of the great mistakes of liberals in recent decades has been the ced-   11
ing of moral concern to right-wingers. Just because one opposes censorship,
one need not be seen as agreeing with pornographers. Why should liberals, of
all people, oppose Gore when she asks that labels be put on products meant
for the young, to inform those entrusted by law with the care of the young?
Liberals were the first to promote "healthy" television shows like *Sesame
Street* and *The Electric Company*. In the 1950s and 1960s they were the leading
critics of television, of its mindless violence, of the way it ravaged the attention span needed for reading. Who was keeping kids away from TV sets
then? How did promoters of Big Bird let themselves be cast as champions
of the Beastie Boys—not just of their *right* to perform but of their performance itself? Why should it be left to Gore to express moral disapproval of a
group calling itself Dead Kennedys (sample lyric: "I kill children, I love to
see them die")?

For that matter, who has been more insistent that parents should   12
"interfere" in what their children are doing, Tipper Gore or Jesse Jackson? All
through the 1970s, Jackson was traveling the high schools, telling parents to
turn off TVs, make the kids finish their homework, check with teachers on
their performance, get to know what the children are doing. This kind of
"interference" used to be called education.

Belief in the First Amendment does not pre-empt other beliefs, making   13
one a eunuch to the interplay of opinions. It is a distortion to turn "You can
express any views" into the proposition "I don't care what views you express."
If liberals keep equating equality with approval, they will be repeatedly forced
into weak positions.

A case in point is the Corcoran Gallery's sudden cancellation of an ex-   14
hibit of Robert Mapplethorpe's photographs. The whole matter was needlessly
confused when the director, Christina Owr-Chall, claimed she was canceling
the show to *protect* it from censorship. She meant that there might be pressure
to remove certain pictures—the sadomasochistic ones or those verging on kid-
die porn—if the show had gone on. But she had in mind, as well, the hope of
future grants from the National Endowment for the Arts, which is under criticism for the Mapplethorpe show and for another show that contained Andres
Serrano's *Piss Christ,* the photograph of a crucifix in what the title says is
urine. Owr-Chall is said to be yielding to censorship, when she is clearly
yielding to political and financial pressure, as Pepsi yielded to commercial
pressure over the Madonna ad.

What is at issue here is not government suppression but government sub-   15
sidy. Mapplethorpe's work is not banned, but showing it might have endangered federal grants to needy artists. The idea that what the government does
not support it represses is nonsensical, as one can see by reversing the statement
to read: "No one is allowed to create anything without the government's subvention." What pussycats our supposedly radical artists are. They not only
want the government's permission to create their artifacts, they want federal
authorities to supply the materials as well. Otherwise they feel "gagged." If
they are not given government approval (and money), they want to remain an
avant-grade while being bankrolled by the Old Guard.

What is easily forgotten in this argument is the right of citizen taxpayers.   16
They send representatives to Washington who are answerable for the expendi-
ture of funds exacted from them. In general these voters want to favor their
own values if government is going to get into the culture-subsidizing area at
all (a proposition many find objectionable in itself). Politicians, insofar as they
support the arts, will tend to favor conventional art (certainly not masochistic
art). Anybody who doubts that has no understanding of a politician's legitimate concern for his or her constituents' approval. Besides, it is quaint for
those familiar with the politics of the art world to discover, with a shock, that
there is politics in politics.

Luckily, cancellation of the Mapplethorpe show forced some artists back   17
to the flair and cheekiness of unsubsidized art. Other results of pressure do not
turn out as well. Unfortunately, people in certain regions were deprived of the
chance to see *The Last Temptation of Christ* in the theater. Some, no doubt,
considered it a loss that they could not buy lettuce or grapes during a Chavez
boycott. Perhaps there was even a buyer perverse enough to miss driving the
unsafe cars Nader helped pressure off the market. On the other hand, we do
not get sports analysis made by racists. These mobilizations of social opprobrium are not examples of repression but of freedom of expression by committed people who censured without censoring, who expressed the kinds of belief
the First Amendment guarantees. I do not, as a result, get whatever I approve
of subsidized, either by Pepsi or the government. But neither does the law
come in to silence Tipper Gore or Frank Zappa or even that filthy rag, the
Dartmouth Review.

Questions for Meaning

1. How does Wills define the difference between *censorship* and *censure?*
2. According to Wills, what is the purpose of free speech?
3. Why does Wills find it ironic when liberals oppose record labeling?
4. In paragraph 15 Wills writes, "The idea that what the government does not support it represses is nonsensical. . . ." Why does he believe this?
5. Vocabulary: reactionaries (1), defamatory (2), denigrating (2), imperatives (4), coterminous (6), opprobrium (8), subvention (15), masochistic (16).

Questions about Strategy

1. Consider the examples Wills cites in paragraph 5. If reported accurately, is either Zappa or *Penthouse* guilty of fallacious reasoning?
2. Could this argument appeal to readers who have different political and cultural values? Or is it likely to appeal only to either liberals or conservatives?
3. How effective is the comparison between Tipper Gore and Jessie Jackson in paragraph 12?
4. This argument contains references to many public figures. Does Wills make any attempt to explain who they are for the benefit of readers who may not recognize some of these names?
5. Why does Wills quote a sample lyric in paragraph 11? What impact did this example have on you?

RICHARD A. POSNER

ART FOR LAW'S SAKE

A judge on the United States Court of Appeals for the Seventh Circuit, Richard Posner is also a senior lecturer at the University of Chicago Law School, where he has taught since 1969. He is a 1959 graduate of Yale, who studied law at Harvard, where he headed the *Harvard Law Review*. His books include *The Economics of Justice* (1981), *Law and Literature: A Misunderstood Relation* (1988), and *The Problems of Jurisprudence* (1990). "Art for Law's Sake" was first published in 1989 by *The American Scholar,* the journal of the Phi Beta Kappa Society.

There is persistent, perhaps intensifying, controversy over offensive art. It is well illustrated by the recent brouhaha over "Piss Christ." A photograph (which I have not seen) by Andres Serrano of a plastic crucifix immersed in a bottle of the artist's urine, "Piss Christ" won a prize funded by a federal grant, sparking proposals to attach conditions to public support of the arts that would prevent future public subsidies of blasphemous, obscene, or otherwise offensive works. The questions raised by the Serrano work were shortly afterward exacerbated by the removal from the Corcoran Gallery of an exhibition, also supported by public funds, of photographs by the late Robert Mapplethorpe on subjects homoerotic and, some have argued, sadomasochistic into the bargain. Among the photographs (which, again, I have not seen) is one that is reported to show a black man urinating into the mouth of a white man. But I shall concentrate on "Piss Christ," which poses the issue of public regulation of offensive art in a particularly useful way. Despite or perhaps because of my being a member of the judiciary, I do not want to discuss the legality of proposals to restrict public funding of offensive art. I want instead to discuss the larger philosophical and jurisprudential issues raised by such art. Concretely I want to argue that nowadays there is no objective method of determining what is art or what is offensive, and to consider whether, if this is right, it implies that offensive art should get a lot, or a little—or even no—protection from governmental interference, however that interference should be defined in this setting. For example, is it interference when the government grants, or when it withdraws, a subsidy to the arts? 1

When we say that lead is heavier than aluminum or that an automobile is faster than a rickshaw, we make a statement that can be verified by methods independent of the tastes or personal values of the people doing the verifying. A Communist, a nudist, a Jehovah's Witness, and a follower of Ayn Rand* will all agree on how to test such propositions and on how to interpret the test results. Such "observer independence" gives the propositions about lead and automobiles truth value, makes them objective. It is quite otherwise if we say 2

*Novelist Ayn Rand (1905–1982) celebrates individualism in works such as *The Fountainhead* (1943) and *Atlas Shrugged* (1957).

that "Piss Christ" has, or does not have, artistic value. The problem is not that artistic value is not a thing which a work either has or has not, for in this respect artistic value is no different from weight or speed, being like them an attribute or property rather than a thing. You don't take apart a Maserati and announce, "This is the carburetor and that is the speed." Similarly, "Piss Christ" is not a composite of urine, a bottle, a crucifix, a photograph, and artistic value.

But while it is possible to make objective measurements of physical properties such as weight and speed, it is not possible to make such measurements of artistic value, because people having different values and preferences do not agree and cannot be brought to agree on how to determine the presence of that attribute or even how to define it. A moralistic critic such as Tolstoy might think that the most important question about "Piss Christ" from an artistic standpoint is its likely effect on belief in Christianity. A Marxist critic might agree, and might further agree with Tolstoy that "Piss Christ" would undermine that belief, yet they would disagree about whether this made the work valuable or pernicious. Even if everyone to whom judges are willing to listen agrees that a work has no artistic value, we know from historical experience that it may; later generations may find such value in the work even though the artist's contemporaries did not. Conversely, a work highly valued in its time, or for that matter in later times, may eventually come to seem thoroughly meretricious. Artistic value is something an audience invests a work with, and as the tastes of audiences change, so do judgments of artistic value. About all that can be said in a positive vein is that the longer a work is held in high repute the likelier it is to continue to be held in high repute. This is the "test of time" that Samuel Johnson, David Hume, and George Orwell thought the only objective test of artistic merit. If, to take a concrete example, the Homeric epics are still being read more than twenty-five hundred years after they were composed, then chances are they will continue to be highly regarded for some time; their appeal is robust and resists cultural change.

So far, though, all we have established is an inductive generalization, not an explanation. We could try to figure out what such durable works as the *Iliad* and *Hamlet* and Raphael's madonnas and *The Marriage of Figaro* and the "Ode on a Grecian Urn" and the Louvre's "Winged Victory of Samothrace" have in common and call that the key to artistic value. But this sort of thing has been attempted for millennia without success, and it now seems clear that the quest is a snipe hunt, so diverse are the durable works of the Western tradition. Conceivably we might identify a *necessary* condition of artistic survival—that a work have a certain "omnisignificance" or, less portentously, a certain ambiguity or generality that enables it to be taken in different ways in different times and places. But the distinction between a necessary and a sufficient condition is critical here, for we would not concede artistic value to every work that crossed some threshold of ambiguity or generality. "Piss Christ" deals with a fundamental concern of humankind, religion, and does so in a distinctly ambiguous way. Serrano denies harboring any blasphemous intent and indeed claims—for all I know, with complete sincerity—that "Piss Christ" is a

Christian commentary on the debasement of religion in modern America. The work may have artistic or even moral value, and then again it may not; it may soon come to be thought a worthless bit of trash. If it seems altogether too slight and ephemeral a work to have *any* chance of winning a secure niche in art history, let us remind ourselves that Marcel Duchamp's toilet seat, one of the objets trouvés of the Dadaist movement, has won such a niche along with Goya's disgusting painting "Saturn Eating His Children."

The conclusion to which I am driven is that ascriptions of artistic value   5
or valuelessness to "works of art"—especially to contemporary works of art—are arbitrary. And so with offensiveness, another property of, not a thing found in, a work. "Piss Christ" is no more a compound of urine, a bottle, a crucifix, and offensiveness than it is a compound of urine, a bottle, a crucifix, a photograph, and artistic value. Again this property, offensiveness, is largely, perhaps entirely, a matter of public opinion rather than of correspondence to or causation by something that is observer independent, something akin to the forces that determine weight and speed in accordance with the laws of physics.

This is not a problem when public opinion is united, as perhaps it is over   6
the offensiveness of certain particularly graphic or degrading types of visual obscenity. With specific reference to "Piss Christ" one might be tempted to argue that, while there may be no consensus on what is art, there is a consensus, in Western societies anyway, that the public display of excreta is offensive. Consensus is a highly fallible warrant of truth, yet we might grant it provisionally objective status, even when it is local and temporary—a consensus in our society today, although not in all others and perhaps not in ours tomorrow. But it is a mistake to suppose that there is a consensus concerning the offensiveness of public displays of excreta. If samples of diabetics' or addicts' urine, or the feces of sufferers from Crohn's disease or cancer of the colon were displayed at a medical convention, we would not think the display offensive. It is all a matter of context and purpose. The question of the offensiveness of "Piss Christ" is therefore connected to the question of its artistic value. Those who find the work artistically valuable will not be offended by the (photographic) presence of urine, which they will consider integral to the work's value. Those who find the work blasphemous and barren of artistic value will consider the display of urine gratuitous and hence, given our culture's feelings about excreta, offensive. A few people may find the work both offensive and aesthetic, as many find Ezra Pound's *Cantos* or Vachel Lindsay's *Congo*. Their judgment on whether "Piss Christ" should be suppressed will depend on how offensive, and on how aesthetic, they find it, and on their personal sense of the proper balance between art and insult.

All this (to turn now from philosophy to jurisprudence) would have lit-   7
tle or nothing to do with law if law had its own values, if it were morally autonomous. But for the most part it does not and is not. The law that entitles the victim of negligence to collect damages from the injurer is parasitic on—has no life apart from—social norms concerning what is careful and what is careless behavior. The prohibition in the First Amendment against government's abridging freedom of speech or freedom of the press, broadly conceived

to include artistic as well as political and scientific expression, is parasitic in
the same sense on social norms concerning artistic as well as other "speech"
values and offensiveness and other speech harms such as violence. If a speaker
urges a mob to lynch a prisoner because his guilt is so plain that a trial would
be a waste of time and money, the speaker will be punishable for incitement
to violence, because the danger of the speech will be felt to outweigh its value
in drawing attention to the problematic character of due process. But if instead he writes a book urging the masses to rise up and liquidate the bosses, he
will not be punishable because such books are thought to have some value and
not to be very dangerous, although citizens of Communist states may want to
dispute both points. If our society thought such books were dangerous, they
would be suppressed. Practical considerations, rather than the text or the
eighteenth-century background of the First Amendment, guide the application of the amendment to today's problems.

Certain forms of obscenity are considered by virtually everyone in our   8
society (including many of the consumers of obscene works) to be completely
worthless and highly offensive, and they are suppressed without much ado, although, it must be added, also without much success. But the consensus that
condemns the extremely obscene does not extend to the class of works illustrated by "Piss Christ," which are thought valuable and non-offensive by
some, worthless and offensive by others, worthwhile but offensive by a handful. If there is no objective way to arbitrate such a disagreement, what should
the courts do? More broadly, what are the implications for law of the kind of
cultural relativism that I am describing?

There are three possibilities here, of which the first two reflect a desire   9
to secure definiteness in law at any price. The first is to forbid *any* governmental interference with "art," no matter how offensive the "art." This approach does not escape subjectivity entirely; rather, it pushes inquiry back a
stage, to the question of whether the work in question *is* art (and also to what
counts as governmental "interference"). If a work is sufficiently offensive, it is
classified as obscene, and therefore as non-art.

At the other extreme is the judicial-hands-off approach: Courts are the   10
forum of principle, there are no principles to apply to questions of aesthetic
merit and offensiveness, so let the political branches do what they want with
these questions. Such an approach is likely to appeal to those who are especially protective of courts—who want the judges to shine and believe that the
judicial escutcheon is tarnished with the judges mess in indeterminate questions such as artistic value and offensiveness.

The third possible approach, the intermediate or pragmatic, is to ac-   11
knowledge that the problem of relativism, moral as well as aesthetic, so strikingly presented by a work such as "Piss Christ," is a general feature of
American, and perhaps of any, legal controversy. Judges need not feel they
must shy off merely because the issues raised by offensive art are spongy. That's
just the way things are in law; the nature of the legal enterprise ensures that
judges will frequently find themselves wrestling with indeterminate questions,
because those are the questions least likely to be settled without recourse to

lawsuits that have to be pressed all the way to the Supreme Court or to another high appellate court before the question can be answered. Judges struggle with such questions all the time yet somehow manage to retain that minimum of public respect which is indispensable to the effectiveness of a court system. They are unlikely to forfeit it if they venture—with appropriate caution—into the controversy that eddies around issues of value and taste in purported works of art. The significance of the qualification will, I hope, become clearer as I proceed.

The first thing to note about this venture is that although artistic value is   12 largely, perhaps entirely, unknowable, there is little doubt that art is valuable. If this seems a paradox, consider: The lesson of history is that many of the scientific theories in which we firmly believe today are almost certainly false, just as Euclidean geometry as a theory of spatial relations, the geocentric theory of the solar system, the luminiferous ether, the spontaneous generation of bacteria, and Newton's laws of motion are now known to be false after having been believed by the scientific community for centuries. Yet the fallibility of scientific theory does not lead a sensible person to doubt the existence, growth, or value of scientific knowledge. Even if every current scientific theory is someday falsified, we will still be able to make atomic bombs, fly airplanes, and immunize people against polio. Likewise it is a fact that art museums are thronged, that works of art command huge prices, that some people devote a lifetime to the study of art, and, more to the point, that many people would feel a profound sense of deprivation if the French Academy had succeeded in suppressing Impressionist art just as they feel that the world is a poorer place because so little classical Greek sculpture has survived.

If we grant that art has value and add that the censorship of art has a   13 dreadful historical record, we can derive, in order to guide judicial review of controversies over offensive art, a presumption in favor of letting the stuff be produced and exhibited to whoever is willing to pay the price of admission. The Supreme Court's recent decision in the flag-burning case illustrates the presumption. Flag burning is an offensive, inarticulate, and immature mode of political communication (at least when the flag is our own), but as long as one is burning a flag one bought and paid for, before a willing audience, the flag burning contributes, however feebly, to the marketplace of ideas without impairing anybody's property rights.

We can bolster the presumption in favor of a permissive judicial attitude   14 toward offensive art by noting that the "test of time" that is the closest we seem able to get to an objective measure of artistic value presupposes, like natural selection in the theory of biological evolution (which the test of time resembles), the existence of variety, from which history makes its selections. The whole thrust of censorship is to reduce variety, to suppress outliers, and by doing this it interferes with the test of time and impoverishes art's legacy to the future.

I don't mean "presumption" in any fancy lawyer's sense. I just mean   15 that judges should be highly suspicious of anything that smacks of censorship. But since it is only a presumption that I am defending, judges should also be sensitive to arguments for rebutting it in particular cases, even at the risk of occasionally being found guilty by history of the sort of folly illustrated by the audience that was scandalized when *The Playboy of the Western World* was first performed in 1907 because Synge used the word "shift" for a woman's slip. There is such a thing as worrying too much about history's verdict on one's actions.

Consider a case in which the presumption in favor of freedom of artistic expression was successfully rebutted. The case was decided by my court years ago, and since it is quite over and done with, I can discuss it without violating professional proprieties.   16

The case, *Piarowski v. Illinois Community College,* involved a small junior college near Chicago that, being public, was subject to the constitutional limitations on restricting free expression. The artist in the case, who was the chairman of the college's art department, made an improbable effort to fuse his two loves—the making of stained-glass windows and the art of Aubrey Beardsley—by making stained-glass versions of some of Beardsley's illustrations from Aristophanes' comedy *Lysistrata.* The illustrations, like the comedy, are bawdy even by today's standards (how fitting that they should be on public display in the Victoria and Albert Museum in London). They are, of course, line drawings of white men and women—Greeks. To transpose the drawings to the stained-glass medium, the artist in my case used pieces of colored glass for each of the figures, and the colors had to contrast. He made the innocent but, as it turned out, unfortunate choice of amber glass for the women and white glass for the men. As a result, one of the stained-glass windows depicts a brown woman, naked except for stockings, on her knees, embracing in an attitude of veneration the huge white phallus of a robed man. The other two windows depict brown women passing wind and masturbating, respectively.   17

The artist hung the windows in the art department's annual exhibition of faculty work, held in an alcove (the "gallery") off the main corridor of the college (the "mall," as it is called), on the ground floor. As the college has only one building, the exhibition was visible to all students, faculty, and visitors, whether or not they wanted to see it—more especially as there is no wall between the gallery and the mall. The first group to complain was the cleaning staff, which was black. Most of the students in the college are black, and they, too, were offended by the stained-glass windows and complained to the president of the college, who ordered the artist to shift the display from the first-floor corridor to a smaller exhibition room on the fourth floor, a room normally used for exhibiting photographs but suitable for exhibiting other works of art as well. When the artist refused, the president took down the stained-glass windows and placed them in his office. The artist sued the college, alleging a violation of the First Amendment.   18

Having studied photographs of Aubrey Beardsley's illustrations for *Lysistrata,* I find the stained-glass pastiches to be essentially free of both artistic value and offensiveness. Beardsley's charm is on the line, and it is lost when lines give way to chunks of colored glass. On the other hand, there was no   19 contention that the chairman of the art department was attempting a commentary on race or sex; he was merely trying to use different colors, vaguely human, to distinguish the figures in the windows from one another. And the very crudeness of the windows neutralizes any obscene impact. For the reasons stated earlier, however, I have no basis for confidence in my or any other judge's ability either to evaluate the artistry of the stained-glass windows or to gauge their offensiveness to a community in which Aubrey Beardsley is not a household word.

A "hands-off relativist" might take the position that since issues of artis-   20
tic and moral taste are not objective, the artist should have lost his suit even if the college had refused to allow him to exhibit his stained-glass windows anywhere on (or for that matter off) the campus. This was not the court's view, but neither did we think the Constitution *entitled* him to exhibit his windows in the most public place in the college. The college's president had offered an alternative place of exhibition that, while indeed less conspicuous, was by the same token less offensive. Racial sensitivities are a fact in our society, and if, as I have argued, offensiveness ultimately is no more objective than artistic value, neither is it less so. The college president's action seemed a reasonable compromise, and the court gave judgment for the college. In so doing, we affirmed that "academic freedom" is a two-way street. It is the freedom of a college to manage its affairs without undue judicial interference no less than it is the freedom of the teacher or scholar to teach or write or, in this case, create works of art without undue interference by the state (for remember that this was a public college, and hence an arm of the state). A further point worth making is that the power of a single junior college to affect the art scene by shunting offensive works to less conspicuous places of exhibition is distinctly limited. But of course the example might prove catching.

So particularistic and fact-specific—so pragmatic—a mode of adjudica-   21
tion that led to the judgment for the college, and that implies that the scope of First Amendment protection may be different for works of art than for political or scientific works, is not to everyone's taste. Lawyers have a predilection for rules, and there indeed are many occasions when hard-edged rules are preferable to fuzzy standards, but controversies over offensive art may not be one of them. It is not even clear that art would be helped rather than hindered by a rule that forbade any and all public regulation of offensive art. Such a rule—a rule that gave privileged status to the *flaunting* of offensive art—might engender public hostility to art that would be out of all proportion to the benefits in artistic freedom gained. On the other hand, a rule that gave government carte blanche to suppress art deemed offensive by any vocal, assertive, politically influential group in our diverse, teeming, and (let us face it) rather philistine society could impair the future of art, a costly consequence. So perhaps the watchword in First Amendment cases having to do with art should indeed be *caution*. ■

Questions for Meaning

1. Why is it that art does not have what Posner calls "observer independence"?
2. What is the role of content and purpose in gauging "offensiveness"?
3. What is the difference between urging a mob to lynch a prisoner and writing a book calling for revolution?
4. Can you explain what Posner means by "cultural relativism" in paragraph 8?
5. Why is academic freedom "a two-way street"? Consider the example in paragraphs 17 through 20.
6. Vocabulary: blasphemous (1), exacerbated (1), homoerotic (1), jurisprudential (1), meretricious (3), millennia (4), portentously (4), ephemeral (4), ascriptions (5), gratuitous (6), escutcheon (10), impairing (13), pastiches (19), predilection (21).

Questions about Strategy

1. Why do you think Posner points out that he has not seen the controversial photographs he refers to in paragraph 1?
2. How does Posner establish his authority to be writing on this topic?
3. Consider the first sentence in paragraph 13. Why would Posner use a word like "stuff" after using a more formal voice in the first half of the sentence?
4. What function is served by alluding to the Impressionists in paragraph 12 and *The Playboy of the Western World* in paragraph 15?
5. In his conclusion, Posner calls for caution. Where has he prepared the way for this conclusion?

ONE STUDENT'S ASSIGNMENT

Writing for an audience of college students, compose an argument of approximately 1,000 words for or against adopting codes that ban hate speech. Draw on at least one source in *The Informed Argument* and one source that you have located on your own. Use APA style documentation and include a Reference List.

Smiling through Clenched Teeth
Doug Micko

Lately scholars have been endorsing the restriction of hate speech   1
through legislation of some kind. Seems like a great cause, doesn't it? After all, it is certainly time we prevent the ostracization of minority groups generations after they have supposedly gained their "rights." And I truly believe it is time that we stop fighting each other and start to smile at one another.

But what happens when the smile is government regulated? Perhaps   2
some would argue that an officially regulated smile is better than no smile at all. To these people, such regulation may seem like a utopia. But to me, the passion that gives birth to a true smile is the same passion we use to get angry, to feel sad, and to hate. I'm not willing to sacrifice this passion, and be left smiling behind clenched teeth.

Regulation of hate speech, it has been argued, is too difficult, for it can-   3
not accurately target only oppressive groups. I'm not sure we'd want to regulate it even if we found a way to specify that only the most awful groups would be prosecuted. In fact, I see hate speech as necessary for humankind.

Regulation of such speech goes beyond the First Amendment to one of   4
the central themes of freedom: expression. We have the right to express how we feel. We have the right to openly criticize policies we don't agree with, and to hear rebuttals for our arguments. Anything less than this sounds suspiciously dictatorial. As Henry Louis Gates, Jr. has written with regard to this exchange of ideas, "you cannot begin to conduct [a] conversation when you outlaw the expression of the view that you would criticize" (1993, p. 367). If we are deprived the ability to disagree, or be disagreed with, we are also depriving ourselves the opportunity for growth and understanding. By streamlining our expressions, we are losing important views that fall outside our artificial boundaries. The loss of any ideas through such oppression is an injustice.

It is also an injustice, to ignore racist speech. As Charles R. Lawrence III   5
writes, "A minority student should not have to risk becoming the target of racially assaulting speech every time he or she chooses to walk across

campus" (1989, p. 351). Very few people I know would disagree with this. No student should have to be the victim of such oppression, and I realize that minorities often bear this cross. Those who practice hate speech are also a minority. What shall we say for the rights of this minority? Shall they undergo not only the scrutiny from their classmates, but also the University? There are differences between each group, and we could, as Mari J. Matsuda (1993) suggests, make regulations that would target certain groups. We must not forget, though, that this country was founded as a means to escape the wrath of governments that oppressed, be it racially, spiritually, or intellectually. It would be a shame if we were now the oppressive government.

It is also argued by Matsuda that we can now not make laws as ambiguous as they have been for we now hold certain universal truths about what is right and wrong and who specifically should be punished. In other words, we can loosen our grip on the First Amendment and instead grab a hold of a "universal truth." "There is no nation left on this planet that submits as its national self-expression the view that Hitler was right" (1993, p. 37) is one such truth she posits. This seems easy to say fifty years after Hitler lost the war, but I wonder what would be written if Hitler had won. If this is one of a number of universal truths, why would there have been conflict regarding it? Was Germany exempt from this universal truth? On ideas of racial supremacy, she writes, "We have fought wars and spilled blood to establish the universal acceptance of this principle" (p. 37). But it's hard to know whether spilling blood leads to true acceptance or merely to the pseudo-acceptance that stems from violent oppression. 6

I believe that it is important to condemn hate speech socially; I also believe that we need to accept it legally. Hate speech will not often bring about understanding, but we need the openness necessary for hate speech, for only through this openness could be reach understanding. When we look at the cases of civil war throughout the world, and the growing sense of nationalism, it is tempting to try to legislate against hate speech. Legislation, though, cannot stop how a person feels, and if the feeling is hatred, I would rather know. If a person speaks of hatred, we can listen and perhaps speak back, and each of us has an opportunity for understanding. If a person feels hatred and cannot speak, we will never understand each other. In simpler terms, if we are all smiling, it will be impossible to identify and understand each other's problems. 7

Grouped with the freedoms of expression and understanding, perhaps the most important value we could have is the ability of free choice, which includes being able to make bad decisions. This may not seem like such a great value to some older, wiser Americans. But as college students we can recognize the significance of being able to make our own mistakes, even about whether to participate in hate speech. And we also do understand the 8 difference between wrong and right. In this instance, the decision seems obvious, and for most it is. What is important is having the ability to make that decision untarnished.

Sometimes we may wonder why we give freedoms that can be abused. 9
But we must realize that unless we are prepared to take the most important rights away from the most important people, unless we are prepared to lose these very rights ourselves, we cannot deprive anyone in our society such a basic gift as this: the ability to talk freely.

We are a nation founded in diversity. Now this diversity is being consid- 10
ered a threat to the civilization it built. We are obligated to not only pre- serve, but to thrive off of the diversity involved in the human race. We must cast off insincere smiles and feel the passion inherent in free expression.

References

Gates, H. L. (1993). Let them talk. In R. Miller (Ed.), *The informed argument.* (pp. 355–75). Fort Worth: Harcourt.

Lawrence, C. R. (1989). On racist speech. In R. Miller (Ed.), *The informed argument* (pp. 350–53). Fort Worth: Harcourt.

Matsuda, M. J. (1993). Public response to racist speech: Considering the victim's story. In M. J. Matsuda, C. R. Lawrence, R. Delgado, & K. W. Crenshaw (Aus.), *Words that wound: Critical race theory, assaultive speech, and the First Amend- ment* (pp. 17–51). Boulder: Westview.

SUGGESTIONS FOR WRITING

1. Are there limits to free speech in American colleges and universities? Should there be restrictions against the use of language that is offensive to historically oppressed groups? Drawing on Lawrence and Gates, ar- gue for the policy you would like your school to adopt.
2. Summarize the argument by Henry Louis Gates, Jr.
3. Research laws governing freedom of expression in Canada or in Eng- land, and write a summary of your findings.
4. Obtain a copy of *Words That Wound* and read the full text of the essays Gates discusses in his article. Draw on this material and write a re- sponse to Gates.
5. Drawing on Williams, Wiener, and Eidus, write an essay explaining how publishers are influenced by social and economic factors.
6. Reread the essays by Garry Wills and Richard Posner. Compare their views about censorship and art.
7. Write an argument for or against public funding for art that can be considered morally offensive. Be sure to define what you mean by both "public funding" and "morally offensive."

8. Research how the arts are subsidized by the National Endowment for the Arts. Report upon how grants are awarded.
9. Can unrestricted freedom of expression lead to violence? Does public well-being justify outlawing certain kinds of expression? Write an argument for or against laws that would put restrictions on images or language that can be published within the United States.
10. Wills and Posner both refer to the photographs of Robert Mapplethorpe. Locate a representative selection of these photographs and evaluate their artistic merit.

COLLABORATIVE PROJECT

In recent years, school boards have faced many challenges from parents concerned about the books to which their children are exposed at school. Research the topic of censorship and school libraries or censorship and textbooks. Choose a specific work that has been challenged, examine it carefully, then prepare a group presentation in which the book will be both opposed and defended.

LITERARY CRITICISM: WHAT DOES A STORY MEAN?

WILLA CATHER

PAUL'S CASE: A STUDY IN TEMPERAMENT

It was Paul's afternoon to appear before the faculty of the Pittsburgh High   1
School to account for his various misdemeanours. He had been suspended a
week ago, and his father had called at the Principal's office and confessed his
perplexity about his son. Paul entered the faculty room suave and smiling. His
clothes were a trifle outgrown, and the tan velvet on the collar of his open
overcoat was frayed and worn; but for all that there was something of the
dandy about him, and he wore an opal pin in his neatly knotted black four-in-
hand, and a red carnation in his button-hole. This latter adornment the faculty
somehow felt was not properly significant of the contrite spirit befitting a boy
under the ban of suspension.

Paul was tall for his age and very thin, with high, cramped shoulders and   2
a narrow chest. His eyes were remarkable for a certain hysterical brilliancy,
and he continually used them in a conscious, theatrical sort of way, peculiarly
offensive in a boy. The pupils were abnormally large, as though he were addicted to belladonna, but there was a glassy glitter about them which that drug
does not produce.

When questioned by the Principal as to why he was there, Paul stated,   3
politely enough, that he wanted to come back to school. This was a lie, but
Paul was quite accustomed to lying; found it, indeed, indispensable for overcoming friction. His teachers were asked to state their respective charges
against him, which they did with such a rancour and aggrievedness as evinced
that this was not a usual case. Disorder and impertinence were among the offences named, yet each of his instructors felt that it was scarcely possible to put
into words the real cause of the trouble, which lay in a sort of hysterically defiant manner of the boy's; in the contempt which they all knew he felt for
them, and which he seemingly made not the least effort to conceal. Once,

when he had been making a synopsis of a paragraph at the blackboard, his English teacher had stepped to his side and attempted to guide his hand. Paul had started back with a shudder and thrust his hands violently behind him. The astonished woman could scarcely have been more hurt and embarrassed had he struck at her. The insult was so involuntary and definitely personal as to be unforgettable. In one way and another, he had made all his teachers, men and women alike, conscious of the same feeling of physical aversion. In one class he habitually sat with his hand shading his eyes; in another he always looked out of the window during the recitation; in another he made a running commentary on the lecture, with humorous intent.

His teachers felt this afternoon that his whole attitude was symbolized by   4
his shrug and his flippantly red carnation flower, and they fell upon him without mercy, his English teacher leading the pack. He stood through it smiling, his pale lips parted over his white teeth. (His lips were continually twitching, and he had a habit of raising his eyebrows that was contemptuous and irritating to the last degree.) Older boys than Paul had broken down and shed tears under that ordeal, but his set smile did not once desert him, and his only sign of discomfort was the nervous trembling of the fingers that toyed with the buttons of his overcoat, and an occasional jerking of the other hand which held his hat. Paul was always smiling, always glancing about him, seeming to feel that people might be watching him and trying to detect something. This conscious expression, since it was as far as possible from boyish mirthfulness, was usually attributed to insolence or "smartness."

As the inquisition proceeded, one of his instructors repeated an imperti-   5
nent remark of the boy's, and the Principal asked him whether he thought that a courteous speech to make to a woman. Paul shrugged his shoulders slightly and his eyebrows twitched.

"I don't know," he replied. "I didn't mean to be polite or impolite, ei-   6
ther. I guess it's a sort of way I have, of saying things regardless."

The Principal asked him whether he didn't think that a way it would be   7
well to get rid of. Paul grinned and said he guessed so. When he was told that he could go, he bowed gracefully and went out. His bow was like a repetition of the scandalous red carnation.

His teachers were in despair, and his drawing master voiced the feeling of   8
them all when he declared there was something about the boy which none of them understood. He added: "I don't really believe that smile of his comes altogether from insolence; there's something sort of haunted about it. The boy is not strong, for one thing. There is something wrong about the fellow."

The drawing master had come to realize that, in looking at Paul, one saw   9
only his white teeth and the forced animation of his eyes. One warm afternoon the boy had gone to sleep at his drawing-board, and his master had noted with amazement what a white, blue-veined face it was; drawn and wrinkled like an old man's about the eyes, the lips twitching even in his sleep.

His teachers left the building dissatisfied and unhappy; humiliated to   10
have felt so vindictive toward a mere boy, to have uttered this feeling in cutting terms, and to have set each other on, as it were, in the grewsome game of

intemperate reproach. One of them remembered having seen a miserable street cat set at bay by a ring of tormentors.

As for Paul, he ran down the hill whistling the Soldiers' Chorus from *Faust,* looking wildly behind him now and then to see whether some of his teachers were not there to witness his light-heartedness. As it was now late in the afternoon and Paul was on duty that evening as usher at Carnegie Hall, he decided that he would not go home to supper.

When he reached the concert hall the doors were not yet open. It was chilly outside, and he decided to go up into the picture gallery—always deserted at this hour—where there were some of Raffelli's gay studies of Paris streets and an airy blue Venetian scene or two that always exhilarated him. He was delighted to find no one in the gallery but the old guard, who sat in the corner, a newspaper on his knee, a black patch over one eye and the other closed. Paul possessed himself of the place and walked confidently up and down, whistling under his breath. After a while he sat down before a blue Rico and lost himself. When he bethought him to look at his watch, it was after seven o'clock, and he rose with a start and ran downstairs, making a face at Augustus Caesar, peering out from the cast-room, and an evil gesture at the Venus of Milo as he passed her on the stairway.

When Paul reached the ushers' dressing-room half-a-dozen boys were there already, and he began excitedly to tumble into his uniform. It was one of the few that at all approached fitting, and Paul thought it very becoming—though he knew the tight, straight coat accentuated his narrow chest, about which he was exceedingly sensitive. He was always excited while he dressed, twanging all over to the tuning of the strings and the preliminary flourishes of the horns in the music-room; but tonight he seemed quite beside himself, and he teased and plagued the boys until, telling him that he was crazy, they put him down on the floor and sat on him.

Somewhat calmed by his suppression, Paul dashed out to the front of the house to seat the early comers. He was a model usher. Gracious and smiling he ran up and down the aisles. Nothing was too much trouble for him; he carried messages and brought programs as though it were his greatest pleasure in life, and all the people in his section thought him a charming boy, feeling that he remembered and admired them. As the house filled, he grew more and more vivacious and animated, and the colour came to his cheeks and lips. It was very much as though this were a great reception and Paul were the host. Just as the musicians came out to take their places, his English teacher arrived with checks for the seats which a prominent manufacturer had taken for the season. She betrayed some embarrassment when she handed Paul the tickets, and a *hauteur* which subsequently made her feel very foolish. Paul was startled for a moment, and had the feeling of wanting to put her out; what business had she here among all these fine people and gay colours? He looked her over and decided that she was not appropriately dressed and must be a fool to sit downstairs in such togs. The tickets had probably been sent her out of kindness, he reflected, as he put down a seat for her, and she had about as much right to sit there as he had.

When the symphony began Paul sank into one of the rear seats with a   15
long sigh of relief, and lost himself as he had done before the Rico. It was not
that symphonies, as such, meant anything in particular to Paul, but the first
sigh of the instruments seemed to free some hilarious spirit within him; something that struggled there like the Genius in the bottle found by the Arab fisherman. He felt a sudden zest of life; the lights danced before his eyes and the
concert hall blazed into unimaginable splendour. When the soprano soloist
came on, Paul forgot even the nastiness of his teacher's being there, and gave
himself up to the peculiar intoxication such personages always had for him.
The soloist chanced to be a German woman, by no means in her first youth,
and the mother of many children; but she wore a satin gown and a tiara, and
she had that indefinable air of achievement, that world-shine upon her, which
always blinded Paul to any possible defects.

After a concert was over, Paul was often irritable and wretched until he   16
got to sleep,—and tonight he was even more than usually restless. He had the
feeling of not being able to let down; of its being impossible to give up this
delicious excitement which was the only thing that could be called living at
all. During the last number he withdrew and, after hastily changing his clothes
in the dressing-room, slipped out to the side door where the singer's carriage
stood. Here he began pacing rapidly up and down the walk, waiting to see her
come out.

Over yonder the Schenley, in its vacant stretch, loomed big and square   17
through the fine rain, the windows of its twelve stories glowing like those of
a lighted card-board house under a Christmas tree. All the actors and singers
of any importance stayed there when they were in the city, and a number of
the big manufacturers of the place lived there in the winter. Paul had often
hung about the hotel, watching the people go in and out, longing to enter and
leave school-masters and dull care behind him for ever.

At last the singer came out, accompanied by the conductor, who helped   18
her into her carriage and closed the door with a cordial *auf wiedersehen,*—
which set Paul to wondering whether she were not an old sweetheart of his.
Paul followed the carriage over to the hotel, walking so rapidly as not to be far
from the entrance when the singer alighted and disappeared behind the
swinging glass doors which were opened by a negro in a tall hat and a long
coat. In the moment that the door was ajar, it seemed to Paul that he, too,
entered. He seemed to feel himself go after her up the steps, into the warm,
lighted building, into an exotic, a tropical world of shiny, glistening surfaces
and basking ease. He reflected upon the mysterious dishes that were brought
into the dining-room, the green bottles in buckets of ice, as he had seen them
in the supper party pictures of the Sunday supplement. A quick gust of wind
brought the rain down with sudden vehemence, and Paul was startled to find
that he was still outside in the slush of the gravel driveway; that his boots were
letting in the water and his scanty overcoat was clinging wet about him; that
the lights in front of the concert hall were out, and that the rain was driving
in sheets between him and the orange glow of the windows above him. There
it was, what he wanted—tangibly before him, like the fairy world of a

Christmas pantomime; as the rain beat in his face, Paul wondered whether he were destined always to shiver in the black night outside, looking up at it.

He turned and walked reluctantly toward the car tracks. The end had to   19
come sometime; his father in his night-clothes at the top of the stairs, explanations that did not explain, hastily improvised fictions that were forever tripping him up, his upstairs room and its horrible yellow wallpaper, the creaking bureau with the greasy plush collar-box, and over his painted wooden bed the pictures of George Washington and John Calvin, and the framed motto, "Feed my Lambs," which had been worked in red worsted by his mother, whom Paul could not remember.

Half an hour later, Paul alighted from the Negley Avenue car and went   20
slowly down one of the side streets off the main thoroughfare. It was a highly respectable street, where all the houses were exactly alike, and where business men of moderate means begot and reared large families of children, all of whom went to Sabbath-school and learned the shorter catechism, and were interested in arithmetic; all of whom were as exactly alike as their homes, and of a piece with the monotony in which they lived. Paul never went up Cordelia Street without a shudder of loathing. His home was next the house of the Cumberland minister. He approached it tonight with the nerveless sense of defeat, the hopeless feeling of sinking back forever into ugliness and commonness that he had always had when he came home. The moment he turned into Cordelia Street he felt the waters close above his head. After each of these orgies of living, he experienced all the physical depression which follows a debauch; the loathing of respectable beds, of common food, of a house permeated by kitchen odours; a shuddering repulsion for the flavourless, colourless mass of every-day existence; a morbid desire for cool things and soft lights and fresh flowers.

The nearer he approached the house, the more absolutely unequal Paul   21
felt to the sight of it all; his ugly sleeping chamber; the cold bath-room with the grimy zinc tub, the cracked mirror, the dripping spiggots; his father, at the top of the stairs, his hairy legs sticking out from his nightshirt, his feet thrust into carpet slippers. He was so much later than usual that there would certainly be inquiries and reproaches. Paul stopped short before the door. He felt that he could not be accosted by his father tonight; that he could not toss again on that miserable bed. He would not go in. He would tell his father that he had no car fare, and it was raining so hard he had gone home with one of the boys and stayed all night.

Meanwhile, he was wet and cold. He went around to the back of the   22
house and tried one of the basement windows, found it open, raised it cautiously, and scrambled down the cellar wall to the floor. There he stood, holding his breath, terrified by the noise he had made; but the floor above him was silent, and there was no creak on the stairs. He found a soap-box, and carried it over to the soft ring of light that streamed from the furnace door, and sat down. He was horribly afraid of rats, so he did not try to sleep, but sat looking distrustfully at the dark, still terrified lest he might have awakened his father. In such reactions, after one of the experiences which made days and nights out

of the dreary blanks of the calendar, when his senses were deadened, Paul's head was always singularly clear. Suppose his father had heard him getting in at the window and had come down and shot him for a burglar? Then, again, suppose his father had come down, pistol in hand, and he had cried out in time to save himself, and his father had been horrified to think how nearly he had killed him? Then, again, suppose a day should come when his father would remember that night, and wish there had been no warning cry to stay his hand? With this last supposition Paul entertained himself until daybreak.

The following Sunday was fine; the sodden November chill was broken   23 by the last flash of autumnal summer. In the morning Paul had to go to church and Sabbath-school, as always. On seasonable Sunday afternoons the burghers of Cordelia Street usually sat out on their front "stoops," and talked to their neighbours on the next stoop, or called to those across the street in neigh-bourly fashion. The men sat placidly on gay cushions placed upon the steps that led down to the sidewalk, while the women, in their Sunday "waists," sat in rockers on the cramped porches, pretending to be greatly at their ease. The children played in the streets; there were so many of them that the place re-sembled the recreation grounds of a kindergarten. The men on the steps—all in their shirt sleeves, their vests unbuttoned—sat with their legs well apart, their stomachs comfortably protruding, and talked of the prices of things, or told anecdotes of the sagacity of their various chiefs and overlords. They occa-sionally looked over the multitude of squabbling children, listened affection-ately to their high-pitched, nasal voices, smiling to see their own proclivities reproduced in their offspring, and interspersed their legends of the iron kings with remarks about their sons' progress at school, their grades in arithmetic, and the amounts they had saved in their toy banks.

On this last Sunday of November, Paul sat all the afternoon on the lowest   24 step of his "stoop," staring into the street, while his sisters, in their rockers, were talking to the minister's daughters next door about how many shirt-waists they had made in the last week, and how many waffles some one had eaten at the last church supper. When the weather was warm, and his father was in a particularly jovial frame of mind, the girls made lemonade, which was always brought out in a red-glass pitcher, ornamented with forget-me-nots in blue enamel. This the girls thought very fine, and the neighbours joked about the suspicious colour of the pitcher.

Today Paul's father, on the top step, was talking to a young man who   25 shifted a restless baby from knee to knee. He happened to be the young man who was daily held up to Paul as a model, and after whom it was his father's dearest hope that he would pattern. This young man was of a ruddy complex-ion, with a compressed, red mouth, and faded, near-sighted eyes, over which he wore thick spectacles, with gold bows that curved about his ears. He was clerk to one of the magnates of a great steel corporation, and was looked upon in Cordelia Street as a young man with a future. There was a story that, some five years ago—he was now barely twenty-six—he had been a trifle "dissi-pated," but in order to curb his appetites and save the loss of time and strength that a sowing of wild oats might have entailed, he had taken his chief's advice, oft reiterated to his employés, and at twenty-one had married the first woman whom he could persuade to share his fortunes. She happened to be an angular school-mistress, much older than he, who also wore thick glasses, and who had now borne him four children, all near-sighted, like herself.

The young man was relating how his chief, now cruising in the Mediter-   26
ranean, kept in touch with all the details of the business, arranging his office hours on his yacht just as though he were at home, and "knocking off work enough to keep two stenographers busy." His father told, in turn, the plan his corporation was considering, of putting in an electric railway plant at Cairo. Paul snapped his teeth; he had an awful apprehension that they might spoil it all before he got there. Yet he rather liked to hear these legends of the iron kings, that were told and retold on Sundays and holidays; these stories of palaces in Venice, yachts on the Mediterranean, and high play at Monte Carlo appealed to his fancy, and he was interested in the triumphs of cash boys who had become famous, though he had no mind for the cash-boy stage.

After supper was over, and he had helped to dry the dishes, Paul ner-   27
vously asked his father whether he could go to George's to get some help in his geometry, and still more nervously asked for car-fare. This latter request he had to repeat, as his father, on principle, did not like to hear requests for money, whether much or little. He asked Paul whether he could not go to some boy who lived nearer, and told him that he ought not to leave his school work until Sunday; but he gave him the dime. He was not a poor man, but he had a worthy ambition to come up in the world. His only reason for allowing Paul to usher was that he thought a boy ought to be earning a little.

Paul bounded upstairs, scrubbed the greasy odour of the dish-water from   28
his hands with the ill-smelling soap he hated, and then shook over his fingers a few drops of violet water from the bottle he kept hidden in his drawer. He left the house with his geometry conspicuously under his arm, and the moment he got out of Cordelia Street and boarded a downtown car, he shook off the lethargy of two deadening days, and began to live again.

The leading juvenile of the permanent stock company which played at   29
one of the downtown theatres was an acquaintance of Paul's, and the boy had been invited to drop in at the Sunday-night rehearsals whenever he could. For more than a year Paul had spent every available moment loitering about Charley Edwards's dressing-room. He had won a place among Edwards's following not only because the young actor, who could not afford to employ a dresser, often found him useful, but because he recognized in Paul something akin to what churchmen term "vocation."

It was at the theatre and at Carnegie Hall that Paul really lived; the rest   30
was but a sleep and a forgetting. This was Paul's fairy tale, and it had for him all the allurement of a secret love. The moment he inhaled the gassy, painty, dusty odour behind the scenes, he breathed like a prisoner set free, and felt within him the possibility of doing or saying splendid, brilliant things. The moment the cracked orchestra beat out the overture from *Martha,* or jerked at the serenade from *Rigoletto,* all stupid and ugly things slid from him, and his senses were deliciously, yet delicately fired.

Perhaps it was because, in Paul's world, the natural nearly always wore   31
the guise of ugliness, that a certain element of artificiality seemed to him necessary in beauty. Perhaps it was because his experience of life elsewhere was so
full of Sabbath-school picnics, petty economies, wholesome advice as to how
to succeed in life, and the unescapable odours of cooking, that he found this
existence so alluring, these smartly-clad men and women so attractive, that he
was so moved by these starry apple orchards that bloomed perennially under
the lime-light.

It would be difficult to put it strongly enough how convincingly the   32
stage entrance of that theatre was for Paul the actual portal of Romance. Certainly none of the company ever suspected it, least of all Charley Edwards. It
was very like the old stories that used to float about London of fabulously rich
Jews, who had subterranean halls, with palms, and fountains, and soft lamps
and richly apparelled women who never saw the disenchanting light of London
day. So, in the midst of that smoke-palled city, enamoured of figures and
grimy toil, Paul had his secret temple, his wishing-carpet, his bit of blue-and-
white Mediterranean shore bathed in perpetual sunshine.

Several of Paul's teachers had a theory that his imagination had been per-   33
verted by garish fiction; but the truth was, he scarcely ever read at all. The
books at home were not such as would either tempt or corrupt a youthful
mind, and as for reading the novels that some of his friends urged upon him—
well, he got what he wanted much more quickly from music; any sort of music, from an orchestra to a barrel organ. He needed only the spark, the
indescribable thrill that made his imagination master of his senses, and he
could make plots and pictures enough of his own. It was equally true that he
was not stage-struck—not, at any rate, in the usual acceptation of that expression. He had no desire to become an actor, any more than he had to become a
musician. He felt no necessity to do any of these things; what he wanted was
to see, to be in the atmosphere, float on the wave of it, to be carried out, blue
league after blue league, away from everything.

After a night behind the scenes, Paul found the school-room more than   34
ever repulsive; the bare floors and naked walls; the prosy men who never wore
frock coats, or violets in their buttonholes; the women with their dull gowns,
shrill voices, and pitiful seriousness about prepositions that govern the dative.
He could not bear to have the other pupils think, for a moment, that he took
these people seriously; he must convey to them that he considered it all trivial,
and was there only by way of a joke, anyway. He had autograph pictures of all
the members of the stock company which he showed his classmates, telling
them the most incredible stories of his familiarity with these people, of his
acquaintance with the soloists who came to Carnegie Hall, his suppers with
them and the flowers he sent them. When these stories lost their effect, and his
audience grew listless, he would bid all the boys good-bye, announcing that he
was going to travel for awhile; going to Naples, to California, to Egypt. Then,
next Monday, he would slip back, conscious and nervously smiling; his sister
was ill, and he would have to defer his voyage until spring.

Matters went steadily worse with Paul at school. In the itch to let his instructors know how heartily he despised them, and how thoroughly he was appreciated elsewhere, he mentioned once or twice that he had no time to fool with theorems; adding—with a twitch of the eyebrows and a touch of that nervous bravado which so perplexed them—that he was helping the people down at the stock company; they were old friends of his.   35

The upshot of the matter was, that the Principal went to Paul's father, and Paul was taken out of school and put to work. The manager at Carnegie Hall was told to get another usher in his stead; the doorkeeper at the theatre was warned not to admit him to the house; and Charley Edwards remorsefully promised the boy's father not to see him again.   36

The members of the stock company were vastly amused when some of Paul's stories reached them—especially the women. They were hard-working women, most of them supporting indolent husbands or brothers, and they laughed rather bitterly at having stirred the boy to such fervid and florid inventions. They agreed with the faculty and with his father, that Paul's was a bad case.   37

The east-bound train was ploughing through a January snow-storm; the dull dawn was beginning to show grey when the engine whistled a mile out of Newark. Paul started up from the seat where he had lain curled in uneasy slumber, rubbed the breath-misted window glass with his hand, and peered out. The snow was whirling in curling eddies above the white bottom lands, and the drifts lay already deep in the fields and along the fences, while here and there the long dead grass and dried weed stalks protruded black above it. Lights shone from the scattered houses, and a gang of labourers who stood beside the track waved their lanterns.   38

Paul had slept very little, and he felt grimy and uncomfortable. He had made the all-night journey in a day coach because he was afraid if he took a Pullman he might be seen by some Pittsburgh business man who had noticed him in Denny & Carson's office. When the whistle woke him, he clutched quickly at his breast pocket, glancing about him with an uncertain smile. But the little, clay-bespattered Italians were still sleeping, the slatternly women across the aisle were in open-mouthed oblivion, and even the crumby, crying babies were for the nonce stilled. Paul settled back to struggle with his impatience as best he could.   39

When he arrived at the Jersey City station, he hurried through his breakfast, manifestly ill at ease and keeping a sharp eye about him. After he reached the Twenty-third Street station, he consulted a cabman, and had himself driven to a men's furnishing establishment which was just opening for the day. He spent upward of two hours there, buying with endless reconsidering and great care. His new street suit he put on in the fitting-room; the frock coat and dress clothes he had bundled into the cab with his new shirts. Then he drove to a hatter's and a shoe house. His next errand was at Tiffany's, where he selected silver mounted brushes and a scarf-pin. He would not wait to have his   40 silver marked, he said. Lastly, he stopped at a trunk shop on Broadway, and had his purchases packed into various travelling bags.

It was a little after one o'clock when he drove up to the Waldorf, and,   41
after settling with the cabman, went into the office. He registered from Washington; said his mother and father had been abroad, and that he had come down to await the arrival of their steamer. He told his story plausibly and had no trouble, since he offered to pay for them in advance, in engaging his rooms; a sleeping-room, sitting-room and bath.

Not once, but a hundred times Paul had planned this entry into New   42
York. He had gone over every detail of it with Charley Edwards, and in his scrap book at home there were pages of description about New York hotels, cut from the Sunday papers.

When he was shown to his sitting-room on the eighth floor, he saw at a   43
glance that everything was as it should be; there was but one detail in his mental picture that the place did not realize, so he rang for the bell boy and sent him down for flowers. He moved about nervously until the boy returned, putting away his new linen and fingering it delightedly as he did so. When the flowers came, he put them hastily into water, and then tumbled into a hot bath. Presently he came out of his white bath-room, resplendent in his new silk underwear, and playing with the tassels of his red robe. The snow was whirling so fiercely outside his windows that he could scarcely see across the street; but within, the air was deliciously soft and fragrant. He put the violets and jonquils on the tabouret beside the couch, and threw himself down with a long sigh, covering himself with a Roman blanket. He was thoroughly tired; he had been in such haste, he had stood up to such a strain, covered so much ground in the last twenty-four hours, that he wanted to think how it had all come about. Lulled by the sound of the wind, the warm air, and the cool fragrance of the flowers, he sank into deep, drowsy retrospection.

It had been wonderfully simple; when they had shut him out of the the-   44
atre and concert hall, when they had taken away his bone, the whole thing was virtually determined. The rest was a mere matter of opportunity. The only thing that at all surprised him was his own courage—for he realized well enough that he had always been tormented by fear, a sort of apprehensive dread that, of late years, as the meshes of the lies he had told closed about him, had been pulling the muscles of his body tighter and tighter. Until now, he could not remember a time when he had not been dreading something. Even when he was a little boy, it was always there—behind him, or before, or on either side. There had always been the shadowed corner, the dark place into which he dared not look, but from which something seemed always to be watching him—and Paul had done things that were not pretty to watch, he knew.

But now he had a curious sense of relief, as though he had at last thrown   45
down the gauntlet to the thing in the corner.

Yet it was but a day since he had been sulking in the traces; but yesterday   46
afternoon that he had been sent to the bank with Denny & Carson's deposit, as usual—but this time he was instructed to leave the book to be balanced. There was above two thousand dollars in checks, and nearly a thousand in the bank

notes which he had taken from the book and quietly transferred to his pocket. At the bank he had made out a new deposit slip. His nerves had been steady enough to permit of his returning to the office, where he had finished his work and asked for a full day's holiday tomorrow, Saturday, giving a perfectly reasonable pretext. The bank book, he knew, would not be returned before Monday or Tuesday, and his father would be out of town for the next week. From the time he slipped the bank notes into his pocket until he boarded the night train for New York, he had not known a moment's hesitation.

How astonishingly easy it had all been; here he was, the thing done; and 47
this time there would be no awakening, no figure at the top of the stairs. He watched the snow flakes whirling by his window until he fell asleep.

When he awoke, it was four o'clock in the afternoon. He bounded up 48
with a start; one of his precious days gone already! He spent nearly an hour in dressing, watching every stage of his toilet carefully in the mirror. Everything was quite perfect; he was exactly the kind of boy he had always wanted to be.

When he went downstairs, Paul took a carriage and drove up Fifth av- 49
enue toward the Park. The snow had somewhat abated; carriages and trades-men's wagons were hurrying soundlessly to and fro in the winter twilight; boys in woollen mufflers were shovelling off the doorsteps; the avenue stages made fine spots of colour against the white street. Here and there on the corners whole flower gardens blooming behind glass windows, against which the snow flakes stuck and melted; violets, roses, carnations, lilies of the valley—somehow vastly more lovely and alluring that they blossomed thus unnaturally in the snow. The Park itself was a wonderful stage winter-piece.

When he returned, the pause of the twilight had ceased, and the tune of 50
the streets had changed. The snow was falling faster, lights streamed from the hotels that reared their many stories fearlessly up into the storm, defying the raging Atlantic winds. A long, black stream of carriages poured down the av-enue, intersected here and there by other streams, tending horizontally. There were a score of cabs about the entrance of his hotel, and his driver had to wait. Boys in livery were running in and out of the awning stretched across the side-walk, up and down the red velvet carpet laid from the door to the street. Above, about, within it all, was the rumble and roar, the hurry and toss of thousands of human beings as hot for pleasure as himself, and on every side of him towered the glaring affirmation of the omnipotence of wealth.

The boy set his teeth and drew his shoulders together in a spasm of real- 51
ization; the plot of all dramas, the text of all romances, the nerve-stuff of all sensations was whirling about him like the snow flakes. He burnt like a faggot in a tempest.

When Paul came down to dinner, the music of the orchestra floated up 52
the elevator shaft to greet him. As he stepped into the thronged corridor, he sank back into one of the chairs against the wall to get his breath. The lights, the chatter, the perfumes, the bewildering medley of colour—he had, for a moment, the feeling of not being able to stand it. But only for a moment; these were his own people, he told himself. He went slowly about the corridors, through the writing-rooms, smoking-rooms, reception-rooms, as though he

were exploring the chambers of an enchanted palace, built and peopled for him alone.

When he reached the dining-room he sat down at a table near a window. 53 The flowers, the white linen, the many-coloured wine glasses, the gay toilettes of the women, the low popping of corks, the undulating repetitions of the *Blue Danube* from the orchestra, all flooded Paul's dream with bewildering radiance. When the roseate tinge of his champagne was added—that cold, precious, bubbling stuff that creamed and foamed in his glass—Paul wondered that there were honest men in the world at all. This was what all the world was fighting for, he reflected; this was what all the struggle was about. He doubted the reality of his past. Had he ever known a place called Cordelia Street, a place where fagged looking business men boarded the early car? Mere rivets in a machine they seemed to Paul,—sickening men, with combings of children's hair always hanging to their coats, and the smell of cooking in their clothes. Cordelia Street—Ah, that belonged to another time and country! Had he not always been thus, had he not sat here night after night, from as far back as he could remember, looking pensively over just such shimmering textures, and slowly twirling the stem of a glass like this one between his thumb and middle finger? He rather thought he had.

He was not in the least abashed or lonely. He had no especial desire to 54 meet or to know any of these people; all he demanded was the right to look on and conjecture, to watch the pageant. The mere stage properties were all he contended for. Nor was he lonely later in the evening, in his loge at the Opera. He was entirely rid of his nervous misgivings, of his forced aggressiveness, of the imperative desire to show himself different from his surroundings. He felt now that his surroundings explained him. Nobody questioned the purple; he had only to wear it passively. He had only to glance down at his dress coat to reassure himself that here it would be impossible for anyone to humiliate him.

He found it hard to leave his beautiful sitting-room to go to bed that 55 night, and sat long watching the raging storm from his turret window. When he went to sleep, it was with the lights turned on in his bedroom; partly because of his old timidity, and partly so that, if he should wake in the night, there would be no wretched moment of doubt, no horrible suspicion of yellow wall-paper, or of Washington and Calvin above his bed.

On Sunday morning the city was practically snow-bound. Paul break- 56 fasted late, and in the afternoon he fell in with a wild San Francisco boy, a freshman at Yale, who said he had run down for a "little flyer" over Sunday. The young man offered to show Paul the night side of the town, and the two boys went off together after dinner, not returning to the hotel until seven o'clock the next morning. They had started out in the confiding warmth of a champagne friendship, but their parting in the elevator was singularly cool. The freshman pulled himself together to make his train, and Paul went to bed. He awoke at two o'clock in the afternoon, very thirsty and dizzy, and rang for ice-water, coffee, and the Pittsburgh papers.

On the part of the hotel management, Paul excited no suspicion. There 57 was this to be said for him, that he wore his spoils with dignity and in no way made himself conspicuous. His chief greediness lay in his ears and eyes, and his excesses were not offensive ones. His dearest pleasures were the grey winter twilights in his sitting-room; his quiet enjoyment of his flowers, his clothes, his wide divan, his cigarette and his sense of power. He could not remember a time when he had felt so at peace with himself. The mere release from the necessity of petty lying, lying every day and every day, restored his self-respect. He had never lied for pleasure, even at school; but to make himself noticed and admired, to assert his difference from other Cordelia Street boys; and he felt a good deal more manly, more honest, even, now that he had no need for boastful pretensions, now that he could, as his actor friends used to say, "dress the part." It was characteristic that remorse did not occur to him. His golden days went by without a shadow, and he made each as perfect as he could.

On the eighth day after his arrival in New York, he found the whole   58
affair exploited in the Pittsburgh papers, exploited with a wealth of detail which indicated that local news of a sensational nature was at a low ebb. The firm of Denny & Carson announced that the boy's father had refunded the full amount of his theft, and that they had no intention of prosecuting. The Cumberland minister had been interviewed, and expressed his hope of yet reclaiming the motherless lad, and Paul's Sabbath-school teacher declared that she would spare no effort to that end. The rumour had reached Pittsburgh that the boy had been seen in a New York hotel, and his father had gone East to find him and bring him home.

Paul had just come in to dress for dinner; he sank into a chair, weak in   59
the knees, and clasped his head in his hands. It was to be worse than jail, even; the tepid waters of Cordelia Street were to close over him finally and forever. The grey monotony stretched before him in hopeless, unrelieved years; Sabbath-school, Young People's Meeting, the yellow-papered room, the damp dish-towels; it all rushed back upon him with sickening vividness. He had the old feeling that the orchestra had suddenly stopped, the sinking sensation that the play was over. The sweat broke out on his face, and he sprang to his feet, looked about him with his white, conscious smile, and winked at himself in the mirror. With something of the childish belief in miracles with which he had so often gone to class, all his lessons unlearned, Paul dressed and dashed whistling down the corridor to the elevator.

He had no sooner entered the dining-room and caught the measure of   60
the music, than his remembrance was lightened by his old elastic power of claiming the moment, mounting with it, and finding it all sufficient. The glare and glitter about him, the mere scenic accessories had again, and for the last time, their old potency. He would show himself that he was game, he would finish the thing splendidly. He doubted, more than ever, the existence of Cordelia Street, and for the first time he drank his wine recklessly. Was he not, after all, one of these fortunate beings? Was he not still himself, and in his own place? He drummed a nervous accompaniment to the music and looked about him, telling himself over and over that it had paid.

He reflected drowsily, to the swell of the violin and the chill sweetness   61
of his wine, that he might have done it more wisely. He might have caught an

outbound steamer and been well out of their clutches before now. But the other side of the world had seemed too far away and too uncertain then; he could not have waited for it; his need had been too sharp. If he had to choose over again, he would do the same thing tomorrow. He looked affectionately about the dining-room, now gilded with a soft mist. Ah, it had paid indeed!

Paul was awakened next morning by a painful throbbing in his head and   62
feet. He had thrown himself across the bed without undressing, and had slept with his shoes on. His limbs and hands were lead heavy, and his tongue and throat were parched. There came upon him one of those fateful attacks of clear-headedness that never occurred except when he was physically exhausted and his nerves hung loose. He lay still and closed his eyes and let the tide of realities wash over him.

His father was in New York; "stopping at some joint or other," he told   63
himself. The memory of successive summers on the front stoop fell upon him like a weight of black water. He had not a hundred dollars left; and he knew now, more than ever, that money was everything, the wall that stood between all he loathed and all he wanted. The thing was winding itself up; he had thought of that on his first glorious day in New York, and had even provided a way to snap the thread. It lay on his dressing-table now; he had got it out last night when he came blindly up from dinner,—but the shiny metal hurt his eyes, and he disliked the look of it, anyway.

He rose and moved about with a painful effort, succumbing now and   64
again to attacks of nausea. It was the old depression exaggerated; all the world had become Cordelia Street. Yet somehow he was not afraid of anything, was absolutely calm; perhaps because he had looked into the dark corner at last, and knew. It was bad enough, what he saw there; but somehow not so bad as his long fear of it had been. He saw everything clearly now. He had a feeling that he had made the best of it, that he had lived the sort of life he was meant to live, and for half an hour he sat staring at the revolver. But he told himself that was not the way, so he went downstairs and took a cab to the ferry.

When Paul arrived at Newark, he got off the train and took another cab,   65
directing the driver to follow the Pennsylvania tracks out of the town. The snow lay heavy on the roadways and had drifted deep in the open fields. Only here and there the dead grass or dried weed stalks projected, singularly black, above it. Once well into the country, Paul dismissed the carriage and walked, floundering along the tracks, his mind a medley of irrelevant things. He seemed to hold in his brain an actual picture of everything he had seen that morning. He remembered every feature of both his drivers, the toothless old woman from whom he had bought the red flowers in his coat, the agent from whom he had got his ticket, and all of his fellow-passengers on the ferry. His mind, unable to cope with vital matters near at hand, worked feverishly and deftly at sorting and grouping these images. They made for him a part of the ugliness of the world, of the ache in his head, and the bitter burning on his tongue. He stooped and put a handful of snow into his mouth as he walked, but that, too, seemed hot. When he reached a little hillside, where the tracks ran through a cut some twenty feet below him, he stopped and sat down.

The carnations in his coat were drooping with the cold, he noticed; all   66
their red glory over. It occurred to him that all the flowers he had seen in the
show windows that first night must have gone the same way, long before this.
It was only one splendid breath they had, in spite of their brave mockery at the
winter outside the glass. It was a losing game in the end, it seemed, this revolt
against the homilies by which the world is run. Paul took one of the blossoms
carefully from his coat and scooped a little hole in the snow, where he covered
it up. Then he dozed a while, from his weak condition, seeming insensible to
the cold.

The sound of an approaching train woke him, and he started to his feet,   67
remembering only his resolution, and afraid lest he should be too late. He
stood watching the approaching locomotive, his teeth chattering, his lips
drawn away from them in a frightened smile; once or twice he glanced nervously sidewise, as though he were being watched. When the right moment
came, he jumped. As he fell, the folly of his haste occurred to him with merciless clearness, the vastness of what he had left undone. There flashed through
his brain, clearer than ever before, the blue of Adriatic water, the yellow of
Algerian sands.

He felt something strike his chest,—his body was being thrown swiftly   68
through the air, on and on, immeasurably far and fast, while his limbs gently
relaxed. Then, because the picture making mechanism was crushed, the disturbing visions flashed into black, and Paul dropped back into the immense
design of things.   ■

MARILYN ARNOLD

AN ALIEN CHILD

A nationally recognized Cather scholar, Marilyn Arnold is professor of English at
Brigham Young University. The following article is an excerpt from her book *Willa
Cather's Short Fiction* (1984). Arnold is also the author of *Willa Cather: A Reference
Guide* (1986). Her recent scholarship has been focused on Cather's letters.

"Paul's Case," the final story in *The Troll Garden,* is drawn from Cather's ex-   1
periences as a high school English teacher and lower-middle–class neighborhood dweller in Pittsburgh. It was the only story for some time that Cather
allowed to be anthologized. Published seven years before Cather's first novel
would appear, it remains one of her most widely read and acclaimed works.

Eccentric, maybe even half-crazy, Paul abhors the dull respectability of   2
his neighborhood on Cordelia Street and his high school. He finds his only
pleasure as an usher at Carnegie Hall and as a hanger-on with the stock theater
company where he can bask in the artificial glow emanating from stage lights

which never play on him, from hotel lobbies he is forbidden to enter, from music and paintings he does not understand, and from the lives of performers he completely misinterprets. By comparison, school and home are drab, unbearable; he cannot be bothered with them. After a minor inquisition in which his teachers "fell upon him without mercy" (244),* Paul still shows no inclination to study or to be agreeable. It is decided finally that he must quit school and go to work, and that he must forego Carnegie Hall and the stock company.

Thus imprisoned in Cordelia Street with all legitimate avenues of escape   3
effectually closed, Paul commits a desperate act. Entrusted to deliver his company's weekend bank deposit, Paul makes his decision and takes flight. Structurally, the story is as bold as Paul. Part 1 ends with the adult collusion that separates Paul from the only things he loves; part 2 begins in abrupt juxtaposition with Paul on a train bound for New York. Once in New York he lives for several marvelous days the life he had always believed he was suited to live, the life of a wealthy boy in a luxurious room at the Waldorf, wearing fine clothes, eating elegant food, and surrounding himself with flowers.[1] But those self-indulgent days make it impossible for him to return to Cordelia Street. When Paul learns from the Pittsburgh newspapers that his father has repaid the stolen money and is en route to New York to retrieve him, he takes a ferry to Newark and a cab out of town. Then he dismisses the cab and struggles through deep snow along the bank beside the Pennsylvania tracks. When the train comes he leaps into its path. In the instant before he dies, however, he suffers a heartbreaking realization: he had been too impatient in grabbing his one moment of splendor; he should have gone to exotic lands across the seas. . . .

Paul knows that he is unsuited for Cordelia Street; what he does not   4
know is that he is unsuited for the worlds of art and wealth as well. Paul is an alien because he has a warped perception of everything; he is unable to see anything in his world as it really is. His mind reconstructs the world in his image of it, and then he tries to inhabit the world he conceives. Since in truth one segment of Paul's world is better than he imagines it to be, and the other is worse than he imagines, he is always out of step no matter where he is. Cordelia Street is repulsive to him, utterly ugly with its "grimy zinc tub[s]" and "cracked mirror[s]" (248) and its insufferable monotony. Cather indicates, however, that Paul's view is not necessarily correct. Cordelia Street is a respectable neighborhood where semisuccessful white collar workers and their wives rear great broods of children and attend ice cream socials at church. The fact that Paul's father can readily make good Paul's theft suggests that he is far from destitute.

Paul wants to believe that Cordelia Street and his high school represent   5
the very antithesis of the world for which he was made, the world of wealth and glamour. What he fails to perceive is that the ideals of Cordelia Street are identical with his own. He only thinks his values are out of place there; in

---

*The page references in this selection refer to the revised edition of *Willa Cather's Collected Short Fiction* edited by Virginia Faulkner and published by the University of Nebraska Press in 1970.

actuality they are not. Cordelia Street, like Paul, worships glamour and money and the things money can buy. Its gods are the wealthy business magnates for whom the men on Cordelia Street work. Up and down the street people like Paul's father sit on their front steps and exchange "legends of the iron kings," tales of their bosses who cruise the Mediterranean but still keep office hours on their yachts, "knocking off work enough to keep two stenographers busy." The street fairly buzzes with "stories of palaces in Venice, yachts on the Mediterranean, and high play at Monte Carlo," stories absorbed greedily by the underlings of the "various chiefs and overlords" (249, 250) whom Paul would like to emulate. Cordelia Street constructs a golden vision of the world Paul longs to enter.

The only thing within Paul's reach that approximates that fairy world is 6 the world of art—music, drama, painting. It seems to offer what he seeks.[2] But he is just as wrong in his perception of that world as he is in his perception of Cordelia Street. He mistakes its stagey glitter for its essence. . . . he knows nothing of true art. Since mere finery is what he craves, "symphonies, as such," do not mean "anything in particular to Paul"; but he loves them for their show just as he loves paintings and the theater. For him art is the soloist's "elaborate gown and a tiara, and above all . . . that indefinable air of achievement, that world-shine" (246). He longs to enter what he perceives to be "a tropical world of shiny, glistening surfaces and basking ease" (247). But not being an artist himself he has no real place in that spangled world.

Cather makes it clear that not only is Paul not an artist, but his perception of the artist's life and the artist's glittering world is miles from the truth. 7 The artists in this story have no delusions—and no wealth. Scarcely the "veritable queen of Romance" that Paul believes her to be, the German soloist is, in fact, "by no means in her first youth, and the mother of many children" (246). Paul's notions about the stock company players is equally distorted, and they, "especially the women," are "vastly amused" when they learn of the romantic stories Paul has told about them. "They were hardworking women, most of them supporting indigent husbands or brothers, and they laughed rather bitterly at having stirred the boy to such fervid and florid inventions" (253). It is a further irony that Paul's idols "agreed with the faculty and with his father that Paul's was a bad case" (253). His alienation from the world of art is complete.

Paul's last desperate effort to find place, to be where "his surroundings 8 explained him" (257), is also destined to failure, again because he mistakes artificial sheen for reality—and because he can make no distinction between the radiance of art and the shimmer of the Waldorf. The latter is just another version of the opera house to him. Art equals shine; shine equals wealth. To him it is all one desire. In New York, with a thousand dollars at his disposal, he believes he is home at last, for "on every side of him towered the glaring affirmation of the omnipotence of wealth." Here, he thinks, is the center of life; ". . . the plot of all dramas, the text of all romances, the nerve-stuff of all sensations was whirling about him like the snow flakes." He glides easily about the Waldorf, at last with "his own people," feeling "as though he were exploring the chambers of an enchanted palace, built and peopled for him alone" (256).

But Paul has merely purchased the sensation of home, played his only ace   9 for a few days of belonging. With stolen money he buys an artificial environment in which to enclose himself—linens, suits, gorgeous people, a fine room, and the hotel itself. Even Central Park is not real, but is "a wonderful stage winterpiece" (256). The Waldorf encasing Paul is the final symbol of his alienation because its artificial splendor isolates him from encroaching reality. Cather represents the Waldorf and its displaced occupant in repeated references to the alien hothouse flowers that bloom "under glass cases" on the streets of New York, all the "more lovely and alluring that they blossomed thus unnaturally in the snow" (256). Like Paul, the flowers can survive for a time if they are protected by artificial light and heat. But even then, their days are limited, and if they are ever removed from their heated cases, they wither and die.

In the story's final scenes, Cather continues to equate Paul symbolically   10 with flowers out of place in a harsh environment. Walking along the tracks, having made the decision never to return to Cordelia Street, Paul notices that

> the carnations in his coat were drooping with the cold, . . . their red glory over. It occurred to him that all the flowers he had seen in the glass cases that first night must have gone the same way, long before this. It was only one splendid breath they had, in spite of their brave mockery at the winter outside the glass; and it was a losing game in the end, it seemed, this revolt against the homilies by which the world is run. (260)

As if prompted by this symbolic description of his own brief moment of splendor and its inevitable end, Paul buries a blossom in the snow, acknowledging his death in a cold world that holds no lasting home for him.

Paul misconceives the garden of art as a glittering world of wealth and   11 ease, and he fails to perceive that the chief difference between Cordelia Street and the Waldorf is the difference between wanting and having—a difference not of kind but of degree. Understanding these worlds so little, he has no home in either of them. Only in his death, when he "drop[s] back into the immense design of things" (261), does the alien child appear to find place.

Notes

1. At least two sources suggest that Cather used two different models for her portraits of Paul in Pittsburgh and Paul in New York. In a 15 March 1943 letter to John Phillipson (Willa Cather archives in Red Cloud), Cather says that the Pittsburgh Paul was a boy she had taught in her Latin class, and the New York Paul was herself. The boy was high-strung and erratic like Paul, and tried to make people believe that he was a favorite of a theater stock company. So far as she knew, he never ran away or jumped under a train. She indicates that the New York Paul reflects her own feelings about New York and the Waldorf-Astoria when as a young woman in Pittsburgh she made occasional visits there. Cather also says that sometimes a character develops from a writer's grafting another person onto herself. Seibel, in his

recollections ("Miss Willa Cather from Nebraska," 205), reports that he read "Paul's Case" and insisted to Willa Cather "that the Paul of the first pages would not act like the Paul of the closing pages." He says, "Paul was not drawn from one boy in her high school classes, but from two boys—hence the dualism I sensed and she later admitted."

2. Slote (*Kingdom of Art,* 96, 97) speaks of Paul's "genuine if expressive feeling for art" and later describes him as "a Forest Child who desires things rare and strange, but to excess and with no one to help him." ■

Questions for Meaning

1. Arnold claims that the structure of "Paul's Case" is "as bold as Paul." What is unusual about the structure?
2. Why does Arnold believe that Paul is an "alien"?
3. According to Arnold, what values does Paul share with the neighbors from whom he feels so alienated?
4. Why is Paul unable to find a lasting place for himself?
5. Vocabulary: abhors (2), emanating (2), antithesis (5), emulate (5), indigent (7), fervid (7), omnipotence (8).

Questions about Strategy

1. Arnold opens her discussion of "Paul's Case" with two paragraphs of summary. Under what circumstances is this an appropriate strategy when writing about literature?
2. Consider the last sentence in paragraph 2: "It is decided finally that he must quit school and go to work, and that he must forego Carnegie Hall and the stock company." Ask yourself, "It is decided *by whom?*" What does the grammar of this sentence reveal about Arnold's point of view?
3. How well does Arnold support her claim that Paul is "half-crazy"?
4. What do the two notes contribute to Arnold's argument?

MICHAEL N. SALDA

WHAT REALLY HAPPENS IN CATHER'S "PAUL'S CASE"?

Michael N. Salda teaches English at the University of Southern Mississippi. In the following article, first published in 1992 in *Studies in Short Fiction,* he argues that the second half of "Paul's Case" happens only in Paul's head. As you read, note the words and passages that Salda uses to build his case, and consider whether you find it convincing.

Critics agree that Paul commits suicide by throwing himself before a train at   1
the end of Willa Cather's "Paul's Case: A Study in Temperament." But is this the only reading possible; in fact, is this reading even likely given the story's details? Bessie du Bois, one of Cather's earliest reviewers, quotes the final paragraphs of "Paul's Case" and then says something that would strike most readers as quite odd: "One feels rather defrauded that the author has omitted to say what came next; it would have been so easy to go on" (du Bois 613).[1] With Paul's broken body hurtling through the air, one wonders what the reviewer might wish Cather to add to the tale. After all, Paul is dead—or is he?

Let us review the day on which we meet Paul. The story opens in late   2
November with Paul, a Pittsburgh High School student under suspension for various ill-defined infractions, about to appear before the faculty's "inquisition" (103). His teachers all take their turns attacking Paul, but he remains composed and unaffected. When the faculty finishes with him, it is so late in the afternoon that he decides to forgo supper at home to go directly to Carnegie Hall, where he has a job as an usher. The concert hall has not opened, so Paul relaxes in the picture gallery. There he is "always exhilarated" by the paintings, and on this particular evening he "sat down before a blue Rico and lost himself" (104) until sometime after seven o'clock. Paul then hurries to don his usher's uniform, feeling, as he invariably does, "always considerably excited" (105) as he dresses for his duties in the concert hall. With great animation he seats the concert-goers, and finally settles into a chair, where "with a long sigh of relief, . . . [he] lost himself" (105) in a reverie brought on by the music. Cather explicitly likens this new fantasy to Paul's hours before the painting and describes it more fully than the first:

> It was not that symphonies, as such, meant anything in particular to Paul, but the first sigh of the instruments seemed to free some hilarious and potent spirit within him; something that struggled there like the Genius in the bottle found by the Arab fisherman. He felt a sudden zest of life; the lights danced before his eyes and the concert hall blazed into unimaginable splendour. (105)

[1]du Bois—whose remarks are entirely unfavorable and generally unjustified by the contents of *The Troll Garden* ("a collection of freak stories that are either lurid, hysterical or unwholesome" [612])—never explains her curious statement.

Paul often daydreams in this way, even in school, where we have all seen 3 the student who "always looked out of the window during the recitation" (103), his mind on something other than what the teacher is discussing. But Cather does not leave us wondering about the specific subjects of Paul's dreams. She takes us into one of them immediately after the concert. He leaves the concert hall early, where with "the feeling of not being able to let down, of its being impossible to give up this delicious excitement which was the only thing that could be called living at all," he paces "rapidly up and down the walk" (106). Paul is waiting: he follows the cab of the soprano who performed that night at Carnegie Hall to the Schenley Hotel. As Paul longs "to enter and leave school-masters and dull care behind him for ever" (106), he imagines himself suddenly swept into the building.

> In the moment that the door was ajar, it seemed to Paul that he, too, entered. He seemed to feel himself go after her up the steps, into the warm, lighted building, into an exotic, a tropical world of shiny, glistening surfaces and basking ease. He reflected upon the mysterious dishes that were brought into the dining-room, the green bottles in buckets of ice, as he had seen them in the supper party pictures of the *Sunday World* supplement. A quick gust of wind brought the rain down with sudden vehemence, and Paul was startled to find that he was still outside in the slush of the gravel driveway; that his boots were letting in the water and his scanty overcoat was clinging wet about him; that the lights in front of the concert hall were out, and that the rain was driving in sheets between him and the orange glow of the windows above him. There it was, what he wanted—tangibly before him, like the fairy world of a Christmas pantomime, but mocking spirits stood guard at the doors, and, as the rain beat in his face, Paul wondered whether he were destined always to shiver in the black night outside, looking up at it. (106–07)

This extended reverie, like the others, shows Paul's ability to inject himself into a story of his own making. During these fantasies, he loses track of time, place, and self. They occur in every case after periods of physical and mental excitement, in moments when Paul is relaxing and allowing his mind to wander. For reality he substitutes images drawn from the newspapers and the stage, from fairy tale and romance. Not that he gets his inspiration from these sources; indeed, he rarely reads (111). In fact, painting and music—good or bad ("from an orchestra to a barrel organ" [111])—inspire Paul's dreams at best indirectly. All he gets from them is "the spark, the indescribable thrill that made his imagination master of his senses, and he could make plots and pictures enough of his own" (111). The periods of excitement and subsequent relaxation help him attain the state of consciousness he requires to create stories, to get past those "mocking spirits," if only temporarily. The narrator's description of Paul's pupils as "abnormally large, as though he were addicted to belladonna, but there was a glassy glitter about them which that drug does not produce" (102), suggests that Paul is in fact addicted to *something,* and that something seems to be this cycle of excitement, relaxation, and reverie, into which Paul falls time and again.

Yet the long day must now end for Paul. He dreads returning to his (al-   4
most literally) colorless[2] life on Cordelia Street, and most of all dreads meeting
his father, explaining why he is so late, and, no doubt, although there is no
mention of it, giving an account of what happened at "the inquisition" that
day. So Paul decides to sneak into the basement to hide until morning. Soaked
through, he huddles near the furnace and stares fearfully into the darkness for
his father to appear at the top of the stairs. After an entire evening of exhilara-
tion, he falls into a now familiar pattern: "when his senses were deadened,
Paul's head was always singularly clear" (108), and, as before, he begins to
imagine, to make plots and pictures. Three scenarios come to mind:

> Suppose his father had heard him getting in at the window and had come down
> and shot him for a burglar? Then, again, suppose his father had come down, pis-
> tol in hand, and he had cried out in time to save himself, and his father had been
> horrified to think how nearly he had killed him? Then, again, suppose a day
> should come when his father would remember that night, and wish there had
> been no warning cry to stay his hand? With this last supposition Paul enter-
> tained himself until daybreak. (108)

Is it possible that the rest of "Paul's Case" arises from these scenarios, especially the last? To put it another way, does Paul, sitting alone in the basement,
imagine all that follows? When Paul drops "back into the immense design of
things" (121) at the end, is that the reader's clue that Paul never actually left it,
that he has been standing, so to speak, outside the Schenley all this time looking up, or, literally, that he has been in his basement all this time looking up
the steps for the arrival of the feared father and yet picturing himself elsewhere? This is the argument I will follow here.

Curiously, we never see Paul's meeting with his father, but are instead trans-   5
ported abruptly in the next paragraph to a typical Sunday afternoon on Cordelia Street. The motif of Paul at the bottom of the basement steps and his
father at the top recurs with Paul on the "lowest step of his 'stoop'" and his
father "on the top step" (109)—both recalling Paul looking up at the Schenley
and contrasting with his superior position later as he gazes down from the
Waldorf. If Paul is imagining all this, one can easily see how his present situation (in the basement) provides materials that he is reworking in this
(day)dream.[3] Now one may argue that all this proves is that Cather consistently develops motifs throughout the story—that (day)dreaming does not enter into it—but that ignores two facts: (1) Paul's obvious preoccupation with
his fantasy world, and (2) the abrupt shift between Paul's beginning to create

---

[2]With few exceptions, descriptions containing color occur in passages describing Paul's excitement and reverie; just as at these moments Paul himself "grew more and more vivacious
and animated, and the colour came to his cheeks and lips" (105).

[3]Given his long day and his exhaustion, perhaps he does fall asleep and dream all that follows.
The narrator says only that Paul "did not *try* to sleep" (108; my emphasis), which leaves open
the question of whether he actually did sleep. Hence I use the ambiguous "(day)dream."

stories about his father and the very next paragraph that starts to tell us a story about Paul and his father. Indeed, one has the feeling that the tale almost begins anew with the description of the day and weather: "The following Sunday was fine; the sodden November chill was broken by the last flash of autumnal summer" (108). Except for the first two words, this could well be a new story.

This new story—Paul's reverie—continues with the tale of his increasing disdain for school until the time, presumably no more than a few weeks after the story opens, when his father and the Principal decide that nothing more can be done with the boy. Paul is withdrawn from school and put to work. His father also makes him quit his position at Carnegie Hall and never again enter the theater.

A shift still more abrupt than the first—and marked by a blank line in the text[4]—signals a new movement. The reader slowly learns that Paul's reverie has shifted to January, that he has become a burglar (recalling the first scenario) by stealing money from his employer, and that he plans to live the high life in New York. The Waldorf replaces—or reconstitutes from the day residue—the Schenley, and again Paul imagines himself inside, enjoying all the opulence New York can offer. He finds himself delighting in each article of new clothing[5] and basking in the luxury of a dream-world where "Everything was quite perfect; he was exactly the kind of boy he had always wanted to be" (115). As in a dream, Paul can even change reality to match the "plots and pictures" he wishes to see: "everything was as it should be; there was but one detail in his *mental picture* that the place did not realize, so he rang for the bell boy and sent him down for flowers" (114; my emphasis).

Yet there is the lingering sense that this is only a reverie. Everything seems a bit *too* perfect to be believed—and Paul, too, recognizes this. He thinks of the Waldorf as "an enchanted palace, built and peopled for him alone" (116). He asks himself, "had he not always been thus, had he not sat here night after night, from as far back as he could remember . . . ? He rather thought he had" (116). The images repeatedly stress the artificial and unnatural aspects of the hothouse life behind the Waldorf's glass windows—all the while an ominous snowstorm rages without. References to Central Park as a "stage winter-piece" (115), the "pageant" (117) that passes before Paul, wine as "a magician's wand for wonder-building" (117), and many others, reinforce this feeling that we are looking into Paul's fantasy, a world created out of those "supper party pictures of the *Sunday World* supplement," a world that finally Paul only observes but cannot join, at least in part because it is not a real world at all but a (day)dream.

[4]Marked by a roman "II" in the magazine version (*McClure's Magazine* 25 [May 1905]: 74–83) that appeared after *The Troll Garden's* publication earlier that year, although the magazine version represents an earlier state of the text; see Woodress (xxvii). Woodress does not, however, list this variant. Subsequent editions of the story also mark the shift with a blank line.
[5]The New York clothes of course recall Paul's acute awareness of the way he dresses for both the faculty inquisition and his ushering job. It is no surprise that Paul's fascination with attire causes him to imagine himself in the role of "dresser" (110) to Charley Edwards.

This reverie, "the plot of all dramas, the text of all romances . . . was   9
whirling about him like the snow flakes. He burnt like a faggot in a tempest"
(116). Such a flame cannot last long. Neither can this fantasy. Although Paul
believes shortly after his arrival in New York that "this time there would be no
awakening, no figure at the top of the stairs" (115), and just as Paul's "golden
days went by without a shadow, and he made each as perfect as he could"
(118), word comes by way of the Pittsburgh newspapers that his father has repaid the money his son had stolen and is en route to New York to retrieve the
errant youth.

Paul now sees that Cordelia Street is inescapable. Just as Paul had known   10
on the way home from Carnegie Hall that "The end had to come sometime;
his father in his night-clothes at the top of the stairs . . ." (107), so, too, this
fantasy is coming to a close. The burglar of the first scenario has already appeared on Paul's stage, the father who figures in each of the proposed plots is
about to appear, and only the pistol remains to be played. It appears suddenly:
we learn, in the sort of narrative afterthought that makes sense only in a
(day)dream, that Paul bought a revolver on his *first* day in New York. Paul (in
the basement) introduces the gun in much the same way he brought the flowers onto the stage: he wills it to be there. But Paul will not shoot himself—that
would be too much like the role he has assigned his father in each of the scenarios—and so he seeks a different end.

He makes his way out of the city, taking a cab, then a ferry, then a train,   11
and finally another cab—all in order to "finish the thing splendidly" (118) by
jumping before a locomotive on Pennsylvania tracks:

> He felt something strike his chest, and that his body was being thrown swiftly
> through the air, on and on, immeasurably far and fast, while his limbs were
> gently relaxed. Then, because the picture making mechanism was crushed, the
> disturbing visions flashed into black, and Paul dropped back into the immense
> design of things. (121)

As Paul had earlier left the Schenley and "walked reluctantly toward the car
tracks" (107) that would return him to Cordelia Street, so now he imagines
himself again using a train to return to the reality of Cordelia Street, the basement, and the father—all of which constitute "the immense design of things"
that Paul can escape only through the power of his imagination. It is an ending altogether bleak, darker than suicide because Paul can only *imagine* that
escape. It is not that Paul must return to Pittsburgh or even that he dies—the
alternatives that he sees before him in the (day)dream—it is that he never
leaves Cordelia Street. His very power to tell stories, to create plots and pictures, is itself annihilated as his cinematic "picture making mechanism" is destroyed and the image fades to black.[6] Paul's imagination is so constricted and

---

[6]It may be worth noting that America's first nickelodeon opened in 1905 in Pittsburgh, the
city in which this story is set and where Cather had been living for a number of years when
"Paul's Case" was first published. The "picture making mechanism" and the "visions [that]
flashed into black" seem to me to derive from the language of cinematography, a language

circumscribed that he can picture himself only within that "immense design" over which he has no control and from which he can find no exit. Even in dreams he finds himself violently thrown back toward his home.

Has Paul succeeded in telling the story he planned: "suppose a day should come when his father would remember that night, and wish there had been no warning cry to stay his hand"? Certainly this reverie goes beyond the first scenario, in which his father simply shoots him because he thinks him a burglar. It is perhaps closer to the second scenario, where the father almost shoots him but stops at the last moment upon recognizing his son's voice. Yet this second plot tries to assign some self-hatred to his father, who would be "horrified to think how nearly he had killed him." Paul refuses to let his story take that turn; the father remains incapable (according to Paul's vision of him) of caring enough about his son to shudder at the thought of almost killing him. The third scenario comes closest to the reverie that Paul actually has. Paul's father removes him from school and bans him from the concert hall and playhouse, and subsequently Paul becomes a thief, runs away, has to have the stolen funds repaid by his father, and ultimately kills himself rather than face his father[7] and return to Cordelia Street. Paul's father has no pity for or understanding of his son's feelings, and (again, according to Paul's vision) would rather have shot his son that night in the basement than allow all the other events to occur. We should perhaps recall that Paul tells this story from his position atop a "soapbox" (108)—a word that almost always suggests someone with a particular point of view and a "case" to present. What better place for him to be as he spins out this tale about a father who cannot understand his son?   12

Works Cited

Cather, Willa. "Paul's Case: A Study in Temperament." *The Troll Garden* 102–21.

—. *The Troll Garden,* Ed. James Woodress. Lincoln: U of Nebraska P, 1983.

du Bois, Bessie. Rev. of *The Troll Garden. The Bookman* 21 (1905): 612–14.

Woodress, James. Introduction. Cather, *The Troll Garden* xi–xxx.   ■

Questions for Meaning

1. If Paul is addicted to something, what is it, according to Salda?
2. What evidence within the story suggests that Paul's life in the Waldorf is "too perfect to be believed"?
3. If Paul does not really commit suicide, why does Salda believe that the conclusion is "bleaker, darker than suicide"?

Cather no doubt would have been accustomed to seeing in the reviews of artistic events published alongside her own. The metaphor is all the more appropriate if Paul is merely creating a fiction.

[7]Still one more reminder that Paul (in the basement) is hiding from his father.

4. According to Salda, why is it significant that Paul sits on a soap box when he is in the basement hiding from his father?
5. Vocabulary: infractions (2), reverie (3), opulence (7), faggot (9), circumscribed (11).

Questions about Strategy

1. Consider the strategy in the opening paragraph. Why is it useful for Salda to establish a point on which critics agree when he himself is about to offer an alternative view?
2. Where does Salda first state his thesis?
3. Does Salda recognize that some readers might question his thesis?
4. Why does Salda emphasize two words in the last quotation in paragraph 7?

CARLOS A. PEREZ

"PAUL'S CASE": THE OUTSIDER

According to one of Paul's teachers, "I don't really believe that smile of his comes altogether from insolence; there's something sort of haunted about it. The boy is not strong for one thing. . . . There is something wrong about the fellow." What could that "something" be? A psychotherapist in private practice, Carlos A. Perez brings a multidisciplinary background to his reflections on this question. The following article was first published in 1989 in a collection of essays devoted to youth suicide prevention. It illustrates the author/date system recommended by *The Chicago Manual of Style*.

"Paul's Case," a classic portrait of alienation, was partially drawn from author   1
Willa Cather's own experiences while she was living in a lower-middle-class area of Pittsburgh at the turn of the century. The story is a vivid portrayal of a youth who is isolated from that culture and of his doomed efforts to seek deliverance. Published in 1905, and appropriately titled for a psychological study, "Paul's Case" remains one of Cather's most widely read and acclaimed works. This short story is admirable not only for its richness of style and detail, but also for its lucid characterization of a complex character—an outsider and a loner.

Although "Paul's Case" is a work of fiction, Cather based the story on   2
individuals from her own work and social environment at that time of her life, and it has been suggested that her sketch derived from an encounter with such

a boy in her high school English class. In that context, it is possible to view the story as a kind of literary "psychological autopsy," a procedure originally developed by the Los Angeles Suicide Prevention Center, which reconstructs the functioning style of a completed suicide. This technique is used to uncover the intention of the deceased as he or she approached death, tracing the evolution of the suicidal process of the individual (McGee 1974, 8).

Although Cather is writing about a culture removed by more than   3
eighty years from the present, this culture nevertheless serves as a psychological profile quite relevant to late twentieth-century America with its more depersonalized society. An assessment of Paul's personality reveals a highly neurotic individual with histrionic and schizoidal tendencies, and looking through the eyes of a suicidologist, one sees the evolution of his self-defeating and self-destructive actions. In the brief time frame of Cather's narrative, we are able not only to identify and to empathize with Paul but are also able to feel pity at his desperation. Cather's duality in sketching Paul's character is a measure of her art and helps the reader, even within the brief confines of a short story, to view Paul as the complicated person that he is.

Paul

The portrait of Paul that emerges from Cather's pages is that of a young man   4
torn by conflicts, ill-adapted to his environment and its people, but desperately practicing an imposture that allows him to survive. In his various spheres of activity, Paul is more an observer than a participant, aggressively working to deceive both himself and the world regarding his lack of integration. His sole pleasures are rooted in his "artistic" endeavors, but even these are counterfeit, for he lacks the depth to comprehend his experiences on anything but a superficial level and contents himself with form rather than substance. Marilyn Arnold (1985) writes:

> Paul is also Cather's ultimate alien. He belongs nowhere, and can never belong. . . . Cather portrays in Paul a being who is alienated by more than environment and lack of human contact and understanding. Paul is an alien because he has a warped perception of everything: he is unable to see anything in his world as it really is. His mind reconstructs the world in his image of it, and then he tries to inhabit the world he conceives. Since in truth one segment of Paul's world is better than he imagines it to be, and the other is worse than he imagines, he is always out of step no matter where he is. (181)

Paul aspires to the arenas of art and wealth, but his participation is pre-   5
dominantly fantasy-inspired. In fact, Paul is a hanger-on, lurking on the fringes of a glittery existence, and his idealized stage sets and imagined characters place no real demands on him, thus allowing him to maintain the illusion that he belongs to that world. His grand internal scenarios are only the substitutes he finds available to compensate for the emptiness of his real-life experiences.

Paul is introduced in the opening paragraphs of the story as he prepares   6
to meet with a disciplinary committee that is convened to pass judgment on

his recurring insubordinate attitudes and disruptive actions in his high school classes. Paul is clever and outwardly calm, but his brittle and aloof defensiveness is apparent:

> His eyes were remarkable for a certain hysterical brilliancy and he continually used them in a conscious, theatrical sort of way, peculiarly offensive in a boy. The pupils were abnormally large, as though he were addicted to belladonna, but there was a glassy glitter about them which that drug does not produce.
>
> When questioned by the Principal as to why he was there, Paul stated, politely enough, that he wanted to come back to school. This was a lie, but Paul was quite accustomed to lying: found it, indeed, indispensable for overcoming friction. His teachers were asked to state their respective charges against him, which they did with such a rancour and aggrievedness as evinced that this was not a usual case. Disorder and impertinence were among the offences named, yet each of his instructors felt that it was scarcely possible to put into words the real cause of the trouble, which lay in a sort of hysterically defiant manner of the boy's; in the contempt which they all knew he felt for them, and which he seemingly made not the least effort to conceal. Once, when he had been making a synopsis of a paragraph at the blackboard, his English teacher had stepped to his side and attempted to guide his hand. Paul had started back with a shudder and thrust his hands violently behind him. The astonished woman could scarcely have been more hurt and embarrassed had he struck at her. The insult was so involuntary and definitely personal as to be unforgettable. In one way and another, he had made all his teachers, men and women alike, conscious of the same feeling of physical aversion. In one class he habitually sat with his hand shading his eyes; in another he always looked out of the window during the recitation; in another he made a running commentary on the lecture, with humorous intention. (Cather 1965, 243–44)

Within the first few paragraphs, the portrait of the youth is vividly   7
drawn: the hysterical brilliance of the eyes, the theatrical gestures and quivering lips, the phobic reaction to being touched. All these behaviors repel his teachers and create puzzlement, thus achieving Paul's desired intention: to manufacture an impassable barrier of disdain between himself and others. He manifests not a reserved or retiring withdrawal but an aggressive defiance, a hostile and cold contempt of authority and values. His passive-aggressive conduct conveys an unmistakable message, one which finally becomes too flagrant and challenging to ignore. Although Paul is given another chance, his recalcitrance becomes completely indigestible, and he eventually forces his ejection from the surroundings he so detests.

As we shortly find out, Paul's aloofness and deceptions are reserved not   8
only for his teachers; his distancing maneuvers with his fellow students take another form, one of elitism. His formidable facade is erected by a continual boasting about world travels, rich relatives, and communion with a "better class" of people than those with whom he has accidentally been misplaced:

> He could not bear to have the other pupils think, for a moment, that he took these people seriously; he must convey to them that he considered it all trivial,

and was there only by way of a jest, anyway. He had autograph pictures of all the members of the stock company which he showed his classmates, telling them the most incredible stories of his familiarity with these people, of his acquaintance with the soloists who came to Carnegie Hall, his suppers with them and the flowers he sent them. When these stories lost their effect, and his audience grew listless, he became desperate and would bid all the boys good-bye, announcing that he was going to travel for a while; going to Naples, to Venice, to Egypt. Then, next Monday, he would slip back, conscious and nervously smiling; his sister was ill, and he would have to defer his voyage until spring. (252)

His transparent pose of association with wealthy, famous, and upper-class people is no doubt seen through and quietly ridiculed by his classmates, but Paul refuses to acknowledge this because his pretense provides him with the means of maintaining a delusion of grandeur, of being special and important, of being worthwhile. Once again Paul functions as an outsider, and his primary form of relating to his peers is a transparent boasting. In his own eyes, he imagines himself to be a misplaced and misunderstood artistic soul, involuntarily imprisoned among the rabble.

As an outsider, Paul does not require the love or acceptance of mere mortals, for he has adopted the belief that he belongs to a better, more cultured world. This posture armors Paul, providing an identity for him to embrace, giving him a fragile sense of meaningfulness in an otherwise barren existence. Although, as Cather later communicates, that meaning is a relatively empty one, it provides for Paul a semblance of an identity and a slender connection to future hopes. Victor Frankl (1967), among others, has written about the necessity of meaningfulness and purpose in one's life, emphasizing that this holds true even (perhaps especially) for a neurotic. Even though the direction taken may be misguided, Paul's belief system and his superficial immersion in the fringes of these idealized worlds supply a reason for being, almost his only reason. This foreshadows Paul's temporary escape through his New York elopement and the suicide that will follow when the structural walls of his impermanent bubble harshly collapse around him.

Paul's Worlds

There are three worlds of experience in Paul's phenomenological existence. First there is the dreary, commonplace "real" world of school, home, and the neighborhood of Cordelia Street. Enduring painfully through the mundane hours of his day, Paul perseveres until the passage of time brings deliverance through flight into his revered second world of art, drama, and music—his aesthetic sanctuaries. Paul spends as much time as possible in the world of the orchestral hall, working evenings as an usher, or in the world of the local theater, ingratiating himself by running errands for the actors or helping out around the theater. Paul's third world is the world of his fantasy, in which he assumes an importance much greater than that which he enjoys in either of his actual worlds. Eventually, what will doom Paul is his inability to separate himself from the third world of his fantasy. Unable or unwilling to break through and make contact with either of his two actual worlds, he resides within his imagination, guardedly content but lacking the nourishment that genuine experience would bring. At the end of the story, when his New York escape proves as ephemeral as his inner world, Paul's tenuous hold on this plane of existence slips and his self-destruction follows.

Paul's intensity of contempt, reserved for those who inhabit the mundane   11 world of reality, signals a pathological defensiveness; his alienation from and rejection of the universe that defines his true identity may be interpreted as a classic psychological defense mechanism, that of projection. As he repudiates the undistinguished middle class he belongs to, Paul vilifies his own ordinariness, an intolerable condition that must be altered through redefinition of reality. Thus, this perceptual reframing requires an all-encompassing denial of his connection to his first world and a subsequent displacement of his self-hatred onto those living out their lives in that niche into which he was accidentally born. For Paul to relate in any substantive way to these inhabitants would be to acknowledge their potential relevance to him; this he must avoid in order to perpetuate his complex concept of superiority. Cather makes this strikingly clear in her description of Paul's arrival at home one evening after having ushered at the orchestral hall:

> Paul never went up Cordelia Street without a shudder of loathing. His home was next the house of the Cumberland minister. He approached it to-night with the nerveless sense of defeat, the hopeless feeling of sinking back forever into ugliness and commonness that he had always had when he came home. The moment he turned into Cordelia Street he felt the waters close above his head. After each of these orgies of living, he experienced all the physical depression which follows a debauch; the loathing of respectable beds, of common food, of a home penetrated by kitchen odours; a shuddering repulsion for the flavourless, colourless mass of every-day existence; a morbid desire for cool things and soft lights and fresh flowers. (248)

Little is explicitly known about Paul's immediate family: his sisters are   12 briefly described playing in the neighborhood, and it is implied that his mother has been dead for some time. His most significant relationship is with his formal and authoritarian father. This relationship is defined by fear and intimidation, engendering a dread within Paul that permeates his emotional consciousness:

> The nearer he approached the house, the more absolutely unequal Paul felt to the sight of it all; his ugly sleeping chamber; the cold bath-room with the grimy zinc tub, the cracked mirror, the dripping spiggots; his father, at the top of the stairs, his hairy legs sticking out from his night-shirt, his feet thrust into carpet slippers. He was so much later than usual that there would certainly be inquiries and reproaches. Paul stopped short before the door. He felt that he could not be accosted by his father to-night; that he could not toss again on that miserable bed. He would not go in. (248)

Paul abhors the plebian respectability and drab surroundings of Cordelia Street—characteristics that are personified by his father. Paul centers the rejection of his own origins on the rejection of his father, thereby further liberating himself, in his own mind, from the prison of this reality and certifying, in his own estimation, that he is there by an accident of fate. Paul's ultimate escape is again foreshadowed by his waking nightmare, in which he is shot by his father following one of his late-night entries.

The energy that fuels Paul's anger and self-rejection and the consequent   13 projection derives from far more than a teenage identity-forming rebelliousness. There is a genuine threat emanating from his father, but it is more accurately the threat of suffocation through the denial of Paul's life-giving escapes. His later flight to New York is precipitated by his father's barring him from his theatrical pursuits and his usher's job at Carnegie Hall and installing him in employment as a menial functionary with a banking establishment.

Ironically, Paul does not really reject the values espoused by his father and   14 the neighbors of Cordelia Street; quite the contrary, he enthusiastically shares many of their much discussed materialistic goals. Like Paul, the inhabitants of Cordelia Street aspire to glamour and wealthy luxuries, and its heroes are the "Legends of the Iron Kings"—powerful business moguls who inhabit palaces in Venice, conduct business in yachts in the Mediterranean, and gamble lavishly in Monte Carlo. But Paul's only ambition is to construct castles in the air, perhaps because he recognizes how far out of reach they really are; except in his fantasies, he does not even wish to enter those castles, but is content to gaze upon them from afar. So Paul must obtain his gratification through a kind of osmosis, by rubbing shoulders with the stock repertory actors, by inhaling the fragrances of the orchestral hall, and by effusively greeting its wealthy and festive patrons. Cather skillfully communicates Paul's relief at achieving this refuge:

> It was at the theatre and at Carnegie Hall that Paul really lived; the rest was but a sleep and a forgetting. This was Paul's fairy tale, and it had for him all the allurement of a secret love. The moment he inhaled the gassy, painty, dusty odour behind the scenes, he breathed like a prisoner set free, and felt within him the possibility of doing or saying splendid, brilliant, poetic things. The moment the cracked orchestra beat out the overture from *Martha,* or jerked at the serenade from *Rigoletto,* all stupid and ugly things slid from him, and his senses were deliciously, yet delicately fired. (251)

Cather graphically depicts the gloominess and claustrophobic confines of   15 Paul's life, at least as he perceives it. What Paul lacks in his everyday existence, in relationships, and in his own personality, he attempts to find vicariously in the world of the arts. His only salvation is an escape into the world of music and theater, experiences which transport him from the grit of Cordelia Street to the glamour of the stage. On certain evenings, Paul works as an usher at Carnegie Hall and in this environment only do we see Paul come alive:

> He was always considerably excited while he dressed, twanging all over to the tuning of the strings and the preliminary flourishes of the horns in the

music-room; but to-night he seemed quite beside himself, and he teased and plagued the boys until, telling him that he was crazy, they put him down on the floor and sat on him.

Somewhat calmed by his suppression, Paul dashed out to the front of the house to seat the early comers. He was a model usher; gracious and smiling he ran up and down the aisles; nothing was too much trouble for him; he carried messages and brought programmes as though it were his greatest pleasure in life, and all the people in his section thought him a charming boy, feeling that he remembered and admired them. As the house filled, he grew more and more vivacious and animated, and the colour came to his cheeks and lips. It was very much as though this were a great reception and Paul were the host. (245–46)

Here, for the first time, Paul is viewed coming to life; he is charming, animated, and colorful, facets of his personality unrevealed in any other side of his character. Like a dormant plant kept too long in the dark, Paul's vibrancy unfolds only in the reflected light of the majestic symphonies and the glittering plays. His basking in the show business glow of the theater is much more intense than that of an ardent fan: Paul in effect transcends spectating and merges with this brilliant display. He is infused with the projected energy and feeds upon and unites with this idealized realm.

For Paul, however, the merger is primarily an escape; he has no genuine appreciation of the artistry, but instead gorges himself on the artificial and temporary ambience created by such events. As an usher at the concert hall and as a hanger-on, a kind of stage-door Johnny at the theater, he is once again an outsider, reacting to the form but not to the substance of the art. He does not understand the paintings that he views for hours on end; the music in which he revels serves simply as a background for his costumed fantasy; and the plays that he attends backstage become merely vehicles to carry him closer to the charmed and glamourous actors and actresses: 16

> When the symphony began Paul sank into one of the rear seats with a long sigh of relief, and lost himself as he had done before the Rico [a painting]. It was not that symphonies, as such, meant anything in particular to Paul, but the first sigh of the instruments seemed to free some hilarious and potent spirit within him; something that struggled there like the Genius in the bottle found by the Arab fisherman. He felt a sudden zest of life; the lights danced before his eyes and the concert hall blazed into unimaginable splendour. (246)

Such a diet serves to provide for Paul his sole emotional sustenance, but the nutritional value of this intake is short-lived. Paul's fantasies, like a binge on empty calories, provide a temporary satiation and pleasure, followed by a depression. Paul experiences an elation similar to a kind of drug high, and were this a contemporary setting, one might well imagine Paul obtaining his transport from a narcotic. Similar to a fleeting, drug-induced euphoria, Paul's imaginative escapes are followed by the inevitable downturn when the effects of this feast wear off:

After a concert was over Paul was always irritable and wretched until he got to sleep, and to-night he was even more than usually restless. He had the feeling of not being able to let down, of its being impossible to give up this delicious excitement which was the only thing that could be called living at all. (246)

Paul is addicted to his escapism; it offers him an illusion of beauty, a respite from earthly demands, but, most importantly, a sense of belongingness, of being a part of a grander, more deserving world. But Paul's membership in that society is his own manufactured fantasy, and the "Beautiful People" themselves are creations of Paul's romantic notions of artists:

The members of the stock company were vastly amused when some of Paul's stories reached them—especially the women. They were hard-working women, most of them supporting indigent husbands or brothers, and they laughed rather bitterly at having stirred the boy to such fervid and florid inventions. They agreed with the faculty and with his father that Paul's was a bad case. (253)

Paul's transparent boastings ensure his role as a dreamer and a loner, an outsider in the world of art as well as in the world of everyday reality. The weary heroes and heroines of his dreams further express an ironic amusement at Paul's tales. His maladroitness and anxieties give rise to the manufacture of a fantasy world in which he can delude himself that he belongs. The delicate balance of forces and counterforces is not to be maintained; it may be that Paul himself, exhausted by the pretenses and fears, brings about this unsettling in an attempt to find desperate relief.

The Escape

Paul's tenuous forays into his contrived sanctuaries are critically endangered as   17
he finally pushes too far with his teachers and his father. Thus, his exasperated father removes Paul from school and places him full-time in a dreary messenger job in a business firm. Unfortunately, his father also sees to it that Paul's job as an usher at Carnegie Hall is ended and his backstage association with the stock theater company is forbidden. Paul's only avenues of escape and acceptance are immediately and permanently cut off. On impulse Paul steals "nearly a thousand" dollars of the firm's money and travels to New York to live out his fantasy life, however briefly. He purchases an expensive wardrobe, checks into the Waldorf, and sets out to indulge in the high style to which he imagines himself to be destined.

There is exultation in the achievement of this dream; the reader feels the   18
lifting of the oppressiveness that makes up Paul's daily life and experiences with him a sense of tranquility as he delights in wintry Central Park, in the opulence of the Waldorf, and in the sanctity of the opera booth. David Stouck (1975) describes Paul as "constricted, tense, tormented by a groping desire for beauty but taken in by mere tinsel and stage properties" (180). Paul is indeed

taken in by this image. But Cather recreates Paul's delight in his illusory experience so powerfully that the reader as well is caught up in the magic of Paul's sense of freedom in his release from maintaining his facade and of keeping up the superstructure of the lies. Cather notes that his deceits were not out of perverseness, but for recognition and admiration. With the removal of this necessity, a measure of self-respect returns, and Paul feels a calm sense of well-being unknown on Cordelia Street.

Yet, in all this splendid living, Paul remains an alien, going through the motions but making no genuine impact on, or contact with, others. Although he avidly consumes concerts, plays, and fine dinners, he does so with no effort to know or to interact with the lives of the people around him. With the stolen money, Paul purchases an artificial environment, a stage set in which he surrounds himself with the props of his dream image, but he is still unable to break through the restrictions of his role; he remains an outsider, merely "dressing the part": 19

> He was not in the least abashed or lonely. He had no especial desire to meet or to know any of these people; all he demanded was the right to look on and conjecture, to watch the pageant. The mere stage properties were all he contended for. Nor was he lonely later in the evening; in his loge at the Metropolitan. He was now entirely rid of his nervous misgivings, of his forced aggressiveness, of the imperative desire to show himself different from his surroundings. . . .
>   . . .
> . . . His dearest pleasures were the grey winter twilights in his sitting-room; his quiet enjoyment of his flowers, his clothes, his wide divan, his cigarette and his sense of power. (257–58)

As Marilyn Arnold explains:

> Paul's last desperate attempt to find place, to be where "his surroundings explained him," is also destined to failure, again because he mistakes artificial sheen for reality—and because he can make no distinction between the radiance of art and the shimmer of the Waldorf. The latter is just another version of the opera because to him, Art equals shine; shine equals wealth. To him it is all one desire. (1985, 182)

The fantasy cannot endure; soon Paul notices in a Pittsburgh newspaper that the crime has been discovered; although restitution has been made by his father and the firm is not pressing charges, he learns that there are reports that he was seen in a New York hotel, and he envisions his enraged father at that moment vengefully seeking him. The inevitable outcome has arrived, and Paul is forced at last to confront the futility of his predicament: 20

> It was to be worse than jail, even; the tepid waters of Cordelia Street were to close over him finally and forever. The grey monotony stretched before him in hopeless, unrelieved years. . . . He had the old feeling that the orchestra had suddenly stopped, the sinking sensation that the play was over. (258)

It is not so much remorse or fear of punishment that causes Paul such   21
distress at the thought of returning, but the prospect of being sentenced to live
out his days in that intolerable, ordinary, drab existence of which he feels no
part. With his money almost depleted, a penetrating numbness overtakes him
and clouds his mind. A wretched fear invades his reason, and his perspective
narrows to a tiny circle of inescapable dread. Nausea accompanies the thought
of girding himself for a future of such daily deprivations, and he feels a weight
of unendurable proportions; his palpable fear drives his thoughts to suicide as
his final evasion:

> It was the old depression exaggerated; all the world had become Cordelia
> Street. Yet somehow he was not afraid of anything, was absolutely calm; per-
> haps because he had looked into the dark corner at last and knew. It was bad
> enough, what he saw there, but somehow not so bad as his long fear of it had
> been. He saw everything clearly now. He had a feeling that he had made the
> best of it, that he had lived the sort of life he was meant to live, and for half an
> hour he sat staring at the revolver. (259–60)

He had lived as gloriously as he knew how, though briefly; in his denial, he
had never consciously looked beyond the point when he would exhaust the
money. Yet, on a deeper level, Paul had always viewed his death as an inescapable companion, waiting for the proper circumstances to emerge; indeed,
he had planned on this alternative to an enforced return, having prepared for
it by bringing the pistol with him to New York.

Although true escape is within his reach, Paul chooses not to take that   22
route. Instead of lavishing his small fortune in New York, he might have gone
abroad to some place where Cordelia Street could never retrieve him. But he
is too needy and emotionally bereft to put off his fantasied escape, and he
never seriously considers other avenues of freedom, turning his back on the
paths that might have saved him. When action is forced through inevitable circumstance, he is too panicked and perhaps too defeated to contemplate further
escape. It seems, therefore, that his self-hatred and destructive urges ines-
capably structure his choice of a brief orgy of wondrous existence, a taste that
dooms him from the moment of his decision to steal the money:

> He might have caught an outbound steamer and been well out of their clutches
> before now. But the other side of the world had seemed too far away and too
> uncertain then; he could not have waited for it; his need had been too sharp. If
> he had to choose over again, he would do the same thing to-morrow. (259)

Deep within himself, Paul recognizes the ultimate futility of his escapade, because, as the outsider, he can never truly belong. Wealth allows him to purchase for a while the exterior trappings of his fantasy, but he is not really of
that world, and the wealth he needs to belong in it is beyond his grasp. Yet, in
his own mind, he is not, nor can he ever be, a part of the world of Cordelia
Street. He is satisfied, he tells himself, with his brief sojourn in the glittering
avenues, which offer a flavor of what life could be. Yet, because this existence

is truly out of his reach, there is no point in continuing with life as he knows it—life as it can only be for Paul.

Paul decides that he will not shoot himself; it is not the way he will   23
choose to play his final scene. It may be that he wishes for a bit more time to reflect, or perhaps he does not wish to despoil the elegance that he inhabited for a time. So he takes a carriage out to the countryside and the woods, and, in his final hour, walking through the snow, remembers the exotic flowers displayed in hothouse cases in New York in mid-winter:

> It was only one splendid breath they had, in spite of their brave mockery at the winter outside the glass; and it was a losing game in the end, it seemed, this revolt against the homilies by which the world is run. (260)

Paul, too, had taken his one splendid breath, and, like a flower removed from its protective case, he would also perish. Prompted by this symbolic representation of his own brief moment of magnificence and its inevitable end, he buries a blossom in the snow, as a way of acknowledging his death in a cold world that holds no lasting home for him. Throwing himself into the path of an approaching locomotive, he recognizes, as he dies, the rashness of his actions:

> When the right moment came, he jumped. As he fell, the folly of his haste occurred to him with merciless clearness, the vastness of what he had left undone. There flashed through his brain, clearer than ever before, the blue of Adriatic water, the yellow of Algerian sands.
>
> He felt something strike his chest, and that his body was being thrown swiftly through the air, on and on, immeasurably far and fast, while his limbs were gently relaxed. Then, because the picture making mechanism was crushed, the disturbing visions flashed into black, and Paul dropped back into the immense design of things. (260–61)

Reflections

Some commentators argue that, in "Paul's Case," Willa Cather intended to   24
make a statement about the inherent beauty of art as compared to the materialistic concerns of the middle class. John H. Murphy and Kevin A. Synnott (1984) write of her depiction of the struggle between "noble artistic ideals and crass commercialism, the theme that would occupy this author for the next forty years" (2). Leon Edel (1984) reports that Cather lived for five years in a series of depressing boardinghouses in neighborhoods much like her descriptions of Cordelia Street, and that "the way in which she escaped from these into the world of theater and music is reflected in 'Paul's Case'" (212). Clearly, some of Cather's sympathies lie in her identification with Paul. From this perspective, Paul is regarded as a sensitive, artistically inclined individual whose innate strivings are in conflict with his environment. The emphasis is on the unresponsiveness, indeed, the deliberate "quashing" of these aspirations by his social milieu; the responsibility for this grinding-down process is clearly placed on that environment, and we are educated by a literary exercise in turn-of-the-century social psychology.

Although this may have been one intentional statement, Cather's other   25
significant message concerning Paul's loneliness and alienation, and his own
role in the maintenance of that detachment, is also of immediate relevance
when viewing the story from a developmental, individualistic perspective.
Cather's profile of an insecure, frustrated, defensive, frightened, and impotent
youth transcends the temporal locale of the story and carries much pertinence
into the present. With the increasing emphasis of style over substance in recent
decades, individuals who possess such fragile identities may end up crushed in
the impersonal jaws of a culture that is insensitive to their needs; their individual struggles may culminate in suicide, anti-social behavior, drug abuse, and a
myriad of other societal ills. The critique of Susan Rosowski (1986) supports
this interpretation:

> Paul is an observer of art. Without talent or ambition to perform, he is forever
> separated from the glittering world he seeks to enter, yet just as separated from
> the common world he seeks to leave. In Paul, Cather has created a charac-
> ter . . . who has lost his soul. Cordelia Street is ugly indeed, with its vulgar
> art, oppressive smells, and near-sighted people; but the fantasy Paul attempts to
> enter is equally inhuman. The story presents the horror of worshipping a false
> idol and the tragedy for one who, having been bewitched by the artificial, has
> no one to save him. (28–29)

If one views "Paul's Case" as a kind of psychological autopsy, Paul's ulti-   26
mate fate can be traced to the lack of genuine interaction between himself and
his worlds. Although it is true that he maintains a formidable shield, this defense is a self-protective mechanism that is perpetuated by a lack of knowledge
of alternative methods of survival. That no one breaks through Paul's armor
plate is testimony not only to the effectiveness of that barrier, but also to the
dehumanizing tendencies of authority, institutions, and social groups en
masse. Nonconformity in any guise is rarely tolerated by power structures, and
few are the individuals who will strive to negotiate such obstacles and reach
out to touch the lonely person at the far end of the gauntlet.

Perhaps the most relevant message communicated in "Paul's Case" is that   27
aggression, anger, hatred, fear, and rejection may simply be symptomatic
shields unwittingly established by outsiders in our societies, and that we must
look beyond and move beyond such distancing surface behaviors in order to
make real contact and prevent destructive consequences. For the outsider
resides within us all, and our own revulsion may be a response to our internal
image that is projected upon those unfortunate individuals who are unable to
find any other disguise for their loneliness and insecurity.

Literature Cited

Arnold, Marilyn. 1985. Two of the lost. In *Willa Cather,* edited by Harold Bloom. New York:
    Chelsea Press.
Cather, Willa. 1905. Paul's Case. In *Willa Cather's collected short fiction,* edited by Virginia
    Faulkner. Lincoln: University of Nebraska Press.
Daiches, David. 1951. *Willa Cather: A critical introduction.* Ithaca: Cornell University Press.

Edel, Leon. 1984. A cave of one's own. In *Critical essays on Willa Cather,* edited by John J. Murphy. Boston: G.K. Hall.

Frankl, Victor. 1967. *Psychotherapy and existentialism.* New York: Washington Square Press.

Gerber, Philip L. 1975. *Willa Cather.* Boston: Twayne.

McGee, Richard K. 1974. *Crisis intervention in the community.* Baltimore: University Park.

Murphy, John J., and Kevin A. Synott. 1984. The recognition of Willa Cather's art. In *Critical essays on Willa Cather,* edited by John J. Murphy. Boston: G.K. Hall.

Murphy, John J., ed. 1984. *Critical essays on Willa Cather.* Boston: G.K. Hall.

Rosowski, Susan. 1986. *The voyage perilous: Willa Cather's romanticism.* Lincoln: University of Nebraska Press.

Stouck, David. 1975. *Willa Cather's imagination.* Lincoln: University of Nebraska Press. ■

Questions for Meaning

1. What does Perez mean when he describes Paul as "passive-aggressive"?
2. According to Perez, what has enabled Paul to persuade himself that he does not need the love or acceptance of the people in his community?
3. What are Paul's "three worlds," according to Perez?
4. Why does Paul settle for a temporary escape in New York City rather than using the money he stole to get far beyond the reach of his father?
5. Why does Perez believe that "Paul's Case" provides insights relevant to current social problems?
6. Vocabulary: alienation (1), duality (3), aloof (6), recalcitrance (7), tenuous (10), pathological (11), plebeian (12), vicariously (15), ambience (16), satiation (16), maladroitness (16).

Questions about Strategy

1. As a psychologist writing about literature, Perez was faced with the need to establish his authority in two separate fields. How does he go about doing so? Is he successful?
2. Consider the quotations drawn from the story. How well do they support the claims that Perez makes? How well does he analyze them?
3. To what extent does Perez rely on Marilyn Arnold? Does he distinguish his interpretation from Arnold's?
4. In writing about "Paul's Case," does Perez have a clear purpose? For what kind of audience do you think he intended this piece? Is a discussion of this story appropriate for the audience in question?

CLAUDE J. SUMMERS

"A LOSING GAME IN THE END": AESTHETICISM AND HOMOSEXUALITY IN CATHER'S "PAUL'S CASE"

Claude J. Summers is the William E. Stirton Professor of English at the University of Michigan, Dearborn. His books include *Gay Fictions: Studies in a Male Homosexual Literary Tradition* (1980), and *E. M. Forster* (1983). He is also the coauthor of *Bright Shootes of Everlastingnesse: The Seventeenth-Century Religious Lyric* (1987). In the following article, first published in *Modern Fiction Studies* in 1990, Summers discusses how Cather responded to Oscar Wilde, the celebrated Irish writer who in 1895 was sentenced to two years in prison with hard labor after a British court decided that he was homosexual.

Willa Cather's homosexuality, for years a well-guarded but scarcely well-kept   1
secret, is by now widely acknowledged. Sharon O'Brien's *Willa Cather: The Emerging Voice* sensitively traces Cather's personal and artistic development, her emergence from the male-identified male impersonator of her adolescence and youth into the mature woman writer who created the first strong female heroes in American literature. Central to this transformation were Cather's eventual liberation from her early internalized male aesthetic after a long and difficult struggle and her acceptance of her lesbianism, even as she recognized the need to conceal her sexual identity as "the thing not named." As O'Brien remarks, "Throughout her literary career, Cather was both the writer transforming the self in art and the lesbian writer at times forced to conceal 'unnatural' love by projecting herself into male disguises" (215).[1]

What has not been sufficiently noted, however, is Cather's early contri-   2
bution to gay male literature and to the debate about homosexuality sparked by the Wilde scandal. More particularly, "Paul's Case," the acclaimed story that marks the beginning of Cather's artistic maturity after a prolonged period of apprenticeship, has not yet been placed in the context of its author's growing awareness of the limits of the masculine aesthetic that she originally espoused. Nor has the story's insight into the homosexual's plight in American society at the turn into the new century been adequately explored. In *Playing the Game: The Homosexual Novel in America,* Roger Austen briefly discusses "Paul's Case" as a depiction of a sensitive young man stifled by the drab ugliness of his environment and places the protagonist in an American literary tradition of "village sissies" (31–33). And more exhaustively, Larry Rubin argues that the title character of the story is "very probably homosexual by nature and temperament" and that "Cather is trying to show us the tragic consequences of the

---

[1]For other discussions of Cather as a lesbian, see Jane Rule (74–87) and Deborah Lambert. Phyllis Robinson discusses Cather's romantic attachments with women but does not use the term lesbian.

450   PART 3 / SOURCES FOR ARGUMENT

conflict between a sensitive and hence alienated temperament, on the one hand, and a narrowly 'moral,' bourgeois environment, on the other" (131). But both discussions tend to sentimentalize the protagonist's gayness and to reduce the story to a simple conflict between the individual and society. Neither study locates "Paul's Case" in the context of Cather's response to the aesthetic movement in general or to the Wilde scandal in particular. Consequently, they fail to grasp the complexity of Cather's story and of her perspective on homosexuality in it.

For the young Cather, Wilde was a profoundly disturbing figure. The   3
target of a number of her early critical remarks published in the *Nebraska State Journal* and the Lincoln *Courier* (now conveniently collected in *The Kingdom of Art*[2]), he unmistakably challenged some of her most deeply cherished social and aesthetic notions and roused her to some of her most visceral expressions of contempt. Cather's attitude toward Wilde and the aesthetic movement in these early newspaper columns and reviews is unremittingly hostile. Regarding him as a poseur who betrayed his talent, she despises his "insincerity," his tendency to mock social conventions, his elevation of art at the expense of nature, and, most important, his "driveling effeminacy" (135). Interestingly, her hostility to Wilde is expressed so vehemently—indeed, so excessively—as to make one suspect that he represented for her not merely an artistic creed with which she lacked sympathy but a personal psychological threat. The early comments on Wilde are extraordinarily revealing of Cather's cast of mind in the mid-1890s, as contrasted with the period some ten years later when she wrote "Paul's Case," and they form an illuminating backdrop against which to explore the story.

In an 1894 review of Robert Hichens' "clever and inane" but insinuating   4
satire on Wilde and his circle, *The Green Carnation,* Cather remarks that "it certainly ought to succeed in disgusting people with Mr. Wilde's epigrammatic school once and for all. It turns and twists those absurd mannerisms and phrases of Wilde's until they appear as ridiculous as they really are" (135). In the same year, in a review of *Lady Windermere's Fan,* she observes that Wilde's "philosophy is so contemptible, so inane, so puny that even with all its brilliant epigrams the club talk in the third act is wearisome" and that through the "little puppy Cecil Graham" (who, like the protagonist of "Paul's Case" and like Wilde himself, sports a carnation in his button-hole) Wilde "vents all his unwholesome spleen and his pitiable smallness" (389). She finds the play artificial and unbelievable because its theme is motherhood, a thing "which a man of Mr. Wilde's ethics and school and life cannot even conceive" (388). Cather's dislike for Wilde in these pieces and the personalizing of her repugnance go beyond measured criticism; clearly, she found his artificiality and iconoclasm, especially his challenge to sex-role conventions and to the hearty masculinity that she embraced at the time, deeply dispiriting. Her references to Wilde in terms of frailty—his "puny philosophy," his "little puppy" of a character, his "pitiable smallness"—are particularly noteworthy. They indicate her contempt

---

[2]All quotations of Cather's journalistic writings are taken from *The Kingdom of Art.*

for any deviance from the masculine ideal that Wilde and his circle mocked and that she celebrated in her effusive praise of such writers as Rudyard Kipling as well as in her commendation of football as a force that "curbs the growing tendencies toward effeminacy so prevalent in the eastern colleges" (213).

In her 1895 columns following Wilde's imprisonment, Cather continues to denigrate him. She begins an essay on Swinburne by noting—almost gleefully—that "his brother in Apollo is picking oakum in prison" (349); and in a column bitterly denouncing the aesthetic movement, she extravagantly hails Wilde's downfall as prefiguring "the destruction of the most fatal and dangerous school of art that has ever voiced itself in the English tongue" (389). She says, "We will have no more such plays as *Lady Windermere's Fan,* no more such stories as *The Portrait* [sic] *of Dorian Gray*"* and adds: "We can do without them. They were full of insanity" (389). She relishes the irony implicit in the "peculiar fact" that a movement that set such store in beauty "has ended by finding what was most grotesque, misshapen and unlovely" (389–390). She accuses Wilde of "the begetter of all evil—insincerity" and in effect congratulates herself on being among the few who were not blinded by the cleverness of *Lady Windermere's Fan,* who "felt in it that falseness which makes the soul shudder and revolt" (390). She explains the rise of the aesthetic school as a consequence" of the artificial way in which men and women are living. . . . Every century or so society decides to improve on nature. It becomes very superior and refined indeed, until right through its surface there breaks some ghastly eruption that makes it hide its face in shame" (390). She finds the aesthetes' insistence that nature imitates art particularly galling. She concludes the essay by saluting the salubrious effects of Wilde's disgrace: "We put on sackcloth and go back to our father's house and become again as little children. Then it is that human endeavor becomes bold and strong and that human art is charged with new life. For it is while we are in that child-like mood of penitence that nature opens her arms to us and God tells us the secrets of heaven" (390). In this conclusion, Cather at once embraces the triumph of the patriarchy, which is implicitly defined as "natural"—in effect, welcoming repression—and yet acknowledges a "shame" that she shares with the aesthetes. This barely concealed acknowledgment of identification with the movement that she vilifies may account for the extremity of her invective here. The tensions and contradictions palpable in this column suggest how thoroughly disturbing Cather found the aesthetic movement's challenge to conventional notions of the relationship of art and nature and to her own aesthetic of hyper-masculinity.

In a reflection on Wilde published later in 1895, Cather accuses him of having wasted his talent and of sinning against the holy spirit in man by having "used the holiest things for ends the basest" (391). "He might have been a poet of no mean order, he might have been one of the greatest living dramatists, he might have been almost anything," she writes, "but he preferred to be a harlequin" (391), thus anticipating Wilde's own clownlike self-representation

*The title of Wilde's book is *The Picture of Dorian Gray*. By inserting [sic], the Latin for "thus; so," Summers indicates that he is quoting Cather exactly and the error is her's, not his.

in *De Profundis* but denying the holiness he was to associate with the harlequin figure there. Although she asserts that the sins of the body are small compared to the sins of the spirit, she nevertheless judges him "most deservedly" imprisoned (392). "Upon his head is heaped the deepest infamy and the darkest shame of his generation. Civilization shudders at his name, and there is absolutely no spot on earth where this man can live" (392), she remarks with some satisfaction. Significantly, she herself shudders at the prospect of naming Wilde: she begins the article by quoting Wilde's "Helas!" and remarking that "I did not know whether to give the name of the author of that lament or not, for he has made his name impossible" (390); and she ends it by quoting lines from Browning's "The Lost Leader" that begin "Blot out his name then" (393). This difficulty with naming may well be the result of Wilde's association with "the Love that dare not speak its name" and with Cather's own preoccupation with her lesbianism, which she would later characterize as "the thing not named."[3] For her, Wilde is a dangerous figure, at once unmentionable yet unavoidably fascinating.

Cather's disparagement of Wilde in the 1890s is especially interesting   7
insofar as it coexists with her own intense admiration for many French *fin de siècle*★ writers, including Verlaine. This coexistence indicates that her contempt for Wilde is not merely an expression of prudish conventionality, a reflection of her Nebraska readership, or evidence of a principled objection to *fin de siècle* preoccupations with immoral or unconventional subject matter. After all, in her warm tribute occasioned by Verlaine's death in 1896, she describes him as profligate and degenerate but nevertheless a supreme artist. "He was imprisoned again and again for unmentionable and almost unheard of crimes. . . . He was a practicer of every excess known to man" (394), she declares, yet proceeds to celebrate him as an artist of genuine inspiration and accomplishment, regarding his personal degeneracy as a necessary ingredient in the creation of his art. Moreover, in defending Verlaine, she attacks those who would denigrate him as "Philistines," that Arnoldian term that Wilde appropriated as his own scornful epithet to hurl against the enemies of art. The point is not that it is necessarily inconsistent to disparage Wilde and to praise Verlaine but that the excesses and terms of Cather's attacks on Wilde are inconsistent with the strategies by which she defends Verlaine. Unlike many turn-of-the-century critics who saw Wilde and Verlaine as equally dangerous figures and who linked them in a common enterprise of decadence, Cather scorns the artificiality of the aesthetes but celebrates the blessed degeneracy of Verlaine. Even as she condemns Wilde's subversive credo as "puny," she finds Verlaine's revolt against bourgeois values heroic, that is, masculine. The conclusion to be drawn from this apparent inconsistency is that Cather's principal objection to Wilde is as much personal as it is literary. More accurately, it is a reaction against his "drivelling effeminacy," his subversive mockery of the

---

[3]On the connection between "the Love that dare not speak its name" and "the thing not named" and on Cather's difficulty in naming Wilde, see O'Brien (126–127 and 142n).

★French for "end of the century" or what in English is called "turn of the century."

masculine ideal, as well as a rejection of his elevation of the artificial and the precious at the expense of the natural and the ordinary. Only when Cather herself came to redefine the masculine aesthetic of her youth could she qualify her attitude toward Wilde and the aesthetes. In a very real, if not altogether obvious sense, "Paul's Case" reflects this modification in her thinking about Wilde and his circle.

The sources of "Paul's Case" are probably many, not least among them Cather's own personal experience as teacher and dreamer. Many years after the story's composition, she claimed that the protagonist was inspired by a student in the Pittsburgh high school at which she taught and that her character's experiences in New York were based on her own feelings about the city.[4] But there is reason to think that the story owes a great deal to her evolving response to the Wilde scandal and to Wilde's role as a symbolic figure, particularly as a discredited aesthete and as a persecuted victim. The story was published in 1905, five years after Wilde's death and soon after the appearance of the first, abridged version of *De Profundis,* at a time when Wilde was once again very widely discussed in literary circles.[5] Most significantly, the protagonist is depicted in easily recognizable terms as a Wildean aesthete, as a dandy who sports a carnation in his button-hole and who found "a certain element of artificiality . . . necessary in beauty" (251). In addition, the story's indictment of the failure of imagination in American society parallels Wilde's stress on imagination in *De Profundis,* although Cather ironically implicates the Wildean aesthete in her indictment.[6] Moreover, placed as it is as the final story in a collection of stories focusing on art and artists,[7] the work invites consideration

---

[4]On the models for her portrait of Paul, see Kathleen D. Byrne and Richard C. Snyder (64–66), James Woodress (xx), and Marilyn Arnold (67n). Woodress suggests that Cather may also have been influenced by an incident widely reported in the Pittsburgh newspapers involving the theft of an employer's money by two boys who ran off to Chicago.

[5]The story was first published in Cather's collection of stories, *The Troll Garden,* and then in *McClure's Magazine* in May 1905. *The Troll Garden* appeared in April or May 1905; it is not known exactly when Cather composed "Paul's Case," but it is generally dated near the end of 1904. Wilde's *De Profundis* appeared in February 1905, so it is unlikely that Cather read *De Profundis* before writing "Paul's Case," and my argument suggesting a similarity between the two works does not depend on the one influencing the other. Nevertheless, involved as she was in literary journalism, Cather would certainly have been aware of so important a literary event as the publication of Wilde's vindication, and this awareness alone may have stimulated her thinking about issues posed by his imprisonment and disgrace; and it is, of course, possible that she may have had access to a prepublication review copy of *De Profundis.*

[6]Imagination is the key faculty in the authentic self that Wilde attempts to create in *De Profundis.* All the charges that he brings against his erstwhile lover Lord Alfred Douglas are subsumed in the accusation that he lacked imagination. The opposite of shallowness, imagination for Wilde indicates a liveliness of the spirit, an awareness of the meaning of experience, a critical alertness to the nature of one's relationships both to others and to society and social institutions, and a constant questioning of established social codes.

[7]Another of the stories in *The Troll Garden,* "The Sculptor's Funeral," also has a homosexual theme. Indeed, "The Sculptor's Funeral" and "Paul's Case" may be viewed as companion pieces. As Alice Hall Petry observes, "The Sculptor's Funeral" is "a remarkably astute study of a family, a town, a society failing to come to terms, not with a young man's artistic inclinations, but rather with his homosexuality" (108–109). In contrast, the emphasis in "Paul's Case" is, as demonstrated below, equally on a homosexual's failure to come to terms with his society.

as a meditation on aestheticism and on the connection between art and nature, the preoccupation of the aesthetes, as well as a consideration of the homosexual's problematic relationship to society.

Central to the full experience of the story is recognition of the fact of 9 Paul's homosexuality, a "fact" that is nowhere stated openly. This lack of explicitness reflects both the difficulty of writing about homosexuality in 1905 and Cather's own preference for insinuation and implication. In her essay on the craft of fiction, "The Novel Démeublé," first published in 1922, Cather calls attention to the presence of absence in her work. "Whatever is felt upon the page without being specifically named there—that, one might say, is created," she remarks. "It is the inexplicable presence of the thing not named, of the overtone divined by the ear but not heard by it, the verbal mood, the emotional aura of the fact or the thing or the deed, that gives high quality to the novel or the drama, as well as to poetry itself" (50).[8] The startling phrase "the thing not named" connotes experience that the author does not, or cannot, express openly. As O'Brien notes, "the most prominent absence and most unspoken love in her work are the emotional bonds between women that were central to her life" (127). In "Paul's Case," however, the thing not named is Paul's homosexuality, a presence made palpable not by direct statement but by numerous hints and a distinct emotional aura and verbal mood.

In his brief article Rubin details some of the most significant clues that 10 the story offers of Paul's gayness, from the youth's slight physique and the "hysterical brilliancy" of his eyes that he uses "in a conscious, theatrical way, peculiarly offensive in a boy" (243), to his dandified dress, his attraction to the young actor in Pittsburgh and the Yale freshman in New York, his fastidiousness and use of violet water, his nervousness and internalized fears. In addition to the clues detected by Rubin, the very title of the story, with its medical and legal overtones, is suggestive, for in 1905 discourse on homosexuality was couched almost exclusively in terms of criminality or psychopathology. The protagonist, the title implies, is a fitting subject for a psychological or criminal case history. The subtitle, "A Study in Temperament," is particularly telling insofar as it implies a psychological condition and insofar as "temperament" is practically a code-word for sexual orientation. But most interesting of all in light of Cather's reference to the importance of verbal mood in her strategy of revelation within concealment is the language of "Paul's Case." Throughout the story, Cather repeatedly uses diction suggestive of homosexuality. Although in almost every instance the words are used with no specific allusion to homosexuality, the startling number and pervasiveness of such terms as *gay* (used four times), *fairy, faggot, fagged, queen, loitering, tormented, unnatural, haunted, different, perverted, secret love,* and so on create a verbal ambience that subtly but persistently calls attention to the issue. However innocently used, these words and phrases appear too often to be merely coincidental. They

[8]Cather's remark in a 1918 interview is also pertinent: "It is always hard to write about the things that are near your heart. From a kind of instinct of self-protection you distort and disguise them" (Overton 259).

function to help establish the overtone by which the ear divines homosexuality in the text. Through this linguistic device, Cather creates a verbal mood that subliminally signals homosexuality as an important aspect of her work, even as she avoids any direct reference to the subject.

In the story, which might be described as a case study of a young aes-   11
thete, Paul's homosexuality is most vividly symbolized as the unnamed fear that has haunted him for years. "Until now, he could not remember the time when he had not been dreading something," he reflects after he has stolen the money. "Even when he was a little boy, it was always there—behind him, or before, or on either side. There had always been the shadowed corner, the dark place into which he dared not look, but from which something seemed always to be watching him—and Paul had done things that were not pretty to watch, he knew" (255). The symbol of his gayness, this "apprehensive dread" pro- foundly shapes Paul's fearful, defensively contemptuous response to life and helps to account for his disaffection from the values of his middle-class envi- ronment. It is also clearly linked to his aestheticism, his preference for the arti- ficial rather than the natural, and his immersion in art at the expense of life. Paul finds freedom from this pervasive fear only when he breaks decisively with his stifling life in Pittsburgh by stealing the money. Then he felt "a curi- ous sense of relief, as though he had at last thrown down the gauntlet to the thing in the corner" (255), Cather writes, describing the break with his past as a kind of symbolic coming out. But although homosexuality in "Paul's Case" is a metaphor for alienation and helps explicate the protagonist's problematic relationship to his society, it is not offered as a sufficient explanation for the youth's tragedy. That is, the cause of Paul's unhappiness and suicide is not his homosexuality but his inability to integrate his homosexuality into real life. This inability is itself the result of the homophobia that pervades his society and that he himself internalizes.

The complexity of the story arises from its skillful, noncommittal narra-   12
tion. The omniscient third-person point of view enables Cather to enter her protagonist's consciousness yet also establishes a crucial distance from him. The narrator evinces and creates sympathy for Paul but never unambiguously endorses his perspective. The distance that Cather achieves by means of her strategy of concealment, dispassionate title, controlled narrative technique, and use of symbols is overlooked by the conventional readings of the story that explain Paul's tragedy as simply the result of an insensitive and uncaring soci- ety. But Cather withholds authorial judgment in the contest she presents be- tween Paul and his environment, and she informs the poignancy of Paul's brief and unhappy life with a peculiar kind of irony. She finally implicates both Bohemia and Presbyteria (to use her private terms for the dichotomy)[9] in the fate of her young aesthete, whose doom is conceived as a bitterly ironic tragedy of errors.

Complicating rather than reducing, Cather transforms the materials of   13
an overly familiar tale of a tormented artist destroyed by Philistines into a rich

[9]On Cather's use of these terms, see O'Brien (225–226).

and complex story that admits of no simple schematization. Her case study of an alienated youth almost mechanically moving to his doom is enriched by an awareness, subtly and delicately conveyed, of missed opportunities that might have saved him. Paul is not merely the homosexual victim hounded to his suicide by a society that persecutes him. Paul's society, including especially his teachers and father, is indeed culpable; but the youth himself partakes of the lack of imagination that culminates in tragedy. Although the understated narration imparts a sense of inevitability to his fate, Paul himself bears a major responsibility for the waste that it represents. In part shaped by the Wilde scandal, the story in effect comments on Wilde's own fate as one that might have been prevented and as one for which he must share the blame.

As in Wilde's *De Profundis,* imagination is a key faculty in "Paul's Case."   14
But in the story it is present by virtue of its almost complete absence, even as the work finally becomes itself an enactment of that imaginative sympathy of which its characters are revealed to be devoid. The lack of imagination on the part of Paul's father, teachers, and neighbors is obvious in their inability to understand the young man and in their simplistic attempts to help him, as well as in their indifference to art and beauty. The father confesses his "perplexity" regarding his son; and the teachers, for all their myriad speculations, admit that "there was something about the boy which none of them understood" (244). The inability of conventional society to understand, and to deal humanely with those who are different, is clearly attacked by the story and exposed as a crucial failure of imagination. This lack of imagination transforms well-intentioned teachers into vicious inquisitors when Paul appears before them to answer various misdemeanors in the story's brilliant opening scene. The teachers are not unkind by nature, but they lack the imagination to understand sympathetically Paul's temperament and consequently allow themselves to be goaded into actions that contradict their own values. What spurs them to their packlike behavior is not merely what Paul actually does but also his defiant attitude and dress. The reaction of the teachers to Paul parallels Cather's own excessive reaction to Wilde's mocking manner in the 1890s and may reflect the author's mature reconsideration of her own earlier lack of imagination in not dealing charitably with Wilde in his disgrace.

A similar failure of imagination leads Paul's father to force the son to   15
break off his relationship with his only friend, the young actor, and to bar him from the theater and concert hall, the scenes of his only pleasures. Instead of regarding Paul's interest in art and in the friend (and potential lover) as possible resources that might be developed to help his son, the father reacts simplistically and increases Paul's isolation and alienation. The father's unimaginative response to his son's difficulties may be said to precipitate (if not to explain) the catastrophe, for, as Paul reflects after stealing the money, "It had been wonderfully simple; when they had shut him out of the theater and concert hall, when they had taken away his bone, the whole thing was virtually determined. The rest was a mere matter of opportunity" (254).

But somewhat less obvious than the failures of those who might have   16
helped him is Paul's own lack of imagination, in the sense that Wilde employs

the term in *De Profundis,* as an awareness of the meaning of one's experience and of one's relationship to others and to society. Yet the power of the story—and its importance as an original contribution to the debate about homosexuality in the first decade of the twentieth century—pivots on this very issue, for it is the exercise of imagination that might have altered Paul's case and allowed him to find a niche in his society. Paul's failure to analyze his society and to perceive possibilities of accommodation within it are personal (although understandable) failures that contribute to his tragedy, but Cather intimates that the failure of imagination may be endemic to aestheticism itself, at least insofar as it became increasingly remote from ordinary life. In this sense, "Paul's Case" subtly criticizes the defiant rejection of society that *De Profundis* enacts (and that may have been a widespread temptation among homosexuals in the wake of the Wilde scandal) and calls for the exercise of imagination as a means of healing the rift between the homosexual and society.

Despite Paul's immersion in art, he is severely deficient in imagination. Art for him is merely a stimulation of the senses and an escape from human engagement. The art to which Paul is most attracted significantly excludes both ordinary reality and human relationships. For example, in the picture gallery he finds Raffelli's studies of Paris streets and Venetian scenes exhilarating, and he "loses himself" in a blue Rico seascape. In contrast, he jeers at the representations of human figures, such as Augustus and Venus de Milo. He is imaginative only in the limited sense of being able to alter mundane reality by fantasizing more exciting, romantic alternatives. Music, about which he is utterly indiscriminating, is simply the spark that ignites his escapist fantasies. In his music-induced reveries, he is able to transform the glamourless, matronly German opera singer—a woman "by no means in her first youth, and the mother of many children"—into "a veritable queen of Romance." In the atmosphere of Carnegie Hall, he is even able to recreate himself temporarily, momentarily feeling "within him the possibility of doing or saying splendid, brilliant, poetic things" (251). Similarly, the stage entrance is for Paul "the actual portal of Romance." It is a "wishing carpet" that whisks him from the realities of "smoke-palled" Pittsburgh to the "blue-and-white Mediterranean shore bathed in perpetual sunshine" (252).

Not surprisingly, after his orgies of romantic escapism, Paul feels increasingly disaffected with mundane existence and alienated from ordinary life. Returning to his Cordelia Street home after an evening at the opera or theater, "he experienced all the physical depression which follows a debauch; the loathing of respectable beds, of common food, of a house penetrated by kitchen odours; a shuddering repulsion for the flavourless, colourless mass of every-day existence; a morbid desire for cool things and soft lights and fresh flowers" (248). As described here, Paul's depression is reminiscent of the neurasthenic morbidity associated with aestheticism and decadence, and exemplified, for example, in Wilde's Dorian Gray and Sir Henry Wotton. Significantly, despite his addiction to the stimulus of art, Paul is himself singularly uncreative. He is neither an artist, musician, writer, actor, nor reader: "He felt no necessity to do any of these things; what he wanted was to see, to be in the atmosphere, float on the wave of it, to be carried out, blue league after blue league, away from everything" (252).

What Paul lacks, of course, is imagination in the sense of sympathy for   19
others, a capacity that is essential both for the creative artist and the successful human being. In the "physical aversion" he expresses toward his teachers, in his refusal to take others seriously or to consider the effect his behavior has on them, in his compulsive lying, and in his complete lack of remorse either for his petty cruelties or his betrayal of trust, Paul signals not merely his revolt against middle-class mores but his contempt for life itself. It is significant that he has almost no relationships with others. He is content to be a voyeur rather than a participant in life. Alone in New York, for example, he feels "not in the least abashed or lonely. He had no especial desire to meet or to know any of these people; all he demanded was the right to look on and conjecture, to watch the pageant. The mere stage properties were all he contended for. Nor was he lonely later in the evening, in his loge at the Metropolitan" (257). His brief fling with the Yale freshman, "a wild San Francisco boy," ends with their "singularly cool" parting (257).[10] In his expensive hotel room, he insulates himself from the winter storm raging outside and from the exigencies of life itself and is thereby subtly connected with the hothouse flowers he so admires, which he finds "somehow vastly more lovely and alluring that they blossomed thus unnaturally in the snow" (256).

Paul's failure of imagination distorts his capacity to perceive clearly his   20
relationship to society and to others. He assesses everyday reality as "but a sleep and a forgetting" (251). His Cordelia Street neighborhood inspires in him only " a shudder of loathing," and he approaches it "with the nerveless sense of defeat" (248). He thinks of his home as repulsive, with "his ugly sleeping chamber; the cold bath-room with the grimy zinc tub, the cracked mirror, the dripping spiggots; his father, at the top of the stairs, his hairy legs sticking out from his night-shirt, his feet thrust into carpet slippers" (248). He rejects his middle-class origins and identifies with the wealthy, thinking of the inhabitants of the Waldorf as "his own people" (256). But Paul's own values—epitomized in his belief in the omnipotence of wealth, in the fact "that money was everything, the wall that stood between all he loathed and all he wanted" (259)—are actually not fundamentally different from the materialistic values of Cordelia Street, which also worships wealth and enjoys the "legends of the iron kings." Like his neighbors, he too relishes "the triumphs of these cash boys who had become famous," but unlike them "he had no mind for the cash-boy stage" (250). Paralleling the tendencies of the aesthetes, including Wilde himself, to identify with upper-class and aristocratic society, Paul's rejection of Cordelia Street values is not based on any probing social analysis but is simply of a piece with his disdain for the ordinary and the everyday. His

---

[10]Rubin conjectures that the frostiness of the parting may have been the result of a sexual overture on Paul's part that the Yale freshman rejects. "Given the lack of any further elucidation of the situation, on Cather's part," Rubin writes, "the reader is left with an unshakable sense of innuendo" (130).

alienation from his own origins bespeaks both self-loathing and a failure to sympathize with the struggles of others.

Similarly, his interpretations of the motives of others are as inaccurate as   21
his romanticization of the opera singer and the members of the acting company, more telling as projections of his disaffection than as reality. An important example of the morbidity of Paul's imagination, of its tendency to distort the motivations of those closest to him, is provided when he returns home from the Carnegie Hall concert near the beginning of the story. Fearful of facing his father in his night-clothes at the top of the stairs, the young man spends the night in the basement. Unable to sleep, Paul creates various scenarios in which his father mistakes him for a burglar:

> Suppose his father had heard him getting in at the window and had come down and shot him for a burglar? Then, again, suppose his father had come down, pistol in hand, and he had cried out in time to save himself, and his father had been horrified to think how nearly he had killed him? Then, again, suppose a day should come when his father would remember that night, and wish there had been no warning cry to stay his hand? With this last supposition Paul entertained himself until daybreak. (249)

The key word in this important passage is *entertained*. It indicates the extremity of Paul's alienation, his failure to take entirely seriously either his own life or his troubled relationship with his father, and it illustrates the youth's almost obsessive need to translate life into art or at least into entertainment. This passage is also significant for its revelation of Paul's expectation that his father will reject him, that he might well someday wish that he had killed his son. This assumption is an expression of Paul's "apprehensive dread," his fear that his father will discover his homosexuality. It reflects the homophobia he feels both in the larger society and within himself.

Rather than the unsympathetic ogre that Paul visualizes, his father is a   22
concerned, though inept and unimaginative, parent faced with a difficult situation, the full extent of which he fails to recognize. Mystified by his son's peculiar devotion to music and theater and disturbed by his problems in school, the father simplistically hopes that Paul will model himself after their much admired young neighbor, who, "in order to curb his appetites and save the loss of time and strength that the sowing of wild oats might have entailed," took his boss's advice and "at twenty-one had married the first woman whom he could persuade to share his fortunes" (250). Ambitious and hard-working, the father embodies the middle-class mores of his neighborhood, "where all the houses were exactly alike, and where business men of moderate means begot and reared large families of children, all of whom went to Sabbath-school and learned the shorter catechism, and were interested in arithmetic; all of whom were as exactly alike as their homes, and of a piece with the monotony in which they lived" (248). These values, symbolized by the pictures of George Washington and John Calvin that hang in Paul's bedroom, are limited, for they presuppose a sameness to human nature that does not admit difference, and

they turn out to be ineffective in helping Paul. But the father's brief appearances in the story, his presence at the top of the stairs, his reluctant provision of car fare, his taking Paul out of school, and, most important, his reimbursement of Paul's theft and his trip to New York to retrieve his son provide evidence not merely of the tyranny that Paul sees but also of love and concern, however mistakenly and unimaginatively applied.

The failures of imagination that the story indicts are epitomized in the   23
ineffective attempts of the father and his neighbors to help Paul after the theft and in Paul's rejection of these attempts. After the theft is discovered, the Pittsburgh newspapers report that

> The firm of Denny & Carson announced that the boy's father had refunded the full amount of the theft, and that they had no intention of prosecuting. The Cumberland minister had been interviewed, and expressed his hope of yet reclaiming the motherless lad, and his Sabbath-school teacher declared that she would spare no effort to that end. The rumour had reached Pittsburgh that the boy had been seen in a New York hotel, and his father had gone East to find him and bring him home. (258)

Clearly, the response of the father and the community to Paul's crime is predicated on a stifling and narrow religiosity. It is unimaginative in its inability to conceive that Paul's needs may be other than those that can be satisfied by home and church. At the same time, it must be acknowledged that the response is unquestionably a generous and forgiving one. Paul, however, reacts to the newspaper report with horror. "It was to be worse than jail, even; the tepid waters of Cordelia Street were to close over him finally and forever," he thinks. "The grey monotony stretched before him in hopeless, unrelieved years; Sabbath-school, Young People's Meeting, the yellow-papered room, the damp dish-towels; it all rushed back upon him with a sickening vividness" (258). Paul's failure of imagination is obvious here. Utterly oblivious to the generous concern expressed by his neighbors and exemplified by his father, he is as unable to imagine human sympathy on the part of others as he is to feel it himself.

The story is placed in perspective by its use of contrasting symbols associ-   24
ated with Paul and his environment. The very name Cordelia Street evokes Lear's daughter, whose death is as pathetic (and unnecessary) as Paul's.[11] Cordelia functions in the story as a complex, double symbol, signifying at once the possibility of both individuality and community responsibility. On the one hand, Cordelia personifies individual integrity and fidelity to one's own vision, the refusal to sacrifice one's sense of self in order to make accommodation with the world. From this perspective, there is considerable irony in evoking Cordelia in connection with the monotonous and conformist neighborhood in which Paul lives, a place whose inhabitants seem unable to comprehend anything beyond their own narrow ken as they look over their multitude of squabbling children and smile "to see their own proclivities

---

[11]It should be stressed that Cather invented the name Cordelia Street: the actual street in Pittsburgh that probably inspired Cather's setting is Aurelia Street. See Byrne and Snyder (83–84).

reproduced in their offspring" (249). But, significantly, despite rejection by her father, Cordelia comes to personify not only individualism but also agape, an association that is strengthened in the story by the framed motto, "Feed My Lambs," that Paul's mother had worked in red worsted and that hangs in Paul's bedroom. Signifying community and family loyalty, caring for others and helping bear their burdens, the symbols of agape underline the story's insistence on the importance of imagination in the sense of a capacity for human sympathy. Moreover, agape is certainly present, at least potentially, in the generosity and forgiveness of the neighborhood's reaction to Paul's escapade. More important, it haunts the story as an unstated presence that promises the possibility of integrating outcasts like Paul—and like Wilde and other homosexuals—into the community, and doing so without violating their individuality. The optimism implicit in the notion of agape inevitably challenges the pessimism of any social analysis—such as that in *De Profundis*—that would lead homosexuals to reject society, or that would sanction society's persecution of gay people.[12]

In contrast to the symbols of agape associated with Cordelia Street is the   25
red carnation favored by Paul. A hothouse flower, unnaturally cultivated and associated with Wilde, homosexuality, and aestheticism, the red carnation that Paul buries in the snow before leaping to his own death is a symbol of life's brevity and fragility and of the artificial mocking the natural. As Paul trudges through the snow, he notices that the flowers displayed in his coat have drooped, their red glory faded. He becomes sadly aware that all the flowers he had seen in the glass cases his first night in New York have similarly failed. "It was only one splendid breath they had, in spite of their brave mockery at the winter outside the glass," he acknowledges; and he concludes, "it was a losing game in the end, it seemed, this revolt against the homilies by which the world is run" (260). In this meditation, soon before Paul's "picture making mechanism was crushed" and he "dropped back into the immense design of things" (261), Paul reaches a conclusion that contradicts his earlier confident assertion that his rebellion "had paid. . . . Ah, it had paid indeed!" (259). In so doing, he enunciates one of the story's central points. The "brave mockery" undertaken by Paul (and by Wilde and the aesthetes) is a losing game in the end. In "Paul's Case," Cather is not so much intent on either prosecuting Presbyteria or defending it from the assaults of Bohemia as on indicating the futility of the battle in the first place.

In "Paul's Case," Cather provides a case study of the Wildean aesthete.   26
Her portrait of the young protagonist as a Romantic artist manqué is, I think, intended as a comment on Wilde and the aesthetic movement, particularly on the movement's celebration of the artificial and mockery of the natural, its privileging of the precious at the expense of the ordinary, and its elevation of

---

[12]At the end of *De Profundis*, Wilde revels defiantly in his exclusion from society, his marginality as homosexual pariah. He rejects the society that has condemned him and looks to nature for comfort and consolation: "Society, as we have constituted it, will have no place for me, has none to offer; but Nature, whose sweet rains fall on unjust and just alike, will have clefts in the rocks where I may hide and secret valleys in whose silence I may weep undisturbed" (238).

art above nature. She tends to explain this phenomenon in sociological terms
and with a measure of controlled sympathy, as when she comments:

> Perhaps it was because, in Paul's world, the natural nearly always wore the
> guise of ugliness, that a certain element of artificiality seemed to him neces-
> sary in beauty. Perhaps it was because his experience of life elsewhere was so
> full of Sabbath-school picnics, petty economies, wholesome advice as to how
> to succeed in life, and the unescapable odours of cooking, that he found this
> existence so alluring, these smartly-clad men and women so attractive, that he
> was so moved by these starry apple orchards that bloomed perennially under
> the lime-light. (251)

In her unflattering depiction of American middle-class life, Cather provides a
context that makes aestheticism understandable and attractive. At the same
time, however, she exposes the unreality on which aestheticism is based and
condemns it for its disdainful rejection of mundane life and human relationships. She convicts in turn both Presbyteria and Bohemia for failures of imagination, the one for its dullness and conformity, the other for its lack of
generosity in divining the motives of ordinary people. But insofar as the story
evinces a more humane and sympathetic response to Wilde as victim than
Cather was able to muster in 1895, "Paul's Case" is also interesting as evidence
of the personal growth its author attained in the following decade, when she
progressed from embracing the masculine ideal to apprehending the need for
diversity and acceptance of others. Her story indicting the failure of sympathy
actually enacts that imaginative response, the lack of which it exposes in its
characters.

   In depicting the futility of the aesthetes' "revolt against the homilies by   27
which the world is run," Cather aims not so much to endorse those homilies as
to indicate the loss involved in the "brave mockery" of them. But it is significant that she shares neither Wilde's pessimism nor his blanket rejection of society. In her tempered optimism, she clings to faith in the possibility of
imagination and in the ideal of agape as antidotes to alienation and anomie.
Moreover, she implies that the solution to the homosexual dilemma in an unac-
cepting society lies in integration rather than separation and in self-acceptance
rather than self-hatred. The homophobia that Paul senses in the larger society is
exacerbated by his internalized homophobia. His perception distorted by his
fears, he fails to realize the possibilities for accommodation within his society
and is thus doomed to his unhappy fate. His symbolic coming out, his defiant
throwing down the gauntlet "to the thing in the corner," is not an acceptance
but a rejection, and it leads not to liberation but to death. In her contribution
to the debate about homosexuality in the wake of the Wilde scandal, Cather
places on society and the homosexual alike the burden of imaginative sympathy, indicting the stifling conformity of American middle-class values even as
she characterizes the homosexual's contemptuous rejection of society as "a losing game in the end."

   "Paul's Case" is complex and resonant. By means of its masterful narra-   28
tion, it achieves an unusual balance of perspective. It vividly depicts what at

first glance may seem the almost inevitable fate of gay people in an unsympathetic, nonpluralistic society, only to deconstruct this pessimistic assessment by subtly implying alternatives to alienation and suicide and envisioning possibilities implicit in those homilies by which the world is run. Embodied most fully in the notions of agape and imagination, these possibilities arise from a social analysis quite different from that offered by Wilde and the aesthetes, one that seeks accommodation rather than confrontation. Cather's social analysis is, however, subject to question. Based as it is on appeals to concepts as inevitably vague as *agape* and *imagination,* Cather's accommodationism is severely limited as a practical response to homophobia; and one may justly complain that in placing equal burdens on an alienated adolescent and an entire society she comes dangerously close to blaming the victim. But by questioning the inevitability of its own plot, "Paul's Case" not only itself enacts an imaginative response but demands that its readers do so as well, both in the process of interpretation and in relating to others in the world beyond the boundaries of fiction. For all its reticence and indirectness, the story is actually surprisingly engaged. A work of unusual power that evokes genuine pathos, Cather's first major achievement is both a moving tale and a significant contribution to the debate about homosexuality sparked by the Wilde scandal.

Works Cited

Arnold, Marilyn. *Willa Cather's Short Fiction.* Athens: Ohio UP, 1984.

Austen, Roger. *Playing the Game: The Homosexual Novel in America.* Indianapolis: Bobbs-Merrill, 1977.

Byrne, Kathleen D., and Richard C. Snyder. *Chrysalis: Willa Cather in Pittsburgh.* Pittsburgh: Historical Society of Western Pennsylvania, 1980.

Cather, Willa. *The Kingdom of Art: Willa Cather's First Principles and Critical Statements 1893–1896.* Ed. Bernice Slote, Lincoln: U of Nebraska P, 1966.

——. "The Novel Démeublé." *Not under Forty.* New York: Knopf, 1936. 43–51.

——. "Paul's Case." *Willa Cather's Collected Short Fiction 1892–1912.* Ed. Virginia Faulkner. Rev. ed. Lincoln: U of Nebraska P, 1970. 243–261.

——. *The Troll Garden.* New York: McClure, 1905.

Lambert, Deborah. "The Defeat of a Hero: Autonomy and Sexuality in *My Antonia.*" *American Literature* 53 (1981–1982): 676–690.

O'Brien, Sharon. *Willa Cather: The Emerging Voice.* New York: Oxford UP, 1987.

Overton, Grant. *The Women Who Make Our Novels.* New York: Moffat, 1918.

Petry, Alice Hall. "Harvey's Case: Notes on Cather's 'The Sculptor's Funeral.'" *South Dakota Review* 11 (1986): 108–116.

Robinson, Phyllis. *Willa: The Life of Willa Cather.* New York: Doubleday, 1983.

Rubin, Larry. "The Homosexual Motif in Willa Cather's 'Paul's Case.'" *Studies in Short Fiction* 12 (1975): 127–131.

Rule, Jane. *Lesbian Images.* New York: Doubleday, 1975.

Wilde, Oscar. *De Profundis. Selected Letters of Oscar Wilde.* Ed. Rupert Hart-Davis. Oxford: Oxford UP, 1979. 152–240.

Woodress, James. "Introduction." *The Troll Garden.* By Willa Cather. Ed. James Woodress. Lincoln: U of Nebraska P, 1983. xi–xxx. ■

Questions for Meaning

1. According to Summers, why was Willa Cather so hostile to Oscar Wilde?
2. What evidence does Summers cite to support his claim, in paragraph 8, that "Paul's Case" was influenced by Cather's "evolving response to the Wilde scandal and to Wilde's role as a symbolic figure . . ."?
3. How does Summers account for the fact that the story makes no explicit mention of homosexuality?
4. Where does Summers locate responsibility for Paul's fate?
5. *Agape* is a Greek word meaning love. Today it is used primarily to describe love that is spiritual rather than sexual. Consider the discussion of agape in paragraph 24. Why is it relevant to Summers' interpretation of "Paul's Case"?
6. Vocabulary: aesthetic (1), espoused (2), unremittingly (3), poseur (3), epigrammatic (4), iconoclasm (4), salubrious (5), harlequin (6), prolifigate (7), fastidiousness (10), explicate (11), endemic (16), neurasthenic (18), homilies (27), deconstruct (28).

Questions about Strategy

1. Summers begins his article with the claim that Willa Cather was lesbian. Is Cather's sexual orientation relevant to the argument Summers makes here or could that argument stand alone if we knew nothing of Cather's private life?
2. What sources has Summers drawn on? Where does he use the work of others to support his interpretation? Does he succeed in convincing you that his interpretation differs from that of other critics?
3. Why does Summers take the trouble to establish that Cather admired the work of the French poet Paul Verlaine?
4. In making assumptions about Paul's sexual orientation, is Summers ever guilty of stereotyping? Does he make any observations that could be offensive to gay or lesbian readers?
5. What is the purpose of this article? Why would it matter whether readers agree with Summers' interpretation of "Paul's Case"?

LORETTA WASSERMAN

IS CATHER'S PAUL A CASE?[1]

The author of *Willa Cather: A Study of the Short Fiction* (1991), Loretta Wasserman has a long-established interest in Cather studies. In the following article, first published by *Modern Fiction Studies* in 1990, she synthesizes recent scholarship and offers an interpretation of her own that draws on the story of Parsifal, a legendary young knight who maintained his innocence through many adventures and eventually became guardian of the Holy Grail. One version of his story is told in an 1882 opera by Richard Wagner, one of Cather's favorite composers.

"Paul's Case" is Willa Cather's most popular story—deservedly so, although one of the reasons for its preeminence is that for many years it was the only one Cather would allow reprinted. It remains still the first choice of anthologists, as a glance at any half dozen current collections will show, and it has been dramatized in a popular public television series. Until recently, however, "Paul's Case" received little critical notice. One reason, doubtless, is that Paul's story seems admirably clear-cut: a sensitive adolescent, attracted to music and the theater, is pushed by a callous, commercial society into a desperate theft. Facing discovery, he takes his own life by falling under the wheels of a locomotive, symbol of the iron industrialism and grinding materialism of the age. Certainly that is how students respond to the story, attracted, naturally, by any picture of misunderstood youth and no doubt inclined to sympathize, too, with Paul's aversion to lady high-school teachers, with their shrill voices and "pitiful seriousness about prepositions that govern the dative" (*Troll Garden* 112).

No doubt a second reason is that "Paul's Case" resists being assimilated to Cather's other work. It seems to lack her stamp. In place of vast prairie horizons or silent cliff dwellings we have a "smoke palled city" (111)—turn-of-the-century Pittsburgh—and a boy who markedly lacks the vibrancy we expect in Cather's central figures. Paul's specialness is a kind of inarticulate stubbornness: his teachers think of him as a cornered alley cat. Further, as this example suggests, the sweep of imagery and allusion that marks Cather's style elsewhere is missing here—the narrative voice feels cribbed and confined like her hero's actions and purposes. In fact, these actions and purposes are the real trouble. Could the Cather who wrote so frequently against materialism regard with sympathy one who spends stolen money on a week of high living in a New York hotel and who, confronting death, reflects that he knew now "more than ever, that money was everything" (119)? The answer from the critics is no; in fact, the gathering consensus is that her story is bathed in irony.

[1]An early version of this essay was read at the conference, "Willa Cather: A Critical Appraisal," Santa Fe, New Mexico, August 1989.

Serious criticism began by confronting a task that has proved trouble-   3
some—fitting the story into the collection where it first appeared, seven stories having to do with art and artists that Cather titled *The Troll Garden,* her
first book of fiction, published in 1905. The title and epigraphs suggest certain dangers in art, the work of not-quite-human trolls, fascinating to "forest
children" peeking into their garden (the epigraph is from Charles Kingsley's
The Roman and the Teuton). Cather made these dangers more puzzling and
ominous by a second epigraph, from Christina Rossetti's "The Goblin Market": "We must not look at Goblin men, / We must not buy their
fruits. . . ." Considerable critical acumen has been expended on this suggested framework. E. K. Brown, Cather's first biographer, asserts rather
lamely that "Paul's Case," the last of seven, makes a "fitting coda" (114).
James Woodress, in his Introduction to his definitive edition of *The Troll Garden,* and in his biography, speaks elliptically of a "forest child destroyed
by . . . the forbidden fruit," the assumption being, it would seem, that Paul
transgresses a moral boundary and that theater and concert hall themselves ex-
ude a malevolency ("Introduction" xvi–xvii, *Life* 172–175).

Other commentators are more explicit or venturesome. Susan Rosowski,   4
in her study of Cather's romanticism, stresses the tempting dangers posed by
the troll/goblin artists and the horror of the "bewitched" boy who has "lost
his soul" to an "inhuman" fantasy (19–23). Marilyn Arnold finds Paul indeed
a case, a psychological one, "eccentric, maybe even half-crazy," mistaken
even about grimy Cordelia Street where Paul, motherless since birth, lives
with his father and two shadowy sisters (43–45). Where Paul sees grey ugliness, Arnold sees a respectable neighborhood of white-collar workers, full of
children and plans for the future. Paul is equally blind about the world of art,
mistaking glitter for real worth. Not unexpectedly, Sharon O'Brien, in her
psychobiography, also stresses psychology—Paul's "probable homosexuality"
may be a thin disguise for Cather's. Cather/Paul yearns for a dissolution of
self, a preoedipal union with the mother—a floating on flowers and music
(the New York scenes) ending in the final dissolution of self in death (282–
283). David Carpenter, in contrast, finds Paul's story a sociological case study
of "an extremely bleak and seemingly irremediable type of determinism"
(591). Paul is a victim of his society, Pittsburgh Presbyterianism, symbolized
by the twin pictures of George Washington and John Calvin over his bed,
icons transmuted by business and industry into signifying the "uncreative, superficial and life-destroying values" that dominate American life (608). Paul
is a debased version of these values: the New York scenes are heavily ironic,
Carpenter maintains, especially Paul's sense of well-being as he luxuriates in
the Waldorf. Nevertheless, Paul remains blameable because he "has consumed
himself morally and ethically by living a lie—one purchased through someone else's hard work" (606). We are back with the "half-crazy" boy who "sold
his soul," however different the etiology of his pathological condition. In
sum, these recent studies all point in the same direction: toward a weak-
willed, morally corrupt, or corrupted youth inevitably enmeshed and destroyed by his own illusions.

That these varying analyses of Paul as a case study in psychology or soci-   5
ology are plausible is proof that Cather has here succeeded in balancing the
competing claims of the old arguments between the opposing determinisms of
nature and nurture. Part of the fascination of Paul's story must inhere in just
this tension. But is this what Cather is telling us about Paul—that he is the
sum of forces impinging on him? I think not, and I think we are alerted to a
less positivistic perspective through the comments of Paul's teachers, who, after the disciplinary hearing aimed at correcting his vaguely impertinent attitude, feel so baffled: "his drawing master voiced the feeling of them all when
he declared there was something about the boy which none of them understood" (104); "each of his instructors felt that it was scarcely possible to put
into words the real cause of the trouble" (102).

One aspect of the story may be agreed upon: it is certainly true, as all the   6
recent commentators stress, that Paul is not a budding artist whose gifts are
being wasted. His fascination with art, music, and theater is of a different order. He uses art as a means; the sounds of the orchestra or painted landscapes
are avenues. When Paul rushes off from the high-school faculty meeting to his
ushering job at Carnegie Hall, he first visits its art gallery where "he sat down
before a blue Rico and lost himself" (104). Later, after helping patrons to their
seats, he falls into a similar dreamy state as the symphony begins: "he lost himself as he had before the Rico" (105). Cather is explicit that his love of the
theater is not based on hidden talent or ambition: "He had no desire to become
an actor, any more than he had to become a musician" (111). Nevertheless,
Charley Edwards, the stock company juvenile, regrets it when Paul's father
forbids Paul to loiter about the dressing rooms because the actor "recognized
in Paul something akin to what churchmen term 'vocation'" (110). What is
meant by this strange term for Paul's obsession? And how likely is it that this
easy-going stock company actor would employ it? It must be that the author is
here signaling to her readers over the head of her character. Blanche Gelfant,
writing on Cather's poetics, notes her technique of "self-reflexivity," of including hints about how to read her story in the story itself. Casting Paul as
one who has heard a summons to spiritual duty must be such a signal. Paul is
serving a master who calls—a master who calls him to life: in clinging to music, art, and theater, Paul is keeping alive intimations of "a world elsewhere,"
a world where he would not be an alien. He is fighting for his life—for the life
of his soul. (Cather once wrote in the *Nebraska State Journal*:[2] "'Soul'—it's too
bad that we have no word but that to express man's innermost ego" [416].)
The life and death nature of his struggle is stressed again and again. When he
ushers, he becomes "vivacious and animated" (105), and color comes into his
usually pale face, the face that one of his teachers found "drawn and wrinkled
like an old man's" (104). The first sound of the orchestra "seemed to free some
hilarious spirit within him; something that struggled there like the Genius in
the bottle found by the Arab fisherman. He felt a sudden zest of life" (105).
His feeling at the concert hall "was all that could be called living at all" (105).

[2]All quotations of Cather's journalistic writings are taken from *The Kingdom of Art*.

"It was at the theater and at Carnegie Hall that Paul really lived; the rest was but a sleep and a forgetting" (110). Conversely, he thinks of Cordelia Street, where his father in his night clothes stands at the head of the stairs demanding explanations, as threatening death, imaged as suffocation by drowning. ("The moment he turned into Cordelia Street he felt the waters close above his head" [107].) When, in New York, he learns that his father has refunded the stolen money and has come to bring him home, he thinks, "the tepid waters of Cordelia Street were to close over him finally and forever" (118). He can confront suicide with equanimity because, it now seems, "all the world had become Cordelia Street" (119).

Further, Paul's crime, the theft, is treated as an act of self-preservation. 7 When Paul's father placed him as a cash boy in a commercial house and forbade the theater and concert hall, "the whole thing was virtually determined" (114). Paul takes the money instinctively, as a salmon swims upstream. He recalls it merely as "simple" and "astonishingly easy" (114). In fact, he has a sense of relief at his "courage" which, before the theft, he had doubted.

Of course no one could argue that Cather intends to condone shiftlessness 8 and thievery, but what does she intend by this extraordinary transvaluation of values? The call that Paul heeds, the call to the soul's life, is—not to put too fine a point on it—the call of Beauty. Paul is that most familiar of Romantic figures—the yearner for an ineffable world, beauty in this one as the promise of the truth of the other. We may say that Paul is on the first rung of Plato's ladder—rather, considering where and who he is, reaching desperately for the rung. Just how grave Paul's situation is can be made clear by comparing him to another of Cather's deprived youths, Clark in "A Wagner Matinee," another *Troll Garden* story. Clark escapes his bleak environment, a frontier farm, but he is helped not only by the music lessons of his devoted Aunt Georgiana but also, however subliminally, by memories of "ploughing forever and forever between green aisles of corn . . . walking from daybreak to dusk" in that vast land (98). What can Paul see in that "smoke palled" city that will speak to him of beauty? Even nature is revealed to him through artifice, through a stage set of "starry apple orchards that bloomed perennially under the lime-light" (111). He must construct beauty from hints—the blue Rico and the stage sets and the tiara that the aged soprano wears. The narrator explains: "Perhaps it was because, in Paul's world, the natural nearly always wore the guise of ugliness, that a certain element of artificiality seemed to him necessary in beauty" (111).

From glitter and stage effects, then, Paul builds a dream world that com- 9 forts and sustains. Music and art are merely a means of entrance, a "portal of Romance" (111). Again Cather hints at religious dedication: "Paul had his secret temple . . . his bit of blue-and white Mediterranean shore" (111). To convey the peculiarly hermetic quality of Paul's "dome in air," Cather alludes through an extended simile to a strange, even lurid, legend that shimmers forth strangely from the usual flat narrative voice: Paul's vision, we are told, "was very like the old stories that used to float about London of fabulously rich Jews, who had subterranean halls there, with palms, and fountains, and soft lamps and richly apparelled women who never saw the disenchanting light of

London day" (111). This odd bit of social rumor is vaguely subversive. It hints at Paul's sense of alienation from his world, at his need for refuge, at the security money can buy, at religious apostasy, or paganism: a temple for the senses. Also—an ironic point, which lifts the story above the sentimental—it hints at Paul's limited imagination: this "pleasure dome" seems modeled after the lobby of a first-class hotel—perhaps the Pittsburgh Schenley.

10   The badge of Paul's fidelity to his dream, his talisman, is the red carnation he wears in the buttonhole of his shabby coat as he confronts his teachers, which they (correctly) interpret as a sign of his unrepentant attitude ("flippantly red"; "the scandalous red carnation" [103]). Cut flowers become a motif: Paul notes that the "prosy" male teachers he despises never wear violets in their button-holes (111). Arriving in his suite at the Waldorf he orders violets and jonquils. Driving down wintry Fifth Avenue he notes the flower stands, "whole flower gardens blooming under glass cases, against the sides of which the snow flakes stuck and melted; violets, roses, carnations, lilies of the valley" (115). Hothouse flowers, being both artificial (raised by human contrivance under unnatural conditions) and yet also natural (they are *real* flowers) appropriately symbolize the limits of Paul's imagination and his plight. They are expensive. Badges of color in a colorless, gray world, they nurture the inarticulate boy's dim sense of a beauty connected to substance and reality but not available to him. He buys carnations again on his last journey to the snowy hill above the railroad tracks.

11   Charles E. May, in his analysis of the generic form of the American short story, locates its dynamic in the confluence of primitive tale and romance on the one hand and the realism of the eighteenth-century novel on the other. "Moreover," May argues, "it is more closely related to the romance than to the realistic mode, and consequently its characters are more apt to be . . . stylized figures rather than 'real people.'" (64) Consider, he says, Goodman Brown in the New England woods, or—a situation closer to Paul's—the stubborn Bartleby up against Wall Street. (Like Bartleby, Paul prefers not to adapt to a deadening normalcy.) Paul's week in New York has this quality of the folk tale made newly local and tame. Realistic enough, the week is also a wish come true, a fairy-tale reward for fidelity. All the little failures are avoided: Paul makes no mistakes. For the first time he is full of energy; he plans appropriate purchases, and he enjoys fully the feel of his clothes, the white linen, the flowers, the red velvet carpets, the sound of popping corks. The experienced clerks at the Waldorf take him at his own estimation, and apparently he could spend an evening on the town with a college boy without betraying ignorance. He is not embarrassed or gauche in the hotel dining room, as an uneducated, callow boy might be: "he wore his spoils with dignity and in no way made himself conspicuous. . . . His chief greediness lay in his ears and eyes, and his excesses were not offensive ones" (117). A slight change Cather made in reprinting the story underscores my contention that Cather here is not writing ironically: in *The Troll Garden* version, Paul, on his last night in the hotel dining room, "drummed a nervous accompaniment to the Pagliacci music" (119). Subsequently she omits the Pagliacci reference,

as though to avoid any hint of clownishness, or masquerade, about the boy.[3] Most intriguing of all is his mental poise. "He was not the least abashed or lonely. . . . He could not remember a time when he had felt so at peace with himself" (117). No qualms about his crime disturb him; apparently the long lessons of Sabbath School had no niche in his consciousness. In fact, he feels virtuous: "The mere release from the necessity of petty lying, lying every day and every day, restored his self-respect. . . . He felt a good deal more manly, more honest, even . . ." (117).

With judgment closing in, and death his only out, Paul still has no regrets, and his final thoughts are put in the only terms his circumscribed life has made available. The truth he knows now, "more than ever," is that "money was everything, the wall between all he loathed and all he wanted" (119). In a theatrical, indeed ritualistic, gesture he buries one of his carnations in the snow before launching himself before the train. As he dies, Paul sees the "folly of his haste . . . with merciless clarity": but the "folly" is not his crime, nor his suicide, nor his false moral sense; rather it is his failure to escape further, to more distant lands, to "the blue of Adriatic water, the yellow of Algerian sands" (121). In part Cather is here taking a sly pleasure in balking the sentimental moralists of her day who expect deathbed guilt and remorse. (In this she resembles her admired Mark Twain.) More to the point is Paul's vision of the temple of beauty that blesses his final moments. Surely this is the "epiphanous moment" of the story, confirming his vision as authentic and his fidelity to it justified. The closing line tells us that a compassionate universe receives him: "Then, because the picture making mechanism was crushed. . . . Paul dropped back into the immense design of things" (121). It is a moment of wonder and absolution.

The pattern beneath Paul's search can now be discerned—it is the ancient Parsifal tale: the clumsy boy whose mistakes and embarrassments melt away in light of the grandeur and mystery of the ideal served. It is possible, too, to see how Paul's motives and sensibilities may reflect his author's. Cather recalled in a letter of 1943 that a part of Paul was owed to her own feelings on first visiting New York (Letter to John Phillopson). The Cather of 1902 was not the self-assured author; she was a young woman from the West trying to enter the great world, as she thought of it. Writing to her friend Elizabeth Sergeant in 1911, she deplored these early stories because "the starvation of a girl avid for a richer environment seemed to stick out, to deform, to make the picture one" (Sergeant, *Memoir* 67). Arriving alone in Pittsburgh in 1896, Cather must often have felt like Paul standing in the cold rain looking in at the warmly lighted Schenley. What sustained her was her blind faith that she was meant to achieve, to be a votary in the divine "kingdom of art" (*Kingdom* 416). In any case, the Parsifal theme was one that stuck in Cather's imagination. She would use it a few years later to structure her novel *One of Ours,* as she wryly admitted in a

12

13

---

[3]This alteration in the text is unaccountably not noted in the "Table of Revisions" for "Paul's Case" in James Woodress' definitive edition of *The Troll Garden,* and David Carpenter, who comments on so many of the revisions, also fails to mention it.

note to a reader who quizzed her on the point (Letter to Mr. Johns). She must have had a fellow feeling for ungainly youth, what with her history of rebellious cross-dressing, her awkwardness as a student at the University of Nebraska, the gaps in her "prairie education," as she called it, and her odd journalistic jobs. A letter to Dorothy Canfield Fisher written in 1921, in which she tries to explain some offense she gave the Canfield family, refers to Paul's defiance as like her own. Here, possibly, is why Cather never disowned "Paul's Case," whereas she discarded so many of her early stories: Paul testifies to an early self and to her own stubborn certainties.

Here also is a link to the other two stories from *The Troll Garden* that   14
Cather included in her collected writings when she assembled them in the late '30s. All three testify to the indestructibility of the soul that knows beauty. Steavens, the young friend of the sculptor in "The Sculptor's Funeral," perceives just how brutal were the circumstances of the artist's boyhood when he accompanies the body back to his home. And yet from all that raw ugliness came a mind that was "an inexhaustless gallery of beautiful impressions" (39). In "A Wagner Matinee" Clark watches his Aunt Georgiana, withered by thirty years of harsh frontier living, melt into tears at the music of the concert, and he reflects, "It never really died, then—the soul that can suffer so excruciatingly and so interminably" (100).

But the immediate appeal of "Paul's Case" does not lie in its relation to   15
the author's personal history or in its relation to other *Troll Garden* stories. It lies, I contend, in our fascination with Paul's transformation of himself, however short-lived, and his discovery, so ultimately wrong, and yet so plausible, so right, "that money was everything." Here is the true accomplishment of the story, the conversion of romantic longing into a devotion to the medium of exchange (of change) itself—currency, the coin of this democratic realm, the glass slipper that can change a sow's ear into a silk purse. It is a very American dream, the romance of money. It was to be given greater and more developed expression a few years after Paul's story in the transformation of James Gatz into Jay Gatsby, who also sought to invent a new self, to find new parents, to create an identity by means of drawers of shirts and opulent surroundings. In fact, there may be a direct line between Paul and Gatsby. In a 1925 letter to Cather, apologizing for what might be seen as plagiarism in the likeness of Daisy Buchanan and Cather's Marian Forrester, Fitzgerald declares himself "one of your greatest admirers" and singles out "Paul's Case," along with her novels, as a favorite (Quirk 579).

Although the beauty Paul served was, like Gatsby's, "vast, vulgar and   16
meretricious," and, like Gatsby, he served it criminally, he served it unswervingly. In her note about the Parsifal theme, Cather refers to the Blameless Fool: a nice epitaph for Paul.

Works Cited

Arnold, Marilyn. *Willa Cather's Short Fiction*. Athens: Ohio UP, 1984.

Brown, E. K. Completed by Leon Edel. *Willa Cather: A Critical Biography*. New York: Knopf, 1953.

Cather, Willa. *The Kingdom of Art: Willa Cather's First Principles and Critical Statements, 1893–1896*. Ed. Bernice Slote. Lincoln: U of Nebraska P, 1966.

——. Letter to Dorothy Canfield Fisher. 8 April 1921. University of Vermont Library, Burlington.

——. Letter to John Phillopson. 15 March 1943. Willa Cather Historical Center, Red Cloud, Nebraska.

——. Letter to Mr. Johns. 17 Nov. 1922. University of Virginia Library, Charlottesville.

——. *The Troll Garden*. 1905. Lincoln: U of Nebraska P, 1983.

Carpenter, David A. "Why Willa Cather Revised 'Paul's Case': The Work in Art and Those Sunday Afternoons." *American Literature* 59 (1987): 590–608.

Gelfant, Blanche H. "Art and Apparent Artlessness: Self Reflexivity in *My Antonia*." In *Approach to Teaching "My Antonia"*. Ed. Susan J. Rosowski. New York: MLA, 1989. 126–133.

May, Charles E. "Metaphoric Motivation in Short Fiction: 'In the Beginning Was the Story.'" In *Short Story Theory at a Crossroads*. Ed. Susan Lohafer and Jo Ellyn Clarey. Baton Rouge: Louisiana UP, 1989. 62–73.

O'Brien, Sharon. *Willa Cather: The Emerging Voice*. New York: Oxford UP, 1987.

Quirk, Tom. "Fitzgerald and Willa Cather: *The Great Gatsby*." *American Literature* 54 (1982): 576–591.

Rosowski, Susan J. *The Voyage Perilous: Willa Cather's Romanticism*. Lincoln: U of Nebraska P, 1987.

Sergeant, Elizabeth Shepley. *Willa Cather: A Memoir*. Philadelphia: Lippincott, 1953.

Woodress, James. Introduction. *The Troll Garden*. Cather xi–xxx.

——. *Willa Cather: A Literary Life*. Lincoln: U of Nebraska P, 1987. ■

Questions for Meaning

1. Wasserman claims that "Paul's Case" has received relatively little critical attention. How does she explain this apparent lack of interest?
2. In paragraph 2, Wasserman refers to "imagery and allusion." What does she mean by these terms?
3. According to Wasserman, what do many critical interpretations of "Paul's Case" have in common?
4. What evidence in the story suggests that Paul's fascination with beauty and splendor could be worthy of respect?
5. Vocabulary: preeminence (1), callous (1), elliptically (3), malevolency (3), etiology (4), positivistic (5), conversely (6), talisman (10), meretricious (16).

Questions about Strategy

1. Does Wasserman ever agree with the other critics she cites? How would you describe her tone when she discusses their views?
2. Why does Wasserman draw attention to the collection of stories in which "Paul's Case" first appeared?
3. Consider the revision that Wasserman discusses in paragraph 11. Does it convince you that Cather wanted readers to regard Paul sympathetically?

4. In her conclusion, Wasserman links "Paul's Case" with *The Great Gatsby,* a novel written twenty years later. What is her purpose in making this comparison?

ONE STUDENT'S ASSIGNMENT

Familiarize yourself with the different interpretations of "Paul's Case" reprinted in *The Informed Argument.* Ask yourself which ones, if any, helped you to understand the story. Assume that some critics will be more helpful than others, but do not feel obliged to agree with anyone else's interpretation. On the contrary, try to offer an interpretation of your own in an essay of approximately one thousand words. Your final draft should include specific evidence from the story to support your thesis. You should also demonstrate that you are familiar with the critical literature and intend your essay to be part of an ongoing conversation about the story. Draw on any sources you decide are appropriate, and use MLA style documentation.

When Someone Touches Him, It Hurts
Jessica Powell

Willa Cather's "Paul's Case" has been interpreted in countless ways in the effort to explain the desperately troubled protagonist. Marilyn Arnold argues that Paul is "an alien because he has a warped perception of everything; he is unable to see the world as it really is" (Arnold 426). A similar view is expressed by Carlos A. Perez.   1

However plausible Arnold's argument may be, it does not explain *why* Paul is "warped." I believe that when Cather's imagery and word choices are placed alongside a profile of a victimized child, they offer a reading of "Paul's Case" that suggests the sexual abuse of a child. Although this interpretation is not definitive, there is enough evidence to render it a feasible explanation of the elusive inner Paul.   2

In their book *Scream Louder,* Barbara Oliver and Marsha Utain present a profile of a typical child-abuse victim. Common symptoms include an inability to trust others, isolation, under- or overreaction to external stimuli, acute startle responses, and physical shaking under extreme stress (209). Paul's manifestation of these symptoms enables the reader to begin to understand "Paul's Case" as one of sexual abuse.   3

The symptoms of distrust and isolation can be found throughout the story. Paul refuses to trust or identify with the members of his neighborhood, his classmates, or any of the people he encounters in New York, and he seeks out isolation in the art gallery, in the basement, and in his hotel   4 room. And although he doesn't react well to people, he overreacts to external stimuli. He responds powerfully to the sound of the symphony, and is keenly aware of the smells, colors, and images in the physical world that surrounds him.

Another symptom can be found in the opening scene's description of an "acute startle response." Paul's English teacher tells of a time she tried to touch his hand, and "Paul had started back with a shudder and thrust his hands violently behind him" (Cather 412). When the hand is raised, even though no harm is intended, Paul does much more than flinch; he instinctively cowers like a beaten dog. This reaction shows that the rejection and hatred of touch have become unconscious, an instinct. Paul has lost his human ability to discern between a threatening touch and a bothersome touch. All he knows is that when someone touches him, it hurts.   5

The same scene shows Paul shaking when he's under extreme stress. When the teachers confront him, he violently shakes and trembles. Paul's entire physical presence exudes nearly constant signals that he cannot effectively cope with stress.   6

Cather provides another clue to the source of Paul's troubling behavior by including sexually suggestive language in the story, the first example coming after Paul's night at the symphony. He dreads going home, knowing that "The end had to come sometime; his father in his night-clothes at the top of the stairs. . . . He felt that he could not be *accosted* by his father tonight, that he could not toss again on that miserable bed [emphasis mine]" (415). The father's position at the top of the stairs controls the entrance to the upstairs and Paul's bedroom, symbolizing Paul's lack of power. It is also significant that the father has changed his clothing, and is now wearing his night-clothes. This implies that he takes on a new persona at night—a persona that Paul reacts to much more fiercely than the father of the daytime.   7

The fear in this passage indicates that Paul is more than a boy merely nervous about breaking curfew. He is a boy who dreads coming home to his father, a boy afraid of being accosted, of being "solicited for sexual immorality" (*Webster's Third New International Dictionary*). It is possible that Paul's bed is miserable because it is the setting for sexual violation.   8

Accosted is by no means the only sexually connotative word in the story. Cather includes even more sexual imagery when Paul returns home from a night at the orchestra: "After each of these orgies of living, he experienced all the physical depression which follows a debauch" (415). Although "orgies of living" and "debauch" presumably refer to Paul's intense experience at the orchestra, the language echoes the sexual complexities that pervade Paul's life.   9

Cather couples the language and images of abuse with haunting refer-   10
ences to a "shadowed corner":

> . . . he had always been tormented by fear, a sort of apprehen-
> sive dread . . . . Even when he was a little boy, it was always
> there—behind him, or before, or on either side. There had al-
> ways been the shadowed corner, the dark place into which he
> dared not look, but from which something seemed always to be
> watching him—and Paul had done things that were not pretty to
> watch, he knew. (420)

Paul recognizes an omniscient and powerful force in his life, but he cannot
yet name or identify it. One critic, however, does name it: "Paul's homosexuality is most vividly symbolized as the unnamed fear that has haunted
him for years" (Summers 455). While Summers' interpretation that Paul is
homosexual may make sense, sexual abuse is also a logical identity of the
unnamed fear, especially because of the distinct presence of another being
who is watching him. The power of this presence, and Paul's lifelong fear of
it, has trapped and surrounded him, making him a prisoner of this darkness in the corner. The final sentence is particularly important because it
articulates the feelings of participation and guilt characteristic of an
abused child; Paul thinks he has sinned rather than been sinned against.

But of course Paul, like any victim of abuse, has not sinned. Instead, his   11
similarity to the profile of an abused child and the language in which his case
is written suggest that Paul is trapped by a sexually abusive father. Nearly a
century after he was created, we finally have the knowledge to recognize the
possibility that Paul's case may be solved if we treat it as one involving the
confusion, pain, and fear felt by a tragic victim of child abuse.

Works Cited

Arnold, Marilyn. *Willa Cather's Short Fiction*. Athens: Ohio UP, 1984.

Cather, Willa. "Paul's Case." *The Informed Argument*. Ed. Robert K. Miller. Fort Worth:
Harcourt, 1995. 411–25.

Oliver, Barbara, and Marsha Utain. *Scream Louder: Through Hell and Healing With an
Incest Survivor and Her Therapist*. Deerfield Beach, Fla.: Health Communications, Inc. 1989.

Perez, Carlos A. "'Paul's Case' The Outsider." *The Informed Argument*. Ed. Robert K.
Miller. Fort Worth: Harcourt, 1995. 436–48.

Summers, Claude J. "'A Losing Game in the End': Aestheticism and Homosexuality
in Cather's 'Paul's Case.'" *The Informed Argument*. Ed. Robert K. Miller. Fort
Worth: Harcourt, 1995. 449–63.

Webster's Third New International Dictionary: Unabridged. Ed. Philip Babcock Grove.
Springfield, Mass.: Merriam-Webster. 1981.

Suggestions for Writing

1. Focusing upon explanations of why Paul is an outsider, synthesize the arguments in this section.
2. Reread "Paul's Case" and then write your own interpretation of it.
3. Read another short story by Cather, such as "The Sculptor's Funeral" or "A Wagner Matinee," and compare it to "Paul's Case."
4. Watch the video of "Paul's Case" and evaluate how effectively it tells Cather's story.
5. Choose a story, poem, or play that you like. Locate at least two sources discussing the work you have chosen, and write an essay exploring your response to both the work and the sources.

COLLABORATIVE PROJECT

Form a group in which each member distributes a short story to read and discuss. After you have discussed each story, decide which ones you want to recommend to other readers. Write a report in which you briefly summarize these works and try to persuade others to read them by showing what you like about them.

P A R T   4

SOME CLASSIC ARGUMENTS

JONATHAN SWIFT

A MODEST PROPOSAL

For preventing the Children of Poor People in Ireland from Being a Burden to Their Parents or Country, and for Making Them Beneficial to the Public

Jonathan Swift (1667–1745) was a clergyman, poet, wit, and satirist. Born in Ireland as a member of the Protestant ruling class, Swift attended Trinity College in Dublin before settling in England in 1689. For the next ten years, he was a member of the household of Sir William Temple at Moor Park, Surrey. It was there that Swift met Esther Johnson, the "Stella" to whom he later wrote a famous series of letters known as *Journal to Stella* (1710–1713). Although he was ordained a priest in the Church of Ireland in 1695, and made frequent trips to Ireland, Swift's ambition always brought him back to England. His reputation as a writer grew rapidly after the publication of his first major work, *A Tale of a Tub,* in 1704. He became a writer on behalf of the ruling Tory party, and was appointed Dean of St. Patrick's Cathedral in Dublin as a reward for his services. When the Tories fell from power in 1714, Swift retired to Ireland, where he remained for the rest of his life, except for brief visits to England in 1726 and 1727. It was in Ireland that he wrote *Gulliver's Travels* (1726), which is widely recognized as one of the masterpieces of English literature, and "A Modest Proposal" (1729), one of the most memorable of all essays.

Ruled as an English colony and subject to numerous repressive laws, Ireland in Swift's time was a desperately poor country. Swift wrote "A Modest Proposal" in order to expose the plight of Ireland and the unfair policies under which it suffered. As you read it, you will find that Swift's proposal for solving the problem of poverty is anything but "modest." Even when we know that we are reading satire, this brilliant and bitter essay retains the power to shock all but the most careless of readers.

It is a melancholy object to those who walk through this great town or travel   1
in the country, when they see the streets, the roads, and cabin doors, crowded
with beggars of the female sex, followed by three, four, or six children, all in

rags and importuning every passenger for an alms. These mothers, instead of being able to work for their honest livelihood, are forced to employ all their time in strolling to beg sustenance for their helpless infants, who, as they grow up, either turn thieves for want of work, or leave their dear native country to fight for the Pretender in Spain, or sell themselves to the Barbados.★

I think it is agreed by all parties that this prodigious number of children 2 in the arms, or on the backs, or at the heels of their mothers, and frequently of their fathers, is in the present deplorable state of the kingdom a very great additional grievance; and therefore whoever could find out a fair, cheap, and easy method of making these children sound, useful members of the commonwealth would deserve so well of the public as to have his statue set up for a preserver of the nation.

But my intention is very far from being confined to provide only for the 3 children of professed beggars; it is of a much greater extent, and shall take in the whole number of infants at a certain age who are born of parents in effect as little able to support them as those who demand our charity in the streets.

As to my own part, having turned my thoughts for many years upon this 4 important subject, and maturely weighed the several schemes of other projectors, I have always found them grossly mistaken in their computation. It is true, a child just dropped from its dam may be supported by her milk for a solar year, with little other nourishment; at most not above the value of two shillings, which the mother may certainly get, or the value in scraps, by her lawful occupation of begging; and it is exactly at one year that I propose to provide for them in such a manner as instead of being a charge upon their parents or the parish, or wanting food and raiment for the rest of their lives, they shall on the contrary contribute to the feeding, and partly to the clothing, of many thousands.

There is likewise another great advantage in my scheme, that it will pre- 5 vent those voluntary abortions, and that horrid practice of women murdering their bastard children, alas, too frequent among us, sacrificing the poor innocent babes, I doubt, more to avoid the expense than the shame, which would move tears and pity in the most savage and inhuman breast.

The number of souls in this kingdom being usually reckoned one million 6 and a half, of these I calculate there may be about two hundred thousand couples whose wives are breeders; from which number I subtract thirty thousand couples who are able to maintain their own children, although I apprehend there cannot be so many under the present distress of the kingdom; but this being granted, there will remain an hundred and seventy thousand breeders. I again subtract fifty thousand for those women who miscarry, or whose children die by accident or disease within the year. There only remain an hundred and twenty thousand children of poor parents annually born. The question therefore is, how this number shall be reared and provided for, which, as I

★The Pretender was James Stuart, the Catholic son of James II. Exiled in Spain, he sought to gain the throne his father had lost to the Protestant rulers William and Mary in 1688. Attempting to escape from destitution, many Irish people went to Barbados and other colonies as indentured servants.

have already said, under the present situation of affairs, is utterly impossible by all the methods hitherto proposed. For we can neither employ them in handicraft or agriculture; we neither build houses (I mean in the country) nor cultivate land. They can very seldom pick up a livelihood by stealing till they arrive at six years old, except where they are of towardly parts; although I confess they learn the rudiments much earlier, during which time they can however be looked upon only as probationers, as I have been informed by a principal gentleman in the country of Cavan, who protested to me that he never knew above one or two instances under the age of six, even in a part of the kingdom so renowned for the quickest proficiency in that art.

I am assured by our merchants that a boy or a girl before twelve years old   7
is no salable commodity; and even when they come to this age they will not yield above three pounds, or three pounds and half a crown at most on the Exchange; which cannot turn to account either to the parents or the kingdom, the charge of nutriment and rags having been at least four times that value.

I shall now therefore humbly propose my own thoughts, which I hope   8
will not be liable to the least objection.

I have been assured by a very knowing American of my acquaintance in   9
London, that a young healthy child well nursed is at a year old a most delicious, nourishing, and wholesome food, whether stewed, roasted, baked, or boiled; and I make no doubt that it will equally serve in a fricassee or a ragout.

I do therefore humbly offer it to public consideration that of the hundred   10
and twenty thousand children, already computed, twenty thousand may be reserved for breed, whereof only one fourth part to be males, which is more than we allow to sheep, black cattle, or swine; and my reason is that these children are seldom the fruits of marriage, a circumstance not much regarded by our savages, therefore one male will be sufficient to serve four females. That the remaining hundred thousand may at a year old be offered in sale to the persons of quality and fortune through the kingdom, always advising the mother to let them suck plentifully in the last month, so as to render them plump and fat for a good table. A child will make two dishes at an entertainment for friends; and when the family dines alone, the fore or hind quarter will make a reasonable dish, and seasoned with a little pepper or salt will be very good boiled on the fourth day, especially in winter.

I have reckoned upon a medium that a child just born will weigh   11
twelve pounds, and in a solar year if tolerably nursed increaseth to twenty-eight pounds.

I grant this food will be somewhat dear, and therefore very proper for   12
landlords, who, as they have already devoured most of the parents, seem to have the best title to the children.

Infant's flesh will be in season throughout the year, but more plentiful in   13
March, and a little before and after. For we are told by a grave author, an eminent French physician,★ that fish being a prolific diet, there are more children

★Francois Rabelais (1494?–1533) the author of *Garganna and Pantagroel,* a five volume satire much admired by Swift.

born in Roman Catholic countries about nine months after Lent than at any other season; therefore, reckoning a year after Lent, the markets will be more glutted than usual, because the number of popish infants is at least three to one in this kingdom; and therefore it will have one other collateral advantage, by lessening the number of Papists among us.

I have already computed the charge of nursing a beggar's child (in which   14 list I reckon all cottagers, laborers, and four-fifths of the farmers) to be about two shillings per annum, rags included; and I believe no gentleman would repine to give ten shillings for the carcass of a good fat child, which, as I have said, will make four dishes of excellent nutritive meat, when he hath only some particular friend or his own family to dine with him. Thus the squire will learn to be a good landlord, and grow popular among the tenants; the mother will have eight shillings net profit, and be fit for work till she produces another child.

Those who are more thrifty (as I must confess the times require) may   15 flay the carcass; the skin of which artificially dressed will make admirable gloves for ladies, and summer boots for fine gentlemen.

As to our city of Dublin, shambles may be appointed for this purpose in   16 the most convenient parts of it, and butchers we may be assured will not be wanting; although I rather recommend buying the children alive, and dressing them hot from the knife as we do roasting pigs.

A very worthy person, a true lover of his country, and whose virtues I   17 highly esteem, was lately pleased in discoursing on this matter to offer a refinement upon my scheme. He said that many gentlemen of his kingdom, having of late destroyed their deer, he conceived that the want of venison might be well supplied by the bodies of young lads and maidens, not exceeding fourteen years of age nor under twelve, so great a number of both sexes in every country being now ready to starve for want of work and service; and these to be disposed of by their parents, if alive, or otherwise by their nearest relations. But with due deference to so excellent a friend and so deserving a patriot, I cannot be altogether in his sentiments; for as to the males, my American acquaintance assured me from frequent experience that their flesh was generally tough and lean, like that of our schoolboys, by continual exercise, and their taste disagreeable; and to fatten them would not answer the charge. Then as to the females, it would, I think with humble submission, be a loss to the public, because they soon would become breeders themselves; and besides, it is not improbable that some scrupulous people might be apt to censure such a practice (although indeed very unjustly) as a little bordering upon cruelty; which, I confess, hath always been with me the strongest objection against any project, how well soever intended.

But in order to justify my friend, he confessed that this expedient was   18 put into his head by the famous Psalmanazar,* a native of the island Formosa, who came from thence to London about twenty years ago, and in conversation

---

*George Psalmanazer (?1679–1763) published an imaginary description of Formosa and became well known in English society.

told my friend that in his country when any young person happened to be put to death, the executioner sold the carcass to persons of quality as a prime dainty; and that in his time the body of a plump girl of fifteen, who was crucified for an attempt to poison the emperor, was sold to his Imperial Majesty's prime minister of state, and other great mandarins of the court, in joints from the gibbet, at four hundred crowns. Neither indeed can I deny that if the same use were made of several plump young girls in this town, who without one single groat to their fortunes cannot stir abroad without a chair, and appear at the playhouse and assemblies in foreign fineries which they never will pay for, the kingdom would not be the worse.

Some persons of a desponding spirit are in great concern about that vast number of poor people who are aged, diseased, or maimed, and I have been desired to employ my thoughts what course may be taken to ease the nation of so grievous an encumbrance. But I am not in the least pain upon that matter, because it is very well known that they are every day dying and rotting by cold and famine, and filth and vermin, as fast as can be reasonably expected. And as to the younger laborers, they are now in almost as hopeful a condition. They cannot get work, and consequently pine away for want of nourishment to a degree that if any time they are accidentally hired to common labor, they have not strength to perform it; and thus the country and themselves are happily delivered from the evils to come. 19

I have too long digressed, and therefore shall return to my subject. I think the advantages by the proposal which I have made are obvious and many, as well as of the highest importance. 20

For first, as I have already observed, it would greatly lessen the number of Papists, with whom we are yearly overrun, being the principal breeders of the nation as well as our most dangerous enemies; and who stay at home on purpose to deliver the kingdom to the Pretender, hoping to take their advantage by the absence of so many good Protestants, who have chosen rather to leave their country than to stay at home and pay tithes against their conscience to an Episcopal curate. 21

Secondly, the poorer tenants will have something valuable of their own, which by law may be made liable to distress, and help to pay their landlord's rent, their corn and cattle being already seized and money a thing unknown. 22

Thirdly, whereas the maintenance of an hundred thousand children, from two years old and upwards, cannot be computed at less than ten shillings a piece per annum, the nation's stock will be thereby increased fifty thousand pounds per annum, besides the profit of a new dish introduced to the tables of all gentlemen of fortune in the kingdom who have any refinement in taste. And the money will circulate among ourselves, the goods being entirely of our own growth and manufacture. 23

Fourthly, the constant breeders, besides the gain of eight shillings sterling per annum by the sale of their children, will be rid of the charge of maintaining them after the first year. 24

Fifthly, this food would likewise bring great custom to taverns, where the vintners will certainly be so prudent as to procure the best receipts for 25 dressing it to perfection, and consequently have their houses frequented by all the fine gentlemen, who justly value themselves upon their knowledge in good eating; and a skillful cook, who understands how to oblige his guests, will contrive to make it as expensive as they please.

Sixthly, this would be a great inducement to marriage, which all wise nations have either encouraged by rewards or enforced by laws and penalties. It would increase the care and tenderness of mothers toward their children, when they were sure of a settlement for life to the poor babes, provided in some sort by the public, to their annual profit instead of expense. We should see an honest emulation among the married women, which of them could bring the fattest child to the market. Men would become as fond of their wives during the time of their pregnancy as they are now of their mares in foal, their cows in calf, or sows when they are ready to farrow; nor offer to beat or kick them (as is too frequent a practice) for fear of a miscarriage. 26

Many other advantages might be enumerated. For instance, the addition of some thousand carcasses in our exportation of barreled beef, the propagation of swine's flesh, and improvements in the art of making good bacon, so much wanted among us by the great destruction of pigs, too frequent at our tables, which are no way comparable in taste or magnificence to a well-grown, fat, yearling child, which roasted whole will make a considerable figure at a lord mayor's feast or any other public entertainment. But this and many others I omit, being studious of brevity. 27

Supposing that one thousand families in this city would be constant customers for infants' flesh, besides others who might have it at merry meetings, particularly weddings and christenings, I compute that Dublin would take off annually about twenty thousand carcasses, and the rest of the kingdom (where probably they will be sold somewhat cheaper) the remaining eighty thousand. 28

I can think of no one objection that will possibly be raised against this proposal, unless it should be urged that the number of people will be thereby much lessened in the kingdom. This I freely own, and it was indeed one principal design in offering it to the world. I desire the reader will observe, that I calculate my remedy for this one individual kingdom of Ireland and for no other that ever was, is, or I think ever can be upon earth. Therefore let no man talk to me of other expedients: of taxing our absentees at five shillings a pound: of using neither clothes nor household furniture except what is of our own growth and manufacture: of utterly rejecting the materials and instruments that promote foreign luxury: of curing the expensiveness of pride, vanity, idleness, and gaming in our women: of introducing a vein of parsimony, prudence, and temperance: of learning to love our country, in the want of which we differ even from Laplanders and the inhabitants of Topinamboo: of quitting our animosities and factions, nor acting any longer like the Jews, who were murdering one another at the very moment their city was taken: of being a little cautious not to sell our country and conscience for nothing: of teaching landlords to have at least one degree of mercy toward their tenants: lastly, of putting a spirit of honesty, industry, and skill into our shopkeepers; who, if a 29 resolution could now be taken to buy only our native goods, would immediately unite to cheat and exact upon us in the price, the measure, and the goodness, nor could ever yet be brought to make one fair proposal of just dealing, though often and earnestly invited to it.

Therefore I repeat, let no man talk to me of these and the like expedients, till he hath at least some glimpse of hope that there will ever be some hearty and sincere attempt to put them in practice.   30

But as to myself, having been wearied out for many years with offering vain, idle, visionary thoughts, and at length utterly despairing of success. I fortunately fell upon this proposal, which, as it is wholly new, so it hath something solid and real, of no expense and little trouble, full in our own power, and whereby we can incur no danger in disobliging England. For this kind of commodity will not bear exportation, the flesh being of too tender a consistence to admit a long continuance in salt, although perhaps I could name a country which would be glad to eat up our whole nation without it.   31

After all, I am not so violently bent upon my own opinion as to reject any offer proposed by wise men, which shall be found equally innocent, cheap, easy, and effectual. But before something of that kind shall be advanced in contradiction to my scheme, and offering a better, I desire the author or authors will be pleased maturely to consider two points. First, as things now stand, how they will be able to find food and raiment for an hundred thousand useless mouths and backs. And secondly, there being a round million of creatures in human figure throughout this kingdom, whose sole subsistence put into a common stock would leave them in debt two millions of pounds sterling, adding those who are beggars by profession to the bulk of farmers, cottagers, and laborers, with their wives and children who are beggars in effect; I desire those politicians who dislike my overture, and may perhaps be so bold to attempt an answer, that they will first ask the parents of these mortals whether they would not at this day think it a great happiness to have been sold for food at a year old in this manner I prescribe, and thereby have avoided such a perpetual scene of misfortunes as they have since gone through by the oppression of landlords, the impossibility of paying rent without money or trade, the want of common sustenance, with neither house nor clothes to cover them from the inclemencies of the weather, and the most inevitable prospect of entailing the like or greater miseries upon their breed forever.   32

I profess, in the sincerity of my heart, that I have not the least personal interest in endeavoring to promote this necessary work, having no other motive than the public good of my country, by advancing our trade, providing for infants, relieving the poor, and giving some pleasure to the rich. I have no children by which I can propose to get a single penny; the youngest being nine years old, and my wife past childbearing. ■   33

Questions for Meaning

1. What do we learn in this essay about the condition of Ireland in Swift's time, and how Ireland was viewed by England? Does Swift provide any clues about what has caused the poverty he describes?
2. What specific "advantages" does Swift cite on behalf of his proposal?
3. Why does Swift limit his proposal to infants? On what grounds does he exclude older children from consideration as marketable commodities? Why does he claim that we need not worry about the elderly?
4. What does this essay reveal about the relations between Catholics and Protestants in the eighteenth century?
5. Where in the essay does Swift tell us what he really wants? What serious reforms does he propose to improve conditions in Ireland?
6. Vocabulary: importuning (1), sustenance (1), prodigious (2), rudiments (6), ragout (9), collateral (13), desponding (19), inducement (26), emulation (26), propagation (27), parsimony (29), incur (31).

Questions about Strategy

1. How does Swift present himself in this essay? Many readers have taken this essay seriously and come away convinced that Swift was heartless and cruel. Why is it possible for some readers to be deceived in this way? What devices does Swift employ to create the illusion that he is serious? How does this strategy benefit the essay?
2. Does the language of the first few paragraphs contain any hint of irony? At what point in the essay did it first become clear to you that Swift is writing tongue in cheek?
3. Where in the essay does Swift pretend to anticipate objections that might be raised against his proposal? How does he dispose of these objections?
4. How does the style of this essay contrast with its subject matter? How does this contrast contribute to the force of the essay as a whole?
5. What is the function of the concluding paragraph?
6. What is the premise of this essay if we take its argument at face value? When we realize that Swift is writing ironically, what underlying premise begins to emerge?
7. What advantage is there in writing ironically? Why do you think Swift chose to treat his subject in this manner?

THOMAS JEFFERSON

THE DECLARATION OF INDEPENDENCE

Thomas Jefferson (1743–1826) was the third president of the United States and one of the most talented men ever to hold that office. A farmer, architect, writer, and scientist, Jefferson entered politics in 1769 as a member of the Virginia House of Burgesses. In 1775, he was a member of Virginia's delegation to the Second Continental Congress. He was governor of Virginia from 1779 to 1781, represented the United States in Europe from 1784 to 1789, and was elected to the first of two terms as president in 1801. Of all his many accomplishments, Jefferson himself was most proud of having founded the University of Virginia in 1819.

Although the Continental Congress had delegated the responsibility for writing a declaration of independence to a committee that included Benjamin Franklin and John Adams as well as Jefferson, it was Jefferson who undertook the actual composition. His colleagues respected him as the best writer among them. Jefferson wrote at least two, and possibly three, drafts during the seventeen days allowed for the assignment. His work was reviewed by the other members of the committee, but they made only minor revisions—mainly in the first two paragraphs. When it came to adopting the declaration, Congress was harder to please. After lengthy and spirited debate, Congress made twenty-four changes and deleted over three hundred words. Nevertheless, "The Declaration of Independence," as approved by Congress on July 4, 1776, is almost entirely the work of Jefferson. In addition to being an eloquent example of eighteenth-century prose, it is a clear example of deductive reasoning.

When in the Course of human events, it becomes necessary for one people to dissolve the political bands which have connected them with another, and to assume among the powers of the earth, the separate and equal station to which the Laws of Nature and of Nature's God entitle them, a decent respect to the opinions of mankind requires that they should declare the causes which impel them to the separation.   1

We hold these truths to be self-evident, that all men are created equal, that they are endowed by their Creator with certain unalienable Rights, that among these are Life, Liberty and the pursuit of Happiness. That to secure these rights, Governments are instituted among Men, deriving their just powers from the consent of the governed. That whenever any Form of Government becomes destructive of these ends it is the Right of the People to alter or to abolish it, and to institute new Government, laying its foundation on such principles and organizing its powers in such form, as to them shall seem most likely to effect their Safety and Happiness. Prudence, indeed, will dictate that Governments long established should not be changed for light and transient causes; and accordingly all experience has shewn, that mankind are more disposed to suffer, while evils are sufferable, than to right themselves by   2 abolishing the forms to which they are accustomed. But when a long train of abuses and usurpations, pursuing invariably the same Object evinces a design to reduce them under absolute Despotism, it is their right, it is their duty, to throw off such Government, and to provide new Guards for their future security. Such has been the patient sufferance of these Colonies; and such is now the necessity which constrains them to alter their former Systems of Government. The history of the present King of Great Britain is a history of repeated injuries and usurpations, all having in direct object the establishment of an absolute Tyranny over these States. To prove this, let Facts be submitted to a candid world.

He has refused his Assent to Laws, the most wholesome and necessary for the public good.   3

He has forbidden his Governors to pass Laws of immediate and pressing importance, unless suspended in their operation till his Assent should be obtained; and when so suspended, he has utterly neglected to attend to them. He has refused to pass other Laws for the accommodation of large districts of people, unless those people would relinquish the right of Representation in the Legislature, a right inestimable to them and formidable to tyrants only.   4

He has called together legislative bodies at places unusual, uncomfortable, and distant from the depository of their public Records, for the sole purpose of fatiguing them into compliance with his measures.   5

He has dissolved Representative Houses repeatedly, for opposing with manly firmness his invasions on the rights of the people.   6

He has refused for a long time, after such dissolutions, to cause others to be elected; whereby the Legislative powers, incapable of Annihilation, have returned to the People at large for their exercise; the State remaining in the mean time exposed to all the dangers of invasion from without, and convulsions within.   7

He has endeavoured to prevent the population of these States; for that purpose obstructing the Laws for Naturalization of Foreigners; refusing to pass others to encourage their migrations hither, and raising the conditions of new Appropriations of Lands.   8

He has obstructed the Administration of Justice, by refusing his assent to Laws for establishing Judiciary powers.   9

He has made Judges dependent on his Will alone, for the tenure of their offices, and the amount and payment of their salaries.   10

He has erected a multitude of New Offices, and sent hither swarms of Officers to harass our People, and eat out their substance.   11

He has kept among us, in times of peace, standing Armies without the Consent of our legislatures.   12

He has affected to render the Military independent of and superior to the Civil power.   13

He has combined with others to subject us to a jurisdiction foreign to our constitution, and unacknowledged by our laws; giving his Assent to their Acts of pretended Legislation: 14

For Quartering large bodies of armed troops among us: 15

For protecting them, by a mock Trial, from punishment for any Murders   16
which they should commit on the Inhabitants of these States:

For cutting off our Trade with all parts of the world: 17

For imposing Taxes on us without our Consent: 18

For depriving us in many cases of the benefits of Trial by Jury: 19

For transporting us beyond Seas to be tried for pretended offences: 20

For abolishing the free System of English Laws in a neighbouring   21
Province, establishing therein an Arbitrary government, and enlarging its
Boundaries so as to render it at once an example and fit instrument for intro-
ducing the same absolute rule into these Colonies:

For taking away our Charters, abolishing our most valuable Laws, and   22
altering fundamentally the Forms of our Governments:

For suspending our own Legislatures, and declaring themselves invested   23
with power to legislate for us in all cases whatsoever.

He has abdicated Government here, by declaring us out of his Protection   24
and waging War against us.

He has plundered our seas, ravaged our Coasts, burnt our towns, and de-   25
stroyed the Lives of our people.

He is at this time transporting large Armies of foreign Mercenaries to   26
compleat the works of death, desolation and tyranny, already begun with circumstances of Cruelty & perfidy scarcely paralleled in the most barbarous
ages, and totally unworthy the Head of a civilized nation.

He has constrained our fellow Citizens taken Captive on the high Seas to   27
bear Arms against their Country, to become the executioners of their friends
and Brethren, or to fall themselves by their Hands.

He has excited domestic insurrections amongst us, and has endeavoured   28
to bring on the inhabitants of our frontiers, the merciless Indian Savages,
whose known rule of warfare, is an undistinguished destruction of all ages,
sexes and conditions.

In every stage of these Oppressions We have Petitioned for Redress in   29
the most humble terms: Our repeated Petitions have been answered only by
repeated injury. A Prince, whose character is thus marked by every act which
may define a Tyrant, is unfit to be the ruler of a free people.

Nor have We been wanting in attentions to our British brethren. We   30
have warned them from time to time of attempts by their legislature to extend
an unwarrantable jurisdiction over us. We have reminded them of the circumstances of our emigration and settlement here. We have appealed to their native justice and magnanimity, and we have conjured them by the ties of our
common kindred to disavow these usurpations, which, would inevitably inter-
rupt our connections and correspondence. They too have been deaf to the
voice of Justice and of consanguinity. We must, therefore, acquiesce in the necessity, which denounces our Separation, and hold them, as we hold the rest of
mankind, Enemies in War, in Peace Friends.

We, therefore, the Representatives of the United States of America, in   31
General Congress, Assembled, appealing to the Supreme Judge of the world
for the rectitude of our intentions, do, in the Name, and by Authority of the

good People of these Colonies, solemnly publish and declare, That these United Colonies are, and of Right ought to be Free and Independent States; that they are Absolved from all Allegiance to the British Crown, and that all political connection between them and the State of Great Britain, is and ought to be totally dissolved; and that as Free and Independent States, they have full Power to levy War, conclude Peace, contract Alliances, establish Commerce, and to do all other Acts and Things which Independent States may of right do. And for the support of this Declaration, with a firm reliance on the protection of divine Providence, we mutually pledge to each other our Lives, our Fortunes and our sacred Honor.

John Hancock	Thomas Lynch Junr.	Th: Jefferson
Button Gwinnett	Arthur Middleton	Benja. Harrison
Lyman Hall	Samuel Chase	Thos. Nelson jr.
Geo Walton.	Wm. Paca	Francis Lightfoot Lee
Wm. Hooper	Thos. Stone	Carter Braxton
Joseph Hewes,	Charles Carroll	Robt. Morris
John Penn	of Carrollton	Benjamin Rush
Edward Rutledge.	George Wythe	Benja. Franklin
Thos. Heyward Junr.	Richard Henry Lee	John Morton
Geo Clymer	Frans. Lewis	John Adams
Jas. Smith	Lewis Morris	Robt. Treat Paine
Geo. Taylor	Richd. Stockton	Elbridge Gerry
James Wilson	Jno Witherspoon	Step. Hopkins
Geo. Ross	Fras. Hopkinson	William Ellery
Caesar Rodney	John Hart	Roger Sherman
Geo Read	Abra Clark	Saml. Huntington
Tho M:Kean	Josiah Bartlett	Wm. Williams
Wm. Floyd	Wm: Whipple	Oliver Wolcott
Phil. Livingston	Saml. Adams	Matthew Thornton ∎

Questions for Meaning

1. What was the purpose of "The Declaration of Independence"? What reason does Jefferson himself give for writing it?

2. In paragraph 1, what does Jefferson mean by "the Laws of Nature and of Nature's God"?

3. Paragraphs 3 through 28 are devoted to enumerating a list of grievances against King George III. Which of these are the most important? Are any of them relatively trivial? Taken together do they justify Jefferson's description of George III as "A Prince, whose character is thus marked by every act which may define a Tyrant"?

4. How would you summarize Jefferson's conception of the relationship between people and government?

5. How does Jefferson characterize his fellow Americans? At what points does he put the colonists in a favorable light?
6. What does Jefferson mean by "the Supreme Judge of the world"? Why does he express "a firm reliance on the protection of a divine Providence"?
7. Vocabulary: transient (2), evinces (2), usurpations (2), candid (2), annihilation (7), render (13), perfidy (26), unwarrantable (30), consanguinity (30), acquiesce (30), rectitude (31).

Questions about Strategy

1. In paragraph 2, why does Jefferson declare certain truths to be "self-evident"? Paraphrase this paragraph and explain the purpose it serves in Jefferson's argument.
2. In evaluating "The Declaration of Independence" as an argument, what do you think is more important: the general "truths" outlined in the second paragraph, or the specific accusations listed in the paragraphs that follow? If you were to write a counterargument to "The Declaration of Independence," on what points would you concentrate? Where is it most vulnerable?
3. Jefferson is often cited as a man of great culture and liberal values. Are there any points of "The Declaration of Independence" that now seem illiberal?
4. Does Jefferson use any loaded terms? He was forced to delete exaggerated language from his first two drafts of "The Declaration." Do you see any exaggerations that Congress failed to catch?
5. For what sort of audience did Jefferson write "The Declaration of Independence"? Is it directed primarily to the American people, the British government, or the world in general?

MARY WOLLSTONECRAFT

THE PLAYTHINGS OF TYRANTS

An English writer of Irish extraction, Mary Wollstonecraft (1759–1797) was an early advocate of women's rights. After working as a governess and a publisher's assistant, she went to France in 1792 in order to witness the French Revolution. She lived there with an American, Captain Gilbert Imlay, and had a child by him in 1794. Her relationship with Imlay broke down soon afterward, and, in 1795, Wollstonecraft tried to commit suicide by drowning herself. She was rescued, however, and returned to London, where she became a member of a group of radical writers that included Thomas Paine, William Blake, and William Godwin. Wollstonecraft became pregnant by Godwin in 1796, and they were married the following year. Their child, Mary (1797–1851), would eventually win fame as the author of *Frankenstein.* Wollstonecraft died only eleven days after Mary's birth.

Wollstonecraft's fame rests on one work, *A Vindication of the Rights of Women* (1792). Although she had written about the need for educated women several years earlier in *Thoughts on the Education of Daughters* (1787), she makes a stronger and better-reasoned argument in her *Vindication.* "The Playthings of Tyrants" is an editor's title for an excerpt from the second chapter, "The Prevailing Opinion of a Sexual Character Discussed." As the excerpt suggests, Wollstonecraft was not especially interested in securing political rights for women. Her object was to emancipate women from the roles imposed upon them by men and to urge women to think for themselves.

To account for, and excuse the tyranny of man, many ingenious arguments   1
have been brought forward to prove, that the two sexes, in the acquirement of virtue, ought to aim at attaining a very different character: or, to speak explicitly, women are not allowed to have sufficient strength of mind to acquire what really deserves the name of virtue. Yet it should seem, allowing them to have souls, that there is but one way appointed by Providence to lead *mankind* to either virtue or happiness.

If then women are not a swarm of ephemeron triflers, why should they   2
be kept in ignorance under the specious name of innocence? Men complain, and with reason, of the follies and caprices of our sex, when they do not keenly satirize our headstrong passions and groveling vices.—Behold, I should answer, the natural effect of ignorance! The mind will ever be unstable that has only prejudices to rest on, and the current will run with destructive fury when there are no barriers to break its force. Women are told from their infancy, and taught by the example of their mothers, that a little knowledge of human weakness, justly termed cunning, softness of temper, *outward* obedience, and a scrupulous attention to a puerile kind of propriety, will obtain for them the protection of man; and should they be beautiful, every thing else is needless, for, at least, twenty years of their lives.

Thus Milton★ describes our first frail mother; though when he tells us   3
that women are formed for softness and sweet attractive grace, I cannot comprehend his meaning, unless, in the true Mahometan strain, he meant to deprive us of souls, and insinuate that we were beings only designed by sweet
attractive grace, and docile blind obedience, to gratify the senses of man when
he can no longer soar on the wing of contemplation.

How grossly do they insult us who thus advise us only to render   4
ourselves gentle, domestic brutes! For instance, the winning softness so
warmly, and frequently, recommended, that governs by obeying. What childish expressions, and how insignificant is the being—can it be an immortal
one? who will condescend to govern by such sinister methods! 'Certainly,' says
Lord Bacon,† 'man is of kin to the beasts by his body; and if he be not of kin
to God by his spirit, he is a base and ignoble creature!' Men, indeed, appear to
me to act in a very unphilosophical manner when they try to secure the good
conduct of women by attempting to keep them always in a state of childhood.
Rousseau‡ was more consistent when he wished to stop the progress of reason
in both sexes, for if men eat of the tree of knowledge, women will come in for
a taste; but, from the imperfect cultivation which their understandings now
receive, they only attain a knowledge of evil.

Children, I grant, should be innocent; but when the epithet is applied to   5
men, or women, it is but a civil term for weakness. For if it be allowed that
women were destined by Providence to acquire human virtues, and by the exercise of their understandings, that stability of character which is the firmest
ground to rest our future hopes upon, they must be permitted to turn to the
fountain of light, and not forced to shape their course by the twinkling of a
mere satellite. Milton, I grant, was of a very different opinion; for he only
bends to the indefeasible right of beauty, though it would be difficult to render
two passages which I now mean to contrast, consistent. But into similar inconsistencies are great men often led by their senses.

'To whom thus Eve with *perfect beauty* adorn'd.
'My Author and Disposer, what thou bidst
'*Unargued* I obey; So God ordains;
'God is *thy law; thou mine:* to know no more
'Is Woman's *happiest* knowledge and her *praise.*'

These are exactly the arguments that I have used to children; but I have   6
added, your reason is now gaining strength, and, till it arrives at some degree
of maturity, you must look up to me for advice—then you ought to *think,* and
only rely on God.

★John Milton (1608–1674) an important English poet best known for *Paradise Lost.*
†Francis Bacon (1561–1626) was an English statesman, philosopher, and essayist.
‡Jean Jacques Rousseau (1712–1778) was an influential philosopher and political theorist best
known for *Discourse on the Inequalities of Men* (1754) and *Social Contract* (1762).

Yet in the following lines Milton seems to coincide with me; when he 7
makes Adam thus expostulate with his Maker.

'Hast thou not made me here thy substitute,
'And these inferior far beneath me set?
'Among *unequals* what society
'Can sort, what harmony or true delight?
'Which must be mutual, in proportion due
'Giv'n and receiv'd; but in *disparity*
'The one intense, the other still remiss
'Cannot well suit with either, but soon prove
'Tedious alike: of *fellowship* I speak
'Such as I seek, fit to participate
'All rational delight—'

In treating, therefore, of the manners of women, let us, disregarding sen- 8
sual arguments, trace what we should endeavour to make them in order to cooperate, if the expression be not too bold, with the supreme Being.

By individual education, I mean, for the sense of the word is not pre- 9
cisely defined, such an attention to a child as will slowly sharpen the senses,
form the temper, regulate the passions as they begin to ferment, and set the
understanding to work before the body arrives at maturity; so that the man
may only have to proceed, not to begin, the important task of learning to
think and reason.

To prevent any misconstruction, I must add, that I do not believe that a 10
private education can work the wonders which some sanguine writers have
attributed to it. Men and women must be educated, in a great degree, by the
opinions and manners of the society they live in. In every age there has been
a stream of popular opinion that has carried all before it, and given a family
character, as it were, to the century. It may then fairly be inferred, that, till
society be differently constituted, much cannot be expected from education.
It is, however, sufficient for my present purpose to assert, that, whatever effect
circumstances have on the abilities, every being may become virtuous by the
exercise of its own reason; for if but one being was created with vicious inclinations, that is positively bad, what can save us from atheism? or if we worship
a God, is not that God a devil?

Consequently, the most perfect education, in my opinion, is such an ex- 11
ercise of the understanding as is best calculated to strengthen the body and
form the heart. Or, in other words, to enable the individual to attain such
habits of virtue as will render it independent. In fact, it is a farce to call any
being virtuous whose virtues do not result from the exercise of its own reason.
This was Rousseau's opinion respecting men: I extend it to women, and confidently assert that they have been drawn out of their sphere by false refinement,
and not by an endeavour to acquire masculine qualities. Still the regal homage
which they receive is so intoxicating, that till the manners of the times are
changed, and formed on more reasonable principles, it may be impossible to

convince them that the illegitimate power, which they obtain, by degrading themselves, is a curse, and that they must return to nature and equality, if they wish to secure the placid satisfaction that unsophisticated affections impart. But for this epoch we must wait—wait, perhaps, till kings and nobles, enlightened by reason, and, preferring the real dignity of man to childish state, throw off their gaudy hereditary trappings: and if then women do not resign the arbitrary power of beauty—they will prove that they have *less* mind than man. . . .

Many are the causes that, in the present corrupt state of society, con-   12
tribute to enslave women by cramping their understandings and sharpening their senses. One, perhaps, that silently does more mischief than all the rest, is their disregard of order.

To do every thing in an orderly manner, is a most important precept,   13
which women, who, generally speaking, receive only a disorderly kind of education, seldom attend to with that degree of exactness that men, who from their infancy are broken into method, observe. This negligent kind of guess-work, for what other epithet can be used to point out the random exertions of a sort of instinctive common sense, never brought to the test of reason? prevents their generalizing matters of fact—so they do to-day, what they did yesterday, merely because they did it yesterday.

This contempt of the understanding in early life has more baneful conse-   14
quences than is commonly supposed; for the little knowledge which women of strong minds attain, is, from various circumstances, of a more desultory kind than the knowledge of men, and it is acquired more by sheer observations on real life, than from comparing what has been individually observed with the results of experience generalized by speculation. Led by their dependent situation and domestic employments more into society, what they learn is rather by snatches; and as learning is with them, in general, only a secondary thing, they do not pursue any one branch with that persevering ardour necessary to give vigour to the faculties, and clearness of the judgment. In the present state of society, a little learning is required to support the character of a gentleman; and boys are obliged to submit to a few years of discipline. But in the education of women, the cultivation of the understanding is always subordinate to the acquirement of some corporeal accomplishment; even while enervated by confinement and false notions of modesty, the body is prevented from attaining that grace and beauty which relaxed half-formed limbs never exhibit. Besides, in youth their faculties are not brought forward by emulation; and having no serious scientific study, if they have natural sagacity it is turned too soon on life and manners. They dwell on effects, and modifications, without tracing them back to causes; and complicated rules to adjust behaviour are a weak substitute for simple principles.

As a proof that education gives this appearance of weakness to females,   15
we may instance the example of military men, who are, like them, sent into the world before their minds have been stored with knowledge or fortified by principles. The consequences are similar; soldiers acquire a little superficial knowledge, snatched from the muddy current of conversation, and, from

continually mixing with society, they gain, what is termed a knowledge of the world; and this acquaintance with manners and customs has frequently been confounded with a knowledge of the human heart. But can the crude fruit of casual observation, never brought to the test of judgment, formed by comparing speculation and experience, deserve such a distinction? Soldiers, as well as women, practice the minor virtues with punctilious politeness. Where is then the sexual difference, when the education has been the same? All the difference that I can discern, arises from the superior advantage of liberty, which enables the former to see more of life.

It is wandering from my present subject, perhaps, to make a political re-   16
mark; but, as it was produced naturally by the train of my reflections, I shall not pass it silently over.

Standing armies can never consist of resolute, robust men; they may be   17
well disciplined machines, but they will seldom contain men under the influence of strong passions, or with very vigorous faculties. And as for any depth of understanding, I will venture to affirm, that it is as rarely to be found in the army as amongst women; and the cause, I maintain, is the same. It may be further observed, that officers are also particularly attentive to their persons, fond of dancing, crowded rooms, adventures, and ridicule. Like the *fair* sex, the business of their lives is gallantry.—They were taught to please, and they only live to please. Yet they do not lose their rank in the distinction of sexes, for they are still reckoned superior to women, though in what their superiority consists, beyond what I have just mentioned, it is difficult to discover.

The great misfortune is this, that they both acquire manners before   18
morals, and a knowledge of life before they have, from reflections, any acquaintance with the grand ideal outline of human nature. The consequence is natural; satisfied with common nature, they become a prey to prejudices, and taking all their opinions on credit, they blindly submit to authority. So that, if they have any sense, it is a kind of instinctive glance, that catches proportions, and decides with respect to manners; but fails when arguments are to be pursued below the surface, or opinions analyzed.

May not the same remark be applied to women? Nay, the argument may   19
be carried still further, for they are both thrown out of a useful station by the unnatural distinctions established in civilized life. Riches and hereditary honours have made cyphers of women to give consequence to the numerical figures; and idleness has produced a mixture of gallantry and despotism into society, which leads the very men who are the slaves of their mistresses to tyrannize over their sisters, wives, and daughters. This is only keeping them in rank and file, it is true. Strengthen the female mind by enlarging it, and there will be an end to blind obedience; but, as blind obedience is ever sought for by power, tyrants and sensualists are in the right when they endeavor to keep women in the dark, because the former only wants slaves, and the latter a plaything. The sensualist, indeed, has been the most dangerous of tyrants, and women have been duped by their lovers, as princes by their ministers, whilst dreaming that they reigned over them. ■

Questions for Meaning

1. What is wrong with treating women as children and expecting "blind obedience"?
2. What causes does Wollstonecraft cite for the degradation of women? On what grounds does she defend their "follies" and "vices"?
3. What does Wollstonecraft mean by "false refinement" in paragraph 11? Explain why she believes it is dangerous to acquire "manners before morals."
4. Where in her essay does Wollstonecraft define the sort of education she believes women should receive? Why does she object to educating women privately in their homes?
5. Wollstonecraft was perceived as a radical by her contemporaries, and relatively few people took her ideas seriously. Looking back on her work after two hundred years, can you find any traditional values that Wollstonecraft accepted without question? Could you argue that she was conservative in some ways?
6. Explain why "the sensualist" has been "the most dangerous of tyrants."
7. Vocabulary: ephemeron (2), specious (2), caprices (2), puerile (2), propriety (2), insinuate (3), docile (3), sanguine (10), desultory (14), corporeal (14), enervated (14), sagacity (14), punctilious (15), cyphers (19).

Questions about Strategy

1. What is the premise of this argument? Where does Wollstonecraft first state it, and where is it restated?
2. What is the function of the last sentence in the second paragraph?
3. Why does Wollstonecraft quote Francis Bacon and John Milton? What do these quotations contribute to her argument?
4. Comment on the analogy Wollstonecraft makes between women and soldiers. What type of soldiers did she have in mind? Is her analogy valid?
5. Do you think Wollstonecraft wrote this argument primarily for men or for women? What kind of an audience could she have expected in the eighteenth century?

DOROTHEA L. DIX

ON BEHALF OF THE INSANE POOR

Dorothea Lynde Dix (1802–1887) was a leading advocate for the poor and the mentally ill. The following article is an excerpt from her most important work, *Memorial to the Legislature of Massachusetts* (1843), in which she argued for much needed reforms in the way the mentally ill were housed and treated in her native state. She subsequently investigated poor houses and insane asylums in several other states and served as superintendent of women nurses during the Civil War.

I respectfully ask to present this Memorial, believing that the *cause,* which ac-   1
tuates to and sanctions so unusual a movement, presents no equivocal claim to
public consideration and sympathy. Surrendering to calm and deep convictions
of duty my habitual views of what is womanly and becoming, I proceed
briefly to explain what has conducted me before you unsolicited and unsus-
tained, trusting, while I do so, that the memorialist will be speedily forgotten
in the memorial.

About two years since leisure afforded opportunity, and duty prompted   2
me to visit several prisons and alms houses in the vicinity of this metropolis. I
found, near Boston, in the Jails and Asylums for the poor, a numerous class
brought into unsuitable connexion with criminals and the general mass of Paupers. I refer to Idiots and Insane persons, dwelling in circumstances not only
adverse to their own physical and moral improvement, but productive of extreme disadvantages to all other persons brought into association with them. I
applied myself diligently to trace the causes of these evils, and sought to supply
remedies. As one obstacle was surmounted, fresh difficulties appeared. Every
new investigation has given depth to the conviction that it is only by decided,
prompt, and vigorous legislation the evils to which I refer, and which I shall
proceed more fully to illustrate, can be remedied. I shall be obliged to speak
with great plainness, and to reveal many things revolting to the taste, and from
which my woman's nature shrinks with peculiar sensitiveness. But truth is the
highest consideration. *I tell what I have seen*—painful and shocking as the details
often are—that from them you may feel more deeply the imperative obligation
which lies upon you to prevent the possibility of a repetition or continuance of
such outrages upon humanity. If I inflict pain upon you, and move you to horror, it is to acquaint you with sufferings which you have the power to alleviate,
and make you hasten to the relief of the victims of legalized barbarity.

I come to present the strong claims of suffering humanity. I come to   3
place before the Legislature of Massachusetts the condition of the miserable,
the desolate, the outcast. I come as the advocate of helpless, forgotten, insane
and idiotic men and women; of beings, sunk to a condition from which the
most unconcerned would start with real horror; of beings wretched in our
Prisons, and more wretched in our Alms-Houses. And I cannot suppose it
needful to employ earnest persuasion, or stubborn argument, in order to arrest

and fix attention upon a subject, only the more strongly pressing in its claims, because it is revolting and disgusting in its details.

I must confine myself to few examples, but am ready to furnish other 4 and more complete details, if required. If my pictures are displeasing, coarse, and severe, my subjects, it must be recollected, offer no tranquil, refined, or composing features. The condition of human beings, reduced to the extremest states of degradation and misery, cannot be exhibited in softened language, or adorn a polished page.

I proceed, Gentlemen, briefly to call your attention to the *present* state of 5 Insane Persons confined within this Commonwealth, in *cages, closets, cellars, stalls, pens! Chained, naked, beaten with rods,* and *lashed* into obedience!

As I state cold, severe *facts,* I feel obliged to refer to persons, and defi- 6 nitely to indicate localities. But it is upon my subject, not upon localities or individuals, I desire to fix attention; and I would speak as kindly as possible of all Wardens, Keepers, and other responsible officers, believing that *most* of these have erred not through hardness of heart and wilful cruelty, so much as want of skill and knowledge, and want of consideration. Familiarity with suf- fering, it is said, blunts the sensibilities, and where neglect once finds a footing other injuries are multiplied. This is not all, for it may justly and strongly be added that, from the deficiency of adequate means to meet the wants of these cases, it has been an absolute impossibility to do justice in this matter. Prisons are not constructed in view of being converted into County Hospitals, and Alms-Houses are not founded as receptacles for the Insane. And yet, in the face of justice and common sense, Wardens are by law compelled to receive, and the Masters of Alms-Houses not to refuse, Insane and Idiotic subjects in all stages of mental disease and privation.

It is the Commonwealth, not its integral parts, that is accountable for 7 most of the abuses which have lately, and do still exist. I repeat it, it is defec- tive legislation which perpetuates and multiplies these abuses.

In illustration of my subject, I offer the following extracts from my 8 Note-Book and Journal:—

Springfield. In the jail, one lunatic woman, furiously mad, a state pauper, 9 improperly situated, both in regard to the prisoners, the keepers, and herself. It is a case of extreme self-forgetfulness and oblivion to all the decencies of life; to describe which, would be to repeat only the grossest scenes. She is much worse since leaving Worcester. In the almshouse of the same town is a woman apparently only needing judicious care, and some well-chosen employment, to make it unnecessary to confine her in solitude, in a dreary unfurnished room. Her appeals for employment and companionship are most touching, but the mistress replied, 'she had no time to attend to her.'

Northampton. In the jail, quite lately, was a young man violently mad, 10 who had not, as I was informed at the prison, come under medical care, and not been returned from any hospital. In the almshouse, the cases of insanity are now unmarked by abuse, and afford evidence of judicious care by the keepers.

Williamsburg. The almshouse has several insane, not under suitable treat-   11
ment. No apparent intentional abuse.

Rutland. Appearance and report of the insane in the almshouse not satis-   12
factory.

Sterling. A terrible case; manageable in a hospital; at present as well con-   13
trolled perhaps as circumstances in a case so extreme allow. An almshouse, but
wholly wrong in relation to the poor crazy woman, to the paupers generally,
and to her keepers.

Burlington. A woman, declared to be very insane; decent room and bed;   14
but not allowed to rise oftener, the mistress said, 'than every other day: it is
too much trouble.'

Concord. A woman from the hospital in a cage in the almshouse. In the   15
jail several, decently cared for in general, but not properly placed in a prison.
Violent, noisy, unmanageable most of the time.

Lincoln. A woman in a cage.   16

Medford. One idiotic subject chained, and one in a close stall for 17 years.   17

Pepperell. One often doubly chained, hand and foot; another violent; sev-   18
eral peaceable now.

Brookfield. One man caged, comfortable.   19

Granville. One often closely confined; now losing the use of his limbs   20
from want of exercise.

Charlemont. One man caged.   21

Savoy. One man caged.   22

Lenox. Two in the jail; against whose unfit condition there, the jailor   23
protests.

Dedham. The insane disadvantageously placed in the jail. In the   24
almshouse, two females in stalls, situated in the main building; lie in wooden
bunks filled with straw; always shut up. One of these subjects is supposed cur-
able. The overseers of the poor have declined giving her a trial at the hospital,
as I was informed, on account of expense.

Franklin. One man chained; decent.   25

Taunton. One woman caged.   26

Plymouth. One man stall-caged, from Worcester hospital.   27

Scituate. One man and one woman stall-caged.   28

Bridgewater. Three idiots; never removed from one room.   29

Barnstable. Four females in pens and stalls; two chained certainly, I think   30
all. Jail, one idiot.

Welfleet. Three insane; one man and one woman chained, the latter in a   31
bad condition.

Brewster. One woman violently mad, solitary: could not see her, the mas-   32
ter and mistress being absent, and the paupers in charge having strict orders to
admit no one.

Rochester. Seven insane; at present none caged.   33

Milford. Two insane, not now caged.   34

Cohasset. One idiot, one insane; most miserable condition.   35

Plympton. One insane, three idiots; condition wretched.   36

Besides the above, I have seen many who, part of the year, are chained or   37
caged. The use of cages all but universal; hardly a town but can refer to some
not distant period of using them: chains are less common: negligences frequent: wilful abuse less frequent than sufferings proceeding from ignorance, or
want of consideration. I encountered during the last three months many poor
creatures wandering reckless and unprotected through the country. Innumer-
able accounts have been sent me of persons who had roved away unwatched
and unsearched after; and I have heard that responsible persons, controlling the
almshouses, have not thought themselves culpable in sending away from their
shelter, to cast upon the chances of remote relief, insane men and women.
These, left on the highways, unfriended and incompetent to control or direct
their own movements, sometimes have found refuge in the hospital, and others
have not been traced. But I cannot particularize; in traversing the state I have
found hundreds of insane persons in every variety of circumstance and condition; many whose situation could not and need not be improved; a less number, but that very large, whose lives are the saddest pictures of human suffering
and degradation. I give a few illustrations; but description fades before reality.

Danvers. November; visited the almshouse; a large building, much out of   38
repair; understand a new one is in contemplation. Here are from fifty-six to
sixty inmates; one idiotic; three insane; one of the latter in close confinement
at all times.

Long before reaching the house, wild shouts, snatches of rude songs, im-   39
precations, and obscene language, fell upon the ear, proceeding from the occupant of a low building, rather remote from the principal building to which my
course was directed. Found the mistress, and was conducted to the place,
which was called '*the home*' of the *forlorn* maniac, a young woman, exhibiting
a condition of neglect and misery blotting out the faintest idea of comfort, and
outraging every sentiment of decency. She had been, I learnt, "a respectable
person; industrious and worthy; disappointments and trials shook her mind,
and finally laid prostrate reason and self-control; she became a maniac for life!
She had been at Worcester Hospital for a considerable time, and had been returned as incurable." The mistress told me she understood that, while there,
she was "comfortable and decent." Alas! what a change was here exhibited!
She had passed from one degree of violence and degradation to another, in

swift progress; there she stood, clinging to, or beating upon, the bars of her caged apartment, the contracted size of which afforded space only for increasing accumulations of filth, a *foul* spectacle; there she stood with naked arms and dishevelled hair; the unwashed frame invested with fragments of unclean garments, the air so extremely offensive, though ventilation was afforded on all sides save one, that it was not possible to remain beyond a few moments without retreating for recovery to the outward air. Irritation of body, produced by utter filth and exposure, incited her to the horrid process of tearing off her skin by inches; her face, neck, and person, were thus disfigured to hideousness; she held up a fragment just rent off; to my exclamation of horror, the mistress replied, "oh, we can't help it; half the skin is off sometimes; we can do nothing with her; and it makes no difference what she eats, for she consumes her own filth as readily as the food which is brought her."

It is now January; a fortnight since, two visitors reported that most   40 wretched outcast as "wallowing in dirty straw, in a place yet more dirty, and without clothing, without fire. Worse cared for than the brutes, and wholly lost to consciousness of decency!" Is the whole story told? What was seen, is; what is reported is not. These gross exposures are not for the pained sight of one alone; all, all, coarse, brutal men, wondering, neglected children, old and young, each and all, witness this lowest, foulest state of miserable humanity. And who protects her, that worse than Paria outcast, from other wrongs and blacker outrages? I do not *know* that such *have been.* I do know that they are to be dreaded, and that they are not guarded against.

Some may say these things cannot be remedied; these furious maniacs are   41 not to be raised from these base conditions. I *know* they are; could give *many* examples; let *one* suffice. A young woman, a pauper, in a distant town, *Sandisfield,* was for years a raging maniac. A cage, chains, and *the whip,* were the agents for controlling her, united with harsh tones and profane language. Annually, with others (the town's poor) she was put up at auction, and bid off at the lowest price which was declared for her. One year, not long past, an old man came forward in the number of applicants for the poor wretch; he was taunted and ridiculed; "what would he and his old wife do with such a mere beast?" "My wife says yes," replied he, "and I shall take her." She was given to his charge; he conveyed her home; she was washed, neatly dressed, and placed in a decent bed-room, furnished for comfort and opening into the kitchen. How altered her condition! As yet *the chains* were not off. The first week she was somewhat restless, at times violent, but the quiet kind ways of the old people wrought a change; she received her food decently; forsook acts of violence, and no longer uttered blasphemous or indecent language; after a week, the chain was lengthened, and she was received as a companion into the kitchen. Soon she engaged in trivial employments. "After a fortnight," said the old man, "I knocked off the chains and made her a free woman." She is at times excited, but not violently; they are careful of her diet; they keep her very clean; she calls them "father" and "mother." Go there now and you will find her "clothed," and though not perfectly in her "right mind," so far restored as to be a safe and comfortable inmate.

Newburyport. Visited the almshouse in June last; eighty inmates; seven   42
insane, one idiotic. Commodious and neat house; several of the partially insane
apparently very comfortable; two very improperly situated, namely, an insane
man, not considered incurable, in an out-building, whose room opened upon
what was called 'the dead room,' affording in lieu of companionship with the
living, a contemplation of corpses! The other subject was a woman in a *cellar.*
I desired to see her; much reluctance was shown. I pressed the request; the
Master of the House stated that she was *in the cellar; that* she was *dangerous to be
approached;* that 'she had lately attacked his wife;' and *was often naked.* I per-
sisted; 'if you will not go with me, give me the keys and I will go alone.' Thus
importuned, the outer doors were opened. I descended the stairs from within;
a strange, unnatural noise seemed to proceed from beneath our feet; at the
moment I did not much regard it. My conductor proceeded to remove a pad-
lock, while my eye explored the wide space in quest of the poor woman. All
for a moment was still. But judge my horror and amazement, when a door to
a closet *beneath* the *staircase* was opened, revealing in the imperfect light a female apparently wasted to a skeleton, partially wrapped in blankets, furnished
for the narrow bed on which she was sitting; her countenance furrowed, not
by age, but suffering, was the image of distress; in that contracted space, un-
lighted, unventilated, she poured forth the wailings of despair: mournfully she
extended her arms and appealed to me, "why am I consigned to hell? dark—
dark—I used to pray, I used to read the Bible—I have done no crime in my
heart; I had friends, why have all forsaken me!—my God! my God! why hast
thou forsaken me!" Those groans, those wailings come up daily, mingling,
with how many others, a perpetual and sad memorial. When the good Lord
shall require an account of our stewardship, what shall all and each answer!

Perhaps it will be inquired how long, how many days or hours was she   43
imprisoned in these confined limits? *For years!* In another part of the cellar
were other small closets, only better, because higher through the entire length,
into one of which she by turns was transferred, so as to afford opportunity for
fresh whitewashing, &c.

Saugus. December 24; thermometer below zero; drove to the poorhouse;   44
was conducted to the master's family-room by himself; walls garnished with
handcuffs and chains, not less than five pair of the former; did not inquire how
or on whom applied; thirteen pauper inmates; one insane man; one woman
insane; one idiotic man; asked to see them; the two men were shortly led in;
appeared pretty decent and comfortable. Requested to see the other insane
subject; was denied decidedly; urged the request, and finally secured a reluctant assent. Was led through an outer passage into a lower room, occupied by
the paupers; crowded; not neat; ascended a rather low flight of stairs upon an
open entry, through the floor of which was introduced a stove pipe, carried
along a *few feet,* about six inches above the floor, through which it was recon-
veyed below. From this entry opens a room of moderate size, having a sashed-
window; floor, I think, painted; apartment ENTIRELY unfurnished; no
chair, table, not bed; neither, what is seldom missing, a bundle of straw or lock

of hay; cold, very cold; the first movement of my conductor was to throw open a window, a measure imperatively necessary for those who entered. *On the floor* sat a woman, her limbs immovably contracted, so that the knees were brought upward to the chin; the face was concealed; the head rested on the folded arms; for clothing she appeared to have been furnished with *fragments* of many discharged garments; these were folded about her, yet they little benefitted her, if one might judge by the constant shuddering which almost convulsed her poor crippled frame. Woful was this scene; language is feeble to record the misery she was suffering and had suffered! In reply to my inquiry if she could not change her position, I was answered by the master in the negative, and told that the contraction of limbs was occasioned by "neglect and exposure in former years," but *since she had been crazy,* and before she fell under the charge, as I inferred, of her present *guardians.* Poor wretch! she, like many others, was an example of what humanity becomes when the temple of reason falls in ruins, leaving the mortal part to injury and neglect, and showing how much can be endured of privation, exposure, and disease, without extinguishing the lamp of life. . . .

Violence and severity do not exasperate the Insane: the only availing influence is kindness and firmness. It is amazing what these will produce. How many examples might illustrate this position: I refer to one recently exhibited in Barre. The town Paupers are disposed of annually to some family who, for a stipulated sum agree to take charge of them. One of them, a young woman, was shown to me well clothed, neat, quiet, and employed at needle-work. Is it possible that this is the same being who, but last year, was a raving madwoman, exhibiting every degree of violence in action and speech; a very tigress wrought to fury; caged, chained, beaten, loaded with injuries, and exhibiting the passions which an iron rule might be expected to stimulate and sustain. It is the same person; another family hold her in charge who better understand human nature and human influences; she is no longer chained, caged, and beaten; but if excited, a pair of mittens drawn over the hands secures from mischief. Where will she be next year, after the annual sale? 45

It is not the insane subject alone who illustrates the power of the all prevailing law of kindness. A poor idiotic young man, a year or two since, used to follow me at times through the prison as I was distributing books and papers: at first he appeared totally stupid, but cheerful expressions, a smile, a trifling gift, seemed gradually to light up the void temple of the intellect, and by slow degrees some faint images of thought passed before the mental vision. He would ask for books, though he could not read. I indulged his fancy and he would appear to experience delight in examining them; and kept them with a singular care. If I read the Bible, he was reverently, wonderingly attentive; if I talked, he listened with a half-conscious aspect. One morning I passed more hurriedly than usual, and did not speak particularly to him. "Me, me, me a book." I returned; "good morning, Jemmy; so you will have a book today? well, keep it carefully." Suddenly turning aside he took the bread brought for his breakfast, and passing it with a hurried earnestness through the bars of his iron door—"Here's bread, a'nt you hungry?" Never may I forget the tone and 46 grateful affectionate aspect of that poor idiot. How much might we do to bring back or restore the mind, if we but knew how to touch the instrument with a skilful hand! . . .

Of the dangers and mischiefs sometimes following the location of insane   47 persons in our almhouses, I will record but one more example. In Worcester, has for several years resided a young woman, a lunatic pauper of decent life and respectable family. I have seen her as she usually appeared, listless and silent, almost or quite sunk into a state of dementia, sitting one amidst the family, 'but not of them.' A few weeks since, revisiting that almshouse, judge my horror and amazement to see her negligently bearing in her arms a young infant, of which I was told she was the unconscious parent! Who was the father, none could or would declare. Disqualified for the performance of maternal cares and duties, regarding the helpless little creature with a perplexed, or indifferent gaze, she sat a silent, but O how eloquent, a pleader for the protection of others of her neglected and outraged sex! Details of that black story would not strengthen the cause; needs it a weightier plea, than the sight of that forlorn creature and her wailing infant? Poor little child, more than orphan from birth, in this unfriendly world! a demented Mother—a Father, on whom the sun might blush or refuse to shine!

Men of Massachusetts, I beg, I implore, I demand, pity and protection,   48 for these of my suffering, outraged sex!—Fathers, Husbands, Brothers, I would supplicate you for this boon—but what do I say? I dishonor you, divest you at once of christianity and humanity—does this appeal imply distrust. If it comes burthened with a doubt of your righteousness in this Legislation, then blot it out; while I declare confidence in your honor, not less than your humanity. Here you will put away the cold, calculating spirit of selfishness and self-seeking; lay off the armor of local strife and political opposition; here and now, for once, forgetful of the earthly and perishable, come up to these halls and consecrate them with one heart and one mind to works of righteousness and just judgment. Become the benefactors of your race, the just guardians of the solemn rights you hold in trust. Raise up the fallen; succor the desolate; restore the outcast; defend the helpless; and for your eternal and great reward, receive the benediction . . . . "Well done, good and faithful servants, become rulers over many things!"

But, gentlemen, I do not come to quicken your sensibilities into short-   49 lived action, to pour forth passionate exclamation, nor yet to move your indignation against those, whose misfortune, not fault, it surely is to hold in charge these poor demented creatures, and whose whole of domestic economy, or prison discipline, is absolutely overthrown by such proximity of conflicting circumstances, and opposite conditions of mind and character. Allow me to illustrate this position by a few examples; it were easy to produce hundreds.

The master of one of the best regulated almshouses, viz. that of Ply-   50 mouth, where every arrangement shows that the comfort of the sick, the aged, and the infirm, is suitably cared for, and the amendment of the unworthy is studied and advanced, said, as we stood opposite a latticed stall, where was confined a madman, that the hours of the day were few, when the whole household was not distracted from employment by screams, and turbulent stampings, and every form of violence, which the voice or muscular force could produce. This unfortunate being was one of the "returned incurables," since whose last admission to the almshouse, they were no longer secure of peace for the aged, or decency for the young; it was morally impossible to do justice to the sane and insane in such improper vicinity to each other. The conviction is continually deepened that Hospitals are the only places where insane persons can be at once humanely and properly controlled. Poorhouses, converted into madhouses, cease to effect the purposes for which they were established, and instead of being asylums for the aged, the homeless, and the friendless, and places of refuge for orphaned or neglected childhood, are transformed into perpetual bedlams.

This crying evil and abuse of institutions, is not confined to our almshouses. The warden of a populous prison near this metropolis, populous, not with criminals only, but with the insane in almost every stage of insanity, and the idiotic in descending states from silly and simple, to helpless and speechless, has declared that, since their admission under the Rev. Stat. of 1835, page 382, "the prison has often more resembled the infernal regions than any place on earth!" and, what with the excitement inevitably produced by the crowded state of the prisons, and multiplying causes, not subject to much modification, there has been neither peace nor order one hour of the twenty-four; if ten were quiet, the residue were probably raving. Almost without interval might, and *must,* these be heard, blaspheming and furious, and to the last degree impure and indecent; uttering language, from which the base and the profligate have turned shuddering aside, and the abandoned have shrunk abashed. I myself, with many beside, can bear sad witness to these things. . . .   51

The master of the Plymouth almshouse writes, in a letter containing many clear views,—"I hope to hear people are awake on this subject, and trust they will not rest till they have compelled the public to provide suitable places for that unfortunate class of demented persons. They should never be received in almshouses."   52

It is not few but many, it is not a part but the whole, who bear unqualified testimony to this evil. A voice strong and deep comes up from every almshouse and prison in Massachusetts where the insane are or have been, protesting against such evils as have been illustrated in the preceding pages.   53

Gentlemen, I commit to you this sacred cause. Your action upon this subject will affect the present and future condition of hundreds and of thousands.   54

In this legislation, as in all things, may you exercise that "wisdom which is the breath of the power of God." ■   55

Questions for Meaning

1. What abuses does Dix call attention to in this argument?
2. Did Dix believe that the abuse she witnessed was intentional or unintentional? How does she account for the suffering she observed?
3. How does Dix believe that the insane should be treated?
4. In paragraphs 41 and 47, Dix refers to the practice of auctioning off inmates. What was the purpose of this practice?
5. Vocabulary: alms-houses (2), alleviate (2), integral (7), culpable (37), traversing (37), imprecations (39), profane (41), wretch (44), infernal (51).

Questions about Strategy

1. In her opening paragraph, Dix refers to her "habitual views of what is womanly and becoming." Why do you think she draws attention to her gender?
2. Why does Dix direct her argument to the men of Massachusetts? What assumptions does she make about them?
3. How does Dix justify reporting information that may be painful to her readers?
4. Paragraph 3 opens with an example of *anaphora:* the deliberate repetition of a word or phrase at the beginning of a sentence or clause. What is achieved through this device?
5. In paragraphs 9 through 36, Dix provides short extracts from her journal. What is her purpose here? How would the effect change if Dix drew closely related examples together in a few long paragraphs?
6. How does Dix respond to people who believe the insane are beyond help?
7. Consider the quotation at the end of paragraph 42. To what is Dix alluding here, and how does this allusion contribute to her argument?

KARL MARX AND FRIEDRICH ENGELS

THE COMMUNIST MANIFESTO

Karl Marx (1818–1883) was a German social scientist and political philosopher who believed that history is determined by economics. Originally intending to teach, Marx studied at the University of Berlin, receiving his PhD in 1841. But, in 1842, he abandoned academics to become editor of the *Rheinische Zeitung,* an influential newspaper published in Cologne. His editorials led the government to close the paper within a year, and Marx went into exile—first in France and Belgium, and eventually in England, where he spent the last thirty-three years of his life.

In 1843, Marx met Friedrich Engels (1820–1895), the son of a wealthy German industrialist with business interests in England. The two men discovered that they shared the same political beliefs, and they worked together closely for the next forty years. Not until 1867 was Marx able to publish the first volume of *Das Kapital,* his most important work. The second and third volumes, published after Marx's death, were completed by Engels, who worked from Marx's extensive notes. *Das Kapital,* or *Capital,* provided the theoretical basis for what is variously known as "Marxism" or "Communism." It is an indictment of nineteenth-century capitalism that predicts a proletarian revolution in which the workers would take over the means of production and distribute goods according to needs, creating an ideal society in which the state would wither away.

Marx and Engels had outlined their views long before the publication of *Das Kapital.* In 1848, they published a pamphlet called *The Communist Manifesto.* It was written during a period of great political unrest. Within months of its publication, revolutions broke out in several European countries. Most of the revolutions of 1848 were quickly aborted, but "the specter of Communism" continued to haunt the world. Here are the first few pages of this classic argument.

A specter is haunting Europe—the specter of Communism. All the Powers of old Europe have entered into a holy alliance to exorcise this specter; Pope and Czar, Metternich and Guizot,★ French Radicals and German police-spies.   1

Where is the party in opposition that has not been decried as communistic by its opponents in power? Where the Opposition that has not hurled back the branding reproach of Communism against the more advanced opposition parties, as well as against its reactionary adversaries?   2

Two things result from this fact.   3

    I. Communism is already acknowledged by all European Powers to be itself a Power.

★Clemens Mettienich (1773–1859) was an Austrian statesman who gained great political influence in early nineteenth-century Europe. He was widely associated with the use of censorship and espionage to suppress revolutionary movements. Francois Guizot (1787–1874) was a French statesman associated with preserving the status quo.

II. It is high time that Communists should openly, in the face of the whole world, publish their views, their aims, their tendencies, and meet this nursery tale of the specter of Communism with a Manifesto of the party itself.

To this end, Communists of various nationalities have assembled in London and sketched the following Manifesto, to be published in the English, French, German, Italian, Flemish and Danish languages.   4

Bourgeois and Proletarians[1]

The history of all hitherto existing society is the history of class struggles.   5

Freeman and slave, patrician and plebian, lord and serf, guild-master and journeyman, in a word, oppressor and oppressed, stood in constant opposition to one another, carried on uninterrupted, now hidden, now open fight, a fight that each time ended, either in a revolutionary re-constitution of society at large, or in the common ruin of the contending classes.   6

In the earlier epochs of history we find almost everywhere a complicated arrangement of society into various orders, a manifold gradation of social rank. In ancient Rome we have patricians, knights, plebians, slaves; in the Middle Ages, feudal lords, vassals, guild-masters, journeymen, apprentices, serfs; in almost all of these classes, again, subordinate gradations.   7

The modern bourgeois society that has sprouted from the ruins of feudal society, has not done away with class antagonisms. It has but established new classes, new conditions of oppression, new forms of struggle in place of the old ones.   8

Our epoch, the epoch of the bourgeoisie, possesses, however, this distinctive feature; it has simplified the class antagonisms. Society as a whole is more and more splitting up into two great hostile camps, into two great classes directly facing each other: Bourgeoisie and Proletariat.   9

From the serfs of the Middle Ages sprang the chartered burghers of the earliest towns. From these burgesses the first elements of the bourgeoisie were developed.   10

The discovery of America, the rounding of the Cape, opened up fresh ground for the rising bourgeoisie. The East Indian and Chinese markets, the colonization of America, trade with the colonies, the increase in the means of exchange and in commodities generally, gave to commerce, to navigation, to industry, an impulse never before known, and thereby, to the revolutionary element in the tottering feudal society, a rapid development.   11

The feudal system of industry, under which industrial production was monopolized by closed guilds, now no longer sufficed for the growing wants   12

---

[1]By bourgeoisie is meant the class of modern Capitalists, owners of the means of social production and employers of wage labor. By proletariat, the class of modern wage laborers who, having no means of production of their own, are reduced to selling their labor-power in order to live. [Marx's note]

of the new market. The manufacturing system took its place. The guild-masters were pushed on one side by the manufacturing middle-class: division of labor between the different corporate guilds vanished in the face of division of labor in each single workshop.

Meantime the markets kept ever growing, the demand ever rising. Even manufacture no longer sufficed. Thereupon, steam and machinery revolution-ized industrial production. The place of manufacture was taken by the giant, Modern Industry, the place of the industrial middle-class, by industrial mil-lionaires, the leaders of whole industrial armies, the modern bourgeois.   13

Modern industry has established the world market, for which the discov-ery of America paved the way. This market has given an immense development to commerce, to navigation, to communication by land. This development has, in its turn, reacted on the extension of industry; and in proportion as industry, commerce, navigation, railways extended, in the same proportion the bour-geoisie developed, increased its capital, and pushed into the background every class handed down from the Middle Ages.   14

We see, therefore, how the modern bourgeoisie is itself the product of a long course of development, a series of revolutions in the modes of production and of exchange.   15

Each step in the development of the bourgeoisie was accompanied by a corresponding political advance of that class. An oppressed class under the sway of the feudal nobility, an armed and self-governing association in the medieval commune, here independent urban republic (as in Italy and Ger-many), there taxable "third estate" of the monarchy (as in France), after-wards, in the period of manufacture proper, serving either the semi-feudal or the absolute monarchy as a counterpoise against nobility, and, in fact, corner-stone of the great monarchies in general, the bourgeoisie has at last, since the establishment of Modern Industry and of the world-market, conquered for itself, in the modern representative State, exclusive political sway. The execu-tive of the modern State is but a committee for managing the common affairs of the whole bourgeoisie.   16

The bourgeoisie, historically, has played a most revolutionary part.   17

The bourgeoisie, wherever it has got the upper hand, has put an end to all feudal, patriarchal, idyllic relations. It has pitilessly torn asunder the motley feudal ties that bound man to his "natural superiors," and has left no other nexus between man and man than naked self-interest, than callous "cash pay-ment." It has drowned the most heavenly ecstasies of religious fervor, of chivalrous enthusiasm, of Philistine sentimentalism, in the icy water of egotis-tical calculation. It has resolved personal worth into exchange value, and in place of the numberless indefeasible chartered freedoms, has set up that single, unconscionable freedom—Free Trade. In one word, for exploitation, veiled by religious and political illusions, it has submitted naked, shameless, direct, bru-tal exploitation.   18

The bourgeoisie has stripped of its halo every occupation hitherto hon-ored and looked up to with reverent awe. It has converted the physician, the lawyer, the priest, the poet, the man of science, into its paid wage laborers.   19

The bourgeoisie has torn away from the family its sentimental veil, and 20
has reduced the family relation to a mere money relation.

The bourgeoisie has disclosed how it came to pass that the brutal display 21
of vigor in the Middle Ages, which reactionists so much admire, found its fitting complement in the most slothful indolence. It has been the first to show
what man's activity can bring about. It has accomplished wonders far surpass-
ing Egyptian pyramids, Roman aqueducts and Gothic cathedrals; it has conducted expeditions that put in the shade all former Exoduses of nations and
crusades.

The bourgeoisie cannot exist without constantly revolutionizing the in- 22
strument of production, and thereby the relations of production, and with
them the whole relations of society. Conservation of the old modes of production in unaltered form was, on the contrary, the first condition of existence for
all earlier industrial classes. Constant revolutionizing of production, uninterrupted disturbance of all social conditions, everlasting uncertainty and agitation distinguish the bourgeois epoch from all earlier ones. All fixed, fast
frozen relations, with their train of ancient and venerable prejudices and opinions, are swept away, all new formed ones become antiquated before they can
ossify. All that is solid melts into the air, all that is holy is profaned, and man
is at last compelled to face with sober senses, his real conditions of life, and his
relations with his kind.

The need of a constantly expanding market for its products chases the 23
bourgeoisie over the whole surface of the globe. It must nestle everywhere,
settle everywhere, establish connections everywhere.

The bourgeoisie has through its exploitation of the world-market given a 24
cosmopolitan character to production and consumption in every country. To
the great chagrin of reactionists, it has drawn from under the feet of industry
the national ground on which it stood. All old-established national industries
have been destroyed or are daily being destroyed. They are dislodged by new
industries, whose introduction becomes a life and death question for all civilized nations, by industries that no longer work up indigenous raw material,
but raw material drawn from the remotest zones; industries whose products
are consumed, not only at home, but in every quarter of the globe. In place of
the old wants, satisfied by the productions of the country, we find new wants,
requiring for their satisfaction the products of distant lands and climes. In place
of the old local and national seclusion and self-sufficiency, we have intercourse
in every direction, universal interdependence of nations. And as in material, so
also in intellectual production. The intellectual creations of individual nations
become common property. National onesidedness and narrowmindedness become more and more possible, and from the numerous national and local liter-
atures there arises a world-literature.

The bourgeoisie, by the rapid improvement of all instruments of produc- 25
tion, by the immensely facilitated means of communication, draws all, even
the most barbarian nations into civilization. The cheap prices of its commodities are the heavy artillery with which it batters down all Chinese walls,
with which it forces the barbarians' intensely obstinate hatred of foreigners to

capitulate. It compels all nations, on pain of extinction, to adopt the bourgeois mode of production; it compels them to introduce what it calls civilization into their midst, i.e., to become bourgeois themselves. In a word, it creates a world after its own image.

The bourgeoisie has subjected the country to the rule of the towns. It   26
has created enormous cities, has greatly increased the urban population as compared with the rural and has thus rescued a considerable part of the population from the idiocy of rural life. Just as it has made the country dependent on the towns, so it has made barbarian and semi-barbarian countries dependent on civilized ones, nations of peasants on nations of bourgeois, the East on the West.

The bourgeoisie keeps more and more doing away with the scattered   27
state of the population, of the means of production, and of property. It has agglomerated population, centralized means of production, and has concentrated property in a few hands. The necessary consequence of this was political centralization. Independent, or but loosely connected provinces, with separate interests, laws, governments, and systems of taxation, become lumped together in one nation, with one government, one code of laws, one national class interest, one frontier and one customs tariff.

The bourgeoisie, during its rule of scarce one hundred years, has created   28
more massive and more colossal productive forces than have all preceding generations together. Subjection of Nature's forces to man, machinery, application of chemistry to industry and agriculture, steam-navigation, railways, electric telegraphs, clearing of whole continents for cultivation, canalization of rivers, whole populations conjured out of the ground—what earlier century had even a presentiment that such productive forces slumbered in the lap of social labor?

We see then: the means of production and of exchange on whose founda-   29
tion the bourgeoisie built itself up, were generated in feudal society. At a certain stage in the development of these means of production and of exchange, the conditions under which feudal society produced and exchanged, the feudal organization of agriculture and manufacturing industry, in one word, the feudal relations of property became no longer compatible with the already developed productive forces; they became so many fetters. They had to burst asunder; they were burst asunder.

Into their places stepped free competition, accompanied by social and   30
political constitution adapted to it, and by economical and political sway of the bourgeois class.

A similar movement is going on before our own eyes. Modern bourgeois   31
society with its relations of production, of exchange and of property, a society that has conjured up such gigantic means of production and of exchange, is like the sorcerer, who is no longer able to control the powers of the nether world whom he has called up by his spells. For many a decade past, the history of industry and commerce is but the history of the revolt of modern productive forces against modern conditions of production, against the property relations that are the conditions for the existence of the bourgeoisie and of its rule. It is

enough to mention the commercial crises that by their periodical return put on its trial, each time more threateningly, the existence of the entire bourgeois society. In these crises a great part not only of the existing products, but also of the previously created productive forces, are periodically destroyed. In these crises there breaks out an epidemic that, in all earlier epochs, would have seemed an absurdity—the epidemic of overproduction. Society suddenly finds itself put back into a state of momentary barbarism; it appears as if a famine, a universal war of devastation, had cut off the supply of every means of subsistence; industry and commerce seem to be destroyed; and why? Because there is too much civilization, too much means of subsistence, too much industry, too much commerce. The productive forces at the disposal of society no longer tend to further the development of the conditions of the bourgeois property; on the contrary, they have become too powerful for these conditions by which they are fettered, and as soon as they overcome these fetters they bring disorder into the whole of bourgeois society, endanger the existence of bourgeois property. The conditions of bourgeois society are too narrow to comprise the wealth created by them. And how does the bourgeoisie get over these crises? On the one hand by enforced destruction of a mass of productive forces; on the other, by the conquest of new markets, and by the more thorough exploitation of the old ones. That is to say, by paving the way for more extensive and more destructive crises, and by diminishing the means whereby crises are prevented.

32 The weapons with which the bourgeoisie felled feudalism to the ground are now turned against the bourgeoisie itself.

33 But not only has the bourgeoisie forged the weapons that bring death to itself; it has also called into existence the men who are to wield those weapons—the modern working class—the proletarians.

34 In proportion as the bourgeoisie, i.e., capital, is developed, in the same proportion is the proletariat, the modern working class, developed, a class of laborers who live only so long as they find work, and who find work only so long as their labor increases capital. These laborers, who must sell themselves piecemeal, are a commodity, like every other article of commerce, and are consequently exposed to all the vicissitudes of competition, to all the fluctuations of the market.

35 Owing to the extensive use of machinery and to division of labor, the work of the proletarians has lost all individual character, and, consequently, all charm for the workman. He becomes an appendage of the machine, and it is only the most simple, most monotonous and most easily acquired knack that is required of him. Hence, the cost of production of a workman is restricted almost entirely to the means of subsistence that he requires for his maintenance, and for the propagation of his race. But the price of a commodity, and also of labor, is equal to its cost of production. In production, therefore, as the repulsiveness of the work increases the wage decreases. Nay more, in proportion as the use of machinery and division of labor increases, in the same proportion the burden of toil increases, whether by prolongation of the working hours, by increase of the work enacted in a given time, or by increased speed of the machinery, etc.

Modern industry has converted the little workshop of the patriarchal   36
master into the great factory of the industrial capitalist. Masses of laborers,
crowded into factories, are organized like soldiers. As privates of the industrial
army they are placed under the command of a perfect hierarchy of officers and
sergeants. Not only are they the slaves of the bourgeois class and of the bourgeois state, they are daily and hourly enslaved by the machine, by the over-
looker, and above all, by the individual bourgeois manufacturer himself. The
more openly this despotism proclaims gain to be its end and aim, the more
petty, the more hateful and the more embittering it is.

The less the skill and exertion or strength implied in manual labor, in   37
other words, the more modern industry becomes developed, the more is the
labor of men superseded by that of women. Differences of age and sex have no
longer any distinctive social validity for the working class. All are instruments
of labor, more or less expensive to use, according to their age and sex.

No sooner is the exploitation of the laborer by the manufacturer, so far at   38
an end, that he receives his wages in cash, than he is set upon by the other portions of the bourgeoisie, the landlord, the shopkeeper, the pawn-broker, etc.

The lower strata of the middle class—the small trades-people, shopkeep-   39
ers and retired tradesmen generally, the handicraftsmen and peasants—all
these sink gradually into the proletariat, partly because their diminutive capital does not suffice for the scale on which Modern Industry is carried on, and
is swamped in the competition with the large capitalists, partly because their
specialized skill is rendered worthless by new methods of production. Thus the
proletariat is recruited from all classes of the population.

The proletariat goes through various stages of development. With its   40
birth begins its struggle with the bourgeoisie. At first the contest is carried on
by individual laborers, then by the workpeople of a factory, then by the opera-
tives of one trade, in one locality, against the individual bourgeois who directly exploits them. They direct their attacks not against the bourgeois
conditions of production, but against the instruments of production themselves; they destroy imported wares that compete with their labor, they smash
to pieces machinery, they set factories ablaze, they seek to restore by force the
vanished status of the workman of the Middle Ages.

At this stage the laborers still form an incoherent mass scattered over the   41
whole country, and broken up by their mutual competition. If anywhere they
unite to form more compact bodies, this is not yet the consequence of their
own active union, but of the union of the bourgeoisie, which class, in order to
attain its own political ends, is compelled to set the whole proletariat in motion, and is moreover yet, for a time, able to do so. At this stage, therefore, the
proletarians do not fight their enemies, but the enemies of their enemies, the
remnants of absolute monarchy, the landowners, the non-industrial bourgeois,
the petty bourgeoisie. Thus the whole historical movement is concentrated in
the hands of the bourgeoisie, every victory so obtained is a victory for the
bourgeoisie.

But with the development of industry the proletariat not only increases   42
in number; it becomes concentrated in greater masses, its strength grows and it

feels that strength more. The various interests and conditions of life within the ranks of the proletariat are more and more equalized, in proportion as machinery obliterates all distinctions of labor, and nearly everywhere reduces wages to the same low level. The growing competition among the bourgeois, and the resulting commercial crisis, makes the wages of the workers even more fluctuating. The unceasing improvement of machinery, ever more rapidly developing, makes their livelihood more and more precarious; the collisions between individual workmen and individual bourgeois take more and more the character of collisions between two classes. Thereupon the workers begin to form combinations (Trades' Unions) against the bourgeois; they club together in order to make provision beforehand for these occasional revolts. Here and there the contest breaks out into riots.

Now and then the workers are victorious, but only for a time. The real   43
fruit of their battle lies not in the immediate result but in the ever-expanding union of workers. This union is helped on by the improved means of communication that are created by modern industry, and that places the workers of different localities in contact with one another. It was just this contact that was needed to centralize the numerous local struggles, all of the same character, into one national struggle between classes. But every class struggle is a political struggle. And that union, to attain which the burghers of the Middle Ages with their miserable highways, required centuries, the modern proletarians, thanks to railways, achieve in a few years.

This organization of the proletarians into a class, and consequently into a   44
political party, is continually being upset again by the competition between the workers themselves. But it ever rises up again, stronger, firmer, mightier. It compels legislative recognition of particular interests of the workers by taking advantage of the divisions among the bourgeoisie itself. Thus the ten hours' bill in England was carried.

Altogether collisions between the classes of the old society further, in   45
many ways, the course of development of the proletariat. The bourgeoisie finds itself involved in a constant battle. At first with the aristocracy; later on, with those portions of the bourgeoisie itself whose interests have become antagonistic to the progress of industry; at all times, with the bourgeoisie of foreign countries. In all these battles it sees itself compelled to appeal to the proletariat, to ask for its help, and thus, to drag it into the political arena. The bourgeoisie itself, therefore, supplies the proletariat with its own elements of political and general education; in other words, it furnishes the proletariat with weapons for fighting the bourgeoisie.

Further, as we have already seen, entire sections of the ruling classes are,   46
by the advance of industry, precipitated into the proletariat, or are at least threatened in their conditions of existence. These also supply the proletariat with fresh elements of enlightenment and progress.

Finally, in times when the class-struggle nears the decisive hour, the   47
process of dissolution going on within the ruling class—in fact, within the whole range of an old society—assumes such a violent, glaring character that a small section of the ruling class cuts itself adrift and joins the revolutionary

class, the class that holds the future in its hands. Just as, therefore, at an earlier period, a section of the nobility went over to the bourgeoisie, so now a portion of the bourgeoisie goes over to the proletariat, and in particular, a portion of the bourgeois ideologists, who have raised themselves to the level of comprehending theoretically the historical movements as a whole.

Of all the classes that stand face to face with the bourgeoisie today the   48
proletariat alone is a really revolutionary class. The other classes decay and finally disappear in the face of modern industry; the proletariat is its special and essential product.

The lower middle class, the small manufacturer, the shopkeeper, the arti-   49
san, the peasant, all these fight against the bourgeoisie, to save from extinction their existence as fractions of the middle class. They are therefore not revolutionary, but conservative. Nay, more; they are reactionary, for they try to roll back the wheel of history. If by chance they are revolutionary, they are so only in view of their impending transfer into the proletariat; they thus defend not their present, but their future interests; they desert their own standpoint to place themselves at that of the proletariat.

The "dangerous class," the social scum, that passively rotting mass   50
thrown off by the lowest layers of old society, may, here and there, be swept into the movement by a proletarian revolution; its conditions of life, however, prepare it far more for the part of a bribed tool of reactionary intrigue.

In the conditions of the proletariat, those of the old society at large are   51
already virtually swamped. The proletarian is without property; his relation to his wife and children has no longer anything in common with the bourgeois family relations; modern industrial labor, modern subjection to capital, the same in England as in France, in America as in Germany, has stripped him of every trace of national character. Law, morality, religion, are to him so many bourgeois prejudices, behind which lurk in ambush just as many bourgeois interests.

All the preceding classes that got the upper hand sought to fortify their   52
already acquired status by subjecting society at large to their conditions of appropriation. The proletarians cannot become masters of the productive forces of society, except by abolishing their own previous mode of appropriation, and thereby also every other previous mode of appropriation. They have nothing of their own to secure and to fortify; their mission is to destroy all previous securities for and insurances of individual property.

All previous historical movements were movements of minorities, or in   53
the interest of minorities. The proletarian movement is the self-conscious, independent movement of the immense majority. The proletariat, the lowest stratum of our present society, cannot stir, cannot raise itself up without the whole superincumbent strata of official society being sprung into the air.

Though not in substance, yet in form, the struggle of the proletariat with   54
the bourgeoisie is at first a national struggle. The proletariat of each country must, of course, first of all settle matters with its own bourgeoisie.

In depicting the most general phases of the development of the proletar-   55
iat, we traced the more or less veiled civil war, raging within existing society,

up to the point where that war breaks out into open revolution, and where the violent overthrow of the bourgeoisie, lays the foundations for the sway of the proletariat.

Hitherto every form of society has been based, as we have already seen, on the antagonism of oppressing and oppressed classes. But in order to oppress a class, certain conditions must be assured to it under which it can, at least, continue its slavish existence. The serf, in the period of serfdom, raised himself to membership in the commune, just as the petty bourgeois, under the yoke of feudal absolutism managed to develop into a bourgeois. The modern laborer, on the contrary, instead of rising with the progress of industry, sinks deeper and deeper below the conditions of existence of his own class. He becomes a pauper, and pauperism develops more rapidly than population and wealth. And here it becomes evident that the bourgeoisie is unfit any longer to be the ruling class in society, and impose its conditions of existence upon society as an over-riding law. It is unfit to rule, because it is incompetent to assure an existence to its slave within his slavery, because it cannot help letting him sink into such a state that it has to feed him, instead of being fed by him. Society can no longer live under this bourgeoisie; in other words, its existence is no longer compatible with society. **56**

The essential condition for the existence, and for the sway of the bourgeois class, is the formation and augmentation of capital; the condition for capital is wage labor. Wage labor rests exclusively on competition between the laborers. The advance of industry, whose involuntary promoter is the bourgeoisie, replaces the isolation of the laborers, due to competition, by their involuntary combination, due to association. The development of Modern Industry, therefore, cuts from under its feet the very foundation on which the bourgeoisie produces and appropriates products. What the bourgeoisie therefore produces, above all, are its own grave diggers. Its fall and the victory of the proletariat are equally inevitable. ■ **57**

Questions for Meaning

1. Comment on the authors' claim in paragraph 5 that the "history of all hitherto existing society is the history of class struggles." What does this mean?
2. In paragraph 9, the authors write: "Society as a whole is more and more splitting up into two great hostile camps, into two great classes directly facing each other: Bourgeoisie and Proletariat." Has history proven them right? How would you describe class relations within the United States? Can American history be seen in Marxist terms?
3. Explain the distinction in paragraph 12 between the feudal and manufacturing systems of industry.
4. Do Marx and Engels concede that modern history has accomplished anything admirable? Do they credit the bourgeoisie with any virtues?
5. Why do Marx and Engels believe that the bourgeoisie is unfit to rule? Why do they believe that the rise of the proletariat is inevitable?

6. What do Marx and Engels mean when they claim "there is too much civilization, too much means of subsistence, too much industry, too much commerce"? Paraphrase paragraph 31.
7. What is "the social scum" that Marx and Engels dismiss in paragraph 50? Why do they believe this class is dangerous?
8. Vocabulary: exorcise (1), patrician (6), plebeian (6), vassals (7), patriarchal (18), nexus (18), slothful (21), indigenous (24), agglomerated (27), presentiment (28), vicissitudes (34), diminutive (39), obliterates (42), precarious (42), augmentation (57).

Questions about Strategy

1. Why do Marx and Engels open their manifesto by describing Communism as "a specter"? Explain what they mean by this and how it serves as an introduction to the political analysis that follows.
2. In interpreting history entirely in economic terms, are there any major conflicts that Marx and Engels overlook?
3. What is the function of paragraphs 29 and 30?
4. Can you point to anything in this work that reveals that Marx and Engels were writing for an international audience?
5. What parts of this essay are the strongest? Where do Marx and Engels make the most sense?
6. Can you identify any exaggerations in *The Communist Manifesto?* If you were to write a rebuttal, are there any claims that you could prove to be oversimplified?
7. Is this "manifesto" an argument or an exhortation? Is it designed to convince readers who have no political opinions, or to rally the men and women who are already committed to revolution? What is its purpose?

MARK TWAIN

FENIMORE COOPER'S LITERARY OFFENSES

Mark Twain is the name Samuel Clemens (1835–1910) assumed in 1863 at the beginning of what would be a long, successful career as a writer. Once called "the Lincoln of our literature," he has remained one of the most widely read of major American writers—admired for his distinctive humor and also for the skill with which he captured the varied forms of American dialect. His best known works include *The Adventures of Tom Sawyer* (1876), *The Prince and the Pauper* (1877), *Life on the Mississippi* (1883), *The Adventures of Huckleberry Finn* (1885), and *A Connecticut Yankee in King Arthur's Court* (1889).

In addition to his achievement as a writer of fiction, Twain is also valued for the penetrating social and literary criticism that can be found in his many essays. "Fenimore Cooper's Literary Offenses," written in 1895, is one of two essays Twain wrote to explain why he objected to James Fenimore Cooper (1789–1851)—an important American novelist whose reputation has never altogether recovered from Twain's charges. Try to read the following essay as an argument on how fiction should be written and not simply as an attack on Cooper.

> *The Pathfinder* and *The Deerslayer* stand at the head of Cooper's novels as artistic creations. There are others of his works which contain parts as perfect as are to be found in these, and scenes even more thrilling. Not one can be compared with either of them as a finished whole.
>
> The defects in both of these tales are comparatively slight. They were pure works of art.—*Prof Lounsbury.*

> The five tales reveal an extraordinary fulness of invention.
> . . . One of the very greatest characters in fiction, Natty Bumppo. . . .
> The craft of the woodsman, the tricks of the trapper, all the delicate art of the forest, were familiar to Cooper from his youth up.—*Prof. Brander Matthews.*

> Cooper is the greatest artist in the domain of romantic fiction yet produced by America.—*Wilkie Collins.*

It seems to me that it was far from right for the Professor of English Literature in Yale, the Professor of English Literature in Columbia, and Wilkie Collins to deliver opinions on Cooper's literature without having read some of it. It would have been much more decorous to keep silent and let persons talk who have read Cooper.

Cooper's art has some defects. In one place in *Deerslayer,* and in the restricted space of two-thirds of a page, Cooper has scored 114 offenses against literary art out of a possible 115. It breaks the record.

There are nineteen rules governing literary art in the domain of romantic fiction—some say twenty-two. In *Deerslayer* Cooper violated eighteen of them. These eighteen require:

1. That a tale shall accomplish something and arrive somewhere. But the *Deerslayer* tale accomplishes nothing and arrives in the air.

2. They require that the episodes of a tale shall be necessary parts of the tale, and shall help to develop it. But as the *Deerslayer* tale is not a tale, and accomplishes nothing and arrives nowhere, the episodes have no rightful place in the work, since there was nothing for them to develop.

3. They require that the personages in a tale shall be alive, except in the cases of corpses, and that always the reader shall be able to tell the corpses from the others. But this detail has often been overlooked in the *Deerslayer* tale.

4. They require that the personages in a tale, both dead and alive, shall exhibit a sufficient excuse for being there. But this detail also has been overlooked in the *Deerslayer* tale.

5. They require that when the personages of a tale deal in conversation, the talk shall sound like human talk, and be talk such as human beings would be likely to talk in the given circumstances, and have a discoverable meaning, also a discoverable purpose, and a show of relevancy, and remain in the neighborhood of the subject in hand, and be interesting to the reader, and help out the tale, and stop when the people cannot think of anything more to say. But this requirement has been ignored from the beginning of the *Deerslayer* tale to the end of it.

6. They require that when the author describes the character of a personage in his tale, the conduct and conversation of that personage shall justify said description. But this law gets little or no attention in the *Deerslayer* tale, as Natty Bumppo's case will amply prove.

7. They require that when a personage talks like an illustrated, gilt-edged, tree-calf, hand-tooled, seven-dollar Friendship's Offering in the beginning of a paragraph, he shall not talk like a negro minstrel in the end of it. But this rule is flung down and danced upon in the *Deerslayer* tale.

8. They require that crass stupidities shall not be played upon the reader as "the craft of the woodsman, the delicate art of the forest," by either the author or the people in the tale. But this rule is persistently violated in the *Deerslayer* tale.

9. They require that the personages of a tale shall confine themselves to possibilities and let miracles alone; or, if they venture a miracle, the author must so plausibly set it forth as to make it look possible and reasonable. But these rules are not respected in the *Deerslayer* tale.

10. They require that the author shall make the reader feel a deep interest in the personages of his tale and in their fate; and that he shall make the reader love the good people in the tale and hate the bad ones. But the reader of the *Deerslayer* tale dislikes the good people in

it, is indifferent to the others, and wishes they would all get drowned together.

11. They require that the characters in a tale shall be so clearly defined that the reader can tell beforehand what each will do in a given emergency. But in the *Deerslayer* tale this rule is vacated.

In addition to these large rules there are some little ones. These require that the author shall

12. *Say* what he is proposing to say, not merely come near it.
13. Use the right word, not its second cousin.
14. Eschew surplusage.
15. Not omit necessary details.
16. Avoid slovenliness of form.
17. Use good grammar.
18. Employ a simple and straightforward style.

Even these seven are coldly and persistently violated in the *Deerslayer* tale.

Cooper's gift in the way of invention was not a rich endowment; but   4
such as it was he liked to work it, he was pleased with the effects, and indeed he did some quite sweet things with it. In his little box of stage-properties he kept six or eight cunning devices, tricks, artifices for his savages and woods-men to deceive and circumvent each other with, and he was never so happy as when he was working these innocent things and seeing them go. A favorite one was to make a moccasined person tread in the tracks of the moccasined enemy, and thus hide his own trail. Cooper wore out barrels and barrels of moccasins in working that trick. Another stage-property that he pulled out of his box pretty frequently was his broken twig. He prized his broken twig above all the rest of his effects, and worked it the hardest. It is a restful chapter in any book of his when somebody doesn't step on a dry twig and alarm all the reds and whites for two hundred yards around. Every time a Cooper person is in peril, and absolute silence is worth four dollars a minute, he is sure to step on a dry twig. There may be a hundred handier things to step on, but that wouldn't satisfy Cooper. Cooper requires him to turn out and find a dry twig; and if he can't do it, go and borrow one. In fact, the Leather Stocking Series ought to have been called the Broken Twig Series.

I am sorry there is not room to put in a few dozen instances of the deli-   5
cate art of the forest, as practiced by Natty Bumppo and some of the other Cooperian experts. Perhaps we may venture two or three samples. Cooper was a sailor—a naval officer; yet he gravely tells us how a vessel, driving toward a lee shore in a gale, is steered for a particular spot by her skipper because he knows of an *undertow* there which will hold her back against the gale and save her. For just pure woodcraft, or sailorcraft, or whatever it is, isn't that neat? For several years Cooper was daily in the society of artillery, and he ought to

have noticed that when a cannon-ball strikes the ground it either buries itself or skips a hundred feet or so; skips again a hundred feet or so—and so on, till finally it gets tired and rolls. Now in one place he loses some "females"—as he always calls women—in the edge of a wood near a plain at night in a fog, on purpose to give Bumppo a chance to show off the delicate art of the forest before the reader. These mislaid people are hunting for a fort. They hear a cannon-blast, and a cannon-ball presently comes rolling into the wood and stops at their feet. To the females this suggests nothing. The case is very different with the admirable Bumppo. I wish I may never know peace again if he doesn't strike out promptly and *follow the track* of that cannon-ball across the plain through the dense fog and find the fort. Isn't it a daisy? If Cooper had any real knowledge of Nature's ways of doing things, he had a most delicate art in concealing the fact. For instance: one of his acute Indian experts, Chingach-gook (pronounced Chicago, I think), has lost the trail of a person he is track-ing through the forest. Apparently that trail is hopelessly lost. Neither you nor I could have guessed out the way to find it. It was very different with Chicago. Chicago was not stumped for long. He turned a running stream out of its course, and there, in the slush in its old bed, were that person's moccasin-tracks. The current did not wash them away, as it would have done in all other cases—no, even the eternal laws of Nature have to vacate when Cooper wants to put up a delicate job of woodcraft on the reader.

We must be a little wary when Brander Matthews tells us that Cooper's 6 books "reveal an extraordinary fulness of invention." As a rule, I am quite willing to accept Brander Matthews's literary judgments and applaud his lucid and graceful phrasing of them; but that particular statement needs to be taken with a few tons of salt. Bless your heart, Cooper hadn't any more invention than a horse; and I don't mean a high-class horse, either; I mean a clothes-horse. It would be very difficult to find a really clever "situation" in Cooper's books, and still more difficult to find one of any kind which he has failed to render absurd by his handling of it. Look at the episodes of "the caves"; and at the celebrated scuffle between Maqua and those others on the table-land a few days later; and at Hurry Harry's queer water-transit from the castle to the ark; and at Deerslayer's half-hour with his first corpse; and at the quarrel between Hurry Harry and Deerslayer later; and at—but choose for yourself; you can't go amiss.

If Cooper had been an observer his inventive faculty would have worked 7 better; not more interestingly, but more rationally, more plausibly. Cooper's proudest creations in the way of "situations" suffer noticeably from the ab-sence of the observer's protecting gift. Cooper's eye was splendidly inaccurate. Cooper seldom saw anything correctly. He saw nearly all things as through a glass eye, darkly. Of course a man who cannot see the commonest little every-day matters accurately is working at a disadvantage when he is constructing a "situation." In the *Deerslayer* tale Cooper has a stream which is fifty feet wide where it flows out of a lake; it presently narrows to twenty as it meanders along for no given reason, and yet when a stream acts like that it ought to be required to explain itself. Fourteen pages later the width of the brook's outlet from the lake has suddenly shrunk thirty feet, and become "the narrowest part of the stream." This shrinkage is not accounted for. The stream has bends in it, a sure indication that it has alluvial banks and cuts them; yet these bends are only thirty and fifty feet long. If Cooper had been a nice and punctilious observer he would have noticed that the bends were oftener nine hundred feet long than short of it.

Cooper made the exit of that stream fifty feet wide, in the first place, for no particular reason; in the second place, he narrowed it to less than twenty to accommodate some Indians. He bends a "sapling" to the form of an arch over this narrow passage, and conceals six Indians in its foliage. They are "laying" for a settler's scow or ark which is coming up the stream on its way to the lake; it is being hauled against the stiff current by a rope whose stationary end is anchored in the lake; its rate of progress cannot be more than a mile an hour. Cooper describes the ark, but pretty obscurely. In the matter of dimensions "it was little more than a modern canal-boat." Let us guess, then, that it was about one hundred and forty feet long. It was of "greater breadth than common." Let us guess, then, that it was about sixteen feet wide. This leviathan had been prowling down bends which were but a third as long as itself, and scraping between banks where it had only two feet of space to spare on each side. We cannot too much admire this miracle. A low-roofed log dwelling occupies "two-thirds of the ark's length"—a dwelling ninety feet long and sixteen feet wide, let us say—a kind of vestibule train. The dwelling has two rooms—each forty-five feet long and sixteen feet wide, let us guess. One of them is the bedroom of the Hutter girls, Judith and Hetty; the other is the parlor in the daytime, at night it is papa's bed-chamber. The ark is arriving at the stream's exit now, whose width has been reduced to less than twenty feet to accommodate the Indians—say to eighteen. There is a foot to spare on each side of the boat. Did the Indians notice that there was going to be a tight squeeze there? Did they notice that they could make money by climbing down out of that arched sapling and just stepping aboard when the ark scraped by? No, other Indians would have noticed these things, but Cooper's Indians never notice anything. Cooper thinks they are marvelous creatures for noticing, but he was almost always in error about his Indians. There was seldom a sane one among them.

8

The ark is one hundred and forty feet long; the dwelling is ninety feet long. The idea of the Indians is to drop softly and secretly from the arched sapling to the dwelling as the ark creeps along under it at the rate of a mile an hour, and butcher the family. It will take the ark a minute and a half to pass under. It will take the ninety-foot dwelling a minute to pass under. Now, then, what did the six Indians do? It would take you thirty years to guess, and even then you would have to give it up, I believe. Therefore, I will tell you what the Indians did. Their chief, a person of quite extraordinary intellect for a Cooper Indian, warily watched the canal-boat as it squeezed along under him, and when he had got his calculations fined down to exactly the right shade, as he judged, he let go and dropped. And *missed the house!* That is actually what he did. He missed the house, and landed in the stern of the scow. It

9

was not much of a fall, yet it knocked him silly. He lay there unconscious. If the house had been ninety-seven feet long he would have made the trip. The fault was Cooper's, not his. The error lay in the construction of the house. Cooper has no architect.

There still remained in the roost five Indians. The boat has passed under   10 and is now out of their reach. Let me explain what the five did—you would not be able to reason it out for yourself. No. 1 jumped for the boat, but fell in the water astern of it. Then No. 2 jumped for the boat, but fell in the water still farther astern of it. Then No. 3 jumped for the boat, and fell a good way astern of it. Then No. 4 jumped for the boat, and fell in the water *away* astern. Then even No. 5 made a jump for the boat—for he was a Cooper Indian. In the matter of intellect, the difference between a Cooper Indian and the Indian that stands in front of the cigarshop is not spacious. The scow episode is really a sublime burst of invention; but it does not thrill, because the inaccuracy of the detail throws a sort of air of fictitiousness and general improbability over it. This comes of Cooper's inadequacy as an observer.

The reader will find some examples of Cooper's high talent for inaccu-   11 rate observation in the account of the shooting-match in *The Pathfinder*.

A common wrought nail was driven lightly into the target, its head having been first touched with paint.

The color of the paint is not stated—an important omission, but Cooper   12 deals freely in important omissions. No, after all, it was not an important omission; for this nail-head is *a hundred yards from* the marksmen, and could not be seen by them at that distance, no matter what its color might be. How far can the best eyes see a common house-fly? A hundred yards? It is quite impossible. Very well; eyes that cannot see a house-fly that is a hundred yards away cannot see an ordinary nail-head at that distance, for the size of the two objects is the same. It takes a keen eye to see a fly or a nail-head at fifty yards—one hundred and fifty feet. Can the reader do it?

The nail was lightly driven, its head painted, and game called. Then the   13 Cooper miracles begin. The bullet of the first marksman chipped an edge of the nail-head; the next man's bullet drove the nail a little way into the target— and removed all the paint. Haven't the miracles gone far enough now? Not to suit Cooper; for the purpose of this whole scheme is to show off his prodigy, Deerslayer-Hawkeye-Long-Rifle-Leather-Stocking-Pathfinder-Bumppo before the ladies.

"Be all ready to clench it, boys!" cried out Pathfinder, stepping into his friend's
tracks the instant they were vacant. "Never mind a new nail; I can see that,
though the paint is gone, and what I can see I can hit at a hundred yards, though
it were only a mosquito's eye. Be ready to clench!"

The rifle cracked, the bullet sped its way, and the head of the nail was
buried in the wood, covered by the piece of flattened lead.

There, you see, is a man who could hunt flies with a rifle, and command   14
a ducal salary in a Wild West show today if we had him back with us.

The recorded feat is certainly surprising just as it stands; but it is not sur-   15
prising enough for Cooper. Cooper adds a touch. He has made Pathfinder do
this miracle with another man's rifle; and not only that, but Pathfinder did not
have even the advantage of loading it himself. He had everything against him,
and yet he made that impossible shot; and not only made it, but did it with
absolute confidence, saying, "Be ready to clench." Now a person like that
would have undertaken that same feat with a brick-bat, and with Cooper to
help he would have achieved it, too.

Pathfinder showed off handsomely that day before the ladies. His very   16
first feat was a thing which no Wild West show can touch. He was standing
with the group of marksmen, observing—a hundred yards from the target,
mind; one Jasper raised his rifle and drove the center off the bull's-eye. Then
the Quartermaster fired. The target exhibited no result this time. There was a
laugh. "It's a dead miss," said Major Lundie. Pathfinder waited an impressive
moment or two; then said, in that calm, indifferent, know-it-all way of his,
"No, Major, he has covered Jasper's bullet, as will be seen if anyone will take
the trouble to examine the target."

Wasn't it remarkable! How *could* he see that little pellet fly through the   17
air and enter that distant bullet-hole? Yet that is what he did; for nothing is
impossible to a Cooper person. Did any of those people have any deep-seated
doubts about this thing? No; for that would imply sanity, and these were all
Cooper people.

> The respect for Pathfinder's skill and for his *quickness and accuracy of sight* [the ital-
> ics are mine] was so profound and general, that the instant he made this declara-
> tion the spectators began to distrust their own opinions, and a dozen rushed to
> the target in order to ascertain the fact. There, sure enough, it was found that the
> Quartermaster's bullet had gone through the hole made by Jasper's, and that, too,
> so accurately as to require a minute examination to be certain of the circum-
> stance, which, however, was soon clearly established by discovering one bullet
> over the other in the stump against which the target was placed.

They made a "minute" examination; but never mind, how could they   18
know that there were two bullets in that hole without digging the latest one
out? for neither probe nor eyesight could prove the presence of any more than
one bullet. Did they dig? No; as we shall see. It is the Pathfinder's turn now; he
steps out before the ladies, takes aim, and fires.

But, alas! here is a disappointment; an incredible, an unimaginable disap-   19
pointment—for the target's aspect is unchanged; there is nothing there but the
same old bullet-hole!

> "If one dared to hint at such a thing," cried Major Duncan, "I should say that
> the Pathfinder has also missed the target!"

As nobody had missed it yet, the "also" was not necessary; but never   20
mind about that, for the Pathfinder is going to speak.

> "No, no, Major," said he, confidently, "that *would* be a risky declaration. I
> didn't load the piece, and can't say what was in it; but if it was lead, you will
> find the bullet driving down those of the Quartermaster and Jasper, else is not
> my name Pathfinder."
> A shout from the target announced the truth of this assertion.

Is the miracle sufficient as it stands? Not for Cooper. The Pathfinder   21
speaks again, as he "now slowly advances towards the stage occupied by the
females":

> "That's not all, boys, that's not all; if you find the target touched at all, I'll own
> to a miss. The Quartermaster cut the wood, but you'll find no wood cut by
> that last messenger."

The miracle is at last complete. He knew—doubtless *saw*—at the dis-   22
tance of a hundred yards—that his bullet had passed into the hole *without fray-*
ing the edges. There were now three bullets in that one hole—three bullets
embedded processionally in the body of the stump back of the target. Everybody knew this—somehow or other—and yet nobody had dug any of them
out to make sure. Cooper is not a close observer, but he is interesting. He is
certainly always that, no matter what happens. And he is more interesting
when he is not noticing what he is about than when he is. This is a considerable merit.

The conversations in the Cooper books have a curious sound in our mod-   23
ern ears. To believe that such talk really ever came out of people's mouths
would be to believe that there was a time when time was of no value to a person
who thought he had something to say; when it was the custom to spread a two-
minute remark out to ten; when a man's mouth was a rolling-mill, and busied
itself all day long in turning four-foot pigs of thought into thirty-foot bars of
conversational railroad iron by attenuation; when subjects were seldom faith-
fully stuck to, but the talk wandered all around and arrived nowhere; when
conversations consisted mainly of irrelevancies, with here and there a relevancy, a relevancy with an embarrassed look, as not being able to explain how
it got there.

Cooper was certainly not a master in the construction of dialogue. Inac-   24
curate observation defeated him here as it defeated him in so many other en-
terprises of his. He even failed to notice that the man who talks corrupt
English six days in the week must and will talk it on the seventh, and can't
help himself. In the *Deerslayer* story he lets Deerslayer talk the showiest kind of
book-talk sometimes, and at other times the basest of base dialects. For instance, when someone asks him if he has a sweetheart, and if so, where she
abides, this is his majestic answer:

"She's in the forest—hanging from the boughs of the trees, in a soft rain—in the dew on the open grass—the clouds that float about in the blue heavens—the birds that sing in the woods—the sweet springs where I slake my thirst—and in all the other glorious gifts that come from God's Providence!"

And he preceded that, a little before, with this: 25

"It consarns me as all things that touches a fri'nd consarns a fri'nd."

And this is another of his remarks: 26

"If I was Injin born, now, I might tell of this, or carry in the scalp and boast of the expl'ite afore the whole tribe; or if my inimy had only been a bear"

—and so on.

We cannot imagine such a thing as a veteran Scotch Commander-in-   27
Chief comporting himself in the field like a windy melodramatic actor, but Cooper could. On one occasion Alice and Cora were being chased by the French through a fog in the neighborhood of their father's fort:

> "*Point de quartier aux coquins!*" cried an eager pursuer, who seemed to direct the operations of the enemy.
> "Stand firm and be ready, my gallant 60ths!" suddenly exclaimed a voice above them; "wait to see the enemy; fire low, and sweep the glacis."
> "Father! father!" exclaimed a piercing cry from out the mist; "it is I! Alice! thy own Elsie! spare, O! save your daughters!"
> "Hold!" shouted the former speaker, in the awful tones of parental agony, the sound reaching even to the woods, and rolling back in solemn echo. "'Tis she! God has restored me my children! Throw open the sally-port; to the field, 60ths, to the field! pull not a trigger, lest ye kill my lambs! Drive off these dogs of France with your steel!"

Cooper's word-sense was singularly dull. When a person has a poor ear   28
for music he will flat and sharp right along without knowing it. He keeps near the tune, but it is *not* the tune. When a person has a poor ear for words, the result is a literary flatting and sharping; you perceive what he is intending to say, but you also perceive that he doesn't *say* it. This is Cooper. He was not a word-musician. His ear was satisfied with the *approximate* word. I will furnish some circumstantial evidence in support of this charge. My instances are gathered from half a dozen pages of the tale called *Deerslayer*. He uses "verbal," for "oral"; "precision," for "facility"; "phenomena," for "marvels"; "necessary," for "predetermined"; "unsophisticated," for "primitive"; "preparation," for "expectancy"; "rebuked," for "subdued"; "dependent on," for "resulting from"; "fact," for "condition"; "fact," for "conjecture"; "precaution," for "caution"; "explain," for "determine"; "mortified," for "disappointed"; "meretricious," for "factitious"; "materially," for "considerably";

"decreasing," for "deepening"; "increasing," for "disappearing"; "embedded," for "enclosed"; "treacherous," for "hostile"; "stood," for "stooped"; "softened," for "replaced"; "rejoined," for "remarked"; "situation," for "condition"; "different," for "differing"; "insensible," for "unsentient"; "brevity," for "celerity"; "distrusted," for "suspicious"; "mental imbecility," for "imbecility"; "eyes," for "sight"; "counteracting," for "opposing"; "funeral obsequies," for "obsequies."

There have been daring people in the world who claimed that Cooper   29
could write English, but they are all dead now—all dead but Lounsbury. I
don't remember that Lounsbury makes the claim in so many words, still he
makes it, for he says that *Deerslayer* is a "pure work of art." Pure, in that connection, means faultless—faultless in all details—and language is a detail. If
Mr. Lounsbury had only compared Cooper's English with the English which
he writes himself—but it is plain that he didn't, and so it is likely that he imagines until this day that Cooper's is as clean and compact as his own. Now I feel
sure, deep down in my heart, that Cooper wrote about the poorest English
that exists in our language, and that the English of *Deerslayer* is the very worst
that even Cooper ever wrote.

I may be mistaken, but it does seem to me that *Deerslayer* is not a work of   30
art in any sense; it does seem to me that it is destitute of every detail that goes
to the making of a work of art; in truth, it seems to me that *Deerslayer* is just
simply a literary *delirium tremens*.

A work of art? It has no invention; it has no order, system, sequence, or   31
result; it has no lifelikeness, no thrill, no stir, no seeming of reality; its characters are confusedly drawn, and by their acts and words they prove that they are
not the sort of people the author claims that they are; its humor is pathetic; its
pathos is funny; its conversations are—oh! indescribable; its love-scenes odious; its English a crime against the language.

Counting these out, what is left is Art. I think we must all admit   32
that. ■

Questions for Meaning

1. What do Wilkie Collins and Twain mean by "romantic fiction"?
2. Demonstrate that you have understood Twain's first eleven rules for literature by paraphrasing them.
3. Why does Twain object to Cooper's use of the device of having a character cause alarm by stepping on a dry twig?
4. Why does Twain believe that Cooper was not observant?
5. What is wrong with Cooper's characterization of the Indians discussed in paragraph 10?
6. Why does Twain object to Cooper's dialogue?
7. Vocabulary: decorous (1), eschew (3), lucid (6), plausibly (7), leviathan (8), ducal (14), attenuation (23), obsequies (28).

Questions about Strategy

1. How important are the quotations that preface this essay?
2. Twain has been much praised for his humor. How does he use humor in this essay to make his point?
3. Did Twain persuade you that he has read Cooper carefully? If so, how? If not, why not?
4. Has Twain assumed that his audience is familiar with Cooper? Could someone who has not read Cooper understand this essay?

CHARLOTTE PERKINS GILMAN

CONCERNING CHILDREN

Best known today for her fiction, especially her story "The Yellow Wall-Paper" (1892), Charlotte Perkins Gilman (1860–1935) was a leading intellectual in the women's movement at the turn of the century. In *Women and Economics* (1898), she offered an extensive analysis of women's role in society and why women have been undervalued. In *Herland* (1915), she described a utopian society of women without men. "Concerning Children" was first published in 1900. As you read, ask yourself whether parents could still profit from Gilman's advice.

The rearing of children is the most important work, and it is here contended   1
that, in this great educational process, obedience, as a main factor, has a bad effect on the growing mind. A child is a human creature. He should be reared with a view to his development and behaviour as an adult, not solely with a view to his behaviour as a child. He is temporarily a child, far more permanently a man; and it is the man we are training. The work of "parenthood" is not only to guard and nourish the young, but to develop the qualities needed in the mature.

Obedience is defended, first, as being necessary to the protection of the   2
child, and, second, as developing desirable qualities in the adult. But the child can be far better protected by removing all danger, which our present civilization is quite competent to do; and "the habit of obedience" developes very undesirable qualities. On what characteristics does our human pre-eminence rest? On our breadth and accuracy of judgment and force of will. Because we can see widely and judge wisely, because we have power to do what we see to be right, therefore we are the dominant species in the animal kingdom; therefore we are consciously the children of God.

These qualities are lodged in individuals, and must be exercised by indi-   3
viduals for the best human progress. If our method of advance were that one person alone should be wise and strong, and all other persons prosperous

through a strict subservience to his commands, then, indeed, we could do no better for our children than to train them to obey. Judgment would be of no use to them if they had to take another's: will-power would be valueless if they were never to exercise it.

But this is by no means the condition of human life. More and more is it   4
being recognized that progress lies in a well-developed average intelligence rather than in a wise despot and his stupid serfs. For every individual to have a good judgment and a strong will is far better for the community than for a few to have these qualities and the rest to follow them.

The "habit of obedience," forced in upon the impressible nature of a   5
child, does not develop judgment and will, but does develop that fatal facility in following other people's judgment and other people's wills which tends to make us a helpless mob, mere sheep, instead of wise, free, strong individuals. The habit of submission to authority, the long deeply impressed conviction that to "be good" is to "give up," that there is virtue in the act of surrender,— this is one of the sources from which we continually replenish human weakness, and fill the world with an inert mass of mind-less, will-less folk, pushed and pulled about by those whom they obey.

Moreover, there is the opposite effect,—the injurious reaction from obe-   6
dience,—almost as common and hurtful as its full achievement; namely, that fierce rebellious desire to do exactly the opposite of what one is told, which is no nearer to calm judgment than the other.

In obeying another will or in resisting another will, nothing is gained in   7
wisdom. A human creature is a self-governing intelligence, and the rich years of childhood should be passed in the guarded and gradual exercise of those powers.

Now this will, no doubt, call up to the minds of many a picture of a   8
selfish, domineering youngster, stormily ploughing through a number of experimental adventures, with a group of sacrificial parents and teachers prostrate before him. Again an unwarranted assumption. Consideration of others is one of the first laws of life, one of the first things a child should be taught; but consideration of others is not identical with obedience. Again, it will be imagined that the child is to be left to laboriously work out for himself the accumulated experiments of humanity, and deprived of the profits of all previous experience. By no means. On the contrary, it is the business of those who have the care of the very young to see to it that they do benefit by that previous experience far more fully than is now possible.

Our system of obedience cuts the child off from precisely this advantage,   9
and leaves him longing to do the forbidden things, generally doing them, too, when he gets away from his tutelage. The behaviour of the released child, in its riotous reaction against authority as such, as shown glaringly in the action of the average college student, tells how much judgment and self-control have been developing behind the obedience.

The brain grows by exercise. The best time to develop it is in youth. To   10
obey does not develop the brain, but checks its growth. It gives to the will a peculiar suicidal power of aborting its own impulse, not controlling it, but

giving it up. This leaves a habit of giving up which weakens our power of continued effort.

All this is not saying that obedience is never useful in childhood. There   11
are occasions when it is; and on such occasions, with a child otherwise intelligently trained, it will be forthcoming. We make a wide mistake in assuming that, unless a child is made to obey at every step, it will never obey. A grown person will obey under sharp instant pressure.

If there is a sudden danger, and you shriek at your friend, "Get up—   12
quick!" or hiss a terrified, "Sh! Sh! Be Still!" your friend promptly obeys. Of course, if you had been endeavouring to "boss" that friend with a thousand pointless caprices, he might distrust you in the hour of peril; but if he knew you to be a reasonable person, he would respond promptly to a sudden command.

Much more will a child so respond where he has full reason to respect the   13
judgment of the commander. Children have the same automatic habit of obedience by the same animal inheritance that gives the mother the habit of command; but we so abuse that faculty that it becomes lost in righteous rebellion or crushed submission. The animal mother never misuses her precious authority. She does not cry, "Wolf! Wolf!" We talk glibly about "the best good of the child," but there are few children who are not clearly aware that they are "minding" for the convenience of "the grown-ups" the greater part of the time. Therefore, they suspect self-interest in even the necessary commands, and might very readily refuse to obey in the hour of danger.

It is a commonplace observation that the best children—i.e., the most   14
submissive and obedient—do not make the best men. If they are utterly subdued, "too good to live," they swell the Sunday-school list of infant saints, die young, and go to heaven: whereas the rebellious and unruly boy often makes the best citizen.

The too obedient child has learned only to do what he is told. If not told,   15
he has no initiative; and, if told wrong, he does wrong. Life to him is not a series of problems to be solved, but a mere book of orders; and, instead of understanding the true imperious "force" of natural law, which a wise man follows because he sees the wisdom of the course, he takes every "must" in life to be like a personal command,—a thing probably unreasonable, and to be evaded, if possible.

The escaped child, long suppressed under obedience, is in no mood for a   16
cheerful acceptance of real laws, but imagines that there is more "fun" in "having his own way." The foolish parent claims to be obeyed as a god; and the grown-up child seeks to evade God, to treat the law of Nature as if she, too, were a foolish parent.

Suppose you are teaching a child arithmetic. You tell him to put down   17
such and such figures in such a position. He inquires, "Why?" You explain the reason. If you do not explain the reason, he does not understand the problem. You might continue to give orders as to what figures to set down in what place; and the child, obeying, could be trotted through the arithmetic in a month's time. But the arithmetic would not have gone through him. He would be not better versed in the science of numbers than a typesetter is in the

learned books he "sets up." We recognize this in the teaching of arithmetic, and go to great lengths in inventing test problems and arranging easy stages by which the child may gradually master his task. But we do not recognize it in teaching the child life. The small acts of infancy are the child's first problems in living. He naturally wishes to understand them. He says, "Why?" To which we reply inanely, "Because I tell you to!" That is no reason. It is a force, no doubt, a pressure, to which the child may be compelled to yield. But he is no wiser than he was before. He has learned nothing except the lesson we imagine so valuable,—to obey. At the very best, he may remember always, in like case, that "mamma would wish me to do so," and do it. But, when cases differ, he has no guide. With the best intentions in life, he can but cast about in his mind to try to imagine what some one else might tell him to do if present: the circumstances themselves mean nothing to him. Docility, subservience, a quick surrender of purpose, a wavering, untrained, easily shaken judgment,—these are the qualities developed by much obedience.

Are they the qualities we wish to develop in American citizens?   ■   18

Questions for Meaning

1. What should be one's goal when raising children?
2. On what grounds does Gilman challenge the value of obedience?
3. What does Gilman mean in paragraph 13 when she writes, "Children have the same automatic habit of obedience by the same animal inheritance that gives the mother the habit of command . . ."? Do you agree with her?
4. Why does Gilman recommend providing children with explanations?
5. Vocabulary: subservience (3), serfs (4), prostrate (8), unwarranted (8), forthcoming (11), caprices (12), glibly (13), docility (17).

Questions about Strategy

1. Where does Gilman anticipate and respond to opposition?
2. Does Gilman make any concessions about the value of obedience?
3. Consider the generalization about college students in paragraph 9. Does it help or injure Gilman's argument?
4. How effective is Gilman's analogy between teaching arithmetic and raising children?
5. Gilman concludes with a rhetorical question. What answer does she expect, and how has she prepared for it?

MARGARET SANGER

THE CAUSE OF WAR

A pioneering advocate of birth control, Margaret Sanger (1883–1966) was one of eleven children. She studied nursing and worked as an obstetrical nurse in the tenements of Manhattan's Lower East Side. She became convinced of the importance of birth control in 1912 when a young woman died in her arms after a self-induced abortion. Sanger went to Europe in 1913 to study contraception, and she is credited with having coined the phrase "birth control." Upon her return to the United States, she founded a magazine, *Woman Rebel,* in which she could publish her views. In 1916, she was jailed for opening a birth control clinic in New York, the first of many times she would be imprisoned for her work. She founded the National Birth Control League in 1917, an organization that eventually became the Planned Parenthood Federation of America. By the time Sanger was elected the first president of the International Planned Parenthood Federation in 1952, her views had come to be widely accepted.

A lecturer and a writer, Sanger published several books. The following essay is drawn from *Woman and the New Race* (1920). Writing at a time when Europe had not yet recovered from the horrors of World War I, Sanger argued that the underlying cause of the war was excessive population growth. Although most historians would argue that the war had multiple causes, you should consider whether Sanger makes a persuasive case.

In every nation of militaristic tendencies we find the reactionaries demanding   1
a higher and still higher birth rate. Their plea is, first, that great armies are needed to *defend* the country from its possible enemies; second, that a huge population is required to assure the country its proper place among the powers of the world. At bottom the two pleas are the same.

As soon as the country becomes overpopulated, these reactionaries pro-   2
claim loudly its moral right to expand. They point to the huge population, which is the name of patriotism they have previously demanded should be brought into being. Again pleading patriotism, they declare that it is the moral right of the nation to take by force such room as it needs. Then comes war—usually against some nation supposed to be less well prepared than the aggressor.

Diplomats make it their business to conceal the facts, and politicians vio-   3
lently denounce the politicians of other countries. There is a long beating of tom-toms by the press and all other agencies for influencing public opinion. Facts are distorted and lies invented until the common people cannot get at the truth. Yet, when the war is over, if not before, we always find that "a place in the sun," "a path to the sea," "a route to India" or something of the sort is at the bottom of the trouble. These are merely other names for expansion.

The "need of expansion" is only another name for overpopulation. One   4
supreme example is sufficient to drive home this truth. That the Great War,

from the horror of which we are just beginning to emerge, had its source in overpopulation is too evident to be denied by any serious student of current history.

For the past one hundred years most of the nations of Europe have been   5
piling up terrific debts to humanity by the encouragement of unlimited numbers. The rulers of these nations and their militarists have constantly called upon the people to breed, breed, breed! Large populations meant more people to produce wealth, more people to pay taxes, more trade for the merchants, more soldiers to protect the wealth. But more people also meant need of greater food supplies, an urgent and natural need for expansion.

As shown by C. V. Drysdale's famous "War Map of Europe," the great   6
conflict began among the high birth rate countries—Germany, with its rate of 31.7, Austria-Hungary with 33.7 and 36.7, respectively, Russia with 45.4, Serbia with 38.6. Italy with her 38.7 came in, as the world is now well informed through the publication of secret treaties by the Soviet government of Russia, upon the promise of territory held by Austria. England, owing to her small home area, is cramped with her comparatively low birth rate of 26.3. France, among the belligerents, is conspicuous for her low birth rate of 19.9, but stood in the way of expansion of high birth rate Germany. Nearly all of the persistently neutral countries—Holland, Denmark, Norway, Sweden and Switzerland have low birth rates, the average being a little over 26.

Owing to the part Germany played in the war, a survey of her birth   7
statistics is decidedly illuminating. The increase in the German birth rate up to 1876 was great. Though it began to decline then, the decline was not sufficient to offset the tremendous increase of the previous years. There were more millions to produce children, so while the average number of births per thousand was somewhat smaller, the net increase in population was still huge. From 41,000,000 in 1871, the year the Empire was founded, the German population grew to approximately 67,000,000 in 1918. Meanwhile her food supply increased only a very small percent. In 1910, Russia had a birth rate even higher than Germany's had ever been—a little less than 48 per thousand. When czarist Russia wanted an outlet to the Mediterranean by way of Constantinople, she was thinking of her increasing population. Germany was thinking of her increasing population when she spoke as with one voice of a "place in the sun." . . .

The militaristic claim for Germany's right to new territory was simply a   8
claim to the right of life and food for the German babies—the same right that a chick claims to burst its shell. If there had not been other millions of people claiming the same right, there would have been no war. But there *were* other millions.

The German rulers and leaders pointed out the fact that expansion meant   9
more business for German merchants, more work for German workmen at better wages, and more opportunities for Germans abroad. They also pointed out that lack of expansion meant crowding and crushing at home, hard times, heavy burdens, lack of opportunity for Germans, and what not. In this way, they gave the people of the Empire a startling and true picture of what would

happen from overcrowding. Once they realized the facts, the majority of Germans naturally welcomed the so-called war of defense.

The argument was sound. Once the German mothers had submitted to   10
the plea for overbreeding, it was inevitable that imperialistic Germany should make war. Once the battalions of unwanted babies came into existence—babies whom the mothers did not want but which they bore as a "patriotic duty"—it was too late to avoid international conflict. The great crime of imperialistic Germany was its high birth rate.

It has always been so. Behind all war has been the pressure of popula-   11
tion. "Historians," says Huxley,* "point to the greed and ambition of rulers, the reckless turbulence of the ruled, to the debasing effects of wealth and luxury, and to the devastating wars which have formed a great part of the occupation of mankind, as the causes of the decay of states and the foundering of old civilizations, and thereby point their story with a moral. But beneath all this superficial turmoil lay the deep-seated impulse given by unlimited multiplication."

Robert Thomas Malthus,† formulator of the doctrine which bears his   12
name, pointed out, in the closing years of the eighteenth century, the relation of overpopulation to war. He showed that mankind tends to increase faster than the food supply. He demonstrated that were it not for the more common diseases, for plague, famine, floods and wars, human beings would crowd each other to such an extent that the misery would be even greater than it now is. These he described as "natural checks," pointing out that as long as no other checks are employed, such disasters are unavoidable. If we do not exercise sufficient judgment to regulate the birth rate, we encounter disease, starvation and war.

Both Darwin and John Stuart Mill recognized, by inference at least, the   13
fact that so-called "natural checks"—and among them war—will operate if some sort of limitation is not employed. In his *Origin of Species,* Darwin says: "There is no exception to the rule that every organic being naturally increases at so high a rate, if not destroyed, that the earth would soon be covered by the progeny of a single pair." Elsewhere he observes that we do not permit helpless human beings to die off, but we create philanthropies and charities, build asylums and hospitals and keep the medical profession busy preserving those who could not otherwise survive. John Stuart Mill, supporting the views of Malthus, speaks to exactly the same effect in regard to the multiplying power of organic beings, among them humanity. In other words, let countries become overpopulated and war is inevitable. It follows as daylight follows the sunrise.

When Charles Bradlaugh and Mrs. Annie Besant were on trial in Eng-   14
land in 1877 for publishing information concerning contraceptives, Mrs. Besant put the case bluntly to the court and the jury:

---

*Thomas Huxley (1825–1895) was an influential English biologist who supported Darwin's theory of evolution but argued that progress could be achieved through scientific control of evolution.

†Best known for *An Essay on the Principles of Population* (1798).

"I have no doubt that if natural checks were allowed to operate right   15
through the human as they do in the animal world, a better result would follow. Among the brutes, the weaker are driven to the wall, the diseased fall out
in the race of life. The old brutes, when feeble or sickly, are killed. If men
insisted that those who were sickly should be allowed to die without help of
medicine or science, if those who are weak were put upon one side and
crushed, if those who were old and useless were killed, if those who were not
capable of providing food for themselves were allowed to starve, if all this were
done, the struggle for existence among men would be as real as it is among
brutes and would doubtless result in the production of a higher race of men.

"But are you willing to do that or to allow it to be done?"   16

We are not willing to let it be done. Mother hearts cling to children, no   17
matter how diseased, misshapen and miserable. Sons and daughters hold fast to
parents, no matter how helpless. We do not allow the weak to depart; neither
do we cease to bring more weak and helpless beings into the world. Among
the dire results is war, which kills off, not the weak and the helpless, but the
strong and the fit.

What shall be done? We have our choice of one of three policies. We may   18
abandon our science and leave the weak and diseased to die, or kill them, as the
brutes do. Or we may go on overpopulating the earth and have our famines
and our wars while the earth exists. Or we can accept the third, sane, sensible,
moral and practicable plan of birth control. We can refuse to bring the weak,
the helpless and the unwanted children into the world. We can refuse to over-
crowd families, nations and the earth. There are these ways to meet the situation, and only these three ways.

The world will never abandon its preventive and curative science; it may   19
be expected to elevate and extend it beyond our present imagination. The efforts to do away with famine and the opposition to war are growing by leaps
and bounds. Upon these efforts are largely based our modern social revolutions.

There remains only the third expedient—birth control, the real cure for   20
war. This fact was called to the attention of the Peace Conference in Paris, in
1919, by the Malthusian League, which adopted the following resolution at its
annual general meeting in London in June of that year:

"The Malthusian League desires to point out that the proposed scheme   21
for the League of Nations has neglected to take account of the important questions of *the pressure of population,* which *causes the great international economic competition* and rivalry, and of the *increase of population,* which is put forward as a
justification for *claiming increase of territory.* It, therefore, wishes to put on
record its belief that the League of Nations will only be able to fulfill its aim
when it adds a clause to the following effect:

"'That each Nation desiring to enter into the League of Nations shall   22
pledge itself *so to restrict its birth rate* that its people shall be able to live in comfort *in their own dominions without need* for territorial expansion, and that it shall
recognize that *increase of population shall not justify* a demand either for increase
of territory or for the compulsion of other Nations to admit its emigrants; so
that when all Nations in the League have shown their ability to live on their

own resources without international rivalry, they will be in a position to fuse into an international federation, and territorial boundaries will then have little significance.'"

As a matter of course, the Peace Conference paid no attention to the reso-   23
lution, for, as pointed out by Frank A. Vanderlip, the American financier, that conference not only ignored the economic factors of the world situation, but seemed unaware that Europe had produced more people than its fields could feed. So the resolution amounted to so much propaganda and nothing more.

This remedy can be applied only by woman and she will apply it. She   24
must and will see past the call of pretended patriotism and of glory of empire and perceive what is true and what is false in these things. She will discover what base uses the militarist and the exploiter made of the idealism of peoples. Under the clamor of the press, permeating the ravings of the jingoes, she will hear the voice of Napoleon, the archetype of the militarists of all nations, calling for "fodder for cannon."

"Woman is given to us that she may bear children," said he. "Woman is   25
our property, we are not hers, because she produced children for us—we do not yield any to her. She is, therefore, our possession as the fruit tree is that of the gardener."

That is what the imperialist is *thinking* when he speaks of the glory of the   26
empire and the prestige of the nation. Every country has its appeal—its shibbo-leth—ready for the lips of the imperialist. German rulers pointed to the com-fort of the workers, to old-age pensions, maternal benefits and minimum wage regulations, and other material benefits, when they wished to inspire soldiers for the Fatherland. England's strongest argument, perhaps, was a certain phase of liberty which she guarantees her subjects, and the protection afforded them wherever they may go. France and the United States, too, have their appeals to the idealism of democracy—appeals which the politicians of both countries know well how to use, though the peoples of both lands are beginning to awake to the fact that their countries have been living on the glories of their revolu-tions and traditions, rather than the substance of freedom. Behind the boast of old-age pensions, material benefits and wage regulations, behind the bombast concerning liberty in this country and tyranny in that, behind all the slogans and shibboleths coined out of the ideals of the peoples for the uses of imperial-ism, woman must and will see the iron hand of that same imperialism, con-demning women to breed and men to die for the will of the rulers.

Upon woman the burden and the horrors of war are heaviest. Her heart   27
is the hardest wrung when the husband or the son comes home to be buried or to live a shattered wreck. Upon her devolve the extra tasks of filling out the ranks of workers in the war industries, in addition to caring for the children and replenishing the war-diminished population. Hers is the crushing weight and the sickening of soul. And it is out of her womb that those things proceed. When she sees what lies behind the glory and the horror, the boasting and the burden, and gets the vision, the human perspective, she will end war. She will kill war by the simple process of starving it to death. For she will refuse longer to produce the human food upon which the monster feeds. ■

Questions for Meaning

1. According to Sanger, what motives have led governments to encourage population growth?
2. From an evolutionary point of view, why is war unacceptable as a "natural check" upon population growth?
3. What are the three policies that Sanger believes nations must inevitably choose among? Are there any alternatives that she overlooks?
4. World War II began less than twenty years after the publication of this essay. Do you know anything about the conditions under which that war began that could be used as evidence to support Sanger's thesis that "militarists" and "reactionaries" favor high birth rates?
5. Vocabulary: belligerents (6), conspicuous (6), turbulence (11), debasing (11), foundering (11), inference (13), base (24), jingoes (24), bombast (26), shibboleth (26).

Questions about Strategy

1. Is Sanger ever guilty of oversimplification? Can you think of any causes of war that have nothing to do with population?
2. How useful are the statistics cited in paragraphs 6 and 7?
3. Of the various quotations that Sanger includes in her essay, which is the most effective?
4. How would you describe the tone of this essay? Is it suitable for the subject?
5. Do you detect any bias in this essay? Does Sanger ever seem to suggest that World War I was caused by one country in particular? Is such an implication historically valid?

ADOLF HITLER

THE PURPOSE OF PROPAGANDA

A frustrated artist, Adolf Hitler (1889–1945) served in the German Army during World War I, and became the leader of the National Socialist Party in 1920, during the turbulent period that followed the German defeat. In 1923, Hitler led a revolt in Munich, for which he subsequently served nine months in prison, using this time to write *Mein Kampf [My Struggle]*. Under his direction, the Nazis gained political influence throughout the 1920s, and, in 1933, Hitler became Chancellor of Germany. Upon the death of President Paul von Hindenburg in 1934, Hitler assumed dictatorial powers and ruled Germany as *Der Führer* [The Leader]. More than any other individual, he is responsible for World War II and the deliberate murder of millions of people during that war.

There are many factors that contributed to Hitler's rise to power, but one of them was the skill with which the Nazis used propaganda. The 1925 publication of *Mein Kampf*, from which the following excerpt is taken, outlined Hitler's views. But at the time, many people did not take them seriously.

Ever since I have been scrutinizing political events, I have taken a tremendous   1
interest in propagandist activity. I saw that the Socialist-Marxist organizations
mastered and applied this instrument with astounding skill. And I soon realized that the correct use of propaganda is a true art which has remained practically unknown to the bourgeois parties. Only the Christian-Social movement,
especially in Lueger's time, achieved a certain virtuosity on this instrument, to
which it owed many of its successes.

But it was not until the War that it became evident what immense results   2
could be obtained by a correct application of propaganda. Here again, unfortunately, all our studying had to be done on the enemy side, for the activity on
our side was modest, to say the least. The total miscarriage of the German
"enlightenment" service stared every soldier in the face, and this spurred me
to take up the question of propaganda even more deeply than before.

There was often more than enough time for thinking, and the enemy   3
offered practical instruction which, to our sorrow, was only too good.

For what we failed to do, the enemy did, with amazing skill and really   4
brilliant calculation. [See illustration on page 581.] I, myself, learned enormously from this enemy war propaganda. But time passed and left no trace in
the minds of all those who should have benefited; partly because they considered themselves too clever to learn from the enemy, partly owing to lack of
good will.

Did we have anything you could call propaganda?   5

I regret that I must answer in the negative. Everything that actually was   6
done in this field was so inadequate and wrong from the very start that it certainly did no good and sometimes did actual harm.

The form was inadequate, the substance was psychologically wrong: a   7
careful examination of German war propaganda can lead to no other diagnosis.

There seems to have been no clarity on the very first question: Is propa-   8
ganda a means or an end?

It is a means and must therefore be judged with regard to its end. It must   9
consequently take a form calculated to support the aim which it serves. It is
also obvious that its aim can vary in importance from the standpoint of general
need, and that the inner value of the propaganda will vary accordingly. The
aim for which we were fighting the War was the loftiest, the most overpower-
ing, that man can conceive: it was the freedom and independence of our nation, the security of our future food supply, and—our national honor; a thing
which, despite all contrary opinions prevailing today, nevertheless exists, or
rather should exist, since peoples without honor have sooner or later lost their
freedom and independence, which in turn is only the result of a higher justice,
since generations of rabble without honor deserve no freedom. Any man who
wants to be a cowardly slave can have no honor, or honor itself would soon fall
into general contempt.

The German nation was engaged in a struggle for a human existence,   10
and the purpose of war propaganda should have been to support this struggle;
its aim to help bring about victory.

When the nations on this planet fight for existence—when the question   11
of destiny, "to be or not to be," cries out for a solution—then all considerations of humanitarianism or aesthetics crumble into nothingness; for all these
concepts do not float about in the ether, they arise from man's imagination
and are bound up with man. When he departs from this world, these concepts
are again dissolved into nothingness, for Nature does not know them. And
even among mankind, they belong only to a few nations or rather races, and
this in proportion as they emanate from the feeling of the nation or race in
question. Humanitarianism and aesthetics would vanish even from a world inhabited by man if this world were to lose the races that have created and upheld these concepts.

But all such concepts become secondary when a nation is fighting for its   12
existence; in fact, they become totally irrelevant to the forms of the struggle as
soon as a situation arises where they might paralyze a struggling nation's power
of self-preservation. And that has always been their only visible result.

As for humanitarianism, Moltke* said years ago that in war it lies in the   13
brevity of the operation, and that means that the most aggressive fighting
technique is the most humane.

But when people try to approach these questions with drivel about aes-   14
thetics, etc., really only one answer is possible: where the destiny and existence
of a people are at stake, all obligation toward beauty ceases. The most unbeau-
tiful thing there can be in human life is and remains the yoke of slavery. Or do

---

*Count Helmuth von Moltke (1848–1916) was a German general who served as chief of staff
during World War I.

these Schwabing decadents* view the present lot of the German people as "aesthetic"? Certainly we don't have to discuss these matters with the Jews, the most modern inventors of this cultural perfume. Their whole existence is an embodied protest against the aesthetics of the Lord's image.

And since these criteria of humanitarianism and beauty must be elimi-   15
nated from the struggle, they are also inapplicable to propaganda.

Propaganda in the War was a means to an end, and the end was the strug-   16
gle for the existence of the German people; consequently, propaganda could
only be considered in accordance with the principles that were valid for this
struggle. In this case the most cruel weapons were humane if they brought
about a quicker victory; and only those methods were beautiful which helped
the nation to safeguard the dignity of its freedom.

This was the only possible attitude toward war propaganda in a life-and-   17
death struggle like ours.

If the so-called responsible authorities had been clear on this point, they   18
would never have fallen into such uncertainty over the form and application of
this weapon: for even propaganda is no more than a weapon, though a fright-
ful one in the hand of an expert.

The second really decisive question was this: To whom should propa-   19
ganda be addressed? To the scientifically trained intelligentsia or to the less
educated masses?

It must be addressed always and exclusively to the masses.   20

What the intelligentsia—or those who today unfortunately often go by   21
that name—what they need is not propaganda but scientific instruction. The
content of propaganda is not science any more than the object represented in a
poster in art. The art of the poster lies in the designer's ability to attract the
attention of the crowd by form and color. A poster advertising an art exhibit
must direct the attention of the public to the art being exhibited; the better it
succeeds in this, the greater is the art of the poster itself. The poster should
give the masses an idea of the significance of the exhibition, it should not be a
substitute for the art on display. Anyone who wants to concern himself with
the art itself must do more than study the poster; and it will not be enough for
him just to saunter through the exhibition. We may expect him to examine
and immerse himself in the individual works, and thus little by little form a fair
opinion.

A similar situation prevails with what we today call propaganda.   22

The function of propaganda does not lie in the scientific training of the   23
individual, but in calling the masses' attention to certain facts, processes, necessities, etc., whose significance is thus for the first time placed within their
field of vision.

The whole art consists in doing this so skillfully that everyone will be   24
convinced that the fact is real, the process necessary, the necessity correct,
etc. But since propaganda is not and cannot be the necessity in itself, since its

*A district in Munich favored by students, writers, and artists.

function, like the poster, consists in attracting the attention of the crowd, and not in educating those who are already educated or who are striving after education and knowledge, its effect for the most part must be aimed at the emotions and only to a very limited degree at the so-called intellect.

All propaganda must be popular and its intellectual level must be adjusted to the most limited intelligence among those it is addressed to. Consequently, the greater the mass it is intended to reach, the lower its purely intellectual level will have to be. But if, as in propaganda for sticking out a war, the aim is to influence a whole people, we must avoid excessive intellectual demands on our public, and too much caution cannot be exerted in this direction.   25

The more modest its intellectual ballast, the more exclusively it takes into consideration the emotions of the masses, the more effective it will be. And this is the best proof of the soundness or unsoundness of a propaganda campaign, and not success in pleasing a few scholars or young aesthetes.   26

The art of propaganda lies in understanding the emotional ideas of the great masses and finding, through a psychologically correct form, the way to the attention and thence to the heart of the broad masses. The fact that our bright boys do not understand this merely shows how mentally lazy and conceited they are.   27

Once we understand how necessary it is for propaganda to be adjusted to the broad mass, the following rule results: 28

It is a mistake to make propaganda many-sided, like scientific instruction, for instance.   29

The receptivity of the great masses is very limited, their intelligence is small, but their power of forgetting is enormous. In consequence of these facts, all effective propaganda must be limited to a very few points and must harp on these in slogans until the last member of the public understands what you want him to understand by your slogan. As soon as you sacrifice this slogan and try to be many-sided, the effect will piddle away, for the crowd can neither digest nor retain the material offered. In this way the result is weakened and in the end entirely cancelled out.   30

Thus we see that propaganda must follow a simple line and correspondingly the basic tactics must be psychologically sound.   31

For instance, it was absolutely wrong to make the enemy ridiculous, as the Austrian and German comic papers did. It was absolutely wrong because actual contact with an enemy soldier was bound to arouse an entirely different conviction, and the results were devastating; for now the German soldier, under the direct impression of the enemy's resistance, felt himself swindled by his propaganda service. His desire to fight, or even to stand firm, was not strengthened, but the opposite occurred. His courage flagged.   32

By contrast, the war propaganda of the English and Americans was psychologically sound. By representing the Germans to their own people as barbarians and Huns, they prepared the individual soldier for the terrors of war, and thus helped to preserve him from disappointments. After this, the most terrible weapon that was used against him seemed only to confirm what his   33 propagandists had told him; it likewise reinforced his faith in the truth of his government's assertions, while on the other hand it increased his rage and hatred against the vile enemy. For the cruel effects of the weapon, whose use by the enemy he now came to know, gradually came to confirm for him the "Hunnish" brutality of the barbarous enemy, which he had heard all about; and it never dawned on him for a moment that his own weapons possibly, if not probably, might be even more terrible in their effects.

And so the English soldier could never feel that he had been misinformed 34 by his own countrymen, as unhappily was so much the case with the German soldier that in the end he rejected everything coming from this source as "swindles" and "bunk." All this resulted from the idea that any old simpleton (or even somebody who was intelligent "in other things") could be assigned to propaganda work, and the failure to realize that the most brilliant psychologists would have been none too good.

And so the German war propaganda offered an unparalleled example of 35 an "enlightenment" service working in reverse, since any correct psychology was totally lacking.

There was no end to what could be learned from the enemy by a man 36 who kept his eyes open, refused to let his perceptions be classified, and for four and a half years privately turned the storm-flood of enemy propaganda over in his brain.

What our authorities least of all understood was the very first axiom of 37 all propagandist activity: to wit, the basically subjective and one-sided attitude it must take toward every question it deals with. In this connection, from the very beginning of the War and from top to bottom, such sins were committed that we were entitled to doubt whether so much absurdity could really be attributed to pure stupidity alone.

What, for example, would we say about a poster that was supposed to 38 advertise a new soap and that described other soaps as "good"?

We would only shake our heads. 39

Exactly the same applies to political advertising. 40

The function of propaganda is, for example, not to weigh and ponder the 41 rights of different people, but exclusively to emphasize the one right which it has set out to argue for. Its task is not to make an objective study of the truth, in so far as it favors the enemy, and then set it before the masses with academic fairness; its task is to serve our own right, always and unflinchingly.

It was absolutely wrong to discuss war-guilt from the standpoint that 42 Germany alone could not be held responsible for the outbreak of the catastrophe; it would have been correct to load every bit of the blame on the shoulders of the enemy, even if this had not really corresponded to the true facts, as it actually did.

And what was the consequence of this half-heartedness? 43

The broad mass of a nation does not consist of diplomats, or even professors of political law, or even individuals capable of forming a rational opinion; it consists of plain mortals, wavering and inclined to doubt and uncertainty. As soon as our own propaganda admits so much as a glimmer of right on the other 44 side, the foundation for doubt in our own right has been laid. The masses are then in no position to distinguish where foreign injustice ends and our own begins. In such a case they become uncertain and suspicious, especially if the enemy refrains from going in for the same nonsense, but unloads every bit of blame on his adversary. Isn't it perfectly understandable that the whole country ends up by lending more credence to enemy propaganda, which is more unified and coherent, than to its own? And particularly a people that suffers from the mania of objectivity as much as the Germans. For, after all this, everyone will take the greatest pains to avoid doing the enemy any injustice, even at the peril of seriously besmirching and even destroying his own people and country.

Of course, this was not the intent of the responsible authorities, but the   45
people never realize that.

The people in their overwhelming majority are so feminine by nature   46
and attitude that sober reasoning determines their thoughts and actions far less
than emotion and feeling.

And this sentiment is not complicated, but very simple and all of a piece.   47
It does not have multiple shadings; it has a positive and a negative; love or hate,
right or wrong, truth or lie, never half this way and half that way, never partially, or that kind of thing.

English propagandists understood all this most brilliantly—and acted ac-   48
cordingly. They made no half statements that might have given rise to doubts.

Their brilliant knowledge of the primitive sentiments of the broad   49
masses is shown by their atrocity propaganda, which was adapted to this condition. As ruthless as it was brilliant, it created the preconditions for moral
steadfastness at the front, even in the face of the greatest actual defeats, and just
as strikingly it pilloried the German enemy as the sole guilty party for the
outbreak of the War: the rabid, impudent bias and persistence with which this
lie was expressed took into account the emotional, always extreme, attitude of
the great masses and for this reason was believed.

How effective this type of propaganda was is most strikingly shown by   50
the fact that after four years of war it not only enabled the enemy to stick to its
guns, but even began to nibble at our own people.

It need not surprise us that our propaganda did not enjoy this success. In   51
its inner ambiguity alone, it bore the germ of ineffectualness. And finally its
content was such that it was very unlikely to make the necessary impression
on the masses. Only our feather-brained "statesmen" could have dared to
hope that this insipid pacifistic bilge could fire men's spirits till they were
willing to die.

As a result, their miserable stuff was useless, even harmful in fact.   52

But the most brilliant propagandist technique will yield no success unless   53
one fundamental principle is borne in mind constantly and with unflagging
attention. It must confine itself to a few points and repeat them over and over.
Here, as so often in this world, persistence is the first and most important requirement for success.

Particularly in the field of propaganda, we must never let ourselves be led   54
by aesthetes or people who have grown blasé: not by the former, because the

form and expression of our propaganda would soon, instead of being suitable for the masses, have drawing power only for literary teas; and of the second we must beware, because, lacking in any fresh emotion of their own, they are always on the lookout for new stimulation. These people are quick to weary of everything; they want variety, and they are never able to feel or understand the needs of their fellow men who are not yet so callous. They are always the first to criticize a propaganda campaign, or rather its content, which seems to them too old-fashioned, too hackneyed, too out-of-date, etc. They are always after novelty, in search of a change, and this makes them mortal enemies of any effective political propaganda. For as soon as the organization and the content of propaganda begin to suit their tastes, it loses all cohesion and evaporates completely.

The purpose of propaganda is not to provide interesting distraction for   55
blasé young gentlemen, but to convince, and what I mean is to convince the masses. But the masses are slow-moving, and they always require a certain time before they are ready even to notice a thing, and only after the simplest ideas are repeated thousands of times will the masses finally remember them.

When there is a change, it must not alter the content of what the propa-   56
ganda is driving at, but in the end must always say the same thing. For instance, a slogan must be presented from different angles, but the end of all remarks must always and immutably be the slogan itself. Only in this way can the propaganda have a unified and complete effect.

This broadness of outline from which we must never depart, in combi-   57
nation with steady, consistent emphasis, allows our final success to mature. And then, to our amazement, we shall see what tremendous results such perseverance leads to—to results that are almost beyond our understanding.

All advertising, whether in the field of business or politics, achieves suc-   58
cess through the continuity and sustained uniformity of its application.

Here, too, the example of enemy war propaganda was typical; limited to   59
a few points, devised exclusively for the masses, carried on with indefatigable persistence. Once the basic ideas and methods of execution were recognized as correct, they were applied throughout the whole War without the slightest change. At first the claims of the propaganda were so impudent that people thought it insane; later, it got on people's nerves; and in the end, it was believed. After four and a half years, a revolution broke out in Germany; and its slogans originated in the enemy's war propaganda.

And in England they understood one more thing: that this spiritual   60
weapon can succeed only if it is applied on a tremendous scale, but that success amply covers all costs.

There, propaganda was regarded as a weapon of the first order, while in   61
our country it was the last resort of unemployed politicians and a comfortable haven for slackers.

And, as was to be expected, its results all in all were zero. ■   62

Questions for Meaning

1. Why did Hitler's interest in propaganda increase after World War I? How important is propaganda in his view?
2. According to Hitler, how did English and American propaganda differ from German propaganda in World War I?
3. Why did Hitler believe that some people do not deserve freedom?
4. How important are truth and aesthetics in propaganda?
5. According to Hitler, what is the key to success in propaganda?
6. How does Hitler characterize the average person?

Questions about Strategy

1. Throughout this argument, Hitler emphasizes that Germany's opponents in World War I used propaganda "with amazing skill and really brilliant calculation." What advantage does he gain from making this point?
2. This argument was first published twenty years before the Allied liberation of Nazi concentration camps. Can you detect any signs of racism within it? Judging from this excerpt, how honest was Hitler in revealing his values before he came to power?
3. In paragraphs 38–40 and 58, Hitler compares propaganda to advertising. Is this a fair comparison? Why is it worth making?
4. Would this argument appeal to the average person? Would it appeal to intellectuals? What sort of audience was most likely to respond favorably to Hitler?

CLARENCE DARROW

THE FUTILITY OF THE DEATH PENALTY

Specializing in labor and political cases, Clarence Darrow (1857–1938) was one of the most famous lawyers in American history. He was especially prominent in the 1920s, a decade that witnessed his two most celebrated cases. In 1925, he was the defense attorney for John T. Scopes, a high school biology teacher who was charged with violating a Tennessee law that prohibited teaching any theory that suggested man may have evolved from a lower species. Although Charles Darwin had published *The Origin of Species* more than a half century earlier, evolution was still regarded as a dangerous doctrine that would undermine the moral authority of the Bible. The Scopes trial attracted worldwide attention as a major test of civil liberties, especially freedom of thought. Darrow lost the case, but his forceful defense of Scopes almost certainly saved teachers in other states from being prosecuted under similar laws.

A year earlier, Darrow had undertaken an even more difficult case when he defended Nathan Leopold and Richard Loeb in a notorious murder case. Although his clients had confessed to an unusually cold-blooded murder and popular feeling demanded that they be executed, Darrow managed to win prison terms for them by arguing persuasively against the death penalty. His objections to capital punishment are best summarized in the following essay, first published in 1928.

1   Little more than a century ago, in England, there were over two hundred offenses that were punishable with death. The death sentence was passed upon children under ten years old. And every time the sentimentalist sought to lessen the number of crimes punishable by death, the self-righteous said no, that it would be the destruction of the state; that it would be better to kill for more transgressions rather than for less.

2   Today, both in England and America, the number of capital offenses has been reduced to a very few, and capital punishment would doubtless be abolished altogether were it not for the self-righteous, who still defend it with the same old arguments. Their major claim is that capital punishment decreases the number of murders, and hence, that the state must retain the institution as its last defense against the criminal.

3   It is my purpose in this article to prove, first, that capital punishment is no deterrent to crime; and second, that the state continues to kill its victims, not so much to defend society against them—for it could do that equally well by imprisonment—but to appease the mob's emotions of hatred and revenge.

4   Behind the idea of capital punishment lie false training and crude views of human conduct. People do evil things, say the judges, lawyers, and preachers, because of depraved hearts. Human conduct is not determined by the causes which determine the conduct of other animal and plant life in the universe. For some mysterious reason human beings act as they please; and if they

do not please to act in a certain way, it is because, having the power of choice, they deliberately choose to act wrongly. The world once applied this doctrine to disease and insanity in men. It was also applied to animals, and even inanimate things were once tried and condemned to destruction. The world knows better now, but the rule has not yet been extended to human beings.

The simple fact is that every person starts life with a certain physical   5
structure, more or less sensitive, stronger or weaker. He is played upon by everything that reaches him from without, and in this he is like everything else in the universe, inorganic matter as well as organic. How a man will act depends upon the character of his human machine, and the strength of the various stimuli that affect it. Everyone knows that this is so in disease and insanity. Most investigators know that it applies to crime. But the great mass of people still sit in judgment, robed with self-righteousness, and determine the fate of their less fortunate fellows. When this question is studied like any other, we shall then know how to get rid of most of the conduct that we call "criminal," just as we are now getting rid of much of the disease that once afflicted mankind.

If crime were really the result of wilful depravity, we should be ready to   6
concede that capital punishment may serve as a deterrent to the criminally inclined. But it is hardly probable that the great majority of people refrain from killing their neighbors because they are afraid; they refrain because they never had the inclination. Human beings are creatures of habit; and, as a rule, they are not in the habit of killing. The circumstances that lead to killings are manifold, but in a particular individual the inducing cause is not easily found. In one case, homicide may have been induced by indigestion in the killer; in another, it may be traceable to some weakness inherited from a remote ancestor; but that it results from *something* tangible and understandable, if all the facts were known, must be plain to everyone who believes in cause and effect.

Of course, no one will be converted to this point of view by statistics of   7
crime. In the first place, it is impossible to obtain reliable ones; and in the second place, the conditions to which they apply are never the same. But if one cares to analyze the figures, such as we have, it is easy to trace the more frequent causes of homicide. The greatest number of killings occur during attempted burglaries and robberies. The robber knows that penalties for burglary do not average more than five years in prison. He also knows that the penalty for murder is death or life imprisonment. Faced with this alternative, what does the burglar do when he is detected and threatened with arrest? He shoots to kill. He deliberately takes the chance of death to save himself from a five-year term in prison. It is therefore as obvious as anything can be that fear of death has no effect in diminishing homicides of this kind, which are more numerous than any other type.

The next largest number of homicides may be classed as "sex murders."   8
Quarrels between husbands and wives, disappointed love, or love too much requited cause many killings. They are the result of primal emotions so deep that the fear of death has not the slightest effect in preventing them. Spontaneous feelings overflow in criminal acts, and consequences do not count.

Then there are cases of sudden anger, uncontrollable rage. The fear of death never enters into such cases; if the anger is strong enough, consequences are not considered until too late. The old-fashioned stories of men deliberately plotting and committing murder in cold blood have little foundation in real life. Such killings are so rare that they need not concern us here. The point to be emphasized is that practically all homicides are manifestations of well-recognized human emotions, and it is perfectly plain that the fear of excessive punishment does not enter into them. 9

In addition to these personal forces which overwhelm weak men and lead them to commit murder, there are also many social and economic forces which must be listed among the causes of homicides, and human beings have even less control over these than over their own emotions. It is often said that in America there are more homicides in proportion to population than in England. This is true. There are likewise more in the United States than in Canada. But such comparisons are meaningless until one takes into consideration the social and economic differences in the countries compared. Then it becomes apparent why the homicide rate in the United States is higher. Canada's population is largely rural; that of the United States is crowded into cities whose slums are the natural breeding places of crime. Moreover, the population of England and Canada is homogeneous, while the United States has gathered together people of every color from every nation in the world. Racial differences intensify social, religious, and industrial problems, and the confusion which attends this indiscriminate mixing of races and nationalities is one of the most fertile sources of crime. 10

Will capital punishment remedy these conditions? Of course it won't; but its advocates argue that the fear of this extreme penalty will hold the victims of adverse conditions in check. To this piece of sophistry the continuance and increase of crime in our large cities is a sufficient answer. No, the plea that capital punishment acts as a deterrent to crime will not stand. The real reason why this barbarous practice persists in a so-called civilized world is that people still hold the primitive belief that the taking of one human life can be atoned for by taking another. It is the age-old obsession with punishment that keeps the official headsman busy plying his trade. 11

And it is precisely upon this point that I would build my case against capital punishment. Even if one grants that the idea of punishment is sound, crime calls for something more—for careful study, for an understanding of causes, for proper remedies. To attempt to abolish crime by killing the criminal is the easy and foolish way out of a serious situation. Unless a remedy deals with the conditions which foster crime, criminals will breed faster than the hangman can spring his trap. Capital punishment ignores the causes of crime just as completely as the primitive witch doctor ignored the causes of disease; and, like the methods of the witch doctor, it is not only ineffective as a remedy, but is positively vicious in at least two ways. In the first place, the spectacle of state executions feeds the basest passions of the mob. And in the second place, so long as the state rests content to deal with crime in this barbaric and 12 futile manner, society will be lulled by a false sense of security, and effective methods of dealing with crime will be discouraged.

It seems to be a general impression that there are fewer homicides in Great   13
Britain than in America because in England punishment is more certain, more prompt, and more severe. As a matter of fact, the reverse is true. In England the average term for burglary is eighteen months; with us it is probably four or five years. In England, imprisonment for life means twenty years. Prison sentences in the United States are harder than in any country in the world that could be classed as civilized. This is true largely because, with us, practically no official dares to act on his own judgment. The mob is all-powerful and demands blood for blood. That intangible body of people called "the public" vents its hatred upon the criminal and enjoys the sensation of having him put to death by the state—this without any definite idea that it is really necessary.

For the last five or six years, in England and Wales, the homicides re-   14
ported by the police range from sixty-five to seventy a year. Death sentences meted out by jurors have averaged about thirty-five, and hangings, fifteen. More than half of those convicted by juries were saved by appeals to the Home Office. But in America there is no such percentage of lives saved after convic-tion. Governors are afraid to grant clemency. If they did, the newspapers and the populace would refuse to re-elect them.

It is true that trials are somewhat prompter in England than America, but   15
there no newspaper dares publish the details of any case until after the trial. In America the accused is often convicted by the public within twenty-four hours of the time a homicide occurs. The courts sidetrack all other business so that a homicide that is widely discussed may receive prompt attention. The road to the gallows is not only opened but greased for the opportunity of killing another victim.

Thus, while capital punishment panders to the passions of the mob, no   16
one takes the pains to understand the meaning of crime. People speak of crime or criminals as if the world were divided into the good and the bad. This is not true. All of us have the same emotions, but since the balance of emotions is never the same, nor the inducing causes identical, human conduct presents a wide range of differences, shading by almost imperceptible degrees from that of the saint to that of the murderer. Of those kinds of conduct which are classed as dangerous, by no means all are made criminal offenses. Who can clearly define the difference between certain legal offenses and many kinds of dangerous conduct not singled out by criminal statute? Why are many cases of cheating entirely omitted from the criminal code, such as false and misleading advertisements, selling watered stock, forestalling the market, and all the dif-ferent ways in which great fortunes are accumulated to the envy and despair of those who would like to have money but do not know how to get it? Why do we kill people for the crime of homicide and administer a lesser penalty for burglary, robbery, and cheating? Can anyone tell which is the greater crime and which is the lesser?

Human conduct is by no means so simple as our moralists have led us to   17
believe. There is no sharp line separating good actions from bad. The greed

for money, the display of wealth, the despair of those who witness the display, the poverty, oppression, and hopelessness of the unfortunate—all these are factors which enter into human conduct and of which the world takes no account. Many people have learned no other profession but robbery and burglary. The processions moving steadily through our prisons to the gallows are in the main made up these unfortunates. And how do we dare to consider ourselves civilized creatures when, ignoring the causes of crime, we rest content to mete out harsh punishments to the victims of conditions over which they have no control?

Even now, are not all imaginative and humane people shocked at the spectacle of a killing by the state? How many men and women would be willing to act as executioners? How many fathers and mothers would want their children to witness an official killing? What kind of people read the sensational reports of an execution? If all right-thinking men and women were not ashamed of it, why would it be needful that judges and lawyers and preachers apologize for the barbarity? How can the state censure the cruelty of the man who—moved by strong passions, or acting to save his freedom, or influenced by weakness or fear—takes human life, when everyone knows that the state itself, after long premeditation and settled hatred, not only kills, but first tortures and bedevils its victims for weeks with the impending doom? 18

For the last hundred years the world has shown a gradual tendency to mitigate punishment. We are slowly learning that this way of controlling human beings is both cruel and ineffective. In England the criminal code has consistently grown more humane, until now the offenses punishable by death are reduced to practically one. There is no doubt whatever that the world is growing more humane and more sensitive and more understanding. The time will come when all people will view with horror the light way in which society and its courts of law now take human life; and when that time comes, the way will be clear to devise some better method of dealing with poverty and ignorance and their frequent byproducts, which we call crime. ■ 19

Questions for Meaning

1. In his opening paragraphs, Darrow claims that capital punishment is supported by "the self-righteous." What kind of people is he referring to? Do you agree with him?
2. Why does Darrow believe that capital punishment does not deter crime? Why does he believe it is still carried out?
3. Darrow argues that "Capital punishment ignores the causes of crime." At what points in his essay does he try to reveal what these causes are?
4. How would you describe Darrow's opinion of human nature?
5. Toward the end of his essay Darrow asks, "Why do we kill people for the crime of homicide and administer a lesser penalty for burglary, robbery, and cheating? Can anyone tell which is the greater crime and which is the lesser?" Can you?

Questions about Strategy

1. For what sort of audience do you think this essay was originally written? Is there any evidence in it that Darrow was not addressing "the great mass of people" or the "mob" to which he refers in paragraphs 5 and 13?
2. In paragraph 9, Darrow argues, "The old-fashioned stories of men deliberately plotting and committing murder in cold blood have little foundation in real life." Consider whether you agree with him. What is his purpose in making this claim?
3. How useful is the comparison between England and the United States?
4. Why does Darrow introduce "fathers," "mothers," and "children" into his second-to-last paragraph?
5. This essay was written more than sixty years ago. Do you think its argument is still valid, or does it seem out of date?

MAHATMA GANDHI

BRAHMACHARYA

The single most important figure in the struggle for Indian independence from British rule, Mohandas Karamchand Gandhi (1869–1948) earned the title "Mahatma," or "Great-Souled" by virtue of an almost saintlike commitment to nonviolence, coupled with a deep belief in the sanctity of all life and an almost complete disregard for his own physical comfort.

Raised in a strict, religious environment, Gandhi traveled to England in 1888 to study law. While there, he met George Bernard Shaw and other British intellectuals concerned with the need for social change. From 1893 to 1914, he lived and worked in South Africa—an experience that had a profound effect on his political development. Shortly after his arrival in South Africa, Gandhi experienced humiliations such as being thrown off of a train because of the color of his skin. After leading the campaign for improving the conditions under which the large Indian population in South Africa lived, Gandhi entered Indian politics in 1919. Throughout the 1920s and 1930s he used nonviolent methods to protest British rule. Gandhi's greatest disappointment was that when independence from Britain was finally secured in 1947, India was partitioned into the separate countries of India and Pakistan (now India, Pakistan, and Bangladesh). When riots broke out that year between Hindus and Moslems, he traveled around the country to bring an end to violence. By fasting in Calcutta in 1947, he managed to end a period of prolonged violence in that city; a subsequent fast in Delhi was also successful. But within a few days of ending the riots in Delhi, Gandhi was shot and killed while on his way to prayer.

Before you read the following selection from 1947, you might note that Gandhi was married at the age of thirteen.

If it is contended that birth control is necessary for the nation because of   1
over-population, I dispute the proposition. It has never been proved. In my
opinion by a proper land system, better agriculture and a supplementary industry, this country is capable of supporting twice as many people as there
are in it to-day.

What, then, is Brahmacharya? It means that men and women should re-   2
frain from carnal knowledge of each other. That is to say, they should not
touch each other with a carnal thought, they should not think of it even in
their dreams. Their mutual glances should be free from all suggestion of car-
nality. The hidden strength that God has given us should be conserved by rigid
self-discipline, and transmitted into energy and power—not merely of body,
but also of mind and soul.

But what is the spectacle that we actually see around us? Men and   3
women, old and young, without exception, are caught in the meshes of sensuality. Blinded for the most part by lust, they lose all sense of right and
wrong. I have myself seen even boys and girls behaving as if they were mad
under its fatal influence. I too have behaved likewise under similar influences, and it could not well be otherwise. For the sake of a momentary pleasure, we sacrifice in an instant all the stock of vital energy that we have
laboriously accumulated. The infatuation over, we find ourselves in a miserable condition. The next morning we feel hopelessly weak and tired, and the
mind refuses to do its work. Then in order to remedy the mischief, we consume large quantities of milk, bhasmas, yakutis and what not. We take all
sorts of "hervine tonics" and place ourselves at the doctor's mercy for repair-
ing the waste, and for recovering the capacity for enjoyment. So the days pass
and years, until at length old age comes upon us, and finds us utterly emasculated in body and in mind.

But the law of Nature is just the reverse of this. The older we grow the   4
keener should our intellect be; the longer we live the greater should be our
capacity to communicate the benefit of our accumulated experience to our
fellow men. And such is indeed the case with those who have been true
Brahmacharis. They know no fear of death, and they do not forget God even
in the hour of death; nor do they indulge in vain desires. They die with a
smile on their lips, and boldly face the day of judgment. They are true men
and women; and of them alone can it be said that they have conserved their
health.

We hardly realize the fact that incontinence is the root cause of most van-   5
ity, anger, fear and jealousy in the world. If our mind is not under our control,
if we behave once or oftener every day more foolishly than even little children,
what sins may we not commit consciously or unconsciously? How can we
pause to think of the consequences of our actions, however vile or sinful they
may be?

But you may ask, 'Who has ever seen a true Brahmachari in this sense?   6
If all men should turn Brahmacharis, would not humanity be extinct and the
whole world go to rack and ruin?' We will leave aside the religious aspect of
this question and discuss it simply from the secular point of view. To my mind,

these questions only betray our timidity and worse. We have not the strength of will to observe Brahmacharya and therefore set about finding pretexts for evading our duty. The race of true Brahmacharis is by no means extinct; but if they were commonly to be met with, of what value would Brahmacharya be? Thousands of hardy labourers have to go and dig deep into the bowels of the earth in search for diamonds, and at length they get perhaps merely a handful of them out of heaps and heaps of rock. How much greater, then, should be the labour involved in the discovery of the infinitely more precious diamond of a Brahmachari? If the observance of Brahmacharya should mean the end of the world, this is none of our business. Are we God that we should be so anxious about its future? He who created it will surely see to its preservation. We need not trouble to inquire whether other people practise Brahmacharya or not. When we enter a trade or profession, do we ever pause to consider what the fate of the world would be if all men were to do likewise? The true Brahmachari will, in the long run, discover for himself answers to such questions.

But how can men engrossed in the cares of the material world put these ideas into practice? What about those who are married? What shall they do who have children? And what shall be done by those people who cannot control themselves? We have already seen what is the highest state for us to attain. We should keep this ideal constantly before us, and try to approach it to the utmost of our capacity. When little children are taught to write the letters of the alphabet, we show them the perfect shapes of the letters, and they try to reproduce them as best they can. In the same way, if we steadily work up to the ideal of Brahmacharya we may ultimately succeed in realizing it. What if we have married already? The law of Nature is that Brahmacharya may be broken only when the husband and wife feel a desire for progeny. Those, who, remembering this law, violate Brahmacharya once in four or five years, will not becomes slaves to lust, nor lose much of their stock of vital energy. But, alas! How rare are those men and women who yield to the sexual craving merely for the sake of offspring! The vast majority turn to sexual enjoyment merely to satisfy their carnal passion, with the result that children are born to them quite against their will. In the madness of sexual passion, they give no thought to the consequences of their acts. In this respect, men are even more to blame than women. The man is blinded so much by his lust that he never cares to remember that his wife is weak and unable to bear or rear up a child. In the West, indeed, people have transgressed all bounds. They indulge in sexual pleasures and devise measures in order to evade the responsibilities of parenthood. Many books have been written on this subject and a regular trade is being carried on in contraceptives. We are as yet free from this sin, but we do not shrink from imposing heavy burden of maternity on our women, and we are not concerned even to find that our children are weak, impotent and imbecile.

We are, in this respect, far worse than even the lower animals; for in their case the male and the female are brought together solely with the object of breeding from them. Men and women should regard it a sacred duty to keep apart from the moment of conception up to the time when the child is weaned. But we go on with our fatal merry-making blissfully forgetful of that sacred obligation. This almost incurable disease enfeebles our mind and leads us to an early grave, after making us drag a miserable existence for a short while. Married people should understand the true function of marriage, and should not violate Brahmacharya except with a view to progeny.

But this is so difficult under present conditions of life. Our diet, our   9
ways of life, our common talk, and our environments are all equally calculated to rouse animal passions; and sensuality is like a poison eating into our vitals. Some people may doubt the possibility of our being able to free ourselves from this bondage. This book is written not for those who go about with such doubting of heart, but only for those who are really in earnest, and who have the courage to take active steps for self-improvement. Those who are quite content with their present abject condition will find this tedious even to read; but I hope it will be of some service to those who have realized and are disgusted with their own miserable plight.

From all that has been said it follows that those who are still unmarried   10
should try to remain so; but if they cannot help marrying, they should defer it as long as possible. Young men, for instance, should take a vow to remain unmarried till the age of twenty-five or thirty. We cannot consider here all the advantages other than physical which they will reap and which are as it were added unto the rest.

My request to those parents who read this chapter is that they should not   11
tie a millstone round the necks of their children by marrying them young. They should look to the welfare of the rising generation, and not merely seek to pamper their own vanity. They should cast aside all silly notions of family pride or respectability, and cease to indulge in such heartless practices. Let them rather, if they are true well-wishers of their children, look to their physical, mental and moral improvement. What greater disservice can they do to their progeny than compel them to enter upon married life, with all its tremendous responsibilities and cares, while they are mere children?

Then again the true laws of health demand that the man who loses his   12
wife, as well as the woman that loses her husband, should remain single ever after. There is a difference of opinion among medical men as to whether young men and women need ever let their vital energy escape, some answering the question in the affirmative, others in the negative. But while doctors thus disagree we must not give way to over–indulgence from an idea that we are supported by medical authority. I can affirm, without the slightest hesitation, from my own experience as well as that of others, that sexual enjoyment is not only not necessary for, but is positively injurious to health. All the strength of body and mind that has taken long to acquire is lost all at once by a single dissipation of the vital energy. It takes a long time to regain this lost vitality, and even then there is no saying that it can be thoroughly recovered. A broken mirror may be mended and made to do its work, but it can never be anything but a broken mirror.

As has already been pointed out, the preservation of our vitality is im–   13
possible without pure air, pure water, pure and wholesome food, as well as pure thoughts. So vital indeed is the relation between health and morals that

we can never be perfectly healthy unless we lead a clean life. The earnest man, who, forgetting the errors of the past, begins to live a life of purity, will be able to reap the fruit of it straightaway. Those who practise true Brahmacharya even for a short period will see how their body and mind improve steadily in strength and power, and they will not at any cost be willing to part with this treasure. I have myself been guilty of lapses even after having fully understood the value of Brahmacharya, and have of course paid dearly for it. I am filled with shame and remorse when I think of the terrible contrast between my condition before and after these lapses. But from the errors of the past I have now learnt to preserve this treasure intact, and I fully hope, with God's grace to continue to preserve it in the future; for I have, in my own person, experienced the inestimable benefits of Brahmacharya. I was married early, and had become the father of children as a mere youth. When at length, I awoke to the reality of my situation, I found that I was steeped in ignorance about the fundamental laws of our being. I shall consider myself amply rewarded for writing this chapter if at least a single reader takes a warning from my failings and experiences, and profits thereby. Many people have told—and I also believe it— that I am full of energy and enthusiasm, and that I am by no means weak in mind; some even accuse me of strength bordering on obstinacy. Nevertheless there is still bodily and mental ill-health as a legacy of the past. And yet when compared with my friends, I may call myself healthy and strong. If even after twenty years of sensual enjoyment, I have been able to reach this state, how much better off should I have been if I had kept myself pure during those twenty years as well? It is my full conviction, that if only I had lived a life of unbroken Brahmacharya all through, my energy and enthusiasm would have been a thousandfold greater and I should have been able to devote them all to the furtherance of my country's cause as my own. If an imperfect Brahmachari like myself can reap such benefit, how much more wonderful must be the gain in power—physical, mental, as well as moral—that unbroken Brahmacharya can bring to us.

When so strict is the law of Brahmacharya what shall we say of those 14 guilty of the unpardonable sin of illegitimate sexual enjoyment? The evil arising from adultery and prostitution is a vital question of religion and morality and cannot be fully dealt with in a treatise on health. Here we are only concerned to point out how thousands who are guilty of these sins are afflicted by venereal diseases. God is merciful in this that the punishment swiftly overtakes sinners. Their short span of life is spent in object bondage to quacks in a futile quest after a remedy for their ills. If adultery and prostitution disappeared, at least half the present number of doctors would find their occupation gone. So inextricably indeed has venereal disease caught mankind in its clutches that thoughtful medical men have been forced to admit, that so long as adultery and prostitution continue, there is no hope for the human race, all the discoveries of curative medicine notwithstanding. The medicines for these diseases are so poisonous that although they may appear to have done some good for the time being, they give rise to other and still more terrible diseases which are transmitted from generation to generation.

No one need therefore despair. My Mahatmaship* is worthless. It is due   15
to my outward activities, due to my politics which is the least part of me and
is therefore evanescent. What is of abiding worth is my insistence on truth,
non-violence and Brahmacharya, which is the real part of me. That permanent
part of me, however small, is not to be despised. It is my all. I prize even the
failures and disillusionments which are but steps towards success.   ■

Questions for Meaning

1. How does Gandhi define *Brahmacharya?*
2. According to Gandhi, what are the advantages of abstaining from sex?
3. What advice does Gandhi offer on the subject of marriage?
4. Does Gandhi believe that men and women experience sexual desire to
    the same degree?
5. In his conclusion, Gandhi predicts the rise of "other and still more terri-
    ble diseases" unless prostitution and adultery are eliminated. Has his-
    tory proved him right?
6. Vocabulary: carnal (2), emasculated (3), incontinence (5), impotent (7),
    progeny (8), evanescent (15).

Questions about Strategy

1. Why do you think Gandhi begins his case by dismissing an argument
    that he could have used when arguing on behalf of celibacy?
2. Where does Gandhi admit to having experienced sexual activity? What
    does he gain from making this admission?
3. How does Gandhi respond to opponents who might argue that there
    would be no future for humanity if everyone practiced Brahmacharya?
4. Does Gandhi make any claims that leave him open to counterargument?
5. In paragraph 7, Gandhi contrasts behavior in his own culture with
    behavior in Western Culture. Is his point useful for the purpose of this
    argument?
6. Why does Gandhi direct part of his argument to parents?

*Mahatma is a Hindu term of respect for a man known for being high-minded and spiritual.

RACHEL CARSON

THE OBLIGATION TO ENDURE

If the environmental movement during the past quarter century can be traced to any single work, it is probably *Silent Spring* (1962) Rachel Carson's widely read analysis of how pesticides and other chemicals were polluting the earth and endangering wildlife. An aquatic biologist for the U.S. Bureau of Fisheries, Carson (1907–1966) became editor in chief of the publications of the U.S. Fish and Wildlife Service. "The Obligation to Endure" is the second chapter of *Silent Spring.* Carson's other works include *The Sea Around Us* (1951) and *The Edge of the Sea* (1955).

The history of life on earth has been a history of interaction between living   1
things and their surroundings. To a large extent, the physical form and the habits of the earth's vegetation and its animal life have been molded by the environment. Considering the whole span of earthly time, the opposite effect, in which life actually modifies its surroundings, has been relatively slight. Only within the moment of time represented by the present century has one species—man—acquired significant power to alter the nature of his world.

During the past quarter century this power has not only increased to one   2
of disturbing magnitude but it has changed in character. The most alarming of all man's assaults upon the environment is the contamination of air, earth, rivers, and sea with dangerous and even lethal materials. This pollution is for the most part irrecoverable; the chain of evil it initiates not only in the world that must support life but in living tissues is for the most part irreversible. In this now universal contamination of the environment, chemicals are the sinister and little-recognized partners of radiation in changing the very nature of the world—the very nature of its life. Strontium 90, released through nuclear explosions into the air, comes to earth in rain or drifts down as fallout, lodges in soil, enters into the grass or corn or wheat grown there, and in time takes up its abode in the bones of a human being, there to remain until his death. Similarly, chemicals sprayed on croplands or forests or gardens lie long in soil, entering into living organisms, passing from one to another in a chain of poisoning and death. Or they pass mysteriously by underground streams until they emerge and, through the alchemy of air and sunlight, combine into new forms that kill vegetation, sicken cattle, and work unknown harm on those who drink from once pure wells. As Albert Schweitzer has said, "Man can hardly even recognize the devils of his own creation."

It took hundreds of millions of years to produce the life that now in-   3
habits the earth—eons of time in which that developing and evolving and diversifying life reached a state of adjustment and balance with its surroundings. The environment, rigorously shaping and directing the life it supported, contained elements that were hostile as well as supporting. Certain rocks gave out dangerous radiation; even within the light of the sun, from which all life draws its energy, there were short-wave radiations with power to

injure. Given time—time not in years but in millennia—life adjusts, and a balance has been reached. For time is the essential ingredient; but in the modern world there is no time.

The rapidity of change and the speed with which new situations are cre-   4
ated follow the impetuous and heedless pace of man rather than the deliberate pace of nature. Radiation is no longer merely the background radiation of rocks, the bombardment of cosmic rays, the ultraviolet of the sun that have existed before there was any life on earth; radiation is now the unnatural creation of man's tampering with the atom. The chemicals to which life is asked to make its adjustment are no longer merely the calcium and silica and copper and all the rest of the minerals washed out of the rocks and carried in rivers to the sea; they are the synthetic creations of man's inventive mind, brewed in his laboratories, and having no counterparts in nature.

To adjust to these chemicals would require time on the scale that is na-   5
ture's; it would require not merely the years of a man's life but the life of generations. And even this, were it by some miracle possible, would be futile, for the new chemicals come from our laboratories in an endless stream; almost five hundred annually find their way into actual use in the United States alone. The figure is staggering and its implications are not easily grasped—500 new chemicals to which the bodies of men and animals are required somehow to adapt each year, chemicals totally outside the limits of biologic experience.

Among them are many that are used in man's war against nature. Since   6
the mid-1940's over 200 basic chemicals have been created for use in killing insects, weeds, rodents, and other organisms described in the modern vernacular as "pests"; and they are sold under several thousand different brand names.

These sprays, dusts, and aerosols are now applied almost universally to   7
farms, gardens, forests, and homes—nonselective chemicals that have the power to kill every insect, the "good" and the "bad" to still the song of birds and the leaping of fish in the streams, to coat the leaves with a deadly film, and to linger on in soil—all this though the intended target may be only a few weeds or insects. Can anyone believe it is possible to lay down such a barrage of poisons on the surface of the earth without making it unfit for all life? They should not be called "insecticides," but "biocides."

The whole process of spraying seems caught up in an endless spiral. Since   8
DDT was released for civilian use, a process of escalation has been going on in which ever more toxic materials must be found. This has happened because insects, in a triumphant vindication of Darwin's principle of the survival of the fittest, have evolved super races immune to the particular insecticide used, hence a deadlier one has always to be developed—and then a deadlier one than that. It has happened also because, for reasons to be described later, destructive insects often undergo a "flareback," or resurgence, after spraying, in numbers greater than before. Thus the chemical war is never won, and all life is caught in its violent crossfire.

Along with the possibility of the extinction of mankind by nuclear war,   9
the central problem of our age has therefore become the contamination of man's total environment with such substances of incredible potential for

harm—substances that accumulate in the tissues of plants and animals and even penetrate the germ cells to shatter or alter the very material of heredity upon which the shape of the future depends.

Some would-be architects of our future look toward a time when it will   10 be possible to alter the human germ plasm by design. But we may easily be doing so now by inadvertence, for many chemicals, like radiation, bring about gene mutations. It is ironic to think that man might determine his own future by something so seemingly trivial as the choice of an insect spray.

All this has been risked—for what? Future historians may well be amazed   11 by our distorted sense of proportion. How could intelligent beings seek to control a few unwanted species by a method that contaminated the entire environment and brought the threat of disease and death even to their own kind? Yet this is precisely what we have done. We have done it, moreover, for reasons that collapse the moment we examine them. We are told that the enormous and expanding use of pesticides is necessary to maintain farm production. Yet is our real problem not one of *overproduction?* Our farms, despite measures to remove acreages from production and to pay farmers *not* to produce, have yielded such a staggering excess of crops that the American taxpayer in 1962 is paying out more than one billion dollars a year as the total carrying cost of the surplus-food storage program. And is the situation helped when one branch of the Agriculture Department tries to reduce production while another states, as it did in 1958, "It is believed generally that reduction of crop acreages under provisions of the Soil Bank will stimulate interest in use of chemicals to obtain maximum production on the land retained in crops."

All this is not to say there is no insect problem and no need of control. I   12 am saying, rather, that control must be geared to realities, not to mythical situations, and that the methods employed must be such that they do not destroy us along with the insects.

The problem whose attempted solution has brought such a train of disas-   13 ter in its wake is an accompaniment of our modern way of life. Long before the age of man, insects inhabited the earth—a group of extraordinarily varied and adaptable beings. Over the course of time since man's advent, a small percentage of the more than half a million species of insects have come into conflict with human welfare in two principal ways: as competitors for the food supply and as carriers of human disease.

Disease-carrying insects become important where human beings are   14 crowded together, especially under conditions where sanitation is poor, as in time of natural disaster or war or in situations of extreme poverty and deprivation. Then control of some sort becomes necessary. It is a sobering fact, however, as we shall presently see, that the method of massive chemical control has had only limited success, and also threatens to worsen the very conditions it is intended to curb.

Under primitive agricultural conditions the farmer had few insect prob-   15 lems. These arose with the intensification of agriculture—the devotion of immense acreages to a single crop. Such a system set the stage for explosive increases in specific insect populations. Single-crop farming does not take advantage of the principles by which nature works; it is agriculture as an engineer might conceive it to be. Nature has introduced great variety into the landscape, but man has displayed a passion for simplifying it. Thus he undoes the built-in checks and balances by which nature holds the species within bounds. One important natural check is a limit on the amount of suitable habitat for each species. Obviously then, an insect that lives on wheat can build up its population to much higher levels on a farm devoted to wheat than on one in which wheat is intermingled with other crops to which the insect is not adapted.

The same thing happens in other situations. A generation or more ago,   16 the towns of large areas of the United States lined their streets with the noble elm tree. Now the beauty they hopefully created is threatened with complete destruction as disease sweeps through the elms, carried by a beetle that would have only limited chance to build up large populations and to spread from tree to tree if the elms were only occasional trees in a richly diversified planting.

Another factor in the modern insect problem is one that must be viewed   17 against a background of geologic and human history: the spreading of thousands of different kinds of organisms from their native homes to invade new territories. This worldwide migration has been studied and graphically described by the British ecologist Charles Elton in his recent book *The Ecology of Invasions*. During the Cretaceous Period, some hundred million years ago, flooding seas cut many land bridges between continents and living things found themselves confined in what Elton calls "colossal separate nature reserves." There, isolated from others of their kind, they developed many new species. When some of the land masses were joined again, about 15 million years ago, these species began to move out into new territories—a movement that is not only still in progress but is now receiving considerable assistance from man.

The importation of plants is the primary agent in the modern spread of   18 species, for animals have almost invariably gone along with the plants, quarantine being a comparatively recent and not completely effective innovation. The United States Office of Plant Introduction alone has introduced almost 200,000 species and varieties of plants from all over the world. Nearly half of the 180 or so major insect enemies of plants in the United States are accidental imports from abroad, and most of them have come as hitchhikers on plants.

In new territory, out of reach of the restraining hand of the natural ene-   19 mies that kept down its numbers in its native land, an invading plant or animal is able to become enormously abundant. Thus it is no accident that our most troublesome insects are introduced species.

These invasions, both the naturally occurring and those dependent on   20 human assistance, are likely to continue indefinitely. Quarantine and massive chemical campaigns are only extremely expensive ways of buying time. We are faced, according to Dr. Elton, "with a life-and-death need not just to find new technological means of suppressing this plant or that animal"; instead we need the basic knowledge of animal populations and their relations to their surroundings that will "promote an even balance and damp down the explosive power of outbreaks and new invasions."

Much of the necessary knowledge is now available but we do not use it.   21
We train ecologists in our universities and even employ them in our governmental agencies but we seldom take their advice. We allow the chemical death
rain to fall as though there were no alternatives, whereas in fact there are
many, and our ingenuity could soon discover many more if given opportunity.

Have we fallen into a mesmerized state that makes us accept as inevitable   22
that which is inferior or detrimental, as though having lost the will or the vision to demand that which is good? Such thinking, in the words of the ecologist Paul Shepard, "idealizes life with only its head out of water, inches above
the limits of toleration of the corruption of its own environment. . . . Why
should we tolerate a diet of weak poisons, a home in insipid surroundings, a
circle of acquaintances who are not quite our enemies, the noise of motors with
just enough relief to prevent insanity? Who would want to live in a world
which is just not quite fatal?"

Yet such a world is pressed upon us. The crusade to create a chemically   23
sterile, insect-free world seems to have engendered a fanatic zeal on the part of
many specialists and most of the so-called control agencies. On every hand
there is evidence that those engaged in spraying operations exercise a ruthless
power. "The regulatory entomologists . . . function as prosecutor, judge
and jury, tax assessor and collector and sheriff to enforce their own orders,"
said Connecticut entomologist Neely Turner. The most flagrant abuses go
unchecked in both state and federal agencies.

It is not my contention that chemical insecticides must never be used. I   24
do contend that we have put poisonous and biologically potent chemicals indiscriminately into the hands of persons largely or wholly ignorant of their poten-
tials for harm. We have subjected enormous numbers of people to contact with
these poisons, without their consent and often without their knowledge. If the
Bill of Rights contains no guarantee that a citizen shall be secure against lethal
poisons distributed either by private individuals or by public officials, it is
surely only because our forefathers, despite their considerable wisdom and
foresight, could conceive of no such problem.

I contend, furthermore, that we have allowed these chemicals to be used   25
with little or no advance investigation of their effect on soil, water, wildlife,
and man himself. Future generations are unlikely to condone our lack of prudent concern for the integrity of the natural world that supports all life.

There is still very limited awareness of the nature of the threat. This is an   26
era of specialists, each of whom sees his own problem and is unaware of or intolerant of the larger frame into which it fits. It is also an era dominated by
industry, in which the right to make a dollar at whatever cost is seldom challenged. When the public protests, confronted with some obvious evidence of
damaging results of pesticide applications, it is fed little tranquilizing pills of
half truth. We urgently need an end to these false assurances, to the sugar coat-
ing of unpalatable facts. It is the public that is being asked to assume the risks
that the insect controllers calculate. The public must decide whether it wishes
to continue on the present road, and it can do so only when in full possession of
the facts. In the words of Jean Rostand, "The obligation to endure gives us the
right to know." ■

Questions for Meaning

1. What is the relationship between living things and their surroundings?
2. Why is Carson concerned about time? What does she mean when she writes, "time is the essential ingredient; but in the modern world there is no time"?
3. Consider the distinction in paragraph 7 between "insecticides" and "biocides." What is the difference?
4. Why does Carson believe that the widespread use of insecticides has become "an endless spiral"?
5. According to Carson, how have different species of insects spread in modern times?
6. Vocabulary: magnitude (2), eons (3), millennia (3), futile (5), vernacular (6), advent (13), mesmerized (22), insipid (22), entomologists (23), unpalatable (26).

Questions about Strategy

1. In paragraph 2, Carson writes that the contamination of our environment "is for the most part irrecoverable." Does this statement encourage you to read further or does it make you lose interest?
2. Why does Carson call attention to the Department of Agriculture?
3. Does Carson ever recognize a need for insect control?
4. Does Carson offer any alternative to insecticides?
5. Consider paragraph 25. What does Carson accomplish by directing attention to the future?

MARTIN LUTHER KING, JR.

LETTER FROM BIRMINGHAM JAIL

Martin Luther King, Jr. (1929–1968) was the most important leader of the movement to secure civil rights for black Americans during the mid-twentieth century. Ordained a Baptist minister in his father's church in Atlanta, King went on to receive a PhD from Boston University in 1955. Two years later, he became the founder and director of the Southern Christian Leadership Conference, an organization he continued to lead until his assassination in 1968. He first came to national attention by organizing a boycott of the buses in Montgomery, Alabama (1955–1956)—a campaign that he recounts in *Stride Toward Freedom: The Montgomery Story* (1958). His other books include *The Measure of a Man* (1959), *Why We Can't Wait* (1963), and *Where Do We Go from Here: Chaos or Community?* (1967). An advocate of nonviolence, King was jailed fourteen times in the course of his work for civil rights. His efforts helped secure the passage of the Civil Rights Bill in 1963, and, during the last years of his life, he was the recipient of many awards, most notably the Nobel Peace Prize in 1964.

"Letter from Birmingham Jail" was written in 1963, when King was jailed for eight days as the result of his campaign against segregation in Birmingham, Alabama. In it, King responds to white clergymen who had criticized his work and blamed him for breaking the law. But "Letter from Birmingham Jail" is much more than a rebuttal of criticism. It is a well-reasoned and carefully argued defense of civil disobedience as a means of securing civil liberties.

April 16, 1963

My Dear Fellow Clergymen:

While confined here in the Birmingham city jail, I came across your recent statement calling my present activities "unwise and untimely." Seldom do I pause to answer criticism of my work and ideas. If I sought to answer all the criticisms that cross my desk, my secretaries would have little time for anything other than such correspondence in the course of the day, and I would have no time for constructive work. But since I feel that you are men of genuine good will and that your criticisms are sincerely put forth, I want to try to answer your statement in what I hope will be patient and reasonable terms. 1

I think I should indicate why I am here in Birmingham, since you have been influenced by the view which argues against "outsiders coming in." I have the honor of serving as president of the Southern Christian Leadership Conference, an organization operating in every southern state, with headquarters in Atlanta, Georgia. We have some eighty-five affiliated organizations across the South, and one of them is the Alabama Christian Movement for Human Rights. Frequently we share staff, educational, and financial resources with our affiliates. Several months ago the affiliate here in Birmingham asked us to be on call to engage in a nonviolent direct–action program if such were deemed necessary. We readily consented, and when the hour came we lived up 2 to our promise. So I, along with several members of my staff, am here because I was invited here. I am here because I have organizational ties here.

But more basically, I am in Birmingham because injustice is here. Just as the prophets of the eighth century B.C. left their villages and carried their "thus saith the Lord" far beyond the boundaries of their home towns, and just as the Apostle Paul left his village of Tarsus and carried the gospel of Jesus Christ to the far corners of the Greco-Roman world, so am I compelled to carry the gospel of freedom beyond my own home town. Like Paul, I must constantly respond to the Macedonian call for aid.   3

Moreover, I am cognizant of the interrelatedness of all communities and states. I cannot sit idly by in Atlanta and not be concerned about what happens in Birmingham. Injustice anywhere is a threat to justice everywhere. We are caught in an inescapable network of mutuality, tied in a single garment of destiny. Whatever affects one directly, affects all indirectly. Never again can we afford to live with the narrow, provincial, "outside agitator" idea. Anyone who lives inside the United States can never be considered an outsider anywhere within its bounds.   4

You deplore the demonstrations taking place in Birmingham. But your statement, I am sorry to say, fails to express a similar concern for the conditions that brought about the demonstrations. I am sure that none of you would want to rest content with the superficial kind of social analysis that deals merely with effects and does not grapple with underlying causes. It is unfortunate that demonstrations are taking place in Birmingham, but it is even more unfortunate that the city's white power structure left the Negro community with no alternative.   5

In any nonviolent campaign there are four basic steps: collection of the facts to determine whether injustices exist; negotiation; self-purification; and direct action. We have gone through all these steps in Birmingham. There can be no gainsaying the fact that racial injustice engulfs this community. Birmingham is probably the most thoroughly segregated city in the United States. Its ugly record of brutality is widely known. Negroes have experienced grossly unjust treatment in courts. There have been more unsolved bombings of Negro homes and churches in Birmingham than in any other city in the nation. These are the hard, brutal facts of the case. On the basis of these conditions, Negro leaders sought to negotiate with the city fathers. But the latter consistently refused to engage in good-faith negotiation.   6

Then, last September, came the opportunity to talk with leaders of Birmingham's economic community. In the course of the negotiations, certain promises were made by the merchants—for example, to remove the stores' humiliating racial signs. On the basis of these promises, the Reverend Fred Shuttlesworth and the leaders of the Alabama Christian Movement for Human Rights agreed to a moratorium on all demonstrations. As the weeks and months went by, we realized that we were the victims of a broken promise. A few signs, briefly removed, returned; the others remained.   7

As in so many past experiences, our hopes had been blasted, and the shadow of deep disappointment settled upon us. We had no alternative except   8 to prepare for direct action, whereby we would present our very bodies as means of laying our case before the conscience of the local and the national community. Mindful of the difficulties involved, we decided to undertake a process of self-purification. We began a series of workshops on nonviolence, and we repeatedly asked ourselves: "Are you able to accept blows without retaliating?" "Are you able to endure the ordeal of jail?" We decided to schedule our direct-action program for the Easter season, realizing that except for Christmas, this is the main shopping period of the year. Knowing that a strong economic-withdrawal program would be the by-product of direct action, we felt that this would be the best time to bring pressure to bear on the merchants for the needed change.

Then it occurred to us that Birmingham's mayoral election was coming up in March, and we speedily decided to postpone action until after election day. When we discovered that the Commissioner of Public Safety, Eugene "Bull" Connor, had piled up enough votes to be in the run-off, we decided again to postpone action until the day after the run-off so that the demonstrations could not be used to cloud the issues. Like many others, we waited to see Mr. Connor defeated, and to this end we endured postponement after postponement. Having aided in this community need, we felt that our direct-action program could be delayed no longer. 9

You may well ask, "Why direct action? Why sit-ins, marches, and so forth? Isn't negotiation a better path?" You are quite right in calling for negotiation. Indeed, this is the very purpose of direct action. Nonviolent direct action seeks to create such a crisis and foster such a tension that a community which has constantly refused to negotiate is forced to confront the issue. It seeks so to dramatize the issue that it can no longer be ignored. My citing the creation of tension as part of the work of the nonviolent-resister may sound rather shocking. But I must confess that I am not afraid of the word "tension." I have earnestly opposed violent tension, but there is a type of constructive, nonviolent tension which is necessary for growth. Just as Socrates felt that it was necessary to create a tension in the mind so that individuals could rise from the bondage of myths and half-truths to the unfettered realm of creative analysis and objective appraisal, so must we see the need for nonviolent gadflies to create the kind of tension in society that will help men rise from the dark depths of prejudice and racism to the majestic heights of understanding and brotherhood. 10

The purpose of our direct-action program is to create a situation so crisis-packed that it will inevitably open the door to negotiation. I therefore concur with you in your call for negotiation. Too long has our beloved Southland been bogged down in a tragic effort to live in monologue rather than dialogue. 11

One of the basic points in your statement is that the action that I and my associates have taken in Birmingham is untimely. Some have asked: "Why didn't you give the new city administration time to act?" The only answer that I can give to this query is that the new Birmingham administration must be prodded about as much as the outgoing one, before it will act. We are sadly 12 mistaken if we feel that the election of Albert Boutwell as mayor will bring the millennium to Birmingham. While Mr. Boutwell is a much more gentle person than Mr. Connor, they are both segregationists, dedicated to maintenance of the status quo. I have hoped that Mr. Boutwell will be reasonable enough to see the futility of massive resistance to desegregation. But he will not see this without pressure from devotees of civil rights. My friends, I must say to you that we have not made a single gain in civil rights without determined legal and nonviolent pressure. Lamentably, it is an historical fact that privileged groups seldom give up their privileges voluntarily. Individuals may see the moral light and voluntarily give up their unjust posture; but, as Reinhold Niebuhr has reminded us, groups tend to be more immoral than individuals.

We know through painful experience that freedom is never voluntarily   13
given by the oppressor; it must be demanded by the oppressed. Frankly, I have yet to engage in a direct-action campaign that was "well timed" in the view of those who have not suffered unduly from the disease of segregation. For years now I have heard the word "Wait!" It rings in the ear of every Negro with piercing familiarity. This "Wait" has almost always meant "Never." We must come to see, with one of our distinguished jurists, that "justice too long delayed is justice denied."

We have waited for more than 340 years for our constitutional and God-   14
given rights. The nations of Asia and Africa are moving with jetlike speed toward gaining political independence, but we still creep at horse-and-buggy pace toward gaining a cup of coffee at a lunch counter. Perhaps it is easy for those who have never felt the stinging darts of segregation to say, "Wait." But when you have seen vicious mobs lynch your mothers and fathers at will and drown your sisters and brothers at whim; when you have seen hate-filled policemen curse, kick, and even kill your black brothers and sisters; when you see the vast majority of your twenty million Negro brothers smothering in an airtight cage of poverty in the midst of an affluent society; when you suddenly find your tongue twisted and your speech stammering as you seek to explain to your six-year-old daughter why she can't go to the public amusement park that has just been advertised on television, and see tears welling up in her eyes when she is told that Funtown is closed to colored children, and see ominous clouds of inferiority beginning to form in her little mental sky, and see her beginning to distort her personality by developing an unconscious bitterness toward white people; when you have to concoct an answer for a five-year-old son who is asking, "Daddy, why do white people treat colored people so mean?"; when you take a cross-country drive and find it necessary to sleep night after night in the uncomfortable corners of your automobile because no motel will accept you; when you are humiliated day in and day out by nagging signs reading "white" and "colored"; when your first name becomes "nigger," your middle name becomes "boy" (however old you are) and your last name becomes "John," and your wife and mother are never given the respected title "Mrs."; when you are harried by day and haunted by night by the fact that you are a Negro, living constantly at tiptoe stance, never quite knowing what to expect next, and are plagued with inner fears and outer resentments; when you

are forever fighting a degenerating sense of "nobodiness"—then you will understand why we find it difficult to wait. There comes a time when the cup of endurance runs over, and men are no longer willing to be plunged into the abyss of despair. I hope, sirs, you can understand our legitimate and unavoidable impatience.

You express a great deal of anxiety over our willingness to break laws.   15
This is certainly a legitimate concern. Since we so diligently urge people to obey the Supreme Court's decision of 1954 outlawing segregation in the public schools, at first glance it may seem rather paradoxical for us consciously to break laws. One may well ask: "How can you advocate breaking some laws and obeying others?" The answer lies in the fact that there are two types of laws; just and unjust. I would be the first to advocate obeying just laws. One has not only a legal but a moral responsibility to obey just laws. Conversely, one has a moral responsibility to disobey unjust laws. I would agree with St. Augustine that "an unjust law is no law at all."

Now, what is the difference between the two? How does one determine   16
whether a law is just or unjust? A just law is a man-made code that squares with the moral law or the law of God. An unjust law is a code that is out of harmony with the moral law. To put it in the terms of St. Thomas Aquinas: An unjust law is a human law that is not rooted in eternal law and natural law. Any law that uplifts human personality is just. Any law that degrades human personality is unjust. All segregation statutes are unjust because segregation distorts the soul and damages the personality. It gives the segregator a false sense of superiority and the segregated a false sense of inferiority. Segregation, to use the terminology of the Jewish philosopher Martin Buber, substitutes an "I-it" relationship for an "I-thou" relationship and ends up relegating persons to the status of things. Hence segregation is not only politically, economically, and sociologically unsound, it is morally wrong and sinful. Paul Tillich has said that sin is segregation. Is not segregation an existential expression of man's tragic separation, his awful estrangement, his terrible sinfulness? Thus it is that I can urge men to obey the 1954 decision of the Supreme Court, for it is morally right; and I can urge them to disobey segregation ordinances, for they are morally wrong.

Let us consider a more concrete example of just and unjust laws. An un-   17
just law is a code that a numerical or power majority group compels a minority group to obey but does not make binding on itself. This is *difference* made legal. By the same token, a just law is a code that a majority compels a minority to follow and that it is willing to follow itself. This is *sameness* made legal.

Let me give another explanation. A law is unjust if it is inflicted on a   18
minority that, as a result of being denied the right to vote, had no part in enacting or devising the law. Who can say that the legislature of Alabama which set up that state's segregation laws was democratically elected? Throughout Alabama all sorts of devious methods are used to prevent Negroes from becoming registered voters, and there are some counties in which, even though Negroes constitute a majority of the population, not a single

Negro is registered. Can any law enacted under such circumstances be considered democratically structured?

Sometimes a law is just on its face and unjust in its application. For instance, I have been arrested on a charge of parading without a permit. Now, there is nothing wrong in having an ordinance which requires a permit for a parade. But such an ordinance becomes unjust when it is used to maintain segregation and to deny citizens the First-Amendment privilege of peaceful assembly and protest.   19

I hope you are able to see the distinction I am trying to point out. In no sense do I advocate evading or defying the law, as would the rabid segregationist. That would lead to anarchy. One who breaks an unjust law must do so openly, lovingly, and with a willingness to accept the penalty. I submit that an individual who breaks a law that conscience tells him is unjust, and who willingly accepts the penalty of imprisonment in order to arouse the conscience of the community over its injustice, is in reality expressing the highest respect for law.   20

Of course, there is nothing new about this kind of civil disobedience. It was evidenced sublimely in the refusal of Shadrach, Meshach, and Abednego to obey the laws of Nebuchadnezzar,* on the ground that a higher moral law was at stake. It was practiced superbly by the early Christians, who were willing to face hungry lions and the excruciating pain of chopping blocks rather than submit to certain unjust laws of the Roman Empire. To a degree, academic freedom is a reality today because Socrates practiced civil disobedience. In our own nation, the Boston Tea Party represented a massive act of civil disobedience.   21

We should never forget that everything Adolf Hitler did in Germany was "legal" and everything the Hungarian freedom fighters did in Hungary was "illegal."† It was "illegal" to aid and comfort a Jew in Hitler's Germany. Even so, I am sure that, had I lived in Germany at the time, I would have aided and comforted my Jewish brothers. If today I lived in a Communist country where certain principles dear to the Christian faith are suppressed, I would openly advocate disobeying that country's anti-religious laws.   22

I must make two honest confessions to you, my Christian and Jewish brothers. First, I must confess that over the past few years I have been gravely disappointed with the white moderate. I have almost reached the regrettable conclusion that the Negro's great stumbling block in his stride toward freedom is not the White Citizen's Counciler or the Ku Klux Klanner, but the white moderate, who is more devoted to "order" than to justice; who prefers   23

---

*Nebuchadnezzar, King of Babylon, destroyed the temple at Jerusalem and brought the Jewish people into captivity. He set up a huge image in gold and commanded all to worship it. Shadrach, Meshach, and Abednego refused and were thrown into a fiery furnace from which they emerged unscathed. (See Daniel:3.)

†In 1956, Hungarian patriots temporarily overthrew the communist dictatorship in their country. Unwilling to confront the Soviet Union, western democracies stood by when the Red Army suppressed the revolt.

a negative peace which is the absence of tension to a positive peace which is the presence of justice; who constantly says, "I agree with you in the goal you seek, but I cannot agree with your methods of direct action"; who paternalistically believes he can set the timetable for another man's freedom; who lives by a mythical concept of time and who constantly advises the Negro to wait for a "more convenient season." Shallow understanding from people of good will is more frustrating than absolute misunderstanding from people of ill will. Lukewarm acceptance is much more bewildering than outright rejection.

I had hoped that the white moderate would understand that law and or-   24
der exist for the purpose of establishing justice and that when they fail in this purpose they become the dangerously structured dams that block the flow of social progress. I had hoped that the white moderate would understand that the present tension in the South is a necessary phase of the transition from an obnoxious negative peace, in which the Negro passively accepted his unjust plight, to a substantive and positive peace, in which all men will respect the dignity and worth of human personality. Actually, we who engage in nonviolent direct action are not the creators of tension. We merely bring to the surface the hidden tension that is already alive. We bring it out in the open, where it can be seen and dealt with. Like a boil that can never be cured so long as it is covered up but must be opened with all its ugliness to the natural medicines of air and light, injustice must be exposed, with all the tension its exposure creates, to the light of human conscience and the air of national opinion, before it can be cured.

In your statement you assert that our actions, even though peaceful, must   25
be condemned because they precipitate violence. But is this a logical assertion? Isn't this like condemning a robbed man because his possession of money precipitated the evil act of robbery? Isn't this like condemning Socrates because his unswerving commitment to truth and his philosophical inquiries precipitated the act by the misguided populace in which they made him drink hemlock? Isn't this like condemning Jesus because his unique God-consciousness and never-ceasing devotion to God's will precipitated the evil act of crucifixion? We must come to see that, as the federal courts have consistently affirmed, it is wrong to urge an individual to cease his efforts to gain his basic constitutional rights because the quest may precipitate violence. Society must protect the robbed and punish the robber.

I had also hoped that the white moderate would reject the myth concern-   26
ing time in relation to the struggle for freedom. I have just received a letter from a white brother in Texas. He writes: "All Christians know that the colored people will receive equal rights eventually, but it is possible that you are in too great a religious hurry. It has taken Christianity almost two thousand years to accomplish what it has. The teachings of Christ take time to come to earth." Such an attitude stems from a tragic misconception of time, from the strangely irrational notion that there is something in the very flow of time that will inevitably cure all ills. Actually, time itself is neutral; it can be used either destructively or constructively. More and more I feel that the people of ill will have used time much more effectively than have the people of good will. We

will have to repent in this generation not merely for the hateful words and actions of the bad people, but for the appalling silence of the good people. Human progress never rolls in on wheels of inevitability; it comes through the tireless efforts of men willing to be coworkers with God, and without this hard work, time itself becomes an ally of the forces of social stagnation. We must use time creatively, in the knowledge that the time is always ripe to do right. Now is the time to make real the promise of democracy and transform our pending national elegy into a creative psalm of brotherhood. Now is the time to lift our national policy from the quicksand of racial injustice to the solid rock of human dignity.

You speak of our activity in Birmingham as extreme. At first I was rather disappointed that fellow clergymen would see my nonviolent efforts as those of an extremist. I began thinking about the fact that I stand in the middle of two opposing forces in the Negro community. One is a force of complacency, made up in part of Negroes who, as a result of long years of oppression, are so drained of self-respect and a sense of "somebodiness" that they have adjusted to segregation; and in part of a few middle-class Negroes who, because of a degree of academic and economic security and because in some ways they profit by segregation, have become insensitive to the problems of the masses. The other force is one of bitterness and hatred, and it comes perilously close to advocating violence. It is expressed in the various black nationalist groups that are springing up across the nation, the largest and best-known being Elijah Muhammad's Muslim movement. Nourished by the Negro's frustration over the continued existence of racial discrimination, this movement is made up of people who have lost faith in America, who have absolutely repudiated Christianity, and who have concluded that the white man is an incorrigible "devil." 27

I have tried to stand between these two forces, saying that we need emulate neither the "do-nothingism" of the complacent nor the hatred and despair of the black nationalist. For there is the more excellent way of love and nonviolent protest. I am grateful to God that, through the influence of the Negro church, the way of nonviolence became an integral part of our struggle. 28

If this philosophy had not emerged, by now many streets of the South would, I am convinced, be flowing with blood. And I am further convinced that if our white brothers dismiss as "rabble-rousers" and "outside agitators" those of us who employ nonviolent direct action, and if they refuse to support our nonviolent efforts, millions of Negroes will, out of frustration and despair, seek solace and security in black-nationalist ideologies—a development that would inevitably lead to a frightening racial nightmare. 29

Oppressed people cannot remain oppressed forever. The yearning for freedom eventually manifests itself, and that is what has happened to the American Negro. Something within has reminded him of his birthright of freedom, and something without has reminded him that it can be gained. Consciously or unconsciously, he has been caught up by the *Zeitgeist,* and with his black brothers of Africa and his brown and yellow brothers of Asia, South 30

*German for "the spirit of the times."

America, and the Caribbean, the United States Negro is moving with a sense of great urgency toward the promised land of racial justice. If one recognizes this vital urge that has engulfed the Negro community, one should readily understand why public demonstrations are taking place. The Negro has many pent-up resentments and latent frustrations, and he must release them. So let him march; let him make prayer pilgrimages to the city hall; let him go on freedom rides—and try to understand why he must do so. If his repressed emotions are not released in nonviolent ways, they will seek expression through violence; this is not a threat but a fact of history. So I have not said to my people, "Get rid of your discontent." Rather, I have tried to say that this normal and healthy discontent can be channeled into the creative outlet of nonviolent direct action. And now this approach is being termed extremist.

But though I was initially disappointed at being categorized as an ex-   31
tremist, as I continued to think about the matter I gradually gained a measure of satisfaction from the label. Was not Jesus an extremist for love: "Love your enemies, bless them that curse you, do good to them that hate you, and pray for them which despitefully use you, and persecute you." Was not Amos an extremist for justice: "Let justice roll down like waters and righteousness like an everflowing stream." Was not Paul an extremist for the Christian gospel: "I bear in my body the marks of the Lord Jesus." Was not Martin Luther an extremist: "Here I stand; I cannot do otherwise, so help me God." And John Bunyan:★ "I will stay in jail to the end of my days before I make a butchery of my conscience." And Abraham Lincoln: "This nation cannot survive half slave and half free." And Thomas Jefferson: "We hold these truths to be self-evident, that all men are created equal. . . ." So the question is not whether we will be extremists, but what kind of extremists we will be. Will we be extremists for hate or for love? Will we be extremists for the preservation of injustice or for the extension of justice? In that dramatic scene on Calvary's hill three men were crucified. We must never forget that all three were crucified for the same crime—the crime of extremism. Two were extremists for immorality, and thus fell below their environment. The other, Jesus Christ, was an extremist for love, truth, and goodness, and thereby rose above his environment. Perhaps the South, the nation, and the world are in dire need of creative extremists.

I had hoped that the white moderate would see this need. Perhaps I was   32
too optimistic; perhaps I expected too much. I suppose I should have realized that few members of the oppressor race can understand the deep groans and passionate yearnings of the oppressed race, and still fewer have the vision to see that injustice must be rooted out by strong, persistent, and determined action. I am thankful, however, that some of our white brothers in the South have grasped the meaning of this social revolution and committed themselves to it. They are still all too few in quantity, but they are big in quality. Some—such

★An important English writer of the seventeenth century, John Bunyan (1628–1688) is best known for his Christian allegory *Pilgrim's Progress from This World to That Which Is to Come.*

as Ralph McGill, Lillian Smith, Harry Golden, James McBride Dabbs, Ann Braden, and Sarah Patton Boyle—have written about our struggle in eloquent and prophetic terms. Others have marched with us down nameless streets of the South. They have languished in filthy, roach-infested jails, suffering the abuse and brutality of policemen who view them as "dirty nigger-lovers." Unlike so many of their moderate brothers and sisters, they have recognized the urgency of the moment and sensed the need for powerful "action" antidotes to combat the disease of segregation.

Let me take note of my other major disappointment. I have been so greatly disappointed with the white church and its leadership. Of course, there are some notable exceptions. I am not unmindful of the fact that each of you has taken some significant stands on this issue. I commend you, Reverend Stallings, for your Christian stand on this past Sunday, in welcoming Negroes to your worship service on a nonsegregated basis. I commend the Catholic leaders of this state for integrating Spring Hill College several years ago. 33

But despite these notable exceptions, I must honestly reiterate that I have been disappointed with the church. I do not say this as one of those negative critics who can always find something wrong with the church. I say this as a minister of the gospel, who loves the church; who was nurtured in its bosom; who has been sustained by its spiritual blessings and who will remain true to it as long as the cord of life shall lengthen. 34

When I was suddenly catapulted into the leadership of the bus protest in Montgomery, Alabama, a few years ago, I felt we would be supported by the white church. I felt that the white ministers, priests, and rabbis of the South would be among our strongest allies. Instead, some have been outright opponents, refusing to understand the freedom movement and misrepresenting its leaders; all too many others have been more cautious than courageous and have remained silent behind the anesthetizing security of stained-glass windows. 35

In spite of my shattered dreams, I came to Birmingham with the hope that the white religious leadership of this community would see the justice of our cause and, with deep moral concern, would serve as the channel through which our just grievances could reach the power structure. I had hoped that each of you would understand. But again I have been disappointed. 36

There was a time when the church was very powerful—in the time when the early Christians rejoiced at being deemed worthy to suffer for what they believed. In those days the church was not merely a thermometer that recorded the ideas and principles of popular opinion; it was a thermostat that transformed the mores of society. Whenever the early Christians entered a town, the people in power became disturbed and immediately sought to convict the Christians for being "disturbers of the peace" and "outside agitators." But the Christians pressed on, in the conviction that they were "a colony of heaven," called to obey God rather than man. Small in number, they were big in commitment. They were too God-intoxicated to be "astronomically intimidated." By their effort and example they brought an end to such ancient evils as infanticide and gladiatorial contests. 37

Things are different now. So often the contemporary church is a weak,   38
ineffectual voice with an uncertain sound. So often it is an archdefender of the
status quo. Far from being disturbed by the presence of the church, the power
structure of the average community is consoled by the church's silent—and often even vocal—sanction of things as they are.

But the judgment of God is upon the church as never before. If today's   39
church does not recapture the sacrificial spirit of the early church, it will lose
its authenticity, forfeit the loyalty of millions, and be dismissed as an irrelevant
social club with no meaning for the twentieth century. Every day I meet
young people whose disappointment with the church has turned into outright
disgust.

Perhaps I have once again been too optimistic. Is organized religion too   40
inextricably bound to the status quo to save our nation and the world? Perhaps I must turn my faith to the inner spiritual church, the church within the
church, as the true *ekklesia* and the hope of the world. But again I am thankful
to God that some noble souls from the ranks of organized religion have broken loose from the paralyzing chains of conformity and joined us as active
partners in the struggle for freedom. They have left their secure congrega-
tions and walked the streets of Albany, Georgia, with us. They have gone
down the highways of the South on torturous rides for freedom. Yes, they
have gone to jail with us. Some have been dismissed from their churches, have
lost the support of their bishops and fellow ministers. But they have acted in
the faith that right defeated is stronger than evil triumphant. Their witness
has been the spiritual salt that has preserved the true meaning of the gospel in
these troubled times. They have carved a tunnel of hope through the dark
mountain of disappointment.

I hope the church as a whole will meet the challenge of this decisive   41
hour. But even if the church does not come to the aid of justice, I have no
despair about the future. I have no fear about the outcome of our struggle in
Birmingham, even if our motives are at present misunderstood. We will reach
the goal of freedom in Birmingham and all over the nation, because the goal of
America is freedom. Abused and scorned though we may be, our destiny is
tied up with America's destiny. Before the pilgrims landed at Plymouth, we
were here. Before the pen of Jefferson etched the majestic words of the Declaration of Independence across the pages of history, we were here. For more
than two centuries our forebears labored in this country without wages; they
made cotton king; they built the homes of their masters while suffering gross
injustice and shameful humiliation—and yet out of a bottomless vitality they
continued to thrive and develop. If the inexpressible cruelties of slavery could
not stop us, the opposition we now face will surely fail. We will win our freedom because the sacred heritage of our nation and the eternal will of God are
embodied in our echoing demands.

Before closing I feel impelled to mention one other point in your state-   42
ment that has troubled me profoundly. You warmly commended the Birmingham police force for keeping "order" and "preventing violence." I doubt that
you would have so warmly commended the police force if you had seen its

dogs sinking their teeth into unarmed, nonviolent Negroes. I doubt that you would so quickly commend the policemen if you were to observe their ugly and inhumane treatment of Negroes here in the city jail; if you were to watch them push and curse old Negro women and young Negro girls; if you were to see them slap and kick old Negro men and young boys; if you were to observe them, as they did on two occasions, refuse to give us food because we wanted to sing our grace together. I cannot join you in your praise of the Birmingham police department.

It is true that the police have exercised a degree of discipline in handling   43
the demonstrators. In this sense they have conducted themselves rather "nonviolently" in public. But for what purpose? To preserve the evil system of segregation. Over the past few years I have consistently preached that nonviolence demands that the means we use must be as pure as the ends we seek. I have tried to make clear that it is wrong to use immoral means to attain moral ends. But now I must affirm that it is just as wrong, or perhaps even more so, to use moral means to preserve immoral ends. Perhaps Mr. Connor and his policemen have been rather nonviolent in public, as was Chief Pritchett in Albany, Georgia, but they have used the moral means of nonviolence to maintain the immoral end of racial injustice. As T. S. Eliot has said, "The last temptation is the greatest treason: To do the right deed for the wrong reason."

I wish you had commended the Negro sit-inners and demonstrators of   44
Birmingham for their sublime courage, their willingness to suffer, and their amazing discipline in the midst of great provocation. One day the South will recognize its real heroes. They will be the James Merediths, with the noble sense of purpose that enables them to face jeering and hostile mobs, and with the agonizing loneliness that characterizes the life of the pioneer. They will be old, oppressed, battered Negro women, symbolized in a seventy-two-year-old woman in Montgomery, Alabama, who rose up with a sense of dignity and with her people decided not to ride segregated buses, and who responded with ungrammatical profundity to one who inquired about her weariness: "My feets is tired, but my soul is at rest." They will be the young high school and college students, the young ministers of the gospel and a host of their elders, courageously and nonviolently sitting in at lunch counters and willingly going to jail for conscience's sake. One day the South will know that when these disinherited children of God sat down at lunch counters, they were in reality standing up for what is best in the American dream and for the most sacred values in our Judeo-Christian heritage, thereby bringing our nation back to those great wells of democracy which were dug deep by the founding fathers in their formulation of the Constitution and the Declaration of Independence.

Never before have I written so long a letter. I'm afraid it is much too   45
long to take your precious time. I can assure you that it would have been much shorter if I had been writing from a comfortable desk, but what else can one do when he is alone in a narrow jail cell, other than write long letters, think long thoughts, and pray long prayers?

If I have said anything in this letter that overstates the truth and indicates   46
an unreasonable impatience, I beg you to forgive me. If I have said anything

that understates the truth and indicates my having a patience that allows me to settle for anything less than brotherhood, I beg God to forgive me.

I hope this letter finds you strong in the faith. I also hope that circum-   47
stances will soon make it possible for me to meet each of you, not as an integrationist or a civil-rights leader but as a fellow clergyman and a Christian brother. Let us all hope that the dark clouds of racial prejudice will soon pass away and the deep fog of misunderstanding will be lifted from our fear-drenched communities, and in some not too distant tomorrow the radiant stars of love and brotherhood will shine over our great nation with all their scintillating beauty.

Yours for the cause of Peace and Brotherhood,

Martin Luther King, Jr.

■

Questions for Meaning

1. What reason does King give for writing this letter? What justification does he provide for its length? How do these explanations work to his advantage?

2. One of the many charges brought against King at the time of his arrest was that he was an "outsider" who had no business in Birmingham. How does King defend himself? What three reasons does he cite to justify his presence in Birmingham?

3. King also responds to the criticism that his campaign for civil rights was "untimely." What is his defense against this charge?

4. What does King mean by nonviolent "direct action"? What sort of activities did he lead people to pursue? Identify the four basic steps to a direct-action campaign and explain what such campaigns were meant to accomplish.

5. Why did King believe that a direct-action campaign was necessary in Birmingham? Why did the black community in Birmingham turn to King? What problems were they facing, and what methods had they already tried before deciding on direct action?

6. What was the 1954 Supreme Court decision that King refers to in paragraph 16? Why was King able to charge that the "rabid segregationist" breaks the law?

7. King's critics charged that he obeyed the law selectively. He answers by arguing there is a difference between just and unjust laws, and that moral law requires men and women to break unjust laws that are imposed on them. How can you tell the difference between laws that you should honor and laws that you should break? What is King's definition of an unjust law, and what historical examples does he give to illustrate situations in which unjust laws have to be broken?

8. What does King mean when he complains of the "anesthetizing security of stained-glass windows"? How can churches make men and women feel falsely secure?

Questions about Strategy

1. Why did King address his letter to fellow clergymen? Why was he disappointed in them, and what did he expect his letter to accomplish?
2. Is there anything in the substance of this letter that reveals it was written for an audience familiar with the Bible and modern theology? Do you think King intended this letter to be read only by clergy? Can you point to anything that suggests King may have really written for a larger audience?
3. How does King characterize himself in this letter? What sort of a man does he seem to be, and what role does his presentation of himself play in his argument? How does he establish that he is someone worth listening to—and that it is important to listen to what he has to say?
4. *Ekklesia* is Greek for assembly, congregation, or church. Why does King use this word in paragraph 40 instead of simply saying "the church"?
5. Martin Luther King had much experience as a preacher when he wrote this famous letter. Is there anything about its style that reminds you of oratory? How effective would this letter be if delivered as a speech?

BETTY FRIEDAN

THE IMPORTANCE OF WORK

Betty Friedan was one of the founders of the National Organization for Women, serving as NOW's first president between 1966 and 1970. Born in Peoria, Illinois, and educated at Smith College, the University of California, and the University of Iowa, Friedan has lectured at more than fifty universities and institutes. Her essays have appeared in numerous periodicals, including the *Saturday Review, Harper's, McCall's, Redbook,* and the *Ladies' Home Journal.* Her books include *It Changed My Life* (1976), *The Second Stage* (1981), and *The Fountain of Age* (1993). The following essay is drawn from the book that made her famous, *The Feminine Mystique* (1963).

More than a quarter of a century has now passed since Friedan published this book, and the leadership of the women's movement has passed to a younger generation. But if the development of that movement could be traced back to the publication of a single work, it would have to be *The Feminine Mystique.* Friedan believed that women needed to escape from the roles they had assumed as wives and mothers, and if her ideas no longer seem as bold as they once were, it is because she anticipated many of the concerns that would dominate the analysis of male/female relations during the 1970s and 1980s. "The Importance of Work" is an editor's title for the concluding pages of Friedan's book, an excerpt that reveals Friedan's conviction that women need to enter the mainstream of the American work force—not simply as typists and file clerks, but as the full equals of men.

The question of how a person can most fully realize his own capacities and   1
thus achieve identity has become an important concern of the philosophers and
the social and psychological thinkers of our time—and for good reason.
Thinkers of other times put forth the idea that people were, to a great extent,
defined by the work they did. The work that a man had to do to eat, to stay
alive, to meet the physical necessities of his environment, dictated his identity.
And in this sense, when work was seen merely as a means of survival, human
identity was dictated by biology.

But today the problem of human identity has changed. For the work that   2
defined man's place in society and his sense of himself has also changed man's
world. Work, and the advance of knowledge, has lessened man's dependence on
his environment; his biology and the work he must do for biological survival
are no longer sufficient to define his identity. This can be most clearly seen in
our own abundant society; men no longer need to work all day to eat. They
have an unprecedented freedom to choose the kind of work they will do; they
also have an unprecedented amount of time apart from the hours and days that
must actually be spent in making a living. And suddenly one realizes the significance of today's identity crisis—for women, and increasingly, for men.
One sees the human significance of work—not merely as the means of biological survival, but as the giver of self and the transcender of self, as the creator of
human identity and human evolution.

For "self-realization" or "self-fulfillment" or "identity" does not come   3
from looking into a mirror in rapt contemplation of one's own image. Those
who have most fully realized themselves, in a sense that can be recognized by
the human mind even though it cannot be clearly defined, have done so in the
service of a human purpose larger than themselves. Men from varying disciplines have used different words for this mysterious process from which comes
the sense of self. The religious mystics, the philosophers, Marx, Freud—all had
different names for it: man finds himself by losing himself; man is defined by
his relation to the means of production; the ego, the self, grows through understanding and mastering reality—through work and love.

The identity crisis, which has been noted by Erik Erikson★ and others in   4
recent years in the American man, seems to occur for lack of, and be cured by
finding, the work, or cause, or purpose that evokes his own creativity. Some
never find it, for it does not come from busy-work or punching a time clock.
It does not come from just making a living, working by formula, finding a
secure spot as an organization man. The very argument, by Riesman and others, that man no longer finds identity in the work defined as a paycheck job,
assumes that identity for man comes through creative work of his own that
contributes to the human community: the core of the self becomes aware, becomes real, and grows through work that carries forward human society.

Work, the shopworn staple of the economists, has become the new fron-   5
tier of psychology. Psychiatrists have long used "occupational therapy" with

★Trained by Sigmund and Anna Freud, Erik Erikson (b. 1902) is an American psychoanalyst
and writer best known for *Childhood and Society* (1950).

patients in mental hospitals; they have recently discovered that to be of real psychological value, it must be not just "therapy," but real work, serving a real purpose in the community. And work can now be seen as the key to the problem that has no name. The identity crisis of American women began a century ago, as more and more of the work important to the world, more and more of the work that used their human abilities and through which they were able to find self-realization, was taken from them.

Until, and even into, the last century, strong, capable women were needed to pioneer our new land; with their husbands, they ran the farms and plantations and Western homesteads. These women were respected and self-respecting members of a society whose pioneering purpose centered in the home. Strength and independence, responsibility and self-confidence, self-discipline and courage, freedom and equality were part of the American character for both men and women, in all the first generations. The women who came by steerage from Ireland, Italy, Russia, and Poland worked beside their husbands in the sweatshops and the laundries, learned the new language, and saved to send their sons and daughters to college. Women were never quite as "feminine," or held in as much contempt, in America as they were in Europe. American women seemed to European travelers, long before our time, less passive, childlike, and feminine than their own wives in France or Germany or England. By an accident of history, American women shared in the work of society longer, and grew with the men. Grade- and high-school education for boys and girls alike was almost always the rule; and in the West, where women shared the pioneering work the longest, even the universities were co-educational from the beginning.

The identity crisis for women did not begin in America until the fire and strength and ability of the pioneer women were no longer needed, no longer used, in the middle-class homes of the Eastern and Midwestern cities, when the pioneering was done and men began to build the new society in industries and professions outside the home. But the daughters of the pioneer women had grown too used to freedom and work to be content with leisure and passive femininity.

It was not an American, but a South African woman, Mrs. Olive Schreiner, who warned at the turn of the century that the quality and quantity of women's functions in the social universe were decreasing as fast as civilization was advancing; that if women did not win back their right to a full share of honored and useful work, woman's mind and muscle would weaken in a parasitic state; her offspring, male and female, would weaken progressively, and civilization itself would deteriorate.

The feminists saw clearly that education and the right to participate in the more advanced work of society were women's greatest needs. They fought for and won the rights to new, fully human identity for women. But how very few of their daughters and granddaughters have chosen to use their education and their abilities for any large creative purpose, for responsible work in society? How many of them have been deceived, or have deceived themselves, into clinging to the outgrown, childlike femininity of "Occupation: housewife"?

6

7

8

9

It was not a minor matter, their mistaken choice. We now know that the   10
same range of potential ability exists for women as for men. Women, as well as
men, can only find their identity in work that uses their full capacities. A
woman cannot find her identity through others—her husband, her children.
She cannot find it in the dull routine of housework. As thinkers of every age
have said, it is only when a human being faces squarely the fact that he can
forfeit his own life, that he becomes truly aware of himself, and begins to take
his existence seriously. Sometimes this awareness comes only at the moment of
death. Sometimes it comes from a more subtle facing of death: the death of self
in passive conformity, in meaningless work. The feminine mystique prescribes
just such a living death for women. Faced with the slow death of self, the
American woman must begin to take her life seriously.

"We measure ourselves by many standards," said the great American psy-   11
chologist William James, nearly a century ago. "Our strength and our intelligence, our wealth and even our good luck, are things which warm our heart
and make us feel ourselves a match for life. But deeper than all such things,
and able to suffice unto itself without them, is the sense of the amount of effort which we can put forth."

If women do not put forth, finally, that effort to become all that they   12
have it in them to become, they will forfeit their own humanity. A woman
today who has no goal, no purpose, no ambition patterning her days into the
future, making her stretch and grow beyond that small score of years in which
her body can fill its biological function, is committing a kind of suicide. For
that future half a century after the child-bearing years are over is a fact that an
American woman cannot deny. Nor can she deny that as a housewife, the
world is indeed rushing past her door while she just sits and watches. The ter-
ror she feels is real, if she has no place in that world.

The feminine mystique has succeeded in burying millions of American   13
women alive. There is no way for these women to break out of their comfortable concentration camps except by finally putting forth an effort—that human effort which reaches beyond biology, beyond the narrow walls of home,
to help shape the future. Only by such a personal commitment to the future
can American women break out of the housewife trap and truly find fulfillment as wives and mothers—by fulfilling their own unique possibilities as separate human beings. ■

Questions for Meaning

1. In her opening paragraph, Friedan writes, "when work was seen merely
   as a means of survival, human identity was dictated by biology." What
   does this mean?
2. Does Friedan believe that all types of work are equally satisfying?
   Where does she define the type of work that has "human significance"?
3. According to Friedan, what is the historical explanation for the identity
   crisis many American women suffered during the twentieth century?

4. What's wrong with "Occupation: housewife"? Why does Friedan believe that women cannot find fulfillment simply by being wives and mothers?
5. Explain Friedan's allusion to "feminists" in paragraph 9. Who were the early feminists, and what did they accomplish?
6. Although you have been given only the last few pages of Friedan's book, can you construct a definition for what she means by "the feminine mystique"?
7. Vocabulary: transcender (2), rapt (3), mystics (3), parasitic (8), deteriorate (8), forfeit (10).

Questions about Strategy

1. What is the premise that underlies Friedan's argument on behalf of meaningful careers for women?
2. Why does Friedan discuss women within the context of psychological "identity"? Why is it important for her to link the needs of women with the needs of men?
3. Comment on Friedan's use of quotation. She refers, for support, to four men (Marx, Freud, Erik Erikson, and William James) and to only one woman, Olive Schreiner. Does her reliance on male authorities help or hurt her argument?
4. When Friedan declares that housewives are "committing a kind of suicide" trapped within homes that are "comfortable concentration camps," is she drawing her work together with a forceful conclusion or weakening it through exaggeration?

SUGGESTIONS FOR WRITING

1. Using "A Modest Proposal" as your model, write a satirical essay proposing a "solution" to a contemporary social problem other than poverty.
2. Write a counterargument to Jefferson, "A Declaration of Continued Dependence" from the point of view of George III.
3. Drawing on the work of Mary Wollstonecraft, Margaret Sanger, and Betty Friedan, write a "Declaration of Independence for Women."
4. Research the relationship between mental illness and homelessness, and write on behalf of today's "insane poor."
5. Marxism seems to have lost most of the appeal it once enjoyed. Evaluate *The Communist Manifesto* in the light of twentieth-century history. Is it entirely out-of-date or does it advance principles that can still be of use?
6. Summarize what Mark Twain taught about good writing style, and apply his criteria to a novel of your own choice.
7. Respond to Charlotte Perkins Gilman by arguing for the principle you believe is the most important when raising children.

8. Research the use of birth control in China, and argue for or against the policies in place there.

9. Clarence Darrow argues that capital punishment does nothing to resolve the causes of violent crime. Identify a social problem that you believe to be a cause of violence and argue on behalf of a specific reform.

10. Write an argument for or against the use of capital punishment in your own state.

11. Compare the propaganda posters reprinted on pages 581–582. How do they reflect the principles outlined by Adolf Hitler in "The Purpose of Propaganda"? Explain the strategy behind each of these posters and determine their relative effectiveness.

12. Research and report upon the conditions in Germany that helped Hitler rise to power.

13. Investigate the fertilizers and pesticides most frequently used by farmers today, and report upon the effect they have on the environment.

14. Compare the current condition of a local river, lake, or forest with how it appeared a generation ago.

15. Drawing on "Letter from Birmingham Jail," defend an illegal act that you would be willing to commit in order to advance a cause in which you believe.

COLLABORATIVE PROJECT

Form a writing group and decide what roles members want to play in creating a dialogue between Thomas Jefferson, Adolf Hitler, Martin Luther King, and Betty Friedan. Focus the dialogue on what it means to be free and how freedom can be achieved.

FIGURE I

Figure 1 is an example of an English poster from the First World War (1914–1919). Figure 2 is a Nazi election poster from the early 1930s. It reads, "Work and Bread through List One." (List One refers to the position of Nazi candidates on the ballot before Hitler seized power.) Figure 3 is a Nazi propaganda poster used in Poland after the German invasion of that country in 1939. The caption, in Polish, reads: "England! This is your work!" The picture shows a wounded Polish soldier pointing to the ruins of Warsaw and addressing Neville Chamberlain, the Prime Minister at the beginning of the war.

FIGURE 2

FIGURE 3

PART 5

A GUIDE TO RESEARCH

If forced to write about an unfamiliar subject, even the most experienced writers can find themselves in difficulty. One of the great advantages of research is that it gives you material for writing. Another advantage is that the search itself can be exciting as you explore resources and make discoveries. You will need to evaluate the material you discover and to decide how you want to organize it. You will also need to know how to handle the mechanics of a researched paper, a type of academic writing governed by a number of rules and conventions. There is nothing especially difficult about writing a paper of this sort if you approach it as a process that begins long before the assignment is due.

Your instructor may allow you to choose your own subject for research. Or you may be required to work on a subject that has been assigned to you. In either case, there are two basic points that you need to remember when undertaking a researched paper: (1) A graceful style cannot compensate for a failure to do adequate research. Even if you are an excellent writer, your paper will be superficial if your research has been superficial. (2) Although research is essential to the process of writing a researched paper, there is more to the researched paper than research alone. You can spend months investigating your subject, but your essay will be a disappointment if it consists of nothing more than one quotation after another. You should remember that you are a writer as well as an investigator, and your own thoughts and interpretations are ultimately as important as the research itself. You may occasionally have an assignment that requires nothing more than reporting on a technical question such as "How is gasoline refined?" or "How do eagles mate?" But most researched papers require that the writer have a thesis and a point of view about the subject under consideration. Unless specifically instructed otherwise, you should think of researched papers as an extended form of argument—arguments that are supported by evidence you have discovered through research.

There are two types of research: primary and secondary. *Primary research* requires firsthand experimentation or analysis. This is the sort of research that is done in scientific laboratories and scholarly archives. Research of this sort is seldom expected of college students, although, if you interview someone, you are doing a type of primary research. An undergraduate paper is usually based on *secondary research,* which means the examination of what other people have already published on a given subject. In order to do this type of research efficiently, you must know where to look. And this means that you must be familiar with the resources that are available to you in your library and develop a strategy for using these resources effectively.

GETTING STARTED

Your primary goal in preliminary research is to get your subject in focus. This usually means narrowing your subject to a specific topic. (See pp. 3–4.) A clear focus is essential if your paper is to have depth and coherence. A ten-page paper on "The Question of Race in *Huckleberry Finn*" is likely to be much more thoughtful than one of that length on "Mark Twain: America's Favorite Writer." And a paper focused on "Is Huck a Racist?" is likely to be better yet. Moreover, your research will probably be easier when you have a clear focus. When you know what you are looking for, you know what you need to read and what you can afford to pass over. This will keep you from feeling overwhelmed as your research progresses. Do not think that you must have a clear focus before you visit the library, however. Your focus may emerge as you look through the resources available to you.

Different instructors make different assignments, and you should always be certain that you have understood what your instructor expects of you. If you have been asked to write a fixed number of pages on a subject of your own choice, a good rule to follow is to narrow your subject as much as possible without narrowing yourself out of the library. Don't put yourself in the position of aimlessly reading dozens of books on an unnecessarily broad subject. On the other hand, don't make your topic so obscure that you will be unable to find enough material to write a paper of the length required.

If you know very little about your topic, you may want to begin your research by reading whatever can be found in a general encyclopedia, such as the *Encyclopedia Britannica* or the *Encyclopedia Americana.* Encyclopedias contain the basic background information that other works may assume you already possess. Within the reference rooms of most libraries, you can also find special encyclopedias and dictionaries for major fields such as art, biography, economics, education, history, law, literature, medicine, music, philosophy, and psychology. Do some preliminary reading in an encyclopedia if doing so will make you feel more comfortable with your subject, but do not spend a lot of time reading in the library at this early stage of your research. Although the reference room may be a good place to begin your work, it has a great disadvantage: The books in this room are seldom allowed to circulate. Your first day in the library should be devoted primarily to finding out what types of material are going to be available to you and to selecting a few sources to borrow for reading later.

LOOKING FOR BOOKS

Never assume that your topic is so new, or so specialized, that your library will not have books on it. A topic that seems new to you may not necessarily be new to others. By looking for books, you will often find sources of great value. There are some topics on which you may not be able to find a book, but you will have more confidence in your research if you have taken the trouble to check.

Using the Main Catalog

One of the first steps in your search strategy should be to consult your library's main catalog. Although some libraries use card catalogs in which cards for each book in the collection are arranged alphabetically in drawers, most college libraries have computerized their catalogs.

Computerized catalogs enable users to search for books by author, title, or subject. Many of these catalogs also enable users to search for material by providing a call number or a "key word," which means a word likely to appear somewhere in the title or description. In addition to providing you with all of the information about a book that you could obtain from a card catalog, computerized catalogs are usually designed to report whether the book is currently available. Computerized catalogs help make research efficient by providing instant access to information that might otherwise be recorded in the different drawers of a card catalog. If you have access to a computerized catalog but are unfamiliar with how to use it, you should be able to find user information posted near the computers. The program will provide instructions on the screen once you begin. And most librarians are willing to help an inexperienced user get started.

If you are limited to a card catalog, do not be discouraged. Until fairly recently, card catalogs were the standard means through which scholars did their research. But you should be prepared to look in more than one place. Card catalogs usually include two or three cards for every book the library owns. This allows you to locate books in a variety of ways, depending on how much you know. You may be looking for books by a particular author, so find your library's *author cards*. You may know the title of the book but not who wrote it, so find your library's *title cards*. These two kinds of card are often filed in the same set of drawers and called an *author/title catalog*. In addition, you may be able to look for books on your subject through a separate *subject catalog*. When you are unable to find material under the heading you have consulted, you should explore alternative headings. Books on the Civil War, for example, might be listed under "War Between the States." You might find a cross-reference directing you to the appropriate heading or you may need to draw on your own ingenuity. If you are sure that the library must have books on your subject and that you are simply unable to find the correct subject heading, ask a librarian for help.

Figures 1 and 2 show how a catalog card compares to an entry on a computer screen. The two entries are very similar despite some minor differences in format. As you do research, you should expect to find variations on these examples. Author cards, title cards, and subject cards will each have slightly different headings so that they can be filed in different places. And the precise format of a computerized entry depends on the program employed by the library you are using.

There is no foolproof method for determining the quality or usefulness of a book from a catalog entry. The best way to judge a book in always to read it. But a catalog listing can reveal some useful clues if you know how to find them. Consider, for example, the date of publication. There is no reason to assume that new books are always better than old books, but unless you are researching a historical or literary topic, you should be careful not to rely heavily on material that may be out of date. Consider also the length of the book. A book with 300 pages is likely to provide more information than a book half that size. A book with a bibliography may help you to find more material. Finally, you might also consider the reputation of the publisher. Any conclusion that you draw at this point should be tentative. But some books are

```
PUBLIC CATALOG                                    Searching:UWSP

Rodriguez, Richard.
    Hunger of memory : the education of Richard Rodriguez : an
      autobiography.
Boston, Mass. : D.R. Godine, 1982.
    195 p. ; 23 cm.


    Rodriguez, Richard.
    Mexican Americans_California_Biography.
    Mexican Americans_Education.
    Education, Bilingual_United States.
    Affirmative action programs_United States.
    California_Biography.



    LOCATION        CALL #/VOL/NO/COPY            STATUS

    STACKS              F870.M5 R62 1982            Available



    (END) Press RETURN to continue or /ES to start a new search:
```

FIGURE I

An entry from a computer catalog

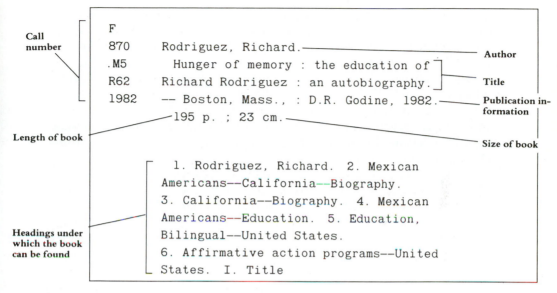

FIGURE 2
An author card from a card catalog

better than others, and it is your responsibility as a researcher to evaluate the material that you use. (For additional information on evaluating sources, see pp. 63–65.) If you are fortunate enough to find several books on your subject, select the books that seem the best.

Understanding Classification Systems

Most American libraries use one of two systems for classifying the books in their collections: the Dewey Decimal system or the Library of Congress system. If you understand how these systems work, you can save valuable time in the library by knowing where to look for material when you are already working in the stacks.

The Dewey Decimal system classifies books numerically:

000–099	General Works
100–199	Philosophy
200–299	Religion
300–399	Social Sciences
400–499	Language
500–599	Natural Sciences
600–699	Technology
700–799	Fine Arts
800–899	Literature
900–999	History and Geography

These major divisions are subdivided by ten to identify specializations within each general field. For example, within the 800–899 category for literature, American literature is found between 810 and 819, English literature between 820 and 829, German literature between 830 and 839—and so forth. Specific numbers narrow these areas further, so that 811 represents American poetry, for example, and 812 American drama. Additional numbers after the decimal point enable catalogers to classify books more precisely: 812.54 would indicate an American play written since 1945. In order to distinguish individual books for others that are similar, an additional number is usually placed beneath the Dewey number.

Most libraries that use the Dewey Decimal system combine it with one of three systems for providing what is called an "author mark." These systems (Cutter two-figure, Cutter three-figure, and Cutter-Sanborn) all work according to the same principle. Librarians consult a reference table that provides a numerical representation for the first four to six letters of every conceivable last name. The first letter of the author's last name is placed immediately before this number, and the first letter of the first significant word in the title is placed after the number. Here is a complete call number for *Cat on a Hot Tin Roof,* by the American playwright Tennessee Williams:

812.54
W675c

Although the Dewey Decimal system remains the most widely used system for the classification of books in American libraries, many university libraries prefer to use the Library of Congress system, which uses the alphabet to distinguish twenty-one major categories as opposed to Dewey's ten:

A	General Works
B	Philosophy, Psychology, and Religion
C	General History
D	Foreign History
E–F	American History (North and South)
G	Geography and Anthropology
H	Social Sciences
J	Political Science
K	Law
L	Education
M	Music
N	Fine Arts
P	Language and Literature
Q	Science
R	Medicine
S	Agriculture
T	Technology
U	Military Science

V   Naval Science
Z   Bibliography and Library Science

Each of these categories can be subdivided through additional letters and numbers. PR, for example, indicates English literature, and PS indicates American. The complete entry will usually involve three lines. Unless you are planning to become a librarian, you will not find it necessary to memorize the complete code. But whether you are using Dewey or the Library of Congress, always be sure to copy down the complete call number for any book you wish to find. If you leave out part of the number you may find yourself wandering in the stacks and unable to find the book you want.

USING PERIODICAL INDEXES

Good researchers want to be aware of the latest developments in their fields. A scholarly book may be several years in the making; publication may be delayed, and another year or two may pass before the book is purchased and cataloged by your library. You may also need to obtain detailed information on a particular subtopic that is discussed only briefly in the books that are available to you. Therefore, you will often need to turn to periodicals after searching for books. "Periodicals" means magazines, newspapers, and scholarly journals: material that is published at periodic intervals. And there are numerous indexes to help you find literature of this sort.

The best known of these indexes is the *Readers' Guide to Periodical Literature,* which is now available not only in the green, bound volumes in which it has been published for several decades but also either on-line or on a CD-ROM disk for use with a computer. The *Readers' Guide* covers approximately 150 magazines and journals, indexing material by subject and by author. Because it indexes popular, mass-circulation periodicals, it will lead you to articles that are often relatively short and accessible. This is also the case for *InfoTrac,* another computerized index for periodicals in general circulation.

Most college libraries have a variety of other indexes that will lead you to more substantial material. Almost every field has its own index, which you should be able to use with little difficulty once you are familiar with the *Readers' Guide.* Detailed lists of such indexes and other reference books can be found in *Guide to Reference Books,* by Eugene P. Sheehy, and *American Reference Books Annual,* edited by Boydan S. Wynar. Among the specialized indexes most frequently used are:

Applied Science and Technology Index   *Index to Legal Periodicals*
Art Index   *Index Medicus* (for medicine)
Biological and Agricultural Index   *Music Index*
Business Periodicals Index   *Philosopher's Index*
Education Index   *Science Citation Index*
Humanities Index   *Social Sciences Index*

Like the *Readers' Guide,* most specialized indexes are now available on-line or on CD–ROM disks that cover several years—a great advantage over bound volumes, which cover only a single year. Anyone doing research in literature should also be familiar with the *MLA International Bibliography* (which includes both books and articles written about English, American, and foreign language literature) and also with the *Essay and General Literature Index,* which indexes essays and articles that have appeared in books rather than in journals.

Although there is occasionally some overlapping from one index to another, you need to realize that each of these indexes covers different periodicals. The references that you find in one will usually be entirely different from the references you find in another. This is worth remembering for two reasons: (1) You should not get easily discouraged when searching for periodical literature. If you cannot locate any material in the past few years of one index, then you should try another index that sounds as if it might include references to your subject. (2) Many subjects of general interest will be found in more than one index, and if you consult more than one index, you are increasing the likelihood of being exposed to different points of view.

You may choose to do research on one of the subjects discussed in Parts 3 and 4 of this book. But let us take an example from outside the book— following the search strategy for a paper on bilingual education and noting how different indexes lead to different material.

The search for periodical literature on this subject began with the *Readers' Guide.* Figure 3 shows an excerpt from the February 1994 volume, identifying only one article on bilingual education. To locate additional sources through the bound volumes of the *Readers' Guide,* you would need to consult volumes covering other periods. (Bound volumes are usually printed annually, although the current year is published in installments.)

If you consulted the *Readers' Guide* on-line, you would find the same sources, but you would find them more quickly. The information is essentially the same as the information in the bound volumes, but the program also identifies the subjects covered in each article—a feature that can help you to evaluate the potential usefulness of sources. Figures 4 and 5 show what your computer screen would look like when conducting an on-line search. Note that the computer identifies the most recent source first and then works backward from it.

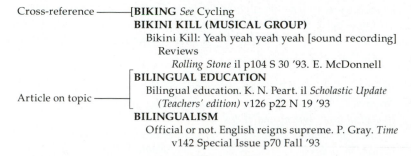

FIGURE 3

An excerpt from the *Reader's Guide* in a bound volume

```
* * * * * * * * * * * * * *  List of Records  * * * * * * * * * * * * * * *
DATABASE:  ReadersGuide              LIMITED TO:
SEARCH:  su:bilingual education FOUND 57 Records

  NO. ___SOURCE _____TITLE _____YEAR _
   1      Sch Update          Bilingual education.                              1993
   2      N Y Times (Late     Los Angeles schools to hire bilingual t           1993
   3      Time                Atte imasuka? (Is that correct?).                 1992
   4      Phi Delta Kappan    Educating the children of immigrants.             1992
   5      Forbes              Promoting alienization.                           1991
   6      McCalls             Why bilingual education fails Hispanic            1991
   7      Sch Update          One language or two?.                             1991
   8      People Wkly         So, you think Latin is tough? Some Virg           1991

HINTS:      More records . . . type F.        View a record . . type record number.
            Decrease number of records . . . . . . . type L (to limit) or A (to 'and').
            Do a new search . . . . . . . . . . . . . . . . . . . type S or SEARCH.

ACTIONS:  Help  Search  And  Limit  Print  Database  Forward  BYE  Reset

RECORD NUMBER (or Action):
```

FIGURE 4

First screen after searching "bilingual education" during an on-line search of *Readers' Guide*

```
* * * * * * * * * * * * * *  Full Record Display  * * * * * * * * * * * * * *
DATABASE: ReadersGuide              LIMITED TO:
SEARCH: bilingual education

 Record 5 of 57___YOUR LIBRARY (MNT) MAY OWN THIS ITEM ___ (Page 1 of 2)
          AUTHOR:  Sowell, Thomas,
            TITLE:  Promoting alienization. (bilingual education and Hispanic activists)
          SOURCE:  Forbes v. 148 (Nov. 25 '91) p. 112 il.
   STANDARD NO:  0015-6914
            DATE:  1991
   RECORD TYPE:  art
       CONTENTS:  feature article
        SUBJECT:  Bilingual education.
                  Spanish language in the United States.

HINTS:    Another page . type F or B.        Another record . type record number.
          Help on 3-letter library symbol . . . . . . . . . . . type H and symbol.
          Return to Record List . . . . . . . . . . . . . . . . . . just press Enter.
ACTIONS: Help  Search  And  Limit  Print  Forward  Back  BYE  Reset
RECORD NUMBER (or Action):
```

FIGURE 5

Second screen of on-line search after user has selected the *Forbes* article in Figure 5

Of the various specialized indexes that can lead you to material in professional journals, the *Education Index* is especially useful for locating information on bilingual education. Like the *Readers' Guide,* it can be consulted in bound volumes or through a computer search. Figure 6 shows what the computer screen looked like when a user searched "bilingual education" in early 1994. If you compare Figure 6 with Figure 4, you will find that the format of these two indexes is the same. But while the *Readers' Guide* led to fifty-seven titles at that time, the *Education Index* led to five hundred and seventy-eight— giving the researcher a much larger pool of potential sources. Note that journals such as *Journal of Instructional Psychology* or *Journal of Reading Behavior* are not indexed in the *Readers' Guide,* so you would not have located these sources if you had limited your search to the *Readers' Guide.* Articles in journals such as these may be longer and more difficult to read than articles in popular magazines. But you can overcome this difficulty through proper preparation: Do not try to read articles in scholarly journals until you have completed some preliminary reading in encyclopedias, books, and magazines.

Continuing your search, you might find additional material on bilingual education through the *Social Sciences Index,* which covers sociology, psychology, and other related fields. And the *Index to Legal Periodicals* might lead to a source discussing laws that help shape the nature of public education. The articles would be different, but the form of the citations would be similar. The

```
* * * * * * * * * * * * * * *  List of Records  * * * * * * * * * * * * * * * *
      DATABASE: EducationInd                      LIMITED TO:
      SEARCH: su:bilingual education FOUND 578 Records

      ┌NO. ──SOURCE ───────────TITLE ─────────────────────────────YEAR ─
      │  1      Urban Educ        The ethics of multicultural and bilingu      1994
      │  2      Top Early Child   Effective and appropriate instruction f      1993
      │  3      Phi Delta Kappan  Where is multiculturalism leading us?.        1993
      │  4      Lang Arts         Emerging biliteracy and cross-cultural        1993
      │  5      J Instr Psychol   Developing writing skills for students        1993
      │  6      Educ Week         O.C.R. threatens Oakland with cutoff in       1993
      │  7      Rev Educ          Points of power: Mexican children in fa       1993
      └  8      J Read Behav      Intergenerational literacy learning wit       1993

      HINTS:     More records . . . type F.        View a record . . type record number.
                 Decrease number of records . . . . . . . type L (to limit) or A (to 'and').
                 Do a new search . . . . . . . . . . . . . . . . . . . . type S or SEARCH.

      ACTIONS:  Help  Search  And  Limit  Print  Database  Forward  BYE  Reset
      RECORD NUMBER (or Action):
```

FIGURE 6

First screen from an on-line search of the *Education Index*

instructions you see on your screen will vary from one program to another, but once you become comfortable with one computer program, you are likely to learn another easily.

USING A NEWSPAPER INDEX

Newspapers are often an excellent source of information, and there are indexes available to help you locate articles in such newspapers as *The Wall Street Journal* and *The Christian Science Monitor.* In addition to bound volumes for specific newspapers, some libraries have CD-ROM disks that can cover a number of newspapers within a single search. Others subscribe to *Lexus/Nexis,* a powerful program that searches for news articles nationwide, often locating material only a day or two after its publication.

If your library has only one index, it is most likely to be the *New York Times Index,* which has been published since 1913. Figure 7 is an example of what you would find if you consulted this index for a paper on bilingual education. Note that the *New York Times Index* gives you a one-sentence summary of each article, rather than article titles.

Although the *New York Times* was not essential to research on bilingual education, the index did lead to a potentially useful article. Bear in mind that the *New York Times* is especially useful when researching historical events or topics that have only recently made news. When using a newspaper index—or any other index—you should always consider whether it is appropriate for the

EDUCATION AND SCHOOLS – Cont

Two Houston, Tex, schools turn gymnasiums into shelters for schoolchildren who have no other place to sleep; eight children, aged 5 to 18, show up first night, leading school officials to believe there are many more who will show up in future; photo (M), Ja 14,I,6:1

Gov Thomas H Kean's call for end to mandatory daily gym classes in New Jersey high schools is attacked by politicians, principals, gym teachers, pediatricians and legislators; many students are with Kean; photo (M), Ja 14, I,27:2

Anthony Reyes, 16, is arrested on charge of bringing unloaded revolver to Immaculata High School in Manhattan and hiding it in his locker (S), Ja 14,I,30:6

New York State Comr of Educaiton, Thomas Sobol, announces broadened policy of bilingual education in state's public schools to meet anticipated needs of growing population of students with limited skills in English (M), Ja 15,I,22:6

Standardized college admission testing is seen as growth industry, one that provided $226 million last year to Education Testing Service, which administers Scholastic Aptitude Test and many others, and $50 million to American College Testing Program, which administers ACT; success continues despite criticism that tests are inaccurate and biased against women and members of minority groups, tests are also being increasingly used for purposes that go well beyond admissions decisions; photo (M), Ja 15,IV,28:4

(M) means that this is of medium length. The date of issue is January 15 (of the year of the volume consulted). "I" means that the article is in section one—on page 22, column 6, in this case.

FIGURE 7

Excerpt from the *New York Times Index*

topic you are researching. An index that did not lead to any articles for your last researched paper may yield several dozen for your next.

USING ABSTRACTING SERVICES

Another type of resource is usually available in a college library: an *abstract,* which means a summary of an article or book (see p. 224 for an example). Among the most important abstracting services are:

Abstracts in Anthropology
Academic Abstracts
Biological Abstracts
Chemical Abstracts
Historical Abstracts
Physics Abstracts
Psychological Abstracts
Sociological Abstracts
Women Studies Abstracts

These abstracts are organized in different ways. If you are searching for abstracts through a computer, you will usually follow a procedure that is similar to a search for periodical literature. When consulting bound volumes of abstracts, you may need to consult the instructions that can be found in the front of most volumes. Given here is an example of what you would find if you looked up "bilingual education" in *Psychological Abstracts*—which requires that you consult an index before you locate any specific summary. Figure 8 (p. 595) shows an excerpt from the subject index for 1993. Reading through the entries in the subject index should help you to identify citations that seem promising. The number that appears at the end of each citation is not a page number. It is the number of the article being summarized. Article summaries can be found in numerical order, either at the front of the volume containing the subject index or in a separate volume (which will be shelved beside it) depending on how your library decides to bind them. Figure 9 (p. 596) shows a partial page of summaries, including one for an article on bilingual education located through the subject index illustrated in Figure 8. Note that it is only at this point that you learn the author(s) of the article, the title of the article, and the journal, volume, date, and pages where it can be found.

Abstracts offer a great advantage. Sometimes it is hard to tell from the title alone whether an article will be useful, and a summary can help you to decide whether you want to read the entire article. A good rule to follow with abstracts is that if you can't understand the summary, you probably won't understand the article. There is one other point to remember when using abstracting services: Many of them are international in scope. Just because the

Bilingual Education—Serials

cloze literacy lessons & student interpretation of use of context clues, bilingual Mexican American 3rd graders & their teacher, 1 yr study, 3352

delayed vs early immersion vs full French medium schooling, French & English & mathematics achievement, anglophone K–6th graders, Canada, 39222

ELS vs special needs placement & educational quality, bilingual Asian vs White 11–16 yr olds, UK, 31294

ethical issues in application of social psychology & self esteem as justification for bilingual education, language minority students, 23471

instruction in native language, receptive acquisition of 2nd language, bilingual 1st graders with language delay, 31400

maintenance bilingual education program, English & Spanish acquisition, Mexican American K–2nd graders with limited language proficiency, 23485

whole language & authentic literature programs & alternatives for educator misconceptions, bilingual students, 43196

Brief description of article (not a title) →

← *The entry number under which you can find the article abstract*

Bilingual Education—Books

Assessing evaluation studies: The case of bilingual education strategies, 8074

Bilingual Education—Chapters

The symbolic politics of opposition to bilingual education, 43244

Bilingualism—Serials

bilingual & bicultural status in hearing oriented society, deaf, 22435

bilingual awareness & characteristics of both languages at time of stuttering onset, bilingual stuttering 25 mo old male, case report, 18161

bilingualism & metalinguistic competence & development, bilingual vs. unilingual Kond tribal 2nd vs 4th vs 5th graders, India, 44864

FIGURE 8
Excerpt from subject index for *Psychological Abstracts*

article summary is written in English does not mean that this is true of the article itself. But if an article is written in a foreign language, that will usually be indicated.

Computers continue to make research easier. Although it does not cover precisely the same sources as *Psychological Abstracts,* the PsychLit database provides easy access to the abstracts of many scholarly articles in the field. Figure 10 shows the first screen when a user recently searched PsychLit for abstracts. Note that the database covered six years and that the user was required to choose between searching for journal articles or searching books and chapters in books. The user chose "K: Journal Articles," and this choice produced the screen reproduced in Figure 11, which, in turn, led to the discovery of eighty-four sources. The abstract for one of these sources is reprinted in Figure 12.

43195. **Fox, Jeremy.** (U East Anglia, Computers in Language Education Group, Norwich, England) **EC research in language learning and IT: Some experiences with LINGUA.** Special Issue: European community R&D in telematics and learning. *Journal of Computer Assisted Learning,* 1993(Jun), Vol 9(2), 100–106.— Discusses ongoing research into the production of a course in Danish for business for native speakers of English. The course will contain both a print course in book form, plus a computer-based multimedia course. The design of multimedia language learning systems is discussed in terms of contributions from applied linguistics, pedagogical theory, and humanistic approaches. An outline is provided of desirable features in a computer-based language learning support system. Underlying principles guiding the writing of the Danish course are discussed. The role and overall philosophy of LINGUA, a European Community Program to promote foreign language competence are also reviewed.

Corresponding entry number (from subject index)

Journal title

Authors and their institutional affiliation

Article title

Date, volume, and page numbers

43196. **Freeman, Yvonne S. & Goodman, Yetta M.** (Fresno Pacific Coll, CA) **Revaluing the bilingual learner through a literature reading program.** *Reading & Writing Quarterly: Overcoming Learning Difficulties,* 1993(Apr–Jun), Vol 9(2), 163–182. —Presents alternatives to 3 misconceptions about bilingual learners to promote the revaluing of these students. In addition, traditional views of literacy instruction for 2nd-language learners are described and a whole-language literature program alternative is suggested. Finally, the difference between inauthentic, controlled, literature-based reading programs and meaningful, authentic literature programs is laid out so that educators can better understand how to draw on the strengths and rich diversity of bilingual students in the classroom.

Abstract

43197. **Gargallo, Bernardo.** (U Valencia, Facultade de Filosofia y Ciencias de la Educación, Spain) **Basic variables in reflection-impulsivity: A training programme to increase reflectivity.** *European Journal of Psychology of Education,* 1993(Jun), Vol 8(2), 151–167.—Observed cognitive impulsivity among 201 children (aged 12–14 yrs) participating in a training program intended to increase reflection. There was no significant difference between sexes on E. Cairns and T. Cammock's (unpublished) Matching Familiar Figures Test 20 items (MFF20) performance. Significant differences between the 3 age groups were found. A reflection increase was observed between ages 12 and 13 yrs and an impulsivity increase was apparent between ages 13 and 14 yrs. Basic Reflection-Impulsivity scores had a higher stability and consistency with MFF20 than the ones from J. Kagan's (1965) Matching Familiar Figures test. There was no confusion in Impulsivity and Efficiency scores between the slow-inaccurate and fast-accurate children.

FIGURE 9

Sample summaries from *Psychological Abstracts*

SilverPlatter 3.1   Journal Articles (1/97 - 6/93)   F10 = Commands   F1 = Help

```
┌─────────────────────────────────────────────────────────────────────────┐
│                      DATABASE SELECTION SCREEN                            │
│     ┌───────────────────────────────────────────────────────────────┐    │
│     │ 1. Use v, ^ to move the cursor to the database you want to search.│  │
│     │ 2. Press [Spacebar] to select the database or databases you want. │  │
│     │ 3. Press [Enter] to load the database or databases you have chosen.│ │
│     └───────────────────────────────────────────────────────────────┘    │
│                                                                           │
│   /K:Journal Articles (1/87 - 6/93)          PsycLIT - APA                │
│    K:Book Chapters & Books (1/87 - 6/93)     PsycLIT - APA                │
│                                                                           │
│                                                                           │
│   SilverPlatter Software Copyright (C) SilverPlatter International N.V. 1992│
└─────────────────────────────────────────────────────────────────────────┘
```

FIGURE 10
Beginning a search on PsychLit

SilverPlatter 3.1   Journal Articles (1/87 - 6/93)   F10 = Commands   F1 = Help

```
┌─────────────────────────────────────────────────────────────────────────┐
│  TITLE SCREEN                                                    1 of 1   │
│  - - - - - - - - - - - - - - - - - - - - - - - - - - - - - - - - - - - -  │
│                     The PsycLIT Database (2 discs)                        │
│                           Journal Articles                                │
│        Copyright 1990 - 1993 American Psychological Assn, all rights reserved│
│                        January 1987 - June 1993                           │
│                                                                           │
│  The PsycLIT Journal Articles Database contains summaries of the world's serial│
│  literature in psychology and related disciplines and is compiled from the PsycINFO│
│  Database. PsycLIT covers over 1300 journals in 27 languages from approximately│
│  50 countries.                                                            │
│     ┌───────────────────────────────────────────────────────────────┐    │
│     │ To learn more about the database               press F3        │    │
│     │ To learn more about the retrieval system       press F1        │    │
│     │ To use the THESAURUS                            press F9        │    │
│     │ To search PsycLIT - type a word or phrase       press ENTER     │    │
│     └───────────────────────────────────────────────────────────────┘    │
└─────────────────────────────────────────────────────────────────────────┘
```

FIGURE 11
The screen when the system is ready to search a topic

SilverPlatter 3.1   Journal Articles (1/87 - 6/93)
No.   Records   Request
1:          468   BILINGUAL
2:        27200   EDUCATION
3:           84   BILINGUAL EDUCATION
Journal Articles (1/87 - 6/93) usage is subject to the terms and conditions of the
Subscription and License Agreement and the applicable Copyright and intellectual
property protection as dictated by the appropriate laws of your country and/or by
International Convention.

                                                                   1 of 84
                                                        Marked in Search: #3

TI   DOCUMENT TITLE: English and Spanish acquisition by
limited-language-proficient Mexican Americans in a three-year maintenance
bilingual program.
AU   AUTHOR(S): Escamilla,-Kathy; Medina,-Marcello
IN   INSTITUTIONAL AFFILIATION OF FIRST AUTHOR: U Colorado, US
JN   JOURNAL NAME: Hispanic-Journal-of-Behavioral-Sciences; 1993 Feb Vol 15(1)
108–120
AB   ABSTRACT: Investigated the long-term effect of a maintenance bilingual
education (MBE) program on the acquisition of Spanish and English for 2 principal,
linguistically homogenous groups of Mexican-American children (kindergarteners and
1st and 2nd graders) who were all limited in English as well as Spanish proficiency.
For purposes of comparative analysis, these program participants were divided into
a most-limited-language proficient group (n = 74) and a limited-language proficient
group (n = 113). Although the primary analysis compared Spanish and English
acquisition, the 2nd analysis examined changes in oral English and Spanish for the
2 principal groups at kindergarten and Grade 2. The most significant overall results
related to the additive effects that the MBE program fostered for the 2 groups' oral
Spanish and English. (PsycLIT Database Copyright 1993 American Psychological
Assn, all rights reserved)
DE   DESCRIPTORS: BILINGUAL-EDUCATION; LANGUAGE-PROFICIENCY;
EDUCATIONAL-PROGRAMS; FOREIGN-LANGUAGE-LEARNING;
MEXICAN-AMERICANS; KINDERGARTEN-STUDENTS;
ELEMENTARY-SCHOOL-STUDENTS; CHILDHOOD-AN PSYC ABS. VOL. AND
ABS. NO.: 80-23485

FIGURE 12

The screen showing number of sources on bilingual education recorded from January
1987 to June 1993 and the first abstract that the user requested

USING OTHER SOURCES

Because of the great amount of material being published, most libraries are now using devices that allow for material to be stored in less space than would be required by its original form. When looking for books or articles, you may need to use some type of microform: printed material that has been reduced in size through microphotography. Libraries that use microform provide users with special readers that magnify the material in question—whether it is available on microfilm or microfiche, which means a flat sheet of microfilm.

Even when space is not an issue, most libraries can afford to purchase only a fraction of the material that is published each year. Although a good college library should give you all the sources you need for most papers, you may occasionally find it necessary to look beyond the library where you normally work. If you live in or near a city, there may be several other libraries that you can use. If this is not the case, remember that most libraries also provide an interlibrary loan service, which will allow you to request a book or journal article that your own library does not possess. When a library offers interlibrary loan, you will be asked to provide bibliographical information about the material you are requesting. Librarians will then do the work of locating and securing a copy of the book or article for you. You should ask for material only if you are reasonably certain that it would be useful for you, and that an equivalent resource is not already available in your own library. You should also recognize that obtaining a source through interlibrary loan can take two weeks or longer, so it will be of no use if you defer your research until a few days before your paper is due.

In addition to interlibrary loan, many libraries subscribe to one or more of the data-base services that link individual libraries with computerized lists of material available throughout the United States and Canada. The most commonly used bibliographic networks are BRS (Bibliographic Retrieval Services), DIALOG (operated by Knight-Ridder), RLIN (Research Libraries Information Network), and OCLC (Online Computer Library Center). A data-base search usually identifies sources that you must then proceed to locate on your own, but there are some programs that also allow for the full retrieval of a short text. Policies regarding data-base searches vary from library to library, and some libraries charge a fee for this service. Inquire about the policy at your own library before requesting a data-base search.

For some topics, you may want to use a nonprint source, such as a personal interview. Although interviews are usually inappropriate for scientific papers, they can be helpful in many other fields. If you are writing a paper on bilingual education, you might decide to interview teachers, children, and members of a local school board. But unless your instructor has encouraged you to do some interviews, you should check to make sure that interviews are acceptable for your assignment. Remember also that interviews need to be planned ahead, and you should have a list of questions before you go. But don't feel compelled to adhere rigidly to the questions you prepared in advance. A good interviewer knows how to ask a follow-up question that is inspired by a provocative response to an earlier question. Do not get so caught up in an interview, however, that you forget to take careful notes. (If you want to use a tape recorder, courtesy demands that you ask permission to do so when you arrange for the interview.) Because you will need to include the interview in your bibliography, record the date of the interview and the full name of the person you have interviewed.

Compiling a Preliminary Bibliography

As you begin locating sources of possible value for your paper, you should be careful to record certain essential information about the books and articles you have discovered. You will need this information in order to compose a preliminary bibliography. For books, you need to record the full title, the full name of the author or authors, the city of publication, the publisher, and the date of publication. If you are using a particular part of a book, be sure to record the pages in question. And if you are using an article or a story included in an anthology edited by someone other than the author of the material you are using, make the distinction between the author and the title of the selection and the editor and title of the book as a whole. When you have located articles in periodicals, record the author(s) of the article, the title of the article, the title of the journal in which it was published, the volume number, the issue number (if there is one), the date of the issue, and the pages between which the article can be found. (For examples of bibliographic form, see pp. 83–91.)

One way to compile a preliminary bibliography is to use a set of 3 × 5 note cards, recording separate sources on separate cards. This involves a little more trouble than jotting references down on whatever paper you have at hand, but it will be to your ultimate advantage. As your research progresses, you can easily eliminate any sources that you were unable to obtain—or that you have rejected as inappropriate for one reason or another. And by using this method, you will later find it easier to arrange your sources in the order in which they should appear in the formal bibliography at the end of your finished paper. Some researchers prefer to use a computer notebook, however, and others work directly from computer print-outs of sources located during their search. Whatever method you use, be sure to keep accurate records. No one enjoys discovering a failure to record an important reference—especially if this discovery comes after the paper is written and shortly before it must be handed in.

Taking Notes

Note taking is essential to research. Unfortunately, few researchers can tell in advance exactly what material they will want to include in their final paper. Especially during the early stages of your research, you may record information that will later seem unnecessary when you have become more expert on your topic and have a clear thesis. So you will probably have to discard some of your notes when you are ready to write your paper. If you have never done a researched paper before, you might benefit from taking notes on 3 × 5 note cards.

The advantage of a note card system is that it allows for flexibility when you are ready to move from research to composition. The odds are against discovering material in the exact order in which you will want to use it. By spreading your note cards out on a desk or table, you can study how they best fit together. You can arrange and rearrange note cards until you have them in a meaningful sequence. This system only works, however, when you have the self-restraint to limit yourself to recording one fact, one idea, or one quotation to a card, as shown in Figure 13. This means that many of your cards will have a lot of empty space that you may be tempted to fill. Don't. As soon as you decide to put two ideas on the same card, you have made an editorial decision that you may later regret. The cost of a set of note cards is minimal compared to the amount of time you must invest in research and writing.

Sorting your note cards is also one of the easiest ways to determine whether you have enough material to write a good paper. If your notes fall into a half-dozen different categories, your research might lack focus. In this case you should do some more research, concentrating on the category that interests you the most. If, on the other hand, your notes fall into a clear pattern, you may be ready to start writing. The point at which you move from research into writing will depend not only on your notes but also on the length of the paper you have in mind: Long papers usually involve more research than short papers.

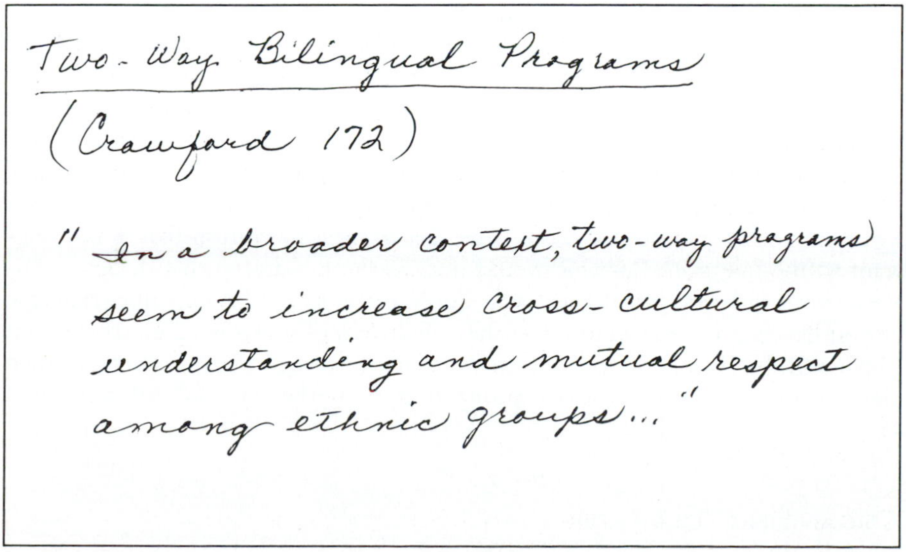

FIGURE 13
Sample note card

If you classify your notes every few days during the process of doing your research, you will be in a position to judge when you have taken as many notes as you will need.

Avoiding Selective Research

Although your research should have a clear focus, and you may have a tentative thesis in mind, you should formulate your final thesis only after your research is complete. Your research strategy should be designed to answer a question that you have posed to yourself, such as "Under what circumstances can bilingual education be most effective?" This is very different from starting your research with your thesis predetermined. A student who is convinced that all Americans should speak English, and nothing but English, may be tempted to take notes only from sources that report problems with bilingual education—rejecting as irrelevant any source that describes a successful program. Research, in this case, is not leading to greater knowledge or understanding. On the contrary, it is being used to reinforce personal beliefs that may border on prejudice.

We have seen that "anticipating the opposition" is important even in short arguments. It is no less important in a researched paper. Almost any topic worth investigating will yield facts and ideas that could support different conclusions. The readings assembled in this book have demonstrated that it is possible to take significantly different positions on gun control, immigration law, and hate speech—among other issues. As you may have already observed, some of the most opinionated people are also the most ignorant. Well-educated people are usually aware of how most problems are complex, and this is because they have been exposed to different points of view during their education. Good students remember this when they are doing research. They allow their reading to influence their thought, and not their thoughts to restrict their reading. Your own research may ultimately support a belief that you already hold, but it could just as easily lead you to realize that you were misinformed. When taking notes, you should remember the question that you have posed for yourself so that you do not waste time recording information that is not relevant to the question. But you should not overlook material that directly concerns your question just because you don't agree with what this material says. If you have a good reason to reject the conclusion of someone else's work, your paper will be stronger if you recognize that this disagreement exists and then demonstrate why you favor one position over another or how different positions can be reconciled.

Organizing Your Paper

If you have used a note card system, you may be able to dispense with an outline and compose your first draft by working directly from your notes—

assuming that you have sorted them carefully and arranged them into an easily understandable sequence. At some point, however, most writers find it useful to outline the ideas they plan to cover. Anyone who lacks experience in writing long papers is especially likely to benefit from taking the trouble to prepare an outline. Depending upon your own writing process, you can outline before attempting to write or after you have completed a rough draft.

If you decide to outline your paper, you might use a formal outline:

I. Major idea
    A. Supporting idea
        1. Minor idea
            a. Supporting detail
            b. Supporting detail
        2. Minor idea
    B. Supporting idea
II. Major idea

And so forth. Subdivisions only make sense when there are at least two categories—otherwise there would be no need to subdivide. Roman numeral I usually implies the existence of Roman numeral II, and supporting idea A implies the existence of supporting idea B. A formal outline is usually parallel, with each part in balance with the others.

An outline may consist of complete sentences or simply of topics, but follow consistently whichever system you choose. (For an example of a topic outline, see p. 607.) The extent to which you benefit from an outline is usually determined by the amount of effort you devote to preparing it. The more developed your outline, the more likely you are to have thought your essay through and considered how it can be best organized. Your outline may show you that you have much to say about one part of your paper and little about another. This could result in a lopsided paper when the parts are supposed to be of equal importance. In this case, your outline may lead you to do some additional research in order to obtain more information for the part of the paper that looks as if it is going to be weak. Or you may decide to rethink your essay and draft another outline, narrowing your paper to the discussion of the part that had most interested you. Either of these decisions would make it easier for you to write a well-organized paper by reducing the risk of introducing ideas you could not pursue.

Many writers prefer to work with less formal outlines. Two widely used alternatives to a formal outline are *listing* and *mapping*. When organizing a paper by listing, writers simply make a list of the various points they want to make without worrying about Roman numerals or indention. They then number the points on the list in the order they plan to discuss them. When mapping, writers create circles or blocks upon a page, starting with their main idea. A different idea is noted in each circle or block, and then lines are drawn to connect ideas that are related. There is no single method that works equally well for all writers. Unless you are specifically instructed to complete a certain type of outline, practice whatever kind of outlining works best for you.

You should remember that an outline is not an end in itself; it is only a device to help you write a good paper. You can rewrite an outline much more easily than you can rewrite a paper, so do not think of an outline as some sort of fixed contract which you must honor at all cost. Be prepared to rework any outline that does not help you to write better.

WRITING YOUR PAPER

When writing a researched paper, you should allow ample time for drafting and revision. Ideas often evolve during the writing process. Even if you have extensive notes, you may discover that you lack information to support a claim that occurred to you when you sat down to write. You would then need to do some more research or modify your claim. The first draft may also include paragraphs that do not relate to the focus of your paper, and these will need to be removed once you realize that they do not fit. Cutting and adding are normal in the writing process, so do not be discouraged if you need to make changes.

One of the challenges involved in writing a researched paper is the need to integrate source material into a work that remains distinctively your own. Many papers suffer because they include too many long quotations or because quotations (be they long or short) seem arbitrarily placed. Make sure that any quotations in your paper fit smoothly within the essay as a whole by providing transitions that link quotations to whatever has come before them. As a general rule, anything worth quoting at length requires some discussion. After you have quoted someone, you should usually include some analysis or commentary that will make the significance of the quotation clear. Let your readers know how you would like them to respond to the material that you are citing. Identify what you agree with and what you question.

To help keep your paper your own, you should try to avoid using long quotations. Quote only what you need most and edit long quotations whenever possible. Use the ellipsis (. . .) to indicate that you have omitted a word or phrase within a sentence, leaving a space before and after each period and including a fourth period with no space before it when the ellipsis comes at the end of the sentence (. . . .). When editing quotations in this way, make sure that they remain clear and grammatical. If the addition of an extra word or two would help make the quotation more easily understandable, you can make an editorial interpolation by enclosing the inserted material within square brackets [ ]. If your typewriter or word processor does not have brackets, you can draw them in by hand.

Remember also that sources do not need to be quoted in order to be cited. As noted in Part 2 (68–69), paraphrasing and summarizing are important writing skills. When revising your paper, use these skills whenever possible.

They can help you to avoid writing a paper that sounds like nothing more than one quotation after another, or using quotations that are so heavily edited that readers start wondering about what you have cut out. When you put another writer's ideas into your own words (being careful, of course, to provide proper documentation), you are demonstrating that you have control over your material. And by doing so, you can often make your paper read more easily.

PREPARING YOUR FINAL DRAFT

After investing considerable time in researching, drafting, and revising your paper, be sure to allow sufficient time for editing your final draft. If you rush this stage of the process, the work you submit for evaluation may not adequately reflect the investment of time you gave to the project as a whole. Unless instructed otherwise, you should be guided by the rules in this checklist:

A CHECKLIST FOR MANUSCRIPT FORM

1. Papers should be typed or word-processed. Use nonerasable $8^{1}/_{2}$ by 11-inch white paper. Type on one side of each page only. Doublespace all lines, leaving a margin of one inch on all sides. If word-processing, use a printer that will produce well-defined letters.
2. In the upper left corner of page 1, or on a separate title page, include the following information: your name, your instructor's name, the course and section number, and the date the essay is submitted.
3. Number each page in the upper right corner, $^{1}/_{2}$-inch from the top. If using MLA-style documentation, type your last name immediately before the number. If using APA-style documentation, type a shortened version of the title (one or two words) before the number.
4. Make sure that you consistently follow a documentation style acceptable to your instructor, and give credit to all of your sources.
5. Any quotation of more than four lines in an MLA-style paper, or more than forty words in an APA-style paper, should be set off from the rest of the text. Begin a new line, indenting ten spaces to form the left margin of the quotation. The indentation means that you are quoting, so additional quotation marks are unnecessary in this case (except for quotations within the quotation).
6. Proofread your paper carefully. Typographical errors or careless mistakes in spelling or grammar can cause your audience to lose confidence in you. If your instructor allows ink corrections, make them as neatly as you can. Redo any page that has numerous or lengthy corrections.
7. If you have word-processed your paper, be sure to separate pages that have been printed on a continuous sheet. Whether your work is word-processed or typed, use a paper clip to bind the pages together.

IN CONCLUSION

The readings gathered in this book have demonstrated the importance of research in the world beyond the classroom. Extensive research is readily apparent in the arguments by Zimring, Riger, and Summers. But research also supports the arguments of Paul, Conover, Gates, and Wiener, among others. None of these works could have been written if their authors had not taken the trouble to become well-informed on their chosen subjects.

Having studied these essays, you should be familiar with the way experienced writers use content notes to clarify various points in their arguments. Individual essays have also illustrated the major documentation styles. Riger and Micko use the APA author/year system. Perez uses a variation of the author/year system recommended by the influential *Chicago Manual of Style.* Jenkins, Lovrien, Fedorczak, Powell, and Summers all use the MLA author/work style.

For another example of the MLA author/work style, consider the following paper by Grace Reyes. It includes material from a range of sources that were located through the use of different tools: the main catalog for books, the *Essay and General Literature Index* for material published in anthologies, the *Readers' Guide* for articles in periodicals such as *Forbes,* and the *Education Index* for periodicals such as *Harvard Education Review.*

As you read the paper, note that it uses sources in order to support an argument. This argument shows that the author has ideas of her own and that her paper is more than a collection of notes. The paper as written, however, is different from the paper Grace originally envisioned. She began by intending to explore whether bilingual education is worthwhile, but she found that this topic was too big for her. She then tried to limit her work to the advantages of two-way bilingual programs only to find that she could not locate sufficient material on that topic. Her solution was to focus her paper on the purpose of bilingual education, a topic that proved to be the right size for her. When you write a researched paper of your own, be prepared to revise your focus when necessary. Although you may be able to write an excellent paper on the topic you set out to research, you could just as easily find it necessary to redefine that topic as your research proceeds.

Bilingual Education in a
Multicultural Nation

Thesis: The purpose of bilingual education needs to be clarified if the controversy surrounding this issue is to
be resolved.

Introduction--why this topic is important
  I. History of bilingual education
      A. Role of federal government
          1. Languages used in bilingual education
          2. Students eligible for enrollment
      B. Range of programs offered
          1. Transitional Bilingual Education
          2. Immersion
          3. English as a Second Language
 II. Issues behind bilingual education
      A. Time necessary for learning language
          1. Quotation from Cardenas
          2. Quotation from Rodriquez
          3. Response to show who is right
      B. Importance of cultural diversity
          1. Languages spoken here
          2. Treatment of minorities
          3. America as a melting pot
III. Challenges facing bilingual education
      A. Segregated classrooms
          1. Integration through two-way programs
          2. Limits of two-way programs
      B. Increased needs
          1. Problems with funding
          2. Larger number of students needing help
      C. Multiple goals
          1. Instruction in English
          2. Instruction in other languages
          3. Instruction in culture
Conclusion--need to set priorities so we can cope with rising
needs

Reyes 1

Grace Reyes
Prof. Lewandowski
English 150
9 May 1991

Double space

Bilingual Education in a Multicultural Nation

Should American public-school children be taught in any
language besides English? Some people might think that this
question was answered a long time ago. After all, the federal
government has been funding bilingual education for over
twenty years. But there is still little agreement over what
"bilingual education" means and how it should be conducted.
Because language is so important in determining what a society is like, the outcome of this debate will affect all Americans, not just students. According to a recent article in
the New York Times, "What's at stake, then, is nothing less
than the cultural identity of the country" (Bernstein 52).

**Student estab-
lishes importance
of the topic**

Most bilingual programs can be traced back to the Bilingual Education Act of 1968.[1] Although the original legislation
was designed to benefit Hispanic children, it was revised to
apply to all non-English speakers as the result of a compromise between Congress and the White House (Stein 31). Spanish
is now only one of 145 languages used for instruction in our
public schools (Thernstrom 46). And since 1974, bilingual
programs have been open to middle-class children whose primary language is English.

**Reference to con-
tent note provid-
ing additional in-
formation**

There is thus good reason to be confused about what
"bilingual education" means. This designation might be used
to describe a program designed to assimilate disadvantaged,
non-English speaking students into American society. It could
refer to a program designed to help middle-class students
maintain a language that is part of their ethnic background
even if they already speak English. Or it could describe a
program with a large number of English-speaking students
whose parents want them to learn a useful foreign language.
Some schools try to pursue all of these goals, and this leads
to another problem: Instruction can suffer when students with
different needs are placed together randomly or with a

**Student identifies
the problems that
concern her**

Reyes 2

teacher who is unprepared to help more than one type of
student.

In addition to enrolling students with different needs,
bilingual programs are organized in different ways. The most
common type of program is called "Transitional Bilingual Education." As its name suggests, TBE offers instruction in both
English and in a student's first language until he or she is
ready to make the transition into regular classes in which
English is the only language of instruction. Much of the debate over bilingual education has focused upon this type of
program, and since 1988 up to 25% of federal funds for bilingual education can be used for alternatives to TBE (Thernstrom 48). These alternatives include Immersion, or classes
in which a teacher speaks only English but nevertheless understands her students' language. (If the teacher occasionally uses the student's language to provide a hint, this is
called Structured Immersion.) Another alternative method of
instruction is teaching English as a Second Language. An ESL
class would normally include students who speak a number of
different languages, and instruction would be offered only in
English. Unlike Immersion, in which regular courses are
taught in English, an ESL class is devoted only to learning
how to read and speak English. Another difference is that
students taking ESL are usually pulled out of their regular
classes for part of the day.

> **Student summa-
> rizes different
> types of bilingual
> education**

Both proponents and critics of bilingual education agree
about the importance of learning English. The controversy
concerns how quickly English should be learned, and what type
of special instruction should be made available. Advocates of
TBE believe that it takes from five to seven years for students with limited proficiency in English to master the formal language necessary for understanding school work taught
in English. José A. Cárdenas, executive director of the In-
tercultural Development Research Association in San Antonio,
warns:

> **Student identifies
> a source**

Failure to allow sufficient language development
before the transition will result in a child's

> **Quotations more
> than four lines
> long are set off as
> a block. Indent 1"
> from left margin
> or leave ten spaces
> blank. Do not add
> quotation marks.**

Reyes 3

being unable to cope with anything but the most
shallow levels of learning and will affect that
child's future capability for learning. (362)

On the other hand, critics of bilingual education believe
that the use of another language in school can delay the
learning of English. In his memoir <u>Hunger of Memory</u>, Richard
Rodriquez writes:

Without question, it would have pleased me to hear
my teachers address me in Spanish when I entered
the classroom. I would have been much less afraid.
I would have trusted them and responded with ease.
But I would have delayed . . . having to learn the
language of public society. (19)

Ellipsis indicates an omission

Rodriquez is often cited as an authority on bilingual education, but he is speculating about what did not happen to him.

Student responds to a quotation

According to Jim Cummins, an internationally recognized expert on bilingual education, "language minority students instructed through the minority language . . . for all or part
of the school day perform as well in English academic skills
as comparable students instructed totally through English"
("Empowering" 20). If this is the case, then it would seem
that neither TBE nor Immersion is clearly preferable strictly
in terms of education.[2]

A shortened version of the title is included because the list of works cited includes more than one work by this author.

But bilingual education is a political issue as well as
an educational issue. Arguing that we need a common language
in order to hold together a society that is ethnically and
culturally diverse, critics of bilingual education often
characterize it as a threat to national unity (Banks 62;
Bernstein 48). According to this reasoning, anyone living
here should learn English as soon as possible, and loyalty to
another language can interfere with this goal. On the other
hand, cultural diversity can also be cited as a justification
for recognizing the importance of languages other than English. The United States "has always been a multilingual nation and indeed was characterized by multilingualism long
before it became a nation" (Paulston 485). Insisting that all
Americans speak English may make sense politically, but pre-

More than one source cited within the same parenthetical reference, indicating that both Banks and Bernstein support the point just made.

Student responds to an argument against bilingual education

Reyes 4

tending that English is the only language ever spoken here
means distorting the past and ignoring important parts of our
national heritage.

Spanish has been spoken in North America since the six-
teenth century, and Native American languages were spoken
here even earlier. It's hard to justify denying anyone the
right to speak the language of his or her ancestors, and it's
especially hard to do so when the language in question has
been spoken here for hundreds of years by people whose ancestors became Americans as the result of military conquest.
Some of the bitterness surrounding the debate over bilingual
education can be understood when we realize that speakers of
Spanish and Native American languages have been the victims
of prejudice. Educators in Texas, for example, used to make
uninvited home visits to persuade parents to stop speaking
Spanish to their children. According to one such teacher:
"Their only handicap is a bag full of superstitions and silly
notions that they inherited from Mexico . . . a lot depends
on whether we can get them to switch from Spanish to English,
when they speak Spanish they think Mexican" (qtd. in Stein
15). I hope that we now realize that it is racist to associate thinking "Mexican" with "superstitions and silly notions." But even if more people are now prepared to recognize
that the United States is a multicultural nation, racism
seems to linger in some of the criticism of bilingual education. For example, a recent article in Forbes magazine defined bilingual education as a "strident political
campaign for separate Spanish teaching," favored by a "loud
minority of Hispanic politicians and leftish liberals"
(Banks 62).

As for immigrants, opponents of bilingual education
often emphasize that the United States was settled by people
from many different countries. But they then argue that their
parents or grandparents received no special treatment after
arriving in the United States, so no one else should either.
This argument implies that the future can never be better
than the past. Late nineteenth-century immigrants were often
crowded into unhealthy tenements and exploited in sweat

**An indirect
quotation**

**As an alternative
to using an ellip-
sis, student uses
her own words to
link together two
short quotations
from the same
paragraph.**

**Student summa-
rizes and re-
sponds to another
argument against
bilingual educa-
tion.**

shops. Child labor was common, and social services were
either minimal or nonexistent. Does this mean that we want
late-twentieth century immigrants to be subject to the same
hardships?

Critics of bilingual education often see the United
States as a "melting pot," implying that people from different cultures were once easily assimilated within the United
States--and that assimilation is being deliberately resisted
by recent arrivals. But I suspect that assimilation was always slow and painful. Even the image of a melting pot is
disturbing once you think about it. I don't think anyone
really wants to get melted down. The racism implicit in this
image can be seen in a pageant once held at the Ford Motor
Company. According to Colman Stein, Jr., a research analyst
who specializes in bilingual education, foreign-born workers
who had taken an "Americanization" program run by Ford carried signs identifying their national origin as they entered
a mock melting pot. Once in the pot, they were "cleaned" by
teachers with large scrub brushes before they could leave the
pot with new signs identifying them as American (5).

Understanding how minorities were treated in the past
should help us to recognize a fallacy in the argument that
bilingual education "sentences too many minority school leav-
ers, particularly Hispanics, to a second-class economic life"
(Banks 64). Minorities were sentenced to a second-class economic life long before the advent of bilingual education.
Bilingual programs may have failed to solve this problem, but
they should not be blamed for creating it. And we would certainly be better prepared to improve the quality of bilingual
education if we eliminated racism and misinformation from
this debate.

A more serious charge against bilingual education is
that it can become a type of segregated education once minority students are grouped together. According to one recent
critic:

> There is often little that is integrated about the
> education of these students. The students may dab-
> ble in paints and dribble a ball together but, for

Student intro-
duces a para-
phrase with a
reference to her
source in order to
show how much
the subsequent
page reference is
meant to cover.

Student responds
to another argu-
ment against bi-
lingual
education.

Reyes 6

> most of the day, a bilingual classroom is a school
> within a school--a world apart. (Thernstrom 48)

This is a problem that must be resolved. One possible solution is to integrate bilingual classrooms with English-speaking students who want to acquire a second language--whatever their own ethnic heritage may be. In fact, one of the most exciting developments in bilingual education is the "two-way" program in which English-speaking students who want to acquire a second language are grouped with language-minority students who are learning English. Although still fairly new, "two-way programs seem to increase cross-cultural understanding and mutual respect among ethnic groups" (Crawford 172). They may also help to improve the quality of foreign language study in the United States, an area in which English-speaking Americans have been traditionally weak. Unfortunately, there is currently a much larger number of students needing to learn English than students who are willing to learn a foreign language by enrolling in a bilingual program. Rosalie Porter, a former member of the National Advisory and Coordinating Council on Bilingual Education, estimates that two-way programs would probably be able to enroll less than 10% of language-minority children (157). Educators will need to explore other ways to make the bilingual classroom a multicultural classroom.

Another problem facing bilingual education is that funding has not kept pace with needs. Although the federal budget for bilingual education increased from $7,500,000 a year in 1968 to $198,625,000 in 1989, funding never reaches many school districts that need it (Porter 224-25).[3] And as the United States becomes more ethnically diverse, bilingual programs are expected to serve an increasing number and variety of students. According to sociologists Kenji Ima and Rubén G. Rumbaut of San Diego State University, 48% of all immigrants to this country during the 1980s came from Asia, and approximately 90% of them had limited proficiency in English. Their needs have only begun to be addressed (54-55).

The number of Americans speaking a language other than English is already higher than ever before in our history

(Bernstein 34), and it is expected to reach 39.5 million by the end of the century (Orvando 567), when approximately 20% of the school population will consist of language-minority children (Porter 5). We cannot ignore these children until they are ready to understand classes conducted exclusively in English, but we may not be able to make instruction available in every language spoken in every district. Although a large school district like that of New York City may be able to offer public education in Chinese, Greek, Haitian Creole, Kymer, Korean, Italian, Russian, and Vietnamese (Bernstein 34), many school systems lack the resources to guarantee instruction in every language spoken within the district.

Student begins to move toward her conclusion.

The debate over bilingual education would not have lasted so long or become so bitter if there were a simple solution to the question of how to help students with special language needs. But if there is no simple solution to this problem nationwide, we should avoid policies that insist upon all school districts offering the same method of instruction. We must also avoid policies that would be so general that school districts could ignore the very real needs of students with limited proficiency in English. It would be one thing to encourage more flexibility in program design and to experiment with different types of instruction; it would be something else to go back to the days when students who could not understand English were allowed to either sink or swim.

Although the list of works cited includes two works by Cummins, the parenthetical reference includes only a page number since the work is identified in the text of the paper.

Overall, the research is inconclusive regarding the various types of instruction currently offered students with limited proficiency in English. We need to keep this in mind when making future decisions. As Jim Cummins argued in Language and Literacy in Bilingual Education, a "rational policy in regard to the education of minority students must abandon conventional wisdoms and acknowledge what is known and what is not yet known" (6).

Since this is the case, the federal government should encourage individual school districts to find the type of instruction that best suits their needs. But the government can define the purpose of bilingual education, and that means establishing priorities among three separate goals. Bilingual

education can be used simply as a means of helping students
with limited proficiency in English become assimilated within
American society. It could become a way of helping all American students become bilingual. Or it could be used as a way
of teaching about the history and value of different cultures.[4]

    Ideally, it would be desirable to pursue all of these
goals. But it is hard to do so in any one classroom, since
students with different needs require different types of instruction. With limited resources and many students, we need
to clarify what goal is our top priority. I believe that lessons in different cultures are important, but they can be incorporated into the regular curriculum in such classes as
history and geography where all students would benefit from
them. The purpose of bilingual education should be to improve
skills in language. We should encourage English-speaking students to become bilingual by developing two-way programs
wherever possible. But our first priority should be helping
language-minority students to learn English through concentrated effort and dedicated teaching. If this goal became
widely understood, the debate over bilingual education would
come closer to being resolved.

Student reaches her conclusion.

1″

Notes

¹Crawford calls bilingual education "a forgotten legacy." He points out that cities like Cincinnati, Milwaukee,
and St. Louis had German-English schools in the nineteenth
century; Louisiana had French-English schools, and Spanish-
English schools were authorized in New Mexico in 1848. But
bilingual education declined during the early twentieth century, in part because learning in other languages seemed unpatriotic during and after the First World War. For
additional information on the history of bilingual education,
see the first chapter in Crawford and the first two chapters
in Stein.

²Cummins argues that one of the most important factors
in helping minority students succeed in school is the attitude educators convey on a daily basis. He also argues that
parents need to get involved in their children's education.
These factors may be more important than whether a school
uses TBE or Immersion.

³Porter argues that the federal government should re-
structure the way it makes money available. She calls for
block grants for every state with minority-language students
instead of the current system which awards money in the form
of grants to successful applicants.

⁴Lessons in culture that would improve the self-esteem
of minority students were considered important when many current programs were founded. See Thernstrom.

**Content notes
supplement the
paper and indi-
cate where read-
ers could get
additional infor-
mation.**

Reyes 10

Works Cited

Banks, Howard. "Do We Want Quebec Here?" Forbes 11 June 1990: 62–64.

Bernstein, Richard. "In U.S. Schools a War of Words." The New York Times Magazine 14 Oct. 1990: 34+.

Cárdenas, José A. "The Role of Native-Language Instruction in Bilingual Education." Phi Delta Kappan 67 (1986): 359–63.

Crawford, James. Bilingual Education: History, Politics, Theory, and Practice. Trenton: Crane, 1989.

Cummins, Jim. "Empowering Minority Students: A Framework for Intervention." Harvard Educational Review 56 (1986): 18–36.

---. Language and Literacy Learning in Bilingual Instruction. Washington: GPO, 1983.

Ima, Kenji and Rubén G. Rumbaut. "Southeast Asian Refugees in American Schools: A Comparison of Fluent English-Proficient and Limited English-Proficient Students." Topics in Language Disorders 9.3 (1989): 54–75.

Orvando, Carlos J. "Bilingual/Bicultural Education: Its Legacy and Its Future." Phi Delta Kappan 64 (1983): 564–71.

Paulston, Christina Bratt. "Bilingualism and Education." Language in the USA. Ed. Charles A. Ferguson and Shirley Brice Heath. Cambridge: Cambridge UP, 1981.

Porter, Rosalie Pedalino. Forked Tongue: The Politics of Bilingual Education. New York: Basic, 1990.

Rodriquez, Richard. Hunger of Memory. 1982. New York: Bantam, 1983.

Stein, Colman Brez, Jr. Sink or Swim: The Politics of Bilingual Education. New York: Praeger, 1986.

Thernstrom, Abigail M. "Bilingual Miseducation." Commentary Feb. 1990: 44–48.

1"

Double-space

Indent 1/2" or leave five spaces blank.

Student cites two works by the same author. Instead of repeating the author's name, type three hyphens followed by a period. In a case like this, arrange the works alphabetically by title.

Two spaces

GLOSSARY OF USEFUL TERMS

ad hominem argument: An argument that makes a personal attack on an opponent instead of addressing itself to the issue that is under dispute.

allusion: An unexplained reference that an audience is expected to understand because of their education or the culture in which they live.

analogy: A comparison that works on more than one level, usually between something familiar and something abstract.

anticipating the opposition: The process through which a writer or speaker imagines the most likely counterarguments that could be raised against his or her position.

audience: Whoever will read what you write. Your audience may consist of a single individual (such as your history teacher), a particular group of people (such as English majors), or a larger and more general group of people (such as "the American people"). Good writers have a clear sense of audience, which means that they never lose sight of whomever they are writing for.

authority: A reliable source that helps support an argument. It is important to cite authorities who will be recognized as legitimate by your audience. This means turning to people with good credentials in whatever area is under consideration. If you are arguing about the economy, cite a prominent economist as an authority—not the teller at your local bank.

begging the question: An argument that assumes, as already agreed on, whatever it should be devoted to proving.

bibliography: A list of works on a particular subject. One type of bibliography is the list of works cited that appears at the end of a paper, article, or book. Another type of bibliography is a work in itself—a compilation of all known sources on a subject. An annotated bibliography is a bibliography that includes a brief description of each of the sources cited.

bogus claim: An unreliable or false statement that is unsupported by reliable evidence or legitimate authority.

claim: Any assertion that can or should be supported with evidence. In the model for argument devised by Stephen Toulmin, the "claim" is the conclusion that the arguer must try to prove.

cliché: A worn-out expression; any group of words that are frequently and automatically used together. In "the real world" of "today's society," writers should avoid clichés because they are a type of instant language that makes writing seem "as dead as a doornail."

concession: Any point in an opposing argument that you are willing to recognize as valid. In argumentation, concessions demonstrate that you are fair-minded and help draw different sides together.

connotation: The associations inspired by a word, in contrast to *denotation* (see below).

data: The evidence that an arguer uses to support a claim. It may take the form of personal experience, expert opinion, statistics, or any other information that is verifiable.

deduction: The type of reasoning through which a generally accepted belief leads to a specific conclusion.

denotation: The literal dictionary definition of a word.

diction: Word choice. Having good diction means more than having a good vocabulary; it means using language appropriately by using the right word in the right place.

documentation: The references that writers supply to reveal the source of the information they have reported.

equivocation: The deliberate use of vague, ambiguous language to mislead others. In writing, equivocation often takes the form of using abstract words to obscure meaning.

evidence: The experience, examples, or facts that support an argument. Good writers are careful to offer evidence for whatever they are claiming (see *claim*).

focus: The particular aspect of a subject on which a writer decides to concentrate. Many things can be said about most subjects. Having a clear focus means narrowing a subject down so that it can be discussed without loss of direction. If you digress from your subject and begin to ramble, you have probably lost your focus.

generalization: Forming a conclusion that seems generally acceptable because it could be supported by evidence. Argumentative writing demands a certain amount of generalization. It becomes a problem only when it is easily disputable. You have overgeneralized if someone can think of exceptions to what you have claimed. Be wary of words such as "all" and "every" since they increase the likelihood of overgeneralization.

hyperbole: A deliberate exaggeration for dramatic effect.

hypothesis: A theory that guides your research; a conditional thesis that is subject to change as evidence accumulates.

induction: The type of reasoning through which specific observations lead to a generally acceptable conclusion.

irony: A manner of speech or writing in which one's meaning is the opposite of what one has said.

jargon: A specialized vocabulary that is usually abstract and limited to a particular field; when used in an argument, it should be defined for the benefit of those outside the field.

loaded term: A word or phrase that is considered an unfair type of persuasion because it is either slanted or gratuitous within its context.

metaphor: A comparison in which two unlike things are declared to be the same; for example, "The Lord is my shepherd."

meter: The rhythm of poetry, in which stressed syllables occur in a pattern with regular intervals. In the analysis of poetry, meter is measured by a unit called a "foot," which usually consists of two or three syllables of which at least one is stressed.

non sequitur: Latin for "it does not follow"; a logical fallacy in which a writer bases a claim on an unrelated point.

paradox: A statement or situation that appears to be contradictory but is nevertheless true; for example, "conspicuous by his absence."

paraphrase: Restating someone's words to demonstrate that you have understood them correctly or to make them more easily understandable.

personification: Giving human qualities to nonhuman objects; for example, "The sofa smiled at me, inviting me to sit down."

persuasion: A rhetorical strategy designed to make an audience undertake a specific action. Although there are many different types of persuasion, most involve an appeal to values, desires, and emotions.

plagiarism: Taking someone's words or ideas without giving adequate acknowledgement.

point of view: The attitude with which a writer approaches a subject. Good writers maintain a consistent point of view within each individual work.

post hoc, ergo propter hoc: Latin for "after this, therefore because of this"; a logical fallacy in which precedence is confused with causation.

premise: The underlying value or belief that one assumes as a given truth at the beginning of an argument.

rhetorical question: A question that is asked for dramatic effect, with the understanding that readers will silently answer the way the writer wants them to answer.

rime scheme (or "rhyme"):   A fixed pattern of rimes that occurs throughout a poem.

simile: A direct comparison between two unlike things that includes such words as "like," "as," or "than"; for example, "My love is like a red, red rose."

stereotype: An unthinking generalization, especially of a group of people in which all the members of the group are assumed to share the same traits; for example, the "dumb jock" is a stereotype of high school and college athletes.

style: The combination of diction and sentence structure that characterizes the manner in which a writer writes. Good writers have a distinctive style, which is to say their work can be readily identified as their own.

summary: A brief and unbiased recapitulation of previously stated ideas.

syllogism: A three-stage form of deductive reasoning through which a general truth yields a specific conclusion.

thesis: The central idea of an argument; the point that an argument seeks to prove. In an unified essay, every paragraph helps to advance the thesis.

tone: The way a writer sounds when discussing a particular subject. Whereas point of view establishes a writer's attitude toward his or her subject, tone refers to the voice that is adopted in conveying this point of view to an audience. For example, one can write with an angry, sarcastic, humorous, or dispassionate tone when discussing a subject about which one has a negative point of view.

topic sentence: The sentence that defines the function of a paragraph; the single most important sentence in each paragraph.

transition: A link or bridge between topics that enables a writer to move smoothly from one subtopic to another so that every paragraph is clearly related to the paragraphs that surround it.

warrant: A term used by Stephen Toulmin for an implicit or explicit general statement that underlies an argument and establishes a relationship between the data and the claim.

COPYRIGHTS AND
ACKNOWLEDGMENTS

AUTHOR-TITLE INDEX